"Uncommonly rich and informative...What makes *Seriously Funny* more than a nostalgia trip, however, is the keenness of the author's judgments....Generously, he packs his pages with excerpts...At his best, Nachman can sum up a whole career in an epigram...In every important way, *Seriously Funny* is as close to a definitive book on the this subject as we're likely to get."

— THE WASHINGTON POST

"Extremely thorough... One [might] protest the minutiae but the minutiae are all the fun."

— THE NEW YORKER

"The story of that [comedy] revolution has now finally been told, and beautifully so...A wonderfully touching book...Each chapter has its own surprise, pleasant and otherwise."

— NEW YORK OBSERVER

"A talented interviewer, and he has a lovely way with an anecdote. *Seriously Funny* kills."

— THE SAN FRANCISCO CHRONICLE

"An inspiring, sprawling book...The research alone is phenomenal. Nachman interviewed everybody. The fruit of his Herculean labor treats these comedians with the intensity usually reserved for politicians and serial killers...I just keep spooning it up because Nachman dishes it out so expertly...I loved this book for the gossip, the social history, the claw-your-way-to-glory stories, the showbiz chestnuts. Nachman not only knows everything about this comic era, he knows how to share his knowledge with zest and grace. *Seriously Funny* brilliantly lives up to its title."

— THE SEATTLE TIMES

"To Nachman, each [comic] is an intricate, invaluable puzzle that must be solved, a continent calling out to be explored to its fullest. Though his underlying affection is clear, Nachman doesn't whitewash the dark sides of his subjects...In these dark days of safe sitcom humor and assembly-line club comedy, *Seriously Funny* is a timely reminder that comedy at its best can be as dangerous, subversive and exciting as rock and roll."

— THE AUSTIN CHRONICLE

"Readers who might imagine that comedy began with John Belushi would do well to read about these comedians who changed the country's cultural landscape. *Seriously Funny* reminds us, most entertainingly, that the bland Fifties had some colorful fringes indeed."

— THE SAVANNAH MORNING NEWS

"Using fresh interviews, his own keen judgment and generous dollops of performance excerpts, the author serves up dozens of fascinating takes on major and minor players. [Nachman is] a shrewd observer."

— THE WEEK magazine

"His essays are dense with fact, anecdote and opinion."

— THE SAN JOSE MERCURY

"If you have affection for comedic giants, then Nachman has written a book you must own."

— KNIGHT RIDDER PAPERS

"A must-have for comedy fans, this book is also a notable study of America as it shed its gray flannel suit and began, finally, to laugh.

— PUBLISHERS WEEKLY

"Remember when comedians got laughs not from rude language or cynical cracks or extreme attitude, but from humor and wit? Remember when comedians were actually funny? Gerald Nachman does, and he revisits that time at length and to great effect in his hugely entertaining and engrossing book."

— JANUARY magazine

"It's been said that analyzing comedy is a bit like dissecting a frog: you arrive at a greater understanding of the frog but the frog does tend to die in the process. The purpose of Gerald Nachman's *Seriously Funny: The Rebel Comedians of the 1950s and 1960s* is not to provide a laugh riot of his subjects' best punch lines, but rather to explore their lives, careers, and influence. Nachman's scope is impressive. He provides detailed biographies not only of household names Sid Caesar, Lenny Bruce, Bob Newhart, and Woody Allen but also comics like Jean Shepherd, Shelley Berman, and Will Jordan whose legacies have far outpaced their name recognition. Nachman has done his research; the book profiles 26 comedians, each in exhaustive detail, and no fan of this era will feel cheated at the end of its 768 pages. There are plenty of entertaining show biz anecdotes (Sid Caesar throwing a lit cigar at young writer Mel Brooks, Bill Cosby punching out Tommy Smothers) along with tales of the darker sides of Mort Sahl, Jonathan Winters, and others whose private lives were far less amusing than their stage acts. But what makes Seriously Funny so compelling…is the author's meticulous attention to each comedian's imprint on the landscape of comedy itself.

— AMAZON.COM

Now that Lenny Bruce is lionized for freeing stand-up from most constraints on material and language, Nachman figures it is time other "rebel" comics of the 1950s and 1960s got some attention, and he certainly knows whom to attend to. Sid Caesar, Ernie Kovacs, and Jonathan Winters are arguably the standouts in the section on the '50s, but even Jean Shepherd, most famous today as creator of the classic Christmas flick *A Christmas Story,* gets his due, in the same chapter as absurdists extraordinaire Bob and Ray. In the '60s section, figures as diverse yet comparably insightful as Bob Newhart and Godfrey Cambridge are profiled. Lenny does, of course, get his chapter, and so do the Smothers brothers, Dick Gregory, and Mel Brooks, plus the now relatively unknown David Frye, Vaughan Meader, and Will Jordan. Rather like aesthetically pondering rock musicians' instrumental techniques, serious discussion of comedy is a chancy proposition. Nachman manages, however, to leaven his content analysis with sheer enjoyment. All entertainment scholarship should be this enjoyable and informative.

— BOOKLIST

Seriously Funny

The Rebel Comedians

of the 1950s and 1960s

GERALD NACHMAN

BACK STAGE BOOKS / *New York*

Senior Editor: Mark Glubke
Production Manager: Hector Campbell
Cover design: Archie Ferguson
Book design: Cassandra J. Pappas

Paperback edition first published in 2004 by Back Stage Books, an imprint of Watson-Guptill Publications, a division of VNU Business Media, Inc., 770 Broadway, New York, NY 10003
www.wgpub.com.com

Library of Congress Control Number: 2004108937

ISBN: 0-8230-4786-5

Grateful acknowledgement is made to Tom Lehrer for permission to reprint excerpts from various song lyrics. Copyright © Tom Lehrer. Reprinted by permission of Tom Lehrer.

Photo credits: Eugene Anthony: hungry i; Photofest: Bob Elliot and Ray Goulding, Shelley Berman, Jonathan Winters, Mike Nichols and Elaine May, Mel Brooks, Dick Gregory, Bob Newhart, Joan Rivers, David Frye, Vaughn Meader, Will Jordan; The Kobal Collection: Sid Caesar, The Smothers Brothers; Ted Streskinsky/TimePix: Tom Lehrer; Meadowlane Enterprises: Steve Allen; Culver Pictures: Stan Freberg, Godfrey Cambridge; © Fred W. McDarrah: Jean Shepherd; Eddie Brandt's: Woody Allen; Michael Rougier/TimePix: Bill Cosby; San Francisco History Center: Ernie Kovacs; Courtesy of Phyllis Diller: Phyllis Diller

Cover photograph of Mort Sahl © Julian Wasser/TimePix

Manufactured in the United States of America

First printing 2004

1 2 3 4 5 6 7 8 9 / 11 10 09 08 07 06 05 04

For Randy Poe and Morrie Bobrow,
sources of infinite merriment

You may humbug the town as a tragedian, but comedy is a serious business.

—DAVID GARRICK,
  eighteenth-century actor-director-producer

Contents

Seriously Funny

SETUP LINES

Introduction

There's a lot to be said for making people laugh. Did you know that's all some people have? It isn't much, but it's better than nothing in this cockeyed caravan.

—JOEL McCREA, in Preston Sturges's *Sullivan's Travels*

NOBODY REALLY REMEMBERS the 1950s, where much of our story is set, with any accuracy. Great sport is still made of the fifties. They're satirized and exploited and even waxed nostalgic about, yet nobody gets them quite right; a sharper close-up of that much-maligned decade is long overdue. The 1950s might have been innocent but they were far from innocuous. Maybe you had to be there. Yet even people who *were* there accept the standard snapshot. The fifties were largely a victim of bad timing—overshadowed by the heroic forties and the histrionic sixties.

Viewed through the lens of its satirical comedians, the fifties were at least as vital and vivid as any flashier decade—and a whole lot funnier. The historians may have been nodding off, but the audiences who flocked to see the new comedians of that time were wide awake. The comedians of the fifties and sixties were a totally different species from any that came before or after, comics whose humor did more than pry guffaws out of audiences. This new post–Korean War comedy poked and prodded and observed, demolishing fond shibboleths left and right; it didn't just pulverize us with a volley of joke-book gags.

Teenagers who grew up watching TV in the early fifties were baffled and bored by the comedians their parents doted on, reverentially trotted out each Sunday night by Ed Sullivan, whose show was almost a wing of the Catskills hotels. Many of them enjoyed a last hurrah on *The Colgate Comedy Hour,* where aging troupers like Eddie Cantor, Jimmy Durante, and Abbott & Costello, refugees from radio, and even vaudeville, grabbed the spotlight week after week. They were consummate entertainers, but they had little to say about the emerging world. Satire then was itself a semiheretical notion, practiced almost exclusively by elite easterners—readers of *The New Yorker,* regulars at swank little Manhattan boîtes, and radical Jewish intellectuals.

Books and documentaries about the 1950s blithely skip over the trenchant satire of the period. In 1971 the *Village Voice* hooted, "A look back at the 1950s is enough to make one's flesh creep; what a dismal decade of cultural rubbish." Arthur Penn, the director, claimed in a TV documentary, "It was an era that was conspicuous for its dullness"—and, as if to illuminate that innate dullness, we get stock shots of Dwight D. Eisenhower, Hula-Hoops, and beach-party movies. But as Norman Podhoretz argued, "The Silent Generation was a term invented by the Leftists of the '60s." Ben Stein wrote in *Brill's Content* in a department called Media Myths: "Journalists have a lazy habit of dismissing the 1950s as a time when life was sterile, stuffy, and dull. They must have seen too many movies. The only problem with this presumption is that it is wildly, comically wrong. The 1950s were an explosive decade, especially culturally."

David Halberstam's not-quite-definitive work, *The Fifties,* mentions Mort Sahl only in passing in a couple of quips about Eisenhower and Werner von Braun, but no mention of Sid Caesar, Lenny Bruce, Nichols & May, Stan Freberg, Shelley Berman, Tom Lehrer, the Second City, or the new cutting-edge comedy they embodied. There are long sections devoted to Elvis Presley, the TV quiz-show scandals, and the Sullivan show, but nothing about the satirical revolution that was as significant as the rock-and-roll revolt that takes up a chunk of Halberstam's tome. In another book about the decade, also titled *The Fifties,* the authors write (after a polite nod to Caesar and Bruce), "In retrospect it was essentially a humorless decade," the prevailing cliché that still shrouds the period. "It was more an era of fear than fun." Oh, yeah? Tell it to the fans of Sahl,

Caesar, Lehrer, Berman, Phyllis Diller, Freberg, Nichols & May, and Steve Allen. Listen to the albums by Allen, Bruce, Sahl, Dick Gregory, and Nichols & May, and you'll know all you need to know about American life in the years 1953 through 1965.

The 1950s, far from fast asleep, helped light the way for many of the cultural eruptions that followed. The sixties had sex, drugs, rock and roll, and civil unrest, but it seems almost culturally drab compared to the fifties' artistic turmoil. Consider the following cultural rebels, with and without causes, who either began or flourished then: Charles Schulz, Elvis Presley, Allen Ginsberg, Jack Kerouac, Dave Brubeck, Miles Davis, Charlie Parker, Marlon Brando, James Dean, J. D. Salinger, Harvey Kurtzman, Paul Krassner, Rod Serling, Paddy Chayefsky, William F. Buckley, Jr., Eric Hoffer, Walt Kelly, Vance Packard, Mickey Spillane, Arthur Miller, William Inge, Tennessee Williams, Truman Capote, Norman Mailer, Jules Feiffer, Hugh Hefner, Pauline Kael, Pete Seeger, I. F. Stone, and Marilyn Monroe. Snoring fifties? There was plenty going on once you take a minute to look around. Rosa Parks boarded a bus, *Sputnik* shot into orbit, Volkswagens rolled off the assembly line, Ray Kroc reinvented the hamburger—and Mort Sahl told a joke about Joe McCarthy. It looks as if the only people snoozing in the 1950s were the historians.

Nearly every major comedian who broke through in the 1950s and early 1960s was a cultural harbinger: Sahl, of a new political cynicism; Lenny Bruce, of the sexual, pharmaceutical, and linguistic revolution (and the anything-goes nature of comedy itself); Dick Gregory, of racial unrest; Bill Cosby and Godfrey Cambridge, of racial harmony; Phyllis Diller, of housewifely complaint; Mike Nichols & Elaine May and Woody Allen, of self-analytical angst and a rearrangement of male-female relations; Stan Freberg and Bob Newhart, of the encroaching, pervasive manipulation by the advertising and public relations culture; Mel Brooks, of the Yiddishization of American comedy; Sid Caesar, of a new awareness of the satirical possibilities of TV; Joan Rivers, of the obsessive catty craving for celebrity gossip and of a latent bitchy gay sensibility; Tom Lehrer, of the inane, hypocritical (and, in Jean Shepherd's case, melancholy) nature of hallowed Americana and nostalgia, and in the instances of Allan Sherman and the Smothers Brothers, of its overly revered folk songs and folklore; Steve Allen, of the late-night talk show as a force in comedy and of the reliance on wit over verbal pratfalls; Shelley Berman, of a generation of obsessively self-confessional humor; Jonathan Winters, of the possibilities of free-form improvisational comedy and of a sardonically updated view of midwestern archetypes; and Ernie Kovacs, of surreal visual effects and the unbounded vistas of video.

Taken together, they made up the faculty of a new school of vigorous, socially aware satire, a dazzling group of voices that reigned roughly from 1953 to 1965, or from Sahl to Rivers. What follows is mainly about their work, what they did, but unavoidably also about their sometimes desperate lives. Much of their humor is as funny, fresh, and unforgettable today as the hour it was first conceived in those allegedly soporific 1950s. The decade left an indelible mark—not the least of which was caused by a revolution of laughter, a muffled explosion that occurred one night in late December 1953 in a small downstairs room in San Francisco called the hungry i. There, a swarthy twenty-seven-year-old Berkeley would-be graduate student wearing a pullover sweater and slacks—Mort Sahl, whose script was the daily newspaper—dared to say what was on his mind. Everything, as it turned out.

Sahl was the acknowledged rebel leader, the mouth that roared, even though the initial rumblings might be traced back to Sid Caesar's *Your Show of Shows* on television in 1950, or even to Caesar's debut on *The Admiral Broadway Revue* in 1949, the same year that an ambitious navy vet appeared on Arthur Godfrey's *Talent Scouts* show and performed imitations of Jimmy Cagney, Humphrey Bogart, and Edward G. Robinson—in a German accent. *That* was different. That was Lenny Bruce.

The 1950s were anything but silent in San Francisco. The city was a cultural hothouse—just as it would be a decade later, when it became the headquarters for rock, hippies, drugs, the antiwar movement, the sexual revolution, and the gay explosion; twenty years later it would be the staging area for a much smaller comedy renaissance led by Robin Williams. If San Francisco was the outpost of the fifties comedy rebellion, Sahl was the first audible sign that something funny was brewing in America. Bob Hope, Jack Benny, and Milton Berle were the comic standard-bearers at the start of the fifties. By the end of the decade, Berle was gone, Benny was old news, and Hope was racing in place, trying to keep up with the new comedians. Clearly there had been a revolt, if not a takeover.

It all started with Sahl, whose entire act, demeanor, language, look, and wardrobe warred against almost everything that had come before. Pre-Sahl was a time in which comedians, clad like band leaders in spats and tuxes, sporting cap-and-bells names like Joey, Jackie, or Jerry, announced themselves by their brash, anything-for-a-laugh, charred-earth policy and by-the-jokebook gags. Catskill refugees, they were *tummlers* and *shpritzers* incubated in resorts, supper clubs, and casinos—mainly members of the comic Jewish Mafia, whose capos included Milton Berle (the Godfather), Henny Youngman, Myron Cohen, Jack Carter, Alan King, Jack E. Leonard, Joe E. Lewis, and Joey Adams, with the occasional non-Jewish ethnic outsider—Danny Thomas, Pat Cooper, Nipsey Russell. It was an exclusive society. Few WASPs or women were allowed entrance, apart from nonthreatening curiosities like Herb Shriner and Orson Bean. The Friars Club was the meeting hall of comedy's made men.

Sahl challenged and changed all that, simply by the unheard-of comic device of being himself and speaking his mind onstage. Everything followed from him. But the Copa comics still ruled. You knew a comic was supposed to be funny if he came out, insulted the orchestra leader or a bald guy in the front row, prowled the stage, and talked about his grotesque mother-in-law, his wife's lousy cooking, or his brother-in-law's inability to hold a job. And how about these kids today! You laughed because you were supposed to laugh, had paid a ton of money, or were seeing a headliner. Not to laugh at George Jessel and Joe E. Lewis was un-American. They might be funny or they might not, but respect was automatically paid them because—well, because they were on *The Ed Sullivan Show* and were thus officially designated funny guys, even if they were plowing tired comic turf, often phoning it in.

Nonetheless, these comics had paid their dues, sweating it out for years in crummy joints ("working the toilets," they termed it), survivors of the fastest and the feistiest. There was little room for individuality, no time for an authentic personality to develop, no leeway for a comedian to traffic in social commentary. Satire was what closed on Saturday night in the thirties and forties, as George S. Kaufman famously said, but come the mid-1950s and '60s, satire was playing to sold-out houses. In small brick-walled cellars, young audiences sought a new comic's take on civil rights, not some moldy comic's made-up in-law problems.

Jules Feiffer, whose cartoons in the *Village Voice* explored the same angst-ridden terrain as Nichols & May, Bruce, and Woody Allen, told me, "If you were in your twenties back in the mid-fifties and living in an urban center, you felt generally unspoken for. If you picked up *The New Yorker,* you felt unrepresented, except perhaps by Salinger, but certainly not in the cartoons, which were for older suburban types, and played it all very safe and genteel." Feiffer was partly responsible for the "sick" label that was slapped carelessly on the humor and comedy of the era.

These rebel forces were heavily backed by Hugh Hefner, whose *Playboy* magazine and nightclub circuit made him a major comedy power broker of the time. *Playboy*'s panels and interviews showcased all the rising, new, socially relevant wits, with Hefner functioning as a kindly Medici behind the renaissance, especially of the Chicago school—Bill Cosby, Dick Gregory, Bob Newhart, Shelley Berman, Nichols & May, the Second City. Hefner provided a major monthly forum in which they could strut and expound.

Like most revolutions, the fifties' comedy overthrow began in a few obscure underground cells, intimate clubs that gave the whole experience an aura of secrecy, even subversiveness. It felt distinctly different—more inside, more personal, more dangerous—than passing through red velvet ropes into the ornate above-ground pleasure palaces. At the copious Copacabanas and lavish Latin Quarters, the plush Persian and Pump Rooms, the imperious Empire Rooms and El Moroccos, and the vast Venetian Rooms, regal Rainbow Rooms, and Royal Boxes, whose very names exuded the sound of money, you were instantly intimidated upon being ushered into a huge forbidding room—and if the room didn't scare you, the waiters would. It was a humiliating experience, usually endured only on birthdays or major anniversaries.

The hothouse rooms of the late 1950s and '60s, where this era's young comic geniuses were planted, nurtured, and bloomed, had little in common with the posh showrooms of America's comic past. These small clubs didn't start out as snug parlors for comedians but as hangouts for folksingers and beat poets. Cheap wine was served in carafes and the price for the evening was a few bucks, no cover charge. People smoked cigarettes (of various composition) and argued politics and poetry. The shock troops who waded ashore and established beachheads in the small rooms were not comedians at all, but folksingers and jazz musicians. They struck the first antiestablishment chords while the comics strummed their own themes mocking the government, suburban life, the sanctity of marriage, and every other hand-me-down value and vaunted institution. The folksingers sang about it and the comedians dissected it.

The small rooms enticed students and Korean War vets who had spent time overseas in little dens of yearned-for iniquity searching for adventure, both sexual and intellectual. The clubs that nursed the subversive satirical comics of the fifties era were dives, basements, storefronts, attics, abandoned Chinese restaurants, rat holes, and mine shafts—Mort Sahl's term for the hungry i, one of the cozier caves. While these dingy clubs were architectural disasters, they were perfect viewing perches— snug and audience-friendly, just right for comedians who had begun at college hangouts, rathskellers, coffeehouses, and jazz joints.

The clubs were cheap but real and alive. You didn't have to fold bills into a maître d's palm, and you weren't hassled by photographers, orchid sellers, and cigarette girls. San Francisco teemed with such rooms. The comic Ronnie Schell, who puts on annual hungry i reunions featuring the old hands, recalls: "Between shows at the Purple Onion, I could go out front and watch Phyllis Diller, or over to the hungry i to see Woody Allen or Mort Sahl. Sometimes I'd run up to Ann's 440 on Broadway for Lenny Bruce, hit Bimbo's to hear Shecky Greene, or slide into Fack's on Bush to see Don Rickles. San Francisco was like a revolving door for all the new comedians."

The hungry i had become by the mid-1950s the Comedy Central of its day, the main staging area of the revolutionary movement. The i was a major feeder of other rooms around the country, with performers bolstered and burnished in part by its rollicking owner, Enrico Banducci. The club with the pink-and-black sign vibrated with poetic intensity; its smoky bohemian aura suggested Sartre and Camus. Outside, on the club's exposed brick wall, the names of that night's performers were daubed in bright pastels. The hungry i got its bizarre name from a hulking ersatz beatnik named Eric (Big Daddy) Nord, a co-owner of the original club; the name actually stood for "hungry id" (not "intellectual," as many thought, due to Sahl). Why "id" was shortened to "i" and the name spelled in lowercase "was to show we weren't white bread," said Banducci.

At the hungry i, which set a style for clubs to come, you jostled and negotiated a steep flight of stairs before entering a beckoning hideout. In this charming wine cellar, the satirical uprising of the fifties and sixties was fermented. After standing in a long anxious line that often wound around the block (the sort of line now seen outside multiplex movie houses), you were marched into the room by a burly man in a beret standing behind a rope—Banducci, nightclub comedy's jaunty CEO— who dropped ticket stubs into a wine vat. Downstairs, you slid into a swayback director's chair, with glass holders built into the arms, as thick cigarette smoke formed clouds under the low ceiling. The club's fabled brick wall was a back-alley backdrop, a *Dead End* set for the raw comic unrest of the era. Every notable comedian (plus future folksinging legends, like the the Limeliters, the Weavers, and Peter, Paul & Mary) stood before that wall and got famous. What the Algonquin Round Table was to American humor in 1935, the hungry i wall was to American comedy in 1955.

The stage was viewed through a bluish haze. Then came a rumbling voice with elegant diction—the light and sound man, Alvah Bessie (he of the Hollywood Ten), announcing: "*The hungry i is very proud to present . . . the next president of the United States . . . Mort Sahl!*" Sahl was titular head of the comic new wave, and with his war cry, "*Are there any groups I haven't offended?*" he cut a swath that made nightclubs safe for political satire, rabid social commentary, and bleak and black humor.

The room also engendered a certain booster mentality among its clientele. "The audience wanted the artist to be a success, to be known; they wanted to be the first to have seen them, to be in on it," Banducci says. Grover Sales, who did publicity for the club in the sixties, notes "They'd been overseas and been exposed to a level of sophistication. They'd read Joyce and Proust and they were ready for something original, for comics who talked up to them, not down to them. No motel or mother-in-law jokes." Sales, who in the late 1960s taught classes in "The American Comedy of Dissent," adds that the i provided a new kind of outspoken antiestablishment humor: "You didn't find it in the legitimate theater, you didn't find it on TV, you didn't find it on the radio, you didn't find it in the movies. The hungry i and the spinoffs of the i were the first signs of opposition to the Cold War conformity." Stanley Eichelbaum, the former *San Francisco Examiner* critic, recalls, "There was no other place like it, not even in New York." Larry King says, "In Miami, we used to think this was some magical place."

Banducci, a former child prodigy violinist from near Bakersfield who was called "the Billy Rose of North Beach," liked to say, "I'm not in the nightclub business, I'm in show business." In his room he was director, producer, and benign dictator. A gifted musician himself, he revered talent. "I wanted to have a club that was fair to the artist—like a theater—to develop and nurture talent," he told me in 1999 at Enrico's Restaurant (upgraded from coffeehouse), where he remains a minor deity. At eighty, Banducci still plays the robust, jovial bohemian emeritus, sporting his signature bespangled black beret and sweatshirt.

A flamboyant, self-created bon vivant rebel, the twenty-seven-year-old Henry (later Enrico) Banducci had made a break from his former life as a wine salesman to take over the club from his partners. Until he met Sahl, the hungry i was just another North Beach wine and espresso bar in a converted Chinese restaurant. Later, it moved a few blocks to a cellar on Jackson Street, where beatniks gathered to hear folkniks like Stan Wilson sing Woody Guthrie songs, dine on spaghetti, and feed their starving ids. Sahl, already dubbed "the thinking man's comedian," became the i's resident id.

The first club, at 149 Columbus Avenue, was an eighty-five-seat hangout for beatniks, junkies, winos, runaway waifs, and wannabe folkies. It was in the bottom of a flatiron building later bought by Francis Ford Coppola, who turned it into an editing studio. When that hungry i closed, Banducci bought out Nord and a third partner and moved the club to its most famous address, 599 Jackson Street, just up the block, where he wangled a ten-year lease at $225 a month. (All that remains of it is a weed-strewn vacant lot; a topless club later bought the name.)

Banducci, himself a ham, became the club's greeter, schmoozer, and impresario, a Barbary Coast Barnum. The show room sat three hundred people and was described by a critic in 1953 as "a drinkery with a Bohemian air." Folksingers were the stars, relieved by earnest poetry readings. Originally, it cost $1.50 to get in. The *San Francisco Chronicle's* jazz critic, Ralph J. Gleason, called the hungry i "probably as important in the history of American entertainment as the Palace was during vaudeville." The club set a style imitated everywhere and copied to this day in the comedy clubs that are its yuppified offspring.

Decreed Banducci, "If you didn't play the i, you didn't exist." In May 1961, the *New York Times* got wind of the revolution that had begun seven years earlier and ran an article under the headline "Spawning Ground of the Offbeat"—with the cautious subhead, "Signs Indicate That New Bohemianism May Be Nascent." Howard Taubman called the hungry i "the most influential night club west of the Mississippi" and said it "expresses California's spirit of informality" and "appears to be determined to set the new style." Taubman noted that Banducci, with his pencil mustache, beret, and barrel chest, looked like "a fat cat out of Montmartre." Indeed, Banducci patterned the club, which cost him $800 to open, after the little cafés he had visited in Paris. The sign outside actually read: "Club des Artistes" and "The Left Bank of San Francisco. Dinners from $1.25." Banducci envisioned the club as part coffeehouse, part cabaret, part salon. "I think sandals and sables ought to mix here," he said. As to the decor, the brick wall seemed existential—"stark, like the Left Bank." One writer commented that the brick wall "suggests the working area of a Cuban firing squad."

Enrico once recalled, "When we opened, everyone said, 'It's not gonna work—not the right people, not the right people.'" Shelley Berman says that the people could not have been more right: "People would shift their interest from jazz to comedy, and the audience didn't mind if you fell on your ass. The most nurturing element was the attention of the audience." Banducci still believes that "the most important thing we had in the room was the quietude, the silence we maintained." The spectators sat around a three-sided stage, adding to its in-the-round intimacy. Irwin Corey remembers how Banducci would yell, "Stop the show. You noisy bunch of mothers! Give 'em back their money. Have respect for the acts or don't come back here."

Banducci terrorized hecklers. He would quickly return their money and pitch them out, bidding them adieu with, "Please don't grace us with your presence again." During a faith-healer routine by Avery Schreiber and Jack Burns, one of a pair of Canadian lumberjacks stood up and yelled, "You stupid bastard—get off that stage! Don't you take the name of the Lord in vain! You're makin' fun of God." He stood up and ripped the chair out of the floor and held it over his head, about to throw it at Burns. Enrico came down the aisle, hustled the men out of the main room, and told them, "If you're gonna fight with anyone, you'll fight with me." "The two guys went into the bar with Enrico and had a fistfight," said Schreiber. "You could hear 'em bangin' and slammin'. While we're inside doing our act, Enrico was fighting these two lumberjacks." Banducci once threw out an entire audience—a Gray Line bus tour of foreigners.

The day-to-day management of the club itself was nothing if not eccentric. Banducci and Alvah Bessie frequently fought for control of the sound-booth mike when one of them decided a comedian was faltering or simply wouldn't get offstage, as in the case of Corey, who would sometimes babble interminably until Banducci was forced to douse the lights and physically haul him offstage—which wound up as part of his act. Once, unable to endure a comic, Bessie turned to Banducci and growled, "How much longer are we expected to put up with this rampant idiocy?" Enrico once cut off a performer in trouble with a quick blackout and the announcement, "Ladies and gentleman, that concludes your show!" He put one faltering young comedian out of his misery, booming, "Thank you from the hungry i and comedian Woody Allen."

The consummate showman, Banducci was a notoriously sloppy businessman who was in serious debt more than once. Corey once reviewed the books, then fired some of Banducci's relatives (his father did the books) and took over managing the club for a while. Enrico's pal Peter Breinig recalls: "Enrico once told a bartender, 'Look, I know you're gonna steal, but can I at least have half?' " On another occasion, Banducci gave Corey a check for $2,000 that bounced, and when confronted by him and a cabaret union representative, Banducci said, "You're showing your true colors, Corey—you tried to cash the check." He sought, whenever possible, to bypass agents and deal directly with the performers, whom he could sweet-talk more easily.

Faith Winthrop, the i's house singer—who also saw checks bounce—recalls: "He was a very eccentric, passionate guy. He looked disorganized, but you could never tell what was really happening with those eyes that were always darting back and forth. He was very excessive in all of his passions. You would hear him fighting with people over the transom. They would throw crystal glasses into the fireplace." Ralph J. Gleason wrote that the hungry i seemed to be run by the Marx Brothers.

When the hungry i was no longer the mother church, it lost some of its cachet among comedians. Dick Cavett recalls that when he played the club, "The alleged sophistication was not there as far as I could see," and around 1965 he got a letter from Woody Allen saying: "Cavett—a fast note to explode the myth of the hungry i. It isn't the hip place it was when Mort Sahl was there." When, in 1968, the original room took its final labored breath—Las Vegas and television had begun to feast on Banducci's menu, and basement boîtes could no longer afford the new comics' fees—it was all over in the wink of an i.

BEYOND SAN FRANCISCO, other would-be hungry i's—intimate rooms that catered to students, professionals, and the certifiably cool—began popping up in Chicago (Mister Kelly's, the Gate of Horn, the first Playboy Club), Los Angeles (the Interlude, the Troubadour), and New York (the Bitter End, the Bon Soir, the Village Gate, the Café Wha?, the Gaslight Club, the Duplex). Here, new comics got their visas stamped, authenticating them as entertainers fit for the masses, permitting them to travel uptown to the Blue Angel, Basin Street East, *The Tonight Show,* and to TV and movie parts unknown.

The fifties club scene attracted misfits and mavericks like Fred Weintraub, a former Wharton School of Business graduate and Scarsdale baby-carriage mogul with sixty stores. He gave it all up to play piano in a Cuban whorehouse and open a club in Havana, where he ran guns for Castro's anti-Batista rebels before being deported. Weintraub returned to play piano in Greenwich Village and took over the lease of a failing Bleecker Street club called the Cock and Bull. He hung some Max Ernst Dada paintings on the walls, brought in a few chairs, and changed the name to the Bitter End. The New York version of the hungry i and the prototype Village club, it began as a coffeehouse where junkies hung out when they weren't asleep across the street in the Bleecker Street Cinema.

Weintraub is a tall, bearded, brutish guy ("I was considered a gruff teddy bear because I never took any baloney—I looked like a bouncer") who became a Hollywood producer. Even in his high-rise office in Los Angeles, the rumpled, baseball-cap-wearing Weintraub still looks the part of a shaggy Village club owner. He makes the claim that "we were the first brick wall. Banducci didn't have it that way at the beginning," even though the Bitter End opened seven years after the hungry i inaugurated the brick wall. Banducci's reply: "He's full of shit up to his ears! The hungry i had a brick wall in 1952." In comedy circles, exactly who first erected the brick wall is like a scholarly dispute among cineastes over who invented the motion-picture camera.

Unlike Banducci, Weintraub concedes, "I had no concept," but, like Banducci, he was up to his ears in folksingers. His policy, like Banducci's, was, "Anybody who was drunk or made noise, we threw 'em out." The audiences were forgiving, says Weintraub. "The audience was not there to say, 'Hey, you stink.' The Bitter End audience said, 'Hey, you're a new performer, let's hear what you have to say.' I had a rule: When audiences came out and said, 'I *hated* that act,' I'd keep it. If they said, 'I *loved* the act,' I'd keep it. If they came out and said, 'That was a nice act,' I never booked 'em again. Indifference was the worst thing."

Bitter End regulars were largely teenagers and college kids, since no liquor was served. The Café Wha? (partly owned by Weintraub), on nearby MacDougal Street, booked comics, but Weintraub calls it a tourist trap, like the Café Au Go Go. "You didn't bring an agent down to the Café Wha?," he says. "You brought him to the Bitter End. You might take him to the Duplex, but the Duplex was never on the map. The Village Gate was on the map." He says, "You know what was special about that era? Nobody was thinking about the big money. There was no talk about what was number one at the movies. It was always, 'How did the performance go? What can we do to improve it?' It was a period when everyone worked together, and performers helped each other. There were jam sessions every night after the club closed." Weintraub sold the club to his employees in the seventies and went to Los Angeles.

Art D'Lugoff, a Village character who never lived downtown but now lectures on Greenwich Village in the fifties and sixties, opened the Village Gate in 1958 as the Village Rathskeller, unsure what he had in mind. "We enjoyed it, made a living, and got laid," D'Lugoff recalls. "People would come from Brooklyn and Queens. They wanted to enrich their lives. Because of its reputation, people gravitated down to the Village musically, artistically. Midtown had nothing like it, and there was a tradition of coffee shops from the old country. The area was ripe for something to happen culturally. Folk music was self-contained; there was not a big expensive group to pay. The business could support itself."

D'Lugoff makes no grand claims to having discovered anyone. In his kitchen on New York's Upper West Side, munching on a banana muffin, the aging guru remarks: "They say Art D'Lugoff or Max Gordon 'discovered' someone. Ninety-nine percent of the people 'discovered' are not discovered. What happens is, they go through a whole series of jobs and eventually, when they pay their dues, at some point, maybe after two years, people realize that this guy is terrific. It's more gradual; it builds up. The biggest thrill is taking a really good talent and moving it along." D'Lugoff had to cope with stars who outgrew the room, falling prey to "greedy managers." Clubs no longer have that kind of star-making power. "In those days, a club was a crucial point for any artist. Now, you can pay your dues in different ways, but comics then were much better trained and had more opportunities to work at the lower level before they made it."

A few Village clubs were mob-run, but Jan Wallman kept her joint, the Duplex, clean. "I was approached a couple of times and I turned them down," she says. James Gavin, the New York cabaret historian, writes that the Duplex had "an erotic environment," a code term for gay. There was no cover charge, and the two-drink minimum would run you about $1.50. Comics were paid fifty dollars a week. Wallman took a chance on wannabe comedians like a middle-aged hack named Rodney Dangerfield, who was making a second run at stardom after years of selling aluminum siding under his original name, Jacob Cohen. Wallman booked performers she liked if she thought they had potential, even if they didn't draw. "It was a labor of love and I really loved it. It was a party every night."

For cave-dwelling agents like Jack Rollins and Charles Joffe, the wizards of the comedy renaissance, a club like the Duplex was the ideal petri dish in which to breed new comics. Woody Allen said, "At the Duplex they put on *anyone* who's not a catastrophe. Twelve people [in the audience] was a big night." Jack Rollins differentiated between the gifted and the needy, between serious talent and, says his longtime partner, "those who are out there looking for love, what Jack called the 'desperados,' making ungainly fools of themselves in a frantic attempt to become loved and popular. Jack refused to handle them and they wondered why and he couldn't tell them why."

The duo would slip into a club like the Duplex and sit in the back so as not to unnerve performers. "Nobody would handle these people in the beginning," Joffe says. "We didn't hand-hold, nor would our clients expect us to. We were always very honest with them. None of us were in the business for the money. Jack used to say 'funny is money'—it's been stolen many times, but he originated it." Joffe adds, "Jack was insightful beyond belief. He could spot these talents in a flash and knew how to speak to them so they would hear him."

Lawrence Christon, the former *Los Angeles Times* critic who patrolled the comedy beat from 1970 to 1995, says Rollins and Joffe "had a great sense of the integrity of those performers. People think of comedy as a light, trivial thing. They realized that a comedian was a discrete entity and every bit as worthy an artist as a soloist at the Philharmonic, and that you had to have a mind there, a creative capacity." Joffe says that the agency never took on two similar comics at the same time, never solicited acts, never had contracts, and never handled more than ten clients at a time. One hopeful comic, Marshall Jacobs, remembers that when he talked his way into Rollins's office, the agent told him that he needed to find a comic persona—"and he was right." Jacobs recalls the mood of their celebrated office: "Woody Allen was in the next room with several guys in suits and it felt like a board meeting of General Motors."

Despite their allegiance to comedy as an ideal in itself, Rollins and Joffe were hard-nosed businessmen. As Wallman recalls: "They used me for their own reasons. They would try out people and then pull Joan Rivers or whoever out of the club on weekends to play bigger gigs. And people would come in from Westchester to hear her after seeing her on the Jack Paar show. I was beginning to get these bridge-and-tunnel types, not just a local crowd. Before that, people came in not to see names but because the *club* had a reputation for having interesting new acts." By the mid-sixties, clubs like the Duplex had lost their cool cachet.

NEW-WAVE COMEDY ALSO SEEPED into the national consciousness via the long-playing record, which first went on the market in 1948 and allowed a comedian's act to be taken home and replayed like an original cast album. The phenomenon called the "comedy album" was a new form that made overnight stars of Berman, Newhart, Lehrer, Mel Brooks, Nichols & May, David Frye, Allan Sherman, Vaughn Meader, and Stan Freberg. Freberg really kicked off the whole trend in 1951 with his recorded soap-opera parody "John and Marsha." Before that, there were only "party records," code for the blue material of raunchy outlaw comics like Belle Barth, Rusty Warren, and Redd Foxx.

Local disc jockeys were then just coming into their own while network radio faded. Many, as relief from playing too much Frankie Laine and Joni James, began spinning albums by unknown young comics, soon unknown no more. The airplay gave the renaissance comedians an electronic comedy circuit, and advance publicity when they went on tour. These newly bright, literate comedy records leaped the generation gap and were the last time that virtually all Americans enjoyed a shared sense of humor; everyone quickly was innoculated by the LP needle.

Both teenagers and parents laughed at Newhart's driving-instructor routine, at Mike Nichols's frantic tangle with a stubborn telephone operator who refused to return his dime, at Berman's fear of flying. If you happened to drop into the conversation a snippet of "*Sarah Jackman, Sarah Jackman, how's by you?*" or muttered, "*We booked him on a 402—overacting,*" everyone knew you were quoting Sherman's "Frère Jacques" parody and Freberg's *Dragnet* takeoff. The records also produced catch phrases, like Freberg's "*Turn off the bubble machine!*" (from his Lawrence Welk parody), Berman's "*Coffee, tea, or milk?*" (soon part of the language), Mike Nichols's "*I would respect you like crazy!*" (from his and Elaine May's necking-teenagers sketch), Steve Allen's standbys ("*Shmock-shmock!*" "*How's your fern?*"), and Joan Rivers's sharp elbow in the ribs ("*Can we talk?*").

The comics of the fifties made comedy records both respectable and trendy. You played them for friends, family, and roommates, memorized entire segments and song snatches—especially the really daring parts, like Tom Lehrer's deliciously rude "Vatican Rag," or the cut on a Nichols

& May album where a pair of passionate, pretentious pillow-talkers philosophize in bed, impressing each other with their sensitivity. Because of comedy records, the new comics got into our heads and became more a part of our lives than comedians had been since the demise of network-radio comedy shows, no longer walled off in nightclubs and on television. "People would buy a record and get some pizza and beer and all sit around and listen to Mike and Elaine," recalls Bob Newhart, whose *Button-Down Mind* LP soon became one of those very records. "The nightclub comedians of that time were all doing jokes anyone could deliver," he observes. "They didn't belong to anybody. Then along came this other kind of humor that had its own stamp. People would say, 'Oh, that sounds like a Nichols and May routine, or a Shelley Berman routine, or a Bob Newhart routine, or Jonny Winters, or Lenny Bruce.'" If a comic tried to steal a Newhart routine, he would instantly be a marked man.

Allan Sherman was hacking away in the lower echelons of TV as a game-show producer when he cut an album of song parodies that he had long performed for fun at parties. The album's instant success typified the comedy-album fad of the early 1960s—"People wanted to be the first on their block to have it," Sherman said. "They wanted to be the first to play it for friends, and they wanted to see their friends' faces when *they* heard it for the first time." But it was his 1963 hit "Hello, Muddah, Hello, Fadduh"—included in his third album, *My Son, the Nut*—that assured his immortality.

No money was spent to promote the first album, but it had a whirlwind word of mouth—first within the immediate showbiz family and then among the general public. Sam Goody's in New York had to limit sales of the album to twelve per customer. The LP's very title, *My Son, the Folksinger,* became a media catchphrase (a play on boastful Jewish mothers who *kvell,* "My son, the *doctor . . .*"): *Time* did a story on Rose Kennedy headlined "My Son, the President"; El Al Airlines ran an ad with the line "My Son, the Pilot." A Ph.D. thesis at the time postulated that its success was due to Americans' deep secret wish to be Jewish. Mused Sherman, "Won't that be news to the New York Athletic Club?" A critic wrote that Sherman "blows a large, loud, and wonderfully resonant Bronx cheer at a very self-conscious and conformist aspect of American taste."

As much as Harry Golden or Philip Roth, Sherman helped Yiddishize America. His 1962 album *My Son, the Folksinger* launched his career as a master parodist of traditional songs, to which he devised ingenious new lyrics, nearly all Jewish-flavored. The album sold half a million copies in four weeks, and eventually a million and a half copies.

At a time when Catskill comics like Sam Levenson, Myron Cohen, and Jackie Mason were timidly wading into the mainstream, roly-poly Allan Sherman jumped into the river with a resounding bellyflop. He looked like a greeter at the Carnegie Deli, a squat, blinky little guy in horn-rim glasses with bulging chipmunk cheeks, warbling, in his ground-glass baritone, "Shake Hands with Your Uncle Moe" (to "McNamara's Band") and "Glory, Glory, Harry Lewis" ("Glory, Glory, Hallelujah!"). The song titles were funny just in themselves—"You Went the Wrong Way, Old King Louie" (from "You've Come a Long Way from St. Louis"), "Shine On, Harvey Bloom" ("Shine On, Harvest Moon"), and "Bye, Bye, Bloomberg" ("Bye, Bye, Blackbird").

Despite the Jewish content in his lyrics, Sherman resisted being branded a "Jewish" performer, as his repertoire played to everyone. All the transcendent fragments that made mid-twentieth-century Jewish family life funny—seltzer, pastrami, matzo balls, the garment trades, phrases like "How's by you?"—were hilariously exploited by Sherman, but he didn't leave things at that, which would have kept him a parochial favorite. He artfully attached his songs to sixties fads—Geritol, Vic Tanny, Sylvia Porter, Bo Belinsky, the Peace Corps, Mitch Miller, the Twist, David Susskind, green stamps, and charge-a-plates. His lyrics spread a generous helping of chopped liver over a slice of American cheese. The playful lyrics were a kick, but they also made fun of Jewish (and, by extension, all) middle-class American life in the early 1960s.

Mainly he seized on the era's folk-song mania. "There must be a deep-seated resentment of folk songs," he concluded. "I always thought folk songs were silly, but I didn't know everyone agreed with me." (Tom Lehrer and the Smothers Brothers made the same discovery.) It helped that most of the folk songs he parodied were in the public domain. When he turned "There Is Nothing Like a Dame" into a hilarious spread of cold cuts ("*We got herring sweet and sour, / We got pickles old and young, / We got corned beef and salami and a lot of tasty tongue, / We got Philadelphia cream cheese in a little wooden box. / What ain't we got? / We ain't got lox!*"), the dour composer Richard Rodgers, with all the humor of a smoked herring, refused to let it be released, snarling, "Allan Sherman is a destroyer."

On an audition reel for Warner Bros. Records made in July 1962, he recorded some revised show tunes from *My Fair Lady* and other musicals—"How Are Things with Uncle Morris?" "Get Me to the Temple on Time," "With a Little Bit of Lox," "Walk on Through the Bronx," and "Seventy-six Sol Cohens" ("*Seventy-six Sol Cohens in the country club,/And a hundred and ten nice men named Levine*"). He had planned an album devoted to show-tune parodies, but couldn't get permission from spoilsports like Rodgers and Meredith Willson.

Many funny elements were at work: you laughed at his improbable recasting of folk songs in Jewish terms; you laughed at the unexpected rhymes, puns, and switches; you laughed at his raspy crooning; and, not least of all, you laughed at the little stories in each lyric. Much of the pleasure was in his inspired plays on the original titles ("Gimme Jack Cohen and I Don't Care," "Won't You Come Home, Disraeli"), but his most inspired, unsurpassable line, in "Glory, Glory, Harry Lewis," a patriotic hymn to a velvet cutter who works for a curtain maker named Roth, reads: "*He was trampling through the warehouse/Where the drapes of Roth are stored./His cloth is shining on!*" Sherman raised the pun and the parody song to witty new heights with "*God rest ye, Jerry Mandelbaum*"; "*Jascha got the bottle of Geritol*"; "*I'm Melvin Rose of Texas*"; and "*Catskill ladies sing this song,/Hoo-hah, hoo-hah,/Sittin' on the front porch playin' mah-jongg/All the hoo-hah day.*" Not to mention this delicatessen ode—"*Do not make a stingy sandwich;/Pile the cold cuts high!/Customers should see salami/Comin' through the rye.*"

Sherman was as unlikely a star as ever was born overnight—a sweet accident, really. Mike Maitland, the head of Warner Bros. Records, made the pragmatic but prescient suggestion that Sherman should parody only folk songs in the public domain and forgo copyrighted pop tunes, a permissions nightmare. A year later, in October 1962, he had gone from the unemployment line to $15,000 a night after *My Son, the Folksinger* became the fastest-selling album in the history of Warner Bros. Records. In two months, half the country was heard singing the silly little ditty about a Jewish kid kvetching at summer camp, written to the singsong melody of "The Dance of the Hours" (from Ponchielli's opera *La Giaconda*), not to mention "*Sarah Jackman, Sarah Jackman, how's by you? How's by you?/How's your brother Bernie? He's a big attorney/How's your sister Rita? A regular Lolita/She's nice, too, she's nice, too . . .*" As he later recalled, "For a few weeks there, I was like the Beatles."

The public brought a new proprietary sense to comics like Sherman. You felt as if you had made a personal discovery and that nobody could possibly dig Steve Allen, Nichols & May, or Tom Lehrer as much as you did. This new comic snobbery certified you as smart enough to grasp all the cultural totems. The new comedians weren't too risqué for TV but were deemed too sophisticated for home viewing. They were permitted on TV only after they had sold hundreds of thousands of records, a way to prescreen new comics feared to be too smart or too inside for the masses. In those so-called golden days, George Gobel, Orson Bean, and Wally Cox were considered cutting-edge comics. All of that changed once Steve Allen took over *The Tonight Show* and introduced bright new comics like himself on late-night TV. He showcased riskier, friskier comedians not yet ready for prime time. Most of the era's groundbreaking comics, who were satirical and critical at a time when TV was at its most banal, had to make their mark in hit-and-run attacks on record albums, late-night talk shows, and the few risk-taking variety shows—Allen's show, *That Was the Week That Was, The Smothers Brother Comedy Hour.* As Sahl was quick to learn, "There's this continuous business of 'They won't get it, you can't do this.' "

Ed Sullivan still ruled, and a comedian was consigned to showbiz oblivion if he didn't turn up on Sullivan's show. As Carol Burnett once put it, "Ed Sullivan was America's taste. When Ed put his arm around you and pulled you over, and said, 'She's a really funny little lady,' America said, 'She's a really funny little lady.' " Sullivan made life both viable and miserable for comics. "He was very vindictive," said Alan King, a Sullivan regular who helped prescreen comics for the show.

Sullivan's comics had all proven themselves elsewhere, but each still had to please the famously square Sullivan, guardian of Sunday nights and gatekeeper of fifties show business. Henny Youngman was banned for five years when he objected to Sullivan cutting some of his jokes. Sullivan supposedly sent Jackie Mason wandering nearly twenty years in the comic wilderness for allegedly flipping him the bird during his act when Sullivan indicated, off-camera, that Mason had only a minute left. The New York gossip columnist took a sharp editor's pencil to comics' acts—sometimes helpfully, says Shelley Berman. But Sullivan's idea of what was funny was considerably to the right of Steve Allen, the anti-Sullivan of the day. Later, Jack Paar and Johnny Carson gave new comics life-changing boosts just by allowing them on their shows, but Allen took the first chances. By the time Carson gained national power, it was rare to find an *older* comic on *The Tonight Show.*

These new comics had something to say, a new slant on American life, and most were ruthlessly honest about themselves. Older comics—the

Berles, Jack Carters, and Morey Amsterdams—had little to say about society, much less about their own real lives. They were, in the purest sense, entertainers who had no public worldview; they presumed the world wasn't interested. They were efficient but anonymous joke merchants. As Joan Rivers observed in the seventies, "Audiences nowadays want to *know* their comedian. Can you please tell me one thing about Bob Hope? If you only listened to his material, would you *know* the man? His comedy is another America, an America that is not coming back."

Of course, we had howled at earlier comedians without knowing the comics' true selves, and no one cared, but all that had changed. The new-wave comedy "came from the bones," as comics say; it was organic to the comedian, not just a generic collection of secondhand gags. Many of the old-wave comics had emerged from "the mountains" (the Catskills in New York, the Poconos in Pennsylvania), where survival was everything. Comics of the 1940s were toreadors who either subdued the beast before a laugh-thirsty throng or died a humiliating death. Hence, the life-or-death jargon of stand-up—"I killed"; "I bombed"; "He died"; "You murdered 'em." There was no room for the insecure or the intellectual. Even after he had succeeded elsewhere, Woody Allen played the Catskills and laid a large nonkosher egg. However primitive, these earlier comics earned every dollar and laugh.

TEMPTING AS IT MAY BE to ridicule the comedians of America's postwar pre-renaissance as dinosaurs, they ruled their world absolutely, and gave the next generation of comics something to revolt against. The comics of that era—of whom Jan Murray, Jack Carter, Shecky Greene, and Alan King are major living examples—had no interest in changing society. They weren't rebels. They were jovial go-along get-along guys whose mandate was to amuse; survival was their foremost worry, not social commentary.

Most of them had scratched their way up from tank-town dives to modest respectability as journeyman performers earning a decent living. They were comic craftsmen. Comedy then was a trade, not a calling. Comics were skillful and resourceful joke-tellers, spielers, showbiz brawlers. The aim was to create hilarity, not humor, much less wit. Jokes were only one piece of the craft. They were not always innately funny, but they acted funny. They were one-liner salesmen, guffaw-dealers, joke-brokers. Comics purchased "material" like it was wholesale piece goods; a joke was a cheap and reusable commodity, easily bought and sold, not a worldview or a political stance. Comics were brokered like sow bellies and soybeans by agents working the phones, persistent Broadway Danny Roses who peddled comics with undimmed passion.

Those comics and their cohorts (the Freddie Romans, Norm Crosbys, Marty Allens, Jackie Mileses, Jackie Gayles, Gary Mortons, Jerry Lesters, Jackie Kahanes, Dick Capris, et al.) had to get your attention in any way possible. Most nightclub, casino, and resort comics were minor players in a larger carnival that featured chorus girls, singers, a dance band, and a conductor-emcee. To grab your ear, they needed to make a racket, verbal and visual. Nightclubbers went out to laugh, and few were fussy about who they laughed at. One comedian was not that different from another, in style or approach—much like today.

There was an explicit resistance among the renaissance comics to their forefathers' coin of the realm—the common gag. "*Good evening, ladies and gentlemen! But why should I call you ladies and gentlemen—you know what you are. But seriously, folks, on behalf of the Copacabana—and believe me, I'd love to be half of the Copacabana . . . I just want to [belches]—I don't remember eating that. But I feel good tonight. I just came over from Lindy's. I always go there for a cup of coffee and an overcoat. All right, these are the jokes. What is this, an audience or an oil painting? Looks like a staring contest out there.*" By the sixties, even the word *joke* had a negative connotation. What separates a joke from a funny insight is often a thin, blurry line. If a joke emerges from a narrative, a situation, or a scene, it assumes a new stature. The hallowed pre-renaissance comics—Youngman, Leonard, Berle, Carter—told smart, clever jokes, but they were more nakedly jokes, unembellished by anecdote, context, or characterization. Mort Sahl told jokes, but they were shrewd, unpredictable, insightful, and informed jokes.

That earlier, brassier breed of Catskill comics was more than the sum of its in-law jokes. They were full-service entertainers, able to sing and dance and do impressions along with the jokes. They clowned, wore funny hats and wigs, and mixed it up with the audience. Arnie Kogen, who wrote for many Catskill comics before moving to TV, remembers driving up to the mountains with comics and working on routines in the car when the cutting-edge crowd arrived on the scene. "The Catskill comics greatly resented the new wave," he says. "They resented the Sahls, the Newharts, the Bermans, who were getting screams, and all of a sudden, what's going on? Some of the older comics might have wanted to change, but some were not capable of changing—they had their own style, they were locked in."

Freddie Roman and Mal Z. Lawrence are typical journeyman Catskill comedians still working there regularly who survived the onslaught of the sixties new-wave comics. Roman contends he felt no rivalry toward the cutting-edge sixties comics: "It never entered my mind that they were competitors, because they were less commercial than we were. We were out there punchin' and makin' a living, so I never felt jealous at all. I *might* have felt threatened, because that's what they were buying on television as opposed to our kind of stand-up."

Mal Z. Lawrence started in the Catskills in 1955 at the Sunrise Manor, as a *tummler*/lifeguard. Like Roman, he wears the label "Catskill comic" as a badge of honor. "Actually, stand-up was defined in the Catskills," he says. The comics who did well in the Catskills "worked big," as Lawrence puts it, using their hands and bodies. "Mort Sahl never moved off a pin spot. Shelley Berman sat on a chair his whole career. You gotta be able to entertain the people—they were tryin' to *inform* the people. They were talkin' down to the people almost. They were good in the coffeehouses, the small rooms, eighty, ninety people. They could see you, so you could be that subtle. You don't see these guys in Las Vegas." Lawrence calls sixties comics "small-room comedians who fell flat on their face" in big-show rooms. "That kind of quiet, little talking humor is not gonna go over. Sahl and Berman used a lot of words because they had to explain things to people who didn't read the paper that day."

Mainstream comics like Joey Bishop scoffed at the likes of Bruce, Sahl, and Berman, telling *Time* magazine, "Those guys tried their hardest to make it our way; when they couldn't, they switched." Joey Adams agreed: "They all act like big nonconformists, but they're all aiming to get on the Ed Sullivan show." The ex-comic Howard Storm recalls that many older comics sneered at the young Woody Allen. "They hated him because he was funny. They resented him because he couldn't perform."

While the older comics were less intellectual, perceptive, or enlightening than later comics, they were fearless *performers* who could hold an audience through sheer dynamic force of personality and technique. "The screamers, the fighters, the pushers had to overcome rough circumstances," says Jackie Mason, citing people like Shecky Greene and Don Rickles, who would come onstage and take over the audience. The new comics are great on TV, he points out, but are unable to command the stage and project a persona—"He's a hit for five minutes with the bit he did on *The Tonight Show,* and for forty minutes he's floundering."

Out of this rigid pre-Sahl comic mold came the "monologuists," joke-tellers who told stories, not isolated one-size-fits-all gags. People like Danny Thomas, Sam Levenson, Myron Cohen, Wally Cox, and a soft-spoken comedienne named Jean Carroll were gentler souls, the over-looked pioneers of the new and more personalized comedy of the fifties and sixties. These understated storytellers took longer to unravel their routines. They were more folklorists than jokesters, creating characters and scenes, kissing cousins of America's humorists, with a distinct point of view. Myron Cohen, in his hushed, controlled voice, peering out through one sly, half-opened eye, told classic tales about "the sweet little Jewish ladies" on their patio chairs in Miami Beach; Levenson, a pickle-barrel philosopher, re-created stories of his former Lower East Side home life steeped in schmaltz; Thomas gave up entirely on jokes and retreated to homespun homilies about his Lebanese family.

As Thomas explained his tactic: "The secret is to get them to listen. With the old-style comics, if you missed a joke or two, three more would be along instantly, but if you missed part of a *story,* you might miss a cru-cial segment and not get the payoff." Thomas and others like him were cannier than they realized. These quieter, more cerebral, personal, often socially aware comedians helped create a new, civilized environment for the wild band of revolutionaries who were slowly gathering on the hori-zon just over the mountains.

Jan Murray, a longtime mountaineer, reflects on all the comic styles he lived through: "The amazing part of comedy is that every era, as it dies, people bemoan it. 'Oh, these new comics aren't like those guys! These guys aren't good like them.' But it's wrong, because every genera-tion breeds its own generation that talks to that generation. You address your generation." Murray never felt threatened by the onslaught of hip, cerebral comics. "What do you mean by hip? We all were hip. *I* was hip. Hey, there's always envy in every line. I'm sure there are guys working in the clubs now who think they're funnier than Seinfeld. Nah, you don't think 'fear' or 'new wave.' You don't dissect it like that. You're in the vor-tex, you're in the middle of it. You do what you do. You survive."

Jack Carter was, in many ways, the definitive comedian of the 1950s. He's what you think of when you think of a comic of that era—brash, fast, invincible, and a little scary. "I have to crush an audience or I'm not happy," he said. "I swarm all over 'em, I give them forty jokes instead of four." Ronald L. Smith writes that Carter would "hand-grenade and strafe the audience with gags and mimicry until they were helpless: instant comic annihilation." On *The All-Star Revue,* which ran from 1951 to '53, Carter was a nonstop robotic funnyman—popping his eyes, delivering puns and one-liners, taking part in sketches, dancing, singing, always moving. Although Carter is only half remembered now, in his circle he remains a daunting presence. In his day there was no more fearless comedian.

Russ Merritt, who teaches film at the University of California at Berkeley, can't forget seeing Carter at New York's Latin Quarter in 1958, when Merritt had to be smuggled into the club by an older pal. "The audience definitely was not there for Carter," he recalls. "They were there, as I was, for the showgirls. Carter was totally undisturbed by all that. He was just like a knife through water. He came out in a hospital gown and did a kind of pre-Twist twist as the gown rode up higher and higher on his legs. To me at that time his jokes seemed pretty racy."

Carter recalls the scene: "The Copa was a tough room. The Murderers Row would come in every show. People eating, gangsters coming in with their broads. The garment center sent their guys—cloak and suiters who knew all the jokes. You had to be ahead of 'em. You had to be smart and brilliant." He doesn't feel his style was obliterated by the sixties comics. "You're sayin' we're dead, we're dinosaurs, but our kind of comedy never went away. Wherever I go I kill audiences."

His response to the new-wave satirical comics is a shrug. "They were good, they were interesting. It was okay. It didn't kill me. They did recordings mostly. It was *recorded* comedy. Everyone said, 'Why don't you record your act?' But I said, 'Me you've got to see. I'm very vital. You have to see me move.' I do a lot of physical humor. It can't be put on tape. The new wave was reciting, really just reading monologues. You could almost read it and laugh, those Newhart things."

Shecky Greene—his very name is so identified with stand-up comedy that an Internet newsletter about the world of stand-up is named *Shecky!*—has pretty much done and seen it all. Like Murray and Carter, little surprises or impresses him—certainly not the socially aware comics who came up with him in the fifties and sixties. "I was very fond of Mort Sahl, but I never laughed. I was never into social satire. I just said, 'That's good, that's good, that's good.' Berman and Newhart never made me laugh. Nichols & May, I would sit there and love 'em to death, but they would not make me guffaw. I would say, 'Wonderful, clever, clever, clever, wonderful.' But Shemp Howard of the Three Stooges going 'Nyuck, nyuck, nyuck'—*that* would make me laugh."

Shecky says he wasn't threatened by the satirical comedy that overtook the older-style comics. "I don't know why anyone is fearful of anyone else. Buddy [Hackett] I knew had a fear about new comedians. Buddy got crazy with Lenny Bruce's success." A case could be made that Shecky Greene, winging it, was as much of an improvisational comic as Bruce or Winters. They just had different agendas. Greene never wanted to change the world or make social observations; he just wanted to give people a good time. "I'd go onstage at the Riviera and never know *what* I was gonna do. I never even had a structure. Sometimes I was sensational, and sometimes I went right in the toilet. The saving grace was that I could sing or do impressions. If I felt I was going into the toilet, I would do an impression." Greene also refuses to wax nostalgic: "People say to me, 'You guys were better in the old days.' *Fuck* the old days! There's no such *thing* as the old days."

Alan King was a contemporary of the satirical renaissance comics of the fifties and sixties, but he wasn't one of them. With his bravura style, waggling cigar, and in-your-face jokes, he performed in the slam-bam manner of the traditional Catskills-Vegas-Miami stand-up comedian. "If a sawed-off shotgun could talk," wrote theater critic Kenneth Tynan, "it would sound like Alan King." When his traditional joke-packed act changed, and he began doing more leisurely, personal material, he became a bridge between the old school of the forties and fifties and the more incisive comics who followed. King was a cranky, conversational comic (one of the first "observational" comics), attired in the slick, silk-tux persona of a cocky Copacabana sharpie.

King played the Catskills while still a child, a fifteen-year-old *tummler* who looked much older. "When I was a kid, my hero was Milton Berle." Every nightclub comic then was a variation of Berle, and King learned the art of comedy and of creative theft. "Great comics—Jackie Miles, Jan Murray, Phil Foster—worked the Catskills, and I soaked them up," he says in his memoirs. "I stole from everyone. I did Milton Berle's act, and Jerry Lester's, I did Danny Kaye." King recalls, "At the Copa, the audience was impressed that you were even *there*. I'd been taught that if they don't like one gag, go to the next. It was all 'But seriously, folks,' and then you'd fill in the holes, do a joke, do a cough, do *something*, because you had to keep going. If you're dying, talk louder and faster." Dying was sometimes an actual possibility in Mafia-run clubs. Howard Storm recalls: "I worked a club in Youngstown, Ohio, owned by the Mafia, and one night a guy ran through the club and shot a gun in the place and I ran out and I asked the owner, a guy named Shakey Naples, what was goin' on, and he looked at me and he said, 'Hey, is he shootin' at you?' 'No.' 'Well, then get back onstage and do your act.' "

After the war, King had a life-changing experience: "I saw a personalized storyteller, Danny Thomas, at the 5100 Club in Chicago, and I saw that this was where it was going. Comedy then wasn't just joke-joke-joke; and it was also third-person. Danny Thomas said, '*I* came home last night,' '*I* was in a bar,' '*My* wife . . .' It became personal humor, and audiences began to identify with it because we were living in a more personal time. It was I-I-I. Thomas told stories about his family, in dialect, and there was no sense of hurry. We were watching somebody in complete control of what he was doing and in complete control of his audience. When I saw Danny Thomas, I knew what I had to do." King abandoned the "My wife is so cheap . . ." one-liners, songs, and impressions to focus on the irritations of modern domestic life.

King's act, unlike the acts of many of his peers, changed with the times. A *Saturday Evening Post* writer called him an "anti-sacred cow," and another scribe tagged him an "angry young comedian." One writer called King the Lenny Bruce of the middle class. "I did not offend people; I offended institutions," said King. "I became not just more topical but more angry. My topicality came from anger—from the telephone company screwing you, or from not being able to get a doctor in the middle of the night. All my personal frustrations were put into my act." He gleefully zinged the AMA and doctors generally, a fairly hostile position in 1963.

King's attack was hard-edged, though his satire was blunter than Sahl's, Berman's, or Newhart's, couched in the old nightclub format he had long practiced. "It was an entirely different approach. Mort Sahl made observations about Eisenhower. My observations came out of the fact that I was upset that the airlines were losing your luggage, or with the telephone company when they started with area codes."

He goes on: "The humanity was going out of our society, and people identified with my anger. I was considered quite controversial. I had a series of lawsuits that *Time* magazine covered—Allstate Insurance, Eastern Airlines. The airlines that sued me—Pan Am, Eastern—are all out of business a long time. And I'm still telling jokes." In 1965 *Newsweek* called him "a bemused victim of commercial society, a middleman of middle-class angst." He doesn't recall ever feeling a rivalry with the new-wave comedians. "If there was anything, I never felt it was threatened. I had enough balls." Like many comics of that time, King didn't burst on the scene overnight with a record album ("You know how smart I was? I said, 'I'm not giving my act away for a dollar ninety-five' ") or a TV shot with Jack Paar. He says, "I was very lucky. I was never 'discovered.' I was ongoing. I just evolved."

Jack Rollins observes: "The big comics [like Jack Carter, Phil Foster, Jack E. Leonard] were stand-up Jewish New York comics, and they were a powerful lot within their contained area. They were good and funny and effective. But if you took them west of the Hudson, you were in trouble. They weren't universal—and television required universality." Sid Caesar's comedy dominion dwindled once mainstream America began buying TV sets and the networks declared that hip satirical humor was beyond the grasp of The People.

INDEED, CAESAR'S SPUTTERING CAREER was a cautionary tale for what was to befall some of the renaissance comedians who came along after him. The life span of too many of these comics was similarly brief and short-circuited. Many later led tortured lives. Like Caesar, several of the great satirists of that era self-destructed. Others, like Lehrer and Gregory, went into self-imposed exile. Sahl went over the edge when he became embroiled in the investigation of the Kennedy assassination, losing his comic distance. His incomparable career peaked in the early sixties, and by the end of that decade he was blacklisted, without a platform.

Lenny Bruce's woeful tale is, like Sahl's, a mixture of genuine injustices, self-destruction, and a mighty ego verging on a savior complex. Sahl would jokingly say that if he had to model himself after somebody, it might as well be God, while Bruce saw himself as a Jesus figure nailed to the cross of hypocrisy. If Bruce and Sahl had pursued the enemy with only their sharp satirical lances, they might have survived their own crusades (and those mounted against them). But something in their dogged natures refused. They felt wronged—by the police, by the public, by politicians, by the press—and were determined to fix things or die trying. In the end, they won the war (overturned court rulings for Bruce, public-opinion reversals on a conspiracy behind JFK's assassination for

Sahl) but lost their careers. They took their mission seriously but took themselves overseriously. Both were laid low at the peak of astonishing successes.

There were other swift rises and falls. Shelley Berman's career blew up on him after a 1963 TV documentary showed him throwing a volcanic backstage tantrum after a phone rang offstage during a dramatic moment in his act. Jonathan Winters had a more highly publicized collapse when, during an engagement at the hungry i in 1959, he was arrested for "bizarre behavior" aboard a ship at Fisherman's Wharf. Partly because of his loopy onstage persona, Winters was perceived by directors and producers as erratic and out of control, a perception that shadowed and shortened his film and TV careers. Master political impressionist David Frye imploded one night onstage, and, because of rumored drinking problems, faded as dramatically as his onstage alter ego, Richard Nixon. Will Jordan, with Frye the other groundbreaking mimic of the era, best known for offbeat impressions of Ed Sullivan, somehow lost his comic traction and vanished, as did Vaughn Meader, whose career fell silent along with his most famous voice, John Kennedy.

Godfrey Cambridge and Allan Sherman each had severe weight, health, and emotional problems that led to their deaths. Ernie Kovacs was another early fatality, but not due to booze, broads, or obesity: he died in an auto accident that cut down one of TV's few acknowledged comic geniuses. Even years before his death, however, he had left TV, an embattled satirist, cast aside by network executives who couldn't figure him out. Jean Shepherd, the rebel radio satirist, was fired in mid-career and slowly sank into rancor.

Only a handful of satirical comics survived in television, a medium not known for playing to the box seats. Steve Allen, one of its swiftest and most convivial comic minds, hung on the longest, until his more serious interests lured him away. For Allen, TV always seemed less of a calling than a lark. The Smothers Brothers, unaccustomed to being hassled for their gentle needling of folk songs in clubs, were chased off TV after three seasons, following one of TV's most lurid political fights.

Most of the renaissance comics like Winters and Sahl and Berman were too big, too brash, or, in many cases, too Jewish and too cutting-edge to earn a sitcom or a variety show in those days of white-bread TV, but they opened up television from the fringes. The networks tried to devise shows for several of the satirical comedians, but none clicked.

The only major TV show—aside from the fairly flashy but short-lived

Smothers Brothers fling—to make a serious attempt at satire on a weekly basis was *That Was the Week That Was,* a British import presided over by the unfunny David Frost. It arrived in 1964 and lasted only a couple of shaky seasons in the United States before being overtaken in 1967 by the more videogenic and giddy *Laugh-In.* Along with Caesar's shows and *The Smothers Brothers Comedy Hour,* that was about it for satire on mainstream TV.

The late-night TV talk shows, however, nurtured the stand-up revolution, as did the afternoon gabfests hosted by Merv Griffin and Mike Douglas, showcases for the new wave. A few maverick comics were badly battered by the time they reached TV as stand-ups, notably Bruce. Comics like George Carlin and Richard Pryor had to redesign themselves away from television before succeeding on the tube in cable, where Carlin became TV's more palatable Lenny Bruce, a groovy seventies guy with newly acquired hippie credentials—beard, ponytail, Levis, T-shirt, vest, and a profane street rap. (As a young comic, he had even once been arrested in a Bruce bust for mouthing off to a cop.)

Probably it was all too funny to last. "Eventually," says Steve Martin, "you just wear out as a stand-up." When it wasn't fun anymore, Tom Lehrer, who hated performing his comic songs, calmly retired on his own terms and returned to teaching math at Harvard and MIT. Dick Gregory gave up full-time comedy for political activism, first in civil rights and then as a health-food advocate. Freberg grew exasperated trying to make a living in the timid TV and recording business and ventured into making funny commercials, where, ironically, he had more freedom. Berman became mainly an actor, his original plan. Steve Allen left full-time performing to write books. Woody Allen scampered into movies. Of the stand-up comedians considered here, only three who came of age in the fifties or sixties stayed with it full-time—Mort Sahl, Phyllis Diller, and Joan Rivers.

While Nichols & May went on to major and minor careers, respectively, their ultimate fame will rest on the four albums that they made four decades ago, a series of brilliant satirical sketches they created out of the anxious fifties air that crystallized that era better than anyone else; their routines are a kind of time capsule of American social life of the period. The early 1900s had Edith Wharton, the mid-1900s had Mike Nichols and Elaine May, who, to their generation, remain forever linked. May made a few movies and zigzagged between play- and screenwriting, but never connected as keenly or as personally with the public as she did when she was teamed with Nichols, who disliked performing.

There are plenty of gifted directors and screenwriters, but there was only one comedy team like Nichols & May. Those who first heard them in the late 1950s have never quite forgiven them for breaking up only a few years later. It seemed a selfish thing to do without first consulting us, but love is like that, irrational and unyielding, and everyone fell in love with Mike and Elaine. Although they may not want to admit it, those little five-minute satirical scenes that they created between 1958 and 1961 were, in sum, more inspired than anything they've done since, all their stage and screen credits notwithstanding. Similarly, Lehrer quit without asking our permission, silencing another urgently needed satirical voice.

COMEDIANS OF ANY ERA are notoriously idiosyncratic, bizarre, and contrary—by calling, by inclination, maybe by birth. They are difficult, elusive, wary, monstrous, jealous, crazy, candid, lovable, angry, curmudgeonly, bitter, paranoid, insecure, brilliant, insufferable, silly, profound—and, oh, yes, funny. The comedians I talked to turned out to be complex and all-too-human characters, full of rich stories, confessions, and regrets. All we've known about them is their comic surface, what they chose to show us. My thought was to move the spotlight into the shadowed corners of these comedians' chaotic and often troubled lives to reveal people we thought we knew, to show not just their genius but to catch glimpses of their demons, damaged souls, and desperate drive.

Why pick these particular comedians? The deciding factor wasn't how funny I thought they were—not all of them are personal favorites of mine—but what they had to say, their unique satirical viewpoint, and their legacy; it's an admittedly fuzzy, subjective line, and open to endless arguments. But in their heyday, all were impact players, each one sui generis. Most of them are as funny now as they were then, despite the passage of time and explosive changes in popular taste in humor.

This blue-ribbon group consists of the major pioneers, performers who challenged the comic status quo and shook up the comedy landscape. Being funny wasn't enough, leading me to leave out some worthy challengers who were funny but not, in the end, lastingly significant—Buddy Hackett, Jackie Vernon, Herb Shriner, and Don Adams, to name a few light-heavyweight contenders.

Other comedians of the period who *did* have something satirical or original to say just didn't make enough of a national splash—characters like Lord Buckley, Irwin Corey, Moms Mabley, Redd Foxx, Dick Shawn,

Larry Storch, Milt Kamen. Many of them, however, influenced comedians who later broke through in a bigger way. For all kinds of reasons—too late, too early, too minor, too derivative, too traditional—they failed to make my personal callbacks. I finally had to raise the curtain and bring down the house lights.

Several comics defied handy compartmentalizing—transitional performers like Sam Levenson, Danny Thomas, and Alan King, who are wedged somewhere between the old and the new comedy; or Robert Klein, Elayne Boosler, Albert Brooks, and David Steinberg, who bridged the new and the newer. Klein was "a hip comic square enough to appeal to middle-of-the-roaders," as one writer put it, but he arrived a little late (*A Child of the Fifties,* to quote the title of his first album) for my core gang of geniuses.

Four major renaissance comedians resisted being squeezed into my time capsule, comics who were visible in the fifties or sixties but didn't burst through until later—Rodney Dangerfield, Jackie Mason, George Carlin, and Richard Pryor. Each had an earlier life in a more primitive form and didn't arrive in a significant way until the seventies, just outside the slightly jagged boundaries of this book. Each one, however, boldly and bravely refutes the cliché that there are no second acts (or sets, in this case) in American lives. Each had a comic second coming that totally overshadowed his original career, and their sagas should give hope to all comedians who knock around for years without finding a niche. These four performers reinvented themselves after either failing miserably (Dangerfield), succeeding only moderately (Mason), or totally refurbishing their comic personae to suit the times and themselves (Carlin and Pryor), fashioning complete overhauls that led to stardom.

Two of the steadiest stars in this comedy cosmos, Phyllis Diller and Joan Rivers, made their initial impact less as a result of their material than on account of who they were: female comedians who broke into a predominantly man's game. Talk about a glass ceiling; they busted through solid iron stage doors, which only partly explains their presence here. Both are strictly joke-tellers, but they changed how women comics (formerly "comediennes") were perceived—as representatives of a new funny female sensibility. They were women who fought to be accepted on an equal footing with men, and on their own terms. Diller and Rivers are the Mother Jones and Betty Friedan of stand-up.

My original scheme was to limit the book to stand-up comics, but it soon became clear that many of the funniest, most original satiric performers of that era were not stand-ups at all—Sid Caesar, Stan Freberg, Tom Lehrer, Steve Allen, Mel Brooks, each one a major mover and shaker impossible to ignore. Nichols & May, though hardly stand-up comics, were the premier comedy team of their time, whose searing insights defined the era by the very nature of what they did with such brilliant consistency. Three comics included here played to smaller constituencies but were so perceptive or so biting that they demanded a place on the marquee: Jean Shepherd, the great radio monologuist, and Bob & Ray, the enduring satirists of the air. Astonishingly, Shepherd and Bob & Ray lingered in radio long after TV humbled that beloved lost medium.

Mythic fifties/sixties TV comedians like Lucille Ball, Carol Burnett, and Jackie Gleason were great sketch comics but not rebel satirists, so they don't belong—though I bent the rules for Sid Caesar, who was grandfathered into this hallowed comic pantheon because his TV *show* broke new ground and jump-started the satirical revolution fifty years ago. Likewise the deceptively vanilla-flavored Smothers Brothers, whose show was a vital part of the sixties revolt. Ernie Kovacs falls into no category, and Steve Allen falls into every category, and both left huge footprints in the comedy of their time while working in the then sterile, satire-free zone of television. Only two of the stand-ups included went on to have long TV careers, Cosby and Newhart, and only two comics had starring movie careers—Woody Allen and Mel Brooks. Winters, Newhart, Diller, Cosby, Rivers, and Elaine May never found their big-screen legs.

SEVERAL OF THESE comedians' sagas are inspiring and others are heartbreaking—and often it's the same saga. A few of the comedians who retreated or had the rug pulled out from under them provide compelling human dramas—Sahl, Berman, Gregory, Winters, Will Jordan, Vaughn Meader, and, of course, Bruce. Many hung in there despite countless bad breaks and setbacks; others were misfits who finally just gave up.

Nobody knows more than Robin Williams about the furies and hazards of the stand-up life. "It's a brutal field, man," he told me. "They burn out. It takes its toll. Plus, the lifestyle—partying, drinking, drugs. If you're on the road, it's even more brutal. You gotta come back down to mellow your ass out, and then [performing] takes you back up. They flame out because it comes and goes. Suddenly they're hot, and then somebody else is hot. Sometimes they get very bitter. Sometimes they just give up. Sometimes they have a revival thing and they come back again. Sometimes they snap. The pressure kicks in. You become obsessed and then you lose that focus that you need. Another thing is, shit grows around you: if someone took a dislike to you—a programmer or an agent—or if someone blackballed you. There once were lists, like the Communist lists. There was a guy at *The Tonight Show*—if he liked you, you got on. If not, you didn't. You could be brilliant but it wasn't his kind of comedy—'That's not what Johnny likes.' "

Abe Burrows once remarked, "The comedian must practice his comedy in order to avoid destroying himself." Some comics here began using humor to escape lethal family situations, to deflect childhood pain: too dumpy, too scrawny, too lonely, too ugly, too shy, too something. "So many diseased souls," sighs one observer of the comedy scene. Howard Storm says, "It's a strange business to be in, to beg people to laugh at you, to bare your soul and to need the laughter. It's as simple as, 'Mommy, please love me.' " Jules Hock, who ran The Horn in Santa Monica, remarks: "I learned early in the game that these folks are a breed unto themselves. If you or I ask someone to pass the saltshaker, there is a high presumption that the saltshaker will be passed. If you ask a comedian, you might get the saltshaker thrown at you. You might be totally ignored. You might get an explosion: 'What the hell do you think I am—a waiter? Get it yourself.' "

The conventional wisdom about comedians is that they all had lousy or lonely childhoods. True enough of Nichols, Winters, Bruce, Sherman, and Dick Gregory; but just as many here had normal, healthy, even pampered, childhoods: Rivers, Newhart, Freberg, Diller, Sahl, Cambridge, Brooks. Samuel S. Janus, a psychologist and former Catskill song-and-dance man who made a study of fifty-five comedians, concludes, "While a lot of these people have deep problems, they're not really sickies. They're really very sweet, sensitive guys. Many of them are very stable people, good family men." (Quite a few—Gregory, King, Caesar, Cosby, Winters, Berman, Newhart, Brooks, Rivers, Carl Reiner, Steve Allen—have had long marriages.)

Janus adds: "If somebody heckles, or walks out, they joke about it, but down deep inside they're crushed. Somebody didn't love them." Arnie Kogen, a writer for Newhart, Carson, Jerry Seinfeld, and David Letterman, says bluntly, "They're all insecure." Many comedians—even megastars—feel un- or underappreciated by the public or by showbiz itself. They never stop running. Rita Rudner says, "Comedy is a business of misfits, and I fit right in. It's where I belong. I'm like the girl in *The Fantasticks* who says, 'Please, God, don't let me be normal.' "

Jackie Mason knows all about that: "It's hard to find a normal comedian. This is a very, very insecure, nerve-wracking business. Everyone's on an ego trip. Most people don't become comedians because they want to entertain people. They only become comedians because they feel rejected and nervous and helpless altogether." Jerry Seinfeld doesn't think you can trace the comic gene quite so easily: "There are a lot of unhappy people driving bread trucks, but when it's a comedian people find it very poignant. Some of them are in pain but I don't see that as a thread."

All comedians, of any era, belong to the same club, and it's not the Friars. It's a secret society. Each one is cut from the same basic cloth. While there's a huge stylistic and content gulf between, say, Shecky Greene and Mort Sahl, or Jonathan Winters and Joan Rivers, they were all manic, high-strung comedians whose fans have stuck by them through thick and thin, and all of them have known more than their share of thin. "Comedy is the only work in the world," says Mike Nichols, "in which the work and the reward are simultaneous. Comedians get laughs on the spot. It's very corrupting to your character. People who become comedians tend to be people who have problems with self-esteem. Some days the pleasure goes and only the fear is left." Jack Carter perhaps put it best: "The funny part, the laughter, is given to the audience, and the comedian is left with the bitter dregs."

Making people laugh may be, right after auto racing, the world's most hazardous occupation. It's tougher than other art forms because there's no shield to hide behind—no book, no canvas, no camera, no orchestra, no script, no costars, no choreographer. It's just you and your wisecracks; if the act fails, *you* have failed. Seinfeld compares stand-up to "going to work in your underwear." The comedian is the whole show, the flesh-and-blood work of art. It's what drives some comics berserk, even the most famous ones, because there's usually a sour aftertaste of early failure. It never leaves them, even after they make it—*especially* after they make it. Every night they start over again and, if they succeed, must face new firing squads. Every audience, every line, tests them again. Comedians exist from laugh to laugh. Lawrence Christon observes: "Comedians don't have any other tools. They live in a tremendous vacuum and most are incredibly neurotic. They're outsiders."

Even though all comics bond on some basic level as wounded veterans

who have been through the wars together, often that's where the cama-
raderie ends. There's a huge envy factor in comedy that Nichols refers to
as a "monster." The hardest thing for a comedian to do is to sit in an audience and listen to another comic getting laughs. He may be laughing
hard, he may love the material and genuinely admire the performer, but
on some gut level he's eating his heart out because it's not him up there.
The comedian Brian Copeland says, half jokingly, "The only time a comedian really laughs is when another comic is onstage dying."

Comedy's leading expert on resentment, Jackie Mason, maintains
that his fellow comics resented his sudden big success. "They still do,"
says Mason with a shrug, as he says everything. Seated backstage before
his one-man show, *Much Ado About Everything,* Mason, something of a
sore winner, told me, "As soon as I walk into the Friars Club, you never
saw such hostility. Alan King with venom, full of vicious hate, Freddie
Roman, full of hate. They don't even try to hide it—it's right in their
faces. I'm not too close to too many comedians. I find there's too much
jealousy among them. Henny Youngman was hated. Alan King in his heyday was not as big as I am now, because of Broadway. It's the thing he
wanted to achieve and never did. He took it out on me with venom and
hate. He'd walk out and say, 'Can you believe what's happening to Broadway? Jackie Mason is being compared to Will Rogers.' " Mason even said
of his discoverer, the sainted Steve Allen, "It's probably killing him that he
gave me my start. He didn't want me to do *this* good."

Warming to the topic, he went on: "A comedian is a very extreme
thing to be. You know how sick you have to be to go up on a stage in Iowa
in front of people who never heard of you and beg people to laugh at you
with jokes that aren't finished yet, and to feel all the rejection and the
contempt that people have for a person who's wasting their time not
being funny? If you sing a song and it stinks, nobody notices it because
they've heard of the song, it's close enough, it's better than nothing. But
if you hear a joke that stinks, you're wasting the guy's time and he's getting nauseous and he wants to throw a chair at you."

Mason's analysis gets a laugh out of Robin Williams, who comments:
"Comedy is a weird fraternity, a weird combination of envy and admiration. They know each other and they cheer each other up and yet they
can't admire each other. You wanna say, 'You won, Jackie, you won!' See,
but these guys can't give up. They're driven by *kvetch.* The school of,
'That fuck, Henny Youngman, I can see that he hates me.' 'But Henny's
dead.' 'God willing!' They can't let go because that's what drove them."

Stand-up comedy is a complex spiderweb of connections that inter-weave and overlap and double back. If you follow the paths long enough, you find that all comedians are linked in some way, consciously or uncon-sciously feeding, or playing, off one another. The DNA of jokes, routines, and premises—of Mel Brooks's "Springtime for Hitler," of Nichols & May's telephone routine, of Johnny Carson's sleazy late-night TV pitch-man—can be traced back across decades from comic to comic to comic; often, it's no more than one degree of separation: David Steinberg tracks a samurai-warrior bit from Sid Caesar to himself to John Belushi. Yet it's not *all* backbiting and backstabbing. Says Jan Murray, "When we're not resenting each other we're loving each other."

Lines, bits, even entire acts routinely get filched; many comedians feel that any rival comic's joke is public property, while stealing an entire "hunk" is considered a treasonous offense. Comedians go to their graves cursing a line, a concept, that made another comic famous. Rip-offs, injustices, and petty grievances are part of any comedian's baggage, often enough to fill a steamer trunk. Like old ballplayers recalling a 1957 two-out double, comedians can remember one another's lines, as they can every slight, slur, and theft. Richard Lewis says that Paul Reiser stole his rhythm. Will Jordan insists that Mel Brooks swiped his Hitler shtick, that Jonathan Winters nabbed his Sabu accent, that Jack Carter made off with his entire Ed Sullivan impression. Redd Foxx claimed that Dick Gregory "stole my cigarette." Alan King, once famous for lifting gags, had a stan-dard retort: "Sue me." The Bitter End's Fred Weintraub refused to book one famous comedian. "I wouldn't even allow him in my club—he would sit in the front row and steal material."

Dick Cavett notes that, until his era, "comedy was pretty much doing stuff other people had done." The habit died hard. He recalls being stunned once seeing a comic doing Shelley Berman's classic father-son piece and another comedian doing Woody Allen's bit about his pet ant. The writer-director Garry Marshall once confronted a comic doing, word for word, one of Berman's routines. The comic explained: "Yeah, *I* do it, too."

PEOPLE WHO LEARNED THAT I'd talked to Woody Allen, Mike Nichols, Bob Newhart, Jonathan Winters, Steve Allen, Joan Rivers, et al. would ask, eyes all agleam, "Were they funny?" I constantly had to disappoint them. Few were funny offstage, which was fine with me. I didn't want a performance; that would be like interviewing a heart surgeon and expecting him to perform a few quick bypasses for my amusement. I'd seen all their moves; I wanted their stories.

The Robin Williams you see on *The Tonight Show* is, mercifully, not the same man analyzing Jonathan Winters in a Chinese restaurant on Ninth Avenue in San Francisco; Jonathan Winters in his study is not "a bag of funnies," to use his phrase. Comedy is what these folks do when an audience is present ("I'm a professional," as Steve Martin used to jokingly boast); it's what pays their bills, but it's just a part of them. "I'm only funny when I get paid," Youngman would say. Yet as Ralph J. Gleason wrote, "Most successful comedians and satirists really are alive only when onstage; the rest of the time is intermission."

Most of the comics discussed here were eager to talk—it's what they do for a living, it's why they became comics. They're articulate about their work; some are even scholarly. But comedians rarely open up in TV and radio interviews. Most comedians are always "on" (generally the lower down on the food chain a comic is, the hungrier he is to be on—anywhere), especially if surrounded by a group or by their fellow comics—but not always. At a gathering of Yarmy's Army, a group of veteran comedians and comedy writers who meet monthly at Jerry's Deli in Beverly Hills, a few minutes of joshing soon gives way to noshing and shoptalk.

During our conversations, the comedians might toss off a funny observation in passing, even an impression, but nobody was going for laughs. Still, they were all great company and in every case I hated to leave. The warmest was Jonathan Winters, who suggested, as we wound up the interview, that we drive into town for lunch. We went to a little Italian place (he in baggy jeans and a yachting shirt, looking like Elwood P. Suggins's rich uncle) where, with my tape recorder discreetly off but my mental Sony running, the interview continued; I took several men's room breaks to jot down his remembrances of a grim childhood. I'd heard how he always jokes with clerks and strangers, but on this particular day, unhappily, he wasn't in the mood.

Phyllis Diller was the oldest comedian I met, and the best sport. When I arrived at her Brentwood, California, home, her daughter called upstairs that a strange man was at the door requesting an interview. Diller had thought we were going to talk by phone, but, ever the game trouper, she padded downstairs sans makeup and wig, almost unrecognizable—a fragile but feisty gray-haired old lady with a pacemaker and a scar she proudly displayed. The only giveaway was her telltale cackle.

Getting to some of these comedians could be more of an adventure than the actual interviews. Easily the most slippery was Dick Gregory. We finally met and had a good heart-to-heart, but not until I had proved my mettle by telephoning him nearly a dozen times in various cities where he was speaking—merely to arrange a *time* to talk. After chasing him to Los Angeles, I eventually cornered him at midnight in the deserted lobby of a Radisson Hotel in Century City, where, while he waxed eloquently about his life and times, a janitor waxed the floor.

Woody Allen in private is famously as sober as a judge, if not more so (Justice Antonin Scalia gives funnier interviews). Our conversation had the no-nonsense, businesslike tenor of a job interview. I met Allen at his three-room editing hideaway and home away from home tucked in the rear of the former Beekman Hotel on Park Avenue and Sixty-third Street. Allen arrived on the dot with his wife-to-be, Soon-Yi Previn, looking wet and windblown upon entering; after her cameo appearance, Soon-Yi vanished. Allen removed his famous floppy hat and mumbled a hello, then offered a limp handshake and half a smile. We chatted in the low-ceilinged screening room, a long, dimly lit cave with olive-green carpet, chairs, and velvet wallpaper where Allen screens films and gives interviews.

Without a word of small talk, the conversation proceeded, congenial but impersonal. Allen, in one of his trademark nerd-power outfits— khakis and dark checked shirt—was straightforward and courteous. He made no jokes, not even banter, but answered everything carefully and candidly. He knew what he wanted to say and didn't once stammer, speaking in confident, well-formed sentences; yet his answers didn't have a boilerplate sound. Once my time was up, Woody offered no personal remarks or pleasant goodbyes. He was instantly back in his own thoughts. By then, a TV crew had already gathered in the waiting area for an audience with the comedy maestro.

Perhaps the most personable comedian I got to was Dick Cavett, whose stand-up career was a blur. A typical dewy-eyed sixties comic, smart and amusing but rough around the edges, or maybe more than just around the edges, Cavett was a failed wunderkind of the comedy renaissance. But he was on the front lines long enough to report on the inner workings and what it was like to be a Rollins & Joffe protégé. Despite his reputation as a flippant know-it-all, he was a warm conversationalist, befitting his talk-show-host résumé, as was the equally down-to-earth Tom Lehrer, who apologized as I left for not offering any refreshment ("I'm very bad at this sort of thing"). A few of the comedians were simply amusing presences—like Shecky Greene, who sat in a big recliner talking to his ailing dog, Cap, while keeping an eye on a stock-market ticker crawling across a TV screen, and, midway through our session, chatting on the phone with his pal Kaye Ballard.

Of all the notable revolutionaries rounded up here, I had most looked forward to chatting with Mort Sahl, who led the charge. Sahl was my idol when I first saw him in college in the fifties, when he blew everyone away with his brilliance at the hungry i. He declined an interview many times in many ways, politely but firmly, despite a cordial professional relationship dating back to the sixties. As even his best friends testify, he's a quirky guy who still marches to his own, increasingly lonely, drummer. Short of candy, flowers, and stalking, I tried every courtship ploy imaginable—letters, phone calls, a list of questions he might simply respond yes or no to—but Sahl is famously stubborn.

"It pains me to say no," he explained. "I just don't want to be in there with all those *other* guys. Who *are* all those guys? I don't consider them in the same league. They didn't do it. I never do the group stuff. I have a policy of not being included. It dilutes what I do. I don't fare well with those people. You should write a book about me!" Sahl laughed, but he wasn't joking. Herb Sargent, the comedy writer and a longtime Sahl ally, translates: "It's ego and pride." Mel Brooks, Sid Caesar, and Carl Reiner also declined to be interviewed, Reiner claiming he was writing his own memoir of that era. After a year of *maybe*'s and *just be patient*'s, word finally came down from Mount Cosby that Bill chose "not to participate," perhaps evidence of Cosby's lifelong distrust of the press—although it generally has been pretty kind to him—and his famously prickly nature.

THE GREAT COMEDIANS collected here changed comedy forever. They rewrote the rules. As a group, they left behind a satirical legacy distinguished by its social and political awareness, literacy, ingenuity, and theatrical flair. Even now, as comic elder statesmen and women, they remain revered names in comedy—myths, icons, and fallen idols.

These comedians were not just produced by their times; they helped produce those times by picking up on cultural-social-political vibes of the 1950s, sounds heard by few others. That luminous and illuminating decade or so produced much of the greatest comedy of the century. Nobody, of course, realized that a major comedy revolt was going on. It's only in retrospect that the outlines of a genuine comedy renaissance begin to appear, in the first sharply defined silhouettes of Caesar, Sahl, Winters, and Freberg.

In the fifties, stand-up comedy was merely a show-business subdivision. By the nineties, stand-up titans like Jay Leno and David Letterman had become so vital culturally that presidential candidates felt obliged to make regular whistle stops on their late-night talk shows to demonstrate what funny guys they were. Until the 1960s, stand-up comedians were viewed as theatrical lowlife, unworthy of serious analysis.

Despite the indelible mark they left, these comedians created a renaissance without a follow-up act: few comics after them carried on what they had begun. Most cultural revolutions produce new blood, but the rebel comedians of the fifties and sixties gave birth to precious few satirical offspring. It's hard to find any traces now, in clubs or on TV, of those brilliant, perceptive, funny comedians. The comics who came later mostly aimed for the gut and the groin, not for the brain or the soul.

By the mid-sixties, the renaissance was about over, and another batch of comedians was being hatched at countless comedy clubs. That next era had begun in 1963 with Budd Friedman's New York room, the Improvisation. The next wave of stand-ups was far more physical and hard-edged, more rowdy and cartoony—perhaps as a counterrevolution to the brainier comedy that preceded it. The comedy clubs transformed comedians into interchangeable performers, warm-ups for rock musicians. It was even dubbed "rock-and-roll comedy." Comics became the stand-up equivalent of garage-band performers, bred not in small intimate nightclubs but in discos, pop concerts, and comedy-only clubs. It was a generation of stand-ups largely weaned on, and heavily influenced by, *Saturday Night Live.*

In the clownish comedy of Steve Martin, Robin Williams, Gilda Radner, Martin Short, and Andy Kaufman, a kind of inspired silliness took over that was almost determinedly antisubstance—comedy about comedy, in a sense. Once the rock-and-roll sensibility took hold, Martin got out: "The problem was the mania. The audiences got wilder. It ruined it. You can't treat comedy like rock-and-roll—it's much more sensitive."

Peter Bonerz, a member of the Second City and The Committee in the 1960s before becoming a regular on *The Bob Newhart Show* (he now directs sitcoms like *Friends*), says: "At comedy clubs now, the people who stand in line outside the Laugh Factory come in, the guy says 'motherfucker,' and everybody laughs. It's an easy gig. It's like bowling—you have a beer, you have a good time." Bonerz continues: "There's no context now, as Mike Nichols says. It's a generation raised on TV. Kids today think comedy started with John Belushi. I look at Sid Caesar's work now and it brings a catch to my throat. I don't think Caesar's stuff will ever disappear."

Why the early 1950s to mid-1960s produced so much bright, incisive, cutting-edge satire is a question without a satisfying answer. Were comedians simply better and brighter? Was the audience quicker? Or were the great comedians highlighted here just anomalies? Jackie Mason contends that the average comedian forty years ago "had the mentality of a used-car salesman." Well into my search for a logical answer, I concluded that the comedy renaissance, like all artistic flowerings—the French Impressionists, the Bloomsbury circle, the Italian and French New Wave cinema, Tin Pan Alley songwriters of the thirties and forties, the 1927 New York Yankees—was just a lucky accident, a happy happenstance we should simply be grateful for and celebrate. Such mystical confluences are inexplicably of the moment—in the writer Louis Menand's words, "a very singular coincidence of circumstances that's not going to recur. The world doesn't accommodate it anymore."

Robin Williams, weaned on the albums of Jonathan Winters and Lenny Bruce, says, "There was just a smarter, more literate audience. When I see Nichols & May, I don't see anyone doing what they did. It was just an incredible high level of wit." Comedy in the fifties and sixties was barbwired and booby-trapped with innuendo and satirical invention. It's now almost as if nothing had happened in the twelve years between Mort Sahl and Joan Rivers, which seems in retrospect to have been almost a mythical period that existed as a kind of misty comic Brigadoon. In a strange way, the stand-up comedians of the nineties and into the early twenty-first century are primitive throwbacks to the hard-sell joke-peddlers of the forties and early fifties. Their jokes seldom connect to the outside world, or to our own real daily (let alone interior) lives. Much recent stand-up comedy has turned into exercises in "attitude," the word that defined eighties and nineties comedians like Dennis Miller, Garry Shandling, Roseanne Barr, and David Letterman.

Murray Horwitz, the head of cultural programming at National Public Radio, says that the old implied contract between audience and performer has been rewritten, if not torn up: "The esthetic changed drastically. What happened in comedy is that cynicism replaced humor. Now, a guy like a Dennis Miller or a David Letterman or Howard Stern will make a cynical remark and people say, "Oh, wow, I can't believe it— did you hear what he said?' But they're not laughing. Was it funny? Was it enlightening in any way? And the answer is *no*. The contract used to be: 'Hey, I am so grateful to you for having paid your twenty dollars and for coming here tonight. Put your cares aside. Relax, I'll take care of you— that's my job. You're either gonna be amused or compelled or moved— some way I'm gonna make this time worth your while. Who knows? Maybe we'll catch lightning in a bottle.' "

What makes the earlier era still resonate isn't just rosy nostalgia, or encrusted age, but something deeper in stand-up comedy that seems to have vanished. Maybe stand-up itself is vanishing as a vital form, or has lost its purpose, existing only as a wing of sitcoms. Only two of this renaissance group transferred to situation comedy, and probably a lucky thing. It boggles the mind to imagine Lenny Bruce, Nichols & May, Mort Sahl, Woody Allen, Shelley Berman, Dick Gregory, or Joan Rivers slogging through a sitcom, though most were approached. Today, we might see Berman as an anxiety-ridden deli owner, Sahl as an investigative reporter, Woody Allen as a geeky dot-commer, Nichols & May as bookish Bickersons, Rivers as a snippy maiden aunt, and Dick Gregory as the proprietor of a radical health-food store.

While some of the more revolutionary comedians were beaten down and destroyed, just as many enjoyed the last laugh. It takes courage to become a comedian, even a bad one; to absorb the emotional whacks and disfiguring pain of working in this most dangerous of knock-about occupations, and to sustain a career for years, let alone decades. For Woody Allen, no less than for the greenest kid on the bill at Funny Bones in Akron, Ohio, the most difficult element of the stand-up life is the grinding pressure to produce consistent laughs. "You have to be great *all* the time," Allen told me. "You've got the pressure of facing an audience and getting them laughing for forty minutes. You go to your dressing room, and then you have to do it again for the second show, or the third, and the next night you have to do it all over again, and this goes on year after year."

According to the critic George Seldes, "The test of a real comedian is whether you laugh at him before he opens his mouth." With a great comedian, he added, "you feel yourself in the presence of a person and of an event. You laugh at his comedy and rejoice in all of him." He specified

Jimmy Durante, but he might have been talking about Woody Allen, Bill Cosby, Bob Newhart, Shelley Berman, Lenny Bruce, Phyllis Diller, or Steve Allen.

Ultimately there is a kind of performing heroism in the personalities profiled here. As I neared the finish of the book, it became all too clear that many of these comedians had led lives of noisy desperation, often full of drama, damaged dreams, even tragedy. Their stories were packed with the rich raw material of a comedy *Chorus Line,* comedians who refused to be denied and demanded to be heard. The laughter they left behind in all of those little underground clubs is long gone, but their legacy still smiles brightly, warmly, and merrily.

The 1950s

A Voice in the Wilderness

Mort Sahl

If you were the only person left on the planet, I would have to attack you. That's my job.

————————

NOBODY SAW Mort Sahl coming. When he arrived, the revolution had not yet begun. Sahl *was* the revolution, at first, although he had no such grand idea in mind. He wasn't plotting the violent overthrow of the conservative comedy government. He was never a rebel, deep down. In thought, yes, but rarely in deed. His vague desire—a pipe dream, really—was to work somewhere as a comedian. He had no experience and little idea where to go to be funny, other than parties and all-night campus hangouts, where he held forth in his motormouth manner.

Of all the great groundbreaking comedians of that era—which officially began with Sahl's inauspicious debut on Christmas Night 1953 before a friend-packed audience at a San Francisco folksinger haven called the hungry i—nobody could have been more different from the standard stand-up comic than Mort Sahl. Even the revolutionary comedians who followed him—Lenny Bruce, Woody Allen, Dick Gregory, Phyllis Diller, Shelley Berman, Jonathan Winters—were cast in a familiar nightclub comic mold; all but Allen, a writer, had worked as actors, or in radio, or as entertainers of some sort. Other comedians labored to find a stage persona, a voice, but Sahl's actual persona was eccentric enough, and his voice was loud and clear. He was a force of nature, a whirlwind whose ideas defined him; behind each joke lurked a sharply etched, cynical worldview.

Everything about him was candid and cool, the antithesis of the slick comic: his casual campus wardrobe (the signature cardigan sweater, slacks, loafers, rumpled hair, open collar, rolled-up shirtsleeves); his material (partly political but heavily laced with social commentary on fads, trends, and the American mind-set at midcentury); his consistently high level of original wit; and, to be sure, his conversational, in-your-face delivery. Unlike the comics of the day, he didn't attempt to ingratiate himself with the audience, yet he connected with them on his own terms.

Often he didn't finish sentences—he spoke in a kind of shorthand and didn't worry about building to a finish or making logical segues; he didn't sing or dance. He was unlike any comedian who had ever been—except that he was stunningly funny. The mere idea of a stand-up comic talking about the real world was in itself revolutionary.

Sahl had "attitude" before it became trendy—and, much later, in the 1980s, before it passed itself off as a substitute for wit. Attitude comedy didn't stem from Steve Martin, David Letterman, and Dennis Miller. It started with Mort Sahl, whose audacious position was that, basically, the fix was in—that life in the 1950s, and politics in particular, was a joke and that he was simply reporting what went on in Washington.

That had also been Will Rogers's pose, but Sahl was citing chapter and verse, and he was no benign, lovable, head-scratching cowboy philosopher. Sahl, it seemed, had never met a man he liked—or, as he cracked, "*I never met a man I didn't like until I met Will Rogers.*" Sahl had read Rogers and concluded, "I'm not flattered when people say I'm the new Will Rogers. You read over some of the old things Rogers wrote and you find out he wasn't very funny." Sahl conceded that Bob Hope "works in some political material," but Hope had no political viewpoint beyond a glib patriotism. Of all the comedians of that time, his closest ancestor—and influence— was the bitter and acidic Henry Morgan, the iconoclastic radio satirist. "He really impressed me," said Sahl. "It was a great blow for freedom that this guy could get it across—it was a rallying point." Sahl was much closer to H. L. Mencken than to any comic—in his ferocity, his lacerating wit, his language, his hyperbole, his imagery, and his impact.

For a time, when he was riding high in the early 1960s, he was almost a fourth branch of government—"the nation's only employed philosopher," said the Hollywood columnist Joe Hyams, and "almost certainly the most widely acclaimed and best-paid nihilist ever produced by Western civilization," wrote *The New Yorker*'s Robert Rice in a 1960 profile. The press's careless comparisons of Sahl to Rogers and Hope were way off the mark. When Rogers or Hope did political material, their jokes weren't meant to wound or to make anyone squirm; Sahl's were, and did. "Will Rogers with fangs," he was labeled, or "the Will Rogers of the beat generation," "the surrealist Montaigne," and "a beat generation Cotton Mather." Sahl was, in fact, virulently anti-beat ("*The beat generation is a coffeehouse full of people expectantly looking at their watches waiting for the beat generation to come on*"). He said, "The beatniks don't want to be involved with society, which is the antithesis of what I do." Pre-Sahl, it was heretical, even career suicide, for a comedian to discuss politics, much less to cut up a sitting president onstage. Rogers and Hope were establishment figures, national heroes, but Sahl was completely out of the Washington loop when he began. Rogers used to say, "All I know is what I read in the papers," a posture close to Sahl's own, though Sahl's slant was that all he knew is what he didn't read in the papers.

Roger Ailes, the head of Fox Cable News, recalled: "I once sat with Mort Sahl in Mister Kelly's, and watched him read a paper in a booth. He got up onstage six hours later that night with forty minutes of new material. With no writers, he just did what he had seen in the afternoon papers. He was a genius." Later, Sahl would tell lengthy stories of attending White House dinners, heavily embellished, that depicted him as an outsider who had snuck in a side entrance to the West Wing when nobody was looking. He was no crony; he didn't hobnob like Hope or wish to be beloved like Rogers, both of whom emerged from vaudeville. Sahl was no show-business baby. He was a guy with things on his mind.

As he later wrote in his memoir, "Something was stirring in the late '50s in America even if people couldn't define it." Sahl defined it. Comics were utterly befuddled by him and what Ralph J. Gleason labeled "the new comedy of dissent." Other comedians, Woody Allen recalled, "became jealous, because Sahl was so natural. They used to say, 'Why do people like him? He just talks. He isn't really performing.'" Not performing in a traditional sense, but his mind did an astonishing tap dance across the front page. "Who wants a comic you gotta have a dictionary on your lap so you can figure out what he's saying, and even then he ain't funny," said Buddy Lester, a paid-up member of the comic rear guard.

Although Sahl clearly loved the attention and later even the friendship of politicians, he didn't seek their approval, only their ears. It cost him dearly when the Kennedy clan—although not John Kennedy himself— mistakenly assumed that, because Sahl had bashed the Eisenhower administration, he was the Democrats' boy. Mort Sahl was nobody's boy. Some took him for a comic hired hand because he had made the mistake of writing jokes for Kennedy during the campaign. Lenny Bruce liked to say, "I am not a comedian, I'm Lenny Bruce," but it was Sahl who truly was not the standard comedian.

Sahl was misjudged as merely a comedian just because he made his living in show business. He embraced fame and success, appearing on major television shows and rubbing elbows with celebrities and collecting all the trinkets of stardom, but he refused to play the logrolling celebrity game—and that conscious rejection would later come back to bite him. He was, like other great comics of that era whose careers skidded off course early, his own worst enemy. He was not just a political rebel, as his later sharp turn to the right revealed, but he had a rebellious personality that cost him friends, colleagues, club dates, managers, agents, wives, and girlfriends. Sahl still goes it alone, with a major ego that assures him he's superior to his fellow comedians. His deeply indignant, contrary streak fires his passion and sparks his wit, but it also burns bridges.

The event that proved he could be as politically committed as, say, Dick Gregory or Lenny Bruce—someone willing to put his name and reputation on the line—was the Kennedy assassination. It scarred his career, and really his life, because his career was his life. In 1963, after blazing across the comedy skies in the 1950s and early '60s, Sahl gradually fizzled out after JFK's death. The Warren Report so traumatized him that he never recovered his footing and still struggles against an ancient stigma that he's a head case.

Sahl was just gaining mainstream acceptance on TV when the assassination brought him down as clearly as it did the Kennedy impressionist Vaughn Meader. Unlike Meader—a novelty item—Sahl, with his boundless and resourceful wit, might be riding high even now if he hadn't got so immersed in the dubious findings of the Warren Commission that it damaged his objectivity. His major tactical mistake was in not maintaining a certain artistic distance, as a wit and commentator, from his material; and he failed, utterly, to recognize that this was how the public viewed him.

He miscalculated the fickle and perverse nature of show business and the copycat media, which hastily and wrongly wrote him off as a radical kook and, with cruel irony, as yesterday's newspaper. By 1966, only six years after he had appeared on the cover of *Time*—a stamp of approval that carried far more clout than it does now, the first true stand-up comedian so honored—and been profiled by *The New Yorker* two months later, Sahl was scrambling for club dates and trying to salvage his career.

His fall from grace was Bruceian. To many he appeared to be preoccupied with the Warren Report, from which he read long excerpts onstage, and it was said that, like Bruce, he had stopped being funny. In fact, most critics felt he was still fresh and funny, but not enough people cared, and the rumor still hounds him. Sahl stalwarts stood by him and showed up religiously whenever he appeared, with decreasing regularity, but he had lost the precious traction that performers need, especially comics with small, hard-core constituencies. A film star or a pop singer has nine lives, a comic only one.

In 1983 Lawrence Christon wrote: "Mort Sahl has charted one of the most precipitous courses in American entertainment for the last thirty years and has gone from celebrity to internal exile. There was no precedent for what he did. There were no prototypes. He's a genuinely self-created man and a true existential in that sense. Once he passes from the scene, people will begin to lionize him and call him the great American and take to heart all the things he's said." Sahl is counting on that. It's what has kept him talking into the next millennium at seventy-five, fifty years after he first kicked the door down.

IT'S HARD TO IMAGINE Mort Sahl as anything but a mature, adult cynic, but in his early recordings in the mid-1950s you can hear the boyish Mort. While the material is richly sardonic, he doesn't sound as deeply cynical as he later became. His voice is lighter and higher than remembered, almost chipmunklike as he delivers his most caustic cracks. He seems delighted with himself, enjoying his own performance, and his sporadic bursts of laughter are infectious yet not self-congratulatory. He sounds surprised when people laugh or applaud a line, and often he responds with a disbelieving "Really?" as if to say, *You actually understand me!* thus spurring him ever "*Onward!*"—his famous battle cry. The monologues were leavened with staccato good-humored guffaws, directed not so much at his own performance as at the general absurdity of American life. No matter how harsh his pronouncements, there was never any hostility in them. It was just that, as Sahl himself put it, "Everything bothers me."

He was born in Montreal as Morton Lyon Sahl (the middle name proved prescient, suggesting its owner's self-approving roar), the precocious only child of a Jewish couple who had moved from New York City to Canada, and finally to Los Angeles when Sahl was seven. His unlikely Canadian roots were quickly shaken off and he grew up a totally Southern California guy—wisecracking, movie-crazed, and, at twenty-three and just out of the service, the embodiment of what a new men's magazine out of Chicago would soon refer to as "The *Playboy* Man." Sahl was all of that—addicted to women, sports cars, jazz, hi-fi equipment, fancy watches, all the fifties talismans of young American manhood.

Although Sahl didn't come from a theatrical background, his father,

Harry, was a leftist and a failed playwright from New York's Lower East Side, and Mort shared much of his father's contempt for show business, if not the entire system. "It's all fixed," Harry Sahl would say. "They don't want anything good." Mort's ebullient mother was "all enthusiasm." Both parents were radicals. His father owned a tobacco store in Montreal before settling in Los Angeles, where he worked as an FBI clerk, one of several low-level bureaucratic positions he held. After making it at the hungry i, Sahl moved his parents to Sausalito and, when his father died, Mort found clippings about Harry Sahl's thwarted career. "My dad was disappointed in his dreams and he distrusted that world for me,"

Even as a kid, Sahl was a precocious talker—standing behind a radio and delivering his own newscast, mimicking Gabriel Heatter and Walter Winchell; by eight, he was hanging around radio stations, fishing discarded scripts out of trash bins and reading them into a fake microphone he had built. His mother said that Mort was talking at seven months and, when he was ten, "spoke like a man of thirty." The young Mort was a teenage patriot during World War II, joining the ROTC in high school and winning a medal for marksmanship and an American Legion Americanism award. At fifteen, he left L.A.'s Belmont High School to join the army, but after two weeks in uniform his mother rescued him. "I was a martinet as a kid," he liked to say. His closest boyhood chum was the actor Richard Crenna. At thirteen, they would sneak into the KFI radio station and try to get on a show called *Boy Scout Jamboree,* but only Crenna was cast; Crenna recalls that Sahl was antiauthoritarian at ten.

Sahl's father tried to get his son a West Point appointment, but Mort was drafted and sent to the Ninety-third Air Depot Group in Anchorage, Alaska. There, his rebel instincts flourished and he grew a beard, refused to wear a cap, and edited a post newspaper, *Poop from the Group,* which won him an eighty-three-day KP sentence for editorials about alleged military payoffs. Thirty-one months later he left the service, still a private but a five-star rebel: "A few months under the heel of authority killed it for me."

Back home in 1947, Sahl—still playing by postwar rules—went to Compton Junior College and then the University of Southern California, where he got a bachelor of science degree in 1950 and went to work on a graduate degree in traffic engineering until the "organization men," as they were then called, repelled him enough to make him quit. "I was no organization cat," he said. "It was Conformity City." England had its surly Angry Young Men, and America's angriest young man was Mort Sahl, whose wit was doused with vitriol—a homegrown cousin of Jimmy Porter in *Look Back in Anger*. At USC, he skipped classes after staying up all night going to jazz joints and following Stan Kenton's band.

Sahl didn't just wander into the hungry i one day and begin performing; he'd had theatrical aspirations much earlier. After USC, he rented a theater with a friend and renamed it Theater X (for "experimental"), writing and staging one-act plays—one of Sahl's was called *Nobody Trusted the Truth*. Meanwhile, he tried breaking into comedy in Los Angeles and applied at some thirty clubs between 1950 and '53, earning about fifty dollars a year as a comedian (one NBC executive told him to just forget the whole idea). Sahl then wore a suit and tie, did impersonations, and called himself, incredibly, "Cal Southern." The wily manner was borrowed from country slicker Herb Shriner, a genial Will Rogers knockoff. "Mort thought he should be rural and folksy but that only lasted about five minutes," says Robert Weide, writer and director of the 1989 HBO documentary *Mort Sahl: The Loyal Opposition*.

Sahl told *The New Yorker* in 1957: "I'd go into the strip joints in L.A. and ask them to let me perform for free during intermission. Despite all the folklore about the faith of friends in the struggling young artist, my friends constantly discouraged me. 'What do you think you're doing? How are you going to make it doing that?' I became very bitter." He wrote film reviews and editorials for a journal published by the Altruistic Artists Foundation, including a piece titled "Art and Poetry, the Siamese Twins of Beauty." He turned out an unpublished novel and short stories while working as a used-car salesman and a messenger. In 1952 he briefly tried to make it in New York, living in a Midtown hotel on eighteen dollars a week and dining on day-old bread. "I couldn't get a thing going. I was working on a novel, I was out of work, and I was out of gas."

He went home, where he realized his one-act plays were more suitable as monologues than dialogues. "I discovered I had to *talk*," he said. "I got the idea that the things I was saying in play form would be less heavy-handed if presented satirically. I tried to sell material to comedians, but they said I wasn't commercial." This angered him enough to make him prove them wrong (Sahl's lifelong credo is: "You know me, I love lost causes"). He recalled, "I listened to just so many refusals, then I evolved a feeling of dynamics. I knew that if I was going to get anything done, I'd have to do it myself." It was easier to perform comedy than to write it and sell it, foreshadowing the emergence of the writer-comic. "A writer has no voice in America," he learned, "but any hooligan can get an audition.

The solution for the writer is simple—he smuggles in his ideas as a performer. The ideas are a lot bigger than the performer anyway." He appeared at the Los Angeles Palladium as an intermission comic for Kenton (for whom he also wrote an oratorio in eighteen stanzas). "I went over fine," he said, but he went unnoticed. "L.A. is a weird town. I was ignored—by managers, by the press, by everybody."

In 1955 the would-be comedian met a girl named Sue Babior on a blind date. "She was perfect," he writes in his autobiography. "She was physically prepossessing, she was a leftist on the campus, she liked jazz, and she was atheist. I remarked to a friend of mine, 'I met a girl who is perfect. I can't seem to find a flaw.' He said, 'I know you and I have every confidence that you will.' " Sahl was stunned to find that she was only sixteen and not a college student, as he had thought, but a junior at Los Angeles High School. He dropped out of graduate school and sold cars until Babior graduated, then followed her to Berkeley (hitchhiking), where she enrolled at the University of California and Sahl audited classes and hung out at campus joints, debating politics, literature, movies, and jazz into the night. (He was never a Berkeley grad student, myth to the contrary.)

"There was a cadre of left-wing-oriented Jewish kids with fervor," Sahl says in his book. "I just sat around and listened." He once described it all in an interview as funny as any routine: "There's a bohemian set there getting degrees by osmosis. They go on for years sleeping on floors, playing chess. They keep meeting for coffee and listening to records. Guys are starving but they own speakers and pre-amps. They don't read publications with dates on them. They read quarterlies. A Trotskyite will come pounding on your door at midnight and tell you the Fascist dogs are hounding him. It turns out he has four tickets on his car for parking."

Sahl broke in at a student hangout in Berkeley, the White Log Tavern, an all-night doughnut and coffee shop near U.C.'s Sather Gate. He haunted campus joints, soaking up Nietzsche and Trotsky. "*Things were simple then,*" he told audiences. "*All there was to worry about was the destiny of man.*" He felt at home in the Bay Area. "I was born in San Francisco," he said, but Sahl was really formed by his experience in Berkeley. When he wasn't sleeping in the back of a friend's 1936 Buick and cadging free hamburgers and pies from a hot-dog joint, the Doggie Diner, managed by a friend, he would sleep in the window seat of the apartment that Babior shared with two roommates. To maintain his dignity he vanished at mealtimes.

When Sahl began searching for a paying gig, Babior suggested the hungry i. "It's in North Beach," she said, "which is the bohemian area—which means a lot of Jewish people acting like Italians." Sahl had tried several clubs before someone in North Beach advised, "Go across the street to the hungry i. Enrico Banducci will talk to anybody." Banducci's risky nature and bravura is what kept the hungry i alive. He took a chance on—took mercy on, really—the young, undernourished Korean war vet. Sahl had been encouraged to try the hungry i specifically, as a result of an off-hand comment by Babior: "If they understand you, you're home free, and if they don't understand you, they'll pretend that it's whimsical humor." Sahl later appreciated her remark as "a veiled attack on phony intellectuals that was quite prophetic."

Sahl was brought to the club by a friend, Larry Tucker, an eighteen-year-old four-hundred-pound fledgling comedian and writer who acted as Sahl's manager when he presented the rail-thin Sahl to Banducci. "I don't deal in comics," said the club owner. "I just have musicians and singers. I don't know about comics." (Sahl didn't either—"I don't have the image of myself as a comedian. It's what I say that's funny, not me.")

Tucker played on Banducci's sympathies, telling him, "He just got out of Veteran's Hospital with malnutrition and a ruptured appendix. He may be a little bit weak and shaky." Banducci told Tucker, "Bring him down and let's hear him." Tucker later recalled, "Enrico just didn't have the heart to tell him he couldn't use him." Banducci now says, smiling, "I didn't tell anyone but I didn't think he was so great. I didn't look at him and say, 'Oh, boy, this guy's gonna be fantastic!' I really looked at him and said, 'Poor kid, he looks so skinny. I thought, for seventy-five bucks a week he can't hurt the place." Sahl had offered to perform for free.

When he started out at the hungry i, Sahl still wore a suit and tie. Banducci (whose recollections, filmmaker Weide warns, "suffer from a lot of historical revisionism—it's hard to know what's true and what's bullshit") claims responsibility for Sahl's historic wardrobe change: "I told him, 'I want you to wear an open shirt, loafers, and a sweater and to put your foot on an apple box.'" (The apple crate was soon cut.) Today, Sahl would be overdressed on a comedy-club stage. Sahl's version: "It occurred to me that you mustn't look like any member of the society you're criticizing. What could I be? I went out and got myself a pair of blue denims and a blue sweater and a white button-down shirt open at the neck: graduate student. And I went out there and I did it and it worked. It let the audience relax." When he wanted to discard the sweater later, it was already part of his image and he was stuck with it.

That first night, he went onstage in a cast-off coat and tie from Kenton musicians, and the audience, full of Berkeley pals, obediently laughed. The next night was a tougher grind. "I thought I was really home free," he recalled. "Then I got up onstage on Monday night without my audience. Dead. People started throwing pennies and peanuts onstage. Boy, they were mad. They were really savage. I was shaken. That's how the newspaper was born in my act."

Banducci also claims the newspaper was his idea, but Sahl insists that the newspaper prop was born of necessity, a security blanket and prompt script on which he wrote key lines and stapled them to the *San Francisco Chronicle,* itself a favorite target. "Then I'd say, 'I see in the paper . . .' But under the harsh lights I couldn't read my own writing, or the silence would make me forget my lines. And then I would digress because I had no discipline. And when I digressed, I got my first laughs."

Sahl was playing to small, bewildered, even semihostile audiences, but Banducci dug him. Seated at a back table, he was out there in the dark, hooting and applauding, hoping to rally the customers. Recalled Sahl: "The audience didn't know what to make of it. It was a strange face, in a new language, with strange ideas. I was expressing what I really cared about. But I've got that negative nature—I thought I must be right. It's never occurred to me to change. The minute everyone agrees with you it's time to move on." He quotes Ibsen: "The majority is always wrong."

Banducci recalls now: "I liked Mort—he was so intelligent, but he was very intense. You had to be careful what you said to him. He listened to me, but he knew what he was doing. He had a few scattered laughs." Michael Stepanian, the i's doorman-cum-bouncer, recalls, "He would say things that would go over the audience. You could see the joke almost literally float three feet above the heads of the audience and go out the swinging doors. I'd say, 'That one's going, going, gone.'" Dick Nolan, a *San Francisco Examiner* columnist, was bewildered by the comedian's avant-garde stand-up style: "He's funny without being much fun. The glitter of Sahl's wit is that of an icicle, full of flash and devoid of warmth." Sahl, he said, was "never satisfied with anything." Precisely.

Laugh by laugh, the act began to build. Sahl would write out his routines across the street at a Chinese restaurant. Much of his commentary was local, with little about national or world politics. Still green, Sahl felt himself floundering as a performer, playing the laughs like any other raw comic. He talked then mainly about movies and sports cars and dating—not unlike comics today, except for the piercing insights. "I didn't dare talk about what was really on my mind. That took a while, that takes some trust. The scene was dominated by Jackie This and Jerry That—those guys were everywhere; they were the ruling class."

On his first album, *Mort Sahl at Sunset,* cut in 1955 (and cited as the first stand-up comedy album), the opening twenty minutes contain nary a political joke. The album—recorded live at Carmel, California's Sunset Auditorium—is, however, a tightly packed time capsule of mid-fifties lore. Sahl jabbers away about hi-fis and speakers so large that one guy "*had to move into the garage and use his house as the speaker.*" He laces the monologue with jargon and brand names. He mentions the jazz singers Jackie & Roy ("*They use their voice as instruments, so they have to ride in the truck with the other instruments*"). He talks about the blue-blazer fad and about students who take their closet door off the hinge and put it on four bricks for use as a coffee table—"*or eight bricks if they want French provincial.*" In engineering class, he designed a bridge without supports—"*I didn't want it to be too busy.*" He discusses the new '55 Jaguars and how he bought one so he could shift gears himself "*and assert my masculinity*"—just the sort of psychobabble he was so adept at skewering in quotes. He alludes to the Oedipus complex and drops in Latin terms like "*ergo*"—the first time *that* word had ever been uttered by a comedian. He reveals early traces of his antifeminism ("*I wanted to impress this girl, but she was a bohemian. I thought she was a girl*") and throughout the act leans on a favorite crutch phrase—"*so there was a lot of that.*"

In high gear, Sahl sounds like an LP playing at 45 RPM, with his piping voice and bursts of laughter. He was such a cheerful cynic. He discusses a CBS documentary about the use of mice for lung-cancer research—"*and the moral question of whether mice should smoke in the first place.*" His closing bit is about three men who held up the Fairmont Hotel and passed a note to the desk clerk. The note says, "'*This is a holdup. If you act normal, you won't get hurt,*' and the clerk—a UC student working nights—wrote a rebuttal: '*Act normal? Define your terms.*'" Woody Allen later devised a suspiciously similar holdup scene in his first major film, *Take the Money and Run.* In Sahl's version, the clerk corrects their illegible note (as in Allen's movie: "Gub? *You have a* gub? *What's a* gub?") and debates the social ills that brought the holdup men to this desperate point.

On side 2, he races through a routine about FBI agents on campus, jazzman Shorty Rogers, General Motors, Corvettes, Berkeley radicals who scrawl "Yankee Go Home!" on buildings, the AMA ("*They're against any cure that is rapid*"), advertising guys in four-button jackets ("*Three but-*

tons aren't sincere enough") and charcoal-gray suits ("*They wanted a color more somber than black*"), the GI bill, Walter Winchell's red-baiting, coeds studying political science, and his time at Fort Ord. He closes with a story about going to a Stanford University poetry club to hear Truman Capote read "Grass" (tossing in a funny Capote impression), "*attended by poets in tattersall shirts reading* Moses and Monotheism."

A fevered energy drives his commentary. Notes Ronald L. Smith, who runs Sahl's official Web site: "Mort was so *wired*. He had so many ideas floating through his head." Sahl once explained where all that energy originated: "I had no one to talk to for twenty-six years, no place to say anything. It all spilled out of me. The second thing was, I was afraid no one would laugh and I wanted to pretend I wasn't noticing the audience. I didn't want the audience to get the idea I was telling a joke and waiting for a laugh"—hence his conversational style. "So the burden was on them to fill that space. I was afraid to pause, afraid of silences. I didn't take that risk. I kept talking through it, kept filling up the gaps—that's where the verbosity comes from. Then I began to take chances."

Between jokes, he would throw in political asides—"and that is when they began to laugh. At the end of the third week, I broke the sound barrier and I was in." His breakthrough and most quoted joke: "*Have you seen the Joe McCarthy jacket? It's like an Eisenhower jacket only it's got an extra flap that fits over the mouth.*" The Eisenhower jokes inspired a contemporary wit to tag him an "Ike-conoclast." Other edgy jokes from the period: "*Joe McCarthy doesn't question what you say so much as your right to say it*"; "*For a while, every time the Russians threw an American in jail, the Un-American Activities Committee would retaliate by throwing an American in jail, too*"; and "*Maybe the Russians will steal all our secrets, then* they'll *be two years behind.*"

That such cracks, mild by today's standards, stirred up so much attention—political journalists regularly spiced up their articles and columns by adding a dash of Sahl—reflects the temper of the times. Banducci remembers Sahl's McCarthy-jacket joke and audiences booing him, even once waiting for him to leave the club. "We had to fight our way out," Banducci claims, chuckling. Yet for such an outspoken guy, Sahl had relatively few hecklers. "It's a funny thing, most of the complaints about me come from recanted leftists," he said in 1955. Grover Sales recalls: "It's hard for the current generation to realize how nobody made jokes about Ike and J. Edgar Hoover. Nobody had ever heard anyone get up onstage and do political humor. It was the laughter of liberation."

Sahl's mother pestered the influential *San Francisco Chronicle* columnist

Herb Caen to go see her son, and in one note gave Caen a Sahl-like jab: "You're Mr. San Francisco but you don't know what's going on because you haven't seen a comic named Mort Sahl." Thus goaded, Caen finally showed up, in Sahl's fifth month, and wrote: "Wound up back at the hungry i to hear a young comedian named Mort Sahl. Sahl has been there eighteen weeks and I like to keep up on things. He's very funny, discussing everything from the difficulty of necking in Jaguars to the reason Horse Trader Ed was sent to prison—they caught him selling a sports car to someone who doesn't live in Sausalito. I don't know where Mr. Sahl came from but I'm glad he's here."

Caen's remarks gave Sahl instant credibility, and the columnist's constant plugs and quotes from the act put his career on track. Caen took Sahl to dinner after first seeing him and decreed, "You are on your way." He had the power to make it happen. Nobody existed in San Francisco until mentioned by Caen, and no celebrity blew into town for more than ten minutes without paying his respects to "the Winchell of the West," who took people like Danny Kaye, Eddie Cantor, and the head of CBS's West Coast division to see the comic. Sahl and Sue Babior were even married in Caen's home in 1955. When they divorced nearly three years later, she took up with the jazz sax player Paul Desmond, Sahl's closest friend, to whom he once gave a cigarette lighter inscribed: "To the sound from the fury."

The hungry i enshrined Sahl, but Sahl also put the club, and Banducci, on the map. Notes Grover Sales: "Sahl made the hungry i. It was just an obscure boîte before him." After Sahl's success there, says Jonathan Winters, "they came to see somebody who was different"—comics like Winters and Woody Allen, who was dismayed when he finally played the place in 1964 and found it filled with bus tours. Banducci was soon devoted to Sahl, and, despite heated arguments, it was a tight bond. Sahl says now, "He had theatrical flair and imagination. I'd be washing cars if it weren't for Enrico."

Even later, when he was earning $3,000 a week, Sahl still lived like a starving graduate student. He would devour armloads of magazines while listening to Kenton on his elaborate hi-fi rig. A *Holiday* magazine profiler remarked, "Mort will sit huddled in an all-night movie, walk back to his hotel at dawn, pick his way to the refrigerator through a litter of newspapers, magazines, books, socks, and sweaters, drink a glass of fruit juice and, when driven to it, sleep."

Sahl stayed at the hungry i for a year, interrupted only by a long run at the Blue Angel in New York. Enrico says, "He wasn't the same comic six months after he was there." Banducci and Sahl had lots of little skirmishes over money, but their first major battle was over a new comic, Dick Gautier, whom Sahl considered a rival. Banducci recalls, "Mort wanted me to fire Gautier. He said, 'I'm your main act,' and I told him, 'Nobody tells me who to hire,' and Sahl said, 'Him or me.' " He left for a year and a half and went from the i to the Village Vanguard, where he broke a house attendance record. Banducci and Sahl had a fourteen-year spat that wasn't patched up until 1981, when Tom Cohen got them together for his documentary film *The hungry i Reunion*. The house pianist, Don Asher, once endured Sahl's wrath when he came in too soon with the comic's exit music ("It's a Grand Old Flag") and Sahl snapped, "Mr. Asher, I suggest you contemplate another means of livelihood." "I was scared," recalls Asher. "He wielded power in those days."

One club owner said, "Make no mistake, Mort's Hostility City all the way." Lainie Kazan recalls, "He was very busy being Mort Sahl at the time." The writer Jerry Mander, then a publicist for the hungry i, recalls: "He was a very strange man, a very difficult man—very angry, very sarcastic, very verbally abrasive; he never had any therapy. He lives by different lights." Paul Goldenberg, who managed the hungry i then and now manages New York's Carlyle Hotel, remembers Sahl as a nervous, high-strung steed and takes credit for the line that always brought him on— "*Ladies and gentleman, the hungry i is very proud to present the next president of the United States!*"

Every celebrity in town dropped by to catch the new phenomenon. Steve Allen, on seeing Sahl for the first time, said, "I was struck by how amateur he seemed. That's a compliment, by the way. All comics of the forties and fifties wore tuxedos, they were all pretty glib, pretty smooth performers who could handle bad audiences. They were very much in control onstage. The first time I saw Mort I wondered what he did for a living. He had none of the nightclub polish, which was indicative of his uniqueness—as if he just stepped out of history class for a minute. His very un-show business manner was one of the things I liked when I first saw him work." When Sahl played the Black Orchid in Chicago, the owners made the comedian leave the club between shows because of his casual garb and return through the kitchen.

Banducci recalled those early audiences' uncertain responses to Sahl: "There was a time when it wasn't smart to laugh at Mort Sahl. He'd use big words and people would say, 'What'd he say? What'd he say?' 'Hey, dummy, didn't you understand what he said? Ha-ha-ha-ha-ha!' They didn't understand either, but they were laughing." Sahl's sardonic chortle, grimace, and eye rolls were laugh cues for audiences who weren't sure they got the joke; at times, he even literally stuck his tongue in his cheek.

Sahl explained to the *Los Angeles Times* critic Charles Champlin how he worked: "I never found you could write the act. You can't rehearse the audience's responses. You adjust to them every night. I come in with only an outline. You've got to have a spirit of adventure. I follow my instincts and the audience is my jury. If I try a joke and they like it, I extend it. The audience is bright, you have to believe that, and they'll know to find the nugget in the story. The audience will always find the joke, but by the time they get around to it, I'm on to something else." In no time, the public caught up with him. "The idea of being hip has pretty well leveled off," he said in 1968. "Today everyone is pretty smart."

Some critics labeled Sahl only a clever phrasemaker, an intellectual *shpritzer,* when in fact he was as crafty a storyteller as Myron Cohen. Sahl's stories weren't couched as "stories," but they were heavily fictionalized versions of his life in Washington and Los Angeles, with real characters—politicians, movie stars, talk-show hosts. Every tale had a beginning, a middle, and eventually an end (capped by his triumphant dry staccato laugh), much of it told in dialogue. It may have been about some political reception he had attended, a movie location he'd been on, a TV show on which he appeared, or a meeting with Robert Redford, a studio head, or some White House functionary. Like any gifted narrator, he was so good at taking you along on his travels that you didn't quite realize until the show was over that you had been on a labyrinthine journey. "He has access to everything he ever thought, felt, read, or knew," says his friend, ex–CBS reporter John Hart, "and it's that access that makes his performance so rich and so enlightening."

Sahl learned to set up jokes as adroitly as any traditional comic. "What he does onstage," notes Robert Weide, "is very clever but very subtle. He will make sure you get the reference before he goes on, and he'll do it in a way that doesn't make you feel stupid. He'll say, 'I'm certain you all know about so-and-so's legislation,' and give you the frame of reference for the joke he's about to tell you. Even if you're someone who never reads the paper, you'll get enough of it just from the way he sets it up." He confided in the audience and made everyone a jolly coconspirator. *"Maybe if things go well this year we won't have to hold these meetings in secret anymore,"* he would say; or, *"I'm just here to take your minds off the fact that we're trapped in this mine shaft.*" It was always Us versus Them; if you were there in the basement club with him, that was proof enough to Sahl that you cared, whatever your politics.

His several albums, unlike many by his sixties peers, are not patched-together segments from various shows but are a continuous flow that never sounds choppy even though he jumps from topic to topic—from Watergate to Michael Dukakis ("*The only colorless Greek in America*"), to himself ("*I generalize with no specific knowledge, so if I wasn't perceptive I'd be a bigot*"). He could drive a stake through any fashionable idea by sharply mocking it with a glib pop catchphrase, tossed off along the way to a conclusion he never quite reaches. "He has thrown away lines other comedians would give their eye teeth to deliver," said one reviewer. Dave Brubeck hated to perform after him: "Mort's impossible to follow. He demands so much from an audience that it hasn't the strength for anyone else." Much of the audience's joy in Sahl lay in being exposed to such a crackling, encyclopedic mind as it darted from topic to topic. The improvisation, wrote the critic Penelope Gilliatt, "goes on a breakneck stammering loop and you think it will never make the circle. It always does. He freewheels a bike on a high-wire tightrope with his brain racing and his hands off the handlebars."

Hearing him now is like reading an old newspaper, edited with smart-aleck footnotes. The rolled-up newspaper in his hand was a perfect defining prop—like George Burns's cigar, Woody Allen's spectacles, or Phyllis Diller's cigarette holder—as he made his way through the news, a brilliant broken-field runner zigzagging through ninety-minute monologues with seeming spontaneity. Even though the general direction of a given routine was pretty well mapped out ahead of time, it rarely sounded rote.

While he clung to a few favorite lines for years, like any ancient vaudeville comic, generally he would rework a piece until he recorded it and then drop it. He was so prolific, and so adept at playing off the news, that he could invent material daily, like a twenty-four-hour cable news channel; he wasn't dependent on writers, only on himself. Sahl could be brutal (on Bobby Kennedy's wiretaps: "*Little Brother is watching*"), but rarely was there a cheap shot or an unearned laugh. He once said, "I have such an oblique personality that when people laugh at a joke I want to discard it. It's a technical problem. I get bored with something before I get to polish it." If he liked a line, however, and it didn't do well, he might stubbornly use it anyway, for weeks.

As he once explained to Paul Krassner, "When I work, I feel a certain cadence, and I feel it coming, I feel rhythms—that's why the jokes sometimes look premeditated, and they seem Bob Hope–ish. You feel a cadence and you find it as you go. But I feel impatient with it and want to start with something else, because every word I do is improvised. I never stress that word 'improvise.' It's become distasteful to me because it's been dissipated by people who don't." Of all the comedians who compare their fifties work to jazz, Sahl was the most jazzlike, with the possible exception of Lenny Bruce; and he was fluent in jazz lingo, sprinkling his early monologues with swinging Sinatraisms like *gasser, chick, drag, cool it, bugged, dig it, the most, weirdo, wild, shakin', wigged,* and, to be sure, *all that jazz*—but he transcended jazz and cult audiences.

His favorite technique was to discuss a news event as if reporting on it, when in reality he was reinventing it for his own satiric purposes. As Robert Rice noted, "Sahl doesn't so much comment on the news as on what he thinks it is." Paul Desmond added that observing the waxing and waning of the comic's bits was "like watching a garden in time-lapse photography." Considering how volatile his material was, it's surprising how rarely audiences attempted to tangle with him—he was too sharp-tongued. One of his standard heckler put-downs was, "*I guess that's not the first time you've failed in the dark*"—about as raw as he ever got. He developed quickly, telling Krassner in a 1963 *Realist,* "The act has gone from children's entertainment to adult education. I have more license. The audience seems to give me a certain credence as an elder statesman." He was all of thirty-six.

A critic wrote that show business and politics made up the prism through which Sahl reflected on all contemporary affairs. He saw their convergence before most others did. With his nose for radical chic crazes, clichés, and brand names, Sahl was a precursor of Tom Wolfe. He has perfect pitch for how Hollywood types talk and can caricature them in one deadly phrase. On egotistical talk-show host Tom Snyder: "*Listen, Pope, I went to Catholic school, too*"; on Ed McMahon after Johnny Carson retired: "*Ed is still laughing in case Johnny has said anything funny at home*"; on Carson's contract with NBC: "*Part of Johnny Carson's new multimillion-dollar deal with NBC is that he doesn't have to be on the program every night but he has to* watch *it.*"

He mimics political/media/showbiz cant with such accuracy that you're certain he really *did* attend a White House party where Republicans danced the minuet as the wives fanned themselves and swooned.

Sahl is the antithesis of a physical comedian, yet he worked with athletic dexterity—the menacing smile, the subversive guffaw, the supple voice that can reproduce, fleetingly, anything from party hack to airhead starlet. His swarthy looks and barking laugh are part of a keen canine intelligence. Before a juicy line, he seemed to lick his chops.

He worked from a deep skepticism that was so ingrained that he could get laughs simply by uttering a name or a trendy phrase—*"standard deviation," "communal guilt," "group needs"*—which, because it came from Sahl's lips, was steeped in sarcasm. Sahl told Ronald L. Smith that he would try to denigrate certain celebrities "even by how I pronounced their name." He had a parodist's eye for the telling detail (Steve Allen reading Walter Lippmann while munching a Mounds bar) and for vivid imagery: in a segment on John Kennedy, after imagining an updated version of the film *North by Northwest,* he describes *"the President climbing over his own face on Mount Rushmore."*

Sahl mastered the contemporary argot—the empty phrases, circumlocutions, euphemisms, and platitudes—not just of politics and show business but of the military, media, academia, feminism, psychology, relationships. He had, noted Lou Gottlieb in a review of a 1960 Sahl album, a "virtuosic command of today's American language that is not merely verbal facility" but a reflection of compulsive reading of everything from *Motor Trend* to *Foreign Affairs,* and he never missed an issue of *Variety.* A voracious skimmer, he was able to quickly absorb a book's gist and run with it. He kept a UPI news ticker in his Beverly Hills den.

Sahl quickly acquired the reputation of being the darling of the intellectuals, an image he disdained: "It was absurd. I was barely a C student. Only in show business would I be considered an intellectual, which I am by default. I *quote* intellectuals." Just as Catskills comics hated being geographically defined, the bright comedians of renaissance comedy resisted being labeled intellectuals, mostly because it narrowed their audience and cut into their bookings. He once noted that "the first thing I used to hear in San Francisco was, 'Well, only intellectuals want to hear it.' Then after that it was, 'They don't want to hear it in the East.' Then, 'They don't want to hear it on TV.' "

"So-called intellectual humor caught on," Sahl remarks in his memoir, "and what is probably my biggest secret is that most Americans look down on other Americans and think they're the only ones that understand the act. All people understand the artist. More than political censorship, or any other kind of censorship, I ran into intellectual censorship against the audience, the most dangerous censorship of all." He would wind up his act saluting the audience, "*Thank you all for your individual perceptions.*"

A certain nineteen-year-old rookie TV comedy writer who first saw him perform in New York, at the Blue Angel in 1954, was stunned and inspired by Sahl's insights. The writer was Woody Allen, who has often said that it was Sahl's style and brains that encouraged him to consider performing: "He was the best thing I ever saw. He was like Charlie Parker in jazz. There was a need for a revolution, everybody was ready for the revolution, but some guy had to come along who could perform the revolution and be great. Mort was the one. He totally restructured comedy. He changed the rhythm of the jokes. He had different content, surely, but the revolution was in the way he laid the jokes down. His jokes were laid down with such guile. He was suddenly this great genius that appeared who revolutionized the medium. He himself was a great funny man. They didn't know that the art was inborn in him, in his intonation. He was highly, highly energetic, like hypermanic."

Before he saw Sahl, Allen had only toyed with the notion of performing, but after seeing him he decided to take the plunge—or forget the idea completely. "I was just so discouraged by how great he was that, for maybe a year or two, I felt that there was nowhere to go," Allen told his biographer Eric Lax. Allen then saw that sheer wit could win the day: "Sahl made it less difficult for all of us who came after him. He was like the tip of the iceberg. Underneath were all the other people who came along: Lenny Bruce, Nichols & May, all the Second City players. I'm not saying that these people wouldn't have happened anyway, but Mort was the vanguard of the enormous renaissance of nightclub comedy that ended not long after Bill Cosby and I came along. Sahl's whole approach was different. It wasn't that he did political comment—as everyone keeps insisting. It was that he had genuine insights. He made the country receptive to a kind of comedy it wasn't used to hearing. He made the country listen to jokes that required them to think."

Allen's manager, Jack Rollins, advised his neophyte client not to be overly dazzled by Sahl. Rollins's position on Sahl and Jonathan Winters in the sixties: "They're popular but they will not be big stars. They have a 'shrill brilliance': they come out and do their material and go off. Yet however much the audience laughs, no person is accessible behind them. Woody's material was all about the person behind it." While Sahl attacked what was wrong with the world, Woody Allen attacked what was wrong with himself—another sea change in stand-up comedy that would occur about six years after Sahl's great breakthrough.

Sahl literally blazed a trail by forging an informal comedy circuit out of jazz clubs through his tours with Kenton and Brubeck, long before there were "comedy clubs." Jazz rooms like Mister Kelly's in Chicago, the Village Vanguard in New York, and the Crescendo in Los Angeles began booking comedians after Sahl played them. "I had to build up my own network of places to play because the others weren't available to me."

The critic Foster Hirsch notes that Sahl's mind, social consciousness, and hip antiestablishment stance also "changed the image of the Jewish comic"—from rowdy Borscht Belt *tummler* to brainy campus philosopher-wit. But Sahl, perhaps the least "Jewish" of all that era's Jewish comedians, said, "I don't have any kinship with a Jewish background. . . . If the role of the Jew is to rock the boat and to be inquisitive—intellectually curious, that is—fine. Classic role." Asked if he considered himself Jewish, he said, "No! I belong to me. And that's *enough*. I don't consider myself anything. You get along with people who have *ideas*, that's all. . . . I'm afraid I will never have a group. My people are never going to be in power, whoever they may be."

When Sahl cracked that "*there are no women in the beat generation, just girls who have broken with their parents for the evening,*" he was discussing a world he knew well; he was a spokesman for—and in a sense against—his generation. The Compass/Second City historian Janet Coleman has observed, "Like any satirist, Sahl's success in show business depended on the good will of a paying audience of people he made fun of: the rich, the powerful, the educated—not the working class." Robert Rice wrote: "He excoriates their mating habits, their avocations, and their intellectual attitudes, he keeps up a drumfire against almost everything they are attracted to—coffeehouses, earnest young women, sports cars, stereophonic jazz, even 'Pogo' " ("*What kind of civilization are we living in when a possum says something and we all say, 'I wish I'd said that' *"). Sahl's most zealous admirers were the targets of some of his most noxious bile. He captured the earnest Zen beatniks he'd met in Berkeley coffee shops in a single deft thrust: "*The Western religions have failed me.*" His very language, noted Rice, "with its thick overlay of jazz and academic jargon, is a deliberate parody of the way his people talk." Sahl collected clichés and flung them back as jokes. "One of the great tools comedians don't use," he noted, "is the English language." Says Coleman, "Sahl was much more than a novelty, he was an alternative press," and she quotes Shelley

Berman's remark that "I write my own material but Mort's is written by William Randolph Hearst."

Unlike most of his colleagues, Sahl ruthlessly engaged and enraged his audiences, who became part of a one-sided conversation punctuated with phrases like, "*Now where was I?*"; "*Oh, yes, back to our theme*"; "*I want to return to that later*"; "*Right!*"; "*Unbelievable!*"; "*I want to talk about that in the next show*"; "*Let's see, what else happened? . . .*" If you listened carefully, you could hear revealing little personal asides—"*I'm essentially a puritan,*" or, following applause, "*I'm not geared for total acceptance.*" Referring to his Asian wife of the time, Sahl would say, "*I actually have empathy with Nixon—we're both trying to live with the Chinese.*"

Like any autobiographical novelist, he telescoped, merged, and embroidered facts and figures from life. Because his material was all current and newsy, people never considered him a folklorist, but he was an urbane teller of tall tales who wasn't above a joke-joke (like pulling into a town in Maine and asking the cabdriver where the action was—"*He took us to a place where they fished illegally*") or even a pun ("*Che's National Bank*"). In his album *On Relationships* he unreels a long story about hiring an assistant from Smith College, larded with dialogue between him and the coed—probably all fanciful. His long-standing defense against any doubters was, "Everything I say is actual, not factual."

He's really no less of a fabulist than Bill Cosby, Woody Allen, or Richard Pryor, all praised for doing much the same thing. Sahl would simply update references in stories and jokes, changing "*God bless George Bush—long may he waver!*" to "*God bless Bill Clinton, long may he waver!*" Both versions got laughs; the joke may have originated with Eisenhower. He interchanged Colin Powell and Bob Dole in his line "*They want to restart the American dream, without waking the American people.*" His White House visits are semiauthentic, says his friend the comedy writer Herb Sargent. "He'll invent things sparked by seeing Kissinger across the room, and then make up a story about him." People who know him well say that his alleged excursions into White House parties are based on a few long-ago dinners there, mainly during the Reagan years. He knew Reagan from his Hollywood days and was friendly with Nancy. "I've seen photos of them all together," says Weide.

How many of the anecdotes in his act are fabrications and how many happened remains a mystery. In Weide's view, "They're all based on a grain of truth or an incident that he blows up to make bigger and bigger," like the lengthy routine he did for years about working on the film *Ordi-*

nary People (in which he quotes its director, Robert Redford, saying, "*I'm exploring Mary Tyler Moore's dark side*"). That was "totally fabricated," says Weide. "Redford may have sent him a script or talked to him on the phone, so there's a basis in reality." While out of power, Sahl worked as a script doctor, and he says on his latest album that he's "written" (i.e., had a hand in) twenty-one movies, from the remake of *Sabrina* to *The Firm, Love Affair, Flashback, Gauntlet,* and a Clint Eastwood film he was to star in that never happened, plus an original screenplay—an autobiographical story of a divorced man who learns that his work is all he has.

A VERY EARLY (July 22, 1954) review in the *San Francisco Chronicle* by Terrence O'Flaherty, the paper's longtime TV critic, commented on Sahl's unique style: "Down at the 'hungry i' they've got a brisk young comedian named Mort Sahl—a refreshing relief after an overdose of folk singers at this North Beach spa. His humor is something very special." O'Flaherty went on to report that Eddie Cantor—to give an idea of the comedy gap that Sahl leaped over in a single bound—"has taken the lad under his wing."

All the old comedy pros tried to straighten Sahl out. Cantor advised him, "Don't wear that red sweater. Wrong associations"; Groucho Marx: "I love your act but it'll never go"; Jack Paar spent two hours before his TV show instructing Sahl to be "less esoteric," but Sahl reports, "The audience was made up of Rotarians. I was on nine minutes and, being esoteric, had to stop six times for applause." He quickly began pulling in an esoteric mix of fans—Adlai Stevenson, Saul Bellow, Lillian Hellman, James Jones, Leonard Bernstein, Marlene Dietrich, S. J. Perelman. Arthur Schlesinger, Jr., said Sahl's popularity was "a sign of a yearning for youth, irreverence, trenchancy, satire, a clean break with the past."

Although he played the Copacabana in 1959 and did so well with a mainstream audience that TV took a second look at him and the movies tossed a cameo crumb his way (*All the Young Men,* in which he answers the phone on Guadalcanal: "*Hello. World War II*"), his audiences were drawn mainly from people who didn't normally go to nightclubs to see comedians. "When I started I did a lot of evangelism, you may remember," he told a *Playboy* panel in 1961. "I've really stuck my neck out. I'm the guy who went to Miami, to Vegas, to the Chez Paree, to the Copacabana—to prove the point. Because I always wanted to challenge the people in the business on their own ground. Not just hide in the little clubs." He said,

"When I hit gold, when I hit a vein, I don't like to talk to three hundred people. I'd like to be talking to three million—but the reason I talk to thirty million on television is because I *built* on the nightclubs. What put me on the cover of *Time*? I had an audience. The *audience* made me a hero." Sahl was confident that in time a mass audience would accept him: "Audiences are in an oxcart until someone chooses to propel it."

But television proved a reluctant, jittery suitor. NBC forced him to wear a suit and tie in his first TV appearance on *The Colgate Comedy Hour,* but later relented and let him appear in his trademark sweater and open collar—the mid-fifties equivalent of wearing shorts and a tank top to church. "In a sweater," noted O'Flaherty, "he has just the right campus touch that took ten years off his age and five years off his act." That "campus touch" set Sahl apart visually from all other stand-up comics. As proof that he was never content to be a fringe voice shouting on the sidelines, in the seventies he even shed his sweater for buckskin jackets, turtlenecks, and other modish attire; the consummate nonconformist let his hair and sideburns grow. He wanted to prove wrong the smart money that said he was a messenger for the intelligentsia. William Morris wouldn't handle him, he claims, because they feared nobody would understand him.

Sahl was considered risky business for TV. He was under contract to CBS and NBC, but he frightened both networks and never made it beyond rehearsals of the Perry Como or Giselle MacKenzie shows. He didn't help matters much by opening an NBC guest shot with the line, "*Well, kids, if we're good today, General Sarnoff might like us, and if he likes us he'll go to Charles Van Doren and get us more money.*" Sahl always bent over backward to show that he couldn't be bought, even if it meant antagonizing the brass. He revealed an early talent for dashing any chances at a mass audience by refusing to compromise. Asked by Eddie Fisher on TV to "say something funny," Sahl memorably replied, "John Foster Dulles." Pretty ballsy stuff in 1958. Considering his impact, it's amazing that he went as far as he did almost entirely without TV, network radio, or films.

In those days, riding high, Sahl had a lot of plans—not just TV but movies; he wanted to make films about the American woman in society and how hard it is for men to deal with smart women. Chicks, as he called them, were Sahl's second favorite subject after politics. For him, females were like liberals—they were always failing him, although he claimed to be their supporter and in favor of "intellectual suffrage" for women, despite lines like "*A woman's place is in the stove.*"

His dark, roguish good looks, intellect, and vitality attracted plenty of women; Herbert Mitgang called him "aggressively virile." He dated a lot of actresses (*"and other female impersonators,"* as he cracks), among them Shirley MacLaine, Tippi Hedren, Julie Newmar, Yvonne Craig ("Bat-girl"), Nancy Olson, and Phyllis Kirk, with whom he had an intense two-year relationship. "Mort feeds on crisis," Kirk later said. "Mort's problem is acceptance. He's not accepted for what he is, and he hasn't yet learned to accept people for what they are." He writes that, while he was dating Hedren, Alfred Hitchcock wouldn't let him on the set of *The Birds*. She told him, "Hitch said you'll ruin things. He said you ruined Phyllis Kirk's life and you ruined Shirley MacLaine's life." Sahl says, "I stopped the car in the middle of traffic and threw her out."

He dated Gloria Steinem for a while, but was, as ever, disenchanted and claimed she "used men [he names Mike Nichols]—all the things she condemns." He also dated waitresses and stewardesses—"Yeah, I've worked that beat, too." Sahl, the idealist, claimed to be a romantic and monogamous, but was capable of such oxymoronic comments as, "I've always paid women the ultimate compliment, which is that I listened to them, whereas Schopenhauer said if women didn't have a unique anatomy there would be a bounty on them." Asked by *Playboy* what women wanted from him, he replied: "Hilarity. Alcohol. Adventure. Escape. Danger. Reflected prestige. They think I'm what I seem to be onstage, and I'm not. Girls say to me, 'You analyze too much. Why don't you follow your feelings?' " He hooted. "That's ridiculous. If I followed my feelings I'd be an outlaw." What he longed for was "a bright, curious, alive girl."

One such bright, curious, alive woman, also attractive and successful, whom he went out with after meeting her on a blind date, recalls: "It was a romantic disaster. Mort is very difficult to be with, incredibly intense. Mort's not bitter about his career. He was and is very bitter about women. He's not a misogynist; he's a totally disappointed romanticist. He has an idealized, very romantic view of women based on the 1950s—someone like a Julie London: a sultry woman in a smoky bar. We didn't always get along, but we liked each other. We had a lot of very intense dinners. I was an anomaly to him. He thought I was very feminist. He likes the girly-girly type. His male side is attracted to Vargas girls; his female side is attracted to take-charge women. That's the duality and complexity of Mort Sahl."

Nonetheless, she warmed to him: "He's such a dear man. He's the sweetest, saddest man—not breaking into sobs, but he needs to be adulated and adored. He wants to be understood and heard. He says men get a raw deal. He believes in every movie he ever saw and the lyrics to all the old songs, and at dinner he quotes those old lines." She adds: "Mort is not one-on-one funny; Mort is provocative. Mort will bark a line at you from a show. But he listens. He's a terrific man, a down-to-earth nice guy, but very, very complex." The reporter Blake Green remembers a less endearing Sahl when she worked at the hungry i in 1968 during a newspaper strike and had dinner once with him and Herb Caen: "He was just an absolute jerk, a very self-important jerk."

Sahl was a woman's guide to Mr. Wrong. But while his romantic views may be stuck in the fourteenth century, he has always been refreshing, however politically incorrect if not emotionally suicidal. As with Mencken or Shaw, the language is cranked up about 50 percent for effect, to stir things up: "Chicks don't want to get old—all they want is to dance all night. Chicks holler for equal rights. What they really mean is they want men's rights and they're willing to give up theirs, which is a dumb bargain. Women want to fight and lose. It's a war and the chicks are waiting to get beaten. Don't believe them—women are *not* like us. Be prepared for surprises no matter how bulky your portfolio of experience. Women are disappointed in American men. And with good reason. Men have collapsed. They're like Cream of Wheat." In one rough riff, he cracks, "Why be a first-class woman when you have a chance to be a second-class man? Women have all the intensity now, but it's rooted in disappointment. The men are all beaten, full of apology. To women, men become the road company of their fathers."

His first marriage lasted two and a half years. "It wasn't a total failure. But she was very Jewish—sensual and neurotic and drowned me in filial obligations. 'First, we'll visit my mother, then we'll visit your mother; then *my* father, then *your* father.' Like many angry women, she had a list of grievances. They present them to you at the door." He didn't get along with his father-in-law, who told him, "We never knew you'd become Mort Sahl." He told the public radio host Sedge Thomson, "I don't lead a racy life. I just run around looking for the perfect woman and watching my satellite dish." Sahl joked that he was *"looking for the perfect woman, someone to grow old with, and I have searched from one end of the bar to the other."* In his act, he cracked, *"About the time they're getting ready to allow priests to marry, the rest of us have given up marrying."*

Sahl views females as gladiators or geishas, and some of his remarks about women place him well to the right of Henry Miller. "I don't expect women to be champions," he has said. "I'm the champion. I don't expect them to be intellectuals." His battle-of-the-sexes jabs sound like excerpts of obsessive Philip Roth characters—Alexander Portnoy, Nathan Zuckerman, Alvin Pepler. But he has always been leery of psychoanalysis, joking, "I haven't exhausted reason yet."

His second and third marriages were to the same woman, the former *Playboy* Playmate Margaret ("China"—pronounced "Cheena") Lee, the magazine's first Asian centerfold. Miss August of 1963 revealed to readers that "being a Bunny is my main career. The popular image of the shy and retiring Oriental female is long overdue for a change." He had once kidded that his ideal woman was a *Playboy* centerfold. *"Once a month you have a paper doll you can call your own. You can unfold her, and fold her up again, but can you live with her?"* In fact, Lee was a strong-minded woman who pushed him to work the material harder ("Don't get bored with it—there's more there," she kept urging him) and the mother of their late son, Mort Jr. She was drawn to him, he said, "because of my independence and she had no mythology about show business. She was bored by it, so that's great *already*." The author and former CBS scribe Gary Paul Gates, a Sahl friend, says, "She was a tough audience. He carried a big torch for China after their second divorce. She was a very strong, no-nonsense kind of woman." Observes Christon: "She was married to a comedian but she had no sense of humor."

Sahl met his current wife, Kenslea, a Delta Air Lines stewardess, on a flight. As a friend tells it, when they first chatted on the plane she had no idea who he was, which charmed him. His new wife is in her forties, says Ronald L. Smith. "She's a stable older woman, not some bimboette trophy wife. She saw him on [the TV shows] *Thriller* and *Richard Diamond* but never as a stand-up. She seems to be a good influence on him and tends to his archives." Weide adds, "She's been great for him. She's very, very sweet. She's taken a lot of the edge off him, the bitterness."

His ideals regarding women, politics, and America come from old movies, often by Frank Capra. "My eyes get moist when I watch *Mr. Smith Goes to Washington* and I realize what they've done to this country since then," he writes in his 1976 memoir. Sahl sees himself as a blend of Jimmy Stewart idealism and John Wayne heroism. His other favorite films include *The Quiet Man, High Noon, Twelve O'Clock High,* and, especially, *One-Eyed Jacks.* Marlon Brando is another of his heroes in an ever-dwindling pantheon. In *One-Eyed Jacks* he identified with both the outlaw

(Brando) and the lawman (Karl Malden), who rob banks together until Malden becomes a sheriff. As Sahl sees it, every time a new president is elected, whoever it may be, "they're the new sheriff and I'm still the bank robber."

He believes in heroes, himself very much included, and one of his favorite early self-mocking lines was that people accused him of having "a Christ-like image of myself." He admitted that he saw himself as an apostle bringing the gospel to the people, one reason he accepted gigs in places that seemed less conducive to his messianic message—Las Vegas and the massive supper clubs; he loved preaching to sinners and saw his lines as sacred text. He's mainly a disappointed patriot, comedy's man without a country, carrying his bent spear and banner, a stand-up Don Quixote. His main real-life hero was Adlai Stevenson—"He doesn't play the game by the rules; Stevenson is a civilized man." Sahl, who spent serious time with Stevenson at the late governor's farm, said, "Of all the people I've known who've run for office, he never once asked for anything but my company."

By 1958 Sahl had arrived with a bang and was booked into a Broadway house (twenty-five years before Jackie Mason's own one-man coup de théâtre), in a show called *The Next President,* which got generally good notices. A group of folksingers calling themselves the "Chorus of the Collective Conscience" opened for him. The *Times*'s Brooks Atkinson reviewed "the pleasant-looking young man with curly hair and regular teeth who has read everything, believes none of it, and talks about it at breakneck speed." He observed that "by curtain time the brightness is wearing off," but noted that Sahl's "conversation was fast, literate, witty, and spontaneous. Name anything that is current in intellectual society and Sahl can make it look either bogus or hopeless. Although he talks in circles, his aim is unerring." Atkinson ended sternly, saying Sahl was not yet "a full-length stage entertainer," whatever that meant. *Newsweek* commented: "Mort Sahl for a full evening in the theater can be a little too much of a good thing. Summing up: A bright new talent with a real gift of gab." *Time* dubbed him "a fresh breath of carbon monoxide" but said he had "too much smugness and too little showmanship," sensing, accurately, that "the danger with anybody as much commentator as jokester is that the mocking will becoming messianic. Already there is an atmosphere in the audience of followers rather than fans."

The *Herald Tribune*'s Walter Kerr regarded Sahl as an early warning signal—"an indication that something in our society has begun—after too many muddy and fearful years—to change. First thing you know, irreverence will be in vogue again, and even satire may wear its old outrageous and becoming smile." Kerr noted Sahl's twitchy mannerisms, his "habit of clenching his teeth fitfully as though he were grinding up something or someone," and observed primly that he "dresses untidily and may not shave regularly." Kerr concluded: "It's nice to know improper things can once more be said in public." Dick Cavett saw the show and recalls: "He was a stunning wonder. I remember wondering if Woody [Allen] would like him as much as I did. So we decided to go and see him at Basin Street East, and we came out and Woody didn't react much. Finally he said, 'When I see him I get this strong feeling that everyone else should quit the business.' He had that intelligence that just dazzled you."

When he was finally canonized by the *Time* cover story in August 1960, the magazine said that, until Sahl, political satire "was caught between social protest and safe, sponsor-tested lampoons." He made lightning connections between seemingly unrelated events, joking that the golf-loving Eisenhower might *"walk a little black girl to school in Little Rock by the hand but couldn't decide whether to use an overlapping grip."* It was one of Sahl's few lines about racial issues, and liberals later accused him of failing to confront race in his act. His reply: "You can be a big hero now by telling a joke about a segregationist. I don't choose to. I *did* that already. I did it when Negroes were out playing the guitar. Now they're all hostile. I thought we were supposed to be eliminating the role of the oppressor; I didn't know we were alternating it." He mocked affirmative action: *"I went to my dressing room between shows and an NAACP attorney was waiting for me. He wanted to know why I didn't have any Negroes in my act."*

Characteristically, Sahl refused to attack easy targets and went after blacks with the same abandon as he did whites. In 1966 he said, "The Negroes bought our insane middle-class dream, instead of trying to reform us. They're saying, 'Baby, move over; I want a place at the trough.' Most Negroes I've talked to want ten percent of the corruption." He also had little to say about Vietnam, maybe because the positions had already been staked out and there was no room for a defensible minority view— or perhaps it just bored him to be on the side of liberals, who had become his easy scapegoats. He disliked conservatives intellectually, but he blasted liberals with a visceral loathing—*"Liberals are people who do the right things for the wrong reasons so they can feel good for ten minutes."* He felt that the liberals had sold out the country, and, even worse, that they had sold him out. As the nation leaned more to the left, the ornery contrarian Sahl leaned more to the right—"*to correct for drift.*" He said in the 1970s: "This is a land of no values, of apathy, even among much of the Left. It's appalling to see how cool, how peaceful, that generation is now. It's like, 'I want to change the world if I can get Dad's permission to use the station wagon.' "

One of the persistently wrongheaded perceptions about Sahl, however, is that he was purely a political comedian, which was much too narrow a box to squeeze him into and which, in a major way, misses the point. "Politics is just the megaphone I talk through," Sahl would say. He easily could talk for half an hour about going to Las Vegas and staying at the Flamingo during an AMA convention, watching Frank Sinatra take the stage at the Sands, all the while tossing off random comments on Billy Graham, actors, Henry Luce, Hedda Hopper, vegetarians, and atheism, with only a quick cutting reference to Harry Truman. He took you inside the bowels of show business to meet pompous network executives, sponsors, lawyers, agents, and the stars ("*Sinatra is an interesting amalgam of ignorance and power—see if you can bring them together in the lab*").

Sahl's only consistent political stance was antihypocrisy and anti–political fashion. "Whoever is elected president I will attack him," he announced. "If you were the only other person left on the planet, I would have to attack you—that's my job." He was an equal-opportunity destroyer, a soldier of fortune with his own agenda. His famous tag line ("*Are there any groups here I haven't offended?*") was never a question but a boast and a taunt. He liked playing the bad guy who is really the good guy—Robin Hood, Zorro, the Lone Ranger. "History will absolve me," he believes. As Ed Linn observed in a *Saturday Evening Post* piece on Sahl in 1964, "The irony is that he does want acceptance, praise, and honor from a world he despises."

Many of his comic contemporaries withheld their acceptance and praise. Alan King says, "I thought he was brilliant onstage, but offstage there was something so arrogant that it affected my appreciation of him onstage. He tried to be evenhanded and do the same thing about the Kennedys he did with Eisenhower, but it didn't work. He didn't have that conviction." Mike Nichols remarks, "I was never a fan and he never seemed funny to me. That was because we worked on the bill with him for a while and he was not generous [i.e., he wouldn't get off the stage], and that was what set in my head. I was always aware of a conflict between this sort of Socialist and the many wristwatches up his arm and the sports cars outside. He was not for me. Lenny was the one for me."

Neil Simon says: "He was not one of my favorite comics. Not that he wasn't good. He was extremely intelligent and on the money all the time, but he didn't deal with what I write about—the behavior of human beings. He was always after the stupidity in the world, and he had his time, but his kind of material needed to be changed constantly."

Milt Kamen, a comic who never quite broke through, told Joan Rivers why he thought Sahl ultimately failed to find a mass audience: "Milt thought Sahl was just a nihilist who cared passionately about nothing but himself. Free of real convictions, he could say anything and he was dazzling. Without a central core of convictions and anger, his act became only the cold sparks of a brilliant mind." His deepest convictions could be gauged by such jokes as, "*I'm for capital punishment. You've got to execute people—how else are they going to learn?*" He sued *Hollywood Close-Up,* a scandal sheet, for libel for calling him a Communist and won; in 1961 he won $5,100 in damages from a Hollywood trade paper for calling him "a phony liberal."

Even in his prime, Sahl was dismissed by many as just a shoot-from-the-hip comedian. Janet Coleman writes: "Sahl was neither complicated nor deep. Other than that of a know-it-all, he had no comedy persona. Sahl made fun of people and events in the news. He never made fun of himself. He used the bullying aspect of his personality to defend his insights. In fact, his sheer bluff and nerviness often concealed scattershot material empty of revelation or insight." The comedy historian Tony Hendra takes issue with such objections: "He was ill served by those who criticized his work as all head and no heart. Sahl went out in the dead of night without support or encouragement, laid down the outline of the structure. He didn't pretend to be a harmless clown, or an eternal kid, or a wacky kook. He went right for the only thing that mattered—the half-wits in charge. By doing that he set the agenda for humor for years."

Sahl didn't just go after liberals—he went after the closest self-satisfied target. As he said, "When I'm in Indianapolis, I don't do any of my material about liberals. I gore *their* sacred cows." He is anti–sacred cow and still clings to unpopular positions. He eagerly took on feminists, blacks, and gays in 1969, at the height of the women's lib, civil rights, and gay pride movements, commenting in one interview, "People are busy tolerating homosexuals, and all the while they are prevailing and having a great time. If you talk about sex three times in the same evening, a girl will refer to you as an animal. But if a homosexual talks about it all day, that's fine, because that's his craft."

Sahl's arrival on the national scene was perfectly timed. He was ideally poised during the Kennedy-Nixon campaign to make his major career move and to become a regular voice during the party conventions. One day in 1960 he got a telephone call that began, "This is Ambassador Joseph Kennedy. I understand that you're preeminent in the field of political humor. I want you to write some things for Johnny." Sahl says he replied, "Well, I'll be happy to, but understand I don't endorse candidates," to which, according to Sahl, the senior Kennedy replied, "I'm not interested in who you endorse; I want you to do this." Flattered, and enamored of JFK, Sahl agreed.

But when he went after the new president once he had taken office, Sahl said, "The Democrats didn't know what to make of me. They felt completely misled by me; I could say the same thing. I kidded Ike for seven and a half years but when I kidded Jack Kennedy the Democrats come backstage, in a committee." In politics, where party loyalty comes above everything, especially candor, the Democrats couldn't fathom an independent intelligent free spirit, a performer who can't be bought and isn't beholden to anyone. They didn't realize that Sahl was a third party that had no politics—"I've been accused of being everything except partisan." JFK quipped that Sahl was "in relentless pursuit of everybody." Christon noted: "He really *is* the loyal opposition. He's like Brando in *The Wild One,* when someone asks him, 'What are you rebelling against?' and Brando says, 'What have you got?' "

Sahl, who laid the groundwork, now led the pack. His main problem with the Democrats was that he was funnier and more quotable than other comics, and his needles had the sting of truth. The jibes weren't nasty—fairly harmless, in fact, often focusing on JFK's youth, which had been candidate Kennedy's major selling point. Sahl observed that in electing Kennedy the country was "*searching for a son figure,*" that Kennedy had appeared on *College News Conference* because "*kids like to talk over problems with someone their own age,*" and that Nixon had sent JFK's father a telegram reading, "*You have not lost a son. You have gained a country.*"

Once Sahl began doing more lethal Kennedy jokes, however, like one about JFK throwing out his back carrying girls upstairs at the White House, Joseph Kennedy called Enrico Banducci and club owners with mob ties who were part of the elder Kennedy's extended family. He reportedly asked Bobby Kennedy to have the IRS close down the hungry i. Banducci was stunned to come to work one day and find the club's doors padlocked by the IRS for unpaid withholding taxes. Sahl's response:

"You know what this is? It's Nazi Germany 1936. Banducci is practically the only guy in America that will hire me now, and now they're getting him." Knowing Banducci's financial snarls, it's likely that he *did* owe the IRS back taxes.

The Kennedy clan, particularly their patriarch, was far more thin-skinned than the president himself and took Sahl's JFK jokes as a slap in the face. "They brought me to the altar as a burnt offering," Sahl said. In the world of Irish-American politics, Sahl had broken the first commandment—loyalty. Perhaps sensing the heat, he joked, "*I have only a few months to tell these jokes before they become treason.*" When he and Kennedy met, JFK wanted to hear Sahl deliver lines to his face. After one (*"Joe Kennedy told Jack he was putting him on an allowance. 'You're not allowed one more cent than you need to buy a landslide'"*), Kennedy asked, "What does that mean?" "It means your father's rich," deadpanned Sahl.

"I was not an advocate for the guy. I didn't even vote for him. I always go in with the proviso that when they get into office I'll be left alone to do what I do. I didn't want any rewards when Kennedy got in; I'm probably the only guy who didn't get any. I didn't want any invitations to the White House. All I wanted was to be left alone. I had nothing against the president, but it's my basic policy to do jokes about the incumbent." But, zingers aide, Sahl was smitten by Kennedy, whom he saw as a kindred spirit and wit. He strongly identified with the president, later saying, "He decided to save America—a dangerous occupation," and chortled. "When he was president, boy did we feel good! That's all gone now."

Sahl told the columnist Mike Royko in 1967 that Kennedy's brother-in-law Peter Lawford had informed the comic, "You're going to get it. You'll see. It would have been so nice if you had laid off." His agent, Milt Ebbins, also Lawford's agent, tried to get him to lay off Kennedy, telling him, "Nobody wants you. You've made lots of enemies." He was told to cool it or "there would be dire consequences." There were. Grover Sales says that Joe Kennedy told Ebbins, "I don't care how you do it, but you get that Jew to shut his fucking mouth!" Ebbins asked Banducci to talk to Sahl about cooling it, saying, "He'll listen to you but he won't listen to me," and Banducci replied, "I'll do no such thing."

The Kennedy pollster Lou Harris told Sahl, "Forget about the Kennedys—that's just the palace guard trying to protect him. Kennedy loves you, he loves the humor, he loves the jokes, and you don't have to stop on his behalf." Sahl confronted Ebbins: "You mean to tell me that the man who faced the Cuban missile crisis and the problem of the Berlin

Wall is worried about a nightclub comedian? I find that hard to accept, even with my ego." As early as 1961 some critics were claiming that Sahl wasn't as funny as he was when Ike was around. It was a bum rap, which, coupled with his later sleuthing for the New Orleans district attorney Jim Garrison to discredit the Warren Report, created a convenient club with which to beat Sahl over the head.

The jobs dried up overnight in the late 1960s, and he couldn't even get work at third-rate nightclubs, saying, "I was indemnifying them by working for practically nothing. And they were not interested." Sahl's income plunged in the 1960s from $400,000 a year to $19,000 during his Warren Report assaults. One of Sahl's agents, Freddie Fields, told his client, "No one can help you in the position you're in. There's interference and resistance. You've built up too much animus." One TV executive ordered Fields not to "bring his name up in these offices."

Gene Norman, former owner of the Crescendo in Los Angeles, confirms that, saying, "There was an attempt [to blacklist Sahl]." When Norman sold his club to Shelley Davis, Sahl says that Davis told him, "I've been told that the White House would be offended if I hired you and I'd be audited on my income tax. I heard that you offended the president." Sahl's wife China blamed Ebbins: "His objective was to ingratiate himself with the Kennedy family."

Amid rumors that he was ill, seeing a shrink seven days a week, even suicidal, Sinatra, albeit the *padron* of Kennedy's extended showbiz family, stuck by Sahl and hired him to record an album, *New Frontiers,* for his new Reprise label. During the early JFK hassles, Sahl said, "I'm not a political flash in the pan. And they can't accept that. They keep treating me like I'm a senator and you better watch out, you're up for reelection. But I've got a lifetime appointment. To this empty bench."

IN 1960 SAHL HAD JOKED, "*Too bad I don't have a cause—I have a lot of enthusiasm.*" Five years later he had his cause.

The assassination was Sahl's undoing, a righteous crusade that wrecked his career and, for a long time, his life. "There's never been anything that had a stronger impact on my life than this issue," he told *Playboy* in 1969. "People ask me if I loved Kennedy. Well, I didn't think he was a saint— just an ordinary mortal. Unfortunately, many of the people who now profess to love him do not serve his memory well." Some claimed that Sahl had gone over the edge on the JFK matter, to which he responded: "If believing—in company with a lot of Americans—that there was a conspiracy to kill my president makes me paranoid, even though I've seen much of the evidence, then so be it. When the show business elite threw me out, it was called 'paranoia.' "

Sahl lived with the word *paranoid* for ten years, from 1966 to '76, during which time he found himself welcome mainly on college campuses. He was so sensitive about being considered paranoid that once, while dining with the actor Robert Vaughn, he asked a waiter why his order was delayed, and when Vaughn kidded, "Maybe the long arm of the CIA has reached into the kitchen," Sahl rose to his feet, fists clenched, and growled, "Stand up and get your time, you son of bitch!" Vaughn said, "Don't get sore. It's a joke. I didn't know you felt so strongly." Sahl accused him of treating "the sum of my life [as a] momentary joke for your amusement." The novelist Herbert Gold recalls, "When I knew Mort Sahl he was almost clinically paranoid, full of hatred for the Kennedys, egomaniacal."

After the assassination, Sahl lost momentum as a comic—lost part of his audience, lost work, lost credibility. The one thing Sahl didn't lose was his wit. Fans who went to see him after he returned to full-time performing walked in worrying that he may have turned into a Kennedy conspiracy nut, some wacko version of Lenny Bruce, only to leave laughing. He did read from the Warren Report onstage and mocked its illogic, turning the more tortured passages into jokes, and he could be funny doing it. Yet for many, the assassination was still too fresh and painful to confront, however wittily.

Worse, he was no longer outside the system but deeply inside it, even though he was trying to correct it, which undermined his objectivity. Like Bruce, by hectoring the public he drove them away instead of winning them over. His persuasive power lay in the wisecrack, but even his best jokes intended to destroy the Warren Report's credibility were undermined by his decision to work for Garrison. Sahl, in brief, was tainted, much as Oliver Stone was by his shrill film *JFK*. As Ronald L. Smith writes, "Sometimes recklessly opinionated, Sahl never stopped throwing grenades, even if some went off in his hands."

Patrick Hallinan, the San Francisco defense attorney, met Sahl during his Garrison period and stayed at his home three times in Los Angeles. "The house was full of assistant DAs and Garrison investigators," recalls Hallinan, whose central memory of Sahl is his round-the-clock chatter. "Forty-five minutes a day—max—was all you could spend with him.

Intense! He was on all the time. He didn't need a whole helluva lot of prep to get going—he'd just pick up that newspaper. But that was Mort. You could engage him in conversation, but it was like lighting a fire-cracker."

By 1967 Sahl was telling the London *Express* in a story carried every-where, "The crime has been solved by Jim Garrison. He has a completely structured case. He knows who pulled the trigger and it was not Oswald. All I can tell you at the moment is that a powerful domestic agency was responsible, and that when Garrison tells his story, the implications will shake the country to its foundations." Some of his early allies in the press had already bailed out. In a 1965 review, Ralph J. Gleason surmised that Sahl no longer had a clear view of where he stood as a satirist. "Mort's edge has been removed by time and the changing world." The columnist Charles McCabe noted, "As his popularity has declined, his ego has swollen"—and he cited Sahl's line, "I've become everyone's conscience." A year later, Gleason, who had been tracking the comic's career since he broke in, finally despaired of him, observing that while "Lenny Bruce could give you flashes of illumination, Sahl doesn't say anything that we don't already know." Gleason, like many liberals, was disillusioned because Sahl wasn't toeing the party line. He also noted that he sensed "a fundamental change in Sahl: his brilliance thirteen years ago has lapsed into bitterness."

The most damaging myth about Sahl was that he stopped being funny after he left full-time performing to work for four years as an unpaid deputy investigator for Garrison. "I thought it was a wonderful quest," Sahl said. He went around the country interviewing witnesses, evaluating evidence, and introducing Garrison to people he might not have met—all at his own expense, he said. Weide comments, "People just thought he'd lost it and wrote him off as not funny anymore and obsessed."

Even though he lost agents, TV talk-show jobs, and his professional footing, he could still kid himself a little. On Hugh Hefner's TV show *Playboy After Dark,* he said, "I don't go out much now because I'm too busy saving America. The last four girls I went out with fell asleep listening to me read the Warren Report." Sahl and Hefner became friends and the comic often stayed at the Playboy Mansion. The perception that Sahl was damaged goods—all it takes in show business to diminish a performer—became cruel reality, and dogs him to this day.

In truth, Sahl was about as bitingly funny through most of the seven-ties, eighties, and even the nineties as he was in the fifties and sixties, and a lot of people wanted to hear what he had to say, yet a crucial and vital voice in the night had been all but silenced. Whenever you located Sahl in some small, offbeat room, you left wondering why he wasn't a regular presence on TV, and as the times became more bizarre, the more he was missed.

To survive, Sahl hosted controversial local TV talk shows in New York and Los Angeles, only to be canceled because of his caustic and at times cruel comments. In 1965 he was fired from WNEW-TV in New York after he said, following an argument with the station bosses, "The problem with Hitler wasn't that he killed six million Jews, but that he missed the ones at Metromedia." For a time, he even did a talk show on the Christian Science cable channel.

Weide concedes, "Mort's hard on people and he's hard on where America is. He talks about America like it's a woman he was once in love with." His actual line: "*Who's gonna get the girl is an American metaphor. The girl is America—that's what the election is all about—who's gonna get the girl.*" In those days, Sahl came off a little like the Dr. Laura of politics, with a brutal ready prescription for what ails the national psyche: "What's really aching Americans is that nobody loves them. If there's no romance, or justice, in your life, life is not worth living."

His on-air commentary turned more bullying and melodramatic: "I charge the government with suppressing the facts. I charge the Chief Justice with distorting the evidence, and I charge the American people with complicity by their indifference to terror. His blood is on your hands. . . . America is down there in the tomb with JFK." On KLAC radio, Sahl called right-wingers "fascists," blasted the left and the middle, and nagged even his most sympathetic callers. He painted a grim picture of the country and cast himself in the role of the nation's sole liberator ("Why am I the only one in America doing this?"). The talk shows brought out the worst of his Mort Sahl–against-the-world mind-set, and he wound up sounding almost hysterical ("Buddy, why don't you buy a paper and *grow up*. Or else go *die* somewhere"). When he filled in on a New York talk show, a woman called in and said, "You evoke such guilt, what do you want us to do? I have a shrine to Jack Kennedy over my mantle and two candles." Sahl replied, "You know what I want you to do? I want you to blow out the candles and curse the darkness."

Don Gregory, Sahl's agent for a time, remarks: "He felt his career was stolen from him, but he helped bury himself. He longed to get back to his success, but the Camelot legend was still aglow and he was getting older—he wasn't the college kid with the rolled-up newspaper any-more." Gregory, however, is sympathetic: "If he's self-destructive he had a great deal of help. He was confronted by either compromising his act and not pissing anyone off or holding on to his ideas; he chose the latter."

He was shunned by his nemesis, Hollywood liberals, most painfully by former pals like Paul Newman and Joanne Woodward ("All my friends looked upon me as lost. Even some of my oldest friends won't have any-thing to do with me now—they say I'm too dangerous to know"). Hedda Hopper denounced him in her syndicated column as un-American. Christon observes further: "One of the things that hurt him is that he likes being part of the power establishment," which he also scorns. "He was the first of the major performers to understand the similarities between Washington and Hollywood. He's had his strongest personal relationships in those worlds. What hurt him is that both those worlds are fueled by fear. The Kennedys wanted an iconoclast, and they got one and couldn't live with him. They can be amused, but beyond a certain point they're not amused. People like Warren Beatty are afraid that he'll turn on them. There's a very wary kind of ambivalence about him. They appreciate him and they want to hear him and they want his good opinion of them, but they're afraid of what he'll say about them. So they want to keep him at arm's length."

In 1976 Sahl's quasi-autobiography, *Heartland,* came out—a bitter book that settled old scores, inflicted new wounds, and made a passionate case for his views on America, politics, women, journalism, and show business but had little to say about Sahl's personal life. It reads like a biog-raphy of someone else, a person the author very much admires but never got to know too well. Essentially, it's a 158-page monologue about a cru-sading comedian, studded with brilliant insights but weighed down by stretches of ponderous diatribe; he fires away at unworthy or trivial tar-gets, fans lost causes, and flogs dead horses.

"In the book's angry rantings," *Newsweek* wrote of it, "the salty Sahl wit is submerged in bitterness." The cover shows a silhouette of a man on a horse, like the Marlboro Man, tall in the saddle—Sahl as lonesome cow-boy, but not at all at home on the range. The book lacks the mocking laugh and slightly maniacal gleam that made his stage monologues, how-ever hostile, hugely entertaining.

Sahl's political turnabout found him praising people he once had clashed with politically, like Bob Hope ("He believes in *something*"), and bashing his old allies, the dread liberals, whom he accused of believing in nothing. He veered right, he said, because if John Wayne says something and shakes your hand, you can take it to the bank. Jack Webb hired him to write scripts for a cop show, *Adam-12*, but the only usable character Sahl created was a guard dog, which Webb later used in a show called *Chase,* earning Sahl a hundred-dollar royalty whenever the dog appeared. Sahl labeled Rod Serling a do-nothing liberal and was hurt when the playwright wouldn't hire him. Larry Kart, who covered comedy for the *Chicago Tribune,* says, "Sahl is always waiting for the betrayal—so many people betrayed him that he's always waiting for the other shoe to drop."

Don Gregory observes: "You never knew if he thought you were a schmuck. Most people to him were banal. People were self-conscious around him, but women loved him. I once told him, 'Maybe you expect too much of people.' His problem was that he had a narrow definition of mankind. Nobody was good enough for him." Jules Feiffer weighs in: "I knew Sahl and I thought he was wonderful until I met him. He's not a very pleasant man." Phyllis Diller's blunt comment on Sahl's flameout: "He thought he was bigger than he was, and more popular than he was, and he wasn't where he thought he was. Arrogance."

Misfortune dogged him. He tried to open a nightclub, in order to have a ready forum, but Mort Sahl's Uprising never opened; he blamed two backers who vanished after a press preview. In 1971 Sahl broke his back twice in what he called "strange" car accidents; concerning one of those instances, he said that the CIA had laced with LSD the cookies he ate at a faculty reception. According to one friend, "The CIA is everywhere, as far as Mort is concerned." To stay solvent, he did a lounge act in Las Vegas, wrote screenplays, and played a small club, Donte's, in North Hollywood; Merv Griffin, a loyal fan, booked him several times on his TV show.

In 1976 even his first and chief cheerleader, Herb Caen, turned against him, partly for personal reasons, and ridiculed Sahl's blacklist claims in a vicious column: "Sahl was no more hounded out of showbiz by the Kennedys than you were," he wrote. "He simply became a b-o-r-e. When you can no longer sell tickets or get jobs, you invent elaborate theories to explain away your shortcomings. I think it's called paranoia. Sahl has his share." Eventually, even Banducci's tolerance for difficult comics was stretched thin: "I never corrected his Warren Commission stuff, only when he attacked Herb Caen," says Banducci. "He kept going on about

Caen"—whose mistress Sahl allegedly stole—and the powerful columnist retaliated in print. "So I cut off the lights and said, 'Thank you very much, Mort Sahl!' "

Sahl insisted that, through it all, he never gave up on his audience, which he said had shifted from the elite to the working class. On Weide's documentary, he comments, "You've got to stay with the people. They're like a jury. If you can wait it out, maybe you can beat it. I don't know. The only way you can die in America is to get into the coffin and hammer it shut from the inside. You don't die. You revise your strategy but you don't die." When he returned to work after his Warren Commission years, people would ask him, " 'Are you all right now?' "—as though I'd come back from a mental institution."

IN THE SEVENTIES, Sahl engineered a partial comeback, aided by Nixon's presidency and Watergate, thus ending his own long national nightmare. He cut a new album, *Sing a Song of Watergate,* and offers began coming his way again—one, incredibly, from the American Bankers Association, to address them. Johnny Carson, David Frost, and Mike Douglas booked him on their TV shows. Carson invited Sahl and Jim Garrison on his show for an entire ninety minutes, giving Carson his highest rating to date, according to Sahl. When a reporter asked him where he'd been, he said, "Since 1961, I was vamping." He played some college concerts to survive ("I'm not eighteen but I'm the angriest man on any campus").

People would hire him for jobs only to get nervous the moment he opened his mouth. When Jerry Lewis got him a gig at the Sands, opening for Patti Page, the casino owner Jack Entratter told him, "Remember, now, you gotta change your act." Ed Sullivan saw him at the Sands and booked him, then changed his mind after hearing him at rehearsal, and replaced him with Jack E. Leonard. When he got a talk show, *Mort Sahl's People,* at the Metromedia station in New York, he wrangled with the management about guests and they pulled the plug.

When Sahl reappeared, he was, like Nixon, "tanned, rested, and ready"—i.e., armed with great jokes. On Nixon's promise to bring the POWs home ("*As soon as he got in office he got two POWs out—Jimmy Hoffa and Bobby Baker. The others took a little longer. I wore a bracelet for Hoffa*"); on Nixon himself ("*He was born sixty-one years ago in a log cabin in Whittier, Cal-*

ifornia, in a blue suit"). In his act, he still took on everyone, from Barry Goldwater (*"The fascist gun in the west"*) and Ronald Reagan (*"Interest rates will go up. Inflation will go up. The sign on his desk will read, 'The half-buck stops here' "*) to Pat Nixon testifying as a Watergate witness (*Q.: "Doesn't the President know he has two daughters?"*; *A.: "He did not ask me and I did not tell him"*).

Sahl's partial return from the dead was part of a resurgence of comedy then astir in the land. Following a humor drought that saw the popularity of elephant jokes, grape jokes, and Polish jokes in the mid-1970s—what one agent dubbed "The Gomer Pyle Era of comedy"—a few edgy new comics came along: Robert Klein, George Carlin, Lily Tomlin, Cheech & Chong, David Frye, and the rough cut of Richard Pryor. Even on TV there was *Rowan & Martin's Laugh-In, All in the Family,* and *That Was the Week That Was.*

Sahl was back, but was he still relevant? A critic in the *New York Times,* noting that the comedian ambled onstage at Michael's Pub with his trademark newspaper in hand, wondered "if it is really today's newspaper." He felt that Sahl's "meandering" monologue dwelled overlong on the Kennedy assassination. Nonetheless, he got off plenty of funny and timely cracks: *"Gerald Ford looks like the guy at Safeway who okays your check"*; *"[New York] Mayor Beame's limo had a decal on the front window that read, 'This City Carries Only $5 in Change' "*; *"Black newscasters look like they were made in a lab by white newscasters."*

His only weakness as a seasoned comedian—surprising given his prolific, teeming mind—was a lazy habit of recycling favorite lines, some from the sixties that his followers know by heart. A related tactical mistake was continuing to refer to people like Stevenson, McCarthy, and Haig, which severely dated him, as well as taking on tired targets— Norman Lear, Paul Newman, Jane Fonda, Ed Asner, Redford. At the same time, he was capable of bitingly topical barbs: *"A girl I know hasn't found her soul mate yet, so she subscribed to* Ms.*,"* and *"They're winding down the war in Vietnam—they're pulling out Bob Hope and Martha Raye."*

The media in the mid-seventies began paying attention to him again. The *Los Angeles Times* even did a Sunday feature in its house-and-garden section, of all places, on the Sahls at home, giving a peek at the human being behind the comic mask. He and his wife then lived in a modest, modern, Japanese-style house with a weathered wood exterior off Benedict Canyon, outfitted with stereo gear and three guard dogs; China, then also her husband's business manager, owned Thoroughbred horses. In 1978, however, the couple filed for divorce for the third time in four years, and after two marriages they finally parted.

An insomniac, Sahl would sleep in two- and three-hour stretches, and when he couldn't sleep he'd wander down to an all-night newsstand or drive out to the beach. He would buy thirty dollars' worth of magazines and newspapers every few days. Then as now, he hung out with politicians, media people, movie directors (Sydney Pollack, John Avildsen), and the screenwriter Robert Towne, and he remained close to Richard Crenna, his old junior high buddy. But people have a way of drifting in and out of his life. As the writer Paul Desruiseaux once neatly put it, Sahl is "a very likable guy who makes ex-friends easily."

In 1980, after a long estrangement, Sahl and Banducci were back on friendly terms when Sahl opened at a new North Beach club, The Entertainers. The club owners had posted a small hopeful sign outside reading, "Enrico Banducci Presents," the idea being to revive the old hungry i spirit. Banducci was hired as consultant–cum–talent scout, but the old chemistry was gone and the club quickly closed, owing Sahl $80,000. His jokes by now had a historical sweep: "*In the sixties, you had to be Jewish to get a girl. In the seventies, you had to be black to get the girl; in the eighties, you had to be a girl to get a girl. What's left?*" As Leonard Feather, the *Los Angeles Times* jazz critic, said in a review of Sahl's most recent album in the late nineties, "His reminiscences are a time capsule of twenty years in American history seen through a broken kaleidoscope." Despite all it had been through, Sahl's ego remained intact. Wesla Whitfield recalls how icy Sahl was when the then-unknown singer opened for him: "He didn't speak to me at all the entire six weeks. I was invisible to him; I just wasn't there."

During a 1980 interview I had with Sahl—Banducci seated alongside, slapping his thigh and howling like a jubilant sidekick, as if discovering him anew—the comic's piercing, hooded eyes peered restlessly about the restaurant; at fifty-seven, an awkward age for an enfant terrible, he still looked like a starved wolf prowling for a choice chunk of raw politician. Talking to Sahl can be an exhilarating but exhausting experience. A formal interview quickly veers off into a wheels-within-wheels conversation in which every question yields six answers, theories, statistics, headlines, parentheses, rhetorical questions, mini Socratic dialogues, one-liners, asides, and Bartlett's quotations. "Yeah, I think it can happen again," he said of his return. "You don't lose your skills. That's a bad movie scenario. 'Judy's great again!' Judy was always great. I do what I always did. In *Tales of Hoffman* Offenbach said, 'You'll always be left with your friend, your talent.' " Sahl observed: "When they felt my star was waning after the assassination, it felt unjust. I was just as good as ever but nobody would admit it. I was untalented retroactively."

Through it all, Sahl never gave up on himself, though others may have: "In the darkest hour, I could find a way to say something—no matter how withering—to sum up my dilemma. If you don't betray the muse, it will never leave you. The muse has not deserted me. You can't betray your trust as an artist. That's what it is—it isn't political. That's not who I am. You have to move the human heart—that's what it is in the last analysis. It's not an intellectual thing, it's an emotional thing."

Sahl still lashed out on all sides with his old moralistic zeal, sounding like I. F. Stone one moment and Spiro Agnew the next, full of low suspicions and high dudgeon, blasting the media and exhorting the nation to speak up. And like Howard Beale, the enflamed newscaster in the film *Network* (a character some think was inspired by Sahl), he could say: "I encourage people to be as mad as they really are, not parrot back the seven o'clock news. The only responsibility is to be a human being. Being a citizen is a full-time job now. I have no time for myself!" Sahl has always earned his living by turning calamity into art, gleefully dancing on the brink of disaster, but even in his darkest hours, he could joke, "I'm not Lenny Bruce. I don't think crucifixion is the answer. I like the resurrection part of the story. I remain optimistic. I want to stay around for the third act. This isn't total darkness; it's just the night approaching." He liked to say, "It isn't that I've changed, it's that America is so hell-bent on suicide that I'm in the unlikely position of standing at the edge of the cliff and saying, 'Wait a minute, have you thought this over?' "

In 1986, back in San Francisco to open Enrico's Restaurant as part of an effort to help bail out Banducci (Bill Cosby and Irwin Corey were other old hungry i hands who came to his financial rescue), Sahl struck up a friendship with Bruce Bellingham, a political reporter for KCBS radio. During that run (Sahl's wife worked the door: "She made sure that cash got to Mort," recalls Bellingham), he was still capable of scathing comments on Gary Hart (*"Kennedy without the batteries"*), Ted Turner (*"He joins hands with himself and sings 'I Am the World' "*), Michael Ovitz (*"The first living heart donor"*), Larry King (*"I loved your book—I read parts of it all the way through"*), and Liz Taylor (*"She devoted her entire evening to AIDS"*).

Bellingham, who met him often for lunch, recounts: "In conversation, when you talk to Mort he's got his lines ready—there isn't too much off the top of the head. It's like a mantra. When you talk to him, you're not quite sure if he's hearing you. I'd say on the phone, 'How you doing?' and he'd say, 'Well, you know, Bruce, down here, the definition of courage is going to a restaurant that hasn't been reviewed yet.' " Bellingham says that the Sahl he knew wasn't bitter about show business. "He was bitter about the world in general. He was bitter about the precipitous drop in the sophistication of the American audience."

It was on the heels of Jackie Mason's 1988 triumph on Broadway in his one-man show that Sahl opened his new show, *Mort Sahl's America,* at an Off-Broadway house, but it didn't catch on, despite good reviews. Even so, the *New York Times* critic raved, "History has returned Mort Sahl to the spotlight when he is most needed. His style has an intuitive spontaneity. His presence is tonic." When the show premiered in Los Angeles, however, Christon wrote tellingly, "It is interesting to note that none of the Hollywood comedy establishment that howled over Jackie Mason last year showed up for Sahl's opening—even though he's always been on-call for Hollywood benefits."

Laurie Stone, the *Village Voice* comedy critic, covered his aborted return to New York. She was unamused: "In the mid-sixties, when I saw Sahl live, he was already a crank, looming over the *Times* as if he were the only person who could decipher it. His upper lip was rising too quickly into a sneer, and he was flashing those pronounced teeth of his, grinning at his own cleverness before anyone else had a chance. That laugh—how to describe it? A foghorn that *wants* you to hit the rocks." She said he was still "a pig" regarding women, and labeled him irrelevant.

SAHL MAY TALK LIKE an anarchist, but he's led a fairly traditional personal life, three wives and sundry female relationships notwithstanding. As performers go, he's almost a Boy Scout. He doesn't drink, smoke, do drugs, curse, or squander his skills. He was always more hostile onstage than off, sounding radical while behaving like a Rotarian. He is a loyal if elusive friend, and was a doting father to his troubled son, who died at nineteen from a mysterious drug-related incident. "He worshiped the kid," says a woman close to Sahl. He often took him on the road with him, and was a devoted father to the boy, whom he called "Mortsky" and "Pal"—Sahl's name for everyone. Yet he never seemed the fatherly type: after his son was born he joked that he'd planted him in a corner and said, "Grow!" His son always told Sahl, "Keep it current, Dad, whatever you do."

Tom Tugend, a writer for a Jewish weekly, met Sahl over a caffè latte at the Glen Deli in Bel Air, in 1996, and asked Sahl about Mort Jr.'s death earlier that year and about his divorce from Lee in 1991. In a rare show of emotion, Sahl said, "My wife touched my heart and my son opened my heart. I've learned that intelligence is no defense against emotional pain." Herb Sargent says, "When his son died, that put him away for a while."

Christon, who was close to Sahl when Mort Jr. died, says: "He never turned his back on the kid, and underwent enormous physical abuse. The kid broke down doors in the house, stole Mort's eighteen-thousand-dollar Rolex, wrecked his stereo, and stole everything. He never disowned him, never said enough is enough. He went to the mat for him. Just when he was coming out of it, the kid had a toxic reaction to something he took. Mort was at the hospital every night, tried to get people to help—he called Nancy Reagan."

Christon says that, despite Sahl's intellectual ferocity, "he's an incredibly gracious decent man who has social instincts for doing the right thing. At a birthday party for him at a steakhouse, he gave a speech, and he went around the table and talked about what he admired about everyone there. I'd never seen anyone do that. He's one of the most complex people I've ever met. I've known him for years and I still can't claim I understand him."

At sixty, he may not have mellowed, but when the actor George Segal saw him after many years, he said, "Mort, something's different. You're easier to take now. You're *rounder.*" Sahl agreed, saying, "Instead of being just that smug guy, I'm now playing Candide." Jim Schock met Sahl in Los Angeles and dined with him. Schock, a former West Coast bureau chief for ABC-TV News, detected something of the aging lion about Sahl, more roar than claws. "He's charming and infectious and all that, but when someone is always on, it's kind of wearing."

Sahl said in 1987 that he hadn't planned to still be at it at sixty, remarking, "I thought I'd do this for a while, then I'd have a TV show, then make movies or maybe be a full-time writer." He's hung in there for nearly half a century, and says, "I thought a young man would come along and relieve me! Where's B Company?" Ed Linn wrote as long ago as 1964, "He's spent his life trying to separate himself from other comics," but noted Sahl's quest for respect: "Despite his scorn of status, he wants recognition so badly that he can't stand the success of other comedians who have followed him into the field of social commentary. The success of Newhart, Berman, Gregory, and his onetime protégé Woody Allen, helps keep him angry and neurotic. In short, functioning at top efficiency." A friend observes, "Mort feels the younger generation doesn't know who he is, but he feels he's an icon."

There were virtually no political comedians after Sahl, maybe because nobody could follow, much less equal, him. No comic since has had his lightning mind, political grasp, and incisive insights, with the possible exception of the late Bill Hicks; *Politically Incorrect*'s Bill Maher, who shares Sahl's outrage, contrariness, and killer instincts; and, yes, occasionally Jackie Mason. But Sahl scoffs at all pretenders to his throne—Don Imus, Will Durst, Mark Russell. There still is nobody to pass the torch to, and the Statue of Liberty already has one. He's said, "Most people who call themselves comedians are no more than a card file. Marlene Dietrich once told me, 'Brando's secret is that he acts [on-screen] like a human being, and most actors act like actors.' Well, I acted like a human being rather than like a nightclub comedian."

Ironically, Sahl made so-called political humor fashionable among much lesser, later comedians, such as the late-night talk-show comics who began to lob jokes at whichever president was in office. Post-Sahl "political humor" was Chevy Chase as Gerald Ford falling down stairs and jokes about Jimmy Carter's sweater, Ronald Reagan's old movies, the George Bushes' (I and II) syntax, and Bill Clinton's appetite for sex and Big Macs. No ideas or political opinions. "The papers are misled because they think when a guy comes on a late-night show and makes a joke about Clinton and girls that that's political satire," Sahl complained to Nick A. Zaino III in an Internet interview in 2000. Sahl told me in 1987: "It's an apolitical generation. They all have this Bruce Willis–Bill Murray attitude, but there's no *wit*. Who have we got? Whoopi Goldberg! Satirists often become a worse cliché than what they once satirized."

Sahl is hard to find these days in clubs, and especially on national TV. He popped up in Denver in 2001 right after the Bush-Gore election and again on *Larry King Live,* where he barely got in a few words edgewise between King and Joan Rivers (on the Supreme Court decision for George W. Bush: "*The American people have spoken—all five of them*"; on modern Jewish mothers: "*My son never faxes*"). With King, who called him "the dean, the pioneer," he appeared the graying elder statesman, with a pained smile and a Bogart-like tic, as he strained to speak. But King wouldn't give him room to roam, so Sahl burst in with a few golden oldies (*"Jesse Jackson—'I have a scheme' . . . Jesse's a man of the cloth— cashmere"*).

Weide says: "Every four years Mort gets hot again. He doesn't work nearly as much as he should. It's all about TV exposure now. If you're not on the tube, people think you don't exist." Christon called Sahl one of America's genuine showbiz mavericks. "He's far above every cliché pandemic in current stand-up, in a class by himself. More than any other major comedian going, he fulfills the definition of the true comedian as a dangerous man. He's an example of the pain in the oyster that produces the pearl. He's the real thing and always has been, as authentic as anyone out there. The act isn't an act."

Ronald L. Smith guesses that Sahl isn't called upon to do network TV because "Leno and Letterman do their ten minutes every night and they don't need Mort"—or maybe fear being upstaged. "Now, there are a number of people doing what Mort does—Bill Maher, Conan O'Brien— so he's not as necessary." Weide says, "Whenever *Nightline* or some show does a political piece, they'll have someone like Al Franken on as the [humorous] commentator. Why *him*? Why aren't people calling up Mort about this stuff? To use musicians' terms, Mort really gets into the quarter notes on these issues. He knows the details and the nuances, and in many cases he knows the players personally, and he knows their histories and how they all intertwine. He's just a valuable natural resource and he is way underused."

SAHL HAS LONG had a strained relationship with Woody Allen, who so revered him. "I've been a shadow over his life," Sahl said in 1987. "He'd always come to the clubs and sit in the front row, and when China [Lee] was in *What's Up, Tiger Lily?*, he was in love with her from afar. He was like flypaper with me. I got a lot of those guys work in the beginning." He once nonchalantly said, "Woody's appropriated some things of mine. All the stuff in *Annie Hall* is really me. The joke about his having a Christ-like image of yourself. That's *me*. The line that goes, 'You're the only guy who'd rather listen to a speech by Adlai Stevenson than make love.' Mine."

His rancor about Allen sounds more like envy: "Woody Allen is funny, but he is dated," he wrote in 1976. "Woody Allen, who said I was his patron saint, sat at my feet at the Copacabana one night and asked me how to get into show business." Allen credits Sahl with getting him into comedy, which years after inspired Sahl to joke that Allen later sent him a note at the Russian Tea Room asking, "Now can you get me out of it?"

He's now seventy-six, but his personal demons continue to rage as he hunts voraciously for a platform. One woman friend notes, "He still has a presence in Los Angeles," if not elsewhere, but he works infrequently—a corporate talk here, a local guest shot there, liner notes for a Kenton CD. Says Christon, "He shows up here and there—at the Jazz Bakery, he hosts the annual Stan Kenton thing, and he did some writing for the [Bill] Bradley 2000 campaign. He's still sharp, just as funny, very alert. He had a line about a Brinks holdup where they stole three hundred thousand dollars and he said the street value of the money was thirty dollars." He performed at a GOP fund-raiser at Alexander Haig's house in March 2001; a more recent Republican ally is the conservative former Wyoming senator Alan Simpson.

In one of those bizarre flip-flops that characterize stand-up comedy fortunes, Allen generously got Sahl his first New York booking in seven years at Joe's Pub in November 2001, for three nights. The previous August, Allen had seen Sahl at the Jazz Bakery, where Allen's New Orleans jazz group was playing. "Sahl volunteered to introduce Woody, and he wound up doing a few minutes," says Weide. "Woody was blown away by Mort. He called up Mort and said, 'Listen, this is crazy—you should be working all the time.' Then he called Jack Rollins and Rollins got the old gleam in his eye again and arranged it." Rollins said, "Woody called me immediately and said, 'Listen, this guy is hilarious. We gotta bring him to New York.' "

Weide goes on: "I had dinner with him a month before the New York gig. Mort told me that he was very, very touched by Woody's gesture. His eyes were almost welling up. Even if it fell apart, he said, 'the fact that Woody made a move to do this means more to me than anything.' He runs into everyone—Warren Beatty and that group, and they all say, 'Oh, God, Mort, you should be working more. There must be something we can do,' and nobody does anything. The fact that Woody did something . . ." So why did it take Allen twenty years? In fact, says Weide, Allen asked Sahl to be in *Manhattan* and was turned down by him. "Mort is probably the only one to ever tell Woody, 'I don't work for scale.' " Or as Robert Rice observed in *The New Yorker* forty-two years ago, "He wants to change the world but he won't take second billing."

In a 2001 interview in the *Los Angeles Times,* Paul Brownfield wrote, "Sahl is a man with a country but not a stage." It seemed a propitious time for his reemergence. After the terrorist attack on the World Trade Center, Sahl had a gig at the New England Jewish Theater and, reports Brownfield, found "his set-ups were playing like applause lines," especially when he mentioned President Bush. "I said, 'Isn't the president a great leader?' And they started cheering"—almost burying his funny pay-off lines—that *"Bush was doing so well it made you embarrassed that he hadn't actually been elected,"* and that *"Bush wants to be the education president and is being home-schooled by Condoleezza Rice."*

Ron Smith went to three shows at Joe's Pub and reported that all three were filled. "There was an advance buzz because of Woody, who probably told a lot of people." But it wasn't just an old crowd of Sahl diehards; at least half of the audience were people in their thirties, who saw him as part legend, part curiosity. Smith overheard one thirty-something say, "I understand he was very in in the sixties, with Lenny Bruce."

Sahl teased his own image, telling the crowd that he had "pioneered the concept of a show where you don't laugh." Smith notes that "Mort's act has changed a little bit. He's not quite the *'Is there any group here I haven't offended?'* guy anymore. He's cleverer now in how to reach an audience without antagonizing them. He didn't go out of his way to annoy anybody, and wasn't as contentious as he was in the late sixties and seventies, when he was so angry about everything. He had the energy, definitely, but it's just a natural evolution—you're not going to be as opinionated or nasty at seventy-four as you are at thirty-four. He didn't really tee off on the liberals and Democrats as savagely as he used to. He mildly attacked George W. Bush. He had the same energy level—he just didn't have that same prickly sense. It was about sixty-forty, new versus old stuff. He wasn't coasting." He didn't mention John Kennedy: "It must have finally sunk in, stay away from that stuff," says Smith. But he did revisit his Redford classic that fans now almost wait for, like Barbra Streisand hauling out "People."

Those who wonder if Sahl is still relevant can pick up a cassette on the Dove label that documents a 1996 appearance seriously marred by the fact that the second half is a love-in between Sahl and crony Eugene McCarthy. Sahl sounds throatier, heavier, older, but he fires away with unerring aim: at Mario Cuomo (*"His grandmother came here from Sicily with thirty dollars in her pocket. Isn't it time to unpack? We're all here"*); at his divorce (*"The judge gave her her space—as well as mine, I might add"*); at relationships (*"It's a country of two hundred and fifty million people and nobody wants to get married except the occasional priest and people of the same sex"*); at a movie he was working on ("*The ad line read, 'Four Years in the Negotiating!'*"); and at Ronald Reagan ("*George Washington couldn't tell a lie, Nixon couldn't tell the truth, and Reagan couldn't tell the difference*"). He tells of running into Michael Caine at the actor's London restaurant, where Caine said, "*Mort Sahl! What are you doing in England?*" to which Sahl replied, "*We're back! The experiment failed.*"

He closes the evening with an audience valedictory: "It's been forty-three years now and I've always approached you all as if you all had Ph.D.s, and it's more than a fair exchange, because you've returned it tenfold to me. Because the first time an audience laughed in San Francisco, I knew I wasn't crazy. After a few days, I realized I wasn't lonely anymore, thanks to the audience. What you do is—all of you make me more honest, because any fool can say what he thinks, but the audience demands that you know what you think before you speak. So you finally arrive at what you really care about, and then you begin to search inside. So it's been very rewarding. Good night, everybody."

As Weide says of him in his documentary, "He opened a door through which few have been able to pass." And Sahl himself told Weide, "I'll tell you what I've learned. It's not: 'Look at my scars.' It's that you can stand up in a society that says, 'Don't rock the boat.' You *can* rock the boat. I'm not afraid to take on anyone. You can have your say in America and really survive. I feel very positive about that. That's the message. Not that you'll get killed for it but that you'll live for it."

Sahl ended a 1968 *Playboy* interview by remarking, "They used to say that no one is above the law. I know a lot of people above the law—and almost everybody is above a lawyer. But I believe no one is above humor. In that sense, my work is never done." Mort Sahl defied the first commandment of comedy—you are there to entertain, not to remind people of their troubles. His entire act was aimed at stirring up trouble, but he was so dazzlingly witty doing it that, with a triumphant laugh, he squelched all the tired and timid show-business dogma of his day.

Rendering unto Caesar

Sid Caesar

*We didn't know we were innovative. We were just looking for
new material.*

———————

WHILE SID CAESAR'S NAME EVOKES an era and provokes involuntary grins, the man who cast a long shadow as one of the towering giants of satirical comedy on TV remains himself a shadowy figure. Caesar's stature heightens our memories of the shows he fronted for a decade and that remain, half a century later, the gold standard for TV sketch comedy. In television's ramshackle hall of fame, he stands on a pedestal with Edward R. Murrow, Walter Cronkite, Jackie Gleason, Rod Serling, and Lucille Ball.

Arriving suddenly on the scene in 1949 in TV's short-lived *Admiral Broadway Revue,* Caesar was never a stand-up comedian. Unlike most major figures of the comedy renaissance, he was a sketch comic, an actor. He conjured ideas and enhanced scenes, but never wrote a word. As sublimely inspired a comic as he was, he was wholly dependent on writers, who, in turn, took inspiration from him. His major weakness, by his own admission, was standing up as himself and speaking—one reason he hid behind his mock German, Japanese, Russian, and Italian accents.

The landmark TV shows he headlined and coproduced for seven years had a satirical flavor different in many ways from that of rival shows. "In temperament, physique, and technique of operation, Caesar represents a new species of comedian," wrote Maurice Zolotow in a 1953 *Saturday Evening Post* profile. The Caesar shows were basically formulaic variety programs studded with satire, and their sketches sharper, edgier, more sophisticated than those on other variety shows. Caesar's shows—*Your Show of Shows* (which ran for four and a half years, 1950–54, on Saturday nights from 9:00 to 10:30 P.M.), *Caesar's Hour, As Caesar Sees It,* plus the occasional special—were heavily fleshed out with singers and dancers, but no dog acts. *Newsweek* noted in 1951, "In the opinion of lots of smart people, Caesar is the best that TV has to offer."

The sketches ran long, up to ten or fifteen minutes, and often were built around two or three acts using dissolves and other film techniques, with a lot of close-ups to catch Caesar's exasperated, horrified, enraged features or to zoom in on one of Imogene Coca's sly winks and leers. Many were tried-and-true domestic routines, such as "The Commuters"—a sort of suburban "Honeymooners"—with Caesar playing off Coca (later Nanette Fabray, and finally Janet Blair) as Charlie and Doris Hickenlooper. In a typical sketch, Fabray is afraid to tell Caesar that she's bought a mink coat and, when he finds out what it costs, he bellows, crosses his eyes, and weeps copious tears in close-up. While brightly enacted, the subject was even then a little worn out. Other sketches were more on the mark, like one in which Caesar bets Carl Reiner that the seventh dwarf was named Weepy; in another, he can't sleep and gets manic, badgers his weary wife (Coca), and winds up taking No-Doz by mistake. "We did reality," said Mel Brooks, "but just bent it an inch or two to the right or left."

The wilder stuff was saved for the movie parodies and for Caesar's and Coca's solo pieces, such as his spaced-out cool jazz musician Progress Hornsby, who explained, Wynton Marsalis–like, the roots of jazz in tangled pseudo-academic babble—writer Larry Gelbart's specialty: *"Hey, man, I got a date in Australia. Like, man, you know, that's on the flip side of the globe."* Caesar's reputation rests mainly on the movie takeoffs, some of them brilliantly wrought. Other variety shows, of course, spoofed films and TV shows, and Jack Benny and Fred Allen had been parodying movies on radio since the early forties; Benny's parody of *Gaslight* even triggered a lawsuit. What distinguishes the Caesar send-ups were that many of them satirized foreign films—a totally new idea. The comedian Richard Lewis recalls, "Even as a child of eight, I knew the difference between watching Milton Berle and watching the Sid Caesar show. Milton was wacky funny but something about Sid was torturously funny." On a 2001 tribute to Caesar on *Larry King Live,* Nanette Fabray observed: "He was the first original TV comedy creation. Milton Berle was a nightclub and radio comic."

Ted Sennett, in his history of *Your Show of Shows,* writes that the comedy-variety program "took a decisive step in turning the 'boob tube' into a reasonably adult medium. For audiences accustomed to TV bowling, Pinky Lee, and Ricky Ricardo, it was a jolt to view takeoffs of *The Blue Angel, Rififi,* and the films of Anna Magnani." Not to mention their movie-musical spoofs, such as "Broadway Rhapsody" (predating real musical pastiches like *Dames at Sea* and *Forty-second Street*) that sent up the backstage musical in grandiose production numbers. Mel Brooks's 2001

Broadway version of his film *The Producers* is really just an old *Your Show of Shows* takeoff, of the kind he wrote for Caesar, but with a gazillion-dollar budget.

Many of the parodies were generic lampoons of gangster films, prison epics, westerns, newspaper dramas, spy movies, and other TV shows, but they were more literate than other shows' spoofs, which simply show-cased their stars—Bob Hope, Jack Benny, Carol Burnett, whose popular seventies show (with its own large share of movie parodies) owed a heavy debt to the Caesar-Coca shows. Because Caesar was a writer's comedian, the dialogue was sharper and funnier: after Coca demurely removes her horn-rimmed glasses, Caesar says, "*Sally! I've never seen you without your glasses,*" then looks her over and cries, "*Put them back on!*"

Their jailhouse film takeoff, "Prison Walls," has Caesar ruminating to his cellmate (Carl Reiner): "*While I was in solitary, I spent a lotta time thinkin'. I did a lot of thinkin'. I got a lot of thoughts. . . . I thought about the walls . . . the bars . . . the guards with the guns. You know what I figured out?*" Reiner: "*What?*" Caesar: "*We're in prison.*" In a *High Noon* parody, Coca asks Caesar: "*I don't understand it! How can you stay here and wait for a man to come and kill you?*" Caesar: "*'Cause I'm stupid, Mary Ellen.*" The show did send-ups of everything from *Cyrano de Bergerac* ("Cyranose") to singing groups (the Haircuts), and specific spoofs of *A Star Is Born, Shane,* and *On the Waterfront,* often seasoned with Catskills jokes. In the *Shane* parody, called "Strange," Coca (as the boy) asks Caesar, "*You seem mighty thirsty. Have a long, dry ride?*"; the buckskin-clad Strange drawls: "*No—I had a herring for breakfast.*"

The foreign film parodies were chancier, since the TV audience wasn't necessarily the same crowd that flocked to *The Bicycle Thief* and *Grand Illusion.* Their versions, titled "La Bicycletta" and "Le Grand Amour" (set in a French bakery), had to work on two levels—as specific parody for the cognoscenti and as broad farce for everyone else. Most of the laughs were generated by Caesar's and Reiner's authentic-sounding Italian/German/French/Russian/Japanese gibberish. One film scholar argues that the parodies helped introduce Americans to foreign films in the 1950s.

Many of the sketches were platforms for Caesar's innate gifts for physical comedy and his pitch-perfect ear for dialects. Caesar, a man of few words off-camera, communicated best through sounds, body language, accents, and facial contortions. Caesar and Coca's pantomime sequences were avant garde by the noisy TV slapstick standards of the time. They ranged from going on a picnic and throwing a party to attending a singles dance and giving a driving lesson. Their more elaborate mime sequences flowered into silent-movie takeoffs, such as "The Sewing-Machine Girl," a *Your Show of Shows* classic.

At heart, Caesar was himself a silent-film comedian working in an alien form, less skillful in sketches dependent on repartee. He was really born to star in Mack Sennett films, with his flickering shadings of joy, sadness, scorn, anger, hatred, or hurt. He could build scenes or shift moods in a flash. In Steve Allen's phrase, he was "born with the ability to write physical poetry," as in a sketch in which he played a discarded Rolls-Royce whitewall tire reclining in a dump and recalling its palmier days. At different times he also impersonated a gumball machine, a lion, a dog, a punching bag, a telephone, a six-month-old baby, an elevator, a railroad train, a herd of horses, a piano, a rattlesnake, and a bottle of seltzer. Like Jonathan Winters, he could people a scene with imaginary characters. Alfred Hitchcock said, "The young Mr. Caesar best approaches the great Chaplin of the early 1920s."

The young Mr. Caesar was then only twenty-seven years old, with just seven months under his belt as a professional comedian who had played a couple of clubs and hotels. He quickly became TV's biggest comedy star after Berle, the hardened pro of vaudeville, radio, Broadway, and movies. As Carl Reiner noted, "Sid went from being a musician at resorts in the mountains to a fully formed star." He came out of nowhere, literally out of the woods—the Jewish mountain resorts.

Caesar was no Chaplin, but he was a new kind of TV clown, the anti-Uncle Milty. Observed a *Collier's* magazine writer: "A gag is as useless to Caesar as a fresh situation is to Milton Berle." *TV Guide* agreed: "Mr. Caesar needs no insult routines, stale gags, shabby sketches to garner his laughs. He is a clown of majesty." He wasn't a warmed-over vaudevillian or a flashy nightclub jokester; like Ernie Kovacs, he was a child of the medium, albeit petrified addressing his own audience.

The critic John Crosby wrote in 1950: "Sid Caesar is one of the wonders of this modern electronic age. Where all the other comics are moaning about the tremendous drain television exerts on material, Caesar has more genuinely funny comedy sequences than he knows what to do with in a week. He could wrench laughter out of you with the violence of his great eyes and the sheer immensity of his parody." In lieu of language, wrote Maurice Zolotow, "Caesar relies upon grunts and grimaces to express a vast range of ideas and emotions." In one sketch, he and Coca, on all fours, played lions in a zoo expressing their innermost thoughts.

Usually, he played a man in pain—a husband dragged to a cocktail party, an expectant father imagining his son as a monster, a bridegroom walking down the aisle worrying about his life as a shackled married man. In a takeoff of *The $64,000 Question,* called "Break Your Brains," Caesar faints inside an oxygen-deprived "humiliation booth." Although Caesar and Coca were mainly physical comedians, some sketches were word-driven, as when the two would meet on a street corner and address each other in a nonstop stream of clichés. In another sketch, he plays a militaristic German whose lackey polishes the medals on his chest as he barks commands for five minutes before he steps outside and blows a whistle for a cab, revealing himself as a hotel doorman. In one tour de force, he compares the simplicity of going on a date a decade earlier (in 1939) with the annoyances of going out in 1949, creating all of the voices—a cabbie, a waiter, his date—and accompanying sounds.

Some of his finest moments are silent solo flights in front of the curtain, such as miming a shy boy at a high school dance who can't figure out where to put his hands or feet. In one of their most remarkable routines, he and Fabray mime a bitter argument in perfect accompaniment to Beethoven's Fifth Symphony, a beautifully worked-out piece of comic choreography that makes you realize, *this* is the sort of thing that kept people home Saturday nights glued to *Your Show of Shows.*

Whenever possible, the writers would toss Caesar a German-professor routine (often written by Brooks), until the character became his trademark, even if it wasn't always Caesar at his most inventive. The addled German expert, such as Siegfried von Sedative, was a vaudeville cliché—a disheveled nutty professor who gabbles non sequiturs in a battered top hat, bedraggled tux coat, loose shirttail, and floppy tie ("Professor" Irwin Corey had his trademark version), but Caesar made it his maniacal own. The fabled costume is on display at the Smithsonian Institution.

Although he didn't write anything, Caesar was a hands-on star and coproducer with the ultimate veto. "After [producer Max] Liebman's original contributions, it all came from Sid," said Howard Morris, the show's third banana, after Reiner. "Once we learned what he had in his skull, we became adjuncts to it. He was the driving force." Said Brooks,

"We all knew we had a great instrument [in Caesar] that we could all play, and we played it very well."

In those famously chaotic sessions, the typist Michael Stewart would wait for a nod from Caesar before recording a joke spinning in the tornado of shouted lines from the writers. If the star didn't like an idea or a joke, he would shoot it down with an imaginary tommy gun. Less literary creator than instigator, Caesar was an inspired idea man who allowed the writers to take more risks than on other variety programs. "Some of the best sketches he has done are not written down at all," noted Zolotow. A script would indicate merely: "Sid does man coming home from business mad."

Caesar was responsible for about a quarter of the material— concepts, details, miming, and rehearsal ad-libs. "Sid would make it ten times funnier than what we wrote," Neil Simon told me. "Sid acted everything out. So the sketches we did were like little plays, like the Hickenloopers sketch, when he's the husband who learns that his wife crashed the car into the liquor store. It's *how* he played it out. It was great for me. It helped me in the theater. I was not writing for a comic who needed jokes. He never did jokes. He was always in character."

Simon further recalls: "The first time I saw Caesar it was like seeing a new country. All other comics were basically doing situations with farcical characters. Caesar was doing life." Caesar did plenty of farce, but it was elevated by superior wit, as when Reiner interviews him as the archaeologist Ludwig von Fossill, who explains how he tried to straighten the Leaning Tower of Pisa by tying a rope from the Tower to the humps of a thousand camels pulling on the building. Reiner: "*Did it straighten out the Leaning Tower of Pisa?*" Caesar: "*No . . . but it straightened out the camels.*"

The tiny smoke-filled writers' room was piled high with food to fuel the writers, who communicated by shouting. "Sid was always food-oriented," said Brooks. He had a mammoth appetite, eating four meals a day, once gorging himself on a whole chicken and a porterhouse steak; he always ordered doubles of everything. At six foot two and two hundred pounds, he was built like a football tackle and burned up calories by hefting hundred-pound barbells over his head.

Stories abound of his Herculean powers, as when he would pick up a steel desk with an electric typewriter on it and set it down, to work off tension. One time in Chicago, claims Brooks, "he picked up a Volkswagen off the street and put it down on the sidewalk so he could have room to park his car." He once punched out a horse, an incident that Brooks re-created in *Blazing Saddles.* Gelbart told him, "Sid, there's only one word I can think of in connection with you. The word is 'gigantism.' Everything you have is the biggest." He adds, "Sid also had the biggest talent." Lieb-man noted that Caesar's size and good looks contradicted the traditional Everyman comic: "The thing Caesar has against him is the very thing that gives him his stamina. Chaplin and the other greats who played little men actually *were* little men. Caesar plays the downtrodden fellow, but it's hard to feel sorry for such a big, strong, handsome ox. It's a tribute to his artistry that his acting is able to overcome this handicap."

Steve Allen said, "Sid's was the show to which all comedy writers aspired. It was the place to be." Gelbart called it "organized chaos." Neil Simon remarks that when Stewart would read back what the writers had been screaming back and forth, "We didn't know who had written the sketch. We didn't realize it was *us*." Even before he wrote for Caesar, Gelbart would come around the set just to watch the famous show rehearse every week. "It was a religious experience."

But, to Mel Brooks, "it was a zoo. Everyone pitched lines at Sid. Jokes would be changed fifty times. We'd take an eight-minute sketch and rewrite it in eight minutes. Then Sid and Coca and Reiner and Morris would relearn it from scratch." Lucille Kallen and Coca were the only women at the sessions. "We suffered from two things," Kallen said, "the smoke of six cigars and the inability to make ourselves heard. I'd have to stand on a desk and wave my red sweater." Sometimes it was like a kid's birthday party—when Caesar or Liebman left the room, everyone would throw spitballs. The sessions might begin with someone shouting an idea and Caesar jumping to his feet to perform it. "More often," though, said a *Collier's* writer who witnessed the process, "the script is dragged out, line by line."

But no jokes, insisted the head writer Mel Tolkin, who recalled, "We didn't think in terms of gags. We were almost a little snobbish about it. Sid could never be a stand-up, one-line comedian. He didn't like one-line jokes in sketches because he felt that if the joke was a good one, anybody could do it. One-liners would take him away from what drove his per-sonal approach to comedy. Caesar insisted on instinctively 'Caesarizing' his material."

Caesar would come up with bizarre ideas based on something he had just experienced, such as observing a fly buzzing around a tray of canapés. "I studied this fly," he told Zolotow. "He kept hopping on that crumb of cheese. I figured he was gloating, 'It's mine, all mine.' " Caesar went into the Monday writers' meeting and announced, " 'Fellas, this week I wanna do a fly.' The writers all looked nauseated. I said, 'I worked out the psychology of a fly. It could be very funny.' I gave them some of my ideas and then I showed them how I could *be* a fly." As the writers tossed out fly jokes and fly shtick, the routine developed into Caesar's fly contemplating the day: "*What a house I live in. It's my house. I was so lucky to find this house. Always something to eat. Crumbs on the table, banana peels on the floor, lettuce leaves in the sink. . . . What a nice sloppy house. Well, I'm hungry. I'll see what there is in the sink. . . .*" He sees a moth and thinks, "*He's crazy, that guy. Eats wool, blue serge . . . yugh. And then every night he throws himself against an electric lightbulb, knocking his brains out.*" And so on, for nine funny minutes.

Max Liebman's place in all of this controlled lunacy gets a bit blurred—often he was busily putting together musical segments of the show and left the writing sessions to Caesar—but it was Liebman's personal vision of a ninety-minute TV revue that gave the show its smart veneer and satirical viewpoint that the writers harnessed for its star.

Caesar's Hour was even wackier backstage than *Your Show of Shows.* Caesar records in his memoirs: "Desks were burned, people's shoes were ripped off their feet and thrown out the window onto Fifty-seventh Street. Writers in disfavor were sent off to work in what was called 'The Jock Room,' " where the male dancers changed. Brooks was regularly hung in effigy on general principles. Contrary to the image of TV comedy writing as wall-to-wall laugh sessions, Woody Allen found it all depressing. He told *The New Yorker*'s Penelope Gilliatt in 1974: "It can make for a terrible atmosphere. When I was writing for the Sid Caesar shows [two specials, actually], they were a mass of hostilities and jealousies." An Allen biographer writes that Woody "chafed under the atmosphere of inspired spontaneity," but Allen once commented, "Writing for Caesar was the highest thing you could aspire to—at least as a TV comedy writer. Only the presidency was above that."

One of Caesar's comic skills was constructing annoying molehills until they became bubbing volcanos. "He was a different sort of a comedian," Gelbart told me. "He was a sketch performer who created his own sketches, like a Richard Pryor"—but without the verbal dexterity of a Pryor. "A sketch comic is in essence an actor, whereas a stand-up comic is a joke-teller. I saw echoes of Harry Ritz in there—a manic energy and strength. He was a pure TV comedian. He was so theatrical. He was not a voice, not a radio performer. He would have been wasted on radio. He couldn't do the straightforward emcee chores, but then why should he? He had no weaknesses." But he had quirks aplenty. For a few weeks, Caesar spoke off-camera in a Polish accent.

The mythic Caesar character is an ogre who flies into rages and browbeats everybody, as in Simon's *Laughter on the 23rd Floor,* in the film *My Favorite Year,* and in Reiner's *Your Show of Shows*–inspired *Dick Van Dyke Show.* And yet, says Gelbart, "I don't remember him being difficult, or if he was I just took it in my stride. I had worked for a lot of comics." Howard Morris acknowledged, "Sid could be difficult, at times he could be rotten," but his anger was never directed at colleagues. "Was he tough to work with?" mused Fabray on *Larry King Live.* "Yes and no. He made me funnier in areas I didn't know I was funny. He said, 'Don't worry, we'll protect you.' And he'd always say, 'You can do that.' "

The Caesar shows were the crème de la crème of fifties television. Fred Allen, radio's great satirist who failed to make the transition from radio to TV, huddled with Caesar backstage in 1950 to learn all he could from the new kid. Gelbart recalls: "We knew it was special—we didn't realize people would continue to think so to this day. We *made* it special. We tried to make it a superior show every week. It was like watching a master class in revue production and comedy." He further reflects: "I look back on it with complete affection. It was a wonderful time for all of us—we were all young, married, in the first six months of psychoanalysis. It was a good time to be in New York, a good time to be alive. It was another life. And we were all with the New York Yankees. We were a bunch of very gifted neurotic young Jews punching our brains out."

What's been forgotten is that *Your Show of Shows* began as the last half of a catchall extravaganza called *The NBC Saturday Night Revue,* which opened with the overshadowed *Jack Carter Show.* The Caesar show became such a Saturday-night must-see habit—the *Saturday Night Live* of its day—that Broadway producers begged NBC to switch the show to midweek. Watching the ninety-minute shows today, it's astonishing to consider that thirty-nine times a year they were conceived, written, rehearsed, and televised in a week, everything performed live on network TV with the benefit of only four rehearsals. There were no TelePrompTers or crib sheets; they learned six sketches in as many days, often editing on their feet during the performance. "You were given two choices," said Morris. "You were funny

or you were dead." A certain amount of "writing" was improvised on camera by Caesar and company during the live telecasts. Caesar often took
liberties with dialogue, but Gelbart insists that these spontaneous changes
were always better than what they had written for him. "He would ad-lib
an attitude not in the script," said Reiner.

What helped give the shows their special theatrical flavor was that
Liebman insisted the sketches be played to the studio audience. "You
worked to them, not to the cameras," said Coca. After the Saturday show,
the cast gathered at Danny's Hideaway for a postmortem. "We'd eat and
drink and carry on like crazy, we had built up such adrenaline during the
week," Gelbart said. Steve Allen once commented that Caesar "burned
up more humor fodder in one season than ten vaudeville comics would
during their entire lifetimes." Bert Lahr was incredulous, saying of the
furious weekly output, "It's impossible." Tolkin said, "We were too young
to know it was impossible. We all were new, we all were poor. That was
an important part of it."

After the Saturday-night show, everyone showed up Monday morning
to gear up for the following Saturday. By Wednesday, the script had to be
written and "sent to mimeo," so that the musicians, set designer, camera
crew, choreographer, and costumer could start work; the cast never saw
the set or worked with props until the day of the show. Friday there was
a camera run-through. On Saturday, there were three rehearsals, from
blocking to full dress at 5:30 P.M.——only hours away from airtime.
Sketches were timed, cut, rewritten, or ditched, and new ones written
on the spot. "We'd throw out a sketch and bang out a new one in thirty,
forty minutes if we were stuck," said Brooks. "We had very talented guys.
We didn't know we couldn't do it, so we did it."

Recalls Simon: "Part of it was frightening and part of it was great
because you were protected by the numbers. They were good guys and
all you had to do was come up with a couple of funny things in the first
week and they said, 'Okay, he's good, we accept him.' We [Neil and his
brother Danny Simon] weren't even in the big room with the guys—
we were sitting on the hallway steps writing things we hoped would get
into the show. Finally we did get things on the show and then we sat in the
big room." Writer Lucille Kallen recalled the setting: "Mel [Tolkin] and I
got the dancers' dressing room. Or we squatted in the hallway." Of her
male colleagues, she said, "Sid boomed, Tolkin intoned, and Brooks,
well . . . let's say that gentility was never a noticeable part of our work-

ing lives. It was a lot of fun." Liebman often hurled a lighted cigar at Brooks. Kallen observes: "Max Liebman was fond of quoting what I think was a Goldwynism: 'From a polite conference comes a polite movie.'"

Simon played Bashful among the seven scribes. "I would say something next to Carl and Carl would say, 'Doc's got it! Doc's got it!' So it would get in. Eventually, it would go around the room and I found you would just wait your turn. We'd break up into groups. Gelbart and I would go downstairs and write a German professor routine, and then we'd come up and pitch it and fix it up. Very often if we'd work on a big sketch we'd all be in there together. There were plenty of arguments, but it was like a family and you could say anything you wanted, like you would to your brother. We were living with each other thirty-nine weeks a year." Brooks said he felt guilty being paid for such a daily frolic: "I thought it was *stealing,* to tell the truth. Gee, fifty bucks for things I'd do on the street corner! Terrific!"

Gelbart admits that "it was a cult show, but there was a niche audience then. People who could afford a TV were likely to be well-educated. As the price of sets came down, so did the IQ of the audience." Coca said, "It never occurred to anyone to talk down to the audience. We just automatically assumed that people would understand what we were doing. And we were doing pretty sophisticated material." Adds Simon: "We were a big hit in all the urban areas, but the minute TV began to spread out into the suburban and rural areas, they didn't get our kind of comedy. We couldn't be as sophisticated as we once were, and the ratings eventually started to drop. One of the big enemies of our show was the *Lawrence Welk Show.* They were getting bigger ratings than us, and there's no mercy at the networks."

The pressures finally took their toll on the easily jangled star. Of Caesar's decline and fall, Simon says, "I can only guess what made him come apart. It was not only the pressure from NBC but also [sinking ratings]." Of Caesar's alcoholism, Gelbart says, "Whatever problems Sid had at that time, we didn't see during a normal working day." Simon recalls that Caesar "was always clear-headed. He took his stuff [liquor] at the end of the day. He had a long drive home." Caesar never drank before or during a show, only afterward, politely asking, after the set was cleared, "Is everything put away?" before opening a bottle. "I couldn't get to sleep, so I'd have a few drinks and fall asleep," he explained. That same pressure gave the show its energy, noted Reiner—"Panic always keeps creative minds working." Morris said, "Somewhere in that marvelous and troubled man was a drive and an instinct, a kind of satiric creativity I can't explain."

Contrary to *Laughter on the 23rd Floor,* Caesar rarely blew up in front of people. "I don't remember him exploding, 'Goddamn it, this is no good!' the way Jackie Gleason would," recounts Simon. "Sid sarcasted you to death. There was an enormous amount of anger, but it would all come out in comedy. When he was angry, he could be very funny about it. Sid loved the writers and paid them better than anyone else. He knew they were his bread and butter." Fabray recalled, "He never showed his anger. He'd say, 'Excuse me,' leave the room, go out and put his fist through a door, then come back as though nothing had happened."

If anything, Simon remembers Caesar's silences. "In my first year, I feared being alone with him, because I wouldn't know what to talk to him about. Because he wasn't very articulate. He wouldn't sit down and be very comfortable saying, 'So Neil, how's your life?' It was all business with Sid. But he cared for everybody; if someone had a problem, Sid was there to help out." Fabray adds, "With his cast he was always generous and gracious, one of the warmest men I've ever worked with."

There was no time on the show for clinical traumas or clashing egos. Everyone was on the same wavelength. Explains Gelbart: "There were some annoyances—Mel's chronic tardiness—but mainly it was a matter of having your lines heard over the creative din. People just spoke up. We didn't mean to be cruel or cutting, but we'd been around; our feelings weren't hurt. But there was no real rivalry. Nobody would stiff anybody. It's hard to sit around and not laugh at Mel Brooks."

Simon remembers, "We were competitive the way a family is competitive to get Dad's attention. We all wanted to be Sid's favorite." Brooks was Caesar's favorite enfant terrible. "Sid could easily throw a bottle at Mel and hit him and still love him, but he loved all of us." Reiner said, "The rest of us were like moths to a flame. We would throw Caesar our best hand and say, 'Here, you can have this.' We were swimming in much more protected waters than he was."

SIDNEY CAESAR WAS NO neighborhood cutup, class clown, or comic in training. He didn't even speak for his first three years in Yonkers, New York, where he was born in 1922. His family feared he might be mute. Caesar recalled, "As a kid, a lot of people thought I was dumb, I used to do such crazy things, but I was just inarticulate." In junior high, he wound up in fights due to his size; he lifted weights in school. Until the age of eighteen, profiled Zolotow, "he is not known to have done or said a single amusing thing. He was a serious, morose, introspective person." One of his teachers later said of Caesar that he "struck me as being one of the slowest-witted human beings I ever encountered. It shows how deceiving appearances can be."

He was only insecure with the English language—so shy he could better express himself through a saxophone, which he began playing at the age of eight. By twelve, Sid was working in swing bands for two dollars a night. "He still grunts and grapples with the language," a reporter wrote years later. A friend remarked, "A hello from Sid is a big conversation." Caesar also isn't terribly articulate about his comedy, but then Fred Astaire fumbled for words to describe his dancing. The young Sid picked up dialects while working between classes as a lunchtime busboy with his brothers at his father Max's cafeteria, the St. Clair Lunch. The Caesars lived above the restaurant, which was located near the railroad depot and was filled with a mix of ethnic factory workers. Years later, when he would dine out with his wife, he enjoyed flummoxing waiters by ordering in French and Italian doubletalk. "He has a musician's ear for languages," says Reiner. Adds Caesar: "Every language has a song."

His shyness may explain why he was a great comic technician but couldn't hold the stage as Sid Caesar. Unlike Danny Kaye, the performer most like him as a pure physical comic, Caesar had no stage personality beyond his characters. He lacked Kaye's natural charm and ebullience. When his TV career ended, he had nowhere to go. He was a creature of his writers. He could give a hungry fly, or a woman putting on makeup, a complex personality, but he had nothing left over for himself.

Before World War II, Caesar played saxophone in the big bands of Charlie Spivak, Claude Thornhill, Shep Fields, and Art Mooney. He had taken some classes at Juilliard and was headed for France to study at the Paris Conservatory ("I was a real longhair") when he stumbled into comedy at the Avon Lodge in the Catskills, working as a waiter and *tummler*. A social director at the Vacationland Hotel in upstate New York, who customarily recruited members of the staff and band for shows, coaxed Caesar, then playing in a six-piece dance band, into taking part. He was finally hooked.

During the war, he switched from sax to comedy: "One day I was at the [USO] canteen in Brooklyn and I got talking with Vernon Duke, the composer, and we decided to form an orchestra for dances at the base. We got the thing going and between numbers I used to kid around a little, doing imitations and doubletalk routines." Caesar's centerpiece was a conversation between Adolf Hitler and Donald Duck, in which he played both roles, but he also broke up the other sidemen with impressions of the officers. "When Vernon was commissioned by the Coast Guard to write a show"—to compete with Irving Berlin's hit *This Is the Army*—"he recommended me to the fellow who was going to stage the production. That was Max Liebman."

Caesar made a splash touring in the Coast Guard revue *Tars and Spars,* whose tour de force was his own war-movie takeoff. In the 1946 film loosely based on it, the tall, strapping, wild-eyed Caesar performs, as "Smiling Jim," a nine-minute parody, "Wings over Bombinschissel," doing all the voices and sounds (three pilots, six airplanes, two machine guns) of an aerial dogfight between the Yanks and the Germans—just the sort of thing he went on to do each week on television.

After the war, Liebman put Caesar in his shows at the upscale Tamiment Hotel, where Liebman had formed a rep company that included Betty Garrett, Jules Munshin, Kaye, and Coca. The weekend shows at Tamiment, in Pennsylvania's Pocono Mountains (less ethnic than the Catskill resorts), were not wobbly amateur nights; they were big-budget events in a raked, twelve-hundred-seat auditorium, staffed with a resident composer, orchestrator, rehearsal pianists, dancers, two writers, and original sets.

Liebman told Ted Sennett, "I was really preparing myself for television at Tamiment. I was doing what you might call television without cameras. Our big performance was Saturday night before a very tough audience." Those revues became a showcase for emerging talent—singers, comics, and writers; the resort's owners were savvy Broadway investors. Certain that he'd found himself another Danny Kaye, Liebman wrote Caesar a nightclub act for the Copacabana (Caesar had never even been in a nightclub before), found him an agent, and guided his early career, counseling him on everything from material to apartment-hunting, and starred him in the 1948 hit Broadway revue *Make Mine Manhattan,* for which he won a Donaldson Award for best debut in a musical (he imitated a gum machine and United Nations delegates).

Liebman then convinced Pat Weaver, NBC's programming visionary responsible for the *Today* and *Tonight* shows, to give him a lavish budget of $15,000 a week to produce *The Admiral Broadway Revue,* which debuted in

January 1949 and was the prototype for *Your Show of Shows*, which premiered a year later, on February 25, 1950. The Admiral show had a different theme for each of its nineteen weeks ("Night Life in New York," "Hollywood," "Signs of Spring"), lampooning such modish fifties topics as modern art, advertising, and psychiatry, very much an extension of the Tamiment extravaganzas (some of whose sketches later turned up on *Your Show of Shows*); it was part TV variety show and part topical satirical revue. Liebman consciously tried to get away from the vaudeville-centered variety shows, to give his version a theatrical flair. "I felt that the one element missing [in TV variety shows] was that of the legitimate theater. I'm referring to sophistication tempered by a sense of showmanship."

The early rave reviews of the Liebman-Caesar-Coca team signaled some of the possibilities of TV comedy. The *Herald Tribune's* John Crosby wrote: "For an hour's entertainment, I can't think of anything better in New York's expensive nightclubs. Come to think of it, there isn't anything much better on Broadway, either." *Time* wrote: "Its jokes and patter are brittle, rowdy, funny, and full of satirical references." (A video compilation of the sketches, *Ten from "Your Show of Shows,"* skims off the cream, but a more complete, satisfying, and representative video anthology, *The Sid Caesar Collection,* was released by Creative Light in 2000.)

Viewing some of the kinescopes of that hallowed series today, it looks a little like a low-budget *Ed Sullivan Show,* featuring guest hosts, the Billy Williams Quartet, singers Bill Hayes and Judy Johnson, and scads of dancers and divas—Russian ballerinas and teams like Mata and Hari, the Hamilton Trio, and Bambi Lynn and Rod Alexander, as well as opera stars Robert Merrill, Lily Pons, and Marguerite Piazza.

"The Commuters," domestic sketches with Caesar and Coca/Fabray as the squabbling Hickenloopers (a more varied, clever, aware version of radio's Bickersons), became the sitcom prototype of the future, foreshadowing the Kramdens. In these sketches, writes Sennett, "tiny disagreements would explode into full-scale warfare." He comments that although Doris and Charlie Hickenlooper "may have seldom indulged in the knockdown slapstick of Lucy and Desi, or the boisterous bickering of Ralph and Alice . . . they were truer, more honestly observed, and funnier." Coca played the exuberant, determined, upwardly mobile wife to Caesar's sullen, housebound, meat-and-potatoes husband inveigled into "new experiences" to please his spouse.

When Coca unwisely left to do her own ill-fated show, Fabray became Caesar's costar. Though a skilled comic actress, she wasn't as winning or as whimsical as Coca, who was part clown and part pixie and whose fey comic style bounced lightly off Caesar's loutish characters. Coca was a blithe spirit too often overshadowed by her more flamboyant costar. (Coca, called "Caesar's Cleopatra," earned $10,000 a week to his $25,000.) Twelve years older than Caesar and with a theater background (she'd begun as a child vaudevillian), Coca was in some ways subtler than her costar and had more range. She was his equal as a mime while also performing funny arias, droll ballerina spoofs (she had trained as a dancer and also been in films and on Broadway), and pixilated versions of *Sleeping Beauty, Giselle, Scheherazade,* and *Afternoon of a Faun.* Some of her most memorable TV routines had originated at Tamiment—the mock striptease, the fur-coat model, the goofball ballets. Lily Tomlin was strongly influenced by Coca.

Imogene Fernandez de Coca was five foot three, almost a foot shorter than Caesar, weighed ninety pounds, and was subdued off-camera. She was every bit as shy as Caesar, fearful of riding in cabs, trains, airplanes, and crowded elevators. Literally afraid of her own shadow, she even avoided watching herself on kinescopes. "Imogene wasn't truly funny in the room," recalled Neil Simon. "She was a great laugher." Reiner called the petite comic "the strongest human being I ever met. She was a frail little thing [but] she could work longer and harder than anyone. I called her a strong bird because she did these musical numbers that took a lot of strength and energy, yet she looked like an elf."

Coca commented later that while she and Caesar weren't social friends, they were comic soul mates. "We had an almost ESP thing going on," she said. After Caesar, she never found anything remotely equal to it, or that used her gifts as well. She told a reporter in 1972, "I'm tired of talking about *Your Show of Shows.* But deep inside, I know I've done nothing as good since. I'd run twenty miles in sheer joy if I'd hear that we would be able to go back on again. It was the most fulfilling time of my life. I'd take fifty bucks a week for the chance to work with him again." Late in her life, Coca wound up at the Actor's Fund Home in New Jersey, suffering from Alzheimer's disease; she died there in 2001, at the age of ninety-two.

As Robert D. McFadden wrote in his *New York Times* obituary of her, "Blending lunatic fantasy and more contortions than a fun house mirror, Coca caricatured the foibles of housewives, spinsters, pouting flappers, and haughty socialites. She could turn a Wagnerian aria into a nightmare of brow-knitted concentration, quavering glissandos, and narrow escapes from tonal disaster." "I never call Coca a comedienne, I call her an artist," said Leonard Sillman, the *New Faces* producer who discovered her in 1936. Liebman, calling her the most disciplined comic on the show, said, "She'd try anything, and she could *do* anything," from oversexed Lola-Lola vamps to overwrought chanteuses (*"I'm yours, only yours. Exclusively yours. No one else's but yours! Because you are mine, this makes us ours!"*).

Describing her rubberized clown features for a *Life* profile, Ernest Havemann wrote that "her left eyelid can droop into the lewdest wink ever allowed on television and her right eyebrow can shoot up an eighth of an inch into the most innocent kind of comic bafflement." To which Sennett adds, "She is the cheerful but not very beautiful girl at the party who wins over the boys with her charm and her eagerness to please. She touches the heart at the very moment she is tickling the funnybone." In her signature number, she sang "Wrap Your Troubles in Dreams" as a hobo; she also did a charwoman who sings about her grande dame fantasies (a bit later revamped by Carol Burnett on her TV show). In finales, Coca would lead the company in a version of an old song like "Glow Worm" or "Peaches Down in Georgia," ending the show on a warm note.

The duo was so well matched, comically, in their pantomimes and the domestic sketches, that many viewers assumed they were a married couple. "There was a deep connection between them that audiences fell in love with," said Howard Morris. Caesar recently explained his and Coca's ESP link: "When we weren't working, we wouldn't say that much to each other. However, when we would rehearse, she would almost feel what I was going to do and I would feel what she was going to do." Even their ad-libs were in sync. "We complemented each other. We weren't in competition, and that was real. When we worked together it was magic and you don't question the magic. She was one of a kind." Said Reiner, "It was an incredible symbiotic thing that happened."

Reiner joined the show in its second season as a foil for Caesar after Liebman saw his work on TV's *54th Street Revue*. As Reiner recalled: "I had such great respect for [Caesar's] talent that I felt there's nothing I do that he can't do better. For example, I used foreign-language doubletalk in my nightclub act. No match for Sid's. I was miserable at first. The writers all were crammed into Max's office, some of them overflowing into the toilet. We were only called in when there was something to rehearse." Like Brooks and the Simon brothers, "I decided I had to get out of the hall and into the inner office. So I began to suggest things." When Reiner suggested a French film parody using himself and other actors—"Until then,

Sid had been doing foreign films alone, playing all the parts himself"—the resourceful performer quickly found himself in the inner circle as an actor-writer.

Two of their cleverest takeoffs were lavish parodies of *From Here to Eternity* ("From Here to Obscurity") and *Sunset Boulevard* ("Aggravation Boulevard"—a riff on squeaky-voiced silent-film stars, with Caesar as a falsetto-voiced John Gilbertesque Valentino and Fabray as a Theda Bara vamp). "On the Docks," though a masterful *On the Waterfront* takeoff with Caesar as Brando's sensitive brute and Reiner as his mobster brother, rambles too long, as all the sketches tended to—and as they so often do today on *Saturday Night Live.* Many of the spoofs, however, were generic and didn't depend on the audience having seen a specific movie. In one, a Vittorio De Sica parody, "The Cobbler's Daughter," Caesar and Reiner enact an elaborate ten-minute scene in Italian gobbledygook, full of flamboyant gestures and emotion, with unexpected phrases in English that were the only "jokes"; the writers' job was to supply the English words, while the actors improvised the rest. Coca, less adept at dialects, had to have the nonsense gibberish written out for her.

Instead of jokes, says Woody Allen, "you wrote situations," as in one of the show's most prized sketches (and Caesar's own favorite), a parody of *This Is Your Life,* with Caesar dragged kicking and screaming onstage to have the intimate details of his life revealed to the viewing audience. The lines themselves aren't funny, but the parody is hilarious thanks to Caesar's physical shtick and because of Morris, who, as a weepy long-lost relative, hurls himself at Caesar and clings to his leg, refusing to let go. Caesar, a thoroughly reluctant subject, is hauled before the TV cameras, still sitting in his theater seat, which two ushers have unbolted from the floor. It's runaway slapstick, without a single joke, but it perfectly nails the Ralph Edwards show's shameless sentimentality.

In 1977 Brooks said: "We wrote things that made *us* laugh, not what we thought the audience would dig. . . . What really collapsed us, grabbed our bellies, knocked us down on the floor, and made us spit and laugh so that we couldn't breathe—*that* was what went into the script." Like this excerpt from *Your Show of Shows,* a preview of Reiner and Brooks's 2,000 Year Old Man: Caesar, a mountain-climbing expert, is explaining the death of a fellow climber, Hans Goodfellow, to Reiner, who asks: *"What should a climber do if his rope breaks?"* Caesar: *"Well, as soon as you see the rope breaking, scream and keep screaming all the way down. This way they'll know where to find you."* Reiner: *"But, Professor, isn't there anything else you can do?"* Caesar: *"Well, there's the other method. As soon as the rope breaks, you spread your arms and begin to fly."* Reiner: *"But humans can't fly."* Caesar: *"How do you know? You might be the first one. Anyway, you can always go back to screaming."* Reiner: *"Was Hans Goodfellow a flyer or a screamer?"* Caesar: *"He was a flying screamer, and a crasher, too."*

Caesar was inspired but often uncontrolled. Even his manager, Leo Morgan, said of him when he starred in the musical *Little Me,* "He's needed this kind of discipline for a long time." One writer commented that he had as many personas as the seven parts he played in *Little Me.* A virtuoso of volatility on- and off-camera, he twice ripped a sink out of a wall and hurled a bucket of sand at his Coast Guard commanding officer. The first time he ever went hunting, he shot a deer and afterward stood over it, weeping. A self-described "gun nut," Caesar collected firearms and sometimes carried one. He worked off his persistent temper by firing salvos at water-filled halvah cans set in trees in the Catskills. He defended his demons, saying, "One guy who *can't* play it cool is a comedian. If he does, he's dead." A musician friend said, "Sid is a man with nothing average or in-between about him. He's either up or he's down."

Despite its revered status, *Your Show of Shows* came to an end in June 1954, after five seasons. NBC wanted to use Liebman on color "spectaculars" and spin off Coca into her own half-hour show. NBC, for purely greedy ends, had busted up a winning team. Liebman wasn't involved with *Caesar's Hour,* which ran from 1954 to 1957 and which Reiner has called "the best work we did"; people now tend to blend all three Caesar series into *Your Show of Shows.* Simon surmised, "Sid was expanding and felt it was time to leave to have more say and more power. Perhaps he wanted to get away from the production numbers Max Liebman was so fond of." But without Liebman, Caesar was lost. He never recovered when *Your Show of Shows* and *Caesar's Hour* ended, followed by thwarted attempts to revive his and Coca's magic in *Sid Caesar Invites You* and *As Caesar Sees It.* Both had hasty burials.

Trying to paint a happy face on events, Caesar told the press: "The truth is that Max, Coca, and myself have to split up because there just isn't time for the three of us to express ourselves on one show anymore. In other words, we've grown up, and we must get out on our own." There was more truth to his next comment: "During the past five years, we've done everything that's possible to do within the confines of one show." He added, "It's time we were given a chance to express ourselves differently.

I know Coca is capable of doing more, and so is Max." In fact, the show gave them all the room they would ever need to express themselves.

The critics who had begun by praising Caesar ended up burying him. Ever since 1952, there had been a few grumbles that TV's most vaunted variety show was growing stale and predictable—"uneven." By the end of the 1953 season, it appeared only on three Saturday nights out of every four; dancers and divas were seen less and celebrity guests more, but the tinkering seemed needless and annoying to the show's fans. The program's built-in problem was that it was so successful that the viewers grew to know it too well. When the cancellation was finally announced, the normally unflappable Coca said, "I made a fool of myself, crying and carrying on." A photo of the final curtain call reveals Coca on the brink of tears and a grim, bottled-up Caesar.

After about a decade of stardom as the head of TV's most cherished prime-time comedy shows, Caesar slid into a personal and career abyss. He, rashly as it turned out, had no interest in movies when Brooks tried to get him to go with him to Hollywood. He would live and die by the tube. His career was short-circuited by alcohol and pills, setting off drunken rages that grew into a twenty-year lost weekend. The pressures of sudden stardom, of headlining and coproducing a weekly hit show, crushed him.

When Liebman first told Caesar's wife that her husband would be a big star, she said, maybe fearing the worst, "Couldn't he be just a *little* star?" Caesar felt it had all come too fast, was too easy, and that he didn't deserve the acclaim. He was as bedeviled as the characters he played on the show—"harassed, haunted, compulsive, bewildered, and frustrated," writes Zolotow, enumerating the terrors that besieged Caesar. "Everybody in show business considers it a sheer miracle that after so many years, Caesar is still able to keep up the mad pace," said the mid-fifties article, whose subhead reads, "For Three Years, Experts Have Expected Him to Crack." About three years later, he cracked.

Brooks said in 1972: "I know of no other comedian, including Chaplin, who could have done nearly ten years of live television. Nobody's talent was ever more used up than Sid's. He was one of the greatest artists ever born. But over a period of years, television ground him into sausages—one sausage a week—until, finally, there was little of the muse left." Once the show folded, Caesar went into "an abrupt, total retreat," said a journalist, "the longest lapse into silence of his adult years." Jack

Carter, who had hung out with Caesar in their NBC heyday, says, "Sid was insane! He was a gigantic drinker. I always used to say that his wife, Florence, would lie next to him on the couch so she could see what he looked like standing up. We became very close. We'd shoot skeet. He had violence on his mind. Guns. He's calm now."

After his long disappearance, he was virtually unemployable and couldn't gain a comic foothold to resume his career in TV, films, or onstage, despite two major hits—a central role in the movie *It's a Mad Mad Mad Mad World* and, in 1962, the lead in *Little Me,* which called upon all of his faceted TV turns. *Ten from "Your Show of Shows"* revived his name long enough for people in 1972 to wonder whatever became of Sid Caesar, who at one time was so famous that people in restaurants would steal uneaten french fries off his plate as souvenirs. Albert Einstein, a huge Caesar fan, invited the comedian to visit him in Princeton in 1955, but the scientist died the following week, before they could meet. Sid's daughter, Michelle, recalled how he would erupt if anyone in the family dared laugh at young comics like John Belushi, a brutish latter-day Caesar, with similar self-destructive tendencies, whose famous Samurai warrior was a cousin to a famous Caesar-Reiner routine. Caesar's son said that during the depths of his alcoholism, his father had a schizoid personality. "Most comedians aren't happy," Caesar remarked on *Larry King Live.*

Years later, his star long fallen, Caesar's former groupie Mel Brooks found a role for his mentor in his 1976 film *Silent Movie.* The reclusive Caesar finally pulled himself out of his black hole. In 1988, at sixty-seven, he attempted a comeback—appearing in a TV movie about three geezers who launch a line of designer jeans. He went on tour with Milton Berle and Danny Thomas, a shadow of his comic self without his old supporting cast, close-ups, and inspired writers. He revived two TV pantomimes (the awkward boy at a dance, a concert pianist) for a cabaret act that he and Coca tried to bring to Broadway. These were valiant efforts to get on his feet. "I had to get back into action," he told me in 1988 at the Fairmont Hotel in San Francisco. "Just to function is all I need. I don't need to knock down any empires." To keep busy, he performed a comic turn as the jailer in a Metropolitan Opera production of *Die Fledermaus,* lectured on "The Importance of Humor Today" (he believed in laughter's healing powers), and did some work for Alcoholics Anonymous.

Caesar never really came back, but at least he was up and about— losing weight, working out, taking care of himself. Part of his cure was talking into a tape recorder every day, a surrogate shrink. "If you don't verbalize things, they get bigger and bigger," he said. "You gotta make friends with yourself, 'cause only you know what can make you happy." He had plenty of time to reflect back on his heyday thirty years earlier. It had all happened so quickly that he didn't have time to savor it then. "The world became my candy store and I didn't have the background to understand what was happening or to appreciate it. I wasn't blasé but I was so busy working. It was very wearing. The main thing was just to get the job done, meet deadlines, and think up ideas." Nobody had any time to sit back and enjoy their genius. "We didn't know we were innovative. We were just looking for new material," he said. He was "surprised, but not *that* surprised" that so many of his writers carved out major careers.

Robin Williams now says of Caesar's shows: "The stuff is precious. I was sitting one time watching a retrospective of *Your Show of Shows* and an old woman sitting there turns to me and she says, 'You'll never be that good.' " Contemporary comedians like Drew Carey still worship Caesar. Appearing with him on *Larry King Live,* Carey said he was humbled to be in Caesar's company. The younger comic paid tribute to Caesar's unflinching on-camera comic presence: "Even while he was just looking bug-eyed, it seemed like the wheels were always turning in his mind." Unlike comics for whom live TV was a license to break up on camera— see Skelton, Hope, Berle—Caesar never broke character. "He was so totally into the scene he never lost it," said Fabray. Reiner added, "He never went to the Actor's Studio, but he has great sense memory," and he remembered a specific rehearsal in which Caesar mimed twisting a stuck lid off a pickle jar. When the idea was killed, Caesar—without realizing it—absently mimed screwing the lid back on the pickle jar.

As his recovery lengthened, Caesar became more scholarly. He delved into physics and history. He traveled with battered paperback copies of an Einstein biography and *The Looking-Glass Universe* and nonchalantly discussed intricate order versus implicit order, quantum mechanics, particles and waves. Two of his heroes were theoreticians Max Planck and Werner Heisenberg. When Heisenberg failed to entertain him, Caesar would pick up a book about the Napoleonic Wars and the Battle of Crécy. He was equally at ease talking about the nuclear arms race, Freud, Jung, drug abuse, and the Japanese economy. Contemporary comedy didn't seem to engage him nearly as much as something Bismarck once said to Krupp. He's an avid watcher of the History Channel and, in 2001, was reading *Hyperspace* to learn about "the superstring theory."

Caesar at nearly eighty was variously reported as "looking like a Dracula victim with too much blood sucked out of him" and as a man "who still has the powerful eyes, warm smile, and trademark expressive face." On the *Larry King Live* tribute, he looked vital and seemed, for him, talkative. His professional life is now largely a matter of taking victory laps to plug DVD video collections of vintage Caesar shows. Since his thwarted comeback of the late 1980s, he's made only a few public appearances, such as showing up at a 2000 Kennedy Center show that paid tribute to Jonathan Winters. The onetime invincible TV comic, now bearded, thin, and fragile, tottered slowly to the podium, waved to the audience, and saluted Winters with a funny and perfectly rendered barrage of French, Italian, Russian, and German gibberish. For just one fleeting moment, it was once again Caesar's hour.

Sing a Song of Strychnine

Tom Lehrer

What good are laurels if you can't rest on them?

─────────

BEFORE POLITICAL INCORRECTNESS had a name, Tom Lehrer gleefully personified it. Like Allan Sherman and Mel Brooks, Lehrer was a party favor who became a favorite—until he'd had enough limelight. A Harvard math student with a delightfully warped mind, Lehrer performed satirical ditties at university parties, smokers, and dances, but soon found a national audience that couldn't get enough of his brilliantly twisted tunes. With demonic wit and delicious rhymes, Lehrer threw derisive jabs at American icons, the Cold War, and do-gooders—from self-righteous folksingers and sanctimonious humanitarians to smug small-town sentimentalists. His songs became passports of a sort, allowing entree into a select society of fans who knew all the words to "Be Prepared" and "The Vatican Rag":

> *First you get down on your knees,*
> *Fiddle with your rosaries,*
> *Bow your head with great respect*
> *And genuflect, genuflect, genuflect!*
>
> *Do whatever steps you want if*
> *You have cleared them with the Pontiff,*
> *Ev'rybody say his own*
> *Kyrie eleison,*
> *Doin' the Vatican Rag!*

Lehrer, an equal-opportunity satirist, spread his acid-tinged humor evenly over banal homilies, social hypocrisies, and folksy humbug. Although a few of the numbers were just fun—like "The Elements," in which he lists every atomic element known at the time, or "Lobachevsky," in which he rhymes unwieldy Russian names, or a salute to the much-married Alma Mahler Gropius Werfel—most of his numbers worked on two levels. They were parodies of musical genres—tangos, rags, reels, hymns, waltzes, lullabies, anthems, ballads—but that was just the packaging.

Neatly tucked inside the jaunty tunes were poison-dipped needles aimed at such noble causes and native rites as racial harmony ("National Brotherhood Week"), the Boy Scouts ("Be Prepared"), the Old South ("I Wanna Go Back to Dixie"), old age ("When You Are Old and Gray"), and true love ("I Hold Your Hand in Mine"). Or as he put it, "something for every depraved taste." But Lehrer had his soft spots, such as smut ("Smut"), dope ("The Old Dope Peddler"), and offing pigeons ("Poisoning Pigeons in the Park"). He took deadly aim at sitting ducks like nuclear testing ("The Wild West Is Where I Want to Be," "So Long, Mom, I'm Off to Drop the Bomb") and the missile program ("M.L.F. Lullaby," "Wernher von Braun"), for which he had a special antipathy after a summer spent working at Los Alamos and entertaining physicists with his joyfully macabre songs.

As he would later prove by walking away from it all at the height of his success, Lehrer was not a professional entertainer—although his work displays great finesse and style, not only his melodies and impeccable rhymes but also his own sly performances of them. He made it look very easy, maybe because he wasn't trying all that hard. He sold his songs by not overselling them. Much of his performing charm lies in his ostensibly amateur manner. But he was in fact an adroit entertainer, warbling his creations in a tart, untrained twang, rich in wicked innuendo, insidious inflections, and insinuating pauses.

His nightclub act, which he did for seven years before giving it up in 1960 (reprising it only in later special reappearances), was more than just funny songs. Each piece featured a droll introduction that displayed his comic narrative skill in mini-monologues as sardonic as his lyrics. He set up each song with an intro so witty that you relished the song before he even got around to singing it. Likewise, his liner notes were models of droll self-deprecation.

Lehrer likes to claim that he was merely "demonstrating the songs," like some 1910 song-plugger in Schirmer's window, but in anyone else's mouth his "demonstrations" would not have been half as amusing. He was just a terrific, polished performer, able to sing in a variety of accents, but his innate showmanship was overshadowed by the lyrics. Peering, indeed leering, through dark horn-rimmed spectacles, he looked and sounded very much like what he was, a smart-ass math major goofing off. Introducing himself in the third person, he'd note: "You'd be *amazed* how much money we save that way."

> *I wanna go back to Dixie,*
> *Take me back to dear ol' Dixie,*
> *That's the only li'l ol' place for li'l ol' me.*
> *Ol' times there are not forgotten,*
> *Whuppin' slaves and sellin' cotton,*
> *And waitin' for the* Robert E. Lee
> *(It was never there on time).*
> —from "I Wanna Go Back to Dixie"

Lehrer's initial album became a popular "party record." His songs were among the first satirical shots across the bow of complacent 1950s America, predated only by Sid Caesar and Stan Freberg a couple of years earlier, though neither Caesar's nor Freberg's satire sliced quite as sharply. Lehrer was out not just for laughs but for blood. Like many new satirical voices of the early fifties—*MAD,* Mort Sahl, Second City—Lehrer became a cult favorite and a collegiate fad. As the writer Leah Garchik observed in a 1982 interview with Lehrer, "It was just the stuff that appealed to the soon-to-be-hatched new lefties, the folks who were turned off by institutions but bored with Alfred E. Neuman. Ten years later, some of them would be burning their draft cards; few would buy into Xerox early."

His stuff was considered too in (as in intellectual), too elitist, and too subversive to interest Americans at large. Radio stations wouldn't touch him. Record companies wouldn't sign him, forcing him to produce his own album. Performing for him, however, was just a detour, a quick way to earn a few bucks to support his grad-study habit. But the popularity of Lehrer's songs got away from him and before he knew it he was shipping albums across the country, being courted by club owners, and, during Christmas week of 1953 (the same week that Mort Sahl was breaking in at the hungry i in San Francisco), opening at the Blue Angel in New York. Never was a man less prepared for sudden success, or more leery of it. As he told the *New York Times,* "I'm completely happy at my research job. I'd almost hate to be a success in comedy." A *New York Times* interview is not the ideal road to anonymity. Against his better judgment, Tom Lehrer was a star.

THOMAS ANDREW LEHRER GREW UP in Manhattan, the son of a successful Jewish necktie manufacturer—"a legend in the industry," in his son's tongue-in-cheek words. Because of the jabs in "The Vatican Rag," people assumed he was Catholic, but Lehrer's ecumenical religious background included Sunday school and Christmas trees, making him, he said, "Jewish by ancestry—more to do with the delicatessen than the synagogue."

Like most Jewish kids then, he obediently took piano lessons, which he abandoned as soon as possible in favor of popular music, pleased "not to have to play music by dead people." Also, he recalls, he "couldn't read the left hand very well, which automatically lets out Bach, Beethoven . . ." Thus his own early works were parodies of show tunes and Tin Pan Alley classics, particularly 1940s novelty songs like "Mairzy Doats." The first tune he learned on his own was "Alexander's Ragtime Band." Lehrer's humor was influenced by the radio comedians he grew up listening to in the thirties and forties—Stoopnagle & Budd, Vic & Sade (whose tapes he collects), and Bob & Ray, radio's foremost send-up artists of the time.

His parents, who divorced when he was fourteen, took young Tom to musicals, to which he remains passionately devoted. "I was exposed in the thirties and forties to the best songs of the time, when grown-ups listened to the same songs as kids." He was crazy about Gilbert & Sullivan and Danny Kaye's triple-tongue patter songs, like "Anatole of Paris" and "Tchaikovsky," Kaye's showstopper from *Lady in the Dark*. He recalls, "I saw *Let's Face It* [songs by Cole Porter and Kaye's wife, Sylvia Fine] eight or nine times because Kaye was in it. Whenever my parents would say, 'What do you want to see?' I'd say, '*Let's Face It.*' I learned his songs and then picked them out on the piano, because they weren't published." He loved the lyrics' intricate rhymes.

"The special material, most of it written by Sylvia Fine, really inspired me tremendously to try to do things like that—later." When Robert Ripley printed the words to Ira Gershwin's and Kurt Weill's "Tchaikovsky" in *Believe It or Not,* stating that Kaye could rattle off the names of fifty Russian composers in thirty-nine seconds, Lehrer says: "I took that as a challenge. I never knew there was a tune to it. I just learned to recite it—[he reels off a few lines]. I did it at parties, and it went over so well that I decided, Gee, I ought to do a list song, too. So I went through the states of the union and the UN countries and a few other lists, but there weren't enough rhymes, so I ended up with the chemical elements, which I then managed to squeeze in as many as I could up to then."

He set his "Elements" to the tune of "Tchaikovsky," explaining, "I tried to write my own tune, but I finally said, why bother when the tune is already there?" That, in turn, inspired his song in praise of plagiarism, "Lobachevsky," about a nineteenth-century Russian mathematician accused of stealing all of his theories, stuffed to bursting with rapidly rhymed Russian names. It was inspired by "Stanislavsky," which Fine also wrote for Kaye."

Lehrer was equally captivated by Abe Burrows's comedy songs, ditties like "The Girl with the Three Blue Eyes." "I knew them very well—'I Gave My Love Golden Earrings and Now Her Ears Are Turning Green,' and 'If You Were the Only Girl in the World and I Was the Only Boy, OK, But Right Now Leave Me Alone.' I started writing little parodies in high school, silly songs, never thinking it would lead to anything you could call a career." His other songwriting idols included E. Y. Harburg and Sheldon Harnick, author of the revue classic "The Boston Beguine." "When I first heard 'Boston Beguine,' in *New Faces of 1952*, I thought, Hey, wait a minute. You can actually get up on a Broadway stage and sing a song like that." All the songs he went on to write were revue tunes minus the revue—until three decades later, when the producer Cameron Mackintosh astutely strung them together in *Tomfoolery*, an anthology of Lehrer's major works.

Lehrer liked to include other people's songs in his act. "One of the problems I had doing songs by other people," he once said, "is that even though I always gave the writers credit, some people would still assume that I had written them." He even parodied Patti Page's "I Went to Your Wedding," changed to "I Went to Your Funeral," which rhymed "funeral" and "sooner'll," later repeated in "We Will All Go Together When We Go":

> We will all fry together when we fry.
> We'll be French-fried potatoes by and by.
> There will be no more misery
> When the world is our rotisserie,
> Yes, we will all fry together when we fry.

Lehrer, who has called himself "a semiprodigy," went to private schools—New York's Horace Mann and Loomis, a Connecticut prep school—and then sped through Harvard in three years, entering at fifteen in 1943 and graduating at eighteen with a math degree. For his admissions essay, he wrote a lengthy verse that wound up: "*I will leave movie thrillers / And watch caterpillars / Get born and pupated and larva'd / And I'll work like a slave / And always behave / And maybe I'll get into Harva'd.*" He went on to get a master's degree, began teaching at eighteen, and then spent the next sixteen years, off and on, studying for a doctorate that purposely eluded him. "I wanted to be a graduate student forever. They want you to be a Ph.D. Unfortunately you can't be a graduate student *and* a Ph.D. at the same time, but I exhausted all the courses."

Lehrer loved campus life (and still does), which he left on a sort of seven-year well-paid show-business sabbatical to perform his songs, happily returning to academia when he'd had enough of full-time entertaining. His colleagues welcomed him back as if nothing had happened. "This was the Math Department—what did they know from show business?" It was, he insists, a decision he's never regretted, despite the clamor of people who have tried to pry him free to write and perform new songs.

He taught calculus, geometry, and statistics, but never regarded himself as a true mathematician. For kicks, he composed songs. "We had plenty of free time then, and in grad school I had even more free time, and I started doing things for parties, never suspecting there'd be any interest beyond the groves of academe." Lehrer, though precocious, was not ambitious, the main reason he majored in math: "It had the fewest requirements. I was going to major in English or chemistry, but when I looked at the list of requirements, I said, 'Forget it.'" He has always taken the path of least resistance. "English would have required reading far too many books," and he recoiled from chemistry ("all those smells and labs to contend with"). Math was a tidier discipline for a fastidious layabout—no homework, papers, or labs. "It was perfect for a lazy student."

Lehrer taught math at Harvard, MIT, and Wellesley (at one point, simultaneously) after serving in the army for two years, before which he worked for defense contractors and spent a year at the Atomic Energy Commission's Los Alamos nuclear test lab as a mathematician and cryptographer.

His campus tunes, a critic wrote in 1959, "were the kind of songs that every sophisticated college boy figures he might have written, but didn't." His first performance, in 1950, was as part of a quartet that sang at a Harvard Law School function; he then performed at the freshman smoker for four years. At the old Howard Theatre in Boston, Lehrer shared the bill with the stripper Sally Rand and sang "The Elements."

The only other Lehrer composition that survived his undergraduate days is "Fight Fiercely, Harvard," the prissy football fight song still played at games by the intrepid Harvard marching band (the band also sings it); a few years ago, the band played "The Vatican Rag" at a Notre Dame game, ruffling feathers all over again. "I wrote 'Fight Fiercely, Harvard' in 1945! Just for the amusement of my friends, never thinking that it would still be selling fifty years later."

> *How we shall celebrate our victory,*
> *We shall invite the whole team up for tea!*
> *(How jolly!)*
> *Hurl that spheroid down the field,*
> *And fight, fight, fight!*

Bob Osserman, special projects director at the Mathematical Sciences Research Institute in Berkeley and a classmate of Lehrer's at Harvard, recalls: "Every year one of the math profs gave a party for all the graduate students and he would entertain, and they were recorded. It was a kind of counterculture humor. I recognized he had this talent and yet there was something sophomoric about it."

Lehrer was a star in the math and physics departments, where his answer to a calculus exam question once took the form of a poem. He also wrote and staged a musical at Harvard on a physics theme; it had a skimpy plot and featured parodies of show tunes like "A Bushel and a Peck," substituting physics terms. Osserman remembers a campus evening when the author of a book on something called Gödel's Theorem was lecturing, to be followed on the program by Lehrer. The lecture drew a crowd of hundreds, but the speaker was annoyed to learn that he was a mere warm-up act for Lehrer. At a Harvard dining hall, says Osserman, there was a math-graduate-student table and a Tom Lehrer table.

Lehrer was something of a campus character, famous for introducing a mixture of vodka and orange Jell-O, later dubbed the "Jell-O shot," which he had perfected in the service as a way to smuggle booze into the barracks. Osserman, still close to Lehrer, says, "He hasn't changed all that much," and his most vivid recollection is: "Tom had this unbelievable photographic memory. In this course we were in together, he never seemed to do any work," and the night before an exam he would speed-read through his notes and ace the test.

Lehrer made his professional debut on a Boston talk show hosted by the "Li'l Abner" cartoonist, Al Capp, who later wrote in a collection of Lehrer-ics, "He is a disillusioned figure, and let us all be grateful for that." For Capp's show, Lehrer would write a topical song and the panel would try to guess the news item that inspired it. One of Lehrer's songs opened, *"This is a story, not a mere allegory, / Of a man and the glory that was his. / This is a story you may find kind of gory, / I admit* a priori *that it is."* The show's producer was shocked, telling him, "You can't say '*a priori*' on television!"

His first actual paid solo gig was in the fall of 1952 at Alpini's Rendezvous in Boston, where he entertained weekends and played intermission piano for fifteen dollars ("They thought I could bring in the college crowd"); he also played at Storyville, a famous Boston club. A year later, he arrived at the Blue Angel in New York, opening for another New England wit, Orson Bean. A *New Yorker* critic failed to mention Lehrer in his review—"out of compassion," claims Lehrer.

He recounts how he got himself recorded: "I had these songs and I thought they might sell a few hundred and it would be nice to have a record. When I made that first record, it was just to sell around Harvard. I worked it all out and I figured if I sold four hundred copies I could break even. Then it began to balloon." He went from earning $3,000 a year at Harvard to half that each week in clubs.

Lehrer produced the LP himself for $700. "I looked up two studios in the Yellow Pages and one was nice and one wasn't, so I went with the one that was nice and for fifteen dollars I got an hour's studio time, editing and everything. No mixing—only one microphone. If I did a take again I just recorded it over the previous song. I had the full twenty-two-minute final edited tape at the end of an hour." He made the recordings on January 22, 1953. It cost him another $700 to have the ten-inch record pressed, and he distributed the albums himself. As he put it, "Every expense was spared." *Songs by Tom Lehrer* came in a jacket designed by Lehrer—the now familiar tacky red cover, edged in hellish flames, with a drawing of a satanic Lehrer at the piano, with horns and a spiked devil's tail uncoiling from under his tuxedo, a pitchfork at his feet. Lehrer's liner notes set the wry tone for what lies within: *"This recording of the imitable songs of Tom Lehrer has been issued in spite of widespread popular demand for its suppression. . . ."*

Indeed, RCA thought the songs too sophisticated and controversial, and Capitol Records responded: "I am sorry to inform you that there is no interest in your 'Album of Songs.' " Lehrer never had an agent until his third album, *That Was the Year That Was,* which, thirty-one years later, in 1996, won a gold record; he might have won one for his first album but wasn't a member of the recording institute that awarded them.

In May 2000 Rhino Records issued a triple-CD box set titled *The Remains of Tom Lehrer,* which includes a few previously unrecorded songs, such as "That's Mathematics." The Rhino box also features four charming numbers from the children's TV show *The Electric Company,* plus the droll "Hanukkah in Santa Monica" (*"I'm spending Hanukkah in Santa Monica / Amid the California flora, I'll be lighting my menorah. / Here's to Judas Maccabeus, / Boy, if only he could see us"*). He semicheerfully promoted the box set despite his usual protestations against returning to the spotlight, for Lehrer wants his songs kept alive simply so that he doesn't have to sing them anymore or even discuss them. "My attitude always was, if you wanna buy it, buy it."

Songs by Tom Lehrer LP arrived long before disc jockeys played funny records on the air. No commercial stations were willing to broadcast such antisocial songs. "I never expected they would be played on radio, but every so often, as an April Fool's joke, some station might play something." His albums sold much better in England and beyond, and he toured Canada, Scandinavia, Australia, and New Zealand. "I was respectable over there, but I was rarely played here on the radio, except by some local FM stations." Mike Nichols, who, pre–Nichols & May, worked as a deejay, played Lehrer's album on a classical station in Chicago.

> *I remember Dan, the druggist on the corner, 'e*
> *Was never mean or ornery,*
> *He was swell.*
> *He killed his mother-in-law and ground her up real well,*
> *And sprinkled just a bit*
> *Over each banana split.*
>
> —from "My Home Town"

"The audience for these records was definitely a cult audience," Lehrer says. "Part of the appeal of it was, '*We* get this, *we* understand this, but the public wouldn't get it,' as if they were not the public. All you needed was a thousand smart people in each major city to make a market. Every university town had that cult. I was very much surprised the records were that popular in England until I realized they have a long university tradition of satirical revues. Peter Cook and Dudley Moore were doing their shows. The BBC played the entire record and did an interview with me, and that spread the word like crazy. In England, standards are presumably lower."

The *New Statesman* said Lehrer was "on his way to becoming a Noël Coward of the 1950s. . . . In his inimitable and ghastly way . . . he has a kind of genius." Not everyone was as amused. The *London Evening Standard* called him "obvious, jejune and remarkably unsophisticated." The *New York Times* wrote, "Mr. Lehrer's muse is not fettered by such inhibiting factors as taste." The *New York Herald Tribune* added, "More desperate than amusing," and the *Christian Science Monitor* sniped, "He seldom has any point to make except obvious ones." One critic raved that Lehrer was "one of the most hilariously caustic iconoclasts to come along since H. L. Mencken and W. C. Fields." A *Saturday Review* critic, however, stifled a yawn: "Of the dozen or so songs, Lehrer's marksmanship is dead center in no more, say, than half."

Lehrer blurbed all of the nastiest reviews on his next album, in 1959, *An Evening Wasted with Tom Lehrer,* and now proudly quotes a new pan from Amazon.com ("He has a grating nasal voice"), laughing, "I wish I'd have known that then—I would've added it." He never became a mainstream fad, which kept him even more in demand on the fringes. "When I was at the Blue Angel," he recently recalled, "the people from *The Ed Sullivan Show* came in and they said, 'Oh, we really love your show. If you ever have anything we can use, let us know.' I think that summed it up."

The word of mouth for Lehrer's songs in America was spread principally via college students who took his album home during semester breaks and played it for friends, reveling in the songs' wicked sentiments but also in their irresistible Ogden Nashian wordplay ("philately / Chatterley," "Tripoli / Mississipoli," "Gustave / must have"), not to mention those sly introductions—"*If a person can't communicate, the least he can do is to shut up!*" and the oft-anthologized, "*It is a sobering thought to realize that, when Mozart was my age, he had been dead for two years.*"

That first album ended up selling 350,000 copies. Nearly half a century later, the syndicated Los Angeles disc jockey Barry Hansen ("Dr. Demento") reports that, apart from Weird Al Yankovic (the rock generation's Tom Lehrer), Lehrer's songs are the most requested by listeners. To date, all of his records have sold a little more than two million copies in fifty years, but sales remain steady. While most topical satire eventually dies, only a few of Lehrer's songs have grown stale. Equally impressive, the songs have been translated into about ten languages, despite their tricky rhymes, puns, and Americanisms. The comedian Greg Proops recalls that Lehrer's album was off-limits in his home and that he had to have a note from his father to play it at a friend's house. Proops, listening to it again for his BBC documentary on American comedy, was impressed by the wit just in the introductions, as in, "*My friend majored in animal husbandry—until they caught him at it.*" Proops says, amazed, "He would throw these lines away, which would be, like, my closer!"

If you were a student yourself in the fifties and sixties, you'll recall the little thrill that came with listening to such subversive titles as "The Old Dope Peddler," "The Masochism Tango," and "Be Prepared," with risqué lines like, "*Don't solicit for your sister, that's not nice, / Unless you get a good percentage of her price.*" In "The Irish Ballad," Lehrer delivered such deliciously Swiftian sentiments as, "*One day when she had nothing to do, / She cut her baby brother in two, / And served him up as an Irish stew.*"

At the time, this was considered pretty wicked stuff, made doubly amusing by Lehrer's agile, surprising rhymes, which one critic said combined "the rhetorical articulation of Vladimir Nabokov, the rhyming virtuosity of W. S. Gilbert, and the perceptive wit of Mort Sahl at his best," adding that Lehrer's "weak spot is in the music. The tunes are not tunes so much as collegiate varsity show vamp-till-ready accompaniments for the verbal tours-de-force." Maybe so, but the tunes were invariably catchy and just right for the composer's higher satirical purposes.

TOM LEHRER HAD STUMBLED upon fame and into the hearts of his countrymen so unassumingly that it was inexplicable to his fans when he decided to walk away from it all as easily as he had backed into it. His almost callous decision to dump his showbiz career has added immeasurably to the Lehrer legend. America loves its celebrity hermits—not just for their un-American audacity of retiring at the height of their success but for the sheer perversity of not giving a damn. It's hard to think of many stars who gave it all up at the height of their success to return to their former humble life. "There's me, Garbo, Salinger, and Deanna Durbin," he jokes.

Lehrer never set out to become a songwriter, which cuts no ice with

Lehrer fanatics who feel shortchanged, even betrayed, believing it was unfair of him to whet their appetite with such brilliant songs only to vanish—as if Cole Porter had hung it up after a couple of hit shows. Lehrer was always openly uneasy about performing, telling *Newsweek* in 1957, "I wouldn't want to do this all my life. It's okay while I'm still an adolescent." He later added, "Occasionally people ask, 'If you enjoyed it'—and I did—'why don't you do it again?' I reply, 'I enjoyed high school, but I certainly wouldn't want to do *that* again.' " He was thirty-two when he opted for early showbiz retirement. Like a lot of musical prodigies, maybe it all just came too easily to him and he didn't value his gift as highly as others did, leaving it all behind after a final performance in Glasgow on July 2, 1960, afraid of turning into a has-been—

> *An awful debility,*
> *A lessened utility,*
> *A loss of mobility*
> *Is a strong possibility.*
> *In all probability*
> *I'll lose my virility*
> *And you your fertility*
> *And desirability,*
> *And this liability*
> *Of total sterility*
> *Will lead to hostility*
> *And a sense of futility . . .*
> —from "When You Are Old and Gray"

An ambivalence about writing and performing runs like a theme through Lehrer's life. He enjoyed singing his songs until he didn't anymore, although he's always liked the writing part—*when* he had an idea. But he squirmed at the thought of coming up with funny songs on demand. He had no need to please the public, or even himself. He saw performing as an annuity: "The main reason I always played was to put some money aside so I could do what I liked—teach and continue writing and lie down a lot and just enjoy myself. I happen to enjoy a low standard of life."

He had, like Noël Coward, a true talent to amuse, but after a few years it no longer amused *him*. Lehrer can write brilliantly but would prefer not to, making him a rare show-business Bartleby. He's at peace with himself, but for his fans it's been infuriating. Perhaps Cameron Mackintosh should have drafted him to write a contemporary show and locked him in a room until he finished new songs. There ought to be a law against someone like Lehrer not using his extraordinary talent to delight us. Who needs more math teachers?

> While married to Gus she met Gropius,
> And soon she was swinging with Walter.
> Gus died, and her teardrops were copious.
> She cried all the way to the altar.
> But he would work late at the Bauhaus
> And only came home now and then.
> She said, "What am I running, a chow house?"
> It's time to change partners again.
>> —from "Alma"

Tom Lehrer sits in his serene seaside apartment in Santa Cruz overlooking the Pacific Ocean. He is still lean, wiry, fit, and bespectacled, a congenial man who looks a good decade younger than his seventy-four years (or as he chooses to think of it, twenty-three Celsius), despite a hearing aid and a slight stoop. Not composing has agreed with him, if with nobody else. As he speaks in bursts, his leg pumps impatiently, surprisingly restless for a man semiretired for forty years. Until 2001 he taught one class in the spring semester at the University of California at Santa Cruz in what he called infinity (math riddles such as: Does .333 truly extend "forever"? Will parallel lines ever meet, and if so, where?), which he calls "philosophy in disguise." He used musical references in his math courses, comparing the mathematical concept of a "fuzzy set" to a line in the song "A Puzzlement" from *The King and I*—"*some things nearly so, others nearly not.*" He told an AP reporter, "It's a real math class. I don't do any funny theorems. So people go away pretty quickly."

He and Bob Osserman discuss math-music links but never why Lehrer gave up entertaining. "He keeps a busy life, but I have no idea what it is," says Osserman. "We talk a lot and e-mail each other about anything mathematical in theater or movies"—such as the plays *Proof, Copenhagen,* and Tom Stoppard's *Arcadia,* the film *A Beautiful Mind,* and the musical *Fermat's Last Tango.*

Lehrer has led a bicoastal life as placid, regular, and unchanging as the surf lapping outside his big window. From 1975 to 1996, he also taught a course in the history of musical theater at UC's woodsy Santa Cruz campus. In 1972 he began dividing his time between there and Cambridge, where he no longer teaches but still lives half the year. He decided on Santa Cruz because it seemed an ideal hiding place. He gave up teaching math in 2001 and resumed coteaching a course in musical-theater history. "We do readings of musicals. I cut 'em down to an hour, no choreography. They just stand up, scripts in hand, and I work with 'em a little."

Given his avowed avoidance of the public eye, Lehrer might fit the profile of a recluse if it weren't for the fact that he is a congenial, accessible man still full of ideas, if not songs. Part of his time is spent adding to a large collection of sheet music and musical-comedy albums and searching out offbeat productions, such as Stephen Sondheim's *Merrily We Roll Along* at a nearby community college ("I'll go *anywhere* to see an unmiked show"). To entertain himself, he noodles at a high-tech upright piano with a built-in computer disc drive, and for years he worked out by tap dancing, until his knee gave out.

Lehrer remains a cheery legend (or, as the *New York Times* dubbed him a few years back, "The Cynic Who Never Soured"), a lifelong bachelor with a strong sense of himself—upbeat but opinionated, self-effacing, and, to be sure, witty. He's a man who seems to have led precisely the life he wanted; a gentler, less autocratic Henry Higgins comes to mind. "He's a very private man," says John Dizikes, a colleague at UC–Santa Cruz. "He's completely his own person. He will meet you halfway, but from then on he will do as he wishes. He's a truly autonomous person." The brief but dazzling career that made him famous lasted barely seven years, during which time he recorded three dozen songs of devastating ingenuity and coruscating wit in four albums before retreating. As he once said, "What good are laurels if you can't rest on them?"

A landmark event for Lehrer devotees came in 1998 when he was briefly pried out of retirement to sing two of his songs to celebrate the televised fiftieth birthday of Cameron Mackintosh, whose London production of *Tomfoolery* was a hit there and in several U.S. cities. ("It spread like herpes," said the astonished author.) His eyes light up as he revels in one moment from Mackintosh's party: "Stephen Sondheim [his idol] introduced *me!*" he cries, pumping a fist in the air. "Now I can take poison and die happily." His other favorite celebrity moment was when he and

Jackie Kennedy were introduced to a woman at a party given by John Kenneth Galbraith and the woman, ignoring the former first lady, cried, "Tom Lehrer!"

As a kid, Lehrer actually attended summer camp with Sondheim in 1939, but they didn't communicate again until meeting at the Mackintosh celebration. "I'm a tremendous fan of Sondheim's songs. He's the greatest lyricist that ever was, and I love his music, too. But the shows are about people I really didn't want to spend that much time with." Sondheim surpasses even the revered W. S. Gilbert, he says, quoting a verse from *Pacific Overtures:* " '*Hello, I come with letters from / Her Majesty Victoria, / Who, learning how you're trading now, sang "Hallelujah gloria!" / And sent me to convey to you her positive euphoria / As well as little gifts from Britain's various emporia.*' "

On the morning of our interview, Lehrer announced merrily, and perfectly in character, "Today is Hitler's birthday, by the way." It was the first of two conversations I had with him at his modest, weathered, gray-shingled condo. On the road outside, people in wet suits lugged surfboards. It's an unlikely place to find an urbane songwriting legend who lives simply and drives a leased Corolla; in Cambridge he hides out in a small house near Harvard Square. Says Osserman, "He lives these two-coast lives and both of them are lovely lives in their own way. It's quite impressive."

In jeans and a pink shirt rolled up partway, Lehrer still looks the career collegiate. Along the wall behind his sofa are hung framed, slightly faded musical-comedy posters and sheet music from Rodgers & Hammerstein shows. There is no hint of his former showbiz career, but then he never considered himself part of show business, just a tourist passing through. "People think I must be dead or committed suicide or am in an asylum," he says with his tentative smile. Indeed, Lehrer starts rumors that he's dead and tries to keep them alive; he even has a file of clippings that refer to him as "the late Tom Lehrer." After *Tomfoolery* temporarily disinterred him, he said, "I'd been dead for many years. Once this blows over, I'll be dead again."

People who meet him at parties, banks, and restaurants usually say one of two things: "There used to be a songwriter with that name" or "Are you any relation to Jim Lehrer?" He doesn't even trust posterity. "There are five quotes by me in *The Penguin Book of Modern Quotations* and four are wrong," he remarks. He also has three quotations in *Bartlett's,* but not his most famous line, which he first uttered when asked why he stopped writing: "*Political satire became obsolete when Henry Kissinger was awarded the Nobel Peace Prize.*" The line is often misquoted as "when Henry Kissinger *won* the Nobel Peace Prize," which bothers a man with Lehrer's keen ear for language. "Won," he explains, is not as funny as "was awarded."

Tracking him down is alarmingly easy; he's listed in the local telephone directory. "People don't call much anymore," he says. "I was always amazed when people said I was hard to find. I said, 'Did you look in the phone book?' " When someone unearths him and asks him to perform, he cracks, "My standard answer is, 'Oh, did hell freeze over?' " There are many reasons he remains in hibernation: "I'd just be doing an impression of myself. It's like looking at baby pictures and saying, 'Oh, isn't he cute!' I don't want to become like people who have lost it, like Carol Channing. I was so relieved I wasn't in that movie [a 1981 documentary reunion of old hungry i entertainers]. Mort Sahl was doing Adlai Stevenson jokes and the Kingston Trio were middle-aged."

Lehrer refers to the perennial clamor for him to return to performing as "The Lenin's Tomb Phenomenon"—a morbid desire to see the remains of anything once famous. "It's like people who say they saw Richard Burton or Stephen Hawking, just to say they were there." He says, "I never regarded writing songs as a career. Thirty-seven songs in twenty years is hardly what I would call a career. I never sat down like a songwriter would do and say, 'Today I am going to write a funny song.' If I got an idea for a song I'd write it, and if I didn't I wouldn't. But it wouldn't bother me. As the years went on, the latter condition prevailed over the former. I wouldn't consider it writer's block or anything like that. If I thought of a funny idea I wouldn't restrain myself from writing it. But even if I wrote more songs, I wouldn't perform them."

Lehrer further explains, "Working nightclubs is not my idea of a good time. For one thing, I'm not a night person. Just when you were looking forward to a nice dinner, that's when you had to go to work. I didn't like that at all. Also, I did not have the temperament of the performer, like Jerry Lewis, where you have to be out there doing something. I'm quite happy to get the royalty checks as a form of adulation instead of people hitting their hands together."

He goes on: "I never set out to be a funny songwriter. I tried that. It didn't work. I just stopped getting funny ideas." But people still came to him with ideas. "Everything has always come to *me*," he points out. Bill Graham wanted him to write protest songs. "I couldn't write a song about Martin Luther King, Jr., or feminists. I can't write songs that have an on-the-other-hand." At one point, however, he was open to offers and even wrote a Hire's root beer jingle that never ran; Columbia Records' Goddard Lieberson asked him to write new songs for Groucho Marx, but he couldn't come up with anything. He wrote songs, oddly, for a Dodge industrial film, and, even more oddly, something about the Strategic Air Command for the movie *A Gathering of Eagles.*

He may have begun to fear "Selling Out," to quote the title of his little-known 1973 song that goes, in part: *"Being rich is no disgrace. / Put on your shoes and join the race. / It has a very soothing voice. / It's up to you to make the choice. / Before you know it, there'll be nothing left to sell."* Moreover, he says, "I'd have to practice. People think, 'Oh, you wrote it, so you just sit down and do it.'" He finally made the decision to retire after a performance at New York's Town Hall when he mixed up two versions of "Fight Fiercely, Harvard." "I blew it twice. I was thinking, 'Did I turn off the oven?' and 'Where would I eat dinner?' My brain was telling me something." He laughs and intones dramatically: *"The maestro laid down his pen."*

Joan Ruderman, who had a brief romance with Lehrer when he was on tour in Chicago in 1955, recalls: "He said then that he wasn't cut out to be a performer, but that he got caught up in all that. It was thrust upon him. He was kind of shy. He was not full of himself at all."

He still sings at parties. Osserman, who coaxed Lehrer into performing for the Math Institute director's eightieth birthday in 1995, muses on Lehrer's retirement: "I think he may have lost the sense of command of the material. He got less sure of himself as a performer. When he performed for us five years ago, he brought the music along, which kind of surprised me. He used to know these things inside and out."

FOR LEHRER, performing simply stopped being fun anymore, a factor seldom acknowledged by performers who keep performing more out of habit or need than fun. Many comedians are all technique and shtick, the joy of it having dried up years ago. James Cagney said he left acting for farming when the kick went out of it, and Garbo presumably got out because it wasn't fun being Garbo anymore.

Lehrer the professional performer was just a much-better-paid version of the singing professor at Harvard parties; he didn't stick around long enough to become slick, cute, or safe. One columnist called Lehrer "lazy," but for him it was more a matter of ennui than inertia. "I was pretty good at it," he once confessed in an uncharacteristic spasm of pride, but to Lehrer the playful writing was the thing.

> *Stories of tortures*
> *Used by debauchers,*
> *Lurid, licentious, and vile*
> *Make me smile.*
> —— from "Smut"

"There were also outside factors," he elaborates. "The times changed. Humor began getting crazy. It was harder to be funny and pointed. You can't be bitter and funny at the same time." He cites Lenny Bruce and Mort Sahl as examples of comics whose bitterness overwhelmed them. "Bruce was funny when he wasn't bitter, and the same with Sahl before the [Eisenhower] administration changed. His Warren Commission shows weren't funny. We didn't come to hear about Clay Shaw and Jim Garrison."

Another major factor in his retirement was his dislike of nightclubs. "My timing was very bad. Concert tours hadn't happened yet." As he told Jeremy Bernstein in *The American Scholar:* "If you said that you were going to do a concert, people assumed that you were going to play the piano or something. The only humorous concerts were given by Anna Russell or Victor Borge." He did his first concert in 1957 at Hunter College in New York—"the same act, only wearing a tuxedo," as he put it; his final professional concert, partly to promote *An Evening Wasted with Tom Lehrer,* was in Copenhagen on September 12, 1967.

Even while performing full-time, he says, "I was very picky. The money was nice but I didn't want to be in Chicago for four weeks at Mister Kelly's. Who wants to spend four weeks in Chicago? People went to shows and talked over the performances. I had no rehearsals. They would just turn a spotlight on me when I came on and turn it off when I'd leave." He played all the major clubs—the Blue Angel, the hungry i, the Interlude, Ciro's—but it now all seems a little remote to Lehrer. "I was on Johnny Carson twice and it was no big deal. Now it's the comics' big moment. Talent is not enough. You need the desire or the temperament. I realized this many times. One manager asked me to cut ten minutes. Other acts screamed, 'I can't cut ten minutes!' It never bothered me. I'd say, 'Sure, cut ten minutes. Cut the whole act. I'll go home.' "

Lehrer pauses. "Look, I don't mean to make it all sound like some kind of torture. I enjoyed meeting new people and traveling. It just wasn't something I imagined myself doing at age forty. A real performer doesn't think that way. I've never understood somebody like Yul Brynner doing *The King and I* or Rex Harrison doing *My Fair Lady* night after night after night and getting something out of it. I added it up recently and I did about a hundred and nine concerts in my career. So I could get the energy up to do that. It was only an hour and a half—fairly painless. I could turn it on and turn it off. I could simulate delight."

The comedy biographer Ronald L. Smith notes, "There are certain barriers to Tom Lehrer that you must respect because he's not a *tummeling* comedian. Even his liner notes have that dry understated professorial manner." Says Lehrer: "I wasn't trying to be Mr. Comedian. In fact, I don't allow them to use the word *comedian. Humorist* is okay. *Satirist* is too strong. I don't consider my songs to be social satire—they just sound like it." He adds, "The difference between me and a comedian is that comics want people to go home and think, 'Wasn't *he* funny.' I wanted people to go home and think, 'Weren't those *songs* funny.' I'd do them until I got the timing right and then I'd make the record and that would be it. They'd go home and play the record. So it didn't make any more sense to me to get out there and do it every night than if I were a novelist and went out there and read my novel every night."

He told the BBC that, before recording songs live for his 1965 *That Was the Year That Was* album, "Many people said to me, 'Oh, you're gonna love it once you get out there again and the audience is applauding and shouting and cheering. You're gonna be hooked again.' I realized after two weeks, no, I wasn't going to be hooked again. I'm really not ready for two weeks at Freddy's in Minneapolis. As I've often said, if you've been to Cincinnati there's no need to go to Cleveland." He adds, "I don't have that need for anonymous affection that performers have. They want people they're never going to meet applauding, and then if the audience does *not* applaud and laugh they get very angry, as if they're entitled to it. So after a while I just wanted to play for a friendly audience."

Lehrer found that doing nothing suited him perfectly: "I putter and I fritter. I dawdle and I shilly-shally. I've even taken up a little loitering." Why does he still teach at all? "I gotta have something to do," he told an interviewer. His albums still bring in a modest amount. "You can just say he makes a comfortable living. Comfortable for a graduate student." Killing time has become a way of life for him: "Didn't you ever have a week or two off when you didn't have to do anything? You don't have to lie down and read Proust and eat bonbons. There's always something to do. I walk around, I talk to people. The time goes by very, very fast." He readily admits, "I don't read books. I'm so delighted to read interviews with Sondheim where he says the same thing. I only read books about popular math and about musicals and theater in particular." In 1986 he told a book critic that the last novel he had read was *Huckleberry Finn*— "but just to see how it compared to the musical version."

People, he adds, tended to confuse the Tom Lehrer who sang the mordant songs with the man himself, and it rankled him a little. "Those songs were written for a different person, just a persona I did. I could do this kind of limited, wry, a-little-bit-aloof person that was singing these songs within my range and capabilities. I was a little more genial, I like to think, than the person who was singing those songs."

The mild-mannered Lehrer had one confrontation with a Catholic clubgoer who objected to "The Vatican Rag." Michael Stepanian, the bouncer at the hungry i, recalls an altercation: "Tom Lehrer was singing 'The Vatican Rag,' and out comes Ricardo Montalban and he was screaming out of his fuckin' mind. He was so offended by 'The Vatican Rag.' He was yelling at Tom Lehrer. I was between them. Montalban's temples are pumping and Lehrer was like this Harvard intellectual with a little black tie. He looked like Mr. Peepers. I said to myself, 'This guy is gonna punch this guy.' Montalban says, 'I love my religion! I will die for my religion!' And Lehrer said, 'Hey, no problem, as long as you don't fight for your religion.' I cooled him down."

By 1982 age had further tamed the already laid-back Lehrer. "I'm more mature—or is it senile?" he mused. "People do their best satirical work when they're young. I'm not interested in saying only the nasty. My mind doesn't run that way anymore. I don't know if the times are changing or I am. On a lot of issues, I don't know where I stand. Sit? Lie? Life used to be much simpler." Years ago he said: "I'm certainly pro-choice. But I couldn't write a funny pro-choice song. I could only write a song about the pro-life people, but . . . I can perfectly understand their position." (Why not a song about the inability to choose?) Decades ago he remarked, "Today, everything just makes me angry, it's not funny anymore," to which he now adds, "Things I once thought were funny are scary now. I have strong convictions, but they're not funny. I often feel like a resident of Pompeii who has been asked for some humorous comments on lava."

What originally sparked his songs was the fiery conviction of youth, which gradually burned away. As he told Jeremy Bernstein in 1984: "At the time I was writing the songs, I was not really aware they would be presented to an audience—at least not in the beginning. So I wasn't self-conscious about them. That's what happens when you are young. You do things without going through all those layers of self-censorship. I was just saying in those songs what I was thinking. Now if I wrote a song, I would think, 'How will this go over with an audience?' "

Like many songwriters, Lehrer performed—"sold"—his own songs better than anyone else, but he wasn't against licensing other people to do his material. "I'd say fine, I wouldn't be against that, but I don't think it's gonna work. It's like Bob & Ray—someone could get up and do them, but it wouldn't be the same." Lehrer even once considered hiring someone to play him. "One of my fantasies was that I could coach someone to go out and sing my songs. I'd stay home and we'd split, fifty-fifty. You'll never guess who I picked. Hold your breath, folks! Roddy McDowall. I just thought of someone collegiate-looking with a bow tie." But the songs really require Lehrer's own sardonic voice.

"When I listen to the box set," he acknowledges, "I realize how much acting I put into it. The weaker the song, the more acting I had to do. If it was funny by itself I wouldn't have to do anything." Even singing in Irish, German, Russian, Spanish, and Calypso, his diction was always perfect. "I'm not a performer—I just sit at the piano," he insists, when in fact he sang with ebulliency, lacing lyrics with self-mocking asides: after finishing one song, he asks, "May I have the next slide, please?"

Even his lesser efforts—"A Christmas Carol," "Send the Marines," "Clementine" as rendered by Cole Porter, Mozart, Gilbert & Sullivan, and a cool jazz singer—make you grin because of his personal panache. Lehrer croons and warbles and knows just when to let his voice crack; lines that look bland on a page are twice as amusing given his droll spin. Even the tempo instructions in his songbook, *Too Many Songs by Tom Lehrer,* are funny: he advises that "Smut" be played "pornissimo"; for "The Wiener Schnitzel Waltz" the composer suggests "*mit schlag*"; at the top of "I Wanna Go Back to Dixie," he writes, "a little too fast"; "The Masochism Tango" should be played "painstakingly."

For his nimble and unexpected verbal acrobatics, Lehrer was called "the Cole Porter of the coffeehouses." To those who claim his songs were nothing but clever rhymes, Lehrer replies that so were Noël Coward's. "In 'Mad Dogs and Englishmen' he doesn't say anything except it's hot and mad dogs and Englishmen don't stay indoors. The rest is dressing, but a lot of people eat salad for the dressing, not the lettuce." His own "Lobachevsky" is a rhymester's holiday, sung in dialect:

> *Plagiarize,*
> *Let no one else's words evade your eyes.*
> *Remember why the good Lord made your eyes,*
> *So don't shade your eyes,*
> *But plagiarize, plagiarize, plagiarize—*
> *Only be sure always to call it please "research."*

As for the lyrics, "It's always fun to come up with an interesting rhyme. To me, that's very important. So many people write humorous songs, but the whole joke is the song. Nothing is really added by making it into a song. Part of the fun is to have internal rhymes. Sondheim is the master of this. He said it makes you want to hear it more than once. Which I think is the criterion of an interesting humorous song. Are there clever rhymes and internal wordplay?"

> *While we're attacking frontally*
> *Watching Brinkally and Huntally,*
> *Describing contrapuntally*
> *The cities we have lost.*
> *No need for you to miss a minute of the*
> *Agonizing holocaust.*
> —from "So Long Mom (A Song for World War III)"

Lehrer is still as intrigued by the intricacies of songwriting as ever. "It has something to do with expectancy. A well-known tune sets up a challenge. There's a template. Now, can he do it? The trick is to avoid what the listener has provisionally guessed. You have to satisfy the task but avoid predictability. That's what is creative—the surprise." Discussing his writing process, Lehrer also told *SF Weekly*'s Jack Boulware in 2000, "The first thing is to get the idea for the song, then to get the title, or the ending, or something. To begin a song is not hard. It's where are you going to end it? You gotta have a joke at the end. Sometimes I'll have an idea for a stanza, but after that, where does it go? So it was mainly getting the idea and then just kind of plugging away at it." His easiest creation, he divulges, was "I Hold Your Hand in Mine."

Lehrer sees a clear connection between math and music. "The construction part, the math, the logical mind, the precision, is the same that's involved in math as in lyrics," he told Boulware. "And I guess in music, too. It's gotta come out right. It's like a puzzle to write a song. The idea of fitting all the pieces so it exactly comes out, the right word at the end of the sentence, and the rhyme goes there and not *there*. It's like an 'elegant proof' in math. It doesn't matter what it proves." He told another reporter, "There's something mathematically satisfying about music. And math has to do with abstractions and making connections."

Lehrer's idea of a good time is something like the Fermat Fest, an event put on in San Francisco by Osserman in 1993 to commemorate Andrew Wiles's proof of Fermat's Last Theorem, for which Lehrer's "That's Mathematics" was the theme song. It was only one of his many, more obscure math-based songs, such as "The Derivative Song," "There's a Delta for Every Epsilon," and his better-known "New Math" (*"Hooray for New Math, / New-hoo-hoo Math, / It won't do you a bit of good to review math. / It's so simple, / So very simple, / That only a child can do it!"*).

By 1980 his songs had pretty much gone unheard for years, but they were hardly forgotten. Lehrer responded to Mackintosh's idea for a revue of his songs, *Tomfoolery,* with his usual enthusiasm: "It's all right with me; it's your money." He regarded the idea with great wariness, yet the show enjoyed a long run in London, after which Mackintosh went on to produce *Cats.* Deadpans Lehrer, "The combined profits from *Cats* and *Tomfoolery* made him a very wealthy man." Even when later productions fell below the London standard, "the material carries it," Lehrer notes, laughing, but maybe only half in jest.

By then a few of the old topics had lost their zing—pollution, the bomb, and dope were talk-show clichés—but the songs still carried a satisfying sting. Once-dead issues were dug up, only to be slain again onstage in engaging graveyard gavottes. A few numbers had become dated, but others were happy rediscoveries, like "New Math" and "I Got It from Agnes"—playgoers made the switch to newer sexually transmitted diseases; "When You're Old and Gray" was updated with the addition of a gay couple alongside the original hetero twosome. Lehrer approved, noting dryly, "I've had my consciousness raised." He willingly changed a "wetback" reference in "Old Mexico" and, because it was deemed too filthy, was happy to replace the word *crud* before Bing Crosby sang "Pollution" on TV, overjoyed that Crosby was singing one of his songs; the "Pollution" album once got as high as number 18 on the *Billboard* charts.

Barry Koron, musical director for the 1982 San Francisco version of

Tomfoolery, recalls how calm Lehrer remained during "a pretty stressful rehearsal when the producer's, director's, and Lehrer's ideas for the show were very different. "He knew exactly how to get laughs on every single line. He was very specific and very precise. This pause has to be 0.8 seconds long, not 0.4 seconds, stuff like that."

Another reason for his theatrical retreat was what Lehrer calls "the challenge issue." He didn't feel audiences were sufficiently challenged by his songs and were just patting themselves on the back for agreeing with his liberal sentiments. "The audience went away feeling self-satisfied." And he felt creatively unchallenged: "To really develop a whole song that has a beginning, middle, and end, and that says something—I couldn't think of anything that would grab me for that length of time. My attention span is really limited" (he says his attention span was shot off during the war), the reason he gives for never marrying: "I couldn't even sit through *Nicholas Nickleby,* let alone a marriage." I don't go to movies anymore because they're so long. That's the first thing I look at—how many minutes it runs. My songs are very short." He once said, "I'm happy to hear one movement of a symphony, and the word *uncut* strikes terror in my heart. I'd rather eat a grape than an apple."

Most people feel that if they had Tom Lehrer's gift they would never stop turning out witty topical songs, but not Lehrer. When pressed on why viable ideas rarely occur to him anymore, he says, "We're not talking about ideas. We're talking about funny ideas for *songs.* I could probably come up with some one-liners, but not a whole idea for a song. There's a lot of funny things happening, but the idea is to do it in a minute and a half." He adds, "And people don't know enough today. Who would get a Schopenhauer reference?" Also, "What was un-PC then is now almost conservative today. You can't say anything now that won't offend an audience. It would be nice to just let 'em have it—feminists and antifeminists and affirmative action and bleeding hearts and knee-jerk liberals, and not be embarrassed about it." Unwittingly, Lehrer touches on juicy potential song topics in conversation and even in a liner note to his box set: "When I was in college, there were certain words you couldn't say in front of a girl. Now you can say them, but you can't say *girl.*"

If any comic deserved to be called "sick" during the ill-named sick-comedy era, it might well be Lehrer; and yet his songs were so jolly and were performed with such amiable zest that they seem the antithesis of sick. When audiences laughed at one of his more wicked lines, he would remark, "You people are sick, you know." In a sense, his songs did have one major theme—celebrating the macabre—and if any criticism can be made of Lehrer, it might be that many of his songs strike the same mock gruesome note, so much so that he was called a musical Charles Addams. "Anything that had to do with death was called sick," he says. "I was morbid, but I wasn't mean." He concedes, however, that, "next to sex, death is the easiest thing to get a laugh on. What I loved best about performing in the dark was I couldn't see whom I'd offended. I'd worry in 'Hold Your Hand in Mine' there'd be someone out there with one arm."

As it happens, Tom Lehrer is a big sloppy romantic—"a sentimentalist at heart," hence his love of Rodgers & Hammerstein. "If a show doesn't make me cry, it's not worth it," he once said, singling out his favorite musical, *The King and I*. "I really like to be moved," he says, and once described himself as "a Rodgers & Hammerstein man in a Stephen Sondheim world." His songs attack what he considers fake or vapid sentiment. "I make fun of sentimentality, not sentiment. I'm positive. If I make fun of something, it's because I wish it were not like that. It would be wonderful if people got married and stayed happy the rest of their lives. Not only doesn't it happen, but why pretend that it does? It's more like 'Help Me Make It Through the Night.' " He once said that he could never write a love song ("I don't feel them"), but, he avers, "I suppose I could write third-rate Rodgers & Hammerstein." Noted Leah Garchik in her 1982 interview: "All this is said as though the mathematician is proving that the sums of the squares of the sides equal the square of the hypotenuse."

Even after Lehrer had had his fill of performing, he was enticed by the prospect of writing new material for *That Was the Week That Was* (a.k.a. *TW3*) when it debuted in 1964. "They were using original songs, and I thought, 'Oh, I can do as well as that,' so I sent in some songs and they used some of them—usually removing the best line." The first song of his that they performed was "National Brotherhood Week," written, by sheer coincidence, a week before the so-named week.

> *It's National Brotherhood Week*
> *National Ev'ryone-smile-at-one-anotherhood Week,*
> *It's only for a week, so have no fear,*
> *Be nice to people who are inferior to you.*
> *Be grateful that it doesn't last all year.*
> —from "National Brotherhood Week"

Like Mort Sahl, Lehrer loved to mock fellow liberals. His own politics, he once said, is "your basic wishy-washy liberal"; he was a 1960s Eugene McCarthy supporter—"until I met him." He performed at political benefits for years for losing candidates, he said, and decided to quit when someone he supported finally won. "I figured I'd better cool it." He called his politics "elitist liberal: I would buy dinner for a poor, dirty, ignorant, starving person, but I wouldn't want to eat it with him."

Songs for *TW3* had to be about something that had occurred during the week, but he managed to slip in more general stuff, like "Pollution." "On TV, they always wanted me to do 'Pollution,' because everyone is against pollution. People liked patting themselves on the back." Nine of the fourteen songs he did for *TW3* were written for the same week's show, but forty years later they're still funny, even prescient. "As a friend of mine once said, always predict the worst and then you will be hailed as a prophet."

The only time Lehrer was asked to write songs that were not political or satirical was for *The Electric Company* in 1971–72. "It was the first time that somebody had wanted me to use my craft rather than just repeat what I had already done," he says. In his classes, he finds, "My students are much more excited to find out I wrote 'Silent E' ('*Who can turn a can into a cane? / Who can turn a pan into a pane? / It's not too hard to see / It's Silent E*') than 'The Vatican Rag' or 'Poisoning Pigeons in the Park.' It's like meeting the guy who wrote 'Jingle Bells.' I don't like to be recognized, but some students know me. They say, 'My grandmother has your record.' "

Lehrer's verses were as skilled as those of any veteran Broadway lyricist, so it seems a further loss that, as well as retiring from writing his own songs, he never gave musicals a whirl—although he and Joe Raposo, the late *Sesame Street/Electric Company* songwriter, took a stab at musicalizing *Sweeney Todd* decades before Sondheim and James Lapine did it. (The Lehrer-Raposo version was to have been a comedy, starring, yes, Jerry Colonna.) The grisly fable of "The Demon Barber of Fleet Street" was custom-tailored for Lehrer's mordant wit and devious wordplay. "We actually started on a couple of songs. Nothing ever came of it, and of course twenty years later Stephen Sondheim beat me to the punch."

In the end, it may simply come down to the fact that Lehrer is a dabbler by nature, not a dedicated artist. He explains that the strictures for writing a show, on a deadline, were just too scary to him, and he's not sure he could work well with others. "I'm not good at collaborating, and it takes a lot of time and then it flops. And I wouldn't want to have to deal with actors." Mainly he felt he "couldn't write music good enough for a book show."

As to the state of contemporary satire, he says: "I watch a lot of [comedy] on TV, and there's very little satire. Carlin I can't watch. He's so mean, which now passes for wit. I don't listen to Leno or Letterman. Today's audiences applaud and hoot and whistle, but they don't laugh." He suspects that the decline of literacy explains the lack of satire today: "It may just be that audiences don't know anything. They're all kids and they've never read a book. If you mention Monica Lewinsky 'going down' it'll get a big laugh. . . . What passes for satire is just easy targets." He also once remarked, "Irreverence has been subsumed by mere grossness." In 1980 he observed, "You have to be extremely vulgar to attract attention now. This is no time for satire."

Surely there are subjects now to inspire a Lehrer song, like gun control or abortion. "What's funny about gun control? To write a funny song you have to be against something—you can't be *for* something. I did write a song about partial-birth abortion called 'Bye, Bye, Baby,' for my own amusement. I played it for a couple of people and they said, 'That's disgusting.' " He explains with a shrug: "Humor isn't going to convince anyone. It wouldn't do any good; it wouldn't work. Satire doesn't move people, it only makes people who are already on your side feel better. You have to be really nasty." He seems not to trust his own satirical instincts or his repressed nasty streak.

These days, Tom Lehrer's songs might be considered mild, however ingenious, but he hasn't gone nearly as soft as he claims. In fact, he may have grown even more macabre but is afraid to face his innermost demonic notions. Surmising about abortion as a possible song topic, he added, casually but devilishly: "I'm not pro-choice, I'm pro-abortion, and I'd like to have it mandatory and retroactive, but you can't really get away with that. It wouldn't be funny. Even infanticide doesn't bother me. I think if a kid comes out rotten, snuff it. It's not a problem for me." Sounds like a terrific idea for a Tom Lehrer song.

The Start of Something Big

Steve Allen

But I digress . . . for a living.

S TEVE ALLEN CARRIED a good time with him wherever he
went. Hilarity was seemingly in the air and his for the taking.
Allen wasn't a stand-up comedian, and yet everything he did
on television in the fifties and sixties was, in its purest sense, stand-up
comedy, even if he did it sitting down at a desk or strolling through an
audience on *The Tonight Show*. He was a freewheeling spirit whose wit
defined the new comic sensibility—satirical, spontaneous, and wildly
self-referential.

Allen, like Mort Sahl, Lenny Bruce, and Jonathan Winters, worked
free-form. Sahl and Bruce were heavily jazz-influenced, and Winters
mocked to his own drummer, but Allen was himself a jazz musician,
which may explain his stream-of-consciousness humor. He was always
many things, several people in one—composer, lyricist, author, actor,
crusader—but his brand of extemporaneous comedy, his anything-goes
notion, is what he's most fondly remembered for. He was an easy entertainer to like, one who didn't present himself as a comedian but as a host.
Wit was such an essential part of Allen, so effortlessly tossed off, that it
never seemed contrived; and even when it was, as in a sketch, there was
always plenty of room for Allen to follow whatever absurd tangent
struck him. He forever shattered television's glass fourth wall.

His ad-lib talent, innate sense of the ridiculous, and an obsessive love
of wordplay ("*I stand corrected—and I should because I'm wearing orthopedic
shoes*") gave him a huge head start on most stand-up comics, and everybody else then on television. He had a massive influence on comedy, not
just because of his own style but because of the comics he presented. Just
to be seen with Allen gave a new comic, or any comic, added stature.
Allen surpassed other genial TV hosts—Ed Sullivan, Garry Moore, Perry
Como, the old boys' variety-show network, all fixtures from the past. He
was an essential part of the future. Sullivan & Co. confirmed your comic
status, but Steve Allen could elevate it and confer coolness upon you.
When Allen howled at a new comic, it was from the gut. He loved com-

edy and the people who created it, and had an insatiable appetite for humor—verbal, physical, surreal, accidental.

He was incubated with the old-school comics. His mother, Belle Montrose, had been a vaudeville performer. (Milton Berle, who once baby-sat the infant Steve, called her "the funniest woman in vaudeville.") His father played straight man to his mother's comic dithering—a primitive Burns & Allen. But Allen junior had something beyond comic credentials and a born-in-a-trunk pedigree. From the beginning, he had intellectual credentials. He wrote books, he reviewed them, he had a mind and a life beyond the TV screen; other hosts, for all their showbiz savvy, never seemed to care much about anything beyond that week's show. So he had the respect of comedians, audiences, and critics. It's almost impossible to find a negative word about Allen, who died in 2000 at seventy-eight after a minor car accident. Shecky Greene put it plainly: "I loved Steve Allen backwards, forwards, and in between. He stands alone."

Allen worked most of his life like the radio disc jockey he began as—making it up as he went along. His gift, and his enduring charm, was that he made it all look nonchalant, unlike so many comedians of that period who seemed tortured individuals. Steve Allen was never tortured, and he downplayed his comic gift as no more than the by-product of a curious mind: "Basically, I just talk like I talk, and if people consider that entertainment it's fine by me." You could almost see his mind clicking away as he sat at his desk on the old *Tonight* show. Half the time he surprised himself along with us, triggering that infectious laugh of high hilarity; cracking himself up, he might dissolve into a fit of giggles.

Allen delighted in the zigzag ways of his own antic, analytical mind. The zanier he got, the more surprising it seemed, because he *looked* so unfunny—with his sincere spectacles, regular features, and low-key demeanor, more like a high school physics teacher than a comedian who, in a twinkling, could become a total goofball. As his trusty discovery, the singer Steve Lawrence, put it, "He appears to be the squarest guy in the room but is the life of the party." Most of his books—numbering fifty-four and including two autobiographies, the first written when he was in his late thirties—are decidedly unamusing. His two books on how to be funny are no-nonsense comedy texts, with stern homework assignments and chapters on everything from delivering funny speeches and ad-libs to writing comic essays, funny letters, even cartoon captions. He hammers out axioms on wit as if explaining how to build a house.

There was always, inside the comic Steve Allen, a teacher/preacher trying to get out. His conversation could take on a professorial tone, stuffy and even self-important, totally at odds with his capering on-camera persona. Allen used that deadpan manner to great comic benefit, assuming a somber voice when, say, reading letters to the editor, becoming a stone-faced inquisitor for nutty man-in-the-street interviews, or reciting rock lyrics a cappella. When he was chosen in 1954 by NBC's programming innovator Pat Weaver to create and host what came to be called *Tonight!,* he looked like a version of his early-morning counterpart, the *Today* show's sober, bespectacled Dave Garroway—another man of many parts, and also a jazz buff, but lacking Allen's playful streak.

Allen's comedy was utterly unencumbered, collegiate without being sophomoric—a mixture of madcap non sequiturs, verbal byplay, and visual horseplay. Even while tied to a talk-show format, he created on his feet—bantering with regulars on the show, interviewing folks in the audience, fooling around with toys and props at his desk, taking part in stunts, making funny phone calls, or just training a camera on folks outside ambling idly by the studio.

The *Chicago Tribune*'s Larry Kart wrote that Allen was perhaps the first comedian "to find ways of being funny on television peculiar to the medium." He and Ernie Kovacs were linked in that way—two comics who made TV their personal plaything. Other comedians danced to TV's tune, while Allen and Kovacs molded the medium to their own Silly Putty purposes, many of which became not just routine devices on late-night shows but have frozen into standard shtick: it will take another Steve Allen to thaw *that* format. He was once called "the most imitated man in television."

David Letterman remains the foremost pretender to the Allen late-night throne, but Letterman is far more tightly wound than Allen and seems to strain to manufacture a madcap mood; Allen genuinely seemed to be having a blast. Meanwhile, Jay Leno, in Allen's old seat, has much of Allen's old breeziness, though he lacks his fertile, ingenious, and intuitive semisurreal mind. Both Leno and Letterman come off as programmed, practicing a hand-me-down form that was indigenous to Steve Allen, the original master of midnight revels. Allen was a precocious child of the television age, developing in front of us on the small screen. Although he had begun in radio, he wasn't a network radio star, or a nightclub or vaudeville carryover.

When Allen did *The Tonight Show*—created it, really, out of the night air—he was improvising it as he went along. Fewer people were watching back in the early 1950s, so a lot less was at stake. It was Allen (and his tiny staff of two) who built *Tonight* into a place where the stakes became very high. By the time he left the show, in 1956, and Jack Paar took over six months later, it had grown into *the* major platform for new comedians. Paar, Allen's emotional opposite, was an uninventive, awkward, twitchy fellow who seemed a nervous wreck on the air. He had none of Allen's loosey-goosey qualities. It was Allen, with his writers Stan Burns and Herb Sargent, who turned an unpromising non-prime-time spot on NBC into a national forum; and the funny thing that happened on the way to that forum was Steve Allen.

He did it by working entirely on instinct, trusting his sense of what was funny. One of his best traits, rare in performers and nearly unknown in comedians, was that, despite a healthy ego, he had no evident envy of other comics. He loved to discover them, boost them, celebrate them, and write about them. The list of comedians Allen championed, or introduced to a national audience, runs from Don Adams to Lily Tomlin.

Unlike many comedians, Allen was comfortable in his own skin, partly because comedy wasn't the only life he had, or maybe because he realized that his brand of comedy was totally his own—not just *by* him but *of* him, even though many of the bits he devised on his shows were blatantly filched by other comics. They might steal his ideas but nobody could ever steal his essential Steve Allenness.

Allen, like Jack Benny before him, realized that he wasn't the whole show and wisely surrounded himself with other comics, not just those he presented on his show who went on to become famous or whom he tried to rescue from oblivion (Jackie Mason, Lenny Bruce), but within the show itself—notably his "Men in the Street": Louis Nye, Don Knotts, Tom Poston, Bill Dana, Pat Harrington, Jr., Dayton Allen, and Gabe Dell. Patterned loosely after Fred Allen's "Allen's Alley" (Dana called it "Allen's Alley sideways"), satirizing TV news's addiction to inane man-on-the-street interviews, Allen would wander over to his lineup of four whacked-out guys and try to elicit their views on something major in the news. Most of the time, the dense interviewees could barely get their names out coherently. (Leno now interviews actual dimwits-in-the-street on historical events, a pale version of the old Allen—both Fred and Steve—routine, which made fun of archetypes, not real people.)

He played off the media in his angry letters to the editor and his bellowing sportscaster, "Big Bill Allen." He toyed just as easily with whatever was in front of him, creating found comic art out of the most mundane items—a goo-goo doll, a salami, a plant, a mug of coffee, a flubbed bit. He was so fast and efficient, on and off his feet, that he became his own foil, with an ability to footnote whatever popped out of his mouth with a rapid comic aside.

Allen had an astonishing skill at seizing on a word or a phrase, on someone's name, occupation, or hometown, and, in a flash, finding its comic essence. Bantering with the audience, Allen was as quick as Groucho Marx sparring with contestants on *You Bet Your Life*. Groucho, however, had the benefit of editing, whereas Allen worked live, sans net. While he was occasionally criticized for making fun of people, Allen was never mean and felt no need to needle or score off guests; he dared to let them be themselves. "It turns out, people are interested in that," he discovered. "One of the biggest laughs in the history of laughs was when I was fitted for a suit of clothes on the show. We brought in a little Italian tailor. He had no sense of being on TV. His total indifference was what made it hysterical."

Letterman has acknowledged his debt to Allen as he tries to channel the old Allen show's rambunctious spirit, but while Allen delighted in people's humanity, no matter how bizarre, Letterman can appear patronizing. Allen had an intuitive sense of taste and decency. Half the time the joke was at his own expense. He sidestepped Letterman's smart-ass edge, explaining, "You have to control yourself to the point where you never become smart-alecky or superior. If I had been rude or cruel, the laughter would have stopped immediately."

Allen wore his cap and bells so lightly that it seemed he didn't much care if you laughed or not. Not that he didn't take himself seriously, for he was famously a man of strong and vocal opinions who suffered fools less gladly off-camera than on. What he didn't take seriously was television, and that was his saving comic grace. He seemed to recognize TV for what it was—a chance to party, to enjoy himself, to shed all those sobering thoughts about nuclear war, racism, pollution, and moral decay. That don't-give-a-damn attitude sparked his wit, relaxed the audience, and created an atmosphere in which comedy could flower.

Great comedians who have attempted to host talk shows—Jerry Lewis, say, or Roseanne Barr—can't sit on their own comic egos long enough to draw anyone else out. Dick Cavett did it, just barely, and Leno manages politely, but for Letterman it seems a supreme act of willpower to stop cutting up long enough to let a guest get a word in. Allen's finely tuned sense of balance and fairness allowed him to lighten things up without getting in the way. No comedian worked on TV so informally, without pushing, yet produced so much pure merriment that went beyond comedy into the wider realm of wit. With no pressure to crack jokes that must pay off, the *Tonight* format was elastic enough to make room for Allen's rambling, uninhibited comic spirit to frolic.

The show and the performer were a perfect fit for the fifties; it was as if Allen constructed the format and all who followed tried to squeeze themselves into it. Paar reconfigured *The Tonight Show,* adding a formal stand-up monologue and making it squirmingly personal, with home movies, emotional pleas, and snits with columnists and critics. After Paar left, Johnny Carson tightened the format even further, turning the show into a rigid ritual as inflexible as a Japanese tea-serving ceremony: monologue, banter with stooge and conductor, bring on guest, do sketch, introduce singer, enter next guest with film clips, bid farewell. Allen simply went wherever his comic nose led him, without an agenda, without a worry, and almost without a clock. Today's talk-show hosts are converted stand-ups working to a talk-show factory time clock, with everybody hemmed into a tight screen no bigger than—well, a bread box.

STEPHEN VALENTINE PATRICK WILLIAM ALLEN grew up the precocious child in a wild Irish family in whose Chicago household humor ran rampant. "I came from a somewhat disorderly background," said the orderly Allen. When his mother was touring (his father, Bill, died when Steve was a year old), the infant Steve stayed with members of his mother's family, shifting from one home to the next while bouncing around to some eighteen schools, usually Catholic parochial schools.

His mother had a drinking problem (or as he put it, "If she didn't have a drink, there was a problem"), which partly accounted for her addled onstage persona. "She wasn't much of a mother, which I say with a smile on my face. She just never went to mother school." Despite all that, and what he has described as a fairly chaotic clan ("flighty Irish," he called them), Allen seemed to have survived his peripatetic boyhood remarkably calm and intact. "I was a part of all that"—the vaudeville life, traveling all night and changing trains at two A.M. in Altoona—"but when you're three and four and five you don't see it as awful, as long as you're with people who love you."

He traced his sense of humor to his family. "I was raised by the Donahues, most of whom had the gift of gab, as they say. It was sort of sarcastic, Irish, side-of-the-mouth, low-volume—not big like Jackie Gleason's humor. I talk as I do largely because I was raised by the Donahues. Most of them were very funny. There was sarcasm that could even get nasty if they were angry, but thank God there was the humor there. I was hardly ever funny at home, even though I grew up among funny people. One nickname for me was the Sphynx, which meant silent. Another was the Philadelphia Lawyer, because when I did communicate with the wacko Donahues, I tended to be reasonable, and they had no sense of reason at all. They were very unstable, highly irrational people. I loved them, but they were nuts." His strongest comic influence was his mother—"her mannerisms, a way of throwing off hand gestures, attitudes, ways of looking and talking, a casual style of comedy."

Amid the humor, he read a lot, took piano lessons, and decided not to go onto the stage but to become a reporter (he resembled Clark Kent); he contributed jokes and light verse to the *Chicago Tribune*. In 1941 Allen went to Drake University in Des Moines, Iowa, where he wrote for the student newspaper, became a popular musician ("I'd sit down to play the piano in a room that was empty and after twenty minutes I'd realize that a hundred and four people had slowly gathered"), and casually signed up for what he thought was a snap course in radio production. At that time, he recalled, "almost anyone not cursed with an annoying speaking voice could find work in radio."

Because of asthma, he transferred to Arizona State Teachers College in Phoenix, but quit a few months later to work at a local radio station, KOY, as an announcer, disc jockey, interviewer, actor, and writer of ad copy, news copy, and even soap operas—a classical radio education. Meanwhile, he played piano in a local steak house and married an Arizona State girl named Dorothy Goodman, with whom he had three sons. (They divorced in 1951, after which he met and married the tall red-haired actress Jayne Meadows, who did much of her performing as a chatty game-show panelist on CBS's *I've Got a Secret,* where she had a seven-year run.)

At KOY, he teamed up with fellow announcer Wendell Noble and, as Noble & Allen, the two began playing gigs around Phoenix, with Allen at the piano, singing, doing crazy voices, and cutting up with his funny partner ("clearly the worst comedy act of all time," Allen said later). Noble moved to Los Angeles, and Allen followed, becoming a staff announcer at KFAC.

Perhaps inspired by a couple of guys on a Boston station called Bob & Ray, he and Noble submitted two audition tapes to executives at KHJ. One was a jokier version of their old Phoenix act of songs and patter, entitled *Smile Time,* which became the basis for a fifteen-minute early-morning show heard up and down the West Coast in 1946 on the Don Lee–Mutual network. "It was cute and clever and fresh. We were like two college-boy types. It was also generally conventional, in that you wrote a script and stood in front of a mike and you played your part." He insisted that show business was "not really my ambition—it was all just for laughs and to meet pretty girls." Allen always shrugged off questions about his ambitious nature by saying, "It's been incredible good luck. Whatever I do now is what I was doing in my teenage years. I wrote poetry and stories for the school magazine. I was in plays, I made speeches. All the same stuff I still do, and it was all there by the time I was sixteen years old. The one thing that never occurred to me, oddly, was show business."

Smile Time was a ragtag thing of shreds and patches—jokes copied from gag books, a recurring character named Claude Horribly, old comic verse from Allen's college days, a silly Mexican, sound effects, zany time checks and weather reports, voices, soap-opera parodies, and the first of his mock band remotes (*"From the beautiful Aragon Ballroom, high atop the fabulous Hotel Fabulous, in the heart of downtown Gallup, New Mexico, just a short forty-five-minute drive from the ball-bearing center of the world, Leaven-worth, Kansas . . ."*)—whatever would fill a twelve-page script every day, much of it imitation Fred Allen and Henry Morgan.

Smile Time was so popular that the team went on the air nationally and added a woman, June Foray, who did funny voices (later Rocky's on TV's *Rocky and Bullwinkle Show*), and an organist named Skitch Henderson, who would be Allen's longtime bandleader. Recalls Foray, "He was very serious and introverted, but, boy, when that mike was turned on. . . . Sometimes we just went on the air cold." Looking back, Allen observed: "The radio experience was invaluable to me in the context of my eventual TV work, in precisely the way it was for Carson, Paar, and Griffin. What we have in common was a radio background, whereas the later generation came out of the comedy clubs." He also credited garrulous guys like Dave Garroway and Arthur Godfrey for "making it possible to work as I do." He adored radio: "Radio was king. It was glamorous and thrilling, so there was no reason to leave that for the grainy world of TV."

When *Smile Time* was canceled after two years ("I loved every minute of it—if I'd had money I would have paid *them*"), Allen went to KNX, a

CBS outlet, as a disc jockey who was told by his boss to "just play records, and in between do a little light chatter." Allen took the cue but didn't trust himself to talk offhand, so he wrote eight-page scripts that were meant to sound extemporaneous. As time went by, he played fewer and fewer records on the show, called *Breaking Records,* and talked more and more, building a devoted following, until an executive memo ordered him to play records and knock off the comedy. The nervy Allen read the memo over the air and got four hundred letters that stated his argument for him—that anyone could spin records but that he offered something original. The ruse worked: his boss backed off and let him do as he pleased, pleading, "But play a *little* music, okay?"

The studio audience grew from a dozen diehards to a hundred—astounding for a small local eleven P.M. show, which became a favorite among comedians like Jack Benny, Fred Allen, Milton Berle, Groucho Marx, Red Skelton, Phil Silvers, and Bob Hope, many of whom wrote encouraging letters or appeared on the program. He counted Al Jolson, Fanny Brice, and Ethel Barrymore among his regular listeners; Jolson called it "the best radio program on the air." The KNX late-night signal carried the show well beyond Southern California, fostering a cult following wherever it was heard.

Another turning point for Allen came the night that Doris Day failed to show up for an interview and Allen was left to his own comic devices with twenty-five minutes of airtime on his hands, which he filled by interviewing people in the studio audience, lugging an old stand-up mike up and down the aisles. "The physical thing of carrying this big mike around the room helped to get laughs. I just horsed around, like with my pals. That opened up a lot of possibilities." He later wrote: "I don't recollect what was said during the next twenty-five minutes, but I do know that I had never gotten such laughs before. When the evening was over I was in a state of high intellectual elation usually associated with an important scientific discovery." Allen had discovered his natural ability to play it as it lays, to talk without a prepared script or format. "For two years I had been slaving away at the typewriter and reading scripts with only moderate success. Now I had learned that audiences would laugh much more readily at an ad-libbed quip, even though it might not be the pound-for-pound equivalent of a prepared joke."

Allen had stumbled upon his greatest comic gift, the thing that unloosed an entire career of flying blind, a revelation for a guy as tightly regimented as Allen. He had unlocked a side of himself he hadn't quite trusted before: "I discovered that engaging an audience in spontaneous banter is the most dependable way of all to strike the magic fire of laughter." Others in radio had wandered into audiences before Allen—gabby guys like Art Linkletter and Bert Parks—but they lacked Allen's ingenuity and verbal dexterity. His background as a jokesmith allowed him to go beyond mere audience chitchat, though it was really his ear for language, an ability to pick up on mangled syntax or an unlikely phrasing, that triggered his funny retorts (woman in the balcony to Allen: *"May I have your autograph?"* Allen: *"Only if you have a very long pencil"*).

He liked to say modestly that everybody speaks extemporaneously all day—but not with a microphone in one hand and millions of people hanging on every word, and not with the demand to be funny, with ratings on the line. The unflappable Allen was funniest when calamity struck the show. Any minor crisis—dead air, a falling ceiling panel, a weird noise, a musical flub—brought out his ad-lib genius. He could put any audience at ease. Hosting an NAACP benefit, he said, *"On this show tonight for the National Association for the Advancement of Colored People we also have in the audience some Negroes, as well as a few blacks. It's admirable that Negroes, blacks, and colored people can come together and work out their differences."*

He was sometimes accused of setting up innocent people, yet quite the reverse was true, he insisted. "When I say to a guest, 'What is your name?' and he answers with calm reassurance, 'Boston, Massachusetts,' he is the funny one and I his willing straight man. Were I to talk for a million years I could never say anything funnier than 'Boston, Massachusetts' in that situation." People loved the byplay, as when a guest said to Allen, *"I'm not sure I follow you,"* and Allen shot back, Groucho-like, *"Well, I'm not sure you don't follow me. Somebody's been following me for the past five days . . . a short, dark man in a green sweater. However, it may be a case of mistaken identity."* In that same interview: *"What business did you say you were in, sir?"* . . . *"Tool and die."* . . . *"Oh, that's too bad, but we all have to go some time."* The guest then asked Allen, *"Say, can my wife see me now?"* to which the host replied, *"I don't know—does she have an appointment?"* Jay Leno notes: "He was the first wiseguy that my mom liked. But he wasn't a wiseguy in that he was mean or nasty. It was just that he was so fast on his feet, so smart. He had that cutting edge, but he wouldn't cut, he would filet. His jokes were like surgical incisions."

What Allen found in these roving interviews was a way to unlock TV's structured format by using its formal façade as a bottomless source for his whimsical turn of mind—which developed into an overall laissez-faire game plan for late-night television, when audiences literally let down their hair at home. Allen was the ideal bedtime host. Indeed, one night he played the piano in his pajamas, explaining that when the show was over he wanted to go straight to bed. He made a distinction between his and others' version of *The Tonight Show:* "When I did *Tonight,* it was a comedy show with lots of music," he said. "Jack Paar brought in the couch and made it a talk show."

To prime his ad-lib wit, Allen booked kooky guests, such as the health-food addict and nature boy Gypsy Boots, not to mention snake charmers, palmists, a lady woodchopper, and a vast assortment of oddballs. He made minor celebrities out of two devoted little white-haired ladies, Mrs. Sterling and Mrs. Dorothy Miller, who came to all his shows and whom he treated with good-natured bemusement. To enrich the mix, he would stir in legends—Carl Sandburg, Harold Arlen, Count Basie. These extemporaneous conversations, which Allen pioneered in TV before Dick Cavett and Charlie Rose made careers of them, is what kept viewers up well past their bedtimes, sleepily awaiting Allen's great unscripted moments.

His shows were gold mines of found humor, such as zeroing in on faces in the audience and running funny captions underneath, or sticking a camera out the back door of the studio and aiming it at innocent bystanders while he ad-libbed comments on people's dress, walk, and demeanor. He once did twenty minutes with a matchbook cover. "Ad-libbing is easier than people think," he maintained. As a young deejay in Phoenix, he would "practice ad-libbing by pretending to be on the air as I drove around, describing the passing scenery to an imaginary audience."

Allen was compelled to ad-lib simply to amuse himself. Steve Lawrence said, "He just loved to laugh." It was almost as if the very act of sitting before millions of people, talking, was in itself an absurd premise. He often looked as if the show had just been handed to him fifteen minutes ago and he was doing his best to bluff his way through it, whereas he was always in full control. Even in a bare-bones interview, he was endlessly inventive: *"What is your name, please?"* . . . *"Mrs. Holt. H-O-L-T."* . . . *"Very well. W-E-L-L."* Allen, ever the scholar, once remarked: "English is an easy language with which to turn normal conversation into nonsense, because it is so full of idiomatic expressions which automatically turn into jokes when subjected to straight-faced analysis. To me, the English language is one big straight line." Easy for him to say, but it takes a finely attuned ear to hear an idiom, see it as a potential joke, pounce on it, and instantly turn it into a gag or a pun—as when a lady in the audience asked him, "*Do they get your program in Philadelphia?*" and he said, "*They see it but they don't get it.*"

Years ago, when doing an on-air commercial for a chair made from the new miracle product Fiberglas, he would hit it with a hammer to show its durability. One night the chair shattered, and Allen, without missing a beat, shouted, "*That's right, ladies and gentlemen, this* hammer *is made of Fiberglas!*" Such on air dexterity requires an extraordinarily fast mind, which Allen displayed night after night for decades. (Roseanne Barr called him "the funniest gentile who was ever born.")

Leonard Feather, the jazz critic, observed that Allen combined several comic gifts in one—Groucho Marx's wisecracking skills, Dick Gregory's hip sense of irony, Bob Hope's "stand-up glibness," Red Skelton's flair for physical comedy, Sid Caesar's satirical exaggeration, and the prose wit of Robert Benchley. Allen's ear for the off-center word or whimsical image also rivaled James Thurber's. For no reason at all except that he liked the sound of a word or a phrase, Allen would get obsessed with it and repeat it because it cracked him up: "*You're under arrest*"; "*How's your fern?*"; "*Kreel*"; "*Watch it, Charley*" (waggling his thumbs menacingly); and his trademark bird cry, "*Shmock-shmock!*" He had a wonderful way of twisting clichés and turning language inside out, like the time he said (in pure S. J. Perelmanese), "*Of all the unmitigated gall—or for that matter, of all the* mitigated *gall. And how does all that gall get mitigated in the first place?*" Allen never needed a straight man, because he simply responded to his own rhetorical questions. As he told me: "I do play straight for myself. Part of my brain is always listening to what the rest of it is doing."

Anyone interviewing *him* was likely to serve up unwitting straight lines that he would hit out of the park, like the time Joe Franklin, the New York talk-show host, remarked to him, "I don't want to put words in your mouth," and Steve replied, "I don't know of a better place." Or when a palm reader told him, "One good thing about you is that you're loyal to a fault," and he answered, "*You're right, I've got a great many faults and I'm loyal to every one of them.*" Someone asked him, "Do you think it's proper for an unmarried girl to sleep with a man?" and Allen said, "*By no means. She should stay awake all night. You don't know what might happen when you're asleep.*" A doctor on his show told Allen, "The only two really instinctive fears in man are the fear of loud noises and the fear of falling," to which Allen responded, "*I have a great fear of making a loud noise while falling.*" When Lucille Ball asked him, "What do you think of working wives?" he said, "*I don't know, I've never worked any.*" His comic rhythms were uncannily Grouchoesque, yet totally his own, as when he told a physician on the show, "*I'm allergic to two things, dogs and cigars, and if I ever meet a dog smoking a cigar I'll be in real trouble.*"

Allen's KNX radio show ("where I worked out all the building blocks for what later became *The Tonight Show*") ran from 1948 to 1950, but it wasn't all ad-lib by any means; he hired two writers, Bob Carroll, Jr., and Madelyn Pugh, who went on to help create *I Love Lucy.* Another Allen gift was his ability to spot original talent—writers (Herb Sargent, Stan Burns, Bill Dana, Don Hinkley, Bill Persky, Sam Denoff), directors and producers (Dwight Hemion, Nick Vanoff, Bill Harbach), singers (Steve Lawrence, Eydie Gormé, Andy Williams), musicians, and, to be sure, comedians. Most went on from there to major careers. "I've always worshiped talent," he said, "but we all have a list of eighty-seven people we've discovered"—plus, he added, all of those who never made it.

When he first began in TV, Allen had trouble booking comedians. They were afraid to go up against an ad-lib wizard, unaware of Allen's love of comics other than himself and his ability to let them take the spotlight. It would have been bad manners and unwise to show up fellow comics, so he eagerly played the straight man to others. "It is a practice that has paid off handsomely," he wrote. When he began his 1956 Sunday-night TV show, he said, "I made the decision to be a 'one-man' show no longer and to surround myself with as many funny people as I could hire." After Allen's death, Don Rickles recalled, "He always looked out for other comedians. He was always interested in how things were going for you, which is rare in this business." Carl Reiner added, "He was responsible for so many comedy careers, including the 2,000 Year Old Man."

When his little local show on KNX became a hit, Allen was hired by ABC-TV to emcee wrestling matches, a situation made to order for his wild and woolly comic mind, allowing him even more freedom to play off events that would seem impossible to make even sillier; Allen found ways. Word quickly got around Hollywood about the bright young TV host, and he was soon hired to appear in two movies (a June Haver musical, *I'll Get By,* and *Down Memory Lane,* a collection of silent-film comedy clips for which he wrote the narration). By 1950 *The Steve Allen Show* on KNX was leading its time slot, playing to four hundred people a night in the studio and many more on weekends. Groucho Marx told Allen, "The trouble with you is, you're too damn good." That year, he was the summer replacement for radio's *Our Miss Brooks,* after which CBS brought him to New York to do a local show five days a week at seven P.M., a blueprint for *The Tonight Show.*

THE TONIGHT SHOW'S PREDECESSOR was *Broadway Open House* (1950–51), a variety show hosted by a rowdy nightclub comic named Jerry Lester, known as "The Heckler of Hecklers," Allen's comic opposite. *Broadway Open House* also featured a va-va-va-voom blonde named Dagmar, TV's first Vanna White—a TV pinup whose twin claims to fame were her breasts, enhanced by her exotic name (in fact, she was born plain old Virginia Ruth Egnor). Her contribution, according to a *Tonight* historian, was "to sit on a stool and breathe" and now and again mouth inane verse while Lester did double takes. This she managed so well that Dagmar become a national byword, even if the show that gave birth to her did not. With her 40D breasts snugly nestled into strapless gowns, Dagmar easily overshadowed everything, including Lester, who finally quit in annoyance.

Allen sealed the deal the night he replaced Arthur Godfrey on his *Talent Scouts* show by making a shambles of the sedate little tea-klatch— steeping his Lipton tea bag in a cup of soup, pouring the soup into Godfrey's ukulele, and mixing up the names of the contest winners. When Allen first ambled out, he stared into the camera and introduced himself to the nation: "*This is Arthur Godfrey. Well, this isn't Arthur Godfrey, really, I was just trying to scare my wife.*" Godfrey loved it, according to Allen, and so did the audience, even if Lipton's ad agency was less ecstatic. The Godfrey appearance launched Allen's network career. "That one accidental hour show," he observed later, "saved me about three years of hard professional work." It also led to a part in a Broadway play, a hosting slot on a look-alike Godfrey show, *Talent Patrol,* and a year's run as a panelist on the highly visible *What's My Line?* A *Variety* critic, knocked out by Allen's antics as a Godfrey fill-in, wrote, "The guy's a natural for the big time. He rates kid-glove attention." He got it.

Allen was on local TV eight hours a week as quizmaster on a summer show and the host of *Songs for Sale,* boosting his national exposure. Meanwhile, NBC's New York station joined with Knickerbocker Beer to produce a nightly program hosted by the young, slender, six-foot-three guy in the horn-rim glasses who was making comic waves in New York. Allen's show began in 1953 with a fifteen-minute New York version that ran from 11:15 to 11:30 P.M.; it was extended to 1:00 A.M. when it went national.

Within a few months, after *Broadway Open House* folded, Pat Weaver told Allen to prepare to go coast-to-coast. Weaver had spelled out in a memo what he said became *The Tonight Show:* "We have plans for a strip [five-night-a-week] show late at night, shot on an ad-lib basis as in the early radio days. . . . We'll run for an hour with fun and songs and jollity and featured and unrehearsed gimmicks. The idea will be that after ten or eleven at night, a lot of people will still want to see something funny." It sounds much like the local show that Allen was already doing, a little romp chock full of jollity. Allen always insisted that, despite Weaver's claims, Weaver did *not* create *The Tonight Show* but simply named it, as a neat match to *Today,* his earlier brainchild.

"He had nothing whatever to do with creating *Tonight,*" Allen states adamantly in his memoirs. "They hired us because we were a big hit, then NBC decided to improve it. They wanted to ditch Steve and Eydie." Weaver envisioned a show that would include theater and movie reviews, comic characters, nightclub-hopping remotes, ski reports, and more of a gadabout spirit, all of which Allen eagerly agreed to. "None of this frightened him," Weaver writes. "He was so good, the show was a colossal hit from the very beginning." After the fifteen-minute local lead-in, the first *Tonight!* show (the "*!*" was later deleted) went on the air at 11:30 P.M. from the stage of the Hudson Theatre. The date was September 27, 1954.

Whoever actually invented it, the show opened with a camera in Times Square, panning the scene (much as the Letterman show now opens), before zooming in on the Hudson Theatre marquee, which dissolved to Allen inside onstage. The host fit the new species of life-size, low-key TV personality embodied by *Today*'s Dave Garroway. As Allen recounted it: "Before me, there were two kinds of announcers on TV. One was the real dumb announcer type—'Say, Mr. Pipe Smoker . . .' Human beings never talk that way. Announcers do. Or there's the other way, the way comedians talk [affects booming voice]: 'Good evening, ladies and gentlemen!' Suddenly Godfrey came along and, like Garroway, he talked just the way people talk on the street. It was so refreshing. Nobody was shouting, nobody was talking like a comic, trying to top you. Just a nice friendly person. That made it possible, when I showed up, to be accepted." In part it was that easygoing guy that audiences responded to so warmly, but there was also that surrogate crazy guy most viewers were too shy to let loose. He could be silly without being dumb or an obnoxious self-indulgent show-off. Judy Holliday once said that Allen was so relaxed it made her nervous.

He began in the quiet, unforced style that quickly gave the show its tone: "*In case you're just joining us, I want to give you the bad news first: this program is going to go on—forever. Boy, you think you're tired now. . . . We especially selected the Hudson Theatre for this late show because I think it sleeps about eight hundred people or so. This is a mild little show. . . . It's not exactly a spectacular; more of a monotonous.*" Whatever it was, Steve Allen's *Tonight* was a new breed of broadcast animal—less than a "variety show" and more than an interview show (the label "talk show" had not yet been coined).

The first show began modestly enough with four new young singers (Lawrence, Gormé, Williams, and Pat Marshall), a comedian (Wally Cox), and one Ink Spot (Bill Kenney). There were always singers, guests, and comedians, and maybe a sketch or two, but it was really what went on *between* the acts that defined the show and glued it all together. Allen was just that crazy glue—crazy but civilized. *Boston Globe* arts columnist George Frazier described the host's humor as "gentle, never savage or petty. Usually satiric in vein, it is casual and well-bred." Jay Leno said in tribute to Allen in 2000: "He always used his intellect. He had smart jokes that rose above the common denominator—that's the thing I most admired about him. I last saw him at the Emmys and he said he was working on a new show, *Touched by an Agent*. It's kind of a lame, silly joke, but the way he said it, with his little 'heh-heh-heh,' it made me laugh. He performed it."

After six months, *Tonight* had replaced old Charlie Chan movies as the midnight TV show of choice, and its bright new host was soon starring in three NBC specials and emceed that year's Emmy Awards show. He popped up as a guest panelist on programs like *This Is Show Business* as the resident intellectual. *Newsweek* was cautious: "To television touts, it seemed that NBC was taking a gamble," the magazine wrote when Allen went network. "Allen's wit might be too New Yorkish and, for some parts of the country, too late in the evening." Explaining why the West Coast saw his show via kinescope, Allen said, "*The program is seen out there three hours later—due to carelessness.*"

Despite his polished veneer and ready repartee, Allen said he was personally "not terribly secure" in those early days. "I somehow had a professional confidence that I never had as a human being," he told Sedge Thomson on *West Coast Live* in 1998. "I was no more secure than any other insecure young fella. But I was aware that I was funny, and I was aware that I could write music, and I somehow saw those as marketable skills. My timing was very fortunate. Radio was *the* big deal. Then TV came along and suddenly there were hundreds or thousands of jobs open for announcers, singers, producers, directors. Whatever you did, TV needed you. So I never had to walk the streets looking for work."

It was Allen's zany streak that, when inspired, gave rise to his gift for non-sequitur gibberish, as in a *Mutiny on the Bounty* parody, when he dashed into the audience and, in full regalia, began ordering everyone around in mock sea-movie lingo, like a mad Captain Ahab/Bligh/Queeg: "*And you, sir, you call yourself an able-bodied seaman? You ought to be Shanghaied to Tokyo, or Tokyoed to Shanghai! And those of you seated on the starboard side, there are no stars on board tonight! But tell the boatswain's mate that I have issued an order to man the women! Ahoy, there! Jib the mains! Swab your tonsils! Save your tinsel!*" It was just this sort of literate nonsense that endeared Allen to millions. Nobody on TV, apart from Sid Caesar & Co., had Allen's consistent sense of inspired lunacy, and nobody else would match it until *Saturday Night Live* landed at NBC a generation later. (*SNL*'s first head writer was Allen's longtime staff writer Herb Sargent.)

The elastic format played to Allen's diverse talents as if he had created the form exclusively for himself, playing the free-style show almost as a series of jazz riffs. He held forth as host, sketch player, pianist, monologuist, interviewer, and whatever else was required of him, from reading the ominous-sounding ingredients off a candy wrapper to engaging in daffy stunts—diving into a vat of Jell-O, being bowled down the street in a plastic ball, and arriving on one show in feathers and flying into a birdcage. He was game for anything—selling hot dogs from a cart, packing the audience with Steve Allen look-alikes, phoning people in offices across the street, stopping cars at traffic lights to inquire if they were carrying any fruits or nuts across the border, or tossing a giant Hebrew National salami (his favorite prop) into the backseat of a taxi and telling the driver, "*Grand Central Station, and step on it!*"

Allen's dignified demeanor made it even funnier. If it all sounds very familiar now, it's because Leno and Letterman have made it so by copying many Steve Allen stunts, but in 1954 it was original, inane, and incredibly inspired stuff. The writers would put Allen into sticky situations he would need to ad-lib his way out of, laughing at the insanity of it all in his manic shriek—of which James Wolcott wrote: "His cackling laugh really did seem torn from all inhibition. He had the true spirit of a comic anarchist fluttering like a red flag in his soul."

Allen's comic devices were ruthlessly stolen by everyone, most of all by Johnny Carson, who had no problem blithely swiping anything he liked from any comedian—Fred Allen, Jackie Gleason, Jonathan Winters. In publishing it's called plagiarism; in commerce it's called copyright infringement; in comedy it's show business as usual. After politely ignoring Carson's larceny for years, Allen finally struck back in his 1992 book *Hi-Ho, Steverino!,* partly a rewrite of his 1960 autobiography *Mark It and Strike It* (the only person Allen steals from is himself, in books that tend to recycle anecdotes and material).

Allen claimed that Carson had stolen his "stump the band" routine, not to mention the even more ruthless pilfering of Allen's late-show movie with resident pitchman, which Carson renamed "The Tea-Time Movie with Art Fern" (*fern* itself being a favorite Allen nonsense word). Carson's "The Great Carnac," in which Carson wrapped himself in a swami's turban, duplicated Allen's Question Man routine ("A precise copy," noted Allen, although Ernie Kovacs had a similar bit), in which his know-it-all wizard provides the questions to answers from Tom Poston. For example: *A. "Butterfield 8-5000"* . . . *Q. "How many hamburgers did Butterfield eat?"* (The more literary version: *A. "Et tu, Brute"* . . . *Q. "How many pizzas did you eat?"*) The routine in which a camera zooms in on someone's face in the audience, followed by a funny caption line, began with Allen ad-libbing silly descriptions; it became a regular fixture under Carson's, and now Leno's, reign. When Allen learned that the reverse-question-man idea had originated with a Los Angeles radio personality named Bob Arbogast, he offered to stop doing the bit or credit and compensate Arbogast; an agreement was reached. Allen sniped, "Perhaps Johnny will leave Arbogast something in his will, in a last-minute paroxysm of guilt."

He never confronted Carson, explaining, "It's too touchy a subject because he's taken so much from so many people." He did, however, write that "Carson's success has provided him with a remarkable Teflon-like protection against the constant charges of plagiarism to which he had been subjected by both other comics and professional critics." He wondered, with thinly concealed scorn, why Carson didn't rely on some of his own talents, such as "his remarkable prowess with a deck of cards."

Letterman has acknowledged the Master in such segments as telephoning people who place strange classified ads, and Allen noted that Jay

Leno was good enough to call him before reworking one classic sidewalk interview into his "Jaywalking" segment (*Would you knowingly vote for a practicing heterosexual?*"). Allen didn't want to be thought a sorehead and appreciated the fact that bizarre minds often think alike; yet he was compulsive about setting the comedy record straight. In 1999 he said, "I oscillate between 'How dare they!' and 'Aw, the hell with it.' The sportscaster Roy Firestone was right when he introduced me as the most borrowed-from man in television." Added Allen, "Personality, thank God, cannot be stolen."

It wasn't evident just *how* good Allen was until he left *The Tonight Show,* when it became a radically less inspired enterprise. "When Paar took over," Allen said, "he ruled out all the music, all the comedy sketches, and turned it into a complete conversation show, and a fine one. He was hip enough to book great talkers. Once he'd made that decision, he could've stayed home some nights and the show would have been just as good."

Unlike Paar, Carson, Leno, Letterman, and Conan O'Brien, Allen needed little big-name celebrity ammunition and very few sketches to ignite the show. "When we first started," he said, "I had no writers at all. Occasionally I would write a comic monologue or a simple sketch for a guest and myself, but all I actually required on a typical night was a piano, a couple of amusing letters from viewers, some unusual toy, a guest or two to chat with, an audience to interview, or a newspaper article that had caught my fancy"—at which point, the Allen fanatic can hear him crack, "And if you've ever had your fancy caught, you know how painful that can be." Years later, watching the Emmys, Allen sat amazed as a dozen David Letterman writers trooped up to accept awards. "To this day I don't understand why it takes that many people to do what little writing such programs require."

Having revolutionized TV on *The Tonight Show,* Allen was given a chance by NBC in June 1956 to go head-to-head in the main event against the acknowledged ruler of Sunday-night television. Or, as Allen put it, "NBC decided I was the solution to a problem they'd had for years, and that was *The Ed Sullivan Show.*" The press covered it as if it were a grudge match, just as the media did forty years later during the Leno vs. Letterman battle for late-night dominance. Sullivan was the Leno figure—a good, solid seasoned champ—and Allen the Letterman figure, a wickedly funny infighter, a promising contender, and a tricky counter-puncher with more than a few clever moves. The smart money was on

Sullivan, who eventually won, but when it ended, four years later, CBS's heavyweight champ knew he'd been in a fight.

Fans of Allen's late-night show were heartbroken when he gave up the weeknight program for crass prime-time reasons—a bigger audience, bigger stakes, and, to be sure, bigger money. "NBC panicked when I finally told them I couldn't keep up with both shows," he said. Pat Weaver later judged it a huge career mistake for Allen. "Steve never again reached the level of popularity he had earned on *Tonight,*" he said, accurately. Allen's son Bill footnotes that NBC persuaded his father by giving him a rare ownership of the Sunday show, but for Allen it was the lure of the center ring: "It's called prime time. Late night is nice, but it's not big time. On a good night, I'd have six million people watching the *Tonight* show and on Sunday night I'd have thirty million watching. Also, the money was five times bigger in prime time, which had a lot to do with it."

Responding to suggestions that he had burned out after burning the midnight oil for four years, he told me: "I wasn't burned out. I could have gone on for forty years—Johnny Carson did thirty. That was not the problem. Those shows are so easy, I wonder why people don't feel guilty about getting a high salary for doing them. A TV talk-show host is no more difficult than being a disc jockey on radio. You don't even need to have any talent yourself. If you have some, that's nice, but it's not a basic requirement. Look at all the people on in the daytime. I could've done that in my sleep." He added: "As I look back, I think the most remarkable thing I did was that, during the eight weeks it took to film *The Benny Goodman Story*"—in which he starred—"I never missed a night of *The Tonight Show.*"

The Sullivan show never had to create material for its guests, but scripts had to be submitted ahead of time for Allen's Sunday show, and NBC quickly got much more involved in the inner workings of what had formerly been a play-it-by-ear, catch-as-catch-can affair for Allen, Burns, and Sargent. Recalls the tall, soft-spoken Sargent: "The network gave us a bad time, and suggested he get rid of Steve and Eydie, and Steve [Allen] said, 'Okay, I'll get rid of them if you get me Dinah Shore and Frank Sinatra.' He was very firm about this. He wasn't sure if he had the clout, he just said it. On the early *Tonight* shows, he'd book people like Zero Mostel and Jack Gilford, who were blacklisted. The network would say, 'Wait a minute, wait a minute,' and Steve would say, 'No, if they don't go on, I don't go on.' He was terrific that way."

Allen admitted that the Sunday-night show was a grind compared to the relaxed weeknight show, which was "pure comedy and wild sketches," whereas Sunday was "big sketches, big stars. It was hard work. Every week we had to put on the equivalent of a Broadway musical-comedy revue, and sometimes on Broadway it takes them a year and they close in one night." The Sunday prime-time show had less of the swinging feeling of the old late-night affair. "He'd hate me for saying this," confides Sargent, "but at some point in the late stages of the Sunday show, he began to feel the audience wasn't getting it. He had a level of communication that was more interesting than Ed Sullivan. That's when he started to over-explain a setup for a sketch or something. He began to get impatient with people who were not thinking quickly. Eventually he wrote these books, like *Dumbth*"—Allen's tome on the dumbing down of America, in which he lists a hundred ways to combat stupidity. (Forever waging war on public ignorance, he was recommending books on TV decades before Oprah Winfrey became America's head librarian.)

Allen actually fared well against Sullivan, even if he eventually lost the Sunday-night ratings battle to the old showbiz general. The show was less wildly inventive than his former late-night hodgepodge, but he kept some of the elements, notably his old "Man in the Street" gang. He left the show in 1960 (the year the show won a Peabody Award) and returned Sunday nights to Sullivan. Allen wasn't devastated. Unlike most funnymen, he wasn't insecure and frantic. In Sargent's words, "He didn't depend on being a comic. He had other things. He didn't care."

Even then, Allen was only a part-time radio-TV personality, spending equal amounts of time writing scripts, short stories, novels, songs, and his longest-lasting literary work, *The Funny Men,* an astute analysis and celebration of comedians; he wrote two sequels, *Funny People* and *More Funny People,* which included a few women, and was working on a fourth volume when he died. He left thirty-six unfinished books—also a collection of romantic poems to Meadows that she hopes to publish. His series of "Steve Allen Mysteries" in the 1980s and '90s were, however, all ghost-written by Walter J. Sheldon and Robert Westbrook, according to the mystery writer Jon L. Breen in the *Weekly Standard.* He wrote a 1963 musical comedy about Sophie Tucker that flopped; he also composed several songs a week, a lifelong regimen. The final total came to more than 8,500, of which only a handful became well known—his theme song "This Could Be the Start of Something Big," "Impossible," the theme from the movie *Picnic,* and the lyrics to "South Rampart Street Parade."

(Lesser-known recorded songs include Louis Armstrong's "Cool Yule," the Grammy-winning "Gravy Waltz," and "Pretend You Don't See Her.") Bill Dana was in awe of Allen's output: "He was an incredibly ambitious, organized guy. If he took a break he walked over to the piano and wrote half a dozen songs."

Frankie Laine once challenged him on his boast that he could write fifty songs in a day; to prove it, Allen sat in a window of a downtown record store, and in seven straight days batted out 350 new songs, most never heard again. The *Guinness Book of World Records* lists Allen as the planet's most prolific composer. His point, he said later, was to show that writing songs was no trick, although getting them published, sung, and recorded was. His own piano playing was featured on thirty albums; he was an equally gifted vibraphonist, and for *The Benny Goodman Story* he learned enough clarinet to mime Goodman's fingering credibly.

Allen was jazz-certified—he both dug it and played it, even lapsing into groovy lingo out of which grew his *Bebop's Fables,* later collected in books and on wax (*"The big bad wolf went to the home of the third little pig. Applying his hairy knuckles to the door, he laid down a crisp paradiddle and said, 'Man, it's a raid!'* . . . *'Pops,' whispered the pig, 'it's after closing' "*). Because he didn't feel that critics considered him a serious jazz musician, just a dabbler, he recorded an album of boogie-woogie piano under the pseudonym "Buck Hammer." (*Downbeat* gave the disc three stars and predicted a bright future for the new artist.) He also cut an album of progressive jazz piano, this time calling himself "Maryanne Jackson."

Had he not gone into broadcasting, Allen might well have had a successful career writing comic essays. His literary bent was apparent when he satirized trends, like the fifties fad in hunky movie-star names (Rock Hudson, Tab Hunter), for which he invented his own stable of macho Hollywood leading men, among them Flash Flood, Chuck Steak, Rock Pile, Zip Code, and Tab Collar. He cooked up a roster of make-believe mobsters off a menu: the gang leader, Oysters Rockefeller; the muscleman, Beef Stroganoff; the moll, Cherries Jubilee; the stool pigeon, Chicken Cacciatore; the waterfront boss, Clams Marinara. He rewrote famous books (*The Bad Seed* by Luther Burbank, *I Led Three Lives* by the McGuire Sisters, *The Sea Around Us* by Lloyd Bridges); and he played with Greek myths (devising such "ancient" heroes as Onus, Parenthesis, Digitalis, Thermos, Virus, and Epidermis). He did parodies of Harold Pinter (entitled *Whatever . . .*), commercials, and TV telethons (his cause was prickly heat). Allen appealed to viewers' brightest and most verbal instincts, which in network TV almost seems subversive. Says the TV critic Ron Miller, "He gave you the feeling he was drawing you into his world and you were going to be brought up a step or two in sophistication."

A large part of Allen's appeal was his diversity (Noël Coward once called him "the most talented man in America"), which placed him in a select company of wits who can do more than make people laugh and may account for the absence of sweaty desperation that oozes from many comedians. Miller notes, "He had to have an ego but you never really saw it." It was as if he was saying, *Laugh or don't laugh, I have books to write, songs to compose, crusades to mount.* His last crusade was an odd one coming from such a famous card-carrying liberal—imploring the public in stern full-page newspaper ads to join him and the Parents Television Council to clean up TV and movies of "the filth, vulgarity, sex and violence [that is] leading children down a moral sewer." Some seven hundred thousand people signed up for his crusade, but the heavy-handed language of the appeal wasn't at all his usual wry style, more like something from Jerry Falwell or Pat Robertson, or from one of those old angry letters to the editor he had always mocked.

His own life was filth-, scandal-, rumor-, and seemingly trauma-free. "Over the years," he said, "I can recall only three or four instances when I couldn't function professionally because of a serious problem." Allen led a placid, highly organized life. Until his death in 2000, he ran Meadowlane Enterprises from a drab, unmarked mustard-colored building in Van Nuys, California, a sort of Steve Allen, Inc., where his assistants bustled about efficiently, monitoring his every move.

In 1999 he still commanded his vast enterprises like a CEO, dressed in a yachting cap and a buttoned-to-the-throat black-and-white plaid shirt, suggesting a tortoise in his shell. He was a hands-on guy who left little to chance and would dispatch his staff to send interviewers batches of clippings in any area of the Allen oeuvre that he felt a reporter wasn't up to speed on; he was equally quick to send off complimentary notes to writers of articles he admired. Despite a seeming modesty (he rated himself as only medium funny next to comics like Mel Brooks and Sid Caesar), he was dismayed that I didn't realize he had also acted in plays (he and Meadows would take shows like *Tonight at 8:30* and *Love Letters* on the road each summer). Allen was well aware of his Mr. Versatility legacy and made sure no facet of it was neglected. Asked which of his creative passions came hardest for him, he leaned forward and confided to me in a whisper, "Nothing," and then laughed. "You see why I feel guilty?"

Steverino, slightly bent but ruddy-faced, sat behind a desk at which he would suddenly, in mid-interview, yank out a pocket tape recorder and capture an idea that occurred to him, lest a fleeting notion flit away; at home, he was said to have a pocket dictating machine in every suit and every room. On the stairway walls leading to his office, like an entrance to a Steve Allen Hall of Fame, were plastered hundreds of magazine covers, album and book jackets, advertisements, posters, and pieces of sheet music, all depicting Allen's docile face staring back, attesting to the depth and breadth of his skills over the past half century. His fans wished he had been as visible on TV in his last twenty years, during which time he all but vanished into his noncomedy projects, only popping up here and there on TV to promote a new book or an old cause.

Two distinct people cohabited within Allen—the quicksilver wit and the fretting schoolmaster. He was a modest comic who disdained showing off, but the scholar part of him had a penchant for displaying his book learning, even to the point of pontificating. In his early autobiography *Mark It and Strike It,* Allen veers off into two-page detours on the sad state of comedy, the plight of the intellectual in America, the struggle between religion and science, the national fear of psychiatry, the need for a nuclear policy, and communism versus capitalism, dropping names like C. P. Snow and Bertrand Russell as casually as he might W. C. Fields or Bert Lahr. His intelligence sometimes ran rampant; a critic complained of his 1962 novel *Not All of Your Laughter, Not All of Your Tears* that an editor should have cut out some of his more "platitudinous philosophical excursions." Equally at home perusing *Variety* or *Commonweal,* he had read widely and he let us know it. Allen wasn't the clown who wanted to play Pagliacci; he was the clown who wanted to discuss *Pagliacci.*

His admired Emmy and Peabody Award–winning PBS series *Meeting of Minds* (1977–81) was an inevitable middlebrow marriage of showbiz and scholar-biz, in which famous historical figures—Darwin, Cleopatra, Karl Marx, Attila the Hun, Emily Dickinson, St. Thomas Aquinas, Socrates, Lincoln, Catherine the Great—sat around a table and discussed the great issues. It was the ultimate talk show, Steve Allen–style. Though it took him eighteen years to get the series on the air, he was spurred on in part by NBC's decision to pass on it and the network's earlier attempts to keep him from discussing certain topics on the air—drugs, crime, the Mafia, capital punishment, the TV and radio blacklists. He explained: "I function as a human being first and do jokes secondly." To a reporter who asked him, when he took on AWARE (a Red-hunting vigilante society), if he worried his ratings might fall: "I'm not worried about my TV rating; I am worried about mankind's rating." He called his politics "radical middle-of-the-roadism."

He seemed almost prouder of *Meeting of Minds* than of all his other work put together. His comedy was transient, he realized, so he was banking on the twenty-four one-hour *Meeting of Minds* programs to leave a permanent mark. "Of all the things I've ever done, that's the one thing that will never lose its importance," he said. He believed he had a second-rate mind compared to the famous thinkers on *Meeting of Minds,* but that it qualified as first-rate by TV standards. His own mentors were Norman Cousins and Robert Maynard Hutchins, whose Center for the Study of Democratic Institutions in Santa Barbara, California—the likely birthplace of *Meeting of Minds*—Allen had regularly attended. "It was pretty much like being back in ancient Greece," he said, "because one was surrounded by capital-P philosophers, great scientists, and political analysts, and I would just sit there at their feet, smiling like a goof."

Between 1960 and 1976, Allen floated around TV. He hosted *I've Got a Secret* for three years and then did a variety of variety shows, the most popular of which was a 1962–64 syndicated series for Westinghouse, *The Steve Allen Show,* that was in the uninhibited spirit of his old late-night NBC show—"much funnier" than the original *Tonight* show, he thought. But on the wild and crazy Westinghouse show, the stunts grew a bit desperately over the top. He once was set afire in an asbestos suit, played the piano atop a crane, was smeared with dog food and set upon by (hungry but friendly) dogs, became a human banana split covered with whipped cream and chocolate syrup, was attached to forty-five tea bags and dunked into a vat of hot water, and walked on the wing of an airplane in flight. The show depended less on Allen's innate comic abilities than on his sheer nerve; there was less and less sketch-playing and more and more giddy gamesmanship, descending at times into lunacy for its own sake. Allen loved invading the Hollywood Ranch Market across the street—just as Letterman delights in visiting, but via camera only, tacky neighboring tourist shops and delis.

Gradually his intellectual pursuits occupied him more than performing, and he became a semistranger to television. By the 1980s, the keyboard he most enjoyed tickling was a typewriter. He hosted *The Steve Allen Comedy Hour* in 1980–81, but after leaving TV, Allen was underused and eventually drifted into guest appearances, speaking engagements, fill-in hosting jobs, concerts, panel shows, a syndicated series called *The*

Start of Something Big (about the origins of commonplace things), and an ill-fated CBS attempt to bring playwrights to prime-time TV, *The Comedy Zone.* In 1988 he returned to his radio roots on a daily three-hour show over NBC and hosted a curious syndicated TV series called *Host to Host,* in which he interviewed *other* TV hosts. The Museum of Television and Radio presented a six-month Steve Allen exhibition in 1984, and two years later he was inducted into the Television Academy's Hall of Fame. On his seventy-fifth birthday, PBS honored him with a ninety-minute tribute, with Allen on-screen nearly the entire time in a cavalcade of Alleniana. Even though semiretired from performing, he still made about fifty personal appearances a year, the last one on the night before he died. (Last year, a ninety-nine-seat theater named for him opened in Hollywood, operated by the Center for Inquiry–West.)

For a comedian, Steve Allen was on the national scene an incredibly long time without ever wearing out his welcome. He eventually soured on the state of TV comedy, due mainly to the filth factor. "He was very disappointed in TV, where he had spent fifty years—particularly in performers like Howard Stern and Jerry Springer," said Jayne Meadows after his death. In a posthumously published book, *Vulgarians at the Gate,* he maintains, in his most finger-wagging fashion, that comedy is "a perfectly functional dipstick to measure the state of our social and ethical collapse," and he goes on to cite the decline of humor, the family, and pop music.

On the last page of his 1992 book on his years in television, *Hi-Ho, Steverino!,* he wrote: "The best humor, when it's not simply purely playful, says something witty and wise about the issues it confronts." Allen's humor was best when it was purely playful, and whether or not it said anything wise or witty about any issue of the day was never the point. For American TV audiences in the fifties and sixties, the laughter that Steve Allen generated was its own reward.

And Now, a Laugh from Our Sponsor

Stan Freberg

Rumble rumble rumble, mutiny mutiny mutiny.

WEARING A BLUE JUMPSUIT and sneakers, Stan Freberg peers over the shoulder of an engineer in a studio at Capitol Records. He chuckles at his fifty-year-old jokes as he oversees the digital remastering of his classic record parodies and commercials for a new four-disc box set. The six-foot-one-inch Freberg, slightly stooped at seventy-five, with an unruly mop of white ringlets, looks like a prominent symphony conductor—his eyebrows arched quizzically, looking cranky and suspicious. A typical resonant Freberg "hel-*lo*" has his old wisenheimer tinge, a familiar nasal voice of manifold skeptical inflections. It's the voice of a thousand voices, and, for much of the fifties and early sixties, it was the voice of satire itself.

Nearly half a century after the fact, the master parodist mouths every lyric and line of dialogue as he listens, sneaking a glance out of the corner of his eye for his interviewer's reaction. He snickers in anticipation of each approaching joke and mutters along with the songs, snatches from his 1966 *Folksongs for Our Time,* like "Oh, Dat Freeway System," with plucked-banjo Stephen Foster music. He asks his engineer to play the songs for me, eager to entertain an audience of one. "It's a compliment to you that I let you in here," he taunts, then adds, "I thought you might be a terrorist and pull out a gun—'*Okay, Freberg, I've waited years for this. . . .*' "

At a time when satirical comedy was found mainly in revues, Freberg was making heavy inroads into the national consciousness via such retro forms as radio and records. Comedy for the ear, which radio had turned into art for decades, was in sudden decline in the early 1950s, when Stan Freberg, a child of radio, produced a series of chart-busting record parodies that put a deliciously wicked spin on pop hits. He became a wunderkind in two fields in the fifties and sixties—first satire and then advertising, a second career that superseded the first.

Opposite, left to right: Composer Walter Schumann, Stan Freberg, Capitol Records president Alan Livingston, actors June Foray and Daws Butler.

Unlike his stand-up comedy counterparts, Freberg rarely worked in nightclubs or on TV, apart from a few appearances with his puppet space-man Orville, who commented on the absurd doings of earthlings. Freberg got into network radio too late, as a 1957 summer replacement for *The Jack Benny Program*. The short-lived *Stan Freberg Show* was in the mocking vein of Henry Morgan's satirical shows, sassy and inventive, but it labored to attract an audience suddenly addicted to television. When the show was canceled by CBS, the resourceful Freberg turned to records, where he could be his own producer and not worry about sponsors or stepping on toes. Indeed, he trounced on toes with both feet. He found a way to skirt the TV networks as deejays everywhere spun his parodies, fresh and daring for their time.

His little 45-RPM spoofs led the way for comedy records. Parodies poured forth from his comedy-record factory, jumping on every pop hit, TV craze, and musical trend—riffs on *The Honeymooners*, Ed Murrow's vapid *Person to Person*, Johnny Cash's "Rock Island Line," payola, Les Paul, Eartha Kitt, "adult westerns" like *Gunsmoke* and *Shane*. There has been nothing comparable to Freberg's ability to seize on a pop fad and, while it was still hot, capitalize on it. Barry Hansen, a.k.a. the deejay "Dr. Demento," says Freberg's spoofs "were the true forerunners of the satirical style of *National Lampoon* and *Saturday Night Live*"—but with many more bull's-eyes. In a review of Freberg's installation at the Museum of Broadcasting's Hall of Fame, in Chicago, the *Wall Street Journal* commented: "Satire is an outlaw art that loves to live dangerously. Mr. Freberg is a satirist who views sacred cows with a presumption of guilt. He has made discontent his living and our amusement for nearly fifty years."

"I was the only guy among all the comedians then who went into a studio and did all original material," Freberg says. "Bob Newhart's and Shelley Berman's albums were simply the sound track of their nightclub act. They were gonna say the same thing in that nightclub whether anyone was recording them or not. Whereas I went into this studio here, with live actors, musicians, sound-effects men, and created audio moments. It's not that my things are any better, just different." The perfectionist in him preferred working in a studio without a live audience. "I rarely had a studio audience. It's easier without an audience. I can time it and futz with it. I don't have to worry about audience reactions."

In the Capitol editing studio, Freberg listens to his "Puffed Grass" commercial (not a marijuana joke but a parody of the Quaker Oats "shot from guns" commercials) with testimony from test pilot Jet Crash ("*I couldn't break the sound barrier if I didn't start out every morning on a stomach full of Puffed Grass cereal"*). He slips in asides over the dialogue—"Nobody ever did this before." . . . "There's a wonderful political-correctness gag at the end of this." He snickers at "Bang Gunleigh, U.S. Marshall Field."

He frets about a dated Adlai Stevenson joke but smacks his lips over original lines restored in his Senator McCarthy hearings send-up, "Point of Order," noting: "They took out lines that I've now put back in. What's so satisfying is to be able to put back what was held up in the vault by lawyers." The CD anthology contains all of his best commercials: "I'm the only guy in advertising who ever owned all his own stuff," says Freberg, always quick to single out personal bests and ideas later adopted by others: "I did the 'I need the eggs' line ten years before Woody Allen used it in *Annie Hall*—*ten years!*" he cries. When "Elderly Man River" plays, he says, "I did this thirty years before anyone invented political correctness." The 1999 box set includes a Monica Lewinsky routine he couldn't persuade the company to bring out as a single—an annoying reminder of his old radio and TV network battles. "Rhino Records was nervous and didn't want to release it as a single, because—once again, thirty years later!—I have a record company telling me [his voice rises sharply] that *nobody buys single records!* I'm back at the beginning!"

Wary at first that a stranger might not appreciate him, he says portentously, "I assume you're familiar with my work." He loosens up over the next few hours as he fine-tunes his golden oldies. "I'm pretty happy with twenty-five to fifty percent of the material," he says. Among that percentage would be "Green Chritma," *Stan Freberg Presents the United States of America, Volume I,* "St. George and the Dragonet," and "Little Blue Riding Hood." Of a Lawrence Welk parody he remarks, "It's perfect. I can't find anything wrong with those things, even now, forty years later." (As one interviewer noted, Freberg "tends to speak of himself in unblushing superlatives," often tossing out asides like "I made *Time* magazine—full page!—seven times.")

His incisive parodies were theatrically, technically, and satirically several cuts above the novelty records of the time, such as Spike Jones's zany hellzapoppin discs and nonsense items like "The Thing," "The Purple People Eater," and "Alvin and the Chipmunks." Freberg's polished creations were carefully produced parodies with savvy musical and media jokes. He himself was a one-man creative band (writer, producer, director, comic, mimic, lyricist, musician) who used a big orchestra and chorus, clever sound effects, and a gifted repertory company of veteran vocal comics from radio and cartoons. Freberg had the record-satire field pretty much to himself. His success was sweet revenge on CBS for canceling his 1957 radio show, but by then radio was too frazzled by TV to handle a smartass whiz kid like Stan Freberg.

STANLEY VICTOR FREBERG GREW UP in South Pasadena surrounded by the pop culture of Los Angeles—movies, radio, TV, records, and, to be sure, animated cartoons—which he sucked up like a vacuum cleaner. "I knew one thing," he says in his memoirs. "I wanted to stand at a network-radio mike someday and be able to write just the right line to skewer some of the absurdities I was already observing in the world." He also wanted to burst the bubbles of everyone on his enemies list: the well-to-do Pasadena classmates whose circle he felt excluded from as the son of a struggling minister (despite his looks and his name, he's not Jewish but a Baptist of Swedish heritage), the revered jocks in his high school, and the pious members of his father's congregation.

"I knew I wanted to write and perform someday, as my idol Fred Allen did, taking potshots at the pretensions and nonsense all around us," he writes. It was Allen who "first opened my mind to the possibilities of satire in the medium of radio, and who first taught me respect for The Word: the precisely correct statement in a sentence of humor." He was also heavily influenced by Henry Morgan, a satiric soul mate whose sardonic attitude and mockery of sponsors foreshadowed much of Freberg's work; by the whimsical radio serial *Vic and Sade,* which helped shape his off-center humor; and by Norman Corwin's compelling, fanciful radio dramas, which taught him how to blend voices, words, and sounds to capture the imagination.

As it did for many housebound kids with no athletic skills, "radio changed forever the life of this introverted Pasadena kid," recalls Freberg. "When other kids went outside to play baseball, I went inside to play the radio." It's hard to imagine an introverted Stan Freberg, but deep inside him beats the heart of a maverick. Ernie Kovacs once called Freberg "a multiple incarnation of Fred Allen, Don Quixote, and Donald Duck."

His first direct connection to radio was via scripts that had been tossed out at CBS, where his Uncle Raymond (a part-time magician) worked the midnight shift in a control room. He'd scoop up used scripts to bring home to the transfixed young Stan, who would take them into the garage and perform before an audience of pet white rabbits. "From

Hollywood!" he would shout. "The Jack Benny Program! With Mary Livingstone, Dennis Day, Rochester, Phil Harris and the orchestra, and yours truly, Don Wilson," followed by his rendition of the Benny theme song, "Love in Bloom." His wit was enhanced by the humor of H. Allen Smith, Thurber, Perelman, and Benchley, but radio, he says, "was my first library."

In high school he asserted himself by starring in variety shows and assemblies, winning trophies in speech and drama. Stan Freberg, jack-of-all-comedy-trades, was born, along with a cocksure attitude that propelled him forward the rest of his life. "I had not yet heard the word *chutzpah,*" he writes, "but somehow I seem to have developed a lot of it growing up, as a means of self-defense." Some years later, at a dinner party in San Francisco, a lady commented to him in the middle of a story, "I don't suppose you know the meaning of the word *chutzpah,*" and Freberg responded, "My dear lady, I am the Southern California distributor."

Ever since his teenage years, Freberg has gone his own way and been his own man. Early success allowed him to be his own boss, free to pick and choose his projects, write and direct as he pleases, and hire and cast whomever he likes, often people he's worked with for decades who know what he wants—a loyal Freberg rep company. Everything broke right for Freberg, at least in his version of the story. Not long after graduating high school, in 1944, while deciding whether to accept a scholarship to Stanford, he took a bus to Hollywood, walked into the Stars of Tomorrow agency in a crumbling building, and, after doing a few voices, got a job interview the next day at Warner Bros. Cartoons. He lay awake that night, thinking, "*Looney Tunes! Merrie Melodies!* This wasn't just being funny in front of an auditorium of high school kids. This was the cartoon big time."

After a brief meeting with the fabled animator Chuck Jones (creator of Bugs Bunny and other Warner's characters), Freberg ran through his standard repertoire of voices and impressions (Franklin and Eleanor Roosevelt, Jimmy Durante, Peter Lorre) and met Bob Clampett, a director putting together a fifteen-minute daily kids' TV show called *Time for Beany.* Clampett felt the young Freberg might fit in as the voice of a Scottie dog (after FDR's Fala) that sounded like Roosevelt. Could he come to a recording session in two days? Stan allowed as how he might be able to squeeze it in. Fritz Freling, Warner's cartoon director, asked him, "Why haven't we heard of you before?" To which the nervy seventeen-year-old Freberg replied, "Beats me. I've been around, ya know." Freling apologized, saying, "Oh, I didn't mean that the way it sounded. I'm sure you didn't just get off the bus." He had, in fact, just done exactly that.

His foot securely in the Hollywood door, he created a menagerie of voices for all of the titans of American animation—Disney, Walter Lantz, UPA (the "Mr. Magoo" studio), Paramount, and, at MGM, the legendary Tex Avery—but his home base remained Warner's, where he worked alongside Mel Blanc on such classics as *Gopher Broke, Lumber Jerks,* and *The Abominable Snow Rabbit,* a parody of Steinbeck's *Of Mice and Men* (in that era, even the cartoons were literate). Freberg mimicked the dimwit Lenny stroking a rabbit (*"I will hug him and pet him and hold him and squeeze him"*) opposite Blanc as Bug's George—a milestone event for Freberg: "I was eighteen years old and standing next to Mel Blanc!"

No matter who or what he portrayed, his distinctive smart-aleck voice, with its characteristic Freberg twang, is unmistakable. During his cartoon days he played everything from marmosets and bumblebees to small dogs and bears, was the voice of Pete Puma, and even had a small part on Jack Benny's radio show, where the overeager young actor stepped on the irked star's punch line.

After a stint in the army, the multifaceted Freberg played guitar for Red Fox (not the comedian) and His Musical Hounds, a sort of poor man's Spike Jones, for whom he began writing monologues, along with sketches for himself and parody commercials (*"Welcome to 'Lox Radio Theater,' brought to you by the makers of Lox soap. Remember . . . Lox is the only soap that swims up-tub"*). Out of this emerged the idea for "John and Marsha," his first hit record, in 1951. At Warner's, he had learned the nuts and bolts of production; with Fox's band, he learned music and performance. He was ready to move on to something else, to a fad called television.

His former boss, Clampett, was working to get *Time for Beany* on TV, and Freberg was hired as a writer, voice actor, and puppeteer for the *Sesame Street* of its day, a groovy children's program that was a huge hit— one of several satirical and ostensible kids' puppet shows and cartoons, such as *Kukla, Fran, and Ollie; Crusader Rabbit;* and *Rocky and Bullwinkle.* Freberg's Muppet-like Orville, the wisecracking green visitor from the moon, was clearly a forebear of Jim Henson's Kermit the Frog. Freberg also played Cecil the Seasick Serpent to his pal Daws Butler's Beany. The daily fifteen-minute show was riddled with puns, song parodies, takeoffs, and ad-libs, an ideal satirical laboratory for the restlessly innovative Freberg.

Meanwhile, he was knocking out special material and comedy songs for comedians, which led to a chance to write adult lyrics—some, he says, good enough to be taken seriously by the songwriter Johnny Mercer, who encouraged Freberg to go into pop-lyric writing. ("I could have easily gone in that direction," he says now.) After five years, Freberg quit *Time for Beany* and signed with Mercer's Capitol Records, where its A&R man Ken Nelson listened to Freberg's "John and Marsha." Hearing the lovers speaking each other's names—the sole dialogue—in varying tones of agony and ecstasy, Nelson said, "This is a very strange record, but I think it could be a hit." Capitol's executives didn't get it, but one of the company's founders, Glenn Wallichs, liked it enough to include it in a group of new unreleased records that the company test-marketed. Nat King Cole's "Nature Boy" was voted number three; number seven was "John and Marsha." Noted one marketer: "I don't know what the heck this 'John and Marsha' thing is supposed to be, but the audience went bananas." Wrote columnist Aline Mosby: "Soap opera, nothing. Freberg put a tape recorder under somebody's bed, and he can't tell me otherwise."

With his keen ear for the sound of Top Ten nonsense, Freberg was launched upon his life work—poking fun at pop culture. "Whatever's on the Hit Parade, I'll satirize it," he told Nelson. He quickly made good with his parody of Johnnie Ray's screechy lament "Cry," retitled "Try." Nervous Capitol executives asked Freberg to get legal clearances. Nelson backed him again, but Ray fans attacked Freberg for "ridiculing an old man with a hearing aid." He says that deejays stopped playing the parody because it supposedly confused listeners.

His satirical re-creations exactly captured the sound of the original. There were (still) funny takeoffs of Les Paul's "The World Is Waiting for the Sunrise," using frenzied electrified banjos in lieu of guitars; Eartha Kitt's "C'est Si Bon," where the faux-Kitt chokes on her throbbing warbles; "Sh-Boom," with its doo-wop gibberish and an engineer screaming for more mumbling ("*I distinctly heard a* word *there—watch it or I'll send ya back to Hugo Winterhalter*"); "The Yellow Rose of Texas," on which an out-of-control snare drummer drowns out the lyrics; "The Great Pretender," all hiccups and obtrusive *ooo-ooo*'s; and a perfectly realized "Rock Island Line" that ridicules the whole precious folk-song craze ("*Are you going to sing this or read it?*" asks an irritated Freberg).

The hits launched catchphrases with long runs, lines like "*I'll take my bongos and go, man,*" from his "Banana Boat" spoof, and "*Turn off the bubble machine!*" from his Lawrence Welk parody, on which every jaunty tune sounds exactly the same and Welk winds up floating out to sea atop the Aragon Ballroom, bobbing through waves of champagne bubbles and shouting, "*Help-uh! Help-uh!*" Some of the parodies had originated on Freberg's radio show before being released as singles.

In his showbiz war stories (with Freberg invariably cast as the hero), he instantly lapses into comic voices. In one anecdote, Welk confronted him at a party, saying, "Why-ah do you-um haff me saying-ah, 'Wun'erful, Wun'erful'? I neffer say that. And why do you haff me cast out to sea? Why didn't you rescue me?' I said, 'Gee, Mr. Welk, sorry about that.' And he said, 'Of course, you could haff rescued me—that's what the Coast Guard is for. That would be a better ending.' Welk had no sense of humor at all. I said, 'Well, yes, Mr. Welk, that might be a better ending.' Welk said, 'Can't you call those records back and redo the ending?' I said, 'Let me check into that.' " Decades later, to Freberg's everlasting joy, Welk titled his autobiography *Wonderful, Wonderful.*

The cheeky parodist then went after bigger game—Ed Sullivan and Arthur Godfrey, national deities. The two stars refused to grant permission, however, and the parodies went unreleased until they finally made it into Freberg's 1999 collected works. Prior to that, Freberg had never sought permission, but Capitol lawyers sent scripts to Godfrey and Sullivan. The takeoffs sound pretty tame today, but at the time the industry was cowed into reverence for such showbiz royalty. Godfrey finally okayed a watered-down version that Freberg refused to release. He liked to say, "My records are not released. They escape."

His Ed Sullivan parody, "The Worst of the Town," in which the mumbly host winds up inside a whale's mouth, was nixed by a Capitol lawyer who asked if it would be possible to revise the sketch so that Ed "comes out of the whale's mouth somehow." After lawyers shot down his Godfrey parody (it's hard to imagine Sullivan or Godfrey being miffed at such good-humored, harmless parodies), the embattled Freberg went to Alan Livingston, a Capitol executive. "I said, 'I want out of here. Your lawyers have made it impossible for me to make a living on Capitol Records. They're making me clear everything.' " He now explains, "I grew up as a satirist in a very nervous time, and I inherited some of the nervousness that Fred Allen had left at NBC, where they were constantly restricting him and making him rewrite scripts."

His parody of a best-seller about the ESP fad, *The Search for Bridey Murphy,* barely survived being censored when Freberg reminded the lawyer that Murphy, if she even *existed,* had died a century earlier. To placate him, Freberg changed his send-up title to "The Quest for Bridey Hammerschlagen." The lawyer thumbed through the phone directory for a Bridey Hammerschlagen, then, finding no such listing, ordered, "Bring me the New York directory! . . . Ah, here, Hammacher-Schlemmer!"

Easily his most controversial creation was "Green Chritma," a poison dart aimed directly at Christmas merchandizing and rampant consumerism that in 1958 was considered not just tasteless but revolutionary. The "curmudgeon of consequence" (as one headline labeled Freberg, to his huge delight) reveled in railing against whatever annoyed him, even when he bit large chunks out of hands that fed him well. The minister's son was genuinely outraged at the corruption of Christianity's holiest day, but masked his outrage. "Outrage in its natural state is not too salable," he once said. "The hard part comes in covering the social message with the candy coating of humor. Otherwise, you end up as just another crackpot on a soap box"—words that Lenny Bruce and Mort Sahl might have heeded. Freberg was always more entertainer than crusader.

Freberg stuffed his satirical stocking, the seven-minute "Green Chritma," with every kind of crass holiday goody—chestnuts today, but Freberg was again first. His reworked version of "A Christmas Carol" parodied carols, "The Twelve Days of Christmas" mocked Yuletide huckstering images, and "Jingle Bells" was accompanied by jingling cash registers. In Freberg's rewrite of Dickens, Bob Cratchitt owns a little spice company in East Orange, New Jersey, but decides not to tie his product to Christmas and Scrooge is a wily advertising man who tries to persuade Cratchitt to get with the program. A chorus chimes in periodically with lines like, "*On the fourth day of Christmas / My true love gave to me / Four bars of soap, / Three cans of peas, / Two breakfast foods, / And some toothpaste in a pear tree!*" Scrooge pipes up: "*Five tube-less tires!*" An announcer breaks in: "*Sayyyy, Mother, as sure as there's an X in Christmas, you can be sure those are Tiny Tim Chestnuts roasting,*" followed by a trio crooning, "*Tin-ee Tim! Tin-ee Tim! Chest-nuts all the way!*"

Capitol's president, Lloyd Dunn, was aghast. This time, the company's best-selling satirist had crossed the line, bashing both business and the sanctity of Christmas advertising. Dunn wouldn't release "Green Chritma," telling Freberg that he himself was offended. As a *Wall Street Journal* writer noted, "It is the knotty dilemma of satire that one's juiciest targets are often one's most fertile patrons." Freberg asked to be released from his contract, then phoned jazz producer Norman Grantz at Verve Records, who agreed to release the parody without even hearing it.

Dunn finally relented, saying Capitol would release it with two small changes: deleting the words *Jesus Christ* and the cash-register bell at the end. But Freberg stood his ground, and Dunn backed down and released the record as written, but without any publicity from Capitol. Still, it went on to be one of his biggest hits.

Freberg was attacked by advertising journals and religious leaders. When New York's leading disc jockey, Martin Block, played the record—twice—the station's sales department threatened to can him if he played it again; a *Time* magazine writer told Freberg that her essay praising the record was killed on orders from the sales department. Despite warnings that the record would destroy his burgeoning advertising career, Freberg notes that two of the companies he had satirized on the record, Marlboro and Coca-Cola, hired him six months later to create ad campaigns—all of which only spurred him on to further controversy.

He soon took on the anti-Communist histrionics of the day in a parody of the Army-McCarthy Hearings with his "Point of Order"—a diluted version of an earlier cut that Capitol was afraid to release. It was sharp and funny, mocking the droning Senator McCarthy character wearily chanting, *"Point of order-rr, Mr. Chairmannn, point of order-r-r. How much longgg-er must this circus continnn-ue?"* Freberg hated the tamer version, in which Baa-Baa Black Sheep is interrogated about how many bags of wool he has, but admits that "the record made me a minor hero." He had to delete the McCarthy character saying, "I hold in my hand the names of twenty-seven black sheep." Freberg recalls the lawyers howling, "Oh, no—no holding in the hand of any lists. That's too much like McCarthy." He now says, "I don't consider it one of my better things. It had to be watered down. It still sold seven hundred and fifty thousand records—even without the 'list.' A Capitol lawyer said, 'Look, if you're investigated by the McCarthy people, we will deny any knowledge of your existence. We're like the State Department.' "

Like all prolific satirists, Freberg's parodies occasionally missed their targets—his takeoffs on TV shows (*The Honeymooners, The Lone Ranger, Person to Person*) lack the finely honed, impudent edge of his musical satires, with the exception of the masterful spin on *Gunsmoke:* simply a series of "realistic" sound effects—cowboys grunting, chewing, sighing, opening and closing doors, more shuffling—with sparse dialogue.

Freberg's finest recorded hour—well, three minutes—was his sublime 1953 imitation *Dragnet,* called "St. George and the Dragonet." *Variety* reported that it was the fastest-climbing record hit in history, selling two million copies in three weeks and winning him his only gold record. Here Freberg assembled all his skills as a mimic and master parodist. It's also something of a tribute to *Dragnet*'s creator and star, Jack Webb, a Freberg fan, who loved the joke and encouraged it, even allowing the use of the show's famous theme music, led by its conductor Walter Schumann. All the parts were played by Freberg, Daws Butler, and June Foray, whose characters' lines absolutely capture the staccato monotone of *Dragnet*:

> ANNOUNCER: *The legend you are about to hear is true—only the needle should be changed to protect the record.*
>
> ST. GEORGE: *This is the countryside—my name is St. George—I'm a knight. Saturday, July tenth, 8:05 P.M. I was working out of the castle on the night watch when the call came in from the chief—a dragon had been devouring maidens—homicide. My job—slay him!*

And later:

> ST. GEORGE: *I'm taking you in on a 502. You figure it out.*
>
> DRAGON: *What's the charge?*
>
> ST. GEORGE: *"Devouring maidens out of season."*
>
> DRAGON: *You'll never pin that rap on me! D'ya hear me—cop!*
>
> ST. GEORGE: *Yeah—I hear you—I've got you on a 412, too.*
>
> DRAGON: *A 412?! WHAT'S A 412?!!*
>
> ST. GEORGE: *Overacting.*

On the flip side, Freberg took a second shot at Joe McCarthy with "Little Blue Riding Hood," told in *Dragnet*-ese: "*The story of Little Blue Riding Hood is true. Only the color has been changed . . . to prevent an investigation.*" The *Dragnet* parodies indelibly established Freberg's reputation as a skilled, edgy satirist, and added the phrase "*Just the facts, ma'am*" to the language. Webb said that he'd only used the phrase a few times but, after the hit spoof, felt obliged to write it into scripts more often, until it became the show's signature line. "Christmas Dragnet" followed, in which Sergeant Friday tracks down a man who doesn't believe in Santa Claus.

Says Freberg: "I was just listening to it again and I realized the writing is flawless. I didn't do that great an impression of Jack Webb, but I got close enough with the music that, if you were in the next room

you would think *Dragnet* was on television. It really is a perfect parody."
While it solidified Freberg's name as a master satirist, it marked almost
the end of his pop-fad parody career. Soon after, he drifted into advertising, using his satirical gifts to peddle products, but not before creating
one last top seller, "Banana Boat," a zinger aimed at Harry Belafonte's
calypso blockbuster, "Day-O." Freberg says that Belafonte wasn't amused.
"He leapt back from me once at a party after it came out. I just felt Belafonte was yelling too much—and today he has terrible laryngitis, so it
turns out he *did* yell too much! If he'd only listened to me. He later
thanked me for helping to keep his career alive."

Freberg maintains that he was driven into advertising by the decay of
the record business, which had been taken over by teenagers, a phenomenon he roundly assailed with "The Old Payola Roll Blues"—a stinging
editorial on corrupt disc jockeys, adolescent pop stars, and the mob-
ridden record business. Not too surprisingly, the record got little airplay.
But Freberg's parodies were rarely savage. Their wit is in the precise
vocal and musical mimicry, and, most of all, in Freberg's canny skewering
of corny showbiz gimmicks and promotional hustles. He gives us an
insider's take not just on a hit song but on the mind-set that produced it.
Freberg had the media's number, which is what later made him such a
canny advertising man.

"BANANA BOAT" HELPED get Freberg the CBS radio show, where he
was given carte blanche. He grabbed it, but his satire was tougher than
CBS had bargained for. He ran aground on the first episode, July 14,
1957, with a "Freberg fable" called "Incident at Los Voraces" ("the greedy
ones"). Las Vegas is destroyed when a casino named Rancho Gomorrah,
in an attempt to outdraw a rival casino, El Sodom, books the hydro-
gen bomb into its big-show room. CBS made him change the bomb to
an earthquake, spoiling his carefully constructed anti-H-bomb theme.
Heard today, with the H-bomb restored, it's long and, for Freberg,
uncharacteristically heavy-handed. He's always worked best as a short-
form guy, from one to five minutes.

Taking on the H-bomb was far riskier than ribbing Lawrence Welk.
He says CBS "went into shock. It was like they were expecting maybe
Henny Youngman and got Jonathan Winters." The unreleased record had
Arab and Gaza Strip jokes (relevant to the 1956 Suez War), all cut by air-
time. Even defused, the "Incident at Los Voraces" show drew admiring

reviews in the New York papers ("He is the man responsible for bringing radio back to life," wrote the *Daily News*'s Kay Gardella). *Time*'s review said Freberg "served up 30 minutes of his exaggerated wildly allusive humor. If the network censors will just stay out of his hair, he promises to deliver a fresh bright new sound that may wrench people away from their TV sets." The *Los Angeles Times* called him "the funniest man currently riding the airwaves." Nevertheless, there was a distinct chill at CBS, which regarded Freberg as a dangerously explosive device.

Another sketch on the program attacked movies and Madison Avenue—much in the *MAD* magazine vein. In "A Gray Flannel Hat Full of Teenage Werewolves," a werewolf turns into a fanged half-monster advertising executive. Freberg told me with delight: "I met Tom Hanks at a black-tie dinner a few years ago. I went up to him and said, 'I admire your work very much. My name is Stan Freberg.' He said, 'Stan Freberg! "A Gray Flannel Hat Full of Teenage Werewolves"!' Everyone stared, looking up at him, like, What is wrong with Tom Hanks? He says, '*I look like a normal werewolf to the other werewolves, but what they don't know is, when the sun comes up, I can feel my fur turning into gray flannel. My hair becomes short and crew cut. . . .*' He did the whole thing! Knew it word for word."

That sort of thing happens a lot, he says. Ann Landers came up to him years ago and said, "Stan Freberg—you're a national treasure!" And he tells of being bowled over at Liza Minnelli's 2002 wedding, where he shyly went over to meet Anthony Hopkins: "Suddenly, this man is on his feet, pumping my hand. He kept saying, 'Stan Freberg! My idol! What an honor, sir! *What an honor!* It was worth coming to this wedding just to meet Stan Freberg!' Who knew? He told me, 'I grew up in England with all of your records. I knew them all by heart. I used to perform "St. George and the Dragonet" all by myself, doing all the voices.' It's a very rewarding thing to think that I'd affected people's lives in different ways."

Freberg went beyond taunting potential radio sponsors. He demanded the power to veto commercials that made him squirm—mainly for deodorants and cigarettes. This didn't further endear him to the network, which killed the show after fifteen weeks—despite good ratings, the star says—claiming that nobody wanted to sponsor him, which planted the seed of Freberg's ongoing love-hate relationship with advertising. He had become, he said, "the snail darter of network radio comedians"—the last network-radio comedy star. A later collection, *The Best of the Stan Freberg Shows,* won a 1958 Grammy. His "St. George and the Dragonet" parody was also the first comedy record to win a gold record.

Undaunted, Freberg proposed a TV show, *Frebergland*. Much too far out for the CBS suits, it was full of wild Ernie Kovacs–style sight gags that targeted sensitive areas—like the corporate logo, the CBS eye. "CBS was very square at this point," he recalls. "I got off on the wrong foot with my own show with the CBS eye logo takeoff." (His producer warned him, "You don't fool around with the eye.") Freberg also took a shot at TV's voracious appetite for salacious material: a producer yells for "a little more sex and gratuitous violence" as scripts are shoveled into the camera lens. "Too esoteric," said the producer. "*Way-y-y* over the audience's head. We may find that funny, but, hey, do they care about that in Peoria?"

That argument, which still pervades TV-think, set the stage for Freberg's lifelong fight on behalf of Peorians everywhere, who would become far more media-smart by the time Freberg got through with them. Like Mort Sahl, Nichols & May, Tom Lehrer, and other renaissance satirists whose material was deemed too cerebral, Freberg trusted the audience to "get it." A perfect example is his prescient anti–political correctness parody, "Elderly Man River," ahead of its time by two generations. In the course of a performance of "Ol' Man River," Freberg is interrupted by a buzzer pushed by a timid network censor whenever he sings a word deemed objectionable, or ungrammatical, with this final, ingeniously sanitized result:

> *Elderly Man River,*
> *That Elderly Man River,*
> *He must know something*
> *But he doesn't say anything,*
> *He just keeps rolling,*
> *He just keeps rolling along. . . .*
>
> *You and I, we perspire and strain . . .*

Freberg recalls that after he used TV's Lone Ranger and Tonto, Clayton Moore and Jay Silverheels, in a Jeno's Pizza commercial, an executive from ABC called and said, "'We need a letter from Mr. Silverheels, saying he's not offended at being cast in a stereotypical role.' I said, 'He's *Tonto*, for God's sake! What do you mean, a stereotypical role? He's made a living all his life being Tonto!' So I called him up. He told me to read it back to him and Jay said, 'You're putting me on! I'll sign the form, and tell that dame to stop screwing around with my residuals.'" In another of Freberg's wry put-downs of political correctness, we hear a Cisco Kid–

like cowboy (Freberg) say, "*Come on, Pedro,*" to which Pedro replies, "*Sí, amigo. We leave mucho pronto.*" A woman asks: "*Where did he come from?*" Cowboy: "*Pedro? He materializes at the end of each episode.*" Woman: "*Is he Mexican?*" Pedro: "*No, señorita. Swees. Thees way we don't offend no-body.*"

Freberg upgraded American satire with inside pop-music jokes about echo chambers, instruments, and singers, with self-referential asides. His "Sh-Boom" parody is about a guy trying to cut a hit record with schlocky electronic tricks. His full-length record masterpiece, *Stan Freberg Presents the United States of America, Volume I,* is loaded with public-relations-speak. He let the audience in on the act itself. Freberg's songs and sketches, jammed with showbiz cant and PR jargon, foreshadowed Mort Sahl, Lenny Bruce, Bob Newhart, and Nichols & May.

An auteur satirist who fussed over every sound and syllable, Freberg took it upon himself to write the copy for his radio show's commercials, which upset his CBS producer, Hubbell Robinson. "We have agencies to do that," Robinson told him, to which Freberg replied acidly, "Yes, I've seen their work." He would later tell an audience at a Museum of Television and Radio tribute, "I went into the advertising business as a totally outraged consumer." His then outlandish position was that the commercials should be as funny as the show. "What if people actually stayed in the room to watch the commercials on purpose?" he proposed. That stumped Robinson, who hadn't heard of Freberg's much-quoted first commercial a year earlier, in 1956, for Contadina tomato paste ("*Who puts eight great tomatoes in that little bitty can?*"), still a landmark jingle and Freberg's first leap onto Madison Avenue. *Advertising Age* dubbed him "the father of the funny commercial," and *Time* said he showed Madison Avenue "that the commercial could be a miniature work of art." His commercials all had the gloss of crafted revue sketches or Broadway moments, with music from a robust chorus and snappy arrangements.

The Contadina campaign ultimately promoted Freberg as much as it did canned tomatoes. Almost overnight he became an advertising virtu-oso. "Without realizing it," Freberg wrote, "I had more or less created a new form." And although the staid agency types chose to regard his funny commercials as flukes, he presented a Frebergian commandment to all advertisers: "They could take an ad or leave it, but they couldn't change it." Freberg's droll writing, delivery, and packaging on radio and TV have since been imitated so often that they've become comic clichés in the hands of others much less deft. "I feel like I opened up a Pandora's box. I want all those creative people to go back in the closet. I just yell at the TV set all the time. My family gave me a rubber brick. I always say to my family, 'Okay, what was the idea of that commercial? What are they trying to say?'"

When he tried to persuade CBS to let him make the commercials as funny as the rest of his 1957 radio show, Freberg recalls, "They told me, 'Look, kid, satire is hard enough to sell in the program area. God forbid we allow you to get it into the commercials. Furthermore, your type of humor is not compatible with the moving of consumer goods.' When I pointed out to him that I'd sold millions of Capitol records to *someone* out there, he said, 'Oh, well, those were record buyers; those weren't necessarily *consumers.*' I dug in my heels."

FREBERG STOPPED PRODUCING parody records when "Capitol drove a spike through my career as a single record artist by telling me, 'Nobody buys singles anymore. If you suddenly want to do a takeoff of someone, just make an album.' I had to lie down. I mean, the idea of doing twelve single-record cuts in an album! Before, if I wanted to do, say, 'Sh-Boom,' or whatever, I could do it and within ten days they could be pressing the record and have it out on the market. After that, I never made any more singles." He laughs his sardonic laugh. "I had to wait another twenty-five years to start becoming a legend."

In a life-changing decision, one day in 1957, while standing in the CBS parking lot, he said goodbye to radio. CBS had canned his summer comedy show, and rather than turn out "an emasculated show with all its satiric teeth removed"—the network wanted him to do a sitcom instead—"I decided to enter the advertising world in all seriousness. But from inside a Trojan horse. I said, 'I'm gonna prove that funny advertising sells products,' and that's when I started Freberg, Ltd. (But Not Very)," which helped him build his antiques-filled mansion, Stan Simeon. Freberg, who was remarried in 2001 to marketing consultant Betty Hunter, has two grown children from his first marriage to his late producer-wife Donna. For the company motto, he chose *Ars Gratia Pecuniae*—"art for money's sake," a takeoff on MGM's *Ars Gratia Artis*—emblazoned on a logo depicting his personal seal: a prototypical Hollywood type in sunglasses.

A few years later, one of his big clients was, yes, CBS. They lured him back to promote *Hogan's Heroes,* a 1965 sitcom about a Nazi POW camp that required a delicate comic touch. The commercial began with Freberg asking the show's star, Bob Crane, "Where does the show take place?" Crane replies, "In a Nazi prisoner-of-war camp in Germany." Freberg (deadpan): "Always a good situation-comedy locale." His *Hogan's Heroes* tag line is a definitive example of Freberg's outrageous style and strategy ("*If you liked World War II, you'll love* Hogan's Heroes").

Humor in advertising was virtually unknown, almost subversive, when Freberg opened up shop on Madison Avenue (Los Angeles branch). "I was the first, except for Bob & Ray," whose Piels Beer commercials were a huge hit. When David Ogilvy published his ten hard-and-fast rules for successful advertising, one of them was: "Humor in advertising doesn't work." So ad man Howard Gossage asked Ogilvy, "What about Freberg?" Ogilvy conceded, "Oh, well, I didn't mean Freberg." Freberg, who howls as he retells the anecdote, broke advertising rules he didn't even know existed.

The conventional Madison Avenue wisdom is that people who laugh at a funny commercial often forget what it's selling, to which Freberg replies, "I defy *anybody* to look or listen to any of my commercials and walk away confused about the name of the product. For example, Sunsweet pitted prunes: just the one TV spot ['*Today the pits . . . Tomorrow the wrinkles!*'], with no radio or magazine support, sales went up four hundred percent." Nobody produced more talked-about commercials—like the Chun King gem that depicts ten doctors, nine of them Chinese, as a voice intones, "*Nine out of ten doctors recommend Chun King chow mein.*" He also dreamed up a group of Chinese folksingers, the Chun Kingston Trio. As in many Freberg commercials, he twits advertising as a kind of secondary joke, a way of having his cake and satirizing it, too.

Freberg saw himself as the brain surgeon of last resort, called in to operate when all hope is gone, who saves the patient. He welcomed lost causes, such as a commercial for churchgoing ("I feel I was destined to do more than just move chow mein off the shelf") and a political commercial on behalf of the 1970 McGovern-Hatfield Amendment to cut off funding for the Vietnam War, his hardest-hitting commercial. In it, a Pentagon spokesman boasts of reducing the body count to thirty-eight American men a week and a spokesman for American Business Machine & Body-Count reports that his firm's new "Vietnamatic 3" can tabulate corpses even faster and give "a quick rundown on left ears for April."

When Freberg was wrong, even his mistakes became classics, notably the famous "white knuckle" fear-of-flying commercial he wrote for Pacific Air Lines. "*Hey, there, you with the sweat in your palms,*" it began, and went on to acknowledge that the pilots themselves were a little scared on occasion. It didn't run long, forced two PAL executives to resign, and soon after the campagn ended the airline merged. But Freberg was back in the news.

He was in and out of trouble with his TV specials. In a sketch with a back-of-the-bus joke, a worried network censor asked him, "Is that an integration joke?" and Freberg responded, "No, it's a carbon-monoxide joke." A series of shows that he coauthored for NBC in 1956 were rejected for lacking "scope," so he wrote one final episode, called "Scope." His epic scheme for a margarine client was thwarted—he had planned to carve three-hundred-foot likenesses of Fats Domino and Mary Margaret McBride out of oleomargarine, in the style of Mount Rushmore. Another idea that went aground was his advertising theme park, Frebergland, featuring a huge glass head with draining sinus cavities.

The hardheaded Freberg has occasionally bumped heads with equally defiant corporate clients. A Kaiser Aluminum executive once slammed him up against a wall and snarled, "Let's get one thing absolutely straight. You work for us, okay?" The downside of hiring him, as one agency man put it, is that "once you hire Freberg, you have no control over him. There's always blood on the wall." He also was expensive (in 1963 he was charging about $55,000 per campaign), which is how he kept control. The *New York Times* dubbed him "the Che Guevara of advertising." He adds, "The amazing part is that I still had to argue with advertisers even after they *came* to me and *hired* me, knowing what I did."

Freberg's most inspired, lasting work was neither his clever jingles nor his hit parody singles, all of which had the transient life of topical satire. Rather, it was *Stan Freberg Presents the United States of America,* a lavish musical-revue LP, a 1961 masterwork that has enjoyed a secure cult status for forty years. It holds up beautifully, not only because it's stylishly produced but because history holds up, and so do Freberg's jokes and references; the songs still pay off, as do the sketches (cowritten with Ken Sullet, who, Freberg says, wrote about 10 percent of the material). *USA* remains Freberg at his best. Finally, under persistent pressure from fans of the original album who had been waiting for that other satirical shoe to drop, Freberg released his long-promised volume II in 1996; subtitled *The Middle Years,* it picks up the story from the end of the Civil War and goes up to the Depression.

Time said volume I was "arguably the best comedy album ever made." The *Los Angeles Times* called it "The *Sgt. Pepper* of comedy albums." But the sequel, like most sequels, is less satisfying than the original; the comparatively limp, drawn-out sketches and thinner songs suggest he perhaps waited too long, until his reliable comic curveball had lost some of its old satirical zing. For the sequel, Freberg used many of the same collaborators—Foray, Peter Leeds, Jesse White, conductor-composer Billy May—but added several contemporary voices: John Goodman, Harry Shearer, David Ogden Stiers, and Tyne Daly, all of whom grew up listening to, indeed memorizing, volume I. (He's now working on volume III.) Daly introduced herself to Freberg by sidling up to him and murmuring in his ear a line from his Columbus-discovers-America sketch, in which a sailor tells Columbus, "*Captain, there are rumblings of mutiny,*" and the crew chants, "*Rumble rumble rumble, mutiny mutiny mutiny.*"

Freberg devotees bond instantly by quoting snatches from the album, such as (after a line of tap-dancing Indians runs through a number in celebration of the first Thanksgiving): "*Hey, you get a pretty good sound outta dem moccasins!*" Or singing a few bars from "Take an Indian to Lunch This Week," needling the National Brotherhood Week slogan. The Beatles, boasts Freberg, knew all his records by heart. In fact, when asked in a 1984 *Playboy* interview where the Beatles got their sense of humor, Paul McCartney said it partly came from listening to Lenny Bruce and Stan Freberg records.

The original album, which took fourteen weeks to record, is Freberg at his most ambitious and surprising. He wrote nearly every line, lyric, and note on it (apart from Billy May's musical bridges), just as he has written the commercials and the lyrics to his parodies. The *USA* numbers are so vivid that you can see them being performed in your head, which may be where they belong, although album diehards still dream of seeing the record produced for the stage in full theatrical finery. The songs are as knowing and tuneful as those of a sparkling Broadway musical. Freberg brought all his gifts into play in such numbers as "A Man Can't Be Too Careful What He Signs These Days," which finds a fusty Ben Franklin reluctant to sign the Declaration of Independence thrust on him by a hot-blooded Thomas Jefferson, who croons, "*Come on and put your name / On the dotted line.*" Franklin: "*I gotta be particular what / I sign.*" Jefferson: "*Come on and put your signature / On the list.*" Franklin: "*It looks to have a very / Subversive twist.*" Jefferson: "*How silly to assume it. / Won't you nom de plume it / Today-y-y . . .*" Jefferson: "*You're so skittish. / Who possibly could care if you do?*" Franklin: "*The Un-British / Activities Committee, that's who!*" In Freberg's routine about the Boston Tea Party, an inept Puritan unwittingly sparks the Revolutionary War by clumsily dumping tea into Boston Harbor. Washington crosses the Delaware but dawdles over which of three rental boats to take, finally settling on the one with Donald Duck painted on the side; then, while posing for the famous painting, he frets that his jacket isn't right for him as an impatient adviser insists, "*It's* you! *It's* you!"

The numbers, characteristically, are laced with showbiz gags and groaners, a Freberg trademark. After a fanfare, a character asks, "*What was that?*" and is told, "*French horns,*" a classic Frebergian joke. An aide tells Freberg's character, "*The natives may be hostile.*" Freberg: "*Well, we're all a little hostile now and then. Some of us try to sublimate, while others . . .*" Freberg (as himself): "*We going out on that joke?*" Indian grunts: "*No, we reprise song. That help.*" Together, singsongy: "*Yeah, but not mu-u-ch.*" On such lines are cults constructed; whenever Freberg speaks, fans, known as "Frebies," arrive clutching battered albums for him to sign.

The most infuriating episode of Freberg's generally happy creative life was his nightmarish experience with producer David Merrick, who optioned the *USA* revue for Broadway and lived up to his reputation as the "Abominable Showman." He jerked Freberg around for a year, changing his mind willy-nilly, humiliating and slowly grinding down the usually ungrindable Freberg. Merrick remarked to him after their first meeting, "I like your arrogance. We'll get along just fine." But Freberg was no match for him. After four years of jumping through hoops for Merrick, he bowed out, a beaten man, unable to please the producer, who at one point ordered him to "take Lincoln out of the Civil War [sketch]. They'll never miss him." Freberg is still determined to mount a production, if only to regain his position as the pop industry's ace satirist.

Whether creating record parodies or pitching products, Freberg stands alone as an innovator in two seemingly opposite comedy worlds without ever having changed either his satirical attitude or his inimitable style. Inherent in almost every Freberg commercial, in fact, is some element that deflates the world of advertising. He used prunes or chow mein or chicken soup as excuses to indulge his wit, giving commercials a playfulness they rarely had before him. Freberg used every sort of literary and theatrical device to frame his commercials: *Moby-Dick*'s Captain Ahab chooses Pittsburgh Paint color chips to help track the white whale; a Gilbert & Sullivan–style patter song peddles Meadowgold Milk; and a thwarted showbiz potato chip, Irving Bell, finally gets to go onstage in a musical when the star potato chip he understudies is injured. Disciple Jeff Goodby, no slouch himself at devising funny commercials ("Got milk?"

etc.), says Freberg was his idol growing up in the late fifties. "Freberg crossed the wires of the grown-up world in ways that got to the truth," Goodby writes. "Freberg was the gatekeeper to this promised land. For a long time, he printed the tickets."

Stan Freberg's deadpan satirical commercials influenced advertising for decades. He could say more in a sixty-second spot than many comedy film directors in an hour. Goodby also remarks on the distinctive Freberg voice, noting, "Consciously or unconsciously, Stan's tone and timing have been emulated by everyone from the Firesign Theater to Garrison Keillor. It's a sound that captures our collective powerlessness in the face of the Big Selling Machine. It is the voice of us—or at least a smarter, wittier version of ourselves. While most advertisers and entertainers talk down to us, Stan treats us as an equal. He presumes we've got a terrific sense of humor. It makes all the difference."

The aging and ever-outraged Freberg, meanwhile, sits in his living room, shouts at the TV set, and regularly hurls his rubber brick at the screen.

Televisionary

Ernie Kovacs

It's no fun if you play it safe all the time.

ERNIE KOVACS RAN his own art form in the 1950s that consisted of scrawling a mustache on the face of television. You can't examine the comedy revolution of the fifties without getting around, sooner or later, to Kovacs, even though he wasn't a stand-up comedian or a standard satirist—or a standard anything. He was an idiosyncratic outsider who never quite conquered the medium he loved. His love for television, despite three Emmy nominations, went largely unrequited.

Kovacs didn't tackle social or political issues; he had no specific targets. He created anarchic comedy out of the raw tools of television—TV clichés, conventional storytelling techniques, movies, and music. A comic surrealist, he was to TV what Dalí was to painting, what Spike Jones was to music, what Busby Berkeley was to choreography. In the words of his widow, the singer Edie Adams, "He had the gift of silliness."

Kovacs can't be boxed into comedy's usual confines, least of all the cramped container that is network TV. Television had no idea what to do with him and barely endured him, although many in TV have been busily praising him since his death, in 1962. It was often said that Kovacs was years ahead of his time, but his time still has not arrived. He was a satirical cosmos unto himself. His visual vignettes, in which he used the TV screen as his personal Etch A Sketch, defy description, just as his objects that danced before our eyes defied gravity. One producer said, "Ernie wasn't in show business at all. He was in Ernie business. He was in his own world." *Time*'s William A. Henry III called him TV's only auteur performer. Robin Williams observes: "It was kind of Dada comedy. Berle was doing his stuff, Sid Caesar was doing great movie parodies, but Kovacs was doing stuff you'd never seen before."

Television was quickly entranced and just as quickly baffled by him. TV gets jittery around genius and has never easily tolerated, let alone nurtured, original comic minds. He came along, alas, too late for silent movies, this Mack Sennett of the airwaves who grappled, à la Chaplin,

Keaton, and Jacques Tâti (a Kovacs hero), with modern life and mechanization. He was totally gag-oriented and might have found a home today on cable TV, which welcomes mavericks and wacky visual jokes.

Kovacs's main problem was that a little of him went a long way, and even his finest humor amounted to variations on the same gag, a virtual unreality in which inanimate objects have a mind and spirit of their own—clock hands come alive, ceramic cows moo, a hydrant squirts a nearby dog, a moose's body is mounted on the other side of the wall from which his head protrudes. His scathing parodies of TV shows were reminiscent of radio's Henry Morgan and Fred Allen—for example, an elaborate game show in which first prize is an appendectomy.

Until 1985, when Edie Adams finally gained control of his tapes, there were only about twenty hours of Kovacs available. Most of his work was lost or destroyed. ABC had erased half of their Kovacs shows and Adams spent $400,000 to buy back the remaining half, some of which is seen sporadically on cable's Comedy Central. Of all Kovacs's astonishing feats, perhaps the most amazing is that he was able to convince stations and, later, networks to give him a show at all. He insisted on free rein to create his own free-form video comedy. He used TV, but was not *of* TV, was never part of the industry mind-set. As Steve Allen noted, "It is odd that a performer who specialized in a humor that absolutely depended upon the television camera was never really taken to television's heart"—neither by the public nor by the industry.

He probably could not have created the work he did at any other time in television history, arriving before TV had become a creative quagmire, and before all the formats had been frozen. At one point, in the early 1950s, he was writing and starring in three separate ventures—a network TV show, a local TV show, and a radio show. Ten years later he likely would have had no shows. As it was, he hung on by his tenacious fingernails; never really popular with the mass audience, he hosted low-rated shows in dead-end time slots. *Kovacs Unlimited, The Ernie Kovacs Show,* and *Kovacs on the Korner* were pitted against entrenched monoliths—Sid Caesar, *Today,* Ed Sullivan. He cultivated small but avid audiences.

Kovacs dashed all conceptions of what TV was supposed to be, breaking the fourth (glass) wall with merry abandon—and always live. He both reinvented television and cut it down to size, reshaping TV's video canvas into his own warped and whimsical image, turning the tube into a funhouse mirror of moving objects that he controlled like an electronic puppeteer. Kovacs and Lewis Carroll were similar warped comic spirits. In his topsy-turvy universe, all the natural laws of visual logic and physics were suspended for an hour. Viewers became a collective Alice, tumbling into a video rabbit hole where water flows uphill, a shooting gallery target fires back, and an angry viewer assaults a lousy TV performer. William A. Henry noticed "a faint aura of menace" and "a tyranny of things" in what he called Kovacs's "dime-store guerrilla theater."

Flipping graphic one-liners, he toyed with time and space, moving images around on the screen with a childlike joy. Bizarre images cascaded out of Kovacs's twisted comic imagination: a saw cuts off a tree limb and the tree falls, not the branch; his beard vanishes the instant a razor touches it; a woman in a tub is invaded by a periscope rising out of the bubbles, and when she pulls the plug the tub putt-putts away (one of his many girl-in-a-bathtub gags); a lady tosses a flower onto a piano and the piano crashes through the floor; a cowboy riddled with bullets lights up a cigar and, as he puffs on it, smoke pours out through the bullet holes.

Kovacs loved musical gags—celery stalks snapping loudly instead of cannon shots during Tchaikovsky's *1812 Overture,* a painting tangoing to "Jealousy." Like Victor Borge and Peter Schickele, he used music as a catapult to launch audacious visual jokes. His most famous and long-running gag was the Nairobi Trio—true gorilla theater—which featured three people in ape suits playing a strangely macabre Kurt Weill–ish tune, "Solfeggio," in the herky-jerky style of a mechanical toy. It became his signature creation, a gag that, like so much of Kovacs, is visually compelling and inspired but defies analysis.

He scoffed at all attempts to analyze his work, saying, "I don't know, I just do it. I just close my eyes and whatever pops out of the back of my head goes down on paper and eventually gets on the screen." Moments fraught with symbolic meaning for serious Kovacs scholars, says Edie Adams, were often just ways of Kovacs killing airtime with whatever prop was at hand. His jokes were totally generic, seldom topical or social; Adams says he had no politics. His major cause was TV, its uses and abuses.

Networks didn't trust him, though he appealed to an audience beyond the bicoastal hip. Adams says, "Everyone—CEOs and milkmen and truckers—felt they were the only ones who truly understood him. He was everyone's subconscious." Kovacs just shrugged and said, "The people I respect get it. It might take everyone else a little longer."

It would be nice to say that Kovacs influenced TV comedians, but *impressed* is much closer to the truth. Nobody in TV ever took up where he left off: when he died, precious few TV shows attempted the kind of sight gags he devised. Kovacs's apolcalyptic cartoons about the world died with him. The zany sight gags that later popped up on *Rowan and Martin's Laugh-In* were faintly Kovacsesque; Dan Rowan later confessed that *Laugh-In* had regularly ripped off Kovacs. But *Laugh-In* relied mainly on revue-style blackouts speeded up for the show's split-second pace; Kovacs's gags built carefully.

Comedy archaeologists search for remnants of Kovacs's whacked-out wit in comedians like Jonathan Winters, John Belushi, Steve Martin, David Letterman, Robin Williams, Garry Shandling, and Chevy Chase, who hired former Kovacs writers and studied his tapes; Letterman's trademark broken-glass sound effect is a particularly Kovacsian touch. But it's hard to find any other traces of Kovacs on anyone else's show today.

Nobody really could imitate Kovacs because nobody *was* Kovacs, with his twisted turn of mind. Biographers cite a few shows—*Monty Python's Flying Circus, SCTV, The Benny Hill Show, Mr. Bean*—as possessing Kovacs-inspired touches: quick cutting, erased images, actors stepping through the screen. At the end of an hour of his wildly surreal gags, he would stare at the camera and, deadpan, sign off with "It's been real."

He was a devotee of the Kitchen Sink school of comedy, in which everything—and especially the kitchen sink—was a resource. For Kovacs, more was more. He hated studio audiences, because they had to watch a monitor to get the visual jokes, and he banned laugh tracks. "If the guys on the crew laugh, you've got a hit," he would say. He cared only about the home audience, but even his network shows had the no-frills informality and intimacy of a local show fattened up with a big budget.

Prior to Kovacs, and forever after him, most TV comedy has been limited to sketches and parodies. Even Sid Caesar's *Your Show of Shows,* the most satirical TV comedy show of that era, remained within the rigid format of the stage revue. In her memoir of her life with Kovacs, Adams observed, "Not having grown up in either vaudeville or nightclubs, he had no perceived notions" of TV comedy's boundaries. His favorite comedian was Shecky Greene, whose comic bravura Kovacs identified with. Kovacs's wit was entirely nonlinear, totally sight- and sound-based. Nobody in any medium has ever blended visual and aural gags as well, wedding radio to television in a new way; his closest disciple was Benny Hill, the British TV comic who created a similar surreal vaudeville.

Kovacs's impressionism and visual puns were like animated Saul Steinberg cartoons, like the kettle drummer who pounds his drum and finds himself up to his elbows in milky goo; Red Skelton later stole the gag. He was especially fond of trap doors, partly because the old stages on which he did his early shows were equipped with them. In the manner of Buster Keaton, a lot of Kovacs's ten-second gags, such as the famous collapsing car (a TV used-car pitchman pats the hood of an automobile that falls to pieces), required elaborate, expensive preparations; he once assembled a full choir to sing two words, "Buy gum." Kovacs was willing to take time to wind up a gag and let it gradually unravel. "He did things with sound effects nobody does today because nobody will *wait* the time that it takes to do them," said Mike Marmer, a veteran Kovacs writer. "It was a much more leisurely paced kind of comedy. He would play a three-minute sound effect for one laugh."

His comedy provoked more grins than laugh-out-loud guffaws. A lot of Kovacs's sight gags and camera tricks can be tracked to silent comedies. Andrew McKay, an early member of Kovacs's crew, once said that the comic must have been affected by Mack Sennett's "nearly surreal comedies, in which Sennett almost penetrated the sacred domain of animation cartoons—by having his actors and the direction, plus photography, do things almost humanly impossible." Kovacs's people and objects obeyed their own rules of behavior: a wristwatch chimes like Big Ben, an hourglass ticks, Ernie twists the knobs on a TV set while contorting his face vertically and diagonally as he tunes himself in. Songs crooned by Adams are interrupted by sight gags playing off the song title; when she mimed singing "Bye Bye Blackbird," out of her mouth flew the voice of Louis Armstrong. The movie critic Jan Wahl called him "the Fellini of TV."

The pert, curvy Adams was ever the good sport, a pretty sitting duck for Kovacs's sight gags, including pies in the face. At first, she felt like a magician's assistant, a human prop. Encouraged by Kovacs, the singer became a wicked impressionist, specializing in Marilyn Monroe. Behind the scenes, Adams was much more than a performer: she also designed costumes, charted musical arrangements, concocted ideas, and pitched in wherever needed.

Adams once remarked, "I spent ten years trying to explain Ernie," a man who, she says, "dedicated his life to staying a child," a ten-year-old in an adult's body who never took anything seriously. "Life for Ernie was recess," and TV his glass-enclosed sandbox. "What Ernie taught me was what he tried to teach the television audience—that life was a romp."

He was also a sentimental lug who wept whenever she sang "Scarlet Ribbons." Kovacs had pursued Adams avidly with jewelry, candlelit dinners in fancy restaurants, and a romantic, larger-than-life personality. When he suddenly pressed an engagement ring on her, she had no answer, so he told her to wear it until she made up her mind. He hired a mariachi band to serenade her backstage at a Broadway musical she was in. Says Adams, "I came from a very uptight Presbyterian family, and I never knew anybody like this."

An NBC executive said Kovacs got ruled out as host of *The Tonight Show* because of his "lack of discipline" (i.e., he couldn't be controlled), but he was far too over-the-top for even a non-prime-time national audience. Steve Allen, a fan of most comics, never found Kovacs all that amusing ("He was more original than he was funny"). Yet Kovacs, despite a naturally rubber face, was, like Allen, the perfect implacable foil for his own manic gags. He was always in the service of the joke, a straight man plugged into himself via Kovacsial cable.

ERNEST KOVACS BEGAN his shenanigans on WTTM radio in his hometown of Trenton, New Jersey, where he also wrote a column, before moving to Philadelphia as the freewheeling host of a local TV cooking show, *Deadline for Dinner*—which he called "Dead Lion for Dinner." He then hosted, in 1950, a local wake-up show, *Three to Get Ready,* a two-hour morning TV program with no format on which Kovacs played records and drew funny sketches during the songs before everything erupted into general horseplay.

"Whatever we wanted to do with those two hours was fine with the station," said Joe Behar, Kovacs's first director. On a local station in the early days of TV, when the stakes were low and few people owned sets, you could do what you pleased and viewers would love it, if only for the novelty. Kovacs tried everything and didn't care if a gag bombed. Few TV performers had any ideas then, and Kovacs had nothing *but* ideas.

Because he couldn't sit still on-camera, he began mixing it up—making funny faces, messing with the set and crew, shinnying up a rope, invading the control booth. "He'd be up all night scribbling things down," an ad man on the show said, "but he would appear to be ad-libbing everything. He actually did a lot of homework. He thought about it a lot. He worked hard at it." Kovacs often worked all night in an office behind a closed glass door on which he had painted *NOT NOW.*

The Ernie Kovacs Show burst onto the national scene in May 1952, pit-ting him against the hottest personality in TV, Milton Berle. Kovacs had all of one week to prepare, plus a low budget and, as usual, no studio audience. But that was fine with him—he hated rehearsing. Adams once said, "I came from a family that had a conference on whether to cross the street. Ernie planned nothing in advance." He rarely mapped out a routine. He carried the entire show around in his head and knew precisely what he wanted. While he may have seemed disorganized to some, everything was organized in his teeming mind.

Kovacs would arrive at production meetings with a precise list of props and bark, "I need two olives six millimeters long. I need two cups of cotton. I need a tiger. And wardrobe, I need a bow tie. I want a toothpick. What size toothpicks do you have?" His personal comic vision ruled out any second-guessing, although some wondered privately why any olives wouldn't do. "It was his voice or no one's," Adams says. "If you didn't agree, he'd leave. Usually, just his threatening to leave would do it."

Kovacs couldn't be cowed. Adams says: "When they wanted to run a talking commercial with his all-silent special, 'Eugene,' he stood up, put his hat on, and said, 'You better get a cowboy film ready.' He didn't care. He really wasn't interested in the money; he was interested in what he was doing, and they couldn't do that to him." During a meeting in which the director vetoed several of his ideas, Kovacs said, "Excuse me, I have to make a phone call," and exited, leaving behind his coat, muffler, and gloves and, in mid-January, walked from Fiftieth Street, Rockefeller Center, to his home on Ninetieth Street in his suit and shirt. Both the critics and the public turned out for his silent show. Jack Gould wrote in the *New York Times,* "Why Mr. Kovacs does not yet have a regular prime evening spot for his efforts is hard to understand. Behind all his foolishness lie both taste and a mind." Harriet Van Horne wrote of *Ernie in Kovacsland* that while some of his nonsense was a "creaky bore," much of it was touched with "true moonlit madness."

He didn't rely entirely on weird imagery and sight gags, the fanciful nonsense he's most remembered for now; he also did his share of parodying movies, TV shows, and commercials: *Mr. Science, Mr. and Mrs. South, Pathetic News* (a riff on the ubiquitous Pathé newsreels of the day), and an evil send-up of *Howdy Doody* in which a drunken puppet-master snips Howdy's strings—the CNN commentator Jeff Greenfield, in an appreciation of Kovacs, called it "one of the great subversive moments of early television." Greenfield argues that Kovacs was saying, in effect, "Don't just lie back passively and let all this wash over you—*pay attention.*" As Armistead Maupin remarked at a 1999 Kovacs tribute at the Mill Valley (California) Film Festival: "The TV was watching back."

He never broke through in a major way because he never had the budget, the network support, or the ratings. His devoted patron was Dutch Masters cigars, whose clever commercials Kovacs created. Adams became a longtime spokeswoman for the company's Muriel label—exhaling, in a slinky Mae West delivery, "Why don't you pick me up and smoke me sometime?" Kovacs's giant (Cuban) cigar was not just a prop; for him it was a way of life. He was offended by cheap cigars. "Everything had to be the best, the latest, and the biggest!" Adams remembers. "He'd get up in the morning and say, 'This is the *greatest* orange juice!' or 'the most *fantastic* coffee!' Manic, you know?"

Kovacs was television's Orson Welles—embattled but unbowed, a genius and a giant, and, to be sure, a prophet without honor in his own medium. Like Welles, he was a large, flamboyant man, one who held conferences while smoking in a bathtub with a drink in one hand; also like Welles, he won awards and praise while still struggling for financial backing. Kovacs was an acquired taste who always seemed to be working at cross-purposes with TV, an avant-garde satirist in a mass medium—Andy Warhol submitting covers to the *Saturday Evening Post.* "Everybody was crazy about him, but he didn't have big numbers," concedes Adams.

A former production assistant said that, for all of his inventiveness, Kovacs could be lazy and undisciplined, often relying on old scripts and not always devoting the time to work out gags or new scripts properly; he spent a lot of time playing poker away from the set. "The skits were hysterically funny when they came off," production assistant Mitzi Matravers told his biographer, Diana Rico. "But he was ill prepared and not putting in the time, and the money was slight."

Midway through the first season of *Kovacs on the Korner,* he tore the set down and went back to New York. One reason Kovacs didn't always put in the time on shows and could be found playing cards with money he couldn't afford to lose was that his personal life was a jumble. He was preoccupied with tracking down the two daughters he had legal custody of; his ex-wife, who had deserted the family, had later kidnapped the girls. In what Rico contends was the first case of a father winning custody from a mother who was alive, well, and not in jail, Kovacs spent a fortune, several years, and much emotional energy trying to locate his children via private investigators. He finally found his daughters, who wound up in his custody after a bitter court battle. Meanwhile, he spent lavishly on himself, Adams, and others.

Out in Hollywood, exiled from TV, he more or less lost his way and was "a hounded man," said Doubleday editor Ken McCormick, a friend, who reported that Kovacs's marriage to Edie was shaky after he moved to Los Angeles to make movies. "They just didn't accept me," Kovacs told the columnist Louis Sobel. When he finally agreed to take any movie work he could get, in order to pay off growing tax and gambling debts (he played in high-stakes card games with Frank Sinatra, Milton Berle, Tony Curtis, Billy Wilder, and Dean Martin), he was cast, oddly, in non-comic secondary best-friend roles in *Our Man in Havana; Operation Mad Ball; Wake Me When It's Over; Bell, Book, and Candle; Strangers When We Meet;* and *Sail a Crooked Ship.* He turned out to be a surprisingly solid, if wasted, dramatic actor. In Hollywood he wasn't impressed by the medium or by its big shots. He once told the iron-fisted producer Harry Cohn to "fuck off!"—the beginning of a beautiful friendship. Kovacs was drawn to showbiz swashbucklers like himself—Cohn, Mike Todd, Jackie Gleason.

To pay his debts, he obediently popped up on panel shows, anthology series, and as a guest on variety programs, but his video comic days were behind him by the close of the fifties. He had a last hurrah in 1960 called *Kovacs on Music,* a charmingly loopy variation on Leonard Bernstein's TV music classes, from "Chopsticks" (dancers leaping on a giant piano keyboard) to Tchaikovsky's *Swan Lake* (ten apes in tutus).

Dutch Masters hired him for three TV specials that he sloughed off as the shows sailed way over budget. One day, Adams got a frantic call from an alarmed producer who told her, "Ernie is goofing off and we're into triple overtime." He was starting to exceed even Kovacs standards for strange behavior. He also began spending money he owed the IRS (some $200,000), plus another quarter of a million dollars owed to ABC for overtime costs to finance his outlandish bits. Then there were huge gambling IOUs. For Kovacs, gambling was his life, his career, and the mark of his comedy. All he had left was $50,000 stashed away in a buried safe in his cellar.

Not long after Kovacs bought a leopard to accessorize Adams's leopard-skin coat, two IRS men turned up at his house, put the couple on an allowance, and ordered them to take any legitimate job offers. Adams recalls, "We got socked for everything. They attached our house, everything we owned," which explains why, in 1958, Ernie Kovacs found himself on a Las Vegas stage with his wife, reviving his old Percy Dovetonsils character, a lisping, silk-bathrobe-wearing poet with painted-on novelty-shop spectacles, said to be based on Alexander Woollcott's epicine persona.

He had several movie projects pending on the night of January 12, 1962, when, returning from a party at Billy Wilder's home, Kovacs reached into a coat pocket for a cigar, took his hands off the wheel momentarily, and his Corvair skidded on a slippery road, jumped a median, and struck a telephone pole. He died a few hours later. Adams relates in her memoir that Dean Martin's wife remembered talking to Kovacs at the party earlier that night: "He told me he felt exhausted and was depressed about his finances, especially because Edie had to go to work. He didn't mind her working, just that she *had* to." Adams says he never felt he would live long. "It's not in the cards, baby," he'd tell her. His gravestone reads: "Nothing in Moderation."

Mom from Mars

Phyllis Diller

I thought I was a normal person.

———————

BEFORE PHYLLIS DILLER FIRST FLAPPED onstage like Big Bird's mother, the idea of a woman standing before an audience and telling jokes was a foreign, almost forbidden, notion. Diller wasn't the first woman stand-up comedian, but she was the first to make it respectable, to drag female comedy out of the gay bars, back rooms, and low-rent resorts and go toe-to-toe with her male counterparts in prime clubs.

She was no card-carrying feminist but, in her own unquiet way, Diller busted down barriers that had kept women stand-up comics in their place in the 1950s—raunchy broads like Belle Barth, Rusty Warren, Ruth Wallis, and Pearl Williams. The few other funny girls around were curiosities—Bea Lillie, Minnie Pearl, Cass Daley, Anna Russell, Judy Canova, essentially music-hall performers and Grand Ole Opry hands— or revue clowns like Martha Raye, Nancy Walker, Imogene Coca, Kaye Ballard, Carol Burnett.

The blue women comics were pioneers, lusty and busty Jewish mamas cut from the Sophie Tucker cloth, and now mostly forgotten. They were verbal strippers, and to succeed they told crude jokes and sang in metallic voices, brassy female *tummlers* who, on small underground labels, recorded so-called party records on a level with Redd Foxx's under-the-counter recordings but laced with Yiddishisms. The album titles told the story—*Knockers Up!, Sin-sational, Rusty Warren Bounces Back*. Their bawdy songs and jokes were laid on with a sledgehammer, full of gags about enemas, foreskins, and a man who sings through his rectum.

Their spicy shows in Miami, Las Vegas, Atlantic City, and the Catskills were after-hours affairs attended by traveling salesmen, showbiz types, and anyone in search of something naughtier than the comic headliners: *"I had my disappointments in the service. I discovered that a twenty-one-inch Admiral was only a television set"*; *"If you think the jury was hung, you shoulda seen the judge."* These burlesque refugees were the X-rated precursors of

Howard Stern and today's shock-jock troops, and, to be sure, of hard-boiled 1980s female comedians like Roseanne Barr, Carrie Snow, Marsha Warfield, Sandra Bernhard, Brett Butler, Paula Poundstone, and Margaret Cho—tough cookies all. (The fat, fearless, foul-mouthed Barr was a throwback to Barth, ridiculing men and flaunting her girth.)

"If I embarrass you, tell your friends," was Barth's refrain and the title of her first album, which sold half a million copies, followed by *My Next Little Story Is a Little Risqué,* her other favorite catchphrase. Discussing hemorrhoids, circumcision, and inflatable dolls, she sold some two million albums in all, collector's items now traded on eBay. There was an unofficial ban on displaying her albums in stores, so the records (labeled: CENSORED. NOT FOR AIR PLAY. FOR ADULTS ONLY) had an added outlaw thrill for people who taped her albums and slipped them to friends—or swiped them. Empty album jackets forced customers to ask clerks for the actual record, sotto voce, as if purchasing condoms.

Labeled "the female Lenny Bruce," Barth's material had no redeeming social anything except guffaws; the only similarity was that she was arrested for obscenity several times. Barth was more like your Aunt Sadie with attitude (*"a maven on dreck,"* as she put it), with a boozy, leather-lunged voice. When the scandalous, five-times-married Belle (born Annabelle Salzman) played Carnegie Hall, she had to tone down her act because of police rumored to be present. Barth, Warren, et al. remained in a sleazy-record ghetto, forced to ply their trade like comic bimbos. Lacking the versatility, pizzazz, and self-promotional skills of a Sophie Tucker, and with no legit outlets for female comics, the only way they could survive was to get down and dirty. There was nowhere for them to go but underground.

Rusty Warren, who billed herself as "The Chippie Off the Old Block," was unabashedly carnal, a blowsy redhead with a scratchy voice whose every joke is scored with a rim shot. Her basic message, and that of her colleagues, was: We want it and we ain't gettin' it. There's an implied pre–Joan Rivers between-us-girls message of "Can we talk?" Warren specialized in breasts (she named hers Gertrude and Agnes) and solicited members for her Knockers-Up Club; she customarily closed her act with a titillating ditty, "Mammaries," sung to the tune of "Memories."

Born Eileen Goldman in 1930, the still robust last of those red-hot vinyl mamas' pastimes today are golf and bridge. As a performer, Warren never indulged in Yiddishisms, played the Catskills, or drew Jewish crowds. "My fans thought I was midwestern Protestant. When I'd go see Belle in Miami, she'd say, 'Oh, look, we have a Jewish shiksa here tonight!' "

Warren was a graduate of the New England Conservatory of Music who taught piano before playing lounges, braying parody songs like "A Hard Man Is Good to Find" and recording on her own label. She played Mister Kelly's, Bimbo's, even the New York Latin Quarter, and made it to Las Vegas in 1962, after *Knockers Up!* hit big. "It was in the Top Fifty for ten years—and it was never played on the radio. It was a phenomenon." Warren made fourteen albums, seven of which went gold, each selling about half a million copies, right up there with the records of male comedy stars. She thinks it's unfair to lump her with Barth & Co.: "We all did totally different things," she told me from her home in Hawaii. "While I talked about sex, they talked about the act. Pearl would talk about how big his thing was. My mentor was Sophie Tucker, but she was more of a singer—a Borscht Belter. Most of my stuff was talking between songs."

Compared to Barth, Warren was almost prim. "I used four-letter words but I never said *fuck.* Oy vey! I could no more do that than stand on my head. My stuff was for Mr. and Mrs. America. But women didn't discuss sex onstage then. My attitude was, What do you mean, women don't like sex? We liked it, we should talk about it. Like when Masters and Johnson came out with their sex book, they talked about three hundred and forty-nine different positions. I said I only knew three, but I knew 'em good." She adds, "I'm called a living legend—can you believe it!" Elayne Boosler gave her a photo years ago and wrote on it: "Thanks for blazing the trail." Lily Tomlin e-mailed her for an autographed photo.

Totie Fields was somewhere in that brassy tradition—she sang and told naughty acceptable jokes—but became a transition figure between Barth/Warren and Diller/Rivers. Fields (born Sophie Feldman) was another rotund Jewish mama, at four feet ten inches and 190 pounds, but she was a kinder, gentler yenta who made fun of herself, not men, and she also "worked clean." Like her nickname, there was something sweet, harmless, and endearing about Totie, of whom someone observed, "How much harm can a 'Totie' do?" With her foghorn voice, jokes about her looks, lack of sex appeal, and romantic bad luck, she specialized in material that might easily have come from Diller or Rivers ("*I've been on a diet now for two weeks and all I've lost is two weeks*").

As women's comedy historian Sarah Blacher Cohen observes, "It's as if, for her and other comediennes, age and ugliness were the credentials required to permit them to be funny." Fields didn't limit herself to mocking her chubby shape and sex life; she talked of other things and closed with a sing-along like many a Catskill comic. Arnie Kogen, who wrote for Fields, says, "She was physical and she was cute and she could deliver a line and she had an attitude, always ending punch lines with, '*Am I right? Am I right?*' "—which Joan Rivers later echoed. "She was a ground-breaker. Being a woman wasn't a difficulty for her. In fact, it may have been a plus—there were so few." Fields, who died at forty-eight in 1978 of complications from plastic surgery, still gamely made fun of herself even after having a leg amputated ("*I never had good legs anyway*"; "*At least I still have a leg to stand on*"), when she finally cracked comedy's glass ceiling.

Bob Shanks, a talent coordinator on the Jack Paar *Tonight* show, claimed he was always on the lookout for funny women. He auditioned some five hundred female comics over three years, but only ten or twenty made the cut. They weren't as funny as the men, he claimed. Elayne Boosler never felt that she had it tougher as a woman: "Nobody's going to say, 'Oh, that's so funny, too bad she's a girl.' Sure there aren't as many women comics as men, but neither are there as many women brain surgeons."

The earliest successful aboveground comedienne of that period, Jean Carroll, is now almost forgotten. Carroll was the opposite of Diller—a smartly dressed, attractive woman who often appeared on *The Ed Sullivan Show* and spoke in a conversational tone about domestic life, sans props or loud whoops. She wasn't self-deprecating and made good-humored fun of her husband, her cooking, and her shopping habits. Shecky Greene says that Carroll "was better than Diller and didn't do the crazy things Diller did." Jan Murray recalls that Carroll was the first woman comedian he ever saw—"a very feminine woman who banged jokes like a guy, which no woman of that era did. She was the first. She was pretty, but she did one-line things."

Lily Tomlin remembers Carroll as the first woman stand-up she ever saw, when she was ten years old—"a woman talking about female things. My favorite line of hers was, '*I'll never forget the first time I saw my husband— standing on a hill, his hair blowing in the breeze, and he too proud to run after it.*" After her husband, Buddy Howe, became head of a major talent agency, in 1954, Carroll vanished, leaving the field wide open for Phyllis Diller's flamboyant entrance a year later.

NOT ONLY HAD THERE never been a woman comedian like Phyllis Diller before, there had never been a woman who looked anything remotely like her, with her fright wig, boa, and even more frightening shriek of a laugh. And that was her first joke—her costume—which became a reliable running gag that kept Diller going for nearly half a century, one of the few stand-up comics of the fifties and sixties to survive every taste and trend in comedy. She is little changed from what she was at the start, albeit more polished and assured. While other comics of that era have faded, folded, or switched direction, Phyllis Diller, love her or leave her, is still and forever herself.

Diller transcended "comediennes" of the day, if not femaleness itself, by announcing her arrival in the mid-1950s in the most outlandish manner imaginable. She landed onstage like a flightless goony bird—wielding her cigarette holder, piercing the nightclub air with her manic squawk, all beak and beady chicken eyes, and dressed in a deliberately garish getup. It was as if Auntie Mame had fled a fire in the middle of the night and, on her way out the door, flung on the first clothes she grabbed.

"I'm a cartoon," she happily admits. "You find the things I say in those little balloons. Everything I do is overdone, a caricature." She would cross her eyes but, one foot still firmly imbedded in cabaret tradition, finish the act with a song like "Every Street's a Boulevard in Old New York." She was a kind of female female impersonator, so it's no wonder that her earliest adoring fans were gay men, who embraced her whacked-out persona and over-the-top style. "The first group that supported me insanely were the faggots," she once said. "They were my maddest fans."

Oh, and one other thing: she was funny. It took a while for that fact to sink in. People were so distracted, even disturbed, by her crazed guffaw and bizarre wardrobe that the wit was upstaged. There must be some mistake here, you thought; this woman does not need an audience, she needs help. She got it. Her original support group, an unlikely coalition of homosexuals and mad housewives, nurtured her career until, gradually, everybody else came around. Diller seemed at first a freak, and later a force of nature, a larger-than-life comedian who wasn't satirical like her cutting-edge peers, nor did she tell stories or reveal her angst.

She was essentially a clown—a rowdy throwback to an earlier day, relying exclusively on jokes rather than her real self. Only in the sense that she dared, and was able, to break through the male stand-up bastion was she in the vanguard. What Diller accomplished was more significant than what she created. She is a superb joke-teller and, over time, became by default a showbiz feminist leader, but as a comedian she was decidedly pre-Sahl—a female Milton Berle, really, a zany *shpritzer*. While she identifies herself with the new-wave comics, the act—which she describes as a thousand one-liners laid end to end—was very old wave.

Yet Diller had little in common with anyone, old guard or new, merrily going her own way where no female comic had gone before—with the exception of Jorie Remus, after whom Diller partly modeled herself, more in manner than in content. Murray Grand, Remus's pianist, told the cabaret historian James Gavin: "Jorie was an extraordinarily creative comedienne, the forerunner of Joan Rivers and Phyllis Diller. Phyllis copied her point-blank after hearing her at the Purple Onion—and admits it." In Diller's first album you can hear a lot of Remus—her italicized delivery, her self-deprecating jokes about her clothes, her general recherché inflections and style. With a saucy, blasé manner and a whiskey Tallulah Bankhead tenor ("*Darlings, I really don't have to do this for a living. I'm dis-gust-ing-ly wealthy*"), Remus was a campy cult cutup, a regular at San Francisco's Purple Onion before playing New York's Bon Soir and Blue Angel.

Remus, the Purple Onion's biggest draw until Diller, delivered lines in a bored, worldly-wise manner that Gavin calls "a low husky purr," her singing voice ravaged by smoking: "*Have you ever had one of those years when everything seems to go all wrong?*" she would croak. "*You wake up in the morning on the wrong side of your life. The first thing you discover is that your husband has run away with your best friend . . . and you miss her.*" She would collapse into languid poses atop the piano and, Bea Lillie–like, manipulate a long red boa parodying Marlene Dietrich. Nat Hentoff remarked on her "slashing sense of the ridiculous" and proclaimed that Remus signaled the end of "the machine-gun one-liner stand-up comic." Not quite. Diller assumed Remus's outrageous style, but took it further into controlled lunacy. She hitched Remus's wicked attitude to a machine-gun barrage of jokes, dropped the songs because they slowed the pace, and left the withering social satire to others. In her personal life, Diller was all that the self-destructive Remus was not—positive, grounded, motivated, organized, and a whiz at self-promotion.

Fields, Remus, Diller, and Joan Rivers were stand-up comedy's rough-and-ready foremothers, but Diller never considered herself a pioneer: "Oh, Jesus, it never entered my mind! No, only in retrospect. I was just trying to make a living." During the heyday of seventies feminism, when a reporter suggested that some women were offended by her portrayal of the modern housewife, Diller argued, "How could they complain about me? I'm one of the spearheads [of women's liberation]." Diller always loved take-my-wife jokes. Her response to her politically correct critics is succinct—"Fuck 'em!" And as for the contributions of those earlier earthier gals—Belle, Rusty, et al.—she scoffs, "I don't count them." Lily Tomlin, a seventies comic with major feminist credentials, wasn't offended by Diller's self-deprecatory lines. "I just liked her because she was so silly. Her material isn't anything I would have necessarily done—some things bothered me—but she made me laugh."

Rivers once remarked that Diller was "basically doing a woman's version of men's acts," and Diller tried hard to emulate her hero, mentor, and, later, costar Bob Hope, hammering jokes home without regard to social comment. For the pragmatic Diller, the bottom line was boffs. Her only difference was that she was a woman, but almost a parody of a woman—overly made-up, arms and legs akimbo, who arrived for work in a bright yellow sailcloth dress festooned with hundreds of cotton poufs, white lizard boots, and long white gloves, with a hairdo described as a wilted artichoke or exposed nerve ends.

Diller admired Remus but says, "She was far too chic, too *New Yorker*." Diller was antichic, indeed she mocked chic, with her cigarette holder, kid gloves, glitzy necklaces, and ersatz exotic gowns. Yet she was hardly your average *McCall's* homemaker. She was a bizarre confusion, a head-on collision, of the two, a merger of cosmopolitan kook and suburban housewife—a sort of alien housewife. Jack Paar, who surrounded himself on his show with dizzy, eccentric dames, once described her as looking "like someone you avoid at the supermarket."

Success was rapid and steady, but it took thirty appearances on Paar's show to implant Diller in the public mind. "I finally did make it. But it only took me five years to get to Carnegie Hall, which I think is some kind of world record." Before Hope, Paar was her main man. "Paar always presented me so beautifully." Not until his show did she graduate to "a total stand-up," she told me. "I always had a piano to lean on and to put my props on. I realized on his show I didn't need the piano, and I decided my next goal was to get rid of the damn props. I had to get rid of the props to get on the Sullivan show." One early prop was a pair of monstrous harlequin eyeglasses (Diller was doing Dame Edna long before Edna was a glint in Barry Humphries's eye). She decided to keep her material smart but not smarty-pants. "It was extremely intelligent, but I never insulted anyone. The material was absolutely current. Like I talked about psychiatry and progressive education. I made fun of fashion; I'd put a hat on and do twenty minutes." Although she says her audience "probably pictures me lying on a chaise lounge covered with feathers with a cigarette holder, they don't know that I'm just a down-home grandmother. My basic thing is still motherhood."

PHYLLIS DILLER WILLED HERSELF to stardom if ever anyone did. She had no show business genes or girlhood stage leanings, and people would say of her, "My God, a woman comedian—she'll never make it"; but once she realized she could make people laugh, and could make a living at it, she persevered. A family friend said of her, "Phyllis could always do anything she put her mind to." As a child (born Phyllis Driver), her main interests were piano and voice. She later went to the Sherwood Music School in Chicago and a religious college, Bluffton, where she entertained dorm mates by walking the halls nude except for curlers, a belt, and a rose between her teeth; that might have been a clue that something was awry.

Aside from such displays, her only performing ambitions lay in music, and after making it as a comic she played several concerts with symphony orchestras around the country; in the 1960s, she also studied ballet. A coloratura soprano with a high note two octaves above middle C, she had wanted to be an opera singer. "I really had a voice," she said. "I took the veil for two years. There was no fooling around." (A *Los Angeles Times* music critic said of a 1975 piano concert: "She got through it [Beethoven's C-Major Concerto] very respectably.") She also loved to write: "I was writing from the third grade on, writing, writing, writing"—romances at first, then humor.

Because of her last name and profession, people often assume she's Jewish: " 'Phyllis Diller' is a terrific stage name—it sounds too good, made up. Most Dillers *are* Jewish and being thought to be Jewish has helped me in many ways, especially in the beginning; I did a lot of benefits for synagogues and they'd say, 'What's your temple?' " She never set them wise, but Diller grew up Methodist in Lima, Ohio, where she was considered plain, funny, and, by Lima standards, a tad quirky; before going on dates, she would memorize jokes. "When I realized I looked like Olive Oyl and wanted to look like Jean Harlow," she once said, "I knew something had to be done. From twelve on, the only way to handle the terror of social situations was comedy—break the ice, make everybody laugh. I did it to make people feel more relaxed, including myself."

She ditched her potential music career to marry Sherwood Diller, a college classmate, and to raise five kids, all of whom provided her with material for the act-to-be; the timid Mr. Diller was later transformed onstage into the beastly husband "Fang." Her only career then was to help support an ever-increasing family by working as an advertising copy-writer for an Oakland, California, department store and a local radio station, KROW ("Out of that tiny independent station came Ralph Edwards, Art Linkletter, Rod McKuen, and me"). She also wrote a shopping column while living in nearby Alameda, where her husband was an inspector at the naval air station and moonlighted as a night watchman. When he lost his job, the first of many such losses, his wife was forced to find work. "He was a talker," Diller said. "He sounded like he would rule the world, but he couldn't hold a job. He just sat there and drank beer all day. He didn't even do *that* well. He had a case of total anxiety. The man was sick. I couldn't get him to take a bath. The barber had to come to the house to cut his hair." If it hadn't been for her husband's sloth, she said, she would only have been the funniest woman in Alameda.

Diller progressed to writing funny ad copy as promotion manager for San Francisco's leading radio station, KSFO, yet she wasn't considered amusing enough for an on-air job. "I was an office girl to them. They couldn't see me at all." The poet Rod McKuen, still a friend, remembered, "I always thought she'd end up in show business, but *she* had no idea." Diller concurs. "I thought I was a normal person. I didn't change. I just went onstage. All my life I was whatever I was. I was funny at parties. In fact, if there was a party, someone would call and say, 'We want something about motherhood,' and I would simply write a bit. I was a pro and didn't know it. First thing you know, I had an act. I was so in demand. This is when my husband started nagging me to become a comic. Push, push, push. I had five little children. I said, 'Are you out of your mind?' It took two years of nagging by my husband to get me onto that stage. He pushed me off the diving board."

The Diller clan lived in a dreary housing development, and Phyllis once told an interviewer, "It was the most painful period of my life." She had to sell her mother's diamonds. The phone was often shut off, and her home teetered on the brink of foreclosure. With five kids, much of her time was spent washing clothes at a local Laundromat, where she became a headliner, entertaining other housewives waiting out the spin cycle.

"I had given up everything to become a stand-up comedian," she has said. "I gave up my house, my kids went to live with relatives, and I went on the road with no home. I had all those kids because I wanted them. But the marriage was no good. I waited until I had gone through all my inheritance, and then I went to work. Nothing was going to stop me. There is no motivation like a mother with her young. Now they've traveled all over the world and they've had everything. I didn't let them down, did I?" To keep the kids from messing up her scripts, she wrote on top of a small upright piano.

PTA gigs followed (Diller on piano, her son on banjo), along with some church groups, the Kiwanis, and women's clubs. Recalls a friend from that time: "She somehow got through to the people at the hospitals. She was so personal." Diller says, "It's amazing how it falls into place and then you know you're ready to open." What propped her up in those gray days was a book, *The Magic of Believing,* a self-help manual by Claude M. Bristol that she clung to like a Bible. The combination of Bristol's message—you can do whatever you choose to do—and an encouraging househusband propelled her forward. Her other testament: "Realize that no one is ever going to help you." She counsels: "Don't take things that seriously. Nothing is permanent. When something goes wrong, it isn't going to stay that way. You've got to have tragedy. Comedy is tragedy revisited."

McKuen said that Diller's husband "gave her the ambition and the drive. Without Sherwood Diller there'd be no Phyllis Diller." Paul Goldenberg, then the hungry i manager (who lured her away from the Purple Onion to play the i), recalls: "Fang was always around, and he was a namby-pamby nerdish kind of guy and she really gave it to him. I didn't like her humor, mind you, but I liked her. What pluck she had!"

For two years she wrote ad copy for Kahn's Department Store in Oakland, until KROW hired her away. "I really knew how to write catchy copy." Terrence O'Flaherty, the longtime TV critic for the *San Francisco Chronicle,* became pals with Diller after he began running her publicity items verbatim. "Early on, she was one of the funniest dames, marvelously brittle," recalled O'Flaherty, who wrote, "She writes some of the best and most delightful commercials in the broadcasting business." For an Oakland restaurant called the Sea Wolf, she wrote, "The chefs are so temperamental that their wolf *du jour* has a psychiatrist in attendance at all times."

Despite her funny items and garb, O'Flaherty had no inkling of her showbiz ambitions. "It surprised me when she broke in her act at the Purple Onion," he said. "We didn't know she could do it, but she had great strength." Certain forces kept prodding her, she explains. "While I was at Kahn's, there was a cute young girl who went out every night. With five children you don't go out *ever*. I'd never *been* in a nightclub. She kept telling me there was a woman over there you gotta see. She saw me as funnier than Jorie Remus. So I went over and saw Jorie. I said, 'My God, look at this—a lady up there being funny.' So one day I said, 'Okay, I'll do it!' She quit work rather than take a leave, deciding that if she was truly serious about selling comedy, it would have to be as an unemployed comic, not as an unemployed copywriter. "It was my grand affirmative gesture," she said.

Wanda Ramey, a former TV anchorwoman, remembers long lunches and serious discussions with Diller when they worked together at KROW. Ramey recalls Diller, *Rocky*-like, looking at the Fairmont Hotel's swank Venetian Room and vowing she would play there someday. "A lot of people talk and never do it, but I knew she would do it. Phyllis just exuded confidence and people loved being around her. Everyone wanted their desk in the same office as Phyllis, because she was fun." In her mid-thirties, Diller was over the hill by showbiz standards, and also broke. "She was very poor," recalls Ramey, who helped buy her clothes and costumes, but when Diller's little girls visited the radio station, they would always be wearing white gloves. Once she made it, Diller paid Ramey back with a mink coat.

Diller wasn't a grotesque until a club owner told her, "You smile too much, be hostile," and she altered her stage demeanor. "I had spent all my life trying to throw hostility out of my personal life, to be a nice, open channel for good. Back then I was too sweet. My voice was sweet. I couldn't understand what he meant." But when she finally got it, she was rewarded with "a review which said 'bitchy,' which is what you gotta do."

It was mainly the self-help manual that spun her around. "If I hadn't read that I'd still be washing the laundry by hand," she says. "It shot me into outer space and absolutely turned me into a dynamo." An old Bay Area friend, the musical-comedy veteran Jane Connell (whose husband Gordon was Diller's pianist), confirms it: "She was out to kill." After seeing the Connells perform, she told them, "Gosh, if you can do it, I can do it!"

Jane Connell told James Gavin, "She worked at it until two or three A.M. Conversations with her were never conversations in those days. She was always honing material with us. If Gordon said something funny she'd write it down."

With the aid of a drama coach, she practiced telling jokes in front of her bedroom mirror after doing the dinner dishes, gags like: "*I'm nine years behind in my ironing. I bury a lot of it in the backyard. But let's face it— if you don't iron it, they'll grow out of it,*" and, "*My Playtex Living Bra died of starvation.*" A year later she auditioned at the Purple Onion, the city's number-two club. To get an audition, she told the hungry i's Enrico Banducci, who owned a slice of the Onion, "I'm so funny you gotta give me a job." He said, "Okay, come down to the Purple Onion." All during her audition they were ordering Chinese food on the phone, but they hired her. When she opened on March 7, 1955, Phyllis Diller was thirty-seven years old.

While Diller broke in her act at the Purple Onion, doing four shows a night, she lived on corn dogs. She wangled an appearance on the TV quiz show *You Bet Your Life,* where her rapid-fire jokes fell flat. Groucho Marx just looked at her oddly. "I had no idea what I was doing. I knew I was good, but I only realize in retrospect there wasn't anyone else. I was *it.* Ten years later, Joan Rivers came along. Then for another ten years, it was just me, Joan, and Totie." (Rivers much later wrote for a short-lived Diller TV series, and, despite journalists' best attempts to stir up a catfight, they only purr admiringly of each other: "I love her and am a great supporter," says Diller of Rivers.)

She worked with an actor-decorator friend who foraged through back issues of *Reader's Digest* in search of material while she snipped out high-fashion photos from *Vogue* to ridicule while wearing her own weird attire. "I always dressed funny, but it was normal for me. I looked like the woman next door with a twist to her mind. Dress off the rack, red hair. I was working in Boston when a guy said, 'You should think about wardrobe.' I didn't know what 'wardrobe' meant."

She describes her original act: "I did German lieder and then a phony translation. It was very Victor Borge. I slithered around the piano like Eartha Kitt. I did *anything.* I did Jeri Southern and a parody of [Menotti's opera] *Amahl and the Night Visitors,* which was pretty esoteric. We had a certain kind of an audience—bright! Here's how I became commercial: the first show I did was for a Gray Line tour—the acid test. They'd never been in a basement bohemian bistro and they were thinking, 'God, this could cave in at any moment.' They were scared! And then I'd come out and scare 'em further. *Ah-hahahaha!* But, look, I'm from Ohio—I understood they were frightened. They were right off the hay wagon." She has never known stage fright—"It was the audience that was frightened."

So she knew how to put the tourists at ease. San Francisco, even then, was famous for its flamboyant characters, and Diller seemed to embody the city's wild reputation. ("It was the best place in the world to start out—they drink!") With her short red hair, drawn-on eyebrows, and heavily painted lips, she wasn't an instant smash, but then she had not yet arrived at the final Phyllis Diller, too busy imitating Yma Sumac or Eartha Kitt singing "Monotonous" (the Diller version was "Ridiculous"), strumming the zither, and mugging with crossed eyes. Singing comedy songs, she would hurl herself across a piano top so violently that she had to wear black leotards to cover the bruises.

It was everything for a laugh, from her opening intro—"*The Purple Onion is pleased, proud, and absolutely terrified to present the one and, God help us, the only dingy dilly delirious doll from Donner Pass, Phyllis Diller!*" She did everything from gun molls and uppity college deans to dancing the cha-cha, in an act heavily reliant on wacky props—tatty furs, glasses, hats, canes—which she later called "the sign of an amateur." As she explains: "Props is not stand-up; it's a crutch. You gotta do something without any help." O'Flaherty recalled her takeoff on the "Modess . . . *Because*" tampon ads, slowly wrapping herself inside a long piece of material and, at the end, whispering, "*Because . . .*" "That was her big number," he said. "It brought down the house, and from then on everybody loved her."

The comedy writer Anne Beatts remarks, "She grabbed hold of the stereotypes and shook them until they rattled"—"*I don't like to cook; I can make a TV dinner taste like radio*"; "*Fang's idea of a seven-course dinner is a six-pack and a bologna sandwich. The last time I said let's eat out, we ate in the garage.*" Beatts adds: "She showed us a kind of female star we'd never seen before: a sloppy loudmouth in a fright wig whose ever-present cigarette holder sprinkled ashes like a benediction on lousy homemakers everywhere." One routine was called "The Homely Friendmaker." Diller was the anti–Harriet Nelson. Stephanie Sarver, who grew up watching Diller on TV and taught a course on female humorists, says: "She was so unlike what we were taught mothers were supposed to be like—her hair all askew, her crazy outfits. She was also an example of marriage gone awry. She was saying: This is how it really is." Diller represented the working-class woman as opposed to Joan Rivers's privileged Jewish American princess in black dress, pearls, and elegant coif.

Although Diller claimed, "What I do onstage has nothing to do with reality; the character I'm playing is all in fun," she truly loathed housework. "I hated ironing. I had the greatest ironing jokes in the world, and women related to them. It was true. I froze my ironing, buried my ironing, anything not to do it." She struck a *Bad Housekeeping* chord later voiced in print by humorists like Jean Kerr, Judith Viorst, Phyllis McGinley, Peg Bracken, and Erma Bombeck. Lawrence Christon comments: "This was the era of suburbia and a lot of women were trapped in the split-level sterile tracts. When she'd put on that boa and the long cigarette holder, it gave women the sense of being a bit vampish, and she was saying outrageous things. The whole culture of grievance has become so mainstream now, but she was a breath of fresh air for those days. What didn't last for her was that her material got to be generic, like Hope."

Diller was dropped by the Purple Onion after a few weeks, but, recalls Ramey, "So many people came in and said, 'Where's that woman?' that they hired her back." An agent had forced another comic on the bill who pushed her out, but she wouldn't be denied. "I said, 'Don't worry about me, baby; I'm gonna make it,' and scared the shit out of him. Like I don't need *you* to make it. That was a new attitude he'd never seen in his life. I was a pit bull." Stanley Eichelbaum, the *San Francisco Examiner*'s theater critic, knew her then. "She was a very amiable motherly type. She would call me every once in a while and we'd have lunch; she carried around a bottle of cracked pepper she would put on everything. I thought her show was very funny then but less so as years went on—and all that nervous laughter. She also was *very* ambitious. I ran into her at a party in L.A. and she grabbed hold of me and said, 'Oh, can I sit with you?' She put her arms around me and suddenly I realized she was hustling me." Diller once said, "I've never wasted a minute of my life."

She stayed at the Purple Onion eighty-nine weeks, a record there, then hit the road alone, leaving her family behind in a home she'd inherited in St. Louis. When the Connells saw her at New York's One Fifth Avenue in the late 1950s, she was playing to half a dozen people. "Talk about rejection!" said Jane Connell. "I would have given up right then, but she went full steam ahead." *Variety* was unimpressed, even misspelling her name, noting: "Phyllis Dillen manages laughs with her rather forced comedy material." At the Blue Angel, remembered the singer Will Holt, "she bombed, bombed, bombed, bombed, night after night. She faced such failure—hostility even."

What drove her, besides fear of poverty, was a wish "to make people cheerful, to make their life less burdensome." The no-nonsense, unsentimental, unself-pitying Diller always maintained her don't-let-the-bastards-grind-you-down attitude: "You stay cool inside. Keep that equilibrium. Most people just panic, they get jangled and they get ugly, they get hostile. They get a bad audience and they get hecklers and they talk back, they get evil, and every time they do that they're weakening and being unprofessional."

Looking back, Diller said: "Whether it's Bill Cosby or Woody Allen—whoever it is—there's a period where you have to find out who you really are. It's extremely painful to get there. All along the way people are saying you'll never make it." Nothing discouraged her. "I learned to accept nothing negative from other people. Negative people are amazing. You can tell them you're going to do something and they have to tell you why you can't." She adds, "Practice is what is so humiliating about becoming a good comic. There's no such thing as a good beginning comic. You have a spark and you want to do it, and you have the material and the material isn't that good in the beginning. All of your training is done in front of people and that's what's so humiliating."

Male comics didn't resist her when she broke in, she says. "I felt no animosity whatever. I was working the big rooms, starring in Vegas, and [Don] Rickles and Shecky [Greene] were working the lounges. Someone asked them, 'Don't you resent her?' And they said, 'Of course we do!' *Ah-hahahahaha!* But they never let *me* know it. I was a fan of theirs." Nobody ever gave her a hard time—not owners or agents? "Nobody ever ever *ever*. I never gave them any reason to. I was on time, I did my best. See, if you're funny, people don't have time to think about that. They accepted me, especially the old guys, Benny and Hope. [Mort] Sahl didn't like me; there's the *one* guy who didn't like me."

Female stand-up comedy then was considered an unnatural act, so Diller felt a certain antagonism from audiences, mainly from males. "Women laugh quicker than men," she learned. "It takes a lot to make men laugh. When the men realized I was a normal human being, they became fans. Old people like me; even children like me. My goal at the very beginning was to get everyone from one to one hundred to like my work." She overcame male resistance, she told the writer Larry Wilde, "by simply being feminine and by understanding it and not hating them for it. I just bided my time and waited for them to come around."

Bob Hope saw her at what she calls "a ghastly little hole" in Washington, D.C. "I was terrible. It was an execution without a blindfold. I tried to sneak out the fire escape but Hope came after me. I stood behind a post all the time we talked. He had seen me on *The Tonight Show* and said he thought I was good." He told her he "saw courage," which gave her plenty. "If Bob Hope likes my work," she thought, "I must be okay. I must have *something*. I went home that night with a new glint in my eye." When she returned to San Francisco to play the city's top club, the hungry i, it had only taken her six years to cross the street, moving from toast-burning housewife to being billed as "The Toast of San Francisco."

By 1961 she was good enough to play the tony Bon Soir in Greenwich Village—a club so sophisticated, she cracked, that "*a nine-year-old boy came in here the other night, and when he left he was thirty-eight.*" Her jokes were burnished to a high gloss, like the line about a mother who told her son, "*Eat, Chester. Have you any idea how many poor people in China would want that oatmeal?*" to which Chester replies, "*Name two.*" At the Bon Soir, she reprised her swankier persona, singing funny songs ("I'd Rather Cha-cha Than Eat"; "Guess Who I Saw Today," with new comedy lyrics) in a surprisingly alluring voice, and cut her first album there, *Wet Toe in a Hot Socket*. In the liner notes, *The New Yorker*'s veteran cabaret critic Rogers Whitaker called her "the thinking man's chatterbox" and "not the avenging angel she sets out to be." He described her laugh as "a wail that approaches in intensity Gabriel's horn."

The *New York Times*'s Arthur Gelb said of her New York debut: "The humor of Miss Diller's lines lies as much in her delivery as in their content, and her delivery, in turn, is based as much on sight gags as it is on timing. There is nothing subtle about her get-up, but a lot of thought and skill have gone into its planning." She wore a tent-shaped metallic dress, a jeweled collar, and shoes with rhinestone buckles.

That first album reveals Diller as a suave performer, and her singing suggests a more real, rounded, and vulnerable person—the very reason she gave it up. The character she settled into was a feisty housewife with delusions of grande dame–deur, with an electrocuted platinum wig and a flashy cigarette holder, cackling like Woody Woodpecker while ripping herself (and all female pretense) to shreds. "I make my living by self-denigration," she said, "then I go on to the denigration of others"—the very route Joan Rivers would follow. "First you do it to yourself, and then you have license to do it to others—your mother-in-law, the neighbors, your kids, your uncle, your brother"—and, of course, your husband.

Her major prop was never her face, figure, cigarette holder, or fashion crimes, but "Fang," the husband who served as foil for all manner of jokes about marriage, sex, and men, many of them standard gagbook boffs ("*Fang was so dumb he was stranded for six hours on a broken escalator*"; "*Fang went up to a map that said 'You are here,' and he wondered how they knew*"). It was a canny comic device that didn't make it seem as though she was attacking all men, just poor old Fang—a neat switch on decades of male comics deriding their presumably hapless wives: Diller was in effect saying, "Take my husband—please!"

She says her husband loved the idea of people thinking he was Fang, but her mother-in-law objected to being called "Moby-Dick" and "the Great White Whale," and her sister-in-law wasn't fond of being called "Captain Bligh"; both asked Diller to drop them from the act when she divorced her husband to marry the actor Warde Donovan, from whom she separated after nine weeks ("*I was so busy getting a divorce I didn't have time to open my wedding gifts*"). Diller sued her in-laws and finally settled out of court.

Fang began as an ad-lib at the Purple Onion and became, over time, "a beloved character," in her words. Comments the comedy critic Judy Brown, "Husbands then were these all-powerful heads of the house, and *her* husband was this inept guy." To Diller "it was therapy, all those years of talking about Fang." Maya Angelou, who began as a singer at the hungry i, once remarked that Diller "transformed the pain of her life and gave it back to us as humor." Diller told Wanda Ramey that "the love of her life" was Robert Hastings, a lawyer whom she met at sixty-four; they were together ten years, until his death in 1991.

A Diller domestic sampler: "*Fang decided that blondes have more fun, so he bleached his hair and asked me for a divorce*" . . . "*I was so ugly when I was born that the doctor slapped my mother*" . . . "*When I go to the beach wearing a bikini, even the tide won't come in*" . . . "*I finally found out how my neighbor gets her laundry so much whiter-looking than mine. She washes it*" . . . "*I spent seven hours today at the beauty parlor; hell, that was just for the estimate*" . . . "*I'm in the fourteenth year of a ten-day beauty plan.*"

The typical Diller joke has more than one laugh. Example: "*I realized on our first wedding anniversary that our marriage was in trouble. Fang gave me luggage. It was packed. My mother damn near suffocated in there.*" Talk about comic efficiency—a line with three solid laughs, each surpassing the last. "I add, add, add, add, add, topper, topper, topper, topper, topper. That's one of my big things. It makes me different." She also paints funny images: "*In my hands food is a weapon. I can louse up corn flakes. I serve it on the rocks.*" Or: "*Oh, I've got a greasy sink. I have watched bugs slide to their death.*" Many of her jokes sound well-thumbed: "*When I was three years old my folks sent me out to buy bubble gum, and while I was out they moved*" is a line that's turned up in versions by everyone from Woody Allen to Rodney Danger-field. Who knows who got there first—probably Henny Youngman.

For Diller, creating an outrageous character was just a fast way to get attention. When she broke in, a comedienne had to be loopy if she wasn't dirty. Shelley Berman says, "A woman doing Mort Sahl [i.e., bright mate-rial] was simply not seen at that time. The guys were so noisy." So Diller was even noisier and caught people's ear and eye, every performer's first obligation. It was all part of her comic bag of tricks: "I always refer to something they're looking at, either my hair or my clothing, and I learned that's the best way to get on," she told me. "Most comics have that *ab-so-lute-ly ri-dic-u-lous* moronic 'Hello, anyone here from Cleveland?' That's so amateur. And they all do it! Getting onstage is the hardest thing in the world, and I worked at it, because I wouldn't sink to that level. Number one, you never ask an audience a question, because from that moment on, they're in charge—'cause you let 'em in. Come on, *you're* supposed to be the leader! You're supposed to know what you're doing. Give no quarter. It took me years and years and years. But I never looked like I was an amateur. I knew to take charge but not *how* to take charge, and I still didn't know how to open."

She's ruthless about finding good jokes, and was known to pay well for them, buying, editing, filing, and cross-referencing gags with a Bob Hope–like meticulousness; for a while, her main supplier was a Wiscon-sin housewife, also with five kids, named Mary McBride. When Joan Rivers wrote for Diller's failed ABC-TV series, she recalled the star fly-ing in from Los Angeles just in time to tape the show, wrapped in a mink coat and followed by a skinny guy carrying a massive joke book: "She would say, 'I need a joke on doors,' and he would turn to *D*. I was very impressed."

Things began to break for her when she dropped the upscale jokes and zeroed in on her own life: "I work right in the center—food, sex, cloth-ing, everyday things," she told Larry Wilde. "I never predicate a gag on the audience having had to read something or to have seen a movie or traveled to a certain place. They can be idiots and I reach them because I know they eat, sleep, and they got a car." Her rule of thumb: "If every person in the audience doesn't get it at the same moment, I don't want it. Because I only want boff, boff, boff, boff! I don't want giggles. I don't want titters." She rarely had hecklers, she explains, because "my timing is so precise, a heckler would have to make an appointment to get a word in."

When Diller walked out onstage, people were laughing before she opened her mouth and emitted the fabled howl. "I now have the most fabulous opening. Look, forty-two years—I got the opening!" She was introduced as "the Madonna of the Geritol set." "Then I'd come out and say, '*You know you're old when your walker has an air bag.*' Then I have seven hot old-age jokes that are *so-o-o* brilliant! Like, '*When I go the beach my grandchildren try to make words out of the veins in my legs. That's why I still take the pill—I don't want any more grandchildren.*' And, '*You want to look younger? Rent smaller children.*' You see, these are hot, hot." She analyzes her delivery with the precision of a sound technician: "The final word should be the joke word and should end in an explosive consonant, like *pop* or *puck* or *kook*—like a shot. You want to do as many [jokes] as you can on one subject. You see, it's economy. It's one setup. If it's tag-tag-tag-tag-tag you don't have to repeat the setup. But there's a limit to how many tags they'll take on one subject." She claims she got twelve laughs a minute to Hope's six.

Like Hope, Youngman, and Berle, she's a perpetual joke machine—someone called her "a joke book on legs"—cranking out wisecracks with well-oiled efficiency, but careful that each one is something her stage character would say; she was like a playwright creating believable dialogue for her role as "Phyllis Diller" as she spewed forth one-liners: "*I put on a peekaboo blouse. He took a peek and booed*" . . . "*It took me three weeks to stuff a turkey—I stuffed it through the beak.*" Despite her jokes as much as because of them, she succeeded, but now and then a joke had the ring of truth—"*Why is it when a couple has reached their fiftieth wedding anniversary, he looks like a little old lady and she looks like a little old man and neither of them knows the difference?*"

It's easy to forget these days, when most comics claim to be simply "themselves," that most of the giants—Jack Benny, Ed Wynn, Groucho Marx, Gracie Allen—created onstage characters. There was a multiple purpose for Diller's shrill crowlike caws—originally to cue laughs and fill any silences between gags ("I was laughing because *they* weren't, trying to prime the pump"), but also to break up the jokes with an oral exclamation point and to enhance and identify the character she plays onstage, which she calls a "literary invention."

Although that maniacal shriek can shred eardrums, the worst advice she ever got was to lose the laugh: "If I told you how many commercials I've been hired to do, with huge money involved, just to get my laugh!" She held on to it as a prop, like the bejeweled cigarette holder she manipulated like George Burns's cigar. It gave her something to do with one hand, enhanced her la-de-da character, and acted as a kind of pointer. "I'll never forget the night in New York at the Left Bank when I first gave that thing a little tap for an imaginary ash and I realized that was *it*—a punctuation mark. And for a woman it's a great thing to always hold up one hand because you get attention. Stop, look, and listen, right?"

Diller never really transferred to other media, despite countless TV guest spots, a sitcom, and twenty-one films, including three fairly grim movies with Bob Hope. Hope had an affinity for Diller, the bipolar opposite of his earlier laid-back leading babes—Dorothy Lamour, Yvonne DeCarlo, Rhonda Fleming, Joan Caulfield. After scores of movies opposite glamour girls, he loved batting jokes around with a gal who gave as good as she got. Hope may have imagined Diller as a sort of wacko Bing Crosby, but it didn't quite work out. Even so, she says, "He taught me a lot, like how to pause and break a line." Diller deliberately didn't watch other comedians, she says, fearful of aping them—only Hope. "I just automatically studied him. I copied him a lot. There is great similarity in our delivery and the way we work." (Christon notes: "When I spoke with her I felt I was interviewing Bob Hope in drag.")

She boasts of more appearances on Hope's TV shows than any other female—twenty-three. Her television career never happened, but, observes TV critic Ron Miller, "she was really a point person for feminism, before it became fashionable, and if they had built a show around that hard persona that she projected, she might have been successful. But instead they made her a crank in *The Prewitts of Southhampton* [in 1966]. It was awful."

Despite Hope's efforts to turn her into a movie/TV comedian, Diller was funniest in clubs and concerts. You had to experience her in the famously problematic flesh to appreciate her overloaded, wired character with the trademark whinny between punch lines—which, people are horrified to learn, is her actual laugh. Since most of her jokes concern her physical self, she needs to be there, on display, to make the lines believable.

THE YOUTHFUL PHYLLIS WAS, she says, "semiattractive" in an off-center way, with a crooked nose from a childhood car accident and piercing eyes. She had to hide her bosom and nice legs with long lamé jackets, high rhinestone-studded boots, ballooning hot pants, and sack dresses, all so she could ridicule her mythical grotesque body. No wonder women loved her instantly: she made every female feel lovelier, and she made men feel that, compared to her, their wives were Aphrodite. "But, oh, Jesus, I had a good figure," she says.

Diller had to wear clownish clothes, "because I wanted to talk about being flat. Then I could tell 'em anything. To make it onstage I had to make fun of myself first. It's mock hostility, of course, or it would be ugly." She looked too good for a proposed satirical *Playboy* layout. "I posed twice, but they found out I had tits. Ruined everything! A lot of the new female comics say, 'Ooo, that's below me, I won't do that.' Let 'em go to hell! *Ah-hahahahaha!*" When the critic Laurie Stone asked her, "Why attack yourself?" she replied, "It got laughs." As Steve Martin used to say, comedy is not pretty.

Phil Berger labeled female comics "hags," "grotesques," and "screech sisters," but Diller says it's almost a woman comedian's obligation to be witchy. "To be a female comic, you *can't* be a beauty. You *mustn't* be a beauty. It goes back to the court jester—the humpback, the clubfoot, and the crooked nose. It helps. That's how you say hello." She was every man *and* woman's worst nightmare, yet she laughed it all away, rising above it.

Diller explains: "I don't know any other way for a female comic to get along. You have to beef about something. If you come out and you're lovely, there's no comedy, so self-deprecation is par for the course." Being odd-looking is standard equipment for most comedians, female or male (Woody Allen: "*I went down to the draft board to take my physical and they took one look at me and* they *burned my draft card*"). She told one interviewer: "Name me one comic who doesn't put himself down. If they didn't, they'd fail. It's classic. You can't look like Grace Kelly and make jokes."

There were always plenty of funny sexy movie actresses—from Mabel Normand and Marion Davies to Lucille Ball, Kay Kendall, Judy Holliday, Carole Lombard, Jean Arthur, Jean Harlow, Eve Arden, and

Marilyn Monroe—but few pretty stand-up comics. Stand-up, unlike movies or theater, is a one-on-one situation where the comic is out there alone and must take charge. Few attractive women in the fifties, sixties, or even much later were able to tame an unruly audience. The sexy exception in the fifties was Elaine May, but she was doing sketches, not stand-up, and she had a partner.

Rita Rudner, one of the two reigning female comics of the 1990s, with Roseanne Barr, her physical and comic opposite, essentially agrees with Diller. Rudner wasn't just clever, she was a totally new kind of female comic—demure, with a delicate doll-like deadpan prettiness, who spoke softly without putting herself or men down. Rudner, who affects a blithe, Gracie Allen–like air, with inverted-logic jokes ("*My boyfriend and I broke up. He wanted to get married and I didn't want him to*"), says: "You always have to make fun of things that are defective. There's nothing funny about a good-looking person doing well. What are you gonna discuss? I find all kinds of things that are wrong with me, and I get excited when I find a new thing—it means another joke." Men still resist funny women, she thinks, but it's better than it was. "Women are much freer to laugh at themselves than men are. We don't think it's a threat to our femininity. To a man, it's a sign of weakness."

Diller skillfully walked the line between assertive and obnoxious, winning men over once she got famous. "Now I don't have trouble with men because I'm a star," she said in 1978. "Everybody likes a winner." She was a feminist without portfolio simply by dint of slugging it out every night for years in the stand-up trenches. She cracked the all-male Friars Club for a Sid Caesar roast; she came dressed as a man, "Philip Downey," and fooled everyone.

Since Diller's basic comic component was her face, it seemed to many people when she had her first face-lift, in 1971, at age fifty-four, that she might literally be cutting off her nose to spite her career. (In 1961 she had told *Time:* "The older I get, the funnier I get. Think what I'll save in not having my face lifted.") She made the crucial decision after seeing herself on *The Sonny and Cher Show:* "I wore a dog-collar necklace and my neck hung out over on one side like I had a horrible growth, and the bags under my eyes had reached the point of no return." It was a brave move in a way, but she publicized it and made it pay off in laughs. The face-lifts gave her a second career, a new reason to make fun of how she *used* to look—but with an updated slant. Her (and Hope's) agent, Frank Lieberman, thought it was a foolhardy plan. "I was against the idea," he said. "She'd spent her whole career as a funny-looking lady." Diller saw no contradiction: "I was ugly and beginning to look old and wrinkled and hangy—we're talkin' droop city. I'm a single woman and I have a private life, which is very important to me. That's my real life. My life onstage is not real. I am a person and I'm real and I want to look good."

Diller explained to Terrence O'Flaherty: "They said, 'It'll ruin you. It'll wreck your career. It's too late for Miss America.' But I didn't look that different. I just looked better. I look younger. Heavens, who wants to look like I used to look?" Once again, she was in the vanguard—a female performer who dared to discuss plastic surgery. And again Joan Rivers followed in her footsteps. No male comic has yet had the courage.

Diller became a poster girl for the plastic-surgery industry and held press conferences, handing out a release detailing each new face-lift, with clinical descriptions of what work had been done. Between 1971 and 1987 she had seventeen reconstructions—everything from chemical peels and brow-lifts to liposuction, cheek implants, a tummy tuck, and a breast reduction ("*There are no two parts of my body the same age*"). How many times, reporters asked, could she have a face-lift? "Until they close the box," she said. Again, Diller was attacked for making looks a high priority in women's lives, and for indulging in a luxury associated with the wealthy. Undaunted, she offered a sensible explanation: "I'll still project the same image when performing. I'm not deserting the housewife. I'll just be showing her it isn't a sin to look better." She draws a sharp distinction between beauty and femininity: "You mustn't give up your femininity. It's not necessary. That's what keeps some [women comedians] from making it. Some of them are so damn butch, you think, 'Well, I'm not gonna be caught in a dark alley with *her.*' *Ah-hahahahaha!*"

Diller seems one of the more balanced comedians around, especially given her manic stage character. She's comfortable in her own skin, however elastic. Of all the comics of that era, Phyllis Diller and Bob Newhart may be the most unneurotic and, many say, among the nicest. Rivers recalls Diller's thoughtfulness toward the staff of a Diller show she wrote for: "What permanently influenced me was her warmth and charm. She made it her business to know everybody's name and go over and say a word to them with no condescension in her voice. She treated me as an equal, as a peer, as a professional in show business—not a nonperson."

Diller lives, as she has for thirty-plus years, in Los Angeles's Brentwood section, where a lone rake scraping leaves on her semicircular driveway is the only sound and the only parked vehicles are gardeners' trucks. Her twenty-two-room house is filled with antiques. The entire upstairs is lined with her own bright, childlike acrylic paintings, which she shows off with her usual joie de vivre, as if displaying her grandchildren's artwork. In her living room, on an easel, stands a huge oil portrait of Bob Hope, a shrine to the man who called her "the Liz Taylor of *The Twilight Zone.*" She lights up the painting and comments, "At night it's so dramatic."

On a divan in her sunny parlor rests a needlepoint pillow that reads: "It's Good to Be the Queen." When the eighty-two-year-old queen enters, it's something of a jolt. She's shorter than expected (five foot three and counting), thinner, and more frail-looking in person than onstage. A daughter pops in daily to look after her. When I arrived to interview her, Diller padded in wearing a print dress, a sweater, no makeup, and hexagonal glasses, her actual hair reduced to wispy white strands ("I never go anywhere with this hair—*Ah-hahahahaha!*"). She looks like, well, a little old lady, yet she sounds much like her stage self, hoot and all. She played her last stand-up date in Las Vegas in May 2002. On *Larry King Live* she explained, "I'm too old to travel and I'm short of breath a lot because of my heart." She told King, "I died three times in the hospital and was brought back to life each time with mouth-to-mouth. It [dying] isn't that bad." Onstage, done up in her Phyllis Diller costume, she still had a certain presence and command, but in person she is, indeed, nothing like her Beulah Witch façade and seems just a good old gal.

No matter how great her gags are, however, there was always something one-note and one-dimensional about her act, and ultimately a little wearying. Christon once observed: "For energy, poise, and delivery, she's a pro at the top of her class, but unlike the great comedians, she offers no humanity in her act. Where others throw a light on the human condition, she attacks it with a blowtorch."

Many liberated women, and men, had problems laughing at her self-abusive persona. Charles Marowitz in a 1970 review in the *Village Voice* speculated that Diller must share Hope's writers "because behind her endless abuse against ugly women, fat women, horrid in-laws, there is something mechanistically routine" about her act. He could praise those mechanics—the timing, delivery, the ability to milk and to mug—but concluded: "And yet one feels, after forty minutes in her company, she is a stranger." He added: "There is more to stand-up comedy than a manic commitment to anatomical derision. She is an odd-looking lady making capital out of being unlovely. But she pushes unloveliness so far. . . . We want her to say something funny about being pretty or wanted or sympathetic."

True, Diller never confronted any real issues behind her jokes, but self-analysis and gender matters were never in her up-from-the-bootstraps nature. You might as well ask Bob Hope to reveal his inner child. Comedians did not disrobe in public in 1955; that wouldn't happen until Shelley Berman, Lenny Bruce, and Woody Allen bared their souls. "She is a true pro," concluded Marowitz, "but I felt her material was preventing me from touching her, from knowing her, and I grew to dislike it."

Diller has refused to dig more deeply into things, to get under that famous sagging skin she joked about, because it would ruin the fun and it was never the point of her act—or of her. If there is any kind of social subtext to her performance, one critic commented, it is "simply that she was living proof that a plain housewife could make good." Phyllis Diller gave comic voice to the cynicism bubbling just below the surface of other restless, overburdened mid-1950s housewives with five kids, an out-of-work husband, and teeming private ambitions. "I was saying all the things women were thinking but not saying."

The Wild Child

JONATHAN WINTERS

I carry a dagger, but it has a rubber blade.

———

A LOOK OF SADNESS settles into Jonathan Winters's face when he's in repose, his eyes and mouth collapsed—he's like a St. Bernard who's lost its way. Then suddenly, unexpectedly, he breaks into one of his thousand faces—a laughing baby, a babbling old lady, a fatheaded farmer, a prissy schoolmarm, a dithering executive, a fatuous general, a cuddly alien. Usually it's someone scared or in big trouble, shooting sidelong glances from worried eyes.

Jonathan Winters was probably the most admired—and the most inimitable—of all the comedians of his time. He was also the least typical of the renaissance comedians—part circus clown and part social observer, a Red Skelton possessed by the spirit of Daumier. While he calls himself a satirist, it isn't traditional satire. Most satirists mock institutions or events or politicians; Winters mocked the yokels next door with a homey (though bizarre) brand of cartoon commentary, sketching and sculpting characters with droll comments that work like balloons above their heads. Alluding to his surreal quality, one album liner note said, "Art has its Jackson Pollock, music its Igor Stravinsky, and comedy its Jonathan Winters." In fact, he also dabbles in art offstage, turning out surrealistic paintings that critics have compared to Klee, Chagall, and Magritte.

Unlike his fellow renaissance comics, what he said seemed less important than what he did or how he did it. Mainly a mimic, Winters preceded the improv movement, but his humor wasn't intellectually or theatrically driven; it was pure instinct. His Silly Putty face reshaped itself endlessly, enhanced by a perfect ear for regional speech and American Gothic tintypes. A *Variety* critic noted in 1961: "His humor is more universally acceptable than any of the current New Comics, with the possible exception of Bob Newhart, because he covers the mass experiences of the U.S. common man—the Army, the gas station, the airport, etc."

There has never been anyone quite like him in comedy. Long before he was officially acknowledged as an American original, he was regarded as "a comedian's comedian," a tag that sounds slightly patronizing. He was a "performance artist" before the phrase was coined. He didn't get off withering one-liners or gore sacred cows; he caricatured people. "I don't do jokes," he remarked. "The characters are my jokes."

Winters shunned the wisecrack, and in TV interviews he seems uneasy, naked without his trunkful of masks to duck behind. Nobody knew what drawer to file him in. Winters couldn't be neatly pigeonholed (he has far too many pigeons to fit in one hole). He doesn't exactly clown, though he's a classic clown in street clothes. He isn't an impressionist, yet everything he does is impressionistic—in a few moves and words, he paints a passing parade of everyone from dimwit garage mechanic attendant to high-tech geek, a rich grab bag of frauds and phonies; he speaks a fluent body language. Winters isn't a comedian in the usual sense, but he makes people laugh. His act—indeed, his entire career—was the very definition of winging it.

In trying to pin him down, people have settled on "humorist," a label he's always been more comfortable with than "comic," which causes him to flinch. In 2000 Washington officially recognized him, awarding him the Mark Twain Prize (a sort of comedians' Nobel) for his enterprising work in the field of laughter. As far back as the 1960s, somebody had tagged him "the Mark Twain of the Missile Age." He was a man doodling caricatures of recognizable national archetypes, small-town eccentrics out of Sinclair Lewis or Ring Lardner, often midwestern but just as likely to be southern or Southern Californian, New Englander, New Yorker— or indeed Martian, as when he landed on *Mork and Mindy* as Robin Williams's spacey son. (The inside joke was that Williams regarded himself—and still does—as the comic son of his idol, Winters, which would make him the illegitimate heir to the throne of the clown prince of improvisation.)

At heart, Winters is a humanist, appealing to a broader audience than most of his more verbal peers. It took a certain antenna to pick up the satiric messages from Mort Sahl, Lenny Bruce, Nichols & May, Dick Gregory, and Stan Freberg, but everyone quickly tuned in to Winters's humor. His characters, no matter how grotesque or goony, are tinged with a comic melancholy. Winters loves his Elwood P. Sugginses and Maude Frickerts, his redneck ballplayers, captains of industry, and blue-haired old ladies, and he makes us love them, too. Beneath the ribbing was a basic humanity. "With all my craziness, there's a lot of sanity down there, too," he says. "I'm not a bad guy." He once explained: "People in general I love. The people I'm really after with my silver bullet are the bully, the bigot, or the Babbitt. I'm not really out to snuff the life out of people. That's no fun for me. But just to watch people operate kills me. I carry a dagger, but it has a rubber blade."

His friend and fellow Ohioan Murray Horwitz, the head of cultural programming at National Public Radio, says: "The accuracy of his satire is just uncanny. He can give you a character in two sentences and in a couple of deft strokes he can paint a whole person and, through that person, often a whole world. Nobody before did this—not even Sid Caesar. At dinner at our house, he got up from the table and said, '*Wal, I wanna thank Mister and Miz Horwitz. We've had Jews at the club before. . . .*' We all knew a dozen guys like that, Dayton [Ohio] Brahmins—some plutocrat who ran National Cash Register."

Lawrence Christon observes: "He was a revolutionary who, with a can opener, opened up the fifties. His antic imagination was so fertile. There was nobody like him. He was like a midwestern lunatic. When a cop pulls him over and asks, '*Where's the fire?*' Winters says, '*In your eyes, officer!*' You didn't know where he was going half the time and often it was pure surreal nonsense." Christon adds: "He was best when he was live. The joy was in the moment. The more it was repeated or institutionalized, the more stale it got. Whenever any of his routines were set in stone they lost their charm. As an actor, in movies or anything scripted, he was very heavy—he overplayed a lot. He wasn't verbal, he wasn't urban, he wasn't intellectual—he was just pure impulse. He's a performer, and a lot of comedians are not performers, they're commentators."

Horwitz maintains that Winters invented a new form: "He took this great leap forward doing sketch comedy as a monologue. What Jonathan did in the mid-fifties was this: he takes Fred Allen—but 'Allen's Alley,' basically—and he takes even Stan Freberg, and he puts it all in one body. He says, 'Put a camera on me and I'll *do* Titus Moody and Senator Claghorn and Mrs. Nussbaum, I'll *do* Mr. Kitzel. I'll *do* all of those radio characters. I'll *be* Mel Blanc.' The guy who comprised it all, in a style, was Jonathan Winters. Fred Allen was Haydn but Jonathan was Mozart."

Horwitz reruns Winters's famous flying-saucer bit (somber interviewer voice): "*We're talking to a man now here, uh, sir, did you actually see it land?*" Switches to swishy lisp: "*Yeth, I did, and I think theeth people are kooks—I think he'th a very attractive man.*" Interviewer: "*Wonderful, wonderful, and what's your name, ma'am?*" In Winters's old-lady voice: "*Maude. Call me Maudie.*" Horwitz explains: "He does all the characters right *there*, without any segues. The point is, the audience will go with you. There's a transition, but it's very short. It's like bebop: when the musicians would hit the chord changes, they'd hit it big, and you'd hear it."

For fifty years, Jonathan Winters has spread his gallery of Main Street figures across America—in movies, TV, recordings, commercials—a parade of off-kilter characters that crowd his imagination and hint at his own complex, all-embracing personality. He peopled an American village with Norman Rockwell figures, but Winters's versions lead twisted interior lives closer to those of the residents of Sherwood Anderson's Winesburg, Ohio.

Whatever he was, he was an anomaly, a satirist with no satirical agenda who was simply reporting the comic news of his fellow Americans. But, for all his originality, or maybe because of it, Winters slipped between the cracks of movies and TV. Nobody knew what to do with all of that bottled-up talent. The thing for which he was most revered—his lightning ability to change characters and improvise the citizens of an entire town—became his albatross. "I've always said versatility is a curse," he remarks. "One-dimensional people [in show business] make a lot of money." The public, the media, the movies, and TV sitcoms feed off famous brand-name commodities. You couldn't hang a sign on Winters as you could on Sahl (Political Comic), Bruce (Dirty Comic), Berman or Newhart (Telephone Comic), Cosby (Family Comic), Gregory (Race Comic), Rivers (Bitchy Comic), and others.

Winters helped rewrite the rules for stand-up comedy, but nobody could quite decipher them. He forged a different connection with his audience, based less on verbal than visual wit, energized by a jumble-shop of sound effects. Where his peers made barbed comments about politics and society, Winters worked the populace, the fringes. Impersonating characters as they came to him (on one album he ran through forty-seven of them), he manufactured real-life voices and precisely accurate sounds—the rapidly ratcheting *click-click-click* of a fishing reel or the authentic *thwip* of a baseball landing in a pitcher's glove.

"In my routines, I always try to speak for the underdog," he says. "I pick on big Babbitts and little Babbitts. I represent those nobody else will. In my sketches on westerns, the Indians are the ones who win. I fight for turtles and dogs. Dogs deserve to be heard." Herb Michelson wrote: "Winters, in an offbeat way, is with *us*. He looks like us and he probably thinks like us. He can sense our foibles and expose them. He leaves an audience totally vanquished—helpless and gasping for breath and spongy from the verbal shock waves. Funny is not a strong enough word for his talent."

Despite his Everyman front, nobody has ever figured out the real Winters, but Horwitz says, "Jonathan was always so disarmingly bare-assed honest. People respond to that. There's a warmth, a kindness there, without being soft or namby-pamby or licking ass. He's a real gentleman and the most professional person I've ever worked with. He's on time, he doesn't throw any diva tantrums, he does his work; he knows his lines. He's a hundred percent true blue."

Although Winters aligns himself with Sahl and Bruce ("There was me, Lenny, and Mort"), he never crested as other mythic comedians of his period did. He first broke through relatively early, around 1956, with a fifteen-minute *Jonathan Winters Show,* for which the director "just let him go." It didn't make much of a dent, although, he said, "I felt I'd arrived." His major breakthrough wouldn't come until 1958, with a series of memorable appearances on Jack Paar's *Tonight* show.

Today, Winters sounds like a man still waiting to arrive. "They're always rediscovering people in this business," he observed in 1969. "They discover you at eighteen and then they discover you again at twenty-seven and then they suddenly find you again at fifty-eight sitting on a park bench with a git-tar." Many people claim they discovered him, but perhaps the first was Joseph Purcell, a TV critic for the *Boston Record,* who wrote in 1956: "Winters is about the freshest, most unique funnyman in the medium today."

Winters never let daily events box him in. As one critic put it, "He made almost no effort to be topically 'relevant.' "What he shared with his fellow renaissance comics was a joyous willingness to create on his feet, to inhabit whoever flew into his head. Wrote Tom Albright in 1980: "Most of his monologue is like a dizzyingly risky high-wire act, with the difference that it cannot be rehearsed. Ideas move in and out of focus, lead to unexpected non sequiturs; moods abruptly change. And, in the end, it all adds up to a peculiar kind of whole." Often his meanderings lead nowhere but into a brick wall. "Sometimes you don't know how you'll get out of a corner," he told me. "It's all part of the game, wondering and fumbling around. I used to always say, shoot your way out. Some form of violence will always get you out—blow up a building."

Audiences are happy to cut him miles of slack, willing to give him the benefit of every comic doubt, laughing politely or assuming they didn't get it, as at a 2000 appearance at San Francisco State University, when he muddled through a fifteen-minute bit as a baseball coach; the crowd laughed at his unerring dialect and reveled in his presence, and even when the lines didn't land, his timing saved him. His comedy is enriched by a lifetime of hard-earned goodwill. When Winters, now seventy-seven, makes a public appearance, wearing a turtleneck and a baseball cap, a beer belly below, he's often preceded by a reel of excerpts from his vast repertoire; it's like watching a flip-book of changing expressions. When he enters, aided by a cane, the audience erupts in warm laughter as he blesses the throng and says, in his doleful deadpan, "Please remain standing."

His first claim to media notoriety was an incident that came to haunt him and that gave directors and producers a convenient cross on which to nail him as a crazy comic. The infamous sighting occurred one spring night in 1959 when he allegedly climbed aboard a ship at San Francisco's Fisherman's Wharf, a little episode that ended with him being carted off to a sanatorium. He had wandered out of his room at the St. Francis Hotel and wound up on the deck of the *Balclutha,* a historic vessel moored at the pier. The event scarred him: it defined, and maligned, him as a nut.

Winters was—is—famous for always being "on." Shelley Berman says, "He's the most 'on' comedian I know. He can't help that. He's always funny and never boring." He once told a reporter, "I was 'on' all the time, always playing the part—in parks, restaurants, wherever I went—and I couldn't get 'off.' Well, I got 'off' "—off liquor, mainly. He comments today: "I'm on when I want to be on. When you go on TV, you're expected to be on. If you sit back, you're considered dull. Robin Williams appears to be always on—take a look at him. You don't see him just sittin' back in a quiet little interview. He's all over the place. And who's more popular? He's making three, four pictures a year, twenty-two million a picture"— a statistic he repeated a couple of times during our interview.

Winters once complained that no matter how he behaves, he can't win. "If I talk like an ordinary person, they write, 'He seemed moody, somber, almost depressed.' If I clown around, they say, 'The poor devil's always on. He probably has to eat alone.' I don't live in a basketful of funnies. Sometimes I'm dark, moody, serious." Winters is incessantly pushed to be on, even when he's not on-camera. People who badger Winters to "say something funny" are totally missing the point. His great gift isn't saying but being.

Stanley Kramer, who directed him in the movie *It's a Mad Mad Mad Mad World,* said, "He fights against being on, but it's hard not to be. Everybody is forever coming to his altar." Kramer called him "the only genius I know" (of which Winters remarks, "That's frightening!"). According to a magazine story at the time (1963), he "awed every big-time comedian in the picture. Between scenes they let his humor take over completely." Winters was terrified, having just come out of rehab. "When I arrived on the set I was in a sweat. I was the new guy on the totem pole and the only one who had never done a film before. It was my big test—and we were working in a hundred and four degrees near Palm Springs. If I disintegrated, I was through. But I got on my feet and bounded away."

Winters was the eye of that frantic film's farcical hurricane, a tribute to his standing in the comedy community. Comics are not known for their generosity toward other comics, especially famous ones who they feel are stealing their lines and spotlight, but comics could afford to love Winters for one basic reason: he had no rivals. Nobody could envy him because nobody could *be* him. He was no threat to anyone; he had come, yes, from another comic planet.

Winters would do thirty minutes for film crews after everyone broke for lunch; even an audience of one in an elevator triggered a minishow. Between takes, actors would amuse themselves by tossing him objects and, like a performing seal, he would improvise something funny with them. Robert Morse, Winters's costar in the film *The Loved One,* said, "Jonny sees things fifty-nine-dimensionally. Give me a hairbrush and I see a hairbrush. Give Jonny a hairbrush and it will be a dozen different things. He could break you up with a paper clip." Toss him a stick and it may inspire him to become an Indian with a bow and arrow, a witch with a broom, a guy paddling a canoe. But sit him down on a TV couch and ask him to discuss himself, and he's stuck.

With his lumpy shape, sagging jowls, squinty eyes, and pliable mouth, he specialized in a variety of hulks, executives, dowagers, geezers, and Indians (he's one-sixteenth Cherokee and has spoken out on Native American causes). He can switch in a twinkling from a Navajo to a red-neck drifter or a lockjawed Boston Brahmin ("*Bahbara and Oi ah racing to Nassau next week. Bahbara's sailing huh yacht and Oi'm sailing moine and who-ever loses has to take the children fah Christmas*"). He has a musician's perfect pitch for native speech patterns and platitudes.

Winters's pièce de résistance, the twangy farmer Elwood P. Suggins, is rivaled by his most famous character, the swinging granny Maude Frickert, whom a critic once called "the most imitated voice in America." Johnny Carson kidnapped her without batting an eyelash—renaming her

"Aunt Blabby," in lacy shawl, black frock, bonnet, and all—and profited from it for decades. Winters says that he never talked to Carson about the TV star's naked theft of his most famous character: "It never bothered me that much—it probably should have." As Winters once explained, Maudie is a cross between Whistler's and Norman Bates's mothers: "She's not quite a dirty old lady, but she's close. People don't stop being hip just because they grow older." He based her on his Aunt Lu Perks and another aunt who taught him to play poker and gave him his first glass of wine. "She was a shut-in, but she always had candy and a glass of wine when you'd visit her. 'Have a little wine,' she'd say. She was feisty."

He finally quit doing Maude in drag because, he explains, "The character can take over and you want to do other things, but they [directors] can't see you any other way." He also tried a Grandpa Frickert, who didn't catch on. Winters finally had to kill Maude off, explaining, "She was taking over." Maude had become his logo and mouthpiece. "She could say things about people that others couldn't, like, 'This man attacked me, but he was attractive.' She was a real rebel, just a wild old lady."

Winters was at his best pegging squares and hicks, probably because he grew up among them, but he was equally deadly skewering their big-city opposites—urban rednecks who sip Manhattans in airport bars at ten A.M. If Jewish comics often indulged in Jewish stereotypes, Winters (and, to a less lethal degree, Bob Newhart) had a keen fix on WASPery. Winters was a comedy minority—a Protestant from a little midwestern town.

MANY OF WINTERS'S most endearing characters are based on the people he had known in Springfield, Ohio, where he grew up in a Huck Finn setting, and, before that, in Dayton, where Jonathan Harshman Winters III was born into a well-to-do family in 1925. That apparent head start soon soured when his parents, who divorced when he was seven, proved to be chilly disciplinarians who not only didn't encourage their gifted son but went out of their way to squash him. If people sense a melancholy in Winters, the roots were solidly planted by his parents, who sound like something out of *Oliver Twist*. As his wife puts it, "With him, his children came first, and with his parents, they came first." His banker father would lock young Jonathan in the car while he was inside a bar getting drunk; Winters called him "a hip Willy Loman."

His mother was a sharp-tongued local radio talk-show host who, notes one family friend, was jealous of her son's success. When Winters's first big movie, *The Russians Are Coming! The Russians Are Coming!*, opened and he proudly called home to tell his parents it was playing at the local movie house, his mother said, "Oh, you know we never go downtown." When he left for the service, she shook hands with him, and after he returned he found that she had given away all his toys, explaining to him, eerily, "We didn't think you were coming back."

The senior Jonathan Winters, after retiring to Florida, once called his son to complain that people were pestering him over the telephone and would Jonathan please change his name. The old man could be malevolent. Once, at their farm, his father saw some dead cows and Jonathan explained, "Dad, I think they're sleeping," and his father said, "No, they're dead, but I want you to milk them anyway." Sydney Goldstein, who has booked Winters in her Bay Area City Arts and Lecture series, recalls, "He once told me his mother said, 'You're the ugliest boy I ever saw,' and his father added, 'And the stupidest.' "

Years after he'd made it, the pain hadn't subsided. In 1963 Winters still carried in his wallet the Emerson quotation "Humor is the mistress of sorrow." And he once imagined an epitaph for himself: "Step on me. Everybody else did." Years later, he said, "I realize now I was always trying to please my father. It didn't matter if everybody else told me I was good. No, I had to hear it from him. And I was never good enough for him. I'd ask myself, Why, why, why? I know the answer now, but I didn't then. I wasn't a problem child—my parents were the problem." He muses, "I always thought that they'd change, and they never did."

He was an only, lonely child who stayed in his room a lot, fantasizing. "I'd talk to myself, interview myself," he says. "I would be a general. I would be a war hero, or whatever I wanted to be. And it was always, 'What is he doing in there?' " Amusing himself. "Humor is a great defense," he says. "In many respects, it's been my salvation. It's not a question of saying, 'Nobody understood me.' A lot of people didn't, and still don't. My old man was an alcoholic, and then my mother went into radio—and I had to amuse myself." He's always regarded himself as an elderly child. "Even though I've been married fifty years, I still sneak off and entertain myself. I have four or five imaginary figures. I play a doctor or a nurse, whatever I want to play."

Winters grew up with one ear glued to the radio, but mainly he was a movie addict, with sensitive comic antennae: "I loved Gleason and Carney on TV, but the only thing I didn't buy about *The Honeymooners,* and I told Jack this—you can't insult anybody for fifteen minutes, especially a woman, and then say, 'Alice, you're the greatest!' " He was also offended by Frank Fontaine's addled barkeep on Gleason's show: "The character's a retard. It's like I ridicule you and then say I was kidding. *Whoa!*"

Winters's boyhood buddy was his grandfather, who had founded the Winters National Bank in Dayton. He, too, was a heavy drinker, but he made time for Jonathan, and the two of them once traveled to Yellowstone National Park together. "Nobody in the world had a grandfather quite like mine," he once said. "We did everything first class. I have a picture of him inscribed, 'To Bozo, my old college chum.' " His granddad "wanted to be in show business in the worst way, and would tell awful jokes," he recalls, assuming his old-timer voice: "*Hey, Carl, it's good to see ya. I see you—do you see me?*" He lists his grandfather, Twain, and James Thurber as his greatest comic influences. "Their humor was based completely on reality. I'm hooked on reality. Thurber was my guy."

The young Jonathan found more appreciative audiences away from home when he was sent off to a boarding school, yet he remained a loner. "Other guys had more security, steady dates, and all that. I didn't. The only thing that kept me going was my comedy. We'd all go to a tavern called O'Brien's, and I would do impressions of the Indianapolis Speedway. I had quite a following." He soon learned that being "on" was a social survival tactic. In lieu of joining the French Foreign Legion, his first choice ("I'd seen Gary Cooper and *he* made out"), in his senior year he enlisted in the navy, partly to get back at his abusive parents and partly to flee school. A slow student, he once bought a book titled *Mathematics Can Be Fun* just so he could burn it. "I hated school, but I wasn't the class clown." He made friends as a boy with a rich old lady of 102 with whom he played Monopoly and who, he says, gave him the best education; he calls himself "an illiterate intellectual."

After Winters left the service in 1946, having served on carriers in the Pacific (where he entertained his biggest crowd to date, two thousand sailors and marines—many of whom later perished on Saipan), he finished high school, then went to Kenyon College "for about an hour and a half." With the hope of becoming a cartoonist, he entered the Dayton Art Institute ("When you choose art, you're in charge"). His father asked him, "Are you a queer?" It was at the Dayton Art Institute that he "learned to observe," he says, and first absorbed the works of Robert Benchley and Charles Addams, other major sources of inspiration.

While working at a variety of jobs, he observed apricot pickers in

California and woodcutters outside Salt Lake City. He also served time as a fry cook at Yellowstone, in a rubber plant, an incubator factory, a bottling plant ("looking for dead mice and white marbles"), and a gas station—the sources of his collection of characters, whose bizarreness he would celebrate. For practice, he studied people at the Greyhound bus station. Many of his characters are reminiscent of the white-trash types found in George Booth's *New Yorker* cartoons—scraggly men and women who sit under bare lightbulbs in their underwear, watching TV with mangy, scratching dogs and cats.

His first lucky break was meeting and marrying a fellow art student, Eileen Ann Schauder, who encouraged him to give up cartooning for comedy. "The first time I heard him talk, my jaw began hanging open," she later recalled. "Did he make up all those things all by himself? So much good stuff was lost on just my ears. He was lively, charming, and the most interesting person I'd met." In his fourth year of art school she encouraged him to try out for an amateur show. "I married you because you were funny," she told him. "You should go down there and win that watch." He won the watch and gave up cartooning (he'd sold one cartoon to the *Saturday Evening Post*). Besides the watch, he also won a job at a Dayton radio station, with the apt call letters WING, as a six A.M. disc jockey. It was only sixty-five dollars a week, and when he waffled about accepting the job his wife ordered, "You take it!" He spun not just records but interviews with people he would conjure up on—and out of—the air, what he termed "miniature vignettes," for which he was finally fired.

With only the deejay job on his thin showbiz résumé, Winters moved to New York in 1953 with fifty-six dollars in his pocket and knocked around for seven months until his new family joined him (by then they had a child). He soon found semisteady work in TV, playing Santa Claus in a Westinghouse commercial, a fireman on *Playhouse 90,* and bit parts in other live TV dramas, plus a shot on *Chance of a Lifetime,* a talent-prize show, where sound effects made up most of his act. With surprisingly little struggle for a comic fish out of water, he got booked at such swanky nightspots as the Blue Angel and Le Ruban Bleu, where Alistair Cooke, the host of the distinguished TV series *Omnibus,* caught his act. An astonished Cooke went backstage afterward and told him, "My, my, you're quite a bundle. I was fascinated by how your mind works. Would you consider appearing on *Omnibus?*" Recalls Winters, "Would I *consider* it?!" Winters was the first stand-up comic to play Cooke's artsy Sunday show.

He worked practically around the clock in TV as a transient guest star—on Jack Paar's morning show, Garry Moore's afternoon show (Moore hired him after seeing him on *Arthur Godfrey's Talent Scouts*), and Steve Allen's late-night show. One writer called him "the darling of the cool people." Winters replaced Orson Bean in the last Broadway edition of John Murray Anderson's *Almanac,* and then became George Gobel's summer TV replacement, which led, in 1956, to the fifteen-minute TV show, half of which featured singers. "It's difficult to come off hilarious in seven minutes," he said.

By now, Winters had perfected the arsenal of sounds that helped make him so distinctive—machine guns, buzz saws, angry dogs, planes taking off, water dripping, car doors closing, horses, explosions, and owls. He has a thing for owls, which he collects in drawings and figurines, along with Civil War artifacts, toy soldiers, ladybug-shaped paraphernalia, coins, tomahawks, beer steins, and nautical paintings. (He was briefly a partner in a Manhattan novelty store.)

A transforming moment occurred when he first came to New York with his act overloaded with impressions and re-creations of war and cowboy movies. It allowed him to employ his vast repertoire of special effects, all achieved with his mouth, but the impressions and sounds became a crutch. "An old guy at the Ruban Bleu gave me some very solid advice. He said, 'I've seen a lot of performers come this way and I think you got an ear, but what you're doing is, you're merely shining their [movie stars'] shoes. You're bringing attention to *them* instead of yourself. You can't break away if you get married to those characters.' "

New York scared him into expanding his talent. "So I started doing characters I'd grown up with. They were always there but they were kind of dormant. I realized there was more to humor than just doing sounds and impressions. I wanted to do little verbal vignettes, pictures right out of my head. I dug deep into my bag of goodies. They tell writers to write what you know, so that's what I did with the characters I knew growing up." Whereupon he segues into: " '*This is Ed Carlisle at station KLBA and this gentleman here is Mr. Murchison, who just witnessed a saucer landing.*' I began to deal with what was happening but timeless, picking out locales people could identify with and incorporating into it this kind of quiet insanity: '*Mr. Murchison, did the man who came out of the saucer look like us?*' . . . '*He was, sort of—wal, he had deep-set eyes, kinda raised eyes, didn't have no slope. He had Caucasian features. He was smokin' something. I don't know what it was, kind of a little pipe there, and a nautical cap. Mah boy had the dowg with him and Whiskers was there and the dowg barked and it musta spooked him. I told him, "You shouldn'ta did that." ' "*

Between the late sixties and the early eighties, Winters's characters and sound effects included an undertaker, former Alabama governor George Wallace, a turtle, a mad doctor, a homecoming queen, Ben Franklin, a gay policeman, a Navajo talking to a tourist, a Brit, a rattling drill, an exploding grenade, an automatic car window, a teenager necking in an old Ford, a TV western, a happy-talk newscast, and Mr. and Mrs. Aristotle Onassis. His centerpiece was "The Cut-Rate Pet Shop," which sold damaged animals. (Woody Allen later did a similar bit about "a used pet store" that featured bent kangaroos and stammering dogs. Even stand-up legends may stoop to a little petshoplifting.)

In a 1976 Bicentennial TV special, he did twenty historical characters, from George Washington and Babe Ruth to Casey Jones and Jesse James. Sylvia Rubin reported on Winters's "childlike guilelessness," noting that "the whole American character seems to pass through him: the macho and the ignorant bigotry and the feckless love of violence, also the candor, the clichés and inconsequentialities, the leery sexuality and the saccharine sentimentality." Winters's comedy doesn't translate well into print, and only barely onto vinyl—how to describe his turtle crossing the Pennsylvania Turnpike? He's almost a totally visceral experience; his records can't convey what he does in the flesh, when his supple face, vocal and body language, sound effects, and running commentary are shaped into something that is more than the sum of the parts—a miscellany of slapstick and satire wound into an indefinable ball of whimsy. As one writer put it in 1965, "He was a you-had-to-be-there kind of performer."

"I'm a satirist," he explains, "but satire has always been an uphill struggle for anyone who gets involved in it. A lot of people just don't understand what you're getting at. Even my old man was against it. He wanted me to get a ukulele and tell jokes. But looking back, doing satire is the one thing I'm sure of. Sure, I've died with it, just like everyone else, but that's the gamble you take. I had some sort of strange fight inside of me with regards to jokes. I didn't like jokes. My dad would tell me jokes all the time. Anytime we'd try to talk, he'd always start, 'Look, I know you don't like jokes, but . . . ,' and I'd say, 'Oh no, here we go again.' "

Murray Horwitz, who once worked briefly with Winters as his straight man, recalls the experience of working in tandem with him: "Jonathan has said to me, 'Just tell the truth and people will laugh.' This deceptively simple phrase is the secret to the whole thing. Say a guy goes into a pharmacy to buy a bottle of Pepto-Bismol. It can go in a couple of obvious ways. If Jonathan does it, it turns out that the guy is his son's lover. Now all of a sudden you've got dramatic irony, and it forces the characters to have an emotional and intellectual life. He's always looking for that extra dimension—the dimension that gives it humanity."

It was Jack Paar who finally hoisted Winters into the big time, heaping praise on him and allowing him the long leash on camera that he's always required. Winters was grateful for the exposure, but the compliments were often left-handed. Paar would always say, "I don't know anyone with greater talent," but, as Winters recalls, there would inevitably be a qualifier: "He always added, '. . . when the moon is right.' " Whenever Winters is lauded, there's usually that madman subtext, the faintly condescending notion that his brilliance wasn't his own nimble mind at work but the result of some out-of-body lunacy.

Steve Allen booked him a lot, unfazed by Winters's personal history. Said Allen: "I didn't give a damn what he may have done on Sunset Boulevard at two A.M. He was always a good egg and a funny one, and that's all there is to it." The give-and-take worked best with himself and with Jack Paar, said Allen: "We were sensible fellows and Jonathan was on another planet." Winters's version: "Paar was a difficult guy. He had this quality, it was like an apology, 'Wha-wha-wha-what am I doin', pal? Why-why-why am I out here?' For the money! I tried to understand this guy as best I could. He was a crybaby, and I get tired of crybabies." Paar would often break in just as Winters was starting to develop a character.

Winters had more genuine fun with Allen, who recalled: "We'd throw him challenges. First we'd say something like, 'Be a German.' Then one of us would say, 'Make him a little effeminate.' A few seconds later, 'Make him an effeminate German nightclub singer.' It didn't matter how many elements we added to the characterization, Jonathan never balked." Allen added, however, that, because Winters was forever cracking up the cast, he could be "a little hard to work with." Allen happily played straight man to him, but he got him talking. Most talk-show interviewers are so convulsed by Winters that they just sit there giggling.

Winters also liked Johnny Carson—"We had a lot of fun together. [He] wanted you to look good. He'd drop into the green room: 'Jonny, what do you want to talk about?' And we talked about it. He liked to play." He's not a fan of Jay Leno and David Letterman, whose appeals perplex him. "I don't understand what they're doing or how they got there.

They don't give you any time. Letterman didn't want to play. I couldn't get going on the show. Letterman is a jar of mayonnaise. He's rude and cold. You start to tell your story and he laughs over your story and kills it. With Carson you were the guest and he was more generous and wanted you to look good."

For all his multifaceted brilliance, TV and films never let Winters chase his comic muse, as the movies once did its Chaplins, Keatons, and Marxes. Too often, Winters was hired only to have his rambunctious spirit hobbled. "Can you imagine writing for guys like Laurel and Hardy and Chaplin and Keaton? Those guys were allowed to do their own thing. What is mindboggling to me is, people say, 'You're a genius,' which is nice to hear, but I always say, 'Yeah, a genius is a man who can do everything but find work.' Or they say, 'You're the king. You're the guy who opened the door to improvisation.' Well, whether I opened it or not, where is it?"

Pauline Kael lamented that Hollywood had handcuffed Winters, whom she called "perhaps the most inventive comedian alive." Horwitz, who wrote a screenplay with Winters, amplifies Kael's judgment: "To set him loose, you could make a movie and put him in it for half a dollar. Would he be difficult to work with? Sure he'd be difficult to work with. W. C. Fields was difficult to work with, but look what happened. Those weren't expensive movies. What they should've done in the seventies is set Jonathan loose, the way they set Pryor loose, or Mel Brooks, and given him a chance to run loose in a movie."

WINTERS DOES MORE THAN just observe characters—he searches them out and eggs them on in conversation, as a kind of comic research project. He loves to mosey into downtown Montecito, near Santa Barbara, and talk to people on the street. When he lived in Mamaroneck, New York, he would stroll into the drugstore and introduce himself as various characters: Jesse James's brother, Phil, shopping for a fancy comb like Jesse carried; or a Mexican outlaw from Mount Kisco called the Kisco Kid; or Mrs. Woodrow Wilson's feebleminded nephew on a day's outing from the sanatorium.

Not everyone was charmed. One neighbor groaned, "When I run into Winters around town, I head the other way. He'll corner you and bore you for hours. He may be great on TV, but in person he's a menace. He doesn't know when to quit." In a lengthy profile, however, the writer

Thomas Berger, author of the novel *Little Big Man,* concluded after two days of following the comic around that most doormen, cabdrivers, waiters, and clerks were enchanted by Winters. "People gravitate to him," said a friend.

There was a time when he would hold court at Manhattan saloons like Toots Shor's, where regulars would buy him drinks to fuel his impromptu characters and other comics would scribble notes as he trotted out characters and ad-libs. "In those days," one writer put it, "Winters's genie was in the bottle." One night he toured Manhattan bistros with a defused hand grenade, shouting, from time to time, "Everybody goes when the whistle blows!" On another occasion he told a friend in a hotel lobby, in a loud voice, "We never should have operated in a hotel room. Granted, he's alive, but you shouldn't have let that brain fall on the rug. Next time, St. Vincent's." Or in a crowded elevator with the comic Pat McCormick: "You don't think we tied him up too tight?"

Winters never felt he was ridiculing his characters or felt any hostility toward them. "I've never really had a chip on my shoulder against anyone. The only chip I ever had was with myself. Elwood Suggins is a quiet redneck who 'tokes lahk this.' My characters, there was an innocent quality to them—a feisty quality, too. I don't put down kids or kick slats out from old people. A lot of things I've been asked to do, that I've shied away from, are gross. I find making fun of somebody—you better know 'em a lifetime, and even then I feel uncomfortable for that other person."

Some critics have carped that his humor trades too deeply in the macabre. "I don't think Jonathan is macabre at all," argues Horwitz. "He tells the truth and exposes the bleak side of human nature, but *all* humorists deal with that. Keaton deals with that. Lily Tomlin deals with that. And that to me is what distinguishes the humorist from the comic." Discussing the universality of Winters's minisketches, Thomas Berger noted, "This is not insipid social satire that will be meaningless within the month, or the synthetic contrivance of the nightclub comic."

Berger's analysis was written in 1965, six years after Winters had returned from his self-imposed exile from clubs and the spotlight generally, after the heavily reported incident aboard the *Balclutha.* He had reemerged in movies with one of his too-rare screen roles as a smarmy cemetery operator in *The Loved One.* But the mad scene on the *Balclutha* was still on people's minds, though Winters insists he never even boarded the ship, let alone climbed the mast. The story did Winters great harm because it confirmed a media stereotype—and a public perception—that

Jonathan Winters must be a nut case. Everything Winters did thereafter was tainted by those ten misunderstood minutes in 1959.

Two days before, he was in a near brawl at the hungry i when hecklers objected to his comments about President Truman. He invited the people to the microphone and then met them later at the bar. The police were called. A few nights later, he began discussing Alcoholics Anonymous from the stage and, during the second show, broke into tears over a cigarette holder that a fan had given him because he was "a good guy." That night, a waiter took Winters back to his hotel room and sat up with him all night drinking coffee. Winters, then thirty-two, had been a heavy drinker—up to two quarts of liquor a day. Many said he'd been sober for years but that the pressures of *not* drinking in a nightclub, surrounded by liquor, caused him to crack. Before that, he was drinking twenty cups of coffee a night to stay up and couldn't sleep afterward. He said, "I can't even make my best friends believe that it was a mental breakdown—not booze—that put me in the psycho ward."

The director Paul Mazursky, then a comic, was on hand the night of Winters's fateful run-in. "Here's what he did," recalls Mazursky. "I was there just to check the room—I was going to open the next night. He was amusing for two or three minutes—not big but getting there—and then he took out his wallet. Pretty soon he's taking out pictures of his family and he's starting to cry. The audience was shocked; they didn't know what to do." Paul Goldenberg, the hungry i's manager at the time, recalls: "Once he called for a candle and I handed it to him and, in total darkness, he spoke of his family and he was welling up onstage."

What happened the night of May 12, 1959, is that Winters hated being on the road away from his family—"six years of never being home except Christmas," he said, "of only seeing my son play one game of baseball a year, and of hardly knowing my daughter." News accounts claim that he scrambled aboard the ship and climbed the mast. Winters insists he didn't climb anything, he only threatened to, but it made a better story to imagine him like a loon up in the crow's nest, so that's how the story has gone down in comedy history. "You can't get rid of it," he says. Winters offered a million dollars to anyone who could produce a photograph of him in the ship's rigging. "People still ask about the time I flipped, and I wonder when is it ever going to end," he said sixteen years later. "It's like doing time."

The *Balclutha* story, as reported in the *San Francisco Chronicle,* has Winters buying a ticket to the square-rigger and claiming it entitled him to climb the mast. When a cop asked him his name, he said, "I'm John Q. What's it to you? I'm in orbit, man! I'm a mooncat on Cloud 9, from outer space." He allegedly resisted arrest, was handcuffed, and taken to San Francisco General Hospital. He was later taken to Belmont, a sanatorium outside of San Francisco, by his wife; the hungry i's Enrico Banducci spent several days with him, and after two weeks he was released. His manager described him as "just an overgrown college kid [who] likes to have fun." Banducci told Abby Wasserman in 1991, "He climbed the mast of the *Balclutha* and yelled, 'Let's get this going, bring out the sail!' He was up there being Captain Frog. He went a little crazy just for that day. I came back to see him and he locked me in the cell and said, 'There he is—now you've got your man.' I made a deal to have him committed to Belmont."

Winters explains now, "I had a breakdown. I wasn't drunk—certainly no drugs. But I never went aboard the ship! I went up to the ticket guy and said something like, 'You oughta get a couple of cannons on this thing.' The next thing I know, the Harbor Police are there. Didn't read me my rights or anything. Just put some irons on me, and the next thing I knew I was in S.F. General. I guess I must have said something that scared him, some remarks. Certainly nothing physical."

He went home to Mamaroneck, quit the road and liquor for good. He explained later that he had been an alcoholic at eighteen, contracted acute nephritis in the navy, and "was given twenty-four hours to live in a naval hospital." Career pressures created new problems—"I always seemed to be just missing out on the big things." He told a TV interviewer, "I was afraid. My time on the road was: get the money, send it home—but how do *I* get home? I took chances, but as free as I wanted to be I became a robot. Once I got that [nightclub] monkey off my back, I could see what improv really could be."

A year into his recovery, he said, "So I don't have a million dollars—or five hundred thousand, or even a hundred thousand. I have my family intact and my skull is working. You've gotta say goodbye to some cash, but I didn't want to say goodbye to my kids." He added, "The episode was a turning point in my life. I learned to quit feeling sorry for myself. Like, a fellow comes up to me and says, 'I see where Bob Newhart's on top now.' I said, 'Listen, I got a new Ford station wagon. And a home. And that's pretty good for a fellow who used to be sitting cross-legged in

Union Square looking at the statues. My favorite line is, 'I quit complaining because I found too many people who could top me.' "

Winters was a memorable booking for the Interlude's Gene Norman, who recalls that, in 1959, "he was on a bill with Jeri Southern and both of 'em flipped out in the same engagement. Both were very neurotic. Every night he became more disconnected. He was obviously a little meshugge. He was kind of unraveling onstage. He'd start talking to himself. One night he walked off the stage onto Sunset Boulevard and directed traffic. That same engagement, Jeri Southern got very melancholy and didn't show up, so I called the William Morris office, which booked both acts, and said, 'May I speak to your staff psychiatrist?' "

Two years after "the San Francisco thing," as he calls it, he had a second breakdown that lasted eight months. Doctors suggested electroshock therapy to erase his painful childhood memories, but Winters refused, saying, "That's one of my big tools, recall." He grew so depressed that "I didn't think I could ever be funny again." His family and friends helped pull him through it; his showbiz pals have included Robert Clary, Louie Nye, Ronnie Graham, Cliff Arquette, and James Cagney, with whom he painted. A close friend now is Gary Owens, the old *Laugh-In* announcer.

Horwitz says emphatically, "This is terrifically important to say about Jonathan Winters: when he had his nervous breakdown and went through AA, remember that was all in full public view at a time when that was not fashionable. He didn't expect to gain anything by it. And now it's a terrific career move—'Geez, weren't you beaten as a child? Can't we sell that? Wasn't your dad an alcoholic?' Can you imagine Bob Hope or Lucille Ball or Nat King Cole going through something like that, and having a breakdown in 1959? They'd have said he's 'suffering from exhaustion.' Jonathan said, 'No, I'm going into a mental institution, I was crazy.' "

Winters reflects, "I haven't had a drink in forty straight years, and I don't mean now and then. But in the eyes of some of these people my age, it's still, 'Oh, you had that problem. . . .' What's confusing today is to have a long track record and then see actors go away for six months [in rehab] and come back and get two or three feature films."

When Winters retired from nightclubs, he was happy to leave it all behind. "Most club audiences ignore you. They're either part of the *Virginia Woolf* crowd that's always playing games or they're sauced out of their heads. But even if everything went perfectly inside a club, I'd still hate it. Clubs are boring." He adds now, "In the beginning it's the audience and the laughter, but if you're raising a family you can't just say, 'How old are you, honey? I'll see you when you're twenty.' I wanted to quit the road—it was my decision. It was late but it wasn't too late."

WITHOUT BIG CLUB DATES, and with TV leery of him, it took Winters several years to arrive again in a substantial sense, when he was signed in 1964 to six one-hour NBC specials and six guest shots on *The Andy Williams Show.* It led to a syndicated series, *The Wacky World of Jonathan Winters,* and his appointment as the Hefty garbage-bag spokesperson, a version of Granny Frickert, in an ad campaign that made "gar-*bage*" part of the slanguage. On TV, he's made his most lasting impression in commercials, first for Hefty Bags and then as a pitchman for the California egg industry. "It pays the rent," he says. "The egg commercial was complete improvisation; they just let me go. Only two times in my career did they let me go like that"—he can't remember the other time.

That clown-on-the-loose quality, which audiences loved, always worried producers, who want predictable performers they can control. Winters wasn't out of control, but he needed room to roam. As far back as 1965, the veteran comedy writer Goodman Ace wrote that he had warned a TV executive that Winters needed special handling. "I volunteered the opinion that Mr. Winters is a TV guest and is not of star quality. Mr. Winters's sense of humor is very special and when expanded to an hour tends to run to the violent and the macabre. And more importantly, it is at its most effective when taken in five-minute doses." Ace added: "Now that Mr. Winters has appeared in five specials it is obvious nobody has been able to persuade him to edit and harness his talent." Lucille Ball said of him, "He was never flexible enough for Hollywood's super egos." Winters's response: "I bent, I just didn't bend over."

Ron Miller, the longtime TV critic, observes: "TV couldn't find a niche for him, but it was more than just his wildness. Robin Williams learned how to do it. I actually was tired of seeing Winters stand in front of an audience and do what he wanted to do. I've seen that and heard all the voices and I wanted to see him in a character. He really needed a structure around him."

Tom Koch, who wrote for a Winters TV show, recalls: "He was a strange man. He played all these different characters because I don't think there was a real person there. He was easy enough to get along with. The hardest thing about working for him was, you'd write a four-minute sketch and he'd go off and do a half hour of material and then you'd have to edit it back down to four minutes again. But some of the stuff he did was much funnier than the stuff that had been written."

Winters necessarily fails some of the time. Viewing a totally improvised 1987 Showtime special, *On the Ledge,* with Milton Berle, Phyllis Diller, Robin Williams, and Mort Sahl all playing straight man to Winters, is like watching improv commit suicide. Piece by piece, every sketch falls thuddingly flat. The comedy agent Jack Rollins had once said that Winters's ability to dazzle an audience momentarily lacked a personality for audiences to latch on to. Woody Allen has commented, "It could be argued that Jonathan Winters is too funny. The world doesn't know the person Jonathan Winters, which denies you the very top rank of success."

He simply may have been, ironically, too off-the-wall for the mainstream Americans he was caricaturing. Whatever the reason, TV never found a series he could be fitted into or a character that could be sustained for more than a few minutes—but, then, TV never found a format for Danny Kaye, either. Even on his various TV specials, Winters was never well served by the writers and was virtually uneditable—his scenes had no seams. He couldn't be contained. Sid Caesar observed: "In TV, you gotta put it in a box, and you couldn't do that with Jonathan, and TV couldn't deal with that."

Winters had lots of ideas for TV shows: "I love history. I wanted to do what I still think could be a helluva sitcom, about a guy who owns an antiques shop. It writes itself: '*Hi, you have antiques from the Revolutionary period?*' . . . '*Sure, this was George Washington's snuffbox. See what it says here?* To George from Martha—*isn't it sweet?*' . . . '*How do ah know thut's real?*' . . . '*Because I told you.*' So I said to this TV guy, 'What about this for a half hour? You're mixing humor with history.' And he said to me, 'After six o'clock it's too heavy.' That's sad. I'm genuinely sorry that I didn't get it across to more people in TV that improvisation could be fun. It's just hard to find someone who you can play with, such as Brooks and Reiner's 2,000 Year Old Man." He plays well with Gary Owens, with whom he cut his first record in thirty years (in 2002), *Outpatients.* For decades now he's been laboring over an autobiography, currently titled *In Search of a Playground*—perhaps a search for his lost boyhood.

With TV dodging him, Winters looked to a career in movies, but that, too, never quite happened, despite his success in *It's a Mad Mad Mad Mad World, The Loved One, Viva Max,* and *The Russians Are Coming! The Russians Are Coming!* He had many offers after *Mad Mad World,* but even films were not the answer. Winters found moviemaking too slow for his racing mind. In

1967 he told a reporter, "Movies are the hardest medium. Your only audience is the director. When you're onstage, you can wander. You're your own editor. If you get bored with a bit, you can just change the subject. Naturally, that can't happen in a film."

Some directors did, in fact, encourage him to improvise, but just as many worried that he would. He adds, "I was always cursed by wanting to improvise. It's very costly, because writers and directors and producers frown on it. Directors and producers and actors talk about their movies and how much they improvise. I always question this. I find if I improvise, they'll say, 'Yes, you go ahead and do your thing, Jon,' and 'That's good, that was funny, that was funny. Now I'll tell you what we'll do, let's go back to the script.' Suddenly you're doing two movies—mine, what I've written, and what they've written." Winters was stunned when he learned that two of his favorite "improvisational" comedy teams, Nichols & May and Bob & Ray, were essentially scripted. "They were always compared to me, but they wrote everything." (Or in Nichols & May's case, froze in.)

His talent was easier to channel into animated films like *The Smurfs, The Rocky and Bullwinkle Movie,* and *The Flintstones.* Time and money are wasted if an improvisation doesn't pay off (increasing the pressure on Winters) and TV executives never knew how far he would go. Michael Morris, who wrote for Winters years ago on a morning TV show, says, "He was a full-fledged nut. He didn't know when to stop. He was on the verge of craziness, in a world of his own. Most of these guys [comics] are that way. It's a world of fantasy. They just think of themselves. They have no relationship to you or me."

Winters sounds wistful about his thwarted movie career, but his talent finally found a part-time home on TV in 1981, when he was reborn on *Mork and Mindy* (he arrived on the show by breaking through a giant egg) as Robin Williams's full-grown fifty-six-year-old son, Mearth, from outer space, a recurring character that refreshed the lagging show and also Winters's flagging career. It was an artistically sweet pairing (a joke in the industry had it that if Lenny Bruce and Jonathan Winters had had a son, it would have been Robin). Williams paid him homage in interviews. Like Winters, he spun out bits with a thousand beginnings and no endings until, Winters-like, he decided to run them together into a stream-of-consciousness act. Winters's endless ingenuity inspired Williams, who says he took from the master improviser the lesson "that anything is possible, that anything is funny—plus he's so visually oriented. And the sounds! He was the first guy before the technology to really morph himself and do all those things." Williams adds: "He gave me the idea that it can be free-form, that you can go in and out of things pretty easily. That's what he did. He just kind of jumps [from bit to bit]." On the occasion of Winters winning the Mark Twain Prize, Williams remarked, "He isn't just Everyman, he literally is *every man.*"

It was the producers who had the idea to hire Winters, not Williams, who told me, "It was in the fourth year and things were kind of in the trenches, and someone said, 'Let's bring in Jonathan.' I thought it was a great idea. Even when it was on, people were, like, 'What the hell is this?' He was, like, playing this big kid and people didn't know what it was." Williams not only revered but trusted Winters's genius. They were totally different comic creatures—Williams didn't do characters in his monologue, just rapid-fire lines and voices—but they were comic brothers under the skin. Winters asked Williams to stop calling him his "mentor," telling him, "That's a bad word in Ohio. Say 'idol.' "

Williams goes on: "A lot of people wouldn't work with Jonathan for years because they thought he was really crazy—and there was that time when he really was. He calls that time he went away 'the great vacation.' Even when we did *Mork and Mindy,* they'd say, 'He can't learn lines.' He would learn lines, he just wouldn't learn the ones he thought were stupid—he would block the ones that weren't funny. He'd come up with lines that were a hundred times funnier." Williams insists, "He's not out of control—he's a brilliant guy who can do anything if you just give him a chance." He paused. "The problem is, sometimes he goes beyond it."

According to A&E's *Biography,* even on *Mork and Mindy* Winters was at odds with the writers and producers—"My hands were bound," he says. His comic gears would shift from inspired to stalled and back again. On a 1964 *Tonight* show, Paar handed him a stick and, for the next five minutes, in a virtuoso display, he used the bare stick as a prop for a wild parade of characters—as a gun, a Zulu spear, a flute, a fishing pole, a golf club, a toreador's sword, a witch's ladle, and a magic wand. Other times, he would vamp while awaiting a reluctant muse, and often the sum was less than its parts.

Williams's first memory of Winters is as a kid of eight: "I saw him on the *Tonight* show, and I remember my father just really laughing. He really let go." (He recalled the actual routine at a Winters tribute: "Jack [Paar] asks Jonathan what he does, and Jonathan says, 'I'm a big game hunter.' 'Well, what do you hunt?' 'I hunt squirrels.' 'And how do you hunt squirrels?' '*I aim for their little nuts.*' ") Williams adds: "Now in the past few years, knowing Jon has been great, hanging out with him, just to take him around the city when he was here." He's also witnessed Winters in action on the streets: "He works a crowd. He goes to antique stores. People in Santa Barbara say he'll do thirty minutes. He does that great thing about the time he parked in the handicapped space and a woman said, '*You're not handicapped,*' and he said, '*Madame, can you see inside my mind?*' "

Williams came to see Winters at an onstage interview in San Francisco in 2000. Sydney Goldstein, the event's booker, recalls Winters saying that "he did not think that Robin Williams was as much like him as other people did, that Robin was so hyper and Jonathan didn't like to think of himself as being hyper." She adds: "I got the sense of a very raw, vulnerable person who has worked out a way of dealing with his vulnerability. He's very attuned to other people. He was very tightly strung—his feelers were out everywhere. I saw also this very self-conscious person who seemed to be baffled by the following that he had."

Only Lenny Bruce has had as much influence on latter-day comedians, who mainly admire Winters's comic abandon. These are comedians who worship at his feet, such as the writer-actor-director Eugene Levy, who has said, "He is the keeper of the holy grail of our craft," and added, "I doubt there would have been an *SCTV,* a *Saturday Night Live,* or an *In Living Color* without Jonathan Winters. This is not only a comic genius at work, this is the epitome of character acting." The comic and actor Richard Belzer commented: "He is the most unique, transformative, revelatory figure in all of comedy," pointing out that Dana Carvey's Church Lady is Maude Frickert's love child.

The comedian Richard Lewis says that he was knocked out when he first heard a Winters album at the age of thirteen: "To me he was like the Jimi Hendrix of comedians. His whole instrument was about being funny. He was like fretting himself. I don't know anyone else who has been so consistently that way. He was put on earth for that reason. I asked to sit next to him at a Stanley Kramer dinner, and just leaning over for a string bean he'd go into a whole riff about where that string bean came from and that I was insane for eating it. Nothing can go by him." Lewis, the comic neurotic and himself an admitted ex-alcoholic, says, "Even though you don't know who he is, you know he's troubled. He channeled his craziness through other people."

The mystery is how much Winters is winging it and how much derives from notes he's written earlier. People question whether his material is all improv. He won't quite reveal whether he writes out his own seemingly spontaneous bits. "I sketch out my ideas," he says, sketchily. In 1981 Murray Horwitz and Winters put together an improvisation routine for their alma mater, Kenyon College. Horwitz says, "He writes constantly. He keeps journals and he'd write and write and write." He also explains the method behind Winters's seeming madness: "He would hold out his hands like two airplanes and he'd say, 'It's like two F-11s—you gotta stay right with me, wingtip to wingtip.' And it's true—that's what it was like. You gotta pay total attention, your concentration has to be as good as his, and you have to follow him. You can have an idea where he's going, but—you know what someone likened it to? Playing chess with a champion player. Most of us think two or three moves ahead, or, if you're real good, seventeen moves ahead, but these guys think *hundreds* of moves ahead."

In the late 1990s, Winters had a brief revival in a sitcom as a retired gunnery officer and grandfather in *Davis Rules,* with Bonnie Hunt and Dennis Quaid, and won an Emmy for it. But, he notes resignedly, "TV has been a problem to me, not movies. I'm not doing that much work, out of choice. The thing is, in a sitcom you've got at least six or seven writers, and a head writer. I was recently asked to do a sitcom, to do the old man or a granddad, and I said, 'I don't want to fight anymore.' And he said, 'What do you mean, fight?' I don't want to fight for my lines, for my humor, for my thoughts. I don't want to do hair-in-the-soup routines. I don't want to grab my pants to see if I have an erection. A lot of TV is leaning toward that stuff. I'm faced with this all the time—'That's what the kids want.' It's very hard not to take the money and run. What I'm saying is, on a Friday you have your head writer coming to you and saying, 'Look, we wanna do this and do that,' and I say, 'I'd like to delete this,' and he says, '*Listen, just do the goddamn lines and if they don't work we'll sweeten it!*' And that's where we are." Lainie Kazan says that Winters seems not so much resigned as defeated—"It's like he's been hammered."

Even today, behind Winters's gentle comedy and gentlemanly demeanor simmers a lingering resentment. He told an interviewer in 2000, "I tried to adhere to the Christian belief of turn the other cheek—only to get cold-cocked." As a kind of delayed response, or maybe as therapy, he's been working for years on a book he calls *Know Thy Enemy,* a compilation of rejoinders to people in his life who rankle him—a guide on "how to handle yourself with assholes," as he puts it. "It has to do with people who come up and feel they've gotta put you down or play with your brains or

go at you. It's how you handle these people. A guy said to me not too long ago, 'Aren't you somewhat of a has-been?' I said, 'No question about it, but I'm an international has-been whereas you're just a local has-been.' "
When people tell him, "I don't see you on TV anymore," Winters replies, "I *never* saw *you* on TV." Lots of little old Maude Frickerts accost him in public with comments like, "You know, you're *crazy.*" His angry, wounded rejoinder: "Are you a doctor? Do I have a crazy look? Am I doing crazy things? By the way, I read your book on sensitivity. Is it still one page?"

He adds, "The standard thing people say is, 'Say something funny.' My answer is, 'I would if I thought you'd get it.' Or, like, you're signing auto-graphs and someone says, 'How do you know you're not signing a check?' It's supposed to be hilarious. Everybody wants to be funny. Atomic scien-tists will say, 'I've got a funny thing I heard the other day.' They want to test you and see what you're all about." Winters lowers his voice and leans in confidentially. "People want to be in competition with you. Peo-ple will admit they couldn't be a doctor—too much blood—wouldn't want to be a lawyer, wouldn't want to be president, wouldn't want to be a test pilot. But nobody admits they're not funny."

In Montecito, where Winters has lived for twenty years, he's treated with a combination of suspicion and condescension. He's like a famous toy. "He's far brighter than people think he is," his daughter, Lucinda, says. Winters remarks, "I don't go to a lot of [Hollywood] parties, because I don't drink and I'm bored. It's a long way to go, an hour and a half, to suit up and go all the way down there. I don't do a lot here, but I'm not a recluse or an antisocial dude. I pick and choose. It's not easy for me to find people to play with here." He frets, "You can't engage a lot of these people. Do they really like me for me or my label? Let them stare at you, stare back at them. Don't be too harsh with them. If they start to stone you, run."

He pauses, then continues: "But I've been fortunate. I have received a few accolades, I've felt a genuine response from the audience, not that I was some sort of freak or offbeat clown." Yet he can't escape the weirdos who chat him up, some seeking him out as a cosmic soul brother. When he went home to Dayton to receive an honor, a funeral director he'd gone to school with came up to him and said (wispy Wally Cox voice), "We did your mother and it would be a feather in our cap if we could do you."

His humor saves him, just barely, but at times the comments have stung and stuck with him, increasing Winters's ever-expanding throng of contemporary Babbitts. "I really get tired of *guys*," he says—" 'Hey, how 'bout that Microsoft?' Who cares! I've still got Pan Am." He prefers female company. "Women are neat. They're so way ahead of men. I just like sittin' there talkin' to 'em." Women seem to sense the human being in Winters, not just the on-call jester. Frances Bergen—the former actress, widow of Edgar Bergen, and mother of Candice—toured with Winters in Vietnam in 1968 to entertain the troops and recalls how he would stop the bus, jump out, and entertain GIs on the side of the road. She said, "He gave and gave and gave of himself."

Through half a century, Winters's fans, friends, and family have accompanied him on a similar zigzag tour of America made smoother by his resilient wit. As he shambles toward eighty, he remains the wild, precocious child with an airborne spirit who prevails. His daughter sums up the ride pretty well: "We've all tried to travel on the tips of his wings with him."

PHOTO BY FRED W. McDARRAH

Out of Thin Air

JEAN SHEPHERD; BOB ELLIOTT AND RAY GOULDING

There's a nostalgia for an unlived past.

—JEAN SHEPHERD

We were sort of one of a kind.

—BOB ELLIOTT

O KAY, GANG, *are you ready to play radio? Are you ready to shuffle off the mortal coil of mediocrity? I am if you are. Yes, you fatheads out there in the darkness, you losers in the Sargasso Sea of existence, take heart, because WOR, in its never-ending crusade of public service, is once again proud to bring you . . . The Jean Shepherd Program!"*

Shepherd was no routine comedian. He was a witty radio raconteur who came of age in the fifties and sixties spinning nocturnal satirical monologues that became their own comic form. Just when network-radio comedy was having its bones picked clean by television, a few comics jumped into the void. None landed more resonantly than the bemused and crackling voice belonging to Jean Shepherd.

With his meandering, real-life fables shot through with sardonic undertones, he reshaped "talk radio." He became a dominant presence in New York before radio was set on today's news/music/sports/call-in autopilot. There had been radio monologuists before him, but nobody who worked as free-form or as fancifully as he did. No satirist covered as many life situations and (except for Bob & Ray) none held forth on the air for as long. He had a brief parallel stand-up comedy career in clubs—mostly at the Limelight Café in Greenwich Village (from 1962 to '67), from which his Saturday-night shows were broadcast. He also spun off his soliloquies into record albums, TV series, magazine pieces, and a shelf of short stories. "I'm a storyteller," he said. "A storyteller can work in any medium."

In his heyday, he became a comic keynote at colleges and concert halls. He gave readings, narrated video documentaries on Babe Ruth, Christmas, Norman Rockwell, Thanksgiving, and the Chicago White Sox, his raging passion. He turned up in a variety of magazines, from *Car and Driver* to *Mademoiselle;* his primary outlet for prose, however, was

Playboy, where he had a fixed pulpit. He devised, produced, wrote, and narrated two TV series for PBS, *Jean Shepherd's America* and *Shepherd's Pie* (the latter spun off from *The Great American Dream Machine*), and appeared in and cowrote *New Faces of 1962.* He was seriously considered as a host for *The Tonight Show*—Steve Allen suggested him—but was felt to be too eccentric.

Most of his writing and TV gigs were versions of his bittersweet radio tales of growing up in Hammond, Indiana, which he brought alive as a community of eccentrics. He could seize upon relics and minutiae from his past—the dismayingly chintzy prize in a box of Cracker Jack, say— and subtly, slowly tease them out into rich cautionary tales with warnings about beguiling come-ons, flimsy promises, childhood naïveté, and life's disappointments in general.

Shepherd may be, with Godfrey Cambridge, the most underrated of all the innovative comic voices of the era; certainly he had the most rabid cult, verging on a fundamentalist religion. For his acolytes, his *Voice in the Night* program was not just a cult, it was a cause, and it remains alive and kicking on the Internet, where his tapes are available and where his memory is still lovingly tended since his death in 1999, at age seventy-eight. His friend and radio colleague Ron Della Chiesa says, "He had probably the largest cult following of any radio personality in America. Of course, Jean would be the first to say, 'What do you mean by *cult,* Ron?' "

Shepherd was mainly a New York/East Coast on-air phenomenon but was heard in a few select syndicate markets, at one point close to twenty. WOR's AM signal carried his voice far afield at night to many surrounding cities. He broke through during the 1960s as an urban folklorist, spinning compelling yarns of growing up in Indiana in the thirties and forties, and saw the American dream reflected in the fun-house mirror of his mind. One grateful listener recalls: "Jean Shepherd had a positive, warm humanity that I didn't experience in my life. It gave me a genuine sense of comfort and peace. For many people who lie in bed alone at night, and feel cut off, he was like a bridge to a hope of some kind, to a connection with other human beings. He created a world that most of us did not inhabit but would like to have inhabited."

Other sixties stand-up comics have been compared to Mark Twain— Bill Cosby, Jonathan Winters, Richard Pryor—but Shepherd perhaps came the closest. He re-created the lay of the land—its sounds, music, smells, and characters, miming the very scenes and scents of his, of everybody's, boyhood; he called them "sensual essays." Invariably, he was likened to midwesterners James Thurber and George Ade, his idol, a fellow Indiana humorist whose ironic voice matched Shepherd's on-air voice, but Shepherd dug much deeper.

The Midwest has long harbored acerbic folk humorists. His closest radio heir is Garrison Keillor, whose whimsy-laden Minnesota memoirs of life in the mythical town of Lake Wobegon are funny and poignant, if much less freewheeling than Shepherd's, whose imagination floated far beyond the Midwest. Shepherd was a more blue-collar, urban comic than Keillor. More in the Shepherd vein was Paul Rhymer, whose thirties and forties radio program *Vic and Sade,* set in a small Illinois town, was a major influence on Shepherd, who, like Rhymer, had a weakness for goofy names—Wanda Hickey, Ollie Hopnoodle, the Bumpus family.

Shepherd recoiled from being tagged a purveyor of nostalgia; he preferred to call himself a "commentator." He ventured farther than nostalgia; he was almost antinostalgia. His every recollection was heavily laced with cynicism. Just because his tales took place in the past didn't make them nostalgic, any more than American history is nostalgia. His relics and references—his use of pop songs, ads, toys, comic books—were evocative, but the scenes were not bathed in amber. For Shepherd, the past was just his jumping-off place. As he once said, "The great American myth is that things used to be wonderful, and the future will be wonderful, too. It's just the present that happens to stink."

His people, noted a *Wall Street Journal* writer, "flirt valiantly but briefly with victory, only to go down in the end to crushing defeat. If there is a constant theme, it is the absolute certainty of daily humiliation in life"—as when his high school coach gave an inspirational pep talk and the fired-up team ran out and lost by a score of 56 to 5. He told one interviewer, "Childhood seems good in retrospect because we were not yet aware of the basic truth: that we're all losers, that we're destined to die."

Della Chiesa says, "He hated that word *nostalgia.* He didn't even like to be pigeonholed as a 'radio personality.' He felt his real genius was in his writing, and yet people constantly brought up radio because they grew up with it. He was a part of their adolescent years." Ironically, Shepherd himself is now a nostalgic memory for his former avid listeners—and there was no such thing as a non-avid Jean Shepherd listener. His audience, says public radio producer Larry Josephson, "were mostly geeks and loners—like me, the smartest kid in high school who had no friends. All of Shepherd's fans are alienated in some way. Mainstream people don't get Jean Shepherd." As Jerry Tallmer wrote in a *New York Post* profile: "His show from the mudflats of New Jersey brought him to the attention of Manhattan's sleepless disciples of deep thought and noncon-formity"—four hundred thousand of them on a good night.

Like a lot of people, Kenneth Turan, the film critic for the *Los Angeles Times,* discovered Shepherd while idly twisting the dial late one night. "When you heard this voice it stopped you. It was such a hypnotic voice. He'd go off on these tangents and he'd somehow bring you back. It was intoxicating. I never talked to anyone about listening to Shepherd because I didn't have any friends who I thought would understand it." Shepherd provided the same sense of private discovery that many of the era's satirists did. "It almost seemed like if I mentioned it, it would go away—like a dream," observed Turan.

Jules Feiffer remembers hearing Shepherd while hunched over his drawing board in his apartment: "I stumbled on this soothing voice of Jean Shepherd, who was remembering all the things from his past." His Indiana boyhood was a universe away from Feiffer's New York, "and yet it seemed to be everything that I knew and recognized. He was the book you picked up in the middle of the night when you felt so lonely, and sud-denly you found the page that relates directly to you. Shepherd was that page."

He was very much of his own time, often playing off the day's head-lines, but the monologues that held listeners most rapt, and for which he was best known, were the wry misadventures of his youth. He claimed, in a 1972 interview with yet another great midwestern radio raconteur, Studs Terkel, that his real interest was in "American rituals," often rooted in the past, but not always. Shepherd could discuss a contemporary Thanksgiving as easily as he could one from his boyhood—or just vamp for an hour on the first Thanksgiving. Or, for that matter, on Mail Pouch Chewing Tobacco, political second bananas, Boy Scout camp, firemen, working in a piano factory, Jack Paar interviewing Zsa Zsa Gabor, druids, the March on Washington, or whoopee parties. Mort Sahl–like, Shep-herd could weave a winding tale that, in its final seconds, would some-how circle back to his opening premise and, in the peroration, build to a climactic moment embedded with a rueful moral.

One typical Jean Shepherd story revealed the kind of Joycean epipha-nies he regularly explored: it began with a seemingly idle remark about realizing, as an adolescent, what a "slob" he was. He discusses all the meat-loaf dinners he ate at home as opposed to the fancy foods he only read about, like raw clams. This early memory of home life segues neatly into a story about a time at college when a girl invited him to dinner with her family. He remembers, among a million other things, her remark to him: "Don't bother to dress." Nevertheless, he dons his Penney's sport coat and Ward's slacks with great care, and as he approaches the girl's address, he sees that the houses are getting bigger and bigger, until he arrives at a large home with pillars and a brass knocker. A butler greets him and he enters to find twenty people present, as Nancy, the girl, runs over and kisses him; nobody ever kissed quite so casually in *his* circles, he notes. Shep takes a drink from a long-stemmed glass, a drink that even has a name—martini. "*My old man would only say, 'How 'bout some booze?' We didn't have any actual names for it—it was just called 'booze.'*"

As they move on to dinner at a table decked with linen and crystal, Nancy asks him, "Have you had any fresh escargot this season yet?" Shepherd: "*Suddenly, in front of me, was this plate of something which had always been rumored in our house—that people somewhere, someplace, ate—and we'd never really believed it—snails. And whenever it was mentioned, it was always, 'Oh, ugh!' And my meat-loaf insides are churning. What am I gonna do? I can't chicken out. And with this little fork, I fished it out and put it in my mouth and, Oh, my God! Oh, my God! It was fantastic! Then I made a total pig of myself and went slurp, slurp, slurp. And then the lesson hit me. I looked around and I saw all these other people who'd been doing this all their lives. They weren't surprised at snails. And then it began to sneak in on me—what other terrible stuff did I learn at home, what other things do I think are awful? I ate the snails, and late that night, when I got home, I'm laying in the dormitory room and I can feel them snails, there's an aftertaste, and I begin to suspect that night that there was a fantastic unbelievable world out there. And I was just beginning to taste it, and God knows where it would lead!*" Classic, definitive, sumptuous Jean Shepherd.

While Shepherd spoke, his voice would rise and crack with intensity and merriment as he approached a crescendo, then fade to a whisper before gathering steam again, plunging forward toward the climax. As you listened in bed, eyes closed, it was like taking a lulling train ride across country. He told Terkel: "I've tried in my writing to do something very few writers have tried to do, and that is to write about American traditions—rather than American sex, or problems, or traumas. We all live a life apart from these problems—we have a race problem, we have this problem, that problem—but we all have a daily life: standing for ice cream at the Carvel's, going into the drive-in at McDonald's, being in the library and seeing that the book you've been waiting for has been stolen."

When Terkel said to him, "You cover an aspect of American life that nobody else ever covers" (meaning the past), Shepherd bristled and said: "You think it's the *past*. Most people who become writers think that everything they used to do no longer happens. I evoke a time past for all people, including a seventeen-year-old's time past, because I'm writing about American rituals. The one thing about a ritual is, it *does* continue."

He went on: "We don't recognize our own rituals—the two-week vacation, the graduation, the Sunday-afternoon dinner. When I say the word *prom,* for people of all ages, from ninety to a guy who's twelve, it evokes a whole series of images. I try to telescope an experience, so I have 'em do everything in absolute detail." At his mention that "county fairs never change," he reels off a catalogue of homemade cakes, pies, and candies at the fair, with every goody's specific name. He continued: "The coffee break is as ritualistic from one end of the country to the other. You go into an office in Tacoma and they're sitting around with the paper cups and the looks on the faces are the same. It's as much a ritual as the English teatime rituals. We're getting old enough now as a country so that we have recognized national rituals."

Shepherd's response to the persistent nostalgia charge: "I don't think there's any one of us, no matter where we live, who doesn't have a secret place, whatever it is. It's like Oz. It's why Americans are so hung up on western movies—it's a dream world. There's a nostalgia for an unlived past." He added: "There's also a small-town myth in America—where people are simply more honest. But most of the people who saw *Our Town* were urban people; it was a Broadway play." He loved upsetting as well as celebrating myths. New York itself was one of his favorite myths, and he could nail it in three lines: "*It's the capital of the world for the disenchanted. It's a goal, Nirvana, for thousands of guys, but they get here and they discover they still have trouble with their chicks. It's like getting to heaven only to find out that heaven is just like the office.*"

Shepherd was emphatically American, and only secondarily a midwesterner or a New Yorker. That unlived past he spoke of he relived and rhapsodized about with a cutting honesty unlike anything Norman Rockwell ever painted. But it was a past that was, for the most part, imaginary, even for those who lived it and who, he joked, longed for an even *earlier* past. His rule of thumb, he said, speaking of his TV series *Jean Shepherd's America:* "I want people twenty years from now to look at my show and feel as if it had been filmed that afternoon."

When fixated, he could drone on (a long-winded monologue on, say, gliding, one of his joys, drifts past the point of interest) or grow too frantic, revving himself up to an overblown climax. He knew how to create in listeners the feeling that he was headed *somewhere,* so he whipped himself into a frenzy to grab ears he might have lost otherwise; when he was all finished, you might wonder, Now what was *that* all about? Edward Grossman wrote a valentine to Shepherd in *Harper's* in 1966, but also noted: "Shepherd's fund of stories is not inexhaustible. He repeats himself and sometimes he serves up just plain cold turkey." Shepherd's amusing personality and persuasive delivery could mesmerize you even when the subject did not. He said, "I believe that the spoken word, the voice itself, is a far more expressive instrument than a typewriter. A typewriter, no matter who the person is behind it, is still a substitute for the human voice."

His radio show's merrily galloping theme song, "The Bahnfrei Overture," by Eduard Strauss, begins with a bugle fanfare calling horses to the gate. It was the perfect blast to bring him trotting out in a burst of excitement. Each show would end with his concluding words, often barely audible under the prancing theme, as you imagined him riding off into the gathering dusk—or into the night, when the show aired at eleven P.M. or one A.M. He was a seductive campfire storyteller, the perfect radio bedtime companion. To build bridges between segments, to augment the narrative, or just to amuse himself, he liked to twang his Jew's harp and hum or sing a favorite song ("Just a Gigolo," "The Sheik of Araby," "Margie," "Ragtime Cowboy Joe," "You Are My Sunshine," "Yellow Dog Blues," "After You've Gone").

There was a primal secret chuckle lurking behind every line, a kind of audible twinkle, and although he wove yarns about his hometown, he manned a postmodern cracker barrel. The bemused voice, whether chortling slyly or in full maniacal cry, was by turns self-mocking, seductive, manic, querulous, and reflective. For all those nostalgia trips back home to Indiana, however, his voice was tinged with quizzical suspicion. Shepherd might wax philosophical, or poetical, but never sentimental— especially when talking about "my old man," a favorite topic.

Shepherd called his "night people" "slobs" and "fat heads," regarded as terms of endearment by the invisible congregation who excused all his affectionate slurs. He was once fired from WOR for writing a piece in *MAD* that the station took to be an attack on advertisers and sheep-like consumers, entitled "The Night People vs. Creeping Meatballism" (the day people). He was quickly rehired when listeners threatened an uprising.

One such night person, Paul Krassner, the editor of *The Realist,* to which Shepherd contributed, recalled: "My idea of a hot date then was to find a girl who also liked Shepherd and lie in bed with her all night listening to him. It ruined my schooling. I'd wake up and he'd be talking about how to explain an amusement park to Venusians." Krassner remembers how, in a moment worthy of *Network,* Shepherd would ask listeners to turn their radios way down, and then, when he signaled, they were to turn the volume all the way up as he screamed some epithet like, "*You filthy pragmatists, I'm going to get you!*" He was convinced that the angry Howard Beale character in *Network* was based on him; yet the film's famous line, "*I'm mad as hell and I'm not going to take it anymore,*" lacks Shepherd's ironic tone. Much closer is the wry Murray Burns character in *A Thousand Clowns,* who also had a penchant for shouting at neighbors out the window and putting on the straight world while sidling through life making grim wisecracks.

Shepherd might slide into the evening's subject with a news item ("Listen to this one! Dateline Hong Kong . . .") and proceed to discuss, in a silly, tasteless Charlie Chan accent, the fact that the Chinese Communists had decreed what shall be the party's official sense of humor. Or he would refer to some phrase he had overheard, before constructing an elaborate sand-castle reverie. There were digressions, footnotes, parenthetical jokes, random observations, and stories within stories, augmented by an occasional sound effect or snatch of music.

Della Chiesa watched him do the show a few times. "He had notes, handwritten, how he would open and where he was gonna end, but there was no script whatsoever. He had the story framed in his mind and a sketchy outline to remind him where he was going—and he'd always end the story *exactly* on time, timed out to perfection. He didn't like anyone in the studio with him, and he didn't want anyone to talk or say anything when he was on the air."

Herb Squire, Shepherd's longtime engineer at WOR, recalled: "You had to pay attention. You learned very quickly it was a one-on-one situation. The engineer was the audience. You had to react and become very animated in your reactions to his material, because if he didn't get a response, it's like any performer—he would feel up the creek without a paddle. Most of the shows were live. No substitute hosts, no reruns. Jean's material was so far ahead of its time. It wasn't the normal radio for the fifties or sixties."

Every night, of course, was different ("I'm antiformat," said Shepherd) and sounded as if he'd decided what he might discuss in the elevator on his way up to the studio. Some nights he would stay on one theme; other nights he zigzagged from topic to topic, at the mercy of demon whims. He dipped at will into his bottomless memory vault of growing up, being in the service, toiling in the steel mills of Gary, Indiana, and working as a pin boy. It was one-third autobiographical, one-third embellished reality, and one-third total make-believe. He had the zeal of a great storyteller and an eye for detail that made everything ring true. And since it all sounded authentic, it really didn't matter what part was fiction. Many of his sagas would begin simply, *"I'm a kid, see . . ."*

The filmmaker Ben Thum remembers sitting transfixed in his car one cold winter night in the late fifties: "Shep was reminiscing about working in a bicycle factory in Hammond, and it was so fascinating that I barely noticed the chill inside my 1957 Ford Fairlane convertible with the broken heater. With maybe fifteen minutes left before sign-off, I chose to shiver in the car rather than enter the warm house, just so I would not miss a second of what had evolved into a highly compelling story."

Shepherd's tales first appeared in revised print form as the story collection *In God We Trust, All Others Pay Cash* (1966), the basis for the now classic 1983 holiday film *A Christmas Story,* narrated by Shepherd—about a kid named Ralphie who yearns for a Red Ryder BB air rifle for Christmas. The movie has achieved *It's a Wonderful Life* holiday cult status on television and later inspired TV's hit *The Wonder Years.* Subsequent story collections emerged, beginning with *Wanda Hickey's Night of Golden Memories, and Other Disasters* (1971), followed by *A Fistful of Fig Newtons* (1981) and *The Ferrari in the Bedroom* (1972), which a Boston TV cable station aired in a nonstop reading for twenty-four hours in 2000 in tribute to the recently departed Shepherd.

Wanda Hickey, a best-seller, plugged into more people than made up his broadcasting base. Wanda, says Shepherd, is the girl that every guy settles for, as opposed to his female fantasy, the cool patrician Diane Bigelow. *"Wanda Hickey,"* he explained, *"is the girl who, at the age of fourteen, is already middle-age and mentally the mother of four kids—the one we all took to the prom. Diane Bigelow is the girl who is always seen from a distance with a guy who looks like John Lindsay."* His hero takes Wanda Hickey to what is "his first social—not sexual—situation" in a story full of richly observed details.

Harry Shearer, who hosts his own ruminative (weekly) program, *Le Show,* on National Public Radio, narrated NPR's tribute to Shepherd, saying: "Shepherd told supercilious easterners stories about the Midwest—not a romanticized Midwest of small-town life, but the Midwest that we never really knew existed—the Midwest of steel mills and tornadoes." As Shearer noted, "Shepherd's home base was not a free forum or even a public radio station; it was about as mainstream a talk station as you could get—friendly, chatty, celebrity-filled talk. Shepherd was the odd man out. That's probably why he appealed to generations of alienated teenagers. His stories evoked the pain and fear of childhood, not 'My favorite toy' or 'My favorite candy.' "

Shepherd's steel-mill days at Inland Steel evoked a Dantean vision of hell, full of roaring furnaces, open "soaking pits," and gruff, beetle-browed coworkers. As *Time*'s Ed Grant noted in 2000: "Despite the infectious exuberance and sharply honed sense of absurdity that always symbolized Shepherd's narration, there is a subtle undercurrent of sadness for the innocent past that can never be recaptured."

He recaptured its wispy memory on the air, but off the air he insisted that none of the stories were from his life, maybe to give them more literary status. Shep's childhood chums claim otherwise. He left Hammond at seventeen and never returned, and his bitterness toward the town increased when he heard that his version of the place wounded its citizens, though few there had ever heard his shows. "My work is not autobiographical. You draw upon all the things that you knew from that period, but more from that *place* than that period." Those who said that he wrote of what Terkel called "the aches and pains of growing up" made Shepherd wince. He claimed, rather, that he wrote of the "cosmic human comedy" and called himself a modern-day Candide.

Marshall McLuhan said that Shepherd had reinvented radio as "a new medium for a new kind of novel that he writes nightly. The mike is his pen and pencil." He compared him to Montaigne. Shepherd readily agreed: "What throws people about me is that they think of me as talking. They don't recognize the fact that what I'm doing is extraordinary. I have a very idiomatic style, which makes every guy who listens to me seriously believe that if he had a microphone that he could do what I do. If you're a writer, people recognize writing as something they can't do. Yet what I'm doing is oral writing. It's taken years for me to learn how to edit, to phrase, to give pause, beat, momentum, and to keep a theme running through the whole thing."

As with any print columnist, the word was Shepherd's oyster. He was as likely to discuss the flying magazines of the 1930s as to salute Jack Benny on his death. He was a nut on the poetry of Robert Service and Lawrence Ferlinghetti, and of Saxe Rohmer, the author of the Fu Manchu stories. Like any great monologuist/writer, he took you into his world, which was eccentric, egocentric, and idiosyncratic. The titles of his individual broadcasts (now available on tape via his Web site, www. flicklives.com) give a flavor of Shepherd's eclectic world: "Tennis Date with First Love," "Americans and Their Cars," "Rude Noises in Company K," "Midwestern Drugstores and Drive-Ins," "Why I'm Such a Sorehead," "The Smell of Homes," "Love at the USO," "Hamburger Binge," "First New Suit Out of the Army," "A&W Root Beer Stand," "Shoplifting," "First Shaves," "Junk in the Basement." When he struck a rich vein, like high school halftime shows, he strip-mined it.

As he explained, "I think that there is a whole area of the wild, swinging anthill that we're all a part of that goes almost completely unreported and unnoticed by the vast body of the press and literature. It's a kind of recording of the daily frustration and the momentary exaltation of the fact of living itself."

Little was beyond his interests—he was also a serious photographer, illustrated his own books, and collected antiques—and it is that wide-ranging unpredictability, curiosity, and passion that grabbed listeners for decades. Somebody called him a "comic anthropologist," sifting through the cultural remains for any jawbone or cracked urn from which he could reconstruct a nation's folkways—a Wimpy doll, a pack of Walnettos, an old vaudeville song.

He evoked the past with precision but never gilded it. Even the stories that sounded merely nostalgic were implanted with a life lesson—"and no lesson ever came cheap," noted Shearer. The stories were studded with epigrams, curbstone philosophy, wistful footnotes, and wisecracks. In one unforgettable Shepherd radio piece, he exhumed an ad in the back of a comic book, "See Through X-Ray Eyes"—"I had a lot of ideas of what I would like to see through. I had all *kinds* of plans." He sent away for the "X-ray eyes" for ten cents and got back a tiny tube that allowed him to see the bones in his hand by holding it up to a bright light. He quickly spies on a girl in the front row of his class but learns, to his dismay, "It does not look through flowered print dresses." Another classic Shepherd shaggy-dog story was of being duped by a commercial on *Little Orphan Annie* when he sent in his money for a decoder trinket, only to learn that the secret message was: "Buy Ovaltine."

He was equally a master at skewering trends and contemporary clichés, as in this profile of a Bennington College girl in 1956 that's as exacting as anything from Mort Sahl, Woody Allen, or Nichols & May: *"She thinks Harry Belafonte is* authentic. *Mabel Mercer is a great actress and does such wonderful things with Cole Porter. Anna Magnani is the only film actress our girl cares to discuss. However, she saw* Marty *twice because it was about* real people."

JEAN PARKER SHEPHERD, Chicago-born but Hammond-bred, and deeply American, set forth on his broadcasting journey early. As a boy, he lay awake nights, twenty miles south of Chicago, listening to "the trains thunder through on their way to somewhere else." He longed to be any-where else.

"Shep," as he was always called, first tuned in to radio as a ham opera-tor, a lifelong obsession, and as a teenager he played Billy Fairfield, Jack Armstrong's pal, on the famous radio show *Jack Armstrong* out of Chicago. His "old man," who loomed large in Shepherd's radio life, was a serious bowler, avid White Sox fan, and beer drinker—an underpaid disen-chanted political cartoonist for the *Chicago Tribune* with a sharp tongue ("Profanity was his medium," said his son; "he hated to hear amateurs swear"), who became a dairyman and deserted the family when Jean was seventeen and moved to Palm Beach, Florida. His mom was "a real mother" who wore a red chenille bathrobe, kept her hair in rollers, and ground out endless meals of meat loaf, red cabbage, and Jell-O. Asked if he ever missed Hammond, his true feelings for the place erupted: "That's like asking, 'Do you miss the cold sores you had last week?' "

Shep's younger brother, Randy, writes Arch McKinlay in the *New York Times* online, was a source of many fables that the monologuist appropri-ated for himself—like those relating to his athletic skills; Randy played professional baseball. McKinlay reveals that Shepherd would "slip into the area" and meet his brother at the Wagon Wheel on Indianapolis Boulevard, where he "pumped him for stories" he'd take back to New York and refashion on the air. Randy, who idolized him, didn't mind.

Shepherd served two years in the Army Signal Corps, a major source of later yarns, and on the GI Bill he went to Northwestern University, the University of Chicago, and Indiana University, but never graduated. He tried the Goodman Theater drama school and selling cars before breaking into radio with his own show in 1949, hosting a hillbilly jamboree and interviewing wild animal acts for a Cincinnati radio station, WSAI-FM, listened to mostly by truck drivers, cabbies, and students. In Cincinnati he later did a wild Ernie Kovacs–style TV show that followed the late movie. From there he moved on to Philadelphia, and finally to New York, beginning his turbulent career at WOR in 1956 doing an all-night show interspersed with jug-band music. Boston's WGBH-FM reran his WOR shows with the commercials snipped out.

"Hip adolescents," noted Edward Grossman, "are particularly sympathetic to him," although "parents are mystified by his programs"—not the subject matter so much as the antic, anticonformist attitude, rarely heard on the air in the 1950s, even late at night. It was the beginning of the era of the wise-guy disc jockey, and nobody was more wisecracking than Jean Shepherd. As Shearer noted, "Radio had to reinvent itself or die." Young, flip deejays like Shepherd—Steve Allen and Don Horsley in Los Angeles, Don Sherwood in San Francisco, Ernie Kovacs in Trenton, and Bob Elliott and Ray Goulding in Boston—were inventing a more personal, intimate, free-form style of radio out of records and their own ad-libbed, on-air comic imaginations.

The critic Charles Strum called Shepherd's programs "part Kabuki, part commedia dell'arte, part Uncle Remus." The *Time* critic Richard Corliss, a childhood fan still bewitched decades later, summoned up the awe listeners felt at Shepherd's mesmeric powers: "Night after night, the words seemed to fall together conversationally, with hardly a pause, a sentence fragment, or a wasted word. How did he do it?"

The radio and the real Shepherd were virtually indistinguishable, recalled Barry Farber, a WOR talk-show legend of another kind. "He was Jean Shepherd *all the time.* He would never relent. There maybe was something manic there." Farber once brought his nephew to the station and introduced him to Shepherd, "who pinned the boy against the wall and gave him a forty-minute show on whatever topic happened to be buzzing around Jean's mind. The Jean Shepherd shows he did for a person that he never saw before and never saw again were every bit as rich as the ones he did on the air."

Shepherd's intimate persona was only his radio character, a mask; off the air, he remained removed, an outsider, secretive and unappreciated by the WOR hierarchy. Farber remarked, "He always felt like a marginal creature because nobody else at the station understood him. Even at the height of his popularity, he told me, 'Barry, the station would like nothing better than for me to tell them I'd like to play the top twenty songs.' They just didn't get it, they didn't realize what they had."

He generally felt that his gift was taken for granted, telling *Newsday*'s Mike McGrady in 1963: "A lot of guys have tried this kind of show, but they find it's a tricky thing. People think you just go out and talk—well, forget it, dad. I'm a dramatist. I know how to build the scene and hold the tension. Some shows I think about for three or four weeks and then one night I come in and just feel that it's right."

His radio show was never listed in the *New York Times,* says Della Chiesa, "and he made a big deal of that on radio, because, apparently, someone at the *Times* said it's not a music show—we don't list those kinds of shows, we have no category for you. So he wrote a pseudo-book. That was his way of getting into the *Times*." The book was a nonexistent bodice-ripper, *I, Libertine,* that wound up on the *New York Times* list of new books as booksellers busily called *Publishers Weekly* to track it down. It later emerged as an actual Ballantine paperback book. In 1962 he wrote a real novel, *What Time Does the Balloon Go Up?*

His Saturday-night gigs at the Limelight Café, listened to again, sound rough-edged due to the room's imperfect acoustics and clatter. Della Chiesa saw him perform there. "He was very animated. He paced around. He got into character." Larry Josephson saw Shepherd at the Limelight several times. "He had the crowd in the palm of his hand, almost like Hitler. He really whipped up the crowd."

He might begin unspooling his spellbinding spiel by saying: "*It's Saturday night and we're here in the Limelight. Have you ever thought what Saturday night is? A very special thing all over America. No other country knows this. . . . You're in the Limelight, gang. You're in Greenwich Village, stretching from Sheridan Square to the river and then, there it is—America! Lying out there in the darkness. There it is: Trenton, Teaneck, places like Circleville, Ohio. Think of waking up in Circleville. . . .*" He would then exhort his young audience, the boys in crew cuts and the girls with velveteen bows in their hair, many from the outer boroughs and New Jersey, in town to witness their invisible weeknight radio roommate: "*We go on the air with an invective that's heard in twenty-seven states, 'Excelsior, you fatheads!' Try it, and don't forget the comma. . . .*" A *New York Times* critic called him "often brilliant and sometimes a trifle mad." The cabaret show and his one-man concerts were racier than the radio shows. One night, he spied a line of graffiti on a men's-room wall before a show and wove it into his monologue.

For a man as intensely public about his every thought, observation, and experience, Shepherd was a major mystery. At the time of his death, even the *New York Times*'s obituary could not determine his age with certainty, or his birthplace. He may or may not have been born in Chicago, they reported, and he had two secret children from an early marriage (to Joan Laverne Warner). But he did indeed grow up in Hammond, Indiana (called "Hohman" in his ongoing saga), and was married for twenty-one years to Leigh Brown, a onetime singer and later his WOR producer, who died in 1998. "He went out of his way not to acknowledge that he even had us," Randall Shepherd, his forty-eight-year-old son, told the *Times* after his father's death. His son, the obit stated, was unaware that Shepherd had remarried the actress Lois Nettleton, his second and third wife.

He remained estranged from his past. "I knew him until three or four years before his death," says Della Chiesa, who visited Shepherd and his wife at their homes on Sanibel Island, Florida, and in Waterville, Maine. "Jean was very private and became at the end quite bitter and reclusive," recalls Della Chiesa. His few friends had once included Jack Kerouac (who fashioned Shepherd into the deejay in *On the Road,* a character to whom the novel's antihero is drawn), a scattering of jazz musicians (he narrated a 1957 Charlie Mingus recording, "The Clown"), and Della Chiesa, the longtime host of jazz and opera shows on WGBH in Boston who met Shepherd in the 1970s. He rarely mentioned his boyhood. "He glossed all that over." But Shepherd did, in fact, own the Red Ryder BB gun that figures prominently in *A Christmas Story,* and, "Rosebud"-like, he still had his first toy fire truck with him in Florida when he died. One of his Sanibel Island haunts was the Bubble Room, a nostalgia haven jammed with artifacts and photos from old-time radio, although almost nobody on Sanibel knew who the bulky, bearded, and balding legend in their midst was.

In the late 1970s, after leaving WOR, he appeared anything but a guy stuck in the past and strained hard to seem a man of his own time, sporting sideburns, turtlenecks, and, alternately, a beard and a Fu Manchu mustache. A Florida writer described Shepherd in his late forties as looking "like your father's country club buddy in a vain eternal search for hipness." Like many a humorist, Shepherd was a crank who grew more cantankerous with age. In his final years, he became a sour cynic who feared being forgotten. Yet, perversely, he mocked the adoring radio fans who cherished work that he dismissed as "just another gig." In the chat with Terkel, however, he expressed his true affection for radio: "Studs, we know something the others don't know—how great it feels to sit before a microphone. There's an excitement in that not matched in any other medium."

THE YEAR AFTER WOR dropped him, he told *People* magazine, "Radio is largely a medium for boobs," and a 1979 interview with him in a small Florida newspaper was headlined, "Jean Shepherd Is Glad to Be Out of the Box." In his last interview, on WEVD radio in New York City in 1998, he told the interviewer Alan Colmes: "Can you imagine four thousand years passing and you're not even a memory? Think about it, friends. It's not just a possibility. It is a certainty." During the interview, he tried to disillusion Colmes and his listeners. He had become radio's man without a country, disowning the place he loved most—behind a microphone.

Josephson said, "He was driven by an intense bitterness about radio, because he was fired from WOR and he never got over it." His way of getting back at WOR for dropping him after twenty-one years, in a housecleaning that included other station veterans whose loyal demographic skewed too gray (John Wingate, Henry Gladstone, Stan Lomax), was to claim he wasn't, in fact, a radio guy at all but a screenwriter and novelist. Josephson remarks: "He would insist to one and all that he wasn't really a radio person. That's all bullshit. The best things he ever did were in radio. The movies, like *A Christmas Story,* were basically schmaltzy."

Shepherd had never viewed the radio industry kindly and once remarked acidly that all the girls in school who wouldn't let you copy their algebra papers were now running public-radio stations. His situation was always shaky at WOR, where he insisted on sponsor approval, and when management tried squeezing in more commercials, Shepherd protested that it broke up the flow of his monologue. Though he mocked advertising, he delivered his own commercials with his usual straight-from-the-heart intensity.

Shepherd required a lot of compliant indulgence. Della Chiesa admits, "He had a big ego. Someone in an audience once said to him, 'You should love radio,' and he snapped, 'No, you've got it all wrong—radio should love *me.*' I remember he once saw Woody Allen on the cover of *Esquire* and remarked that Allen had ripped off a lot of his stuff. He said that a lot of the comics ripped him off. It makes sense to me. He was on five nights a week telling all kinds of stories, all kinds of material. He really felt he was abused by a lot of guys." He had to have envied Garrison Keillor's greater radio fame, but conceded, "I've often felt I lacked the drive to become famous. I like going my own way." He was also envious of Mort Sahl and blasted Sahl's autobiography in a review in the *New York Times.*

Richard Corliss understood why Shepherd disparaged radio and indeed his own legend: "In his day, the novel was the standard of artistic achievement; a hit movie was the standard of popular culture. Yeah, and talking on the radio—what respect did that get you? It was the Rodney Dangerfield of media. It awarded no Pulitzer, no Oscar, not even an Emmy. All radio gave Shepherd was an underground notoriety and a fan base whose adulation probably gave him the creeps." Adds Corliss: "Still, he should have been a nicer guy. His rudeness to his admirers is one more object lesson in the futility of searching for gurus. Trust the talk, not the talker"—a sentiment straight out of Shepherd's philosophy.

Della Chiesa adds: "One of the things that embittered him was that he never felt really appreciated until *A Christmas Story,* a major turning point in his life. He had struggled hard to get to that point." But he disliked how the director had softened it considerably from its author's original vision—"Dickens's *Christmas Carol* as retold by Scrooge." He said the father, clearly based on his own, was not dear old dad: "He's a flesh-and-blood father who hates his kids intensely because they have tied him down." He'd wanted to call it *Santa's Revenge* and have "Silent Night" played on a kazoo and washboard. He said his fans were sentimental, but he saw himself as a misanthropic Mark Twain.

Della Chiesa recalls that Shepherd "enjoyed the challenge of a good argument, but sometimes he could bear down on people real hard. When you were in conversation with Shepherd you had to lay back. It could be hard to get a word in. But in unguarded moments he could turn very quiet. You could just see another person coming out. It was very odd to see. He would get philosophical"—like when the Red Sox blew the 1986 World Series to the New York Mets after a ball dribbled through Bill Buckner's legs at first base.

Often, as on the air, it was hard to know when Shepherd was saying something for effect, gilding the facts, or revealing his deepest feelings. "Sometimes he'd create stories just for the benefit of the people around him that you knew were not true," says Della Chiesa. He would make a lot of claims—that he was "responsible" for everything from a certain perfume to LeRoy Neiman's fame. He would often put people on and, adds Della Chiesa, "he was fantastic at one-upmanship." He talked a lot about music, especially jazz, which he had absorbed from his nights at the Limelight, after which he would hang out in the Village jazz clubs; he knew Mingus and Miles Davis. "He also loved classical music, and boy, did he know his opera. He used a lot of classical music on *Jean Shepherd's America.*"

Of Shepherd's last years, Della Chiesa recounts: "When he lost Leigh, the whole bottom fell out. He just became more and more reclusive, he wasn't in the best of health and his weight was out of control." The only other close friend of Shepherd's that Della Chiesa knows of was his accountant, Irwin Zwillig, whom Shepherd would ask to bring him bagels and pastrami sandwiches from the Carnegie Deli. "He once said to me, 'Y'know, Leigh and I don't have any friends except you guys.' He felt Joyce and I really understood him. We'd send him a Christmas card and then visit him and see that our card was the only one he had up."

Josephson notes: "Leigh was his friend and protector, she organized his life"—and became his primary audience in his postradio years. "After she died, I spent a day with him. He had a nice house; presumably he had money. But he sounded disoriented. He was extremely bitter. He died of a broken heart, actually—about her and about how the world had treated him. The final end was bizarre. In his will, he said he had no issue. It's one thing to be cut off, but can you imagine what it must be like to find in your father's will that you don't exist?"

Josephson first met Shepherd after one of his annual Carnegie Hall concerts, which he would end by rolling out a stuffed bear on roller skates. "When I went backstage to meet him, I discovered that this man who I thought was brilliant and deep was kind of shallow. He would make allusions to deep intellectual concepts like existentialism or references to Ionesco and Kirkegaard, and yet when you tried to approach him on that level he didn't have anything to say. These were buzzwords, but, again—it doesn't matter. What matters is the work."

Shepherd never had the crucial network radio show that would have ingrained him more deeply into the national consciousness and brought him a deserved wider listening audience. His fame spread slowly, by word of mouth, fan by fan, ear to ear, and he became an icon to people in radio itself. He was a national treasure even though virtually unknown in the small towns that provided so much of the raw material that inspired his humor. Those who found him, through whatever lucky accident, became lifelong devotees, no matter where they lived. New York was just a point of origin. For Jean Shepherd, all of America lived in Hammond, Indiana.

*

OF ALL THE SATIRICAL COMICS who came of age during the fifties and sixties, only Bob Elliott and Ray Goulding straddled radio's golden age of the forties, whose shows they kidded with deadly affection. They weren't out to draw blood, though, just to needle radio's pretentiousness, sentimentality, and silliness.

The team's parodies spoofed every kind of program in a free-form improvisational manner. "*From approximately coast to coast,*" to quote their own introduction, Bob & Ray mocked soap operas, farm reports, science experts, news correspondents, cop shows, sportscasters—nearly everything that went out over the air. They were two of the most inventive comics on radio (or anywhere), whose dry, laid-back, on-target sensibility transcended broadcasting and their own time. Astonishingly, they lasted nearly half a century and remained funny long after radio comedy was dead and buried.

It's a long way comically from *Amos 'n' Andy, The Life of Riley,* and even the smart, self-referential *Jack Benny Program* to Bob & Ray's inspired parodies. Their humor was both anachronistic and contemporary and their satire generic enough to span generations. While the radio programs they spoofed were ancient history, their formats and conventions carried over to TV, where the interviewers were (are) just as fatuous and phony and their subjects just as banal, predictable, and self-important. In an increasingly clamorous comedy era, Bob & Ray were finely nuanced satirical minimalists who never altered their style to compete, become more current, or branch out, sticking resolutely to their radio roots. "It kind of stood out on its own," says Elliott now, in his tentative, self-effacing way. "We were sort of one of a kind."

Elliott and Goulding showed stand-up-comics-to-come that sharp satire constituted vital and viable new comedy ground, and they broke acres of it themselves. All of the comics who grew up listening to Bob & Ray were infected with their brand of satire that skewered the vapid and knuckleheaded with a poker-faced style. They didn't bother with social or political matters, with the exception of their Joe McCarthy send-up, the prickly "Commissioner Carstairs."

Neither Bob nor Ray was a straight man; each guy was hilarious in his own way, although Ray tended to play blowhards and loopy ladies, while Bob was usually the befuddled, boring expert or windy dimwit interviewer, best personified as the snuffly Wally Ballou, "winner of seven international diction awards." They generally avoided accents, finding enough variety in their own flexible voices, ranging from gruff to flutey. In their routines, the obtuse keep coming voice-to-voice with the overblown. As Kurt Vonnegut described them in the introduction to a collection of their scripts, "Ray was the big bluffer, Bob was the smaller, more easily disappointed one."

ROBERT BRACKETT ELLIOTT AND Raymond Walter Goulding had been in radio since 1946, but they didn't come into their own nationally until the fifties and sixties, via NBC's weekend *Monitor* show, right about the time when radio comedy was running aground. Like Jean Shepherd, they were truly creatures of the airwaves, and, like Shepherd, they were more humorists than comedians. When their star first began to rise, all the radio comedians, led by Jack Benny, were jumping ship for TV, which left Bob & Ray almost alone as radio satirists; they had the entire field to themselves.

The pair first met after the war, in '46, at station WHDH in Boston. Elliott recalled their meeting for me: "I was doing a morning record show and Ray was doing the news every half hour, and we would just start to kibitz before he went back to the newsroom, and it grew and became kind of a regular thing. It just happened. We knew that we were on the same wavelength, that's for sure. We'd been doing the morning stuff for six to eight months. That's when the station acquired the Red Sox and did a show prior to the games. We put a little more effort into planning those shows, but they were still pretty much ad-lib."

Bob & Ray left Boston for New York in 1951 to substitute for *The Gloom Chasers,* a Morey Amsterdam show. In July of '51, they got their own network-radio show on NBC for two years (which opened with, "*Bob Elliott and Ray Goulding present the CBS Radio Network*"), plus a different fifteen-minute TV show that ran until 1953. An agent heard a tape of some bits they had done for Amsterdam and took it to the network. "Pat

Weaver liked us very much, and when he did *Monitor* in 1955 he thought we might be a good buffer for the serious stuff. They put us in a little studio and when they'd run out of stuff they'd go to us and we'd come up with something—almost on the spot live—connected to what they were doing. We'd spend the weekends up there."

They never did jokes as such, but they were not strictly an ad-lib radio phenomenon, as most people believe; part of their genius was that it all sounded so breezily spontaneous. "I think we were the first people to go on the air at NBC without prior script approval," says Elliott. They hired an actress—Audrey Meadows—on their 1951–53 TV show to play all the women's parts, like Linda Lovely. When Jackie Gleason saw Meadows on their show, he stole her away (Cloris Leachman took over).

Before and after that, Goulding would play all the women—Mary McGoon, Agatha Murchfield, Mary Backstayge ("Noble Wife")—specializing in puffed-up dowagers who spoke in a sort of Julia Child–ish falsetto, though the occasional femme fatale was not beyond his range. They added a few sight gags, but as Elliott says, "Nobody knew what was happening in TV. We had an outline but a good part of it we winged."

One of the mysteries surrounding this very private duo is: How much of their stuff was ad-libbed? "Basically we were ad-lib," Elliott says of the team's beginnings. But even in their early ad-lib days, adds Larry Josephson, their last radio producer and the man who runs their Web site, sells their tapes, and tends to their legend, "the best things got written down. They would refresh the references. They stopped ad-libbing sometime in the fifties." Although Bob & Ray were winging it long before the Second City packaged improvisation and made it trendy, they also had a valuable silent partner in Tom Koch. "Tom did a tremendous amount of stuff for us," says Elliott, which may startle their fans. "Once he got the format for a bit, he was able to churn those things out, things we had originally ad-libbed." They still improvised here and there, but not nearly as freely as their listeners assumed—a notion of which they never disabused their fans.

Jonathan Winters, one of the few comedians who literally created on his feet, was shocked when he discovered that Bob & Ray worked mainly from scripts. "I idolized Bob & Ray," he recalls. "They were so clever, and I assumed that they were improvised. But they wrote everything down! That was so amazing. It was so well done that I thought everything they ever did was improvised. I hired them to do a Bicentennial special, 'cause I loved them. I told them I'd been looking forward to this like a little boy.

So I said to them on the set, 'Okay, here's what's gonna happen. I'll ride up as George Washington and you'll be two Minutemen and I'll interview you.' They just looked at me. Then I finally realized, nothing was happening. They were stumped. They needed lines. I never dreamed! I was just wiped out."

Tom Koch had never written comedy before he wrote for Bob & Ray. He had been a "semiserious" news- and sportswriter for radio and was writing for Dave Garroway on *Monitor* when Bob & Ray began doing their own pieces, ten spots per weekend. Koch (pronounced "Cook") was asked by NBC in the fall of 1955 to write a few spots on spec for the team, which had begun on *Monitor* in June. "I'd loved 'em. They were unique. They had a kind of a chemistry. Each one would know what the other one was gonna do—when to pick it up and keep the thing alive. It wasn't anything they could've planned." Koch wrote for them, on and off, between 1955 and 1988. Later, he wrote for *MAD* magazine, which had reprinted his scripts in a comic strip version of Bob & Ray.

NBC was nervous about the ad-libbing of the young team from Boston. "The network preferred to have something written down so they knew what was going out on the air," recalls Koch. "So I wrote ten spots and they used eight of them. Then I did another ten and from that point on I don't think they ever rejected a script." Koch only recalls one script they ever sent back—a *Waltons* parody. "The kids were really mean and one was baby-sitting and let his little brother drown. They didn't really like that." He wrote nearly three thousand Bob & Ray spots, each about three pages long. "They took everything I wrote. They didn't change 'em at all, at least the ones I heard." He wasn't their only writer; Tony Webster was also a regular contributor.

Koch was simply tuned in to Bob & Ray's subtle wavelength. "I guess I had a small-town midwestern background and many of the characters they did seemed like that. Also, I'd been a newswriter at NBC, and many of Bob & Ray's characters were just pompous versions of real people. It was a gentle humor. We weren't taking digs at anyone." He goes to the heart of their drollery: "It always started out fairly straight. You didn't know it was humor and it would just slowly veer off into something that was hilariously funny. Some people didn't think it was funny at all. They had a group of really ardent fans. Either people never heard of 'em or they loved 'em."

Koch then lived in St. Louis and rarely spoke with the comics. "I guess we had a couple of phone conversations, but that was pretty much it." He never got to watch them at work behind the mike, but he met them in New York a few times and once was invited to Bob's summer home in Maine. "You would never take them to be comedians," says Koch, whose flat midwestern drawl sounds like someone you would never take to have been Bob & Ray's head writer. "I've worked with a lot of other comedians, and they're all very outgoing, always on. You would take Bob and Ray for two businessmen, soft-spoken and pretty serious except when they were performing—Bob, I'd say, more so than Ray. Bob was the studious type, kind of shy, a creature of habit. Ray had a little more flair and was more the actor than Bob. . . ."

Koch modestly owns up to the great Bob & Ray bits he created: "Oh, I did mainly satires of the radio shows," he says, half dismissively, and mentions *The Gathering Dusk, Squad Car 119,* and a *Dragnet* spoof in which the two cops never get to any of the crimes. He also invented such Bob & Ray classics as the Slow Talkers of America, the mock commercials for Einbinder Flypaper and Monongahela Foundry, and *Garish Summit,* based on TV's *Dallas,* as well as many Wally Ballou reports; but the opening upcut, "——ly Ballou here," was Bob's idea.

Throughout his four decades of writing for them, on and off, Koch remained a freelancer paid by the sketch. "That's the odd thing about it: I wrote just short of three thousand spots and we never had a contract. Sometimes they would give me some money and sometimes they wouldn't." He says he received no residual payments for all the shows that ran on NPR or that have been sold since. "I never got paid for it and don't think I have any claim to get paid for it," he says, laughing shyly when asked if it bothers him. "Well, it would be nice to get something."

While he never had a cross word with Bob or Ray, Koch sounds a little hurt that they didn't acknowledge him publicly—until now, anyway. "Throughout their whole career, Bob & Ray kept it pretty quiet that they had a writer. I think it was on purpose." When Koch and his wife were on a motor trip, they played some tapes from Bob & Ray's NPR shows. "They would give credit to their sound man, the organist, the guy who went out for sandwiches, but never mention that they had a writer," he says.

In one of their many incarnations, a New York City station asked them to use a studio audience, but audiences just got in their way. "We had a small audience for a while, but I always thought it worked better without one," says Elliott. Audiences threw their timing off, forcing them to alter their natural comic rhythms and messing up a sketch's continuity. A live audience laughing at their deadpan sketches also tended to sound canned. An audience and a small band was far too much production, all wrong for the low-budget and audience-free radio shows they parodied; all they ever needed was an organist (Paul Taubman, who had played for real radio soaps) to get them in and out of a routine. Their sketches seem to begin and end almost willy-nilly. They don't build toward a clever or socko tag line. As Andy Rooney observed, "Their sketches are just as funny in the middle as they are at the end."

Kurt Vonnegut, who also submitted a few pieces, compared their satire to Dalí's melted wristwatches: "Their jokes turn out to be universal, although deeply routed in old-time radio, because so much of life itself presents itself as the same dilemma: how to seem lusty and purposeful when less than nothing is going on."

Ad-lib or scripted, with or without a studio audience, TV or no TV, locally or approximately coast to coast, Bob & Ray remained undaunted and undistracted. They were true to their original satirical vision—that almost everything on the air is fair game—throughout their entire forty-four-year career, nearly a world record for comedy teams. Although often forced to relinquish their microphones for brief stretches, the team invariably returned in some new-but-familiar format—whether it was a daily afternoon show out of New York or their final rebirth on National Public Radio in the early eighties, when they were rediscovered by a third generation of rabid fans.

"A lot of people think, as I do," said Rooney, who wrote a few pieces for them, "that they appreciate Bob & Ray more than anybody else does." Even so, they were less famous than they were influential: they played a major part in the creative lives of comedians who made more noise nationally during the fifties–sixties renaissance. They were subdued wits in an era of comic hubbub. Their names pop up again and again as major influences—on the comedians who came out of radio (Steve Allen, Stan Freberg, Ernie Kovacs), but also on Bob Newhart, Jonathan Winters, Tom Lehrer, and many others. For years in radio they were out there almost alone on a witty wing and a prayer (only Fred Allen, *Vic and Sade,* and Henry Morgan rivaled them on the air), but people like Lenny Bruce, Mort Sahl, Mike Nichols and Elaine May, and Woody Allen clearly got their message.

Bob & Ray never felt a need to destroy their targets, preferring to tickle them to death with a well-aimed feather, a tactic unknown today; their satire was devastating without being crude, crazy, cranky, or sarcastic. Their satire is so understated that it sounds almost British, in the *Beyond the Fringe* spirit, but, oddly, they never caught on in England. In their early days on WHDH, they did fairly wicked satire for that time, such as zinging the iconic Arthur Godfrey, whom they called "Arthur Sturdly." Josephson says, "One of the myths about Bob & Ray is that their humor was nice, which it isn't. Bob & Ray were nasty. They did parodies of *Strike It Rich,* where somebody needed an iron lung and they gave them a wardrobe from Frederick's of Hollywood. They were your basic liberals, but they were very anticapitalist. Wally Ballou visiting the paper-clip factory is about as anticapitalist as you can get. The employees are bending them by hand, earning fourteen cents a week. There was a real tinge of bitterness."

Bob & Ray were never as famous as they should have been, which seems not to have bothered them terribly much. "We had a very thriving commercials business, starting with the Piel's beer commercials," says Elliott, the classic ads in which they played Bert and Harry Piel. "We did a load of them—Alcoa, GE, General Motors Guardian Maintenance. Once we got the commercials business, we kinda laid back. We were basically lazy." Although they were heard only sporadically over the years, Elliott says he was hardly distraught—"I wasn't ready to jump out of any windows."

Observes Josephson: "They didn't have the fire in the belly—that's why they weren't world-class stars. They were essentially very shy people. This whole house sort of fell on them and they adapted nicely. It was people running after them, the fans like me. And also their humor is intellectual. You have to have a very keen understanding of language and of media. Is Kmart America or Wal-Mart America gonna get that? No. In *Garish Summit,* there's a kidnap note and someone asks, 'What does it say?' and Bob says, 'Well, it's written in Garamond semibold sans-serif,' and he analyzes the fucking type font! Ultimately, Bob & Ray were not mass phenomena because their humor, like Tom Lehrer, and like Stan Freberg to some extent, went over the heads of the average American."

Bob saw himself and Ray as a kind of mom-and-pop comedy shop. "We treated our career as a business. We had an office in the Greybar Building in New York and came in around eleven o'clock and worked till late afternoon. And then either we went to a studio or we went home. Ray lived in the suburbs and I stayed in the city. So there wasn't much socializing, and neither one of us was very social, anyway. We made a few business trips with our families." Attempting to branch out a little at first, they played a few nightclubs in 1949 and '50, but gave it up quickly. When comedy records got hot in the sixties, they gave the fad a pass, perhaps unwisely, and also never parlayed their act into films, TV, or concert tours, though they played some colleges. "We didn't want to travel—that was another thing we let go by."

Josephson adds: "They were comfortable—they both had two homes—but they weren't wealthy either. They had eleven kids between them [among them, the comic actor Chris Elliott]. They turned down a lot of gigs. They had high standards, and God bless 'em for it. They wouldn't be interviewed by TV hosts they didn't like. They used to say, and it's true, that they were very boring people. There are no scandals. At the same time, they would complain to me that people with lesser talent became millionaires. A lot of people have ripped off Bob & Ray, like Garrison Keillor. If I were them, I'd be furious."

Ray, a year older than Bob, now eighty, worked with his partner almost to the end, despite a ten-year battle with kidney disease before his death in 1990. Elliott, the more reserved of the two, is less easy to know than the gregarious Goulding. "Ray was a wonderful man," recalls Josephson. "He had a violent temper but he was basically sweet and outgoing. Ray was on dialysis. He'd come to rehearsals white as a sheet, walk through the rehearsals, and then, when it was time to go on, he'd hit it. Ray was a great hero to me. But he had a volcanic temper; if there was a page missing from the script he'd go nuts, and then he'd forget about it." Goulding was a beloved figure in his hometown of Manhasset, Long Island, where he was active in Little League. On the day of his funeral, the police stopped traffic all across Manhasset for the cortege—"an amazing tribute to him," says Josephson. "I was deeply impressed with that. Me, I'm gonna have to take a cab to the funeral home."

The team's vast loyal underground following never expanded enough to give them a leap to mass popularity, but their 1981 Carnegie Hall appearance drew enough fans to fill the hall three times over. They had been afraid of not attracting enough for even one night. Says Josephson: "Bob & Ray were a strange mixture of insecurity and ego. They said, 'Nobody will pay to see us in Carnegie Hall,' even though they'd sold out their Broadway show for six months. They limited the top to thirty-five dollars when scalpers were getting seventy dollars. And I couldn't extend it—it was an ordeal for Ray." In their last live gig, they were on the air four hours a day at WOR, often re-creating classic routines. "Four hours is an enormous strain when you're fifty and have kidney disease," says

Josephson, but Goulding wouldn't give in to it. Once when Josephson told Ray that he sounded tired, he barked at him, and when they met a year later he chided Josephson, "Do I sound tired today, Larry?"

When the undynamic duo starred on Broadway in 1971 in their show *The Two and Only,* which ran six months and toured a year, the critics wondered collectively, "Where have they *been* all these years?" The answer, of course, was: here, there, everywhere, even occasionally popping up on *The Tonight Show,* whose host, Johnny Carson, was a devoted Bob & Ray fan (there is no other kind). "They were big stars in a certain way," observes Josephson. "The people who loved 'em, loved 'em to death. But a lot of people under the age of forty-five never heard of 'em. Bob & Ray is for smart people. Bob & Ray is not for people who like the Three Stooges or Abbott & Costello or Red Skelton."

Do any comedians make Bob Elliott laugh? "Not too many," he says in his polite, low-key way. He doesn't know why there are few comedy teams now but notes, "People's taste in humor has really gone down the drain, and I think that's where the teams went."

They had, in fact, almost faded away themselves when Josephson got them back on radio, on NPR, in 1982. "They'd been on everywhere, then all of a sudden, it stopped," he recalls. "They were dropped in 1976 by WOR," when the station changed formats, also dumping its longtime star Jean Shepherd. From 1976 on, explains Josephson, "they had been doing nothing except commercials. So here comes this kid in 1981 from something called National Public Radio, which in 1981 no one had ever heard of. They said, 'Oh, sure, kid.' I paid 'em five hundred dollars for a six-month option, shopped them around, and got major backing from NEA."

Josephson is justifiably proud of reviving their careers, saying, "I've basically kept them out of the dustbin of radio history for twenty-one years. I've kept them alive. I've kept them out of the realm of old radio geeks—the people who have conventions and restage old radio shows. Bob & Ray is a fresh, contemporary product. I've kept them on the active market, in Borders and Barnes & Noble, and in all the major [record] catalogues." (Their tapes are available via www.bobandray.com or from 1-800-laugh-24.) The Grammy Awards gave him a small grant to collect everything they ever did for its archives.

When Ray died, Bob went into a reluctant semiretirement. He took his lifelong partner's death very badly, says Josephson. "He was severely depressed. They were Siamese twins. It's a marriage, and it's like being half of a stage horse—two people in one costume. People call all the time who want to 'perform Bob & Ray,' and I tell them to forget it. The material is only half of it."

Like Jean Shepherd, Elliott and Goulding never got all the fanfare they had coming to them, but to their followers (including the more celebrated comedians they inspired) there was no more famous comic during the fifties and sixties who was any funnier, or who now is more fondly revered. As I said of them in a 1998 book on the golden age of radio, Bob & Ray began more than half a century ago and nothing about them has aged except their listeners.

Unlike almost every other comedy team in history, Bob & Ray remained friends to the last and never had a falling out, not even any major creative disagreements. "We ended up agreeing," says Bob. "If somebody said they didn't think it was funny, one of us would usually have a suggestion that might be better." On some tapes they would totally lose it. Comments Josephson: "People are always asking me, 'Did they really like each other? Did they hate each other?' So I once asked 'em, 'How did you guys get along all these years?' and they said, 'Well, we make each other laugh.' "

Call Interrupt

SHELLEY BERMAN

I got up there on a stool and I made a little phone call and the audience screamed.

———————

S OMETHING ABOUT SHELLEY BERMAN made you want to throw your arm around the guy and tell him that everything was going to be all right. Even forty years later, it's impossible to forget that anguished whine in his voice. A comedian whose neuroses helped define the revolutionary comedy of the fifties and sixties, Berman was a scary jolt of reality for the jolly stand-up comics who had come before. To start with, he didn't stand up during monologues; he sat.

He was several laps ahead of comics of his own era, founding father of the school of persecuted comedians—the first of the method comics. Before Woody Allen bumbled along a few years later to captivate audiences as the neurotic frog-prince, Berman laid the cornerstone. He wasn't an obvious schlemiel like Woody, but a man in agony over modern life—over his *own* life. He sat there on his bar stool, clinging to his sanity. "*Coffee, tea, or milk?*" was a stewardess's insipid reply when he informs her that the plane's wing seems to be on fire. It became a national catchphrase, but when Berman uttered it, it sounded more like, "Coffee, tea, or morphine?" and captured the corporate cluelessness of the airline industry.

While Woody Allen fidgeted, Berman tried to remain calm on his stool, squirming as his personal demons escaped in a desperate, highly strung voice once described as "a novice violin." One writer said it sounded as if Berman were "trying to curl up inside himself." He *appeared* in good mental health, in his sober dark suit and neatly barbered façade, but he sounded like he might unravel at any moment. He sat, exhausted from the trauma of simply making it to the stage, as if standing was too problematical.

Berman may have been the first major comedian to work sitting down, probably because to actually lie down on a couch onstage would have been too embarrassing. The bar stool was his security blanket during his ninety-minute public self-analysis. As the spotlight played over his wincing, weatherworn face, he appeared to be a man undergoing a third-degree grilling, a Kafkaesque figure called upon to justify his life. During these tense sessions we became Berman's surrogate shrink as he spilled his jittery guts. The audience recognized a fellow in far greater misery than they were.

Berman's civilized observations about the terrors of getting through the day—flying in a plane, choking on a popcorn kernel, or contemplating a glass of milk with suspicious black specks in it—illuminated a bedeviled soul (*"Those black specks are smart as hell!"*). The poet and critic Louis Untermeyer called the black-specks piece "a saga of the grotesque." Here was a man who sent a shirt to be cleaned with a Hershey bar in the pocket, who tripped when entering rooms and, to hide his humiliation, pretended it was on purpose. His minor embarrassments were funny, but Berman and his people were in pain. He flashed a sunny amiability ("I may have neuroses," he once said, "but at least I'm not an unhappy man"), but his pieces were edged with shame. Consider his morning-after phone call (as the phone is ringing, he mutters, *"My tongue is asleep and my teeth itch; Oh, God, God, God—c'mon, God,* will *ya?"*) to the host of a party at which Berman feared he has made a total ass of himself. Or his manic call to a store across the street where a person is poised to leap from a ledge—who might well have been Berman himself.

Even coaxing a nephew to call his mother to the phone became, in Shelley Berman's world, an adventure in horror that built from annoyance into full-blown paranoia. In some sketches, Berman moaned as if undergoing physical torture. "My whole act is confession," he once confessed. "Every word I say, I'm admitting something." *Time* called him "Everymanic-depressive." In 1961, at the height of his fame, he revealed, "My insecurity goes on and on." Everything for Berman was fraught with potential disaster. His first album, *Inside Shelley Berman,* hinted at the comic's stressed-out interior. By the third album, *The Edge of Shelley Berman,* he drew closer to his buried fears and rage. Two pieces deal with rejection, first by a girlfriend, then by an old buddy; his characters were teenage souls in torment. Wrote Untermeyer: "Berman is neither a biting cynic nor a buffoon. He is one of us." Said Berman, "Once I have acknowledged my humanity, I have already touched the funny bone of somebody in Tibet."

Even his asides dug deep—about the nostalgic value of the phrase "skate key," or "those *tiny* embarrassing moments" (spinach between the teeth, a cigarette falling out of his mouth onto his lap)—and helped make him the most purely "observational" comic on the scene years before the term was in vogue. Much of it was Benchleyesque (Berman has long wanted to do a one-man Robert Benchley show but can't get the rights).

He was an original in other ways—the first comic whose recorded act became a major hit album, selling well over a million copies. *Inside Shelley Berman* is often regarded as the first comedy LP to win a gold album, though in fact it won in the "spoken word" category; Stan Freberg won for comedy. Berman's album instantly created a new industry as well as a promotional device for comedians. As he likes to say, "If it hadn't been for my record . . . you would never have had the comedy record business. I made it happen." He was the first improvisational actor to break free of a comedy ensemble and fly solo successfully.

With his live-performance record, he reinvented the comedy wheel. One hit album could overnight do the work of a thousand nightclub gigs or a few Ed Sullivan shows—as Bob Newhart, Bill Cosby, and Allan Sherman quickly discovered. The Chicago columnist Irv Kupcinet, in a liner note, confided, "This album is a recording of Shelley Berman actually doing one of his nightclub acts. It's a new idea in records." Kupcinet advised, "Take *Inside Shelley Berman* home, put the record on your gramophone, turn the lights down low, and there you are—a do-it-yourself nightclub, with guaranteed laughs."

When his first record appeared, Berman became a phenomenon, an instantaneous comedy success. He had found a new nationwide audience seated in their living rooms. Until then, record companies assumed that people would only pay to hear comics live, in clubs. Nobody would pay to hear one at home, or so went the industry wisdom, afraid that a record would pall after one playing. Berman's repertoire would become so entrenched that audiences' lips would move silently along with his. As Ralph J. Gleason observed, "Part of the fun was anticipating the laughs, and knowing the jokes was considered a status symbol." More than that, commented Albert Goldman, "records got comics into places they could never reach, like the college dorm or the Bohemian-Beatnik pad. People played the discs over and over again, until they really *heard* what the comic said."

Soon after *Inside Shelley Berman* was a colossal hit, another new comedian—also from Chicago, also doing telephone routines—cut his first album, *The Button-Down Mind of Bob Newhart*. When asked about the chronology of Berman and Newhart, and their similarities, Berman gave a derisive laugh: "To see someone sitting on a stool doing phone calls, I mean . . . I had a woman across the street in a department store window and suddenly I hear about a comedian who has a guy in a sports jacket on a roof across the street. I even did a driving lesson with Elaine May"—as did Newhart alone later. Berman told the writer Jeffrey Sweet: "Somehow this comedian [unnamed] thought of it at exactly the same time or a little bit afterward." He stops himself. "I don't know how much good it's going to do to dwell on this. I saw some things that looked similar, but I couldn't and I won't make that case." Berman also performed a bit about the world's most important booking agent on the phone with Albert Schweitzer, Picasso, Hemingway, and the pope, which bears a striking resemblance to Lenny Bruce's later "Religions, Inc." piece.

Berman discovered a way of presenting material via the telephone that was distinctively fresh, a method expanded on—and skillfully exploited—by Newhart a year or so later with his own fantasy phone calls from historic figures. Earlier comics had done bits on the phone, but Berman presented the telephone as a forbidding weapon, not the friendly device it had always seemed before. In his sweating hands, the telephone receiver became a symbol of terror. (Imagine what he might have done with call waiting, answering machines, call interrupt, telemarketing, speed dialing, and automated "menus.") His routines revealed that the telephone was making people paranoid, agitated, and cranky. "His search for the perfect telephone call," Mort Sahl said, "is like my search for the perfect woman."

Berman turned his pieces into seriocomic sketches, somewhat in the style of the monologuist Ruth Draper, that went way beyond routine one-liners. They were solidly funny and studded with jokes but always pushing a dramatic point, an approach that grew out of his work as an improvisational actor with Chicago's Compass Players. He created credible characters for himself and for the unseen person at the other end of the telephone. He developed a daringly long twenty-minute "Insomniac's Soliloquy," set entirely in the dark, about a troubled man lying awake at night ruminating on his life, which one critic called "Joycean."

He created classics, most memorably the fear-of-flying sketch that launched an entire genre, the blueprint for hundreds of airplane sketches by other comics, none nearly as funny (especially his pilot-on-the-intercom imitation). He said that the airplane scene "contributed more to my success that any other thing I've ever done." What begins as a casual observation (*"I never have the slightest doubt about my safety in a plane until I walk into an airport terminal and realize that there is a thriving industry in this building selling life insurance policies*") descends into a nightmare.

The monologue begins with Berman's stewardess asking (in his most obsequious voice), "*Care for a pillow?*" Berman: "*Oh, Miss, the wing is on fire out there.*" "*Oh, really?*" "*Yes, really. Take a look out there. The wing is a* sheet of flame. *Take a look.*" "*Coffee, tea, or milk?*" "*We don't have time for coffee, tea, or milk. We're doomed!*" "*Well, then, how about a martini?*" After a few airline crashes, he retired the sketch for a time, but the album was allegedly used in stewardess training classes and probably led to them being upgraded to "flight attendant." In that same bit, Berman introduced the word *stewardi* into the language as a logical plural for *stewardess* and further postulated that the plural of Kleenex should be *Klenecees.* Moreover: "*It seems to me that the plural of yo-yo should be yo-yi. How about one sheriff, several sheriffim? Or goof—a group of geef. One blouse, two blice. Two jackeye.*" (George Carlin would work this same vein of language riffs twenty years later.)

While Mort Sahl, Lenny Bruce, Jonathan Winters, Joan Rivers, Phyllis Diller, and Woody Allen did high-speed monologues, Berman took his time. He slowly unveiled, in great detail, the horrors of visiting the dentist. Of the moment when the nurse clips a bib around his neck, he observes, "*You know you're going to* ble-e-e-e-d. *You know you're not going to be eating lobster.*" He mastered not just the dread moment but the imagined slight and the minor triumph, often narrated in an interior monologue. The routines reveal a Rolex sense of timing and control that could be disrupted by a dropped pin. Berman's chamber pieces were meant for attentive playgoers, not nightclubbers. On *Inside Shelley Berman,* a father tries to advise his fifteen-year-old daughter about men in preparation for her first date ("*A young boy is . . . a young boy is . . . a young boy is . . .* rotten"), a subject seemingly exhausted, except that Berman made it a daughter, not a son (the usual premise), which gives it added sweetness. His elastic face and vocal control fleshed out the scenes.

Two set pieces on *The Edge of Shelley Berman* are insightful sketches about two losers, one named Alvin, who phones his girlfriend, Shirley, to see why she's been ignoring him, only to discover she wants to break up: "*The last few months, Shirley, it's been so, so, so . . . yech,*" says Alvin, an adenoidal adolescent. Berman portrays his poor *schlubs* with such depth and understanding that you can only assume they plumb his own boyhood. It's not much of a leap to imagine the young Berman as Alvin or Sammy, sensitive loners. Alvin asks Shirley if anything's wrong with him, and all we hear is, "*Uh-huh . . . uh-huh . . . uh-huh . . . uh-huh,*" then, "*Gosh, Shirley, a* lot *of guys breathe through their mouths. Hey, c'mon, I think yer reachin' now, Shirley.*"

There are a few funny lines (like the memorable "*When two people are holding hands, can anyone really be sure whose hand is doing the sweating?*"), but it's wrenching to eavesdrop on Alvin as the truth slowly dawns on him that he's been dumped. He still tries for a date, and we hear: "*Okay, then, how 'bout the Saturday-or-Sunday after that? . . . How about the Saturday-or-Sunday after that? . . . And what about the Saturday-or-Sunday after that? . . . That gets us into November.*" Alvin at last gives up and signs off, "*Listen, I'll call ya next November, okay?*" Berman was not truly a comedian. He was an actor in comic's clothing, an early performance artist.

In the album's final piece, Alvin becomes Sammy, another of Berman's poignant losers. Sammy calls his pal Davy to say hello only to learn that he didn't get invited to a party and that the girl who turned him down for a date because she was ill was at that party—and, what's worse, that Davy had four tickets to a ballgame and didn't ask him. It's never maudlin, though, just bittersweet as Berman relates it: "*Nah, I'm not* ma-a-a-ad *or anything like* tha-a-a-t," Sammy singsongs, afraid of upsetting his so-called friend. Like Alvin with Shirley, Sammy is undaunted, finally asking, "*Hey, Dave, how come ya never call me?*" Long pause. "*Okay, if not, then I'll call you . . . an' what I'll do is . . . I'll see ya.*"

This was totally new territory, and Berman had it all to himself. Joan Rivers says: "He was amazing to me. He did funny skits that ended sad. Hoo-hoo, I liked that! That was acting. What a wonderful thing to be able to do." No comic twisted comedy into pathos as he did. Mike Nichols and Elaine May performed similar reality-based sketches, but they were clearly—and specifically—satirical. Berman went for laughs, of course, but he also went for something richer and rounder. Because the routines are rooted in universals, snapshots of the human comedy, his albums hold up better than those of many breaktrough fifties and sixties comics.

Not everyone was on his wavelength, however. In a 1974 review in the *Los Angeles Times,* Dennis Hunt wrote that Berman's show at the Playboy Club was "only mildly funny and featured few routines that generate belly laughs. It is full of the kind of jokes that you applaud for being clever, incisive, and perceptive. But few of them inspire all-out laughter." To such criticisms Berman would concede: "Occasionally I come on too strong. When I come on too strong, I fall flat on my face." Alan King says, "I always thought Berman was wonderful. I thought he was very clever.

But I thought it was one-dimensional. That *sound* in his voice, an hour of that . . ." Jack Carter wasn't overly impressed: "He does good stuff, but he thinks he's Marlon Brando. He's so affected. He thinks he's Actors Studio, Lee Strasberg's gift to the Jewish people."

One headline summed him up nicely as a "Cheerful Sufferer," and Berman half-agreed, saying, "I'm a suffering man and we're all suffering together. The whole concept of my comedy is founded on a person suffering in an unbearable circumstance of some kind." He felt this was tied to his Jewishness: "A comic may not be Jewish, but if he suffers in his comedy, he's in the Jewish category. Every misfortune carries the same intensity of grief—losing a nickel or losing the girl." (Lenny Bruce called him "a Reform rabbi.") Many stand-up comedians have enjoyed second careers as actors—from Ed Wynn to Robin Williams—but few were as well trained as Berman, who studied in New York under Uta Hagen.

Berman's most endearing routines were autobiographical, or felt like they were, most notably the sketch in which he plays himself as a teenage boy phoning his father at the family delicatessen to ask him for money so that he can go to acting school in New York. Berman fashioned the essential facts into a touching monologue and reveals how he re-created it novelistically: "I wanted to go to acting school, and neither of my parents understood my desire to go to acting school, absolutely convinced if I went to study acting I would become a 'sissy boy.' That, in essence, is what happened, about my having to get my family's blessing. If I was going to dramatize it, I increased the cultural gulf by giving my father a dialect. Ultimately, both my parents did see me through and help." It's a beautifully nuanced piece, still effective. The father is funny but loving, and the last line still packs a wallop (*"Sheld'n, one t'ing—when you get to New York and you're a famous ectah . . . dun't change your name"*).

Robert Klein recalls that "in 1970 I had a summer show. Shelley and I went out to lunch and we had two double martinis. I asked if he wanted some pot, nothing heavy, and he said, 'No, no, I don't like marijuana. My father smoked marijuana.' I said, 'The guy in the deli? *"Sheld'nnn"?'* It was all a myth! His father was a cabdriver and a pimp, he told me. But you know something? It doesn't take one iota away from it—it was so believable." Berman admits, "Yes, I've fantasized it considerably."

GROWING UP IN CHICAGO, where he was born in 1924, Sheldon Leonard Berman was considered the smart son in his family, and his brother the nice son. "My mother would say to me, 'Why can't you be nice like Ronnie?' and to my brother, 'Why can't you be smart like your brother?' " His mother died at forty-seven, too soon to see her bright, unruly son succeed, but his father lived long enough to enjoy his fame. Berman wrote a play about his immigrant grandparents, in whose home he was raised and where his first language was Yiddish.

His family life sounds like a scene out of a Woody Allen movie, everyone living together in a small flat "full of bickering on a massive scale. I couldn't be heard! There was never a discussion, always an argument. No one ever paid any attention, let alone deferred to another's point of view. I was a little boy, and I stood there in this chaos, trying to make myself known, to be heard saying anything. Then I got to school. I found there were silences, and I filled them." He has variously described his young self as "smart aleck," "clod," "show-off," and "wisecracking punk," although he felt that his friends considered him a "pansy" since he wrote short stories and sculpted in wood. His later pursuits included sonnet writing and stargazing (he carried a telescope with him on the road).

After high school, he did indeed set out to be an "*ectah*" and, on the way, stumbled into comedy. "I was struggling to be an actor, but I could not get arrested," he said of the period when he was performing in stock and attending Chicago's Goodman Theater drama school (where a classmate recalled him as "the greatest Iago I've ever seen"). He joined a suburban company and taught dancing at an Arthur Murray studio before moving to Los Angeles. Nothing happened there except three collisions in four weeks as a cabdriver, so he left for New York, where he became friends with Geraldine Page, who called him "a wonderful brilliant actor, especially in Shakespeare." But he couldn't get an agent. "I would freeze at auditions. I was God's worst at auditions. To this day my hands shake."

Between auditions, he sold some sketches to Steve Allen's *Tonight* show. About that time, the late 1950s, a friend, the actor Martin Landau, told him about a new avant-garde group in Chicago called the Compass that did something called "improvisation," and that they had a summer opening in 1956. "I went down there and replaced Severn Darden, a great comedy actor." Until then he'd never considered performing comedy as a way to make a living, although he was already writing comedy. He told Larry Wilde, "I'd been funny at parties, which is a colossal bore, but I was the lampshade man. I was moderately humorous—nothing memorable, funny much more than witty. I knew I could be amusing onstage, but I was a straight actor."

The Compass kept him on and he began working with that later-famous core company, which included Mike Nichols, Elaine May, Barbara Harris, Darden, Alan Arkin, et al. "I didn't know improvisation, so I started to learn what to do. I just thought you were supposed to go out there and try to be funny—which is the *worst* thing an improvisationalist can do." As he told Jeffrey Sweet, "If you have funny in you, the funny will happen. To trust that and not to work for funny was the thing I had to learn." Berman recalls, "I made a fool of myself the first few times. I had to remember to 'play my action.' I started to learn what all those terms meant and I started to deliver. It was incredible!"

Slightly older than the others, Berman didn't fit into the group, which he later called "a bunch of extremely young smart-asses. They weren't a clique, but I wasn't a part of the group." Even so, he adds now, "I think the greatest joy I ever had in my life was working with them. We were doing the best work of our lives." He especially liked "The Panhandler's Apprentice," in which he instructs Darden in the art of begging. Darden later said of him, "He was absolutely great to work with. You could work on a really thin wire with Shelley and know that you wouldn't fall down."

Berman is remembered by his colleagues as a quivering ball of energy and ambition, who offended company members with his insistent on-stage gambits. "I was hungry for recognition," he told Janet Coleman in her book on the Compass, which later evolved into the Second City. "I wanted to get somewhere. I was looking at thirty years old, and nothing was happening in my life. It was scaring the hell out of me. My energy was that of a man running. I was always inclined to go for the laugh. I was very pushy about that. I always wanted to be onstage. I really *was* a stage hog." Berman eventually learned to tone himself down at the Compass, where a fellow actor asked him, "Why do you have to reach? Why does it *always* have to be funny?"

To save a scene that he thought was dying, he would occasionally interrupt it with an imaginary phone call. He stole laughs from others and once upstaged Elaine May, who took no guff and told him, according to Compass director David Shepherd, "The next time you fuck me up onstage, I'll pull down your zipper and pull out your dick." Berman heightened the level of competition onstage, said fellow Compass member Bobbi Gordon, who recalled that before Berman, there had been "a reaching out for each other. Shelley really broke that chain. It became *me*. And once that *me*—and a very powerful *me*—began to take over, then it was, 'I've got to protect myself,' and everybody began to withdraw."

Berman's swift rise to fame soon after leaving the group changed the group's esprit de corps; the new prospect of stardom altered the group dynamic. Performers now wanted to be showcased, to show off, to shine.

The telephone vignettes that made Berman famous were created out of necessity while he was at the Compass. "I was an actor," he told me. "I didn't know beans about being a comedian. There was no way I could be funny directly to the audience. So I wrote this little monologue where I wouldn't have to talk directly to anyone. It wasn't a gimmick or a calculated technique. I came up with the idea of selling myself to the mirror. I'd be a teenager and call one of my buddies. On the phone, I would find out lots of things. Then I would hang up and go to the mirror and sell myself to myself." One night, the audience exploded after he hung up the phone, so Berman decided to end the piece there. Thus did Shelley Berman reinvent the telephone.

His classic morning-after routine began when Berman suggested to Elaine May that they do the scene together, with her as the hostess and he as the drunken guest, but she told him, "I'm doing a thing with Mike." So, he recalls, "I just figured I'd go out and do it myself. I did it, and that became a routine"—with a small but crucial assist from Darden, who suggested that Berman's character apologize for flinging a *cat* instead of a lamp. While Berman was at the Compass, he, Mike Nichols, and May did several sketches together, such as *Hamlet* set in a Jewish deli, with Berman as Uncle Claude, May as Gertrude, and Nichols as Hamlet, smoking and kvetching. May did her Jewish mother bit—"*Mrs. Rosencrantz and Mrs. Guildenstern, their sons don't act like this.*"

Berman imagined the three going on to form a trio, but Nichols and May were already working as a team, and Berman, who felt an instant rapport with May, became the Other Man in a comic ménage à trois. "I had a few things I did with Elaine, like the lost dime"—Berman as a harried man trying to persuade a dubious operator that he had deposited his last dime—"which became part of *their* act. But that was *our* scene." Berman's solo version, called "Franz Kafka on the Telephone," "was never really a dynamite routine, but their duet version was a dynamite routine."

Recounting what turned into a traumatic experience for him, Berman explains: "The three of us would work on a thing"—such as May interviewing him as a famous playwright, based on Tennessee Williams, which also later became a Nichols & May staple, or a child psychologist taking questions from the audience, which Berman later used in *his* act. "For several weeks we worked as a group. We'd kill 'em."

He goes on: "Every week I would keep asking, 'Could we please do more things together?' One day I said, 'I keep coming up with suggestions for names for a group and you keep saying they're no good.' I said, 'C'mon. We're a trio. Let's get a name for a trio.' And Mike says, 'What trio?' " Berman was devastated. Forty years later, he still chokes up retelling the incident: "I had so much *hope*. I'd put so much stock in it. But I'm sure Mike had good reasons, and I'm sure she did. I can't make any claims. There's no villain in this piece. But I *do* know that happened and it was perhaps the worst kick in the gut that I can recall"—his voice breaks—"and I've had some in my time. This was really bad, and so unexpected. It still hurts."

Former Compass director Walter Beakel has recalled: "Mike didn't want to work with him. It was more and more apparent as we went along that Mike and Elaine were a pair. They were more cerebral than Shelley." Berman would later admit to Janet Coleman that "I was a bit more vulgar than Mike, in fact a bit more vulgar than all the others. I found myself working less from my head than my gut." Beakel said Berman's only flaw was his propensity for going over the top. "You almost had to go in there with a riding crop to keep him in line, or he'd go too far."

Berman's feelings about Nichols remain unresolved. Commenting on Nichols's often icy façade, he says, "I think the *Titanic* ran into him," then adds: "There are few men on this earth I admire more than Mike. I have always always loved his work, and I've always *always* wished he'd loved me as I love him. I've never been intimidated by him, just felt he was slightly out of reach, as she [May] was. I always looked up to him, even though I was a few years older. Even to this day, if he gave me a tumble, I'd be right there." Even so, Berman looks back today on that whole period more in pride than pain: "I was in on the ground floor, which went from the Compass to Second City to *SCTV* to *Saturday Night Live*."

Berman, Nichols, May, David Steinberg, Robert Klein, Joan Rivers, and others who went on to become stars using material conceived—often by them—at Compass/Second City were considered disloyal by some in the company. The producers argued that all sketches were company property, as they are now, but it caused ethical and legal rifts that lasted decades and still rankle alumni like Nichols.

A major irritant to the rebel comedians was being confused with one another. It seems impossible to mix up Mort Sahl with Shelley Berman and Lenny Bruce, but it happened all the time and does even today. "I gotta tell ya something—it hurt us terribly," Berman says. "Since we were so different from our predecessors, we were lumped as the same. We lost our individuality. That's a *ver-r-ry* serious problem. The most precious possession we had was ourselves. Mort's edges were also being blurred—I was sort of folded into his territory and he into mine. In reality, our edges were very, very sharp. But the press and the public didn't see it that way." People still confuse them. "I went to an engagement in Maryland, and the house booker says to me, 'You'll do your topical stuff,' and I said, 'I don't really do topical stuff,' and he said, 'You know, the political stuff, the stuff about Clinton.' I know who he thought I was. Only when I was performing did they realize I'm *not* Mort Sahl."

When *Time* magazine stamped the "sick" label on the new wave of satirical comedians in their July 13, 1959, issue, it stuck and was impossible to peel off. Berman rebelled against having it slapped on *him*. In 1960 he told *Newsweek:* "It connotes the mocking of tragedy. It is *so* offensive to me. Damn it, comedians for the past two decades have made jokes at the expense of spastics, people with cleft palates, homosexuals; they have violated the bedroom—and I just don't do that!" He noted, later: "You have no idea how it affected me. When I first heard 'sick' I thought I was all washed up."

Being a comic rebel in the late fifties took far more guts than it does now, says Berman. "You have to remember, there was a man out there *scaring the shit* out of the world, a senator from Wisconsin named McCarthy. We were really very much afraid. You had to be damned careful." One example: "Ike had had a heart attack, and in one routine I was on the phone saying to Nixon, '*Well, better luck next time, kid.*' And Mike Nichols said to me, 'I thought that was very poor taste.' That tells you about our time. I was scolded! So when the senator got his comeuppance we felt free to really *speak*! We were the first to break the constraints in a new way, very early in that new freedom. We were gathering steam."

Berman still wasn't sure what he eventually wanted to do. He wasn't a traditional comedian and had no idea how he would make it in the nightclub world. In his first solo gig in Chicago, at the Gate of Horn, he was fired after two weeks. "I never said 'Good evening,' I never said 'Thank you.' I never acknowledged the audience. I was introduced, 'Shelley Berman, bum-bum-bum,' got on the bar stool, sat down immediately, and dialed the phone. I didn't do joke, joke, joke, I didn't ask what town you were from. I didn't know how to say hello to an audience." Then he saw a new comedian who broke the rules, and it confirmed his own approach: "I watched this guy come on wearing a sweater and carrying a newspaper under his arm and the son of a bitch never told a joke. God, I didn't realize that was possible. And he got us laughing and he was bright and he was exciting and I thought, 'Jeez, I use big words, too, and I know what's going on in the world, however I don't know what he knows. But at least I know something and can do something.' That guy was, of course, Mort Sahl."

Sahl had a huge impact on Berman—"He was a major inspiration because he showed me that *humor* will sell, not stand-up jokes. I was a fourth-wall actor. You get up and do your thing and you don't talk to the audience. So I wangled an audition at Mister Kelly's, and I got up there on a stool and I made a little phone call and the audience screamed."

Berman did something else that few comedians had ever done before on a nightclub stage—he sat down while he made his phone calls, simply because it felt right. "We'd all sat on chairs at the Compass. When you make a phone call you don't always stand up, you sit down. Also, Mister Kelly's had this low stage, so if I'd sat in a chair nobody would've seen me. So I asked if I could borrow a bar stool. They said, 'Well, they're all taken.' The boss said to me, 'Ya know, if you're a comedian you lose a lot of authority sitting down—you lose control.' I said, 'It's what I do.' So they got a guy to get off his bar stool."

His first nightclub piece was a sketch about dialing a department store across the street to tell them that a woman was hanging out the window. "The audience laughed and laughed and laughed. I did two things and came off the stage, and the next day I got a call that they wanted me to go on in the summer for three hundred fifty dollars a week for four weeks with an option for the following year for four weeks at seven hundred and fifty dollars. It was like the *Reader's Digest* sweepstakes. It was incredible to me! I was making fifty-five dollars a week."

Berman's act, more than most, required a high level of attention. People listened because they had to catch all the references and asides. Unlike the work of earlier comics, with their predictable rhythms, the new comedy depended on inflection and nuance. Hecklers were rare, and apart from the occasional table of drunks, comics now commanded respect. Club owners like Enrico Banducci at the hungry i and Oscar Marienthal at Mister Kelly's made sure that they got it; Banducci, although a famously sloppy bookkeeper ("He gave me a bonus," says Berman, smiling—"it's still bouncing"), was quick to rout loudmouths.

Younger audiences began flocking to see specific, not generic, comics, who, like Berman, were literate, different—and often difficult. Says

Berman, "I knew I was different, but I didn't know that different meant better. I knew that what I did sold in Mister Kelly's, a jazz room with everybody looking and listening and appreciating everything you do. They were used to listening to jazz players and singers, and what I was doing was also the result of improvisation. It was the right audience in the perfect room, with college grads, people who would shift their love for jazz to us."

Berman explained to Larry Wilde how he came upon his own style. "The biggest problem in our time was the hurdle of introducing a new comedy form. I was essentially a monologuist. I did the routine, finished that, took a bow, then started the next routine. I had nothing *between* them. So I was not, in the strict sense of the word, a comedian. I was unable at first to cope with the atmosphere in a nightclub." Berman, the sedate opposite of the raucous Borscht Belt *tummlers,* grafted a theatrical form onto a nightclub stage that had been home to old-style comics.

Satirical comedians of Berman's era began in little rooms with hip, well-educated audiences—and then, once officially decreed funny by the media, were embraced by a wider audience. Some crossed over to the masses—Berman, Winters, Cosby, Diller, Rivers, Newhart—but just as many did not: Woody Allen (except in urban markets), Bruce, Dick Gregory, Nichols & May, Sahl. Berman admits that at first he "was a darling of a certain select cult," but then went for a national audience, once acknowledging, "I'll trip over my feet. I'll do hokum. I'll do farce. I'll do anything to make people laugh as long as I think it's funny." Sahl once said, "They wanted to turn him into Red Skelton."

When Berman first appeared at the Thunderbird Hotel in Las Vegas, he was a disaster. "I never heard a titter. For twenty-seven days, I didn't hear a laugh. I didn't know how to deal with an unreceptive audience, or a heckler. I didn't know how to address the audience. I could only do these little playlets on the phone by myself." The singer Billy Eckstein told Berman, when the comic opened for him in Montreal, "Shelley, tonight I'd like you to try something just once. I'd like you to smile at the audience and say 'Good evening' before you go to work." Berman answered, "I can't do that. I don't know how to do that." He explains: "I thought I was different. I wasn't different. I just wasn't a comedian. I became a comedian along the way. But it was not a willing or a happy thing. It was terrifying." He objected to being called a "comic," which he considered an insult until he finally stopped fighting it.

Berman always had an unusually fragile relationship with audiences, even letting them know how much he needed them to survive. All comics realize this; few are so frank about it. Berman would sign off his act by nakedly exposing his dependency on the customers: "You don't need me but I sure as hell need you. It's a *stinking* situation! You can laugh by yourself without my help. I am not funny alone in my bathroom. So the act is strewn with several tiny little lies to ingratiate myself to you. . . . So here's the logic: if I've been funny tonight, it must be because of *you*. The lines are negligible. If you weren't here, I would not hear anything. So together we did it! In essence, you're not an audience, but you've been a helluva act and I am deeply beholden to you. Good night."

WITH THREE GOLD RECORDS BY 1963, Berman was the hottest comedian in the country. At one point he was asked to lead the creative department of a major studio and to take over several failing TV comedy shows. Then everything went sour. Suddenly he wasn't around so much. It wasn't that the public rejected him or cooled off. Berman's comedy career flamed out, almost as fast as it had erupted, through a bitter set of circumstances that he finds difficult to discuss even today.

He was important enough in 1963 to be spotlighted in a prime-time TV documentary that focused on the behind-the-scenes life of a comic. The film, titled *Comedian Backstage,* was aired March 3 on NBC's *Du Pont Show of the Week,* and virtually destroyed Berman's career, or at least sent it reeling for years. He never fully recovered.

Did Shelley Berman murder his ex-wife? Rape a minor? Get caught shoplifting? Set himself on fire freebasing cocaine? Drive off a bridge with a young girl who drowned? No, what Berman did was blow his stack backstage after a telephone had rung offstage during a crucial moment in his act. It was a cruel irony—he who had lived by the phone died by the phone. It didn't take much then for a show-business career to be destroyed. The incident had the impact of Arthur Godfrey firing Julius La Rosa on the air or Jackie Mason reportedly flipping Ed Sullivan the bird off-camera. Today, it might be worth a Jay Leno joke. But the incident stained Berman's career, much as Jonathan Winters's manic few moments aboard a ship on Fisherman's Wharf left a scar that people refuse to forget. To those who wonder whatever happened to Shelley Berman, *Comedian Backstage* is what happened. As one headline put it: "For Shelley Berman, the Phone Stopped Ringing."

"That very destructive time in my life took all the pleasure out of working," he says. Berman took a huge cut in pay but found it hard to scale down his affluent ways (*Time* reported in 1961 that Berman was the wealthiest of the new comics and owned a dozen expensive suits, all with jackets bent at the elbow from holding a mock telephone). "I wanted it and needed it," he told an interviewer—the autograph signing, the best tables. "It was such a grand sensation, a great way to live."

He began claiming that comedy had become "laborious" and that he got a bigger kick from theater, largely because stand-up comedy jobs were suddenly fewer and lower-paying. "I turned to acting both from love and necessity." All he ever wanted out of comedy, he said once, was a good part in a play. In 1990 Berman remarked, "Being a comedian wasn't a blessing. I think it was a very bad idea, the worst thing I ever did."

Among the bizarre things that befell Berman, all of which sound like one of his own stage nightmares, was how one brief moment in a documentary distorted people's (even old friends') memories of him. "I have had to live with this legend of being exceptionally difficult to work with. The gossips and the self-fulfilling prophesy [among employers] is, 'Oh, you're gonna find yourself in trouble.' So you have people watching you. Yes, even today, people say, 'Shelley, believe me, I tell those people *I* know how to talk to you.' I say, 'Man, you don't know how to talk to me either. Because if you think I need to be talked to in a special way, you're making a mistake.' "

When he went back to play Mister Kelly's after *Comedian Backstage* had aired, the staff treated him as if Godzilla had returned. "The waiters, waitresses, people who saw me time and time again and *knew* I wasn't like that—now were behaving as if I were." Four years afterward, he noted, "People are genuinely surprised that I say 'please' and 'thank you' and that I don't have saber teeth." For years he was afraid to send a steak back.

Berman feelingly re-created for me the backstage incident behind his career obituary: "There were two phone calls ringing offstage. The first time the phone rang offstage I finished my show, everything's fine and I go to my new road manager and I said, 'Make sure this doesn't happen again, okay, because it could upset the act.' So everything was swell. The second time, in the middle of the father-son routine, which is my most important routine, the phone rang again. *Then* I got angry."

In the documentary, the two phone calls were reversed. "For dramatic purposes, they took the second phone call and showed that first, took the first phone call and showed that second. I said, 'That's wrong, they're gonna get the wrong idea.' They said, 'No, no, it'll show you're a good sport.' I argued with them and was convinced by them, by the silence of everyone around me, that maybe it was right." He later said, "I thought the public would understand that I am a human being who loses his temper once in a while when things go wrong." After watching the rough cut: "The silence around me was deafening! Everyone was there—my personal manager, my business manager, my wife, close friends. I turned around to say, 'People, this has been screwed up, it's twisted around chronologically. It makes a dramatic show, but you know what could happen to me here.' And I'm not hearing anybody saying *anything*."

Bob Newhart, who shared the same manager with Berman, now says, "There is a story that it was a setup, that it was intentional on the part of whoever was doing the documentary to *arrange* for the phone to ring, to see how he would react." Berman concurs: "I'm pretty sure it was intended. Everyone was ready for me to be upset. They also knew *when* to do it, during the most critical portion of the routine. I can't come out and say it for sure, but I can sure think it. These people wanted an exciting program."

What mostly tears Berman apart is that he could have canceled the show had he obeyed his gut instinct. "I told everyone there, 'I don't have to let this go on. Could someone just tell me what you think?' 'Well, it's you,' they said. 'I know, but do you see what's happening? What do you think I should do? *Help me out!*' Silence. Not one word of advice." He laughs. "Maybe they saw what was going to happen and sort of liked it. I didn't see it when it went on. I didn't know that the next day I would be a pariah. I had no idea."

He continues: "There are people who *still* say I tore a phone off the wall. If you look at that thing you'll see that I did *not* tear a phone off the wall. But I'm famous for having torn a phone off a wall, which is a fucking lie." In fact, he yanked it off the hook and let it dangle. "And I paid pretty good. Jesus, it cost me dear. Such a costly, costly thing. You're talking about a man who has paid a *helluva* price for letting the audience see something that wasn't even true in the first place. That was it. It was gone."

A *New York Herald Tribune* critic wrote a scathing review, saying that the show revealed Berman to be "extremely nervous, a chronic worrier, full of self-pity, self-deception and a colossal ego, a spoiled child with a nasty temper, a petty disposition and a taste of tyranny, and a blind insensitivity to others." Everyone seemed to have a Shelley Berman story—that he once insulted the management in curtain speeches and used obscene gestures, that he refused to go onstage unless his beard was trimmed and his boots shined. People refused to hire him, not much caring whether he was a tiger or a pussycat, and walked on eggshells around him. It got so bad that he worked with out-of-tune pianos, lousy lighting, and crummy sound systems rather than complain; he once paid out of his own pocket to rent a new spotlight, only to hear later that he'd been "uncooperative." In one engagement, the price of the drinks he held onstage was subtracted from his fee.

Grover Sales, then the hungry i's publicist, says, "He was quite mad. Of all the people I did PR for, he was by far the most unappreciative, difficult, and paranoid. He did a concert at the Masonic Auditorium in the early sixties and there were two empty seats out of thirty-six hundred and he threw a tantrum at me before the show, asking, 'Can you explain this?' " In an interview, he blew up at a disc jockey who mentioned two fellow comics ("What do Lenny Bruce and Mort Sahl have to do with me?"). Paul Goldenberg, the former manager of the hungry i, recalls: "It was a difficult relationship. He was a very nice guy but extremely neurotic. Because of a few [noisy] people in the audience, he didn't want to go on for the second show. He put his arm around the safe and sobbed." The former TV sitcom writer Bob Schiller says, "He was considered a pain in the ass by everybody." Gene Norman, who hired Berman at the Interlude, says: "I would accommodate him. I think of all acts as tall children, but Shelley Berman was a big baby. You couldn't run the mixing machine when he was on. He was scared to death." Although Don Gregory calls him "a lovely lovely man," he wonders, "Why that one TV show should destroy his career and not others with similar incidents, I don't know, but they missed a great talent." Lily Tomlin, who grew up admiring Berman's character monologues, says, "It's so ironic that that TV thing could cause his career to spiral when he should be celebrated."

Lawrence Christon reflects: "That documentary had to have been the match to the tinderbox. Everyone has idiosyncrasies, particularly show-biz people. Everybody can be unpleasant. They must have been waiting for him. They must have just heard that this guy was impossible. Once he actually came down in the audience and said [of himself], 'I wanna see how this sonofabitch is doing.' I think he's got control of it now. He had an almost virulent uncontrollable self-hatred. A friend of mine who's a psychotherapist said, 'He doesn't believe he deserves his success.' " Phyllis Diller said, "If it happens too fast it goes to your head. He had a bodyguard, but nobody ever bothered him."

Berman once said, in his defense, "I am not a taut mainspring ready to crack at the slightest jar, but timidity has no place in the creation of any artistic work. There are points in the act where a spoken word from a heckler can be a blow. If there is an interruption, that moment is lost." He has conceded, "Sure, I'm difficult," but added, "Who gets cheated if things aren't right? The audience—because they see less than the best possible show. Nothing occurs in front of an audience that is undetectable. I call it the perceptibility of the imperceptible. Like the hum of an air conditioner is only noticed when it goes off. Often an audience can't quite pin down what is wrong, but it affects their reaction." A dance floor between the stage and the tables, or a floral centerpiece that blocks people's views, can ruin a show. "And you know that even while you're breaking your head to do the job, some people are gonna walk out of that room and say, 'Gee, it was a terrible show. I remember him as being funnier.' "

Marty Kummer, Berman's onetime manager, told the writer Phil Berger that Berman would make fun of his own wired temperament. "But the truth was, he was temperamental and went out of his way, unknowingly, to make himself a bad guy. He destroyed himself. He didn't mean to. He was troubled. He couldn't stop imagining and second-guessing things and finding fault." Added Kummer: "This is the same fellow who would take an hour of his time to talk to you because your mother wasn't feeling well." People who attest to Berman's humanity—his writing letters to a comedy writer he barely knew who'd had a stroke, his working quietly for Jewish causes—admit that he could erupt over shoddy service, sending outraged letters to airlines and telephone and electric companies. Kummer would say to Berman: "The time you spent on that, why don't you write a new piece of material?"

Others in show business vividly remember Berman as a man of at least as many sides as his album titles proclaim. In 1975 a critic called him "innovative, paranoid, hostile, insecure, earnest, friendly, and brilliant." A promoter was quoted in 1961 as saying, "You have to keep patting him and telling him he's good"—not unlike most performers. Mort Sahl wrote in a liner note: "He is a perfectionist who worries about everything in 'his theater,' from the hospital plan for the backstage employees to the off-street parking for the audience."

The disc jockey Dan Sorkin, who helped advance the careers of Bob Newhart and Allan Sherman by playing their records in Chicago, recalls emceeing a show at the Chicago Opera House where Berman shared the bill with the Kingston Trio. "He was backstage roaring, 'The Kingston

Trio is going on too long! They're wearing out the audience. They're the backup act, for chrissake! I'm the star.' He was really grousing and screaming, and when he came stomping out, still angry and muttering, he walked off the stage and fell into the orchestra pit. When he got back onstage, his toupee was on at an angle, he was smudged, and he looked like a madman. Then when he got to the punch line of his father-son piece, 'Don't change your name, Sheldon,' the lights didn't black out. He looked up at the light man and yelled, 'You cocksuckers!' And then the lights went out. The audience thought it was a punch line."

When Lainie Kazan ran Lainie's Rooms in New York and Los Angeles, she booked Berman, and recalls: "Shelley Berman was the most anxious, nervous, uptight, neurotic person I ever worked with. He'd say, 'Am I on yet? Am I on yet?' I'd say, 'You got five minutes,' and he couldn't wait. He'd go, 'Ladies and gentlemen, Shelley Berman!' He would announce himself and go on!" Paul Mazursky recalls, "Shelley followed me at the hungry i. I saw the show, it was very successful. I went backstage and said, 'Shelley, it was fabulous.' He said, 'Was it good? Was it good?' I said, 'Shelley, did you hear them applauding and laughing?' He said, 'I didn't hear it.' He wasn't joking."

Berman's intensity lessened after the death of his twelve-year-old son from a brain tumor. "I used to think of my performances as life-and-death," he said in 1977. "They are not life-and-death. This I know. I used to be antagonistic, arrogant, and far too worried about my own performance. If an audience didn't laugh, I was devastated! It's a good thing I'm not a critic or I'd wipe out my entire career." Then he added, in a burst of Bermanesque candor: "But I haven't been cleansed. I still think I'm a son of a bitch. When I'm working I don't want anyone to screw me up. I don't want anyone to play around with my lights, my microphone."

Berman was the first of the publicly vulnerable, let-it-all-hang-out performers—the Judy Garland of comedians. As he once said, "I allow everyone to see everything about me. I let them see my height, my width, my depth. I'm a man of good words and bad words, kindness and cruelty. I have arrogance and humility. I do have a real flaw. It's called humanity." Berman paved the way for comics riddled with angst, like Woody Allen and Richard Lewis, who strongly identified with Berman. Lewis, known for his onstage woe, says, "He was a huge influence. He was very, very tortured, as I was. He was a real craftsman—he was almost like a funny Monty Clift. He was very wired. God forbid you heckle him, he'll hang himself."

Berman has watched comedy grow meaner, rougher, and grislier over the years. He has lots of theories as to why, part of a master's-level course in creative writing he's taught for nearly two decades at the University of Southern California. In that course, titled "Humor Writing: Literary and Dramatic," he unfolds his theory of what he calls "decadent relativity": "George Carlin took off the jacket and tie, let his hair grow long, gave us the seven words you're not supposed to say and he articulated our anger. Carlin is a comedian of today, but he's one of us, at least in years. He made the transformation and he made it well, but I don't care for the word *fuck* as punctuation; there are other ways to punctuate. Richard Pryor is another of them. Then, when the anger ceased and blacks started getting their share of the pie, when there wasn't acute anger, there were comedians smart enough to at least pick up the packaging—Eddie Murphy and the comediennes who talk about going down on their boyfriends. These people were just taking on the packaging."

Irreverence, Berman says, became a commodity efficiently packaged by television. "*We'd* been the guys with the irreverent humor before. We were the torchbearers of irreverent humor for a long, long time. Then some guy put a show on TV called *All in the Family,* and all of the irreverent humor now went to TV . . . and it almost put us all out of work. We had to go one better. The comedy hasn't changed, but the *packaging* has changed."

Like many other renaissance comics of the fifties and sixties, Berman is discouraged by what passes for stand-up comedy today. "What's happening now is that there is no life after teen age. Not everyone can laugh at going to the toilet or diddling with oneself or whatever seems to amuse today—catching your penis in a zipper, which of course is *so* brand-new. I can't look at this. I don't know what's going on. I can't tell about this phenomenon, but I know that this comedy is called for by our time, though I'm not sure what our time is. All I know is, I feel very left out. Not only as a performer but as a member of the audience."

Although Berman has been out of the limelight for decades, he hasn't been inactive—nor has he died, as some people assume. The actor Larry Hankin says, "I went to see Shelley Berman about three years ago and his comic mind is alive. I've never heard such timing. He's surgical in his timing." Berman seems to have lightened up, or at least grown more tolerant of audiences. He still does his classic sketches, but he doesn't do many comedy engagements now. After his headliner comedy career imploded in the mid-sixties, he returned—if not in quite the way he had imagined—to his original career, acting, and began popping up in movies and TV series, portraying various anguished middle-aged men. More recently, he's acted in summer-stock shows and at regional theaters, playing Tevye in *Fiddler on the Roof,* Nathan Detroit in *Guys and Dolls,* and Armand in *La Cage aux Folles,* also in *Damn Yankees* and *Where's Charley?* "I've broken house records all over the country with the dinner-theater circuit," he said in 1977. "I'm still a mighty good draw." He starred as the troubled antihero in *The Prisoner of Second Avenue;* in a play about Jonathan Pollard, the convicted spy for Israel; and in *The Eleventh,* a parable of Jewish history. Today he teaches, directs, speaks, and performs occasionally.

Berman is not a comic force anymore at seventy-nine, but neither is he living in a dimly lit one-bedroom apartment in downtown Los Angeles, flipping through old scrapbooks. He lives comfortably in a spacious ranch-style house in a gated community in the San Fernando Valley. On the way downstairs to his study (many books, photos of Berman in various shows and toupees), he points out glass cases that house a collection of knives and daggers whose psychological significance for him can only be imagined. When you sit down with him, his wife of fifty-three years, Sarah, arrives with coffee and cookies and discreetly vanishes.

The longer he's performed—or just lived—the mellower he's become. Howard Storm, a member, with Berman, of a comedy old-timers' dinner group called Yarmy's Army, says: "Shelley was always a loner until he joined, and he's in shock. He can't believe there is this bunch of comics who care about each other. He just loves being there and having these relationships. It's an amazing group of guys. Shelley closes our show and he's sensational—they adore him." Says Budd Friedman of the Improv: "He's completely changed now. Couldn't be nicer. He does the Improv in Vegas—I use him all the time. He does very well with our crowd."

He now plays a couple of stand-up dates a year in Las Vegas, plus assorted one-nighters and benefits, and reflects how he's changed as a comedian: "What happens is a confidence that comes out of the affection you feel for the people who are there. The mature performer knows that the most wonderful people in the world are the people who come to see him or her. It's very rare for me to slip, very rare for me to say, 'Now that was a tough audience.' You don't figure anyone's to blame, or yourself either. Sex isn't great every single time, but that doesn't put you off sex. You don't start blaming your partner. Fear of performance failure is absurd, and it doesn't help. It doesn't do anything.

"When I was younger, the first thing I did was blame myself. 'What am

I doing wrong?' One of the things I did wrong when I was younger was expect the audience to respond as I expected them to respond. I've had audiences that were thrilled but weren't the biggest laughers. My performances now, as opposed to my performances as a very young performer, are characterized by my affection for the people." A tempered Shelley Berman says today: "I tell every audience that I have a problem—that my audiences are now made up of people too young to know who I am and too old to *remember* who I am."

He smiles, but a faint melancholy shadows his face. His laughs are a grateful release. He still seems intense and fragile, as if he might dissolve into wistfulness, and now and then his voice will erupt with emotion or his eyes moisten. He speaks candidly but often uneasily and urgently, and his voice cracks when discussing hurts from long ago. But there remains a sweetness about him. He has survived a collapsed career, bankruptcy, his son Joshua's death. A month after that, he told an interviewer: "I've been taught a profound lesson—the future is a breaker of promises."

Double Jeopardy

MIKE NICHOLS AND ELAINE MAY

Sometimes each of us would be thinking, "Oh, God, I know where we're going," and both of us would race to get there first.
                                                          —MIKE NICHOLS

H E WAS SLIM, pasty, sensitive, meek, and wary, somewhere between helpless and haughty. She was dark, pretty, sensuous, strange, and wired, with her come-hither drop-dead look. Between them, Mike Nichols and Elaine May made a formidable team that demolished the pretensions of American life at midcentury, in particular the shifting and increasingly iffy relationships between men and women.

Their characters were fraught with uncertainty and peril, delivered with a sardonic, often devastating, and always precisely aimed wit not seen in a comedy team before or since: from a sniggering after-hours rendezvous between secretary and boss to a romantic spat between dentist and hygienist during oral surgery; from confused oversexed teenagers necking in a car to a pair of blasé overeducated lovers in bed; from a martyred mother berating a thoughtless son for not calling to a telephone operator humiliating a hapless customer. Like Shelley Berman, they created full-blooded characters.

Nichols & May made a major noise in American comedy overnight when they first emerged from the original Compass Players in Chicago (which would become the Second City). They reigned for only four years until their unexpected breakup in 1961, at the height of their fame, following a Broadway run that confirmed their place in comedy history. On just four albums, and in a few appearances onstage and on television, Nichols & May established themselves as the leading social satirists of their generation, a title never seriously threatened in the forty years of sketch comedy since. Mort Sahl, Lenny Bruce, and Woody Allen left huge lasting imprints, but Nichols & May are perhaps the most ardently missed of all the satirical comedians of their era. When Nichols & May split up, they left no imitators, no descendants, no blueprints or footprints to follow. No one could touch them.

In their satirical scenes, they subtly captured the sound of terribly earnest and sensitive young sophisticates flashing their badges of sophistication for each other, as in a pillow-talk routine heard over the sound of a piano piece by Bartók—the definitive Nichols & May sketch. May: "*There is, always, another dimension to music. And it's apart from life. I can never believe that Bartók died on Central Park West.*" Nichols: "*Isn't that ugly?*" May: "*Ugly, ugly, ugly . . . Oh, I love this part! Listen.*" Nichols: "*Almost hurts.*" May: "*Yes, beauty often does.*" Nichols: "*When I discovered Nietzsche, and he* said *that, in a way.*" May: "*In many ways, when I read* Thus Spake Zarathustra *a whole world opened for me.*" Nichols (excitedly): "*I know exactly what you mean!*" May: "*Do you know what I mean?*" Nichols: *Exactly!* May: "*Did that happen to you?*" Nichols: "*I know* exactly *what you mean!*"

Mike Nichols and Elaine May somehow had absorbed much of high and low culture and folded it into routines about real people in which they effortlessly, ironically, dropped in literary-musical-historical references that kidded those cultures in a way that both flattered and tickled their equally alert audiences. They mocked the mind-set of the way we—well, some of us—lived then. Mike and Elaine addicts dug the humor, but they dug equally the kick of belonging to a select circle that knew who Bartók was—and, more important, who the people were who would drop Bartók's name into a seemingly casual postcoital discussion as earnest as the sex itself. Those people, hilariously, were *us.*

The theater critic Robert Brustein, writing in *The New Republic* in 1960, compared Nichols & May to TV's Sid Caesar, "their less sophisticated mentor," observing that the team was part of a movement of "Comedians from the Underground," along with Sahl, Bruce, and Jules Feiffer. Brustein said that, by employing "extraordinary powers of observation to locate clichés of conventional middle-class life," they strip them "to their essential absurdity, so that the action tends to criticize itself." Caesar's show might satirize foreign films, but Nichols & May would ridicule the artistic pretensions of the people who went to them.

Brustein noted that May was so accurate that "she often threatens to break out of comedy altogether." He was less enamored of their improvisation segment, calling it "the least impressive thing in the program since it only suggests the remarkable ingenuity of this team; the [prepared] sketches demonstrate they have brilliance, irreverence, and wit as well." He called them "the voice of outraged intelligence in a world given over to false piety, cloying sentiment, and institutionalized stupidity." That pretty well covers it.

Nichols & May took the core elements of improvisational theater—the back-and-forth intellectual Ping-Pong matches, the literate cultural allusions, and the seemingly simple children's gamesmanship ("You be the Joker and I'll be Batman")—and shaped them into digestible comic form, frequent as we watched. They were in no way stand-up comics—they were funny actors—yet their goal was the same: laughs, as many as possible, within a theatrical setting.

In 1964, after they were no longer working together, Nichols said, "We weren't *really* a comedy team. Elaine and I kept thinking we'd be found out. We developed an act without really meaning to. We were actors, writers, and directors, all at once. We'd think up a situation and then play it just like it would be in real life. If either of us broke up laughing, we knew we'd hit on something true. So we'd keep that line in the routine." May's explanation: "It just happens. On good nights it's as though a dybbuk had entered us. On bad nights—well, we've never both been in a slump at the same time." Nichols added, "Since we're not competitive—between ourselves, that is—we never try to throw each other."

What they did was totally new. It wasn't a nightclub act, though they performed mainly in clubs, nor was it really a theater piece, although it worked as well at the Golden Theater on Broadway as it did at the Blue Angel. It wasn't a revue, yet the routines were revue-style sketches. Neither was it, truly, even improvisation, since most of what they did became pretty well frozen—if not on paper, then in their heads, although it was originally all extemporaneous, and it did change a little nightly. They didn't rely on jokes per se. Tom Lehrer said: "Nichols & May are still just as funny to me as ever because they wrote the kind of things that you can listen to over and over again, as opposed to a comedian telling a joke. Because once you've heard the joke, you don't want to hear it again. But Nichols & May have such wonderful routines that even if I know them by heart, I want to savor the next line."

They relied, instead, on joking references and, most of all, on the audience recognizing clichés and character types, for most of what Nichols & May did was to make fun of the new intellectual, cultural, and social order that was just emerging at the time. Young Americans in the late 1950s *were* their main joke in an era when America still took itself seriously. Nichols & May merged comedy and reality and helped shape their generation's satirical sensibility. They represented yet another new direction that comedy was going in—away from conventional forms and toward the conversational, not just in its subject matter and satirical attitude, but in its very tone.

Their partnership was a new kind of comedy team, nothing at all like the traditional duos—Laurel & Hardy, Fibber McGee & Molly, Burns & Allen, Abbott & Costello, Martin & Lewis—with a smart one and a stupid one. Steve Martin, who remarked that their humor seemed totally uninfluenced, once rhapsodized, "They were like music"—less a comedy duo than a wry duet, verbal comic musicians jamming with each other: challenging, each tearing off a new lick and topping the other or heading off into an unexpected place, quoting a famous work or social banality in joking italics and then moving on, but always maintaining the rhythm, tempo, and melody of normal speech.

They had no rigid gender or comic roles—neither one played straight for the other; if you had to identify a "straight man," it might have been Nichols. David Shepherd, cofounder of the Compass, noted, "Elaine broke through the psychological restrictions of playing comedy as a woman." They were equals in every way—equally smart, equally funny, with the laughs pretty equally divided, if tipped a shade toward May. Also, unlike most comedy couples, they did neither physical comedy nor even verbal comedy like the 1960s British teams of Flanders & Swann, BBC radio's *Goon Show* trio of lunatics, or the *Beyond the Fringe* quartet.

They didn't sing, they didn't do malapropisms or shtick, they didn't even do dramatic "characters" in the style of Berman or, later, Lily Tomlin. Nichols & May mostly did *scenes,* deliciously satirical, often hilarious vignettes that commented on life around them, with no pokes in the rib. Their closest comic cousin was, yes, Jonathan Winters, who was a comedy team, if not an entire company, unto himself. The only team even remotely like them, Jerry Stiller and Anne Meara, who came along soon after, were funny and endearing, but not biting. Nichols & May were never endearing. Nichols's benign stage persona was an antidote to May's typically darker, more vitriolic streak, as in their funeral home sketch in which a cheery May greets Nichols, a weeping mourner, with, "*I'm Miss Loomis, your grief lady*" (long before actual "grief counselors" or Jessica Mitford's *The American Way of Death*), then tries to peddle him a lavish funeral: "*Before you go, I was just wondering—would you be interested in some extras for the loved one?*" Nichols: "*What kind of extras?*" May: "*Well, how about a coffin?*"

Nichols's specialties were the needy esthete, the frustrated loser, the blithe phony, and the nebbish with an annoying wheedling whine, while

May specialized in pushy or handwringing Jewish mothers, pretentious WASP club ladies, ding-a-ling secretaries and starlets, and bratty teenage girls. Some were stereotypes, but the team's genius was in particularizing them with platitudes that perfectly fit the time. May had more range than Nichols (she had so many characters inside of her that somebody said nobody was ever sure exactly *what* she actually looked or sounded like) and freer improvisational skills, but Nichols—the latent director at work—labored to shape the pieces, steer them, and know when to end them and, for their records, what to delete. The first album didn't do as well as Berman's or Bob Newhart's, which sped to the top of the charts. Nichols & May's *Improvisations to Music* got in just under the Top Forty wire.

Like their satirical contemporaries, Nichols & May could skewer a character or a situation in a phrase, even a word—for example, May (intensely): "*Too many people think of Adler as a man who made mice neurotic. He was more.* Much *more*"; or Nichols (as an office lothario trying to impress a secretary over cocktails): "*I'll bet you don't know your postal zone, Miss Leamis—not many people do.*" The two of them could string clichés together into an unbroken sequence of ironic dialogue.

The Age of Irony, later personified by comics like Steve Martin, Bill Murray, and David Letterman, really began with Nichols & May batting contemporary banalities back and forth, as in a devastating echo of watercooler piety over the quiz-show scandals. In one sketch, even more apt today, a mother tells her child's teacher, "*We work at least one and a half hours a night on respecting the rights of others,*" but worries that her daughter has failed a Relationships course ("*After all, she can always take remedial reading, but it looks very funny if you're at a football game alone*").

Anyone who has heard the team's albums can recall their precise tone of voice. They captured the attitudes of their time, the language, the nuances of the vain or vapid people uttering them, mostly people rather like themselves—bright, articulate, serious, neurotic. Steve Martin noted that Nichols & May satirized "a new thing then, which was 'relationships.' The word came into being in the early sixties. Now we can't get rid of the word, but it was the first time I ever heard it satirized. I remember one of Elaine's lines—they're talking about their family life—and she said, '*Oh, we didn't relate. There was proximity but no-o relating.*' I can still hear the tone of her voice from listening to it as a punk."

Martin, introducing Nichols & May at the U.S. Comedy Arts Festival in Aspen, Colorado, in February 2000, recalled how he first heard about them: "I had a friend who was a fan of comedy and he said, 'Have you heard these new comedians?' And I said no and he gave me some records. And one of them was Nichols & May. I went to sleep at night listening to these records for weeks, for months. And the rhythm of their voices rocked me to sleep. I was listening to their voices—the sound, the intonation. Not so much the jokes. They influenced us all and changed the face of comedy." Lily Tomlin recalls: "The nuances of the characterizations and the cultured types that they were doing completely appealed to me. They were the first people I saw doing smart, hip character pieces. My brother and I used to keep their *Improvisations to Music* on the turntable twenty-four hours a day."

When Nichols & May suddenly split up, it was as if everybody's perfect couple had announced their divorce. Many fans had assumed (or wished) they were married, but they were mainly intellectual soul mates—despite a brief fling when they first met, which they've never quite confessed to but teasingly hinted at. Their professional breakup came as a startling and depressing blow to everyone who had savored their routines as satirical touchstones of the time; their recordings belong in any time capsule of the decade, to give everyone an idea of what was funny in 1961, but also to give people something to laugh at a hundred years from now.

Nichols first met May in 1954, while both were halfheartedly attending the University of Chicago. She was auditing courses when she felt like it, having dropped out of school in Los Angeles at fourteen; May never enrolled but majored in hanging out. She would sit in on a philosophy class, said Nichols, say something outrageous, and leave. He described her as "extremely rude, a very dark bohemian girl in a trench coat." They soon learned of each other. "I heard she was great-looking and very dangerous," said Nichols. "It was said that she and I had the cruelest tongues on campus."

As May has recounted it: "Paul Sills [the Compass's cofounding director] said, 'I want you to meet the only person at the University of Chicago who is as hostile as you.' And then he took me to see Mike in a play." That historical meeting was a production of *Miss Julie,* during which Nichols, onstage, noticed "this evil, hostile girl" glaring at him from the front row "with a look of utter contempt." They made eye contact. "She had big eyebrows and stared at me coldly. It made a tremendous impression on me." May later denied it, saying (with utter contempt), "I didn't regard him at all." Of the production, she recalled, "I laughed straight through it. We loathed each other on sight." He said, "I knew she hated it and I hated *her* because I knew it was shit but there was no way I could let her know that I knew." A few days later, the *Chicago Daily News* in hand, Nichols saw Sills with May and showed him the review. May read along and then pronounced her verdict: "Ha!" It was not exactly an example of meeting cute, but for Nichols and May it seems perfect. He says now, "Elaine was very important to me from the moment I saw her."

Their more legendary, and cuter, meeting came six weeks later in the waiting room of the Illinois Central Railroad in Chicago, when Nichols, in what he later termed "half spy, half pick-up," slid onto a waiting-room bench next to May and, before an audience of commuters seated nearby, began their first improvisational scene as secret agents—later recorded. Nichols (in a sinister Central European accent): *"May I seet down, plis?"* May: *"If you veesh."* Nichols: *"Do you haff a light?"* May: *"Yes, zertainly."* Nichols: *"I had a lighter, but . . .* [insidiously] *I lost eet on Fifty-seventh Street."* May: *"Oh, of course, zen you are . . . Agent X-9?"*

The little railway-station routine, May would say later, "took the place of a lot of chitchat and coffee cups." The spy parody drew them together and, as they began to talk with each other in the weeks that followed, led to a lifelong alliance. "We had instant rapport," Nichols once said, "which is like instant coffee." After their waiting-room scene, she invited Nichols back to her place, where Nichols was treated to her house specialty—a hamburger with cream cheese and ketchup.

The two were alike in all kinds of crucial ways—both were eventual dropouts and both were, as a mutual friend put it, "on the lam from their childhoods," his in New York City, hers in Los Angeles. They were dead-broke theater junkies and, as Nichols boasted, "We both had big reputations on campus as being dangerous-to-vicious." They had superior intellects, and knew it, with a tendency to lord it over lesser minds; they were intellectual snobs—"fresh eggheads," *Time* would later dub them.

MIKE NICHOLS WAS BORN in 1931 into a prosperous Jewish family in Berlin, where his father, Paul Peschkowsky, was a prominent Russian-born doctor. His mother's family were intellectuals active in Germany's Social Democratic Party, headed by his grandfather, Gustav Landauer (one of the first Jews killed by the Nazis); Landauer's wife had written the libretto to Richard Strauss's opera *Salome,* and the philosopher Martin Buber was a family friend. As a boy in Nazi-era Berlin, the young Michael Igor Peschkowsky went to religiously segregated schools, until the family emigrated in 1938. The family sailed to America, on the *Bremen,* when Mike was seven, he knowing only two English phrases—"I do not speak English" and "Do not kiss me" (the latter to keep him away from other, presumably diseased, immigrants). When he got off the *Bremen,* he saw a delicatessen with a sign in Hebrew and asked his father, "Is that allowed here?"

In the United States, the family adopted the name Nichols, from his father's Russian patronymic, Nicholaiyevitch. Until his father got established, they were "very poor," says Nichols. He and his younger brother, Robert (later a physician), stayed with an English family in America who bid the boys good night by shaking hands. Once reunited with his parents, who had what would now be called an "open relationship," the family fought a lot. His mother was ill and his father, he told *The New Yorker*'s John Lahr, "wasn't too crazy about me. I had a mouth. I loved him anyway. What I loved him for was that he had great vitality and joy of life. I feel linked to him in many ways."

His sickly mother, Brigitte, wallowed in martyrdom. "Everything wounded her to the quick," Nichols recalled. " 'I raised you so you could say that to me? Thank you very much. I deserve that.' It went on for days." Elaine May, he discovered, "had the same mother," out of which grew their classic sketch about the guilt-ridden rocket scientist who neglects to phone his martyred mother, who says she hasn't eaten in days for fear of having her mouth full should he call (*"Someday you'll have children of your own. And, honey, when you do, I only pray that they make you suffer the way you're making me. That's a mother's prayer"*).

After his father died, his mother worked at odd jobs to keep the family afloat, but their rooms were bug-infested. Nichols, who grew up in Manhattan's West Seventies (in "one of those tiny apartment houses with a podiatrist on the first floor"), attended progressive private schools (Walden, Dalton) on scholarships (he reportedly had an IQ of 180) and squeaked through. "I was quietly unhappy," he once said. "I felt strange and solitary. I didn't fit"—largely because he had lost all his hair at four due to a reaction to a whooping-cough injection and had to withstand the gibes of classmates, who called him "poor boy." It didn't help that he had a German accent and wore a cap indoors. "I was that little bald kid, the most popular of the unpopular kids."

He shook off most of his childhood traumas in college. "I began to think, 'Yes, I had a tough childhood. I had all those problems—but enough already! Let's get on with my life. Let's start now.' " As he told

Lahr, "All the shit was in the beginning." Heyward Ehrlich, who knew Nichols at college, told Janet Coleman that Nichols "really thought the world had fucked him over. His family had made money, lost money. He had been through several identities. He had lost his hair. He was bleeding on the inside and trying not to show it." Nichols loves to tell about the night a guy who had bullied him in school came backstage to see him. Nichols asked what he was doing, and when told he was selling cars, Nichols, flashing his lethal grin, said, "Oh, I am so glad."

After high school, Nichols had no idea what to do next, though he loved theater, had read all of Eugene O'Neill at fourteen, and was further inspired by a life-changing performance of *A Streetcar Named Desire* he'd seen at sixteen on a date—"We just sat there. We didn't talk. We couldn't believe there was such a thing." After that he decided, "I just wanted to be around theater." After school, Nichols gave horseback-riding lessons (later, as a showbiz sultan, he raised Arabian horses).

When it was time for college, he decided against New York University's school of drama ("I knew I was bright, but I didn't think I had any talent; I simply couldn't imagine a part anyone would cast me for"), opting instead for the University of Chicago, where he discovered there were "other weirdos like me." In line at registration there, he met the fifteen-year-old Susan Sontag, who became a lifelong friend. "I thought he was terrific," she told Lahr. "He was totally alive and incredibly verbal. We talked about books, about feelings, about how to get free of our pasts. I would happily have become his girlfriend physically, except I was intimidated by the hair problem and felt he was untouchable." Even so, an old college roommate remembered, "Despite the strangeness of his appearance he did very well with girls. He was courtly and he was well read, which got you a long way at the university." He stayed two years, describing it as a place "where everybody talked a lot and nobody ever went to class."

He went to a few classes but busied himself acting in campus plays. "I spent a lot of time sleeping," he says, up to sixteen hours a day. Off campus, he got a job as a staff announcer at the country's first all-classical FM station in Chicago, which gave him a taste of celebrity. "They fired him a number of times," reports his ex-roommate. "He was funny and knowledgeable but totally unreliable." He also drove a post office truck and worked as a filing clerk, a job he fled after excusing himself to go to the men's room. Nichols has always painted himself as a wastrel in college, but when confronted with evidence to the contrary, he told me, "Until a month ago I would have said I've never been ambitious—until I ran into a Chicago friend from before I came to New York to study with Strasberg. He had with him a letter I'd written to him, and I was stunned by the ambition in the letter. It was all about 'Strasberg is really interesting and there are things to be done in the theater and I like this girl I'm with and we're talking about doing blah-blah.' I was full of plans for the future. I had no *idea*."

Semi-poverty-stricken at college, he ate leftovers at a coffee shop where Paul Sills was a waiter. At the school cafeteria, he'd walk through the line backward or eat off other plates. He stole cheese from supermarkets and wondered "why my rich friends didn't just give me some of their money, since they had so much of it." An old friend later said that Nichols "loved to magnify his sense of adversity so that he could triumph over it." Nichols once dined on an entire jar of mustard, created tomato soup at the Automat out of hot water and ketchup, and could make a meal out of butterscotch Metrecal and canned corn. Whenever he had a few dollars, he dined on pâté and caviar, but even after he'd made it, he still ate bologna sandwiches and doughnuts. While directing *Barefoot in the Park,* recalls playwright Neil Simon, "he could walk into rehearsal, look around, and say, 'Is it possible there are no doughnuts? There's no point in rehearsing if there are no doughnuts.' "

Janet Coleman contends that the young Nichols was—quoting his colleagues—"cold," "insecure," "ambitious," "hungry," and "insufferable." Omar Shapli, a Compass actor, told her, "Not too many people got along warmly with Mike. He had an edge about him that put people off." Nichols's manner, said another Compass player, was that of "a princeling deprived of his rightful fortune." Heyward Ehrlich recalled, "Mike was like the abused child who turns the abuse on others. I liked him, but you had to endure him. He was a pain in the ass. Mike Nichols was not Mike Nichols in those days. He was the person he came to satirize, and he wasn't laughing at it. He felt the world had treated him so cruelly. In some ways, the theater was his revenge." At college, he shed much of his childhood angst through free campus therapy and by joining the Compass, where he met other radical theater types—Ed Asner (his roommate for a time), Barbara Harris, Severn Darden, Anthony Holland, Zohra Lampert—who hung out at Jimmy's, a bar near school where Nichols was a minor campus celeb thanks to his FM radio show.

After their railroad-station vignette, Nichols and May became fast friends. May was catnip. "Everybody wanted Elaine, and the people who got her couldn't keep her," Nichols told John Lahr, who writes that "her juicy good looks were a particularly disconcerting contrast to her sharp tongue." They formed a tight union, a kind of platonic marriage. "Elaine held me like an autistic child," he said. "We were safe from everyone else when we were with each other. And also safe from each other. I knew somehow that she would not do to me the things she'd done to other guys. I knew she wouldn't lose interest and move on. I knew instantly that everything that happened to us was ours." Outsiders admired, envied, and were even disturbed by their strong connection. Elaine once said: "People are always telling us they feel left out."

Men who dated May had vivid memories of her, and Coleman catalogues them in her 1990 book *The Compass.* The director Tom O'Horgan remembered "a kind of scarifying lady" who spoke out of the side of her mouth with a cigarette dangling out the other side. Coleman says May arrived at the Compass with great advance publicity and "absolutely lived up to everything." Omar Shapli was also "struck by her piercing, dark-eyed, sultry stare. It was really unnerving. After we were introduced, she said, 'Omar, will you marry me?' If I'd said, 'Of course,' we would have been married that afternoon. But I went to pieces and she wrote me off. She was quite playful but vicious. She was like Carmen. She seemed like a potential black widow." Marvin Piesner called May a "manizer," saying, "In some of these affairs, she destroyed the man."

Herbert Gold, the novelist, dated May in the late fifties and recalls, "She was very cute, a lot like Debra Winger, just a pretty Jewish girl. She treated everything funny that men take seriously," but she had to ration her men. "She told me, 'If I kiss, I fuck, and I don't want to fuck.' " Gold once took her to one of George Plimpton's salon gatherings. "She was always very funny—she had a funny take on everything. It was all natural. She was never serious. Her life was a narrative." But Gold couldn't cozy up to Nichols: "I was a little bit in awe of him. There was something about him—but he was clearly the sharpest knife in the drawer."

One of her ex-beaus, James Sacks, remembered: "Elaine had a genuine beautiful madness, a raw unpolished intelligence, and an unbalanced education. She knew everything about the theater and psychoanalysis. She didn't know about anything else. She didn't know if Eisenhower was a Republican or a Democrat." May would hold court, discussing her days as a child actor in the Yiddish theater, as men hung on her every word. Every guy who knew her was in love with her, said Bob Smith—"You'd have been stupid not to have been."

Men were drawn to her smart, sexy edginess, but women were less enamored. Annette Hankin, who studied with May, told Coleman, "I think she saw love in a cruel light and all things as trade-offs. It was a terrible, awesome vision, that of a person who has survived an emotional holocaust. That may have been why she was so distant. I saw her cry more than once. I thought it had something to do with the fact that her mother was raising her child." Another woman depicted May as "one of these women who likes to think they're very vulnerable, but she was a tough cookie." May was also a gifted caricaturist, but dismissed her drawings as mere doodles; if a subject wanted to keep one, she tore it up. Nancy Ponder, a Compass actress, recalled, "She was the strongest woman I ever met." Ponder credits May with giving novices chances, helping to bring in a black actor, making the group more democratic, and taking creative leaps that improved everyone's work.

An actress who lent May a dress said she lived "like a gutter rat" and went around in creative disarray, wearing sneakers and a black dress hemmed with a green thread, and had an annoying habit of snapping her bra strap at rehearsals. May taught Barbara Harris how to beg ("She kept saying, 'We have to do it in Brechtian style,' " recalled Harris) and once got a crate and shined shoes outside the Ambassador Hotel. May lived in a cellar with one piece of furniture in the living room—a Ping-Pong table. She wore basic beatnik black and, like her film characters, was a brilliant disheveled klutz. Harris, the only other woman at the Compass who became a star, told Coleman, "Elaine was so incompetent in terms of being able to get her clothes on. I was always running and getting her pins." But once safety-pinned together, May was transformed from a near bag lady into a compelling, radiant presence.

Some who knew them then were surprised that Nichols and May ever became a cohesive team, because they were such creative and stylistic opposites. As the director Ted Flicker sorted out the duo: "Mike is a superficial man of great taste and wit. Elaine is a passionate artist and an archetypal slob. Mike likes to dominate and control everyone around him. Elaine needs to dominate and control men. She trusts nobody." He added, "They routinely manipulated the hell out of each other."

Nichols admitted that the pair were "insanely judgmental" snobs, bound "by tremendous hostility to everyone else," but that May's toughness was an illusion. Severn Darden said: "Working with me onstage, she was wonderful, but she had this fierce competitiveness. You have the feeling that at any moment she might kill you. Other than that . . . When

Elaine and I worked together, we had such arguments that we wouldn't even go onstage together. It's hard to explain. She's just terrifying." Compass colleague Eugene Troobnick added, "She's about fifty percent more brilliant than she needs to be, for one thing." Richard Burton, who met her while starring in *Camelot,* recalled: "Elaine was too formidable, one of the most intelligent, beautiful, and witty women I had ever met. I hoped I would never see her again."

May was famous for her nasty lightning retorts. Nichols warned, "Generally, it was unwise for people to start trouble with her." Once, followed by two men on the street blowing her noisy kisses, she wheeled and said, "What's the matter? Tired of each other?" When one of the man yelled, "Fuck you!" she responded, "With what?" (Nichols was no slouch himself as put-down artist. Once, on the set of *The Odd Couple,* he gave Walter Matthau what the actor took to be an emasculating direction, and Matthau said, "Mike, can I have my cock back now?" Nichols shouted, "Props!")

When a brawl broke out with some drunken steeplejacks at a Compass show, May was the only performer willing to confront them. She ignored all taste and language taboos at the Compass; the actor Andrew Duncan remembered that she liked to sit cross-legged onstage, flashing the audience. Bobbi Gordon recalls: "The first time I met her was at Compass. She was chewing apple cores. Her hair was down to her knees practically. I was frightened of her. She was very distracted, rather annoyed about everything. You saw that she and Mike could destroy you with a word, but neither of them was out to do that. In fact, they were both most helpful and sweet, Mike more so than Elaine initially. Elaine was this grande dame of letters. With people sitting around her feet, staring up at her, openmouthed in awe, waiting for The Word."

ELAINE MAY WAS BORN in Philadelphia in 1932 and took to the road early with her father, Jack Berlin, in a traveling Yiddish theater company, playing a generic little boy named Benny; when they appeared together on radio, she played a sort of Yiddish Baby Snooks called Baby Noodnik. She began school late, at eight, and hated everything about it except diagramming sentences, often spending her days at home reading fairy tales and mythology.

Her rebel streak continued when she dropped out of Hollywood High School at fourteen and at sixteen married Marvin May, an engineer and toy inventor; their daughter, who grew up to be the actress Jeannie Berlin, was raised for a while by her grandmother. May's second husband, for all of two months (somebody cracked that "she got custody of the cake"), was the *Fiddler on the Roof* lyricist Sheldon Harnick; she later married her psychoanalyst, David Rubenfine.

After studying acting with Maria Ouspenskaya, May heard she could go to the University of Chicago without graduating from high school. She disliked most of her childhood, especially the years she spent in Los Angeles. In 1961 she told a *New Yorker* profiler: "I feel in opposition to almost everything anyway, but it comes to its height in Los Angeles." She didn't want to be an actress ("or be anything") but wound up drifting into college theater groups. Edmund Wilson, who was smitten by her, called her "something of a genius"—and he had known a few.

At Chicago, she acted in a group called Tonight at 8:30, until it was shut down by fire laws, at which point (in 1955) Paul Sills and David Shepherd organized the Compass theater, a café of sorts patterned after European cabarets. The Compass, of which May was a charter member, hired Nichols in late 1955. They resumed their friendship on the Compass stage, where the pair developed many of the pieces that they would take with them to New York as a team after leaving the company—later a matter of great controversy when the group's producer, Bernard Sahlins, claimed that the sketches developed at the Compass belonged to the company.

Given the scores of famous comedians and comic actors it spawned, the Compass was the urban Catskills of the 1960s. "Chicago is not a fashion-driven place," Nichols points out. "Nobody said, 'Oh, you've got to come and see these fabulous people!' Nobody cared. They're not impressed with anything, which is the best possible training for anybody." Chicago, he continues, is "a safer, quieter place"—not like New York, "full of pride and excitement over its art. New York and Los Angeles and other big cities are so fashion-driven, but in Chicago they're grounded. Their own lives are what occupy them." Even so, the University of Chicago was full of bright academics and students who loved their sketches. "It was the most referential community that I think ever existed in this country," he says.

Nichols felt nothing momentous about their work: "We were winging it, making it up as we went along. It never ever crossed our minds that it had any value beyond the moment. It was great to study and learn and work there. We were *stunned* when we got to New York, which is not only fashion-driven but fashion-obsessed—and stunned to become a fashion. And we became a fashion in the usual way—we were written about in *The New Yorker*. The first week or two at the Blue Angel, nobody much laughed at us. But when *The New Yorker* came out, *how* they laughed. We were horrified. We didn't know such things were possible. We'd just been in Chicago, where people laughed if it was funny; if it wasn't they didn't. We had to be approved, accredited. Once they said we were like the Lunts, they laughed when we came out onstage."

NICHOLS WAS REBORN at the Compass: "The entire Chicago experience was the beginning of my life as myself. I hadn't had friends, really. I certainly hadn't had a circle of friends. I hadn't ever met anybody who was also as weird as I thought myself. Nobody said to you, 'You read too much,' which I'd heard a lot of—not at home, at work. When I went back to Chicago after truly starving in New York—especially after I got okay at improvising, I think you could say it was the first happy time in my life. I was making a living, to my surprise—first twenty-eight dollars and over the years it went up to sixty-five dollars a week. I had all day free. Did these shows at night. Had a life. It was very nice. I was still plenty weird, but now it was fine."

When he first joined the Compass, Nichols was blocked—unable to improvise until he linked up with May. He thought, "I can't do this at all," but she sparked his latent gift. Their first scene was a dramatic situation about a man who has to choose whether or not to rat on his friends. Nichols felt secure because it was a serious premise. From then on, he told me, "it became mostly pleasure because of Elaine's generosity. The fact of Elaine—her presence—kept me going. She was the only one who had faith in me. I loved it. Of all the people in Compass, Elaine was the one who excited me most at the time—in every sense. Elaine and I didn't know each other very well, but I was at that time drawn to her in every possible way. I was more interested in talking to her, being with her, working with her than anybody else." It sounds suspiciously like love. "In some way, I think that's true. I don't know. I just knew I wanted to be around her."

Nichols also credits Paul Sills with loosening him up onstage. "Paul was a great spiritual soil. You could do awful scenes, good scenes, fifty scenes. And if you really screwed up, you could run down to Lake Michigan and jump in, and run back and do another scene. Paul believed in you no matter what. I kept saying, 'I want to go home. I'm terrible.' He'd say, 'Stay, it's all right. You'll be fine.' " Nichols adds, "Theater is so much about exclusion: 'We're doing a play but I'm *afra-a-aid* there isn't anything for you.' " Neither he nor Barbara Harris got the hang of it for weeks. "I was a disaster! For a month I cried in scenes because that's what I thought I'd learned from Strasberg." One colleague said Nichols wasn't a natural actor but compensated with his agile mind.

After a month of improv fright, he became one of the company's resident geniuses; the rivalry was stiff. His and May's connection was, if not exactly romantic, kinetic. "We had a similar sense of humor and irony. So we became friends and would go to her room. I was very attracted to her. She was beautiful. She was sexy, but she had a dangerous edge. She made a big gap in the edge for me—I don't know why. We both had read the same things, we were both heavy into the Russians. We both had sort of fallen into Dostoyevsky, and our jokes had to do with Russian novels and also Joyce, and we were in a kind of ecstasy over literature. It was something we did with each other and talked about."

When later prodded about their personal relationship, Nichols always gave his standard reply: "We live very quietly and we date occasionally. Right now we are seeing Comden and Green." Asked once point-blank if he was in love with May, he said, deftly sidestepping the issue, "I was in love with Elaine, and I still love Elaine." Another time, he said, "Elaine and I like each other. When you consider how much we're together, it's fairly surprising. We kept marrying other people." Though only a year older, he called her "the kid." When Tom Smothers popped the question at the Aspen tribute—"I wasn't sure, were you lovers or not?"—May replied, "I will answer that. We were lovers or not." They were lovers, but for only three days, according to David Shepherd.

Marriage was never in the cards, someone close to them said—"They understand and respect each other, but marriage would be a kind of incest." Added Nichols, "It was much too serious for marriage." Friends thought that his second wife, Margot Callas, bore a striking resemblance to May. (His first wife was the jazz singer Pat Scot, and his third wife was the Anglo-Irish novelist Annabel Davis-Goff; since 1988 Nichols has been married to the TV news anchor Diane Sawyer. He has a daughter, Daisy, by his second wife and two children, Max and Jenny, from his marriage to Davis-Goff; he also had a favorite horse named Max, one of the Arabians raised on his 375-acre ranch in California.)

Discussing his onstage relationship with May, he said: "I would never have been a performer without her, and I don't think she would have without me. Elaine and I are, in some weird way, each other's unconscious. It didn't feel as funny with other people. For me, it depended on a certain connection with Elaine and a certain mad gleam in either her or my eyes when we knew something was starting." He adds, "*I* interested me when I was with her. It wasn't only that she was so great, but that when I was with her I became something more than I had been before."

They had only a rough idea of any given routine's general route. "We usually know we're heading toward a last line. And when we were on television we had certain checkpoints—things in the middle that we were getting to. We improvised around a set of ideas." He added, "It was both bliss and just as funny as it gets when something occurred to Elaine and me—when we'd both look at each other and sometimes each of us would be thinking, 'Oh, God, I know where we're going,' and both of us would race to get there first."

Nichols goes on: "Somehow we could talk in shorthand. If one of us said, or someone in the audience said, 'Two teenagers in the backseat of a car,' we had the scene. We didn't have to know more than that sentence. We first did the scene pretty much as it is now. And there was the time my mother called me and said, 'Hello, Michael, this is your mother—do you remember me?' and I said, 'Mother, let me call you right back,' and I called Elaine and I said, 'I've got a really good piece for us tonight.' And I gave her that line and we did the piece that night exactly as it exists now. We found a few gags later, but basically that was it."

They shared similar disruptive childhoods. "We had extremely difficult Jewish mothers. In finding them funny, we began to free ourselves. But until you free yourself—which only takes about fifty years—it's not all that funny, and of course the part that isn't in the sketch is the part that isn't so funny. These two mothers had a pretty devastating, long-long-lasting effect on both of us. We were not lost souls but we were difficult people and we were difficult for others. And we had not entirely successful relationships with a string of people, but kept returning to each other, as it were. We were the steady relationship and the others came and went." In 1961 Nichols told an interviewer, "The secret we share is that neither of us likes people very much—they have no reality to us."

Eugene Troobnick analyzed their chemistry: "When you practice improvisation, you learn that funny lines aren't it. The rule is to be truthful to the moment, and the funny stuff will flow from that. With Mike and Elaine, those rules did not apply. They could get up and say one funny line after another. Verbally, Mike Nichols was the fastest person I've ever known. He was a consummate wit." Geraldine Page said: "They clanked together with great efficiency. Like a juggernaut." With May, Nichols could tap into his own unconscious and buried resentments, but mainly he just enjoyed making smart jokes. "When a joke comes to you," he says, "it feels like it's been sent by God." He often broke up onstage and his infectious laugh could collapse them. Coleman claims that Nichols would deliberately break up as a scene-stealing device, sometimes even faking it by turning his back to the audience and shaking his shoulders.

At the Compass, he absorbed the fundamentals of scene construction—theme, conflict and tension, resolution—and discovered that jokes had to evolve from a central idea; otherwise, you were only as good as your last line. Furthermore, in a well-constructed scene, a line can refer back to another line to create a new joke. The improv sketches evolved semiaccidentally out of a grand plan to do improvised plays, but when nobody could think of any, the audience was asked to suggest ideas.

Having to produce before an audience was a major creative spur. "It's why improvising is such a great teacher," Nichols explains. "The pressure of the expectation of the audience teaches you that you'd better get something started very fast that's a situation. The thing that improv teaches you, which is what I teach, is what makes a scene. That's why it was such good preparation for direction and, in Elaine's case, writing. If you say black, I've gotta say white. There are only a few ways of making things happen—conflict is one, seduction is another."

Many of their pieces, said May, came out of offstage conversations, "almost the way people exchange stories when they meet. We were sort of just meeting each other. Even the teenage scene, it was, 'Do you remember when . . . ?' or, 'Did you ever . . . ?' "

Nichols, unlike most of the Compass players, was not political. "I have nothing I want to tell people," he said. "Mike's politics are the politics of J. D. Salinger," said the Compass's Larry Arrick. "He would rather do style. He would rather do that *New Yorker*–esque thing that Michael did so well, like a sketch called 'How to Appear Cultured.' " Shepherd agreed, saying that Nichols seemed interested mainly in "finely sharpened barbs. You present these barbs to the audience. And you pop balloons as big as you can."

May had a far deeper, blacker, Swiftian view of satire. In a classic Compass sketch, "Georgina's First Date," she played a fat girl asked to the prom by a stud just so he can win a bet that he can seduce her, which he does—

to her grief. She goes home afterward and, sobbing, tells her delighted parents what a great time she had. May cracked the stereotype of what roles a woman could play then, for her own personality was so against the fifties female grain. Said Shepherd: "She was not an ingénue. She rarely chose traditional female roles. She played challenging, sophisticated, worldly women. She was the doctor, the psychiatrist, the employer, the wicked witch." Even so, said Del Close, "I never got the sense that she was a feminist." Walter Beakel told Coleman, "Bill Shakespeare said, 'Hold the mirror up to nature.' Elaine held the mirror up to Elaine."

A colleague once compared them: "Michael knows about everything that exists. He has read everything. He can tell you the difference between a Wall Street broker and a Nairobi tribesman. Elaine can tell you what they have in common." One friend noted that Mike had "an acute sense of manners and appearances. He believes you can tell a book by its cover. Elaine is interested in the inside of the book and even more in the jelly stains and finger smudges on the pages." In any case, they saw the lay of the social landscape as one; said another friend—"Mike was the left eye and Elaine was the right eye."

Their great strength—the complementary yin and yang that welded their work together—ultimately led to their undoing. Nichols always needed to know what the point of a sketch was, whereas May liked exploring ideas as the scene progressed. It was a classic case of creative differences between an endlessly noodling actor-writer (May) and a director without portfolio but with a tough commercial sense (Nichols). He explained to Jeffrey Sweet in his oral history of the Compass/Second City: "I'd done improvisations with Strasberg, but never with the pressure from the audience. Over the months, that pressure taught everyone to answer the unspoken question the audience asked—'Why are you telling us this?' You learn various answers to that main question. 'Because it's funny' is a very good answer. If you can't answer, 'Because it's funny,' then you'd better have a damn good other answer. You can't have *no* answer."

Nichols was discovering how to tell a story onstage and how to convey an authority: "What was so good about it was that after doing it months and months and years, it became almost a reflex." He felt a new creative force stirring within him. "Once every six weeks you would literally be possessed. I don't mean to sound mystical, but such things did happen, like speaking languages you didn't speak and doing twenty minutes of iambic pentameter that just came pouring out. That was thrilling, and you'd be drained and amazed afterward, and you'd have a sense of your possibilities. You could become more than yourself and say things you hadn't thought and become people you didn't know."

Nichols and May became an informal team at the Compass and performed on off-nights at a little place on Chicago's North Side. They briefly worked as a trio with Shelley Berman, but Nichols squelched the idea. Nichols's pragmatic version: "We were a trio for a little while and that worked all right, but the truth is that, for performing, two is a lot more felicitous number than three. There was only so much material that would work for three, and then we'd have to go back to our two, or Elaine with Shelley, who was an *enormously* competitive person. Shelley was the first person at Compass *ever* to count who had how many sketches in a set, and I still think of it as the first bite of the apple at Compass. We were in Eden in some way until that."

After Berman left the group and became a comedy star, the other players saw the commercial potential of what they were doing for intellectual kicks—Nichols far more than May, who remained committed to fresh work while Nichols was more content to rerun routines. "She was very pure," recalled Mark Gordon. "She had a commitment to improvisation and was not going to let it go." As Shepherd put it, "Elaine was interested in playing to the drunken sailor in the audience. Or nun. She always knew that last night is not tonight."

Nichols moved on to New York to study acting with Lee Strasberg, whom he once called the only great man he ever met, while May stayed behind with the Compass and wrote a movie treatment of Plato's *Symposium,* in which everyone is drunk. She worked as a roofing salesperson, private eye (on one job she sat in a bar, eyeing the bartender to determine if he was honest), advertising copywriter, and, astonishingly, performed in a hillbilly act as "Elly Mae." In New York, Nichols worked as a waiter at Howard Johnson's until he was fired for telling a customer that the ice cream flavor of the month was chicken.

In 1957, when the Compass opened a potential branch in St. Louis, at the Crystal Palace, Nichols rejoined the company, mainly to work again with May. Jay Landesman, who ran the Crystal Palace, says in his memoir that Nichols & May "were so good, they eventually threw the company off balance, leaving the other members out on a limb." Ted Flicker, suspecting they were using the Compass to prepare their own act, accused Nichols of hogging the action. Flicker told Landesman to fire him. There was added tension in St. Louis because Nichols had just married, and even after his marriage he and May shared a room, platonically, during the week. Nichols was informed that he had "too much talent" and was dismissed. It was the end of the Compass Players and the beginning of Nichols & May.

Once Nichols and May and other Compass comics began going out on their own, the company claimed they weren't entitled to use material developed there. Nichols snorted fire when I raised the issue: "The whole thing is so horrifying to me. For David Shepherd to *dare* to think that any of that material was his outraged me then and it does now. And for [producer] Bernie Sahlins to sign people to years of servitude and then keep the material that they developed is monstrous to me—*monstrous!* You can't do it. It's against any union that ever existed to protect people, except that nobody tried to protect people who were improvising." Paul Sills says that today "Second City owns all the material that's invented there, whereas Mike and Elaine went off and made their careers with material that David Shepherd, who had paid for all this, never got a nickel out of." Though he sees some merit in Nichols's argument, he concludes, "You know, there's a commandment—thou shalt not steal."

In her Compass study, Coleman, who contends that Nichols was "violating a trust," lays out a complex scenario of how the Nichols & May duo came to be, full of intrigue and betrayal straight out of *The Treasure of the Sierra Madre*. (Neither Nichols nor May ever spoke with her, although she says she tried many times to contact them; when she finally met Nichols at a party and cornered him, she adds, he cringed. Nichols refers to her as "that awful woman who wrote that awful book.")

Her version of how Nichols & May was born involves an aborted plot by four Compass members (Nichols, May, Del Close, and Nancy Ponder) to break away and form their own company in New York, with Nichols and May going on ahead to meet with Jack Rollins, whom Nichols had heard of from a former Strasberg student. As Nichols tells it: "Elaine and I weren't mad at each other even after I was fired, and then this strange audition came up with Jack Rollins. I called and said, 'Do you want to audition for this guy?' and she said sure, and we were famous three weeks later. It took no time at all."

Precisely how, when, and why Close and Ponder were dropped along the way remains a mystery. Close later claimed, "We were conned into betraying Ted [Flicker] and we were in turn betrayed." Exactly what happened is anyone's guess. Did Nichols (as Coleman implies) hatch a nefarious scheme to get back at the Compass for firing him, with Close and Ponder as pawns who then were dumped while Nichols arranged a Rollins meeting for just himself and May? Whatever the truth, when the dust had settled, only two of the Chicago four were left standing in New York: Mike Nichols and Elaine May.

In Nichols's version of how they splintered off from the Compass, he said: "As the years went by, we began to have a body of material with each other, and not that much with the other members of the group. We loved them and it went great with them, but we somehow built up scenes that we would repeat, like the teenage thing. But at no point, including when we went on TV, did it occur to us that we would ever do this profession-ally." This might be a little revisionist history, for it's hard to believe that after Nichols had pursued agents, he was as indifferent to show business success as he claims. Their original agent, Charles Joffe, says that Nichols had been to several agencies and was turned down by all of them. Even when Nichols was at the Compass, Flicker said, "Mike was interested in only one thing: getting ahead."

Nichols called Rollins, who met them for lunch at the Russian Tea Room. "We walked in and had a scoop of borscht while wildly improvis-ing a set of ad-libbed little skits we not only had never rehearsed but had never even thought of until that desperate minute," Nichols told the *New York Morning Telegraph* in 1959. "When the coffee came, I remember with some relief that he not only signed us but also sprang for the lunch check. That had us pretty worried until he grabbed it." Rollins was knocked out by them: "Their work was so startling, so new, as fresh as could be. I was stunned by how really good they were, actually as impressed by their act-ing technique as by their comedy." Rollins adds: "They were totally adventurous and totally innocent, in a certain sense. That's why it was accepted. They would uncover little dark niches that you felt but had never expressed." He was blown away by their style: "I'd never seen this technique before. I thought, My God, these are two people writing hilar-ious comedy on their feet!"

He told me: "They were so un–show business they didn't know to be scared. They were remarkable immediately. They were complete. I knew they had something odd and wonderful, but I didn't know whether to laugh or cry." Joffe's first impression, when they opened at the Blue Angel for Shelley Berman: "I saw pure intelligence and absolute funny. Original. Nobody was doing boy-girl things." Rollins got them a one-night shot at the Blue Angel, following the Smothers Brothers and Eartha Kitt. When they told Rollins that they were broke and needed work, he found a spot for them at the Village Vanguard with Mort Sahl. Joffe recalls that he and Rollins took the team in hand, literally. "They were totally broke and had no idea what they should wear at the Blue Angel. Jack bought Mike a new shirt and Jack's wife took Elaine out and bought her a dress."

Tom Lehrer, opening for them soon after at the Blue Angel, told a friend, "Watch these guys, they're really good." *Variety* agreed. In its first review, the paper's critic declared: "Mike Nichols & Elaine May are hipsters' hipsters. Their thought patterns are Cloud No. 7 inspired and their comedic routines are really far out. It's an act that requires plenty of 'digging' on the audience's part. In a setting such as the Vanguard, with its hip music policy, the duo is in a favorable environment. However, in average exposure spots the act will have trouble finding its mark." *Theatre Arts* said that their art lay somewhere between Ruth Draper and the Marx Brothers. They auditioned for Jack Paar's *Tonight* show, but their improvisations bombed before a studio audience. Paar cut them off and wanted nothing else to do with them—until they'd been a hit on other TV shows and *Life* did a story on this new hot comedy act. Paar invited them back, but they wanted more money, and he was shocked by their ingratitude: "They won't come on with me even though I discovered them," he said.

Rollins neatly engineered the ploy that brought Nichols & May to national TV prominence when he got them on the prestigious *Omnibus* as part of a special theme show called "The Suburban Review." As he recalls now: "I knew it was very difficult to present them on television at the time, because TV is a medium of twenty-second bites. Nobody is on longer than five minutes. They needed to be on *fifteen* minutes. Where are you gonna get that in TV? But it came along, because there was a show called *Omnibus,* a very classy cultural show on Sunday afternoon with high ratings, with Alistair Cooke as the host. So I made a deal that they do two pieces—and that nobody had the right to do any editing. The producers were delighted. They wanted a sense of class, but it wasn't so easy [to find a classy comedy act]. Well, they were a smash and that did the trick. If that set of circumstances hadn't happened, it would have been a slow development for Nichols & May in the clubs." Joffe told Eric Lax that after they had appeared on *Omnibus,* "the world broke open for them." That night there were lines around the block. Milton Berle came three times and couldn't get in.

Rollins notwithstanding, their shot on *Omnibus* came about after the program's producer, Robert Saudek, had seen them on a Steve Allen show performing a sketch about a ditsy name-dropping starlet (*"the very wonderful, the very talented Barbara Musk"*) talking to a fatuous deejay, Jack Ego (i.e., Chicago disc jockey Jack Eigen), about her close personal friendship with Albert Schweitzer: *"Jack, I think you know that I think Al is just a great guy. Al is a lot of laughs. I personally have never dated him,"* adding, *"Bertie* [Bertrand Russell] *also is a heck of a good kid. I think a pushy philosopher is always a drag."*

Nichols recalls the impact of their *Omnibus* debut: "We were not on that long, but the next day there were these headlines—'New Comedians Have Arrived'—and all this stuff, and it was very big, and Elaine says I called her at four in the morning and said, 'What do we do now?' " He reiterates, "Never for a moment did we consider that we would do this for a living. It was just a handy way to make some money until we grew up." He said, "Everyone thought we were in show business, but we knew we weren't—we were snobs. Suddenly, I had sharkskin suits and Jack Rollins calling us the hottest team in showbiz. And we kept thinking, 'How the fuck did we get *here?*' "

Jules Feiffer, whose film *Carnal Knowledge* Nichols later directed, remembers first seeing them on *Omnibus:* "I couldn't believe what I was watching because it was as if I was watching stuff completely out of my own mind in a style that was quite advanced from mine—they were much more finished than I thought I was."

Rollins says that the duo required very little tinkering with when they arrived. "All they needed was some editing, cutting mainly." Pieces that had gone on for twelve minutes at the Compass needed to be trimmed for nightclubs. He recalls, "It was a question of lopping and polishing what they already had. But that was the only thing. Elaine would go on forever if you let her. She is insanely creative, but she had no sense when to quit. Really, the editor was Mike, because he lives in this world—I call him Mr. Practical—and she lives in her own world, completely disconnected from the practical world." Adds Joffe: "Everyone who saw them thought that she was the backbone of the act, and we knew it was him."

Joffe says that Nichols & May were the first comics they made money with. Lax writes, "Because of Nichols & May, Jack Rollins was considered the best comic manager in the business." The team was a New York hit from their first uptown appearance at the Blue Angel in December 1957, when *The New Yorker*'s Douglas Watt was impressed enough with what he called "their little dialogues" to return twice. "On one of my visits they took off on Euripides, and I'm sure that the Greek theatre was never more fun." In comparing them to Alfred Lunt and Lynne Fontane, Watt cited "the bantering tones, the repeated phrases, the artful covering of each other's lines," and "the ease with which they slipped into and out of" scenes. He described Nichols as "a fair youth with an alert and friendly mien" and May as "a brunette with lustrous eyes and an abject air that would fool nobody." Her face was a subject of great fascination among reviewers. She was described by one critic as possessing a "long, beautiful, yawning dromedary face." *Time* called her "a dark-eyed Columbine of many moods." *Look*'s Betty Rollin said Nichols looked pale and soft, like the boy who never played ball, adding: "Except the eyes. They have played ball."

Lawrence Christon calls their instant success "one of those instances when everything comes together at the right time and you realize that you're in some miraculous moment, that this is the next big thing. It was like when *Beyond the Fringe* hit—you just knew it was a defining moment. They caught the urban tempo, like Woody Allen did." After their Broadway show opened, Rollins said he was turning down about eight TV offers a week. Nichols was characteristically, if deceptively, blasé, claiming, "My ambitions are not concerned with success. I perceive nothing operationally different in my life." May was uncharacteristically excited, exclaiming that having money was "an enormous adventure," allowing her to shed her usual black stockings, tennis shoes, and trench coat wardrobe for Lord & Taylor splurges and even a session with Kenneth, hairdresser to the Kennedys. She told *Newsweek:* "When we came to New York, we were practically barefoot. And I still can't get used to walking in high heels."

The team hated discussing how they did what they did, and *The New Yorker*'s Robert Rice observed, "They cherish the spontaneous nature of their work so fiercely that . . . their instinctive reflex when one of the scenes is analyzed in their presence is not to listen." It could break the spell—the fragility of whatever it was that made their work so instinctive, mysterious, and funny. The cautious Nichols learned from May's riskier approach to life. "Elaine has a wonderful motto," he told the *New York Times*'s Barbara Gelb. " 'The only safe thing is to take a chance.' " His own life motto was embroidered on a pillow in his home at one time— "Nothing Is Written," a quote by and from *Lawrence of Arabia,* a favorite Nichols movie and a dictum for their improvisational work.

The team's literary parodies, which set them apart from their comic peers, ranged from a ten-second version of Dostoyevsky (following ten seconds of uproarious laughter from May, Nichols shouts: "*Unhappy woman!*"—blackout), to Tennessee Williams (renamed Alabama Glass, whose heroine has "*taken to drink, prostitution, and puttin' on airs*" and whose husband, Raoul, has killed himself "*on bein' unjustly accused of not bein' a homosexual*"), to *Oedipus Rex* ("*Look, sweetheart, you're my mother*"). In their famous Pirandello parody, an eighteen-minute sketch that toyed with the illusory nature of life and theater, Nichols and May pretended to be themselves and wound up in a brutal fight. The sketch fooled audiences into thinking they really were scrapping with each other until the couple abruptly stopped and concluded with a one-word tag ("*Pirandello!*") that sent audiences home shaking their heads in awe.

The stage scrap brought to the surface some of their pent-up frustrations from working together—her tardiness was an ongoing irritation for Nichols. "We had huge fights about that," he said. "I never could understand why she found it so difficult. Two hours out of twenty-four. It's a perfect job. It wasn't that way for her." After shows, reported Rice, they often sniped at each like a married couple on the way home from a cocktail party. "How-dare-you-treat-me-this-way is a recurrent theme," he noted, perhaps a foreshadowing of Nichols's fascination with Edward Albee's *Who's Afraid of Virginia Woolf?*—his first film-direction job.

"The thing we battled about the most was 'Pirandello,'" Nichols recounts. "The piece created hostility. The whole scaring of the audience was based on a battle between us, the two performers. Without even knowing it, we drew on real things, and we argued and fought about that scene all the years we did it. How long this beat was, when to start the next beat—we just could never leave it alone. We tortured ourselves over it, and all that time it never occurred to us that what was really happening was that the scene was taking us over a little bit. And it went very far. When we were in Westport in tryout, I must have blanked out or something, 'cause I was hitting Elaine, back and forth on both sides of her face, and she had clawed open my chest, which was pouring blood, and we didn't know how we had got there. They brought the curtain down and we burst into tears and embraced and sort of controlled it after that. It was scary; it really got away from us. Even after that, we still argued about it."

Their other classics included a sketch about a panic-stricken man in a phone booth whose last dime has been swallowed as he pleads for its return with a suspicious operator: "*Your di-yem has been returned. Sir, Bell Telephone doesn't need your di-yem. When you hang up, your di-yem will be auto-*

matically returned to you." "No, it won't, Operator. I know that sound. I've heard it all my life. That dime is in there." "Sir, Information cannot argue with a closed my-ind." In another, a quasi-parody of *Brief Encounter* set during a dental appointment (a favorite theme was physicians and nurses, captured in their album *Nichols & May Examine Doctors*), Nichols, in a clipped British accent, says with stiff-upper-lip passion to his female patient: *"I knew, even then, that I loved you. There— I've said it. I do love you, you know. . . . Let's not talk about it for just a moment. Rinse out, please."* Although May had never seen *Brief Encounter,* she followed Nichols's lead and picked up on his tone of doomed English lovers; similarly, she was able to parody Faulkner without ever having actually read him.

The team's best-known routine, seen on *Omnibus,* was the empassioned teenagers in a car who become too physically entwined to kiss: *"Isn't the lake suicidally beautiful tonight?"* sighs May's young girl. *"That lake out there, it's just a lot of little water and then, bang, all together it's a lake. That just kills me. You know, like, have you ever gone into your kitchen or your bathroom and you turn the faucet on and water comes out of it into your glass and did you ever stop to realize that that water is that lake? It just knocks me out. . . ."* Nichols, as her doltish, on-the-make date: *"I go right along witcha. That whole deal is very rough."* Later, trying to calm her fears of going too far, she's reassured by Nichols's panting would-be Romeo, *"I know what you're going to say. You're going to say I won't respect you, right? Well, let me tell you right here and now, you have no idea how I'd respect you. I'd respect you like crazy!"*

While much was made of their innate improvisational talents, the bulk of their routines were as worked out as any Sid Caesar–Imogene Coca sketch. On Broadway, they did only one improv piece per evening, in the second half, as if to demonstrate they could do it. The sketch put their dazzling minds on display. They would ask for a first line, a last line, and a literary or theatrical style, then spin out parodies of Proust, *Reader's Digest,* Beckett, Al Capp, whatever. *Time* wrote that the improvisation was a show-off stunt that "seems a mistake" and noted a gap between their freewheeling style and crafted routines. The improvs, though rarely their best stuff, became their trademark, and, later, part of their legend. When one worked, it sent audiences away shaking their heads and created the impression that everything they did was improvised.

The sketches might change slightly, but once they hit Broadway the routines were all but frozen. "When we repeat an improvisation," May explained, "it's not by rote but by re-creation of the original impulse."

Skeptics claimed even the improv pieces were all preset, but Nichols maintained they almost always took the first audience suggestion rather than choose from several shouted ideas. "There are simply too many styles," he argued. "We couldn't possibly have formulas for every one." It was a kind of magic trick: they knew, though we didn't, that people almost always suggested the same things—Shakespeare, Williams, Chekhov, a handful of others—and they were ready for nearly every literary style. According to Joffe, Rollins was planted in the audience each night to "suggest" the Pirandello parody.

When I interviewed him for the *New York Post* in 1966, Nichols willingly unraveled their mystical creative process: "I have an image of how we worked, though I've never discussed it with Elaine. Elaine can turn herself into a mother, say, and do a million things. She can fill and fill and fill. What I did was push it on. I think I brought a sense of form to us— what points should be made, what kind of conflict, and so forth."

He goes on: "We never even stated a premise on the [NBC radio] *Monitor* things. She'd say, 'You want to start one?' and I'd say, 'No, you start one.' It was like a game. One time we did fifty-two pieces for *Monitor* in three hours"—without notes, just ashtrays and coffee cups. The radio pieces were ad-libbed; they had to come up with five every weekend. One writer estimated that the team had taped some six hundred radio bits, of which three hundred were usable, although only a dozen or so were vintage Nichols & May. The statistic reveals their incredibly prolific and playful minds, and doesn't even include the many ten-second uncredited vignettes they improvised for a series of animated Jax Beer commercials.

The creative part was fun but, Nichols said, "it was work when we had to do it over and over." He learned to trust his instincts with May, growing more adroit at getting out of tight corners onstage: "Elaine had a great rule, 'When in doubt, seduce,' which I've passed on to my acting students." He chuckles. "And it's a great rule for life, too." May had another rule for playing comedy—the laughs are in the details: "The difference between comedy and romance and tragedy is that in comedy you do every detail and in romance and tragedy you do a sweep. If you kill yourself in a drama, you take the gun and you shoot yourself. If you kill yourself in a comedy, there are no bullets. You have to go buy some. You don't have any money, you have to borrow some. You have to have your ID. It just goes on."

May said in 1961, "I have no sense of mission about our work, I have nothing to tell people," which might account for her refusal, since 1966, to give interviews. Forty years ago, May teased an interviewer trying to pry a few facts out of her about their real selves: "I will tell you something but I warn you it is a lie"; the most intimate fact she revealed was that Nichols subscribed to *Dog World*. Nichols handled all the nuts and bolts of their career—dealing with the press and producers. He was a major worrier, famous for calling up with dire emergencies, and once wailed to the producer Alexander Cohen that their theater was "in total darkness" after one bulb had burned out.

Some years later, Nichols claimed that he gave up performing satirical sketches with May because it got so trendy. In 1966 he said, "Satire is 'in' now. It's like discotheques. Everyone's a satirist. A lot of people leaped into it because it's very commercial now to be noncommercial." He told *Playboy,* "At first I thought, Jesus, I'm *in*. How do I get out? And then I realized all I have to do is wait ten minutes and it'll take care of itself."

LOOKING BACK FROM today's dumbed-down comedy era, it's worth noting that audiences had no difficulty at all understanding Nichols & May's reference-studded routines, however "intellectual" they may have seemed compared to the typical nightclub act in 1960. When the team broke in, comedy's wiseguys figured the couple would never find an audience smart enough to dig their humor, but it soon became clear that Nichols & May had that rarest of things, both snob *and* mob appeal, funny both to the literati and the lumpen.

Even so, television was not to be their medium, confirmed by an Emmy Awards telecast they hosted. May came out and praised all the people who had been honored for creative excellence before saying, "*But what about others in the industry? Seriously, there are men in the industry who go on, year in and year out, quietly and unassumingly producing garbage,*" and she called Nichols up from the audience to accept his award as "*the Most Total Mediocrity in the Industry.*" Portraying a producer with a silly lopsided smile, Nichols clutches the award and, in a loopy voice, says, "*This is the proudest moment of my life. I'd like to say briefly how I did it. Firstly, no matter what suggestion the sponsors make, I take them. Last and most important, I have tried to offend no one anywhere on earth. In ten years of production, we have received not one letter of complaint.*"

Dick Cavett recalls being transfixed by the couple: "You can't get any better than they were, and the miraculous thing is, they appealed to everybody, enjoyed by every kind of person. You never heard anyone say,

'They're too weird' or 'I don't understand the words they're using.' Because of them, other comics not of their caliber spoke of Kafka in their act. I could name any number of comics I saw who were trying to hit that note of elitism. They were one of the comic meteors in the sky." Steve Martin likewise has pointed out that the high IQ of their sketches was not their main appeal. "Smart is not necessarily funny," he said. "You can go through a whole evening of smart and have laughed completely perfunctorily. Smartness is death to comedy. It was just plain funny. However smart it was, it never got smug."

Nichols always protested the highbrow label: "I object to the whole thing about 'intellectual' comedians," he said in 1961. "These days you can be an intellectual in twenty seconds just by saying certain names: Nathanael West, Djuna Barnes, Dostoyevsky, Kafka. Intellectual used to mean a process of thinking, or a body of knowledge. For some nutty reason, it doesn't anymore." The team resisted the "intellectual" label because it made them sound pretentious and difficult to grasp, and their success proved that theirs was hardly a cult following. Nichols told an Aspen comedy festival audience: "The most interesting thing that we discovered when we came from the University of Chicago, and then did the Blue Angel in New York and thought, 'Well, these are sophisticated smart-asses,' was when we went on television, where the audience consisted of mostly ladies who waited in line to see a TV show, and they were just exactly as sharp and as hip and as alive and as with it."

The two of them laughed at their instant success, and both were wary of it. "I think people try to become famous, because they think: 'If you can get the world to revolve around you, you won't die,' " Nichols told me in 1964. He says today that success was a little disappointing, but liberating, like graduating. "It's like when you get out of high school— and Laura Biddleford wouldn't go out with you but Lorna Winkelstein would. And then you get out and you find it's wide open." Those who would go out with him, later, included Gloria Steinem, Suzy Parker, Jackie Onassis, and, of course, Diane Sawyer, his fourth wife. Nichols wallowed in success, living in the mid-1960s in a Billy Bigelow—decorated penthouse with white carpets, white furniture, and paintings by Matisse, Picasso, Rousseau, and Vuillard; in the 1980s, he had an all-white tower penthouse at the Carlyle Hotel. A friend once said that Nichols could live on a loaf of bread but would need a staff of ten to keep the loaf.

Nichols basked in his celebrity status but eyed it with his usual cynicism. He said, "Having fame is wonderful," but "it can make you feel like a baby. Part of it is wonderful and exciting. Part of it is a terrible kind of posing and a seeping away of yourself." He told *Playboy* in 1966, "For a while I thought success is a great danger to sensation, to feeling. I went through periods of asking, what's the matter, why don't I taste anything, why don't I feel it? Somehow I thought I would be taller."

Nichols found himself becoming a showbiz brat: "I was narcissistic. I would get mad. I bitched about our billing. I did all the things I dislike. We had troubles, but it's the trouble that teams have. You have all this paraphernalia—managers and agents and accountants and producers and people saying, 'What about this spot on the *Dinah Shore Show,* and what about playing D.C.—and we have this standing offer from blah-blah-blah.' Pretty soon you want to do different things. One of you wants to go to D.C. and the other doesn't. One of you never wants to go on *Dinah Shore* again and the other thinks it would be nice to get a lot of money." Their lives, he said, had become "a million deals."

The team's breakup caught everyone but them by surprise. In 1961, just as the world was discovering them, they decided to call it quits, stating that they wanted to pursue separate careers—he as a director, she as a writer—which was only partially true. What triggered their parting was far more complicated and emotional. While May wanted to invent, Nichols only wished to please. "The more we became the talk of the town," revealed Nichols, "the more I was afraid to try something new when we had so many things that worked well." In John Lahr's words, "May cared more about process, Nichols more about results." Nichols told Barbara Gelb: "Several things happened. One was that I, more than Elaine, became more and more afraid of our improvisational material. She was always brave. We never wrote a skit, we just sort of outlined it: I'll try to make you, or we'll fight—whatever it was. We found ourselves doing the same material over and over, especially in our Broadway show. This took a great toll on Elaine."

May, to stay interested, would extend a sketch or go off on a tangent that would throw and annoy Nichols. The sketches changed a little, he says, "if for nothing else than to keep us interested. Elaine could get me laughing helplessly by changing a digit in a telephone number." He says that he never snapped his fingers at her to speed up, as she claimed, but admits, "I nagged the hell out of her. I was always saying, 'You're taking too long over this.' It taught me about beginnings, middles, and ends. I had to push the sketch ahead, because I couldn't invent as she could. I'm a chicken and I don't like doing something new, because what if it doesn't work? . . . After all, other performers repeated their act. Why the hell should we have to have a new one every night?" But then of course they *weren't* other performers.

Explained Nichols further: "I wasn't happy with getting paid a fortune for something and not having tried it out in advance. The audience didn't give a shit whether you were improvising or not. They'd come to see good comedy." He boasted, "We never got a negative review. We never had an empty seat. Everybody loved us. Everybody felt they had discovered us." He told an interviewer, "We stopped because Elaine couldn't stand it anymore. She told me she was tired of doing what we had been doing for so many years. It was always a rule between us that we would respect the other's wishes. The longer you go, the harder it is. What happened is what happens to all long runs. It got so dehumanized and so unreal by the time we'd played it a year. You begin doing by rote. I would start playing games, like, 'Let's see how fast I can make it go.' "

The specific event that caused their personal split was May's play *A Matter of Position,* about a man who will not get out of bed. It was based on Nichols, and he starred in its Philadelphia tryout in 1961; she also was supposed to be in the play but backed out. "That's what fractured our relationship," he told me. The experience damaged their old dynamic. "The biggest problem was, we had done everything together, and now I was onstage and Elaine was in the audience watching me, judging me, and whispering to the director, Fred Coe, who was a stranger." Nichols told Jeffrey Sweet, "It divided us in some terrible way, and we never quite recovered from that. It's like that thing in *Nineteen Eighty-Four*—once they betray each other they can be friendly, but it's never quite the same. And we did, in fact, betray each other. Things arose. She was trying to get another actor. I was saying, 'Get her to cut the play or I'm leaving.' Once we'd gone through that experience, of trying to screw the other one, out of panic and discomfort, it was sort of over."

The critics blasted the play and the audience was bored by it. May wanted to replace Nichols when he agreed with Coe that the play needed to be cut by forty minutes. She felt embattled; Nichols said, "I behaved very badly toward Elaine." "The fights were just terrible," remembers Joffe, who sums them up: "He was arrogant, she was nuts." Coe once commented, "Elaine is a very talented girl. Elaine is a very difficult girl. I have found the two are synonymous." She took legal steps to enjoin Coe from changing so much as a comma, reports Coleman. The play closed after seventeen performances.

"It was cataclysmic," Nichols later said of the breakup. He fell into a state of depression. His ex-agent, Robert Lantz, told Lahr, "He really wasn't functioning. He went to bed. Period." Nichols said, "I didn't know what I was or who I was." A friend commented, "Mike has no tolerance for failure." Looking back now, Nichols says, "When it was over it was really over. Once we got over being mad at one another, we would come together for this or that ratfuck, and that was fun. We enjoyed it, people enjoyed it." They wouldn't reunite as a creative team until 1996, when Nichols directed the movie *The Birdcage,* which May adapted from the play, film, and musical *La Cage aux Folles;* earlier she had worked, uncredited, on screenplays of some Nichols films.

Five years after the breakup, Nichols could only tell me, "I don't know what to say. We had done it, created a body of work, and there it was. God knows we presented it enough. The way I feel is, we did it and we should shut up." May felt that they could never top themselves after the Broadway smash. Nichols added, "The kicks diminished a little, too. In the old days, I was always nervous as hell before a show. Then I got to be sort of super-casual and I didn't like it. The odd thing is, neither of us ever felt at home acting. We'd be backstage and there'd be all these dancers running around in their tights, and Elaine would ask, 'Can I borrow your comb?' and I'd say, 'Oh, don't be silly.' " Rex Reed's epitaph for the brilliant duo read: "They stopped throwing crumbs at a begging audience of millions of discriminate fans who had previously asked politely for cake." Arthur Penn summed it up: "They set the standard and then they had to move on."

Following the breakup, Nichols was creatively and psychologically crushed. "I felt I was the leftover half of a comedy team. I really felt for a long time that what I was able to do came from my special connection with Elaine. Without her, there was not much I could do. I was in a slough of despond." While they were together he'd said, "There are things we want to do apart—and we will someday. But not comedy. We could never be funny without each other." Rollins says that he didn't even try to talk them out of it. "They did what they had to do. I think they'd just reached a point where they were driving each other a little nuts." Perhaps dubious about their solo commercial futures, Rollins and Joffe declined to handle them except as a comedy team.

A year later, Nichols read a new comedy by a young writer, Neil Simon, called *Nobody Loves Me* and agreed to fix it and stage it. Retitled *Barefoot in the Park,* it was his first Broadway play and a huge hit. (Prior to that he had only staged *The World of Jules Feiffer,* a revue based on Feiffer cartoons with music by a new composer, Stephen Sondheim, that never reached New York.) When the producer Arnold Saint-Subber handed him the Simon play, Nichols said to himself: " 'Well, let's see if I can do it'—and from the first hour of the first day I knew instantly I was home. I knew that's what I could do. I felt adult for the first time. This was a grown-up job. I think the role of director satisfies me partly because I am creating a father that I miss." (Nichols was twelve when his father died of leukemia.)

In directing, he found his life work—and himself. When asked later if directing on Broadway was an unsettling experience, he remarked, "It was a settling experience." He said in 1966, again invoking his pet parenting analogy: "The difference between performing [and directing] is the difference between a child and a daddy. There's a secret about directing and it's this—you're trying to help people. As long as the thing is taking place, it doesn't matter who's doing it. I don't mean to come on, but you can't beat Aristotle, who said that one of the great joys in life is to give order to things. That's why we have theater. You can control it more than you can life."

Nichols exerted his control over Neil Simon, who writes in his memoir that a phone call from the director "would immediately raise my IQ by fifty points and speed up my thought processes by seconds." Simon never quite decoded Nichols: "He's still a hard guy for me to read. I sat behind him in five plays of mine he directed, trying to learn what he did, and I didn't learn anything." If Simon suggested an idea Nichols didn't like, "Mike didn't say a word. He just looked at me poutingly like a child, as if to say, 'Poor baby. Came up with a dumb idea.' "

Some of his old Compass colleagues felt that, apart from films like *The Graduate,* the 1967 movie that made him a national name, he had sold out to safe comedies; that his unique cutting-edge wit had been dulled by exposure to Broadway audiences. The high gloss he gave to shows like *The Odd Couple* in 1965 had hugely enhanced his fame, but the critic and director Robert Brustein was unimpressed, commenting, "Nichols is becoming famous directing precisely the kind of spineless comedies and hopeless musicals that he once would have satirized." (An interviewer once asked Nichols what was wrong with Broadway, and he replied, "You can never get a cab.") Nichols himself was uneasy with his golden-boy luster. "It's very depressing to be described as a Success. A Maker of Hits.

Who wants to be a Success? That's an odd profession." A few knocks brought him back to earth. In 1966, in the first flush of success, he remarked, "It's a beginning. Now we'll find out if I can do anything. Wait! You're going to see such failures you wouldn't believe it!"

Indeed, after two highly touted films, *Carnal Knowledge* and *Catch-22*, failed financially, Lahr writes that Nichols felt he had lost his way, that the golden "Nichols touch" had turned to lead. He once said, "If I could have any wish it would be to be free of caring about the opinions of others. Did they like me? Was I rude?" Apart from producing and guiding *Annie* to hit status in 1977, he drifted for a dozen years but laid his Midas hand on Whoopi Goldberg, whom he discovered doing a one-woman show in San Francisco; he saw in her an Elaine May gift for satirical characterization, as he did in Gilda Radner, whose one-woman Broadway show he also directed.

Nichols sank into creative limbo from, roughly, 1977 until 1983, when he again directed a series of hits—*Silkwood, Biloxi Blues, Working Girl, The Birdcage*—that placed him back on his showbiz throne, partly thanks to May. Working with her on *Primary Colors* and *Birdcage*, he said, "was like coming home, like getting a piece of yourself back that you thought you'd lost." May was never consulted on his earlier films—"We weren't very close at that point." Curiously, he's never cast her in any of his movies, explaining a bit uneasily, "I cast for the character. It just never came up." After *Birdcage* became his first big hit in years, he told a friend, "My reaction, instantaneously, was, 'Fuck you, bastards. You thought I couldn't do this anymore. Well, look at this!' "

Most of his post–*Catch-22* movie comedies were well-crafted, comfortable successes; Roger Bowen, a Second City alumnus, called *Working Girl* "a Republican fairy tale." Lahr observed, stingingly, "The early pictures said new things in an ironic, challenging way, and the later work ruffles no feathers." Buck Henry agreed that Nichols "should be doing more *Hurlyburly*s." William Goldman, the screenwriter, told *Time* in 1970: "Mike is one of the most famous directors in the U.S., but he hasn't made one significant contribution to the theater. But Mike doesn't want to do anything badly. He takes a risk on things he knows he can do better than anyone else." Goldman earlier had sniped in *The Season*, his book about the Broadway season of 1967–68: "Nichols's work is frivolous—charming, light, and titanically inconsequential. What Nichols is is brilliant. Brilliant and trivial and self-serving and frigid. And all ours."

Whether a movie is serious or trivial doesn't matter to him, Nichols says in his defense. "I can only follow my excitement. It's either alive for me or it's not. If you're funny, and you stay funny, I think that's already doing pretty good." His movie-producing friend John Calley told Lahr that, because Nichols can command $7.5 million a film plus 12 percent of the gross, "it's hard for him to say no. He knows I don't like a lot of the stuff he does. I think it's beneath him."

Elaine May never spoke on the record about Nichols until she rambled for a full three minutes to Lahr in 2000, saying, "So he's witty, he's brilliant, he's articulate, he's on time, he's prepared, and he writes. But is he perfect? He knows that you can't really be liked or loved if you're perfect. You have to have just enough flaws. And he does. Just the right perfect flaws to be absolutely endearing." Then she coyly clammed up. "Your three minutes are up. If I had another four seconds I'd tell you every one of those flaws."

In 1966, only five years after Nichols & May broke up, *Life* wondered, "Whatever Happened to Elaine May?" In what was her last serious magazine interview, the writer surmised that Hollywood was suspicious of her. May's journey since the split has been much more erratic and subterranean than Nichols's—a few acting jobs, screenplay doctoring (*Reds, Tootsie,* TV specials for her pal Marlo Thomas), some movie directing (easily the best of which was the hilariously cynical 1972 comedy *The Heartbreak Kid,* costarring her daughter), and the occasional play or screenplay, such as *Heaven Can Wait, A New Leaf* (which she directed, playing a geeky botanist opposite Walter Matthau), and the landmark forty-million-dollar flop *Ishtar,* which entered the language as a synonym for disaster.

A close friend of May's said, in that where-is-she-now piece in *Life:* "I feel sad for Elaine. She could sell out—write gag plays like Jean Kerr and make a fortune, and be on magazine covers like Mike Nichols. She could take pratfalls and be funnier than Lucille Ball. She could hole up somewhere and write tragedies blacker than Lillian Hellman's. Hell, she could teach philosophy at Radcliffe. She has so many things going for her that, in a curious way, I don't think she'll ever be happy."

After *Luv,* a lackluster 1967 re-creation of Nichols's stage hit that he declined to direct on-screen, her movie roles have squandered a unique comic talent, from playing a sleazy actress in the film *Enter Laughing* to portraying a dumb-cluck cookie clerk in Woody Allen's *Small Time Crooks* in 2000. After leaving Nichols, she was offered what she called "female Tony Randall roles." Carl Reiner once said she could be a major movie star if she wanted, but she didn't want: "I think she's either the sexiest funny woman I ever saw or the funniest sexy woman."

Her own plays have not had much luck since her first solo work, *Adaptation*—a sardonic sixties one-acter about life as a game show (anticipating today's "reality" TV shows), heralded as the debut of a sparkling new playwright. In the short play, really a lengthy sketch, a female character blathers, "I have this problem—I can give but I can't take," ridiculing the psychobabble of the era. She also twitted patronizing liberal piety in a scene (*"Mother, what is a Negro?" "You must think of the Negro as something very, very beautiful that God gave white people to enjoy"*). Last fall, her play *Adult Entertainment* debuted off-Broadway, costarring her daughter.

May has remained the eccentric woman of her youth. Some of the crew on 1971's *A New Leaf* described her as "brilliant but spooky." Matthau's take on working with her: "She makes Hitler seem like a little librarian." She reportedly fired two producers, ran way over budget (and was herself fired and rehired), and cast old friends and her mother. She sued to keep *A New Leaf* from opening after Paramount took it away from her, and her lines in the film's final five minutes were dubbed by another actress. She held on to the last two reels until Barry Diller pried them out of her. The film was millions of dollars over budget and about four years overdue, according to *New York* magazine. May's six-year pet project, *Mikey and Nicky,* a 1976 movie about two small-time hoods, became an equally celebrated production nightmare when it took her a year to cut it while she subsisted on health foods and pills. *New York* reported, "May's rooms were hopelessly strewn with candy wrappers, half-eaten sandwiches, and months of accumulated cigarette butts."

Colleagues have simply learned how to decipher her thoughts and to tolerate her quirks as best they can. Neil Simon, who worked with her on *The Heartbreak Kid,* says of her: "I don't know much about her. She has her own method of working. Sometimes I don't understand it, then I would watch it and say, 'Gee, that's good.' She speaks her own language; you don't always know what she's thinking. I never had a conversation with her that sounds like a real conversation."

May has always lived by her own lights and, like the CIA, never explains and never complains, but her careers as a writer, director, and occasional actor never jelled as firmly as Nichols's did into what seemed an almost nonstop series of stage and screen successes; even his flops somehow are forgotten, excused as aberrations or absorbed into his general rosy aura of celebrated genius.

IN HIS NO-FRILLS OFFICE on West Fifty-seventh Street in Manhattan, Nichols exudes an air of mellow well-being. At seventy-one, he has lost the wispy "elfin" look and assumed a ruddier, paunchier bearing; Candice Bergen calls him "a poster child for unhealthy living," and Lahr observed that "he never met a calorie he didn't like." Seated in a swivel chair and sucking on a hard candy, he stretched out his legs as he looked back over a long, busy, and charmed career. Sirens screeched through an open window as he chatted in his cool, unperturbed way, happy to have just heard that day that the studio liked his new comedy *What Planet Are You From?* (It later quietly flopped.)

In his *New Yorker* profile, Lahr painted Nichols as a kind of show-business pasha, but his longtime friend Buck Henry said, "He knows when his ass is being kissed and when it isn't, although it is most of the time. He casts a baleful eye on all of it, but in his heart he wants it and needs it." Richard Avedon added, "He's on an island that belongs to him, manned on the turrets by men with machine guns. People can only get in with a passport, and then only his friends."

In person, Nichols can be an intimidating presence, with his aura of genius, success, power, and aging wunderkind. One also tends to feel a bit dull around him, which can render nearly mute anybody not used to his enigmatic Cheshire cat smile—verging on a smirk—and the secret chuckle and the "off-putting glacial stare that could shatter a producer's sunglasses at fifty paces," to quote a *Playboy* interviewer. Woody Allen called him "supercilious in the way we all wish we had the genius for. He's a nice version of George Sanders in *All About Eve*." Indeed, at a retrospective for him, Nichols blew a poisoned dart at his old protégé Dustin Hoffman for not attending: "It's like the monster not showing up at the tribute for Dr. Frankenstein."

You're not always sure when he's kidding or if he's secretly mocking you. Barbara Goldsmith wrote: "Nichols has two smiles. The one he wears most frequently is not unlike the mask of Comedy that decorates theater prosceniums." Another writer remarked: "When faced with the clear-eyed Nichols stare, whatever you say sounds like a clumsy cliché in italics but that when he uses a cliché it's got these knowing, built-in, deprecating quotation marks" around it. His intelligence, the writer added, was like a giant amplifier that played back remarks "with just enough distortion so that they seem hilarious. This was his genius as a performer." Alan Arkin, who was directed by Nichols in *Luv* and *Catch-22,* said, "He has a way of speaking that avoids passion, but he feels very deeply."

That implacable manner may be part of Nichols's defense system from years of playing power games with New York and Hollywood: "Never let people see what you want, because they will not let you have it," he told Lahr. "Never let anybody see what you feel, because it gives them too much power. You're better off not showing weakness whenever you can avoid it, because they'll go for you." He once told Lillian Hellman, "The butterflies in my stomach won't stop fluttering until I have thirty million dollars."

His former agent, Lantz, comments: "He's ruthless when he wants to be, or sometimes maybe even when he doesn't want to be." When aspects of his Broadway staging showed up in movie versions of plays he had directed, Nichols took action and became the first film director to get a cut of the playwright's royalties. He argued with a producer over whether *Who's Afraid of Virginia Woolf?* should be shot in color or black and white, Nichols insisting on the latter. When the producer balked, Nichols flicked on the ice machine and said, "Well, okay, I'll tell you what. You make it in color. I'll go home. I like it at home." He prevailed, of course; when he was later thrown off the movie as it was being sound-mixed, Nichols calmly gave mixing directions to the sound editor by phone. He even cooked up a scheme to have the film passed by the Catholic Church's Legion of Decency by having Jackie Kennedy sit next to the monsignor and, when it was over, turn to him and say, "How Jack would have loved it!" To the studio's astonishment, the Legion passed it. Nichols was once more a hero.

From Elizabeth Taylor on, Nichols loved working with big stars and was rarely cowed by them. (The *New York Observer*'s John Heilpern, reviewing Nichols's star-studded production of *The Seagull* in 2001, with Meryl Streep, Kevin Kline, Christopher Walken, John Goodman, Natalie Portman, and Marcia Gay Harden, wondered if Nichols ever directed anything that wasn't jammed with Hollywood names; see also Nichols's 1988 staging of *Waiting for Godot* with Robin Williams and Steve Martin.) George C. Scott vanished for three days during rehearsals of *Plaza Suite,* and when he returned, recalled Neil Simon, Nichols turned to Scott and said coolly, "Hi, George. We're on Act Two, page twenty-one." When

Jules Feiffer asked Nichols if the young, inexperienced Candice Bergen could act, Nichols said, "She'll act for me."

Diane Sawyer fell for his seductive wiles when they first met at a Paris airport. Before boarding, she asked him to lunch, ostensibly with an interview in mind (she was then dating Richard Holbrook, the former assistant secretary of state). As she told a beauty magazine in a 1999 cover story, "He was so intimately, mouth-droppingly fascinating that there was no time to think about flirting. I just tried to keep up with him." She says, "All that light in his eyes is some sort of invitation. He's just full of invitation. It's like, 'Let's be young together. Let's see things for the first time and tell each other the absolute truth, want to?' "

Chirpy as a newlywed, she proclaimed it "a great marriage, so much more than I thought it would be. He makes you feel the truth. You feel you can say anything, because he redeems everything." Sawyer did the pursuing and the proposing—only days after they began dating, undaunted by his previous three marriages. "It's like you feel this big resounding 'Yes!' inside you."

His Royal Cuteness, as Sawyer calls him, says of her: "She's so many different people. The siren, the candy striper, the wilderness heroine, and there's Captain Baby"—a game they play. Sawyer explained the rules: " 'I am a baby and you must do as I say.' It's those days when you need nursery pleasures, like chocolate syrup over ice cream in bed. We take turns being Captain Baby." In *More* magazine, Sawyer said: "He wakes up in the middle of the night funny. I don't mean a little funny. You know that no matter what happens you won't be bored." She wanted no kids, just Nichols all to herself: "That's what I waited for and that's what I wanted." He still dotes on her after fourteen years, saying, "All of her is available all the time." He told a TV interviewer, "True love made Pinocchio a real boy. If you're very lucky, along comes someone who loves you the right way, and then you're real."

Looking back on what has become a historical time in comedy and in his life, Mike Nichols finds no evidence that what he and Elaine May did was very influential. "I don't know about any of that. It's the old gag— I'm the bird, you're the ornithologist. I do know that, since Compass and Second City, improvisation became a kind of industry that led to so many things, like *Saturday Night Live*. Although that's all carefully written, the people all came out of improvisation." He adds, "I find improvisation very, very painful to watch. I can't bear to see bad improvisation, because when people have things prepared, you wonder why bother with this?"

He has, however, watched improv's slick TV version—*Whose Line Is It, Anyway?*—and "was surprised that I liked it very much. The people are remarkable." He adds, "The mistake is to place too much emphasis on the improvising. I watched Lenny Bruce every night for six months when he opened for us, because nothing on earth is funnier than a great joke when it first occurs to someone. Lenny Bruce was just a *really funny man,* when he still was. And it was more about that than it was about improvising."

For May, says Nichols, improv was innate: "There are very few people who have the gift of Elaine." He offers an example from a long-forgotten bit they did on the 1950s TV quiz-show scandals, in which two people meet at the office watercooler and the Nichols character says, with self-righteous indignation, "*It's a moral issue,*" and May replies, "*Yes, and it's so much more interesting than a* real *issue.*" He now remarks, smiling, "Well, there aren't a lot of people who can do *that.* And when you have a mind like that, saying such startlingly funny things, it's something different from almost anyone else improvising. It just is."

Of their brief but shining career together, Nichols says, "The thing about Nichols & May is, neither of us ever looked at ourselves except to see if our hair was okay. We didn't actually look at what we were doing. I never thought I was that good an actor, and now it turns out I may have been wrong. Maybe I was better than I thought. I think we're still funny— God help me, touch wood, *kinehorah*—because we did not do topical scenes; we did what, at Compass, we called 'people scenes.' And now when I look back at our work, I think: Look at that—we were good."

The 1960s

Charlie Everybody

Bob Newhart

All of my humor is based on the fact that I'm the only sane person in a world gone completely mad.

I F NORMALCY IS a gimmick, Bob Newhart had one of stand-up comedy's greatest hooks. The most unusual thing about him was that he was the least unusual of the renaissance comedians of the fifties and sixties. A minimalist, he wasn't a fast-talking radical like Mort Sahl, a ball of nerves like Shelley Berman, a neurotic dweeb like Woody Allen, a frenzied profane hipster like Lenny Bruce, a sophisticated observer of social manners like Nichols & May, or a zany like Jonathan Winters and Phyllis Diller. He was the real Mr. Clean, in word and deed—the classic little man caught in the system. One critic called him "a spokesman for the Walter Mittys in our midst." Almost alone among the premier satirists of his generation, he was the embodiment of the fresh-faced, squared-away 1950s, in his neatly barbered "buttoned-down" look, like a college boy modeling Arrow shirts.

Nor was it just a sly façade. By every account, he was very much the way he looked, the straightest guy in the room—a conservative, golf-playing, martini-sipping, hardworking, tax-paying, law-abiding family man whose career has never been touched by personal scandal—unless you count his close ties to Don Rickles. When Newhart told us in his act that he had been an accountant, the corporate cypher persona fit him as snugly as his three-button suits, and when interviews revealed that he had grown up in a Catholic family, been married but once, and is the father of four fine kids, it enhanced the Ozzie-and-Harriet image.

As it happened, Newhart's comedy routines were mainly *about* images and image-making at a time when the general public was learning about the nefarious schemes of Madison Avenue in books like *The Image-Makers, The Hidden Persuaders, The Man in the Gray-Flannel Suit,* and *A Nation of Sheep.* In his act, and later on TV, he was himself the stereotypical fifties "organization man." The cultural critic Steven D. Stark noted, "What he really just kept portraying was the same bemused, ironic, and somewhat boring embodiment of conventionality he played so well for so long. A lot of his appeal obviously lay in his grayness," what another social critic called "that perfect averageness which is American." In 2002 Newhart won the fifth annual Mark Twain Prize for humor, awarded by the Kennedy Center, and the citation read: "His trenchant comedy signaled the end of the complaisant fifties. He found the befuddling lunacy that lurks beneath the surface of deceptive calm."

When he first arrived on the scene in 1960, however, even he was not quite what he seemed—a stand-up nightclub comedian. That was his first and last lie. He had never worked as a professional nightclub comedian when he cut his first album, the record that launched his career in April 1960. *The Button-Down Mind of Bob Newhart* was an early "concept" album, a new way to create a persona and market him to the public as a hot new stand-up comedian. He was not yet hot (although the record would make him so instantly), he was utterly unknown, and he was not a stand-up comedian. The record company's plan was to imitate the success of the recent torridly successful comedy album *Inside Shelley Berman,* which was released a year earlier and had made Berman an overnight star.

It worked perfectly all over again with Newhart, who was, in many ways, Berman's opposite. Both were from Chicago, but Berman was Jewish, the son of immigrants, who attended the (rather Jewish) University of Chicago, whereas Newhart was a devout Catholic who went to Loyola University. Berman was a dedicated, New York–trained actor, while Newhart had done only small roles in amateur theater groups. Berman created sketches using a telephone and always sat on a stool; Newhart created sketches using a telephone and rarely used a stool.

What's more, Berman's characters, all of whom he himself portrayed, were realistic people riddled with angst, while most of Newhart's characters, whom he almost never actually portrayed but only reacted to, were historical concoctions. Berman presented himself as a comic performer, making faces and employing a wide array of voices, body language, and acting techniques in semidramatic scenes, whereas Newhart was a deadpan straight man who reacted to distant (or invisibly present) people on the other end of the telephone in comic situations. Berman acted, Newhart reacted. Berman sweated, Newhart fretted. Berman emoted, but Newhart just listened, nodding and smiling uncomfortably until finally and reluctantly responding, usually in a little stammer. ("By the way," he takes pains to point out, "it's a stammer, not a stutter, which I think is a sign of higher intelligence.")

If Berman was the troubled patient, Newhart was his therapist—the role he seemed born to play on his long-running situation comedy *The Bob Newhart Show*. His Middle American—ness is part of what kept him such a steady presence in sitcom America for two decades. When Lenny Bruce first saw Newhart on *The Ed Sullivan Show*, he sensed his wide appeal and cracked that there was an audience for "a funny goy"; and when he saw him in person at Mister Kelly's, Bruce predicted, "He'll make more money than me, Sahl, and Berman because Paar, Sullivan, and [Garry] Moore need a goy comic so bad their teeth ache." Bruce said, "The gentiles had to have someone speak for them."

It's hard to know whether Berman influenced Newhart's telephone routines (a lot, Berman strongly suggests, but stops short of accusing him of outright poaching), yet the question is almost irrelevant. At the time, the issue was never raised, because the two comics had such totally different styles, personally and comically. Only in retrospect do you realize that they both became household names in the early 1960s through routines involving telephones. "I was certainly aware that Shelley preceded me," Newhart now says. "We weren't doing the same material. It was a form that had been around, since George Jessel and 'Cohen on the Telephone.' It's a comedy technique. There are just certain routines that lend themselves to a telephone."

Among the renaissance comics, there was more coincidental overlapping than calculated thievery. You couldn't have found two more opposite comic personas than Bob Newhart and Lenny Bruce, yet they rubbed creative elbows, attacking subjects from a similar angle, although with vastly different attitudes. Bruce took on image-making in his famous "Religions, Inc." piece, in which he plays a canny agent talking on the telephone to the pope as he tries to shape the pontiff's image—something Newhart might have concocted had he not been an observant Catholic and a more tasteful guy. Bruce did other routines on the telephone, playing the shrewd, cynical manipulator. Both comics had a bead on the Madison Avenue mentality. Bruce's stuff was, of course, tougher and more daring than Newhart's (or anybody's), cutting closer to the bone. While Newhart needled quietly, Bruce gouged under the skin, creating juicier, Jewishier characters in his gallery of gargoyles and showbiz sharks, and made much more racket.

Newhart was the most Everyman of them all—nonethnic, nonabrasive, non-angst-ridden, non-you-name-it. Unlike many of his new-wave peers, he wasn't on the attack but was, in fact, in retreat. His mild-mannered, quizzical nature worked like a sedative for the increasing craziness of the time. He seemed to be apologizing for his presence onstage. At a time when many of his peers were labeled "sick" comics, Newhart was an undeniably healthy comic, although he claims that some of his stuff verged on the unhinged.

Bruce took it all much further by going beyond mere image-handlers to the corrupt personalities *themselves,* but Newhart's characters were innocents, just as Newhart himself seemed to be. His fellow satirists were iconoclasts and malcontents; however, Newhart was not fighting the establishment so much as razzing it. He was very much a part of it, actually, a swell fellow who just didn't quite understand the establishment and simply was trying to fit in, a bewildered company man. Newhart laughs. "I have that kind of face. Guys think they were in the army with me and women think I was their first husband. I look like everybody."

Newhart, with Jonathan Winters, was almost a comic relief from the intense, introspective satirical comedians. In some respects he was a fifties holdover; his pieces were really acted-out comic essays. Even the well-behaved and equally buttoned-down Smothers Brothers turned into concerned, issue-oriented comics on their controversial TV show. The issue that most upset Newhart, he said, was "the impersonal corporate bigness in modern life, and the individual getting lost." In his routines he never blows his stack; he always remains—well, buttoned-down.

One exception was his drunken company man, Chuck Bedloe, who at his retirement dinner finally tells off the bosses; but even Bedloe is really just miffed and a bit surly (also smashed): "*I don't suppose it ever occurred to any of you that I had to get half-stoned every morning to get down to this crummy job. . . . You put in your fifty years and all they ever give you is this crummy watch. I figure it works out to about twenty-eight cents a year. If it hadn't been for the fifty bucks a week I glommed out of petty cash, I couldn't have made it.*" Newhart was the Dilbert of his day, gently ribbing the corporate life. "I resent large corporations," he said in 1962. "They flatten personalities. When I worked for a huge accounting firm, that's what happened to me. So I quit." And as he later remarked, "All of my stuff is full of anachronisms, a longing for the past, a less mechanical time."

Newhart shied away from provocative issues and politics because, as he told me, "the subjects I like to needle need jabbing, regardless of politics." He was never tempted to do political material: "It's laziness. You devote so much time to a new piece, and you want it to last, and it lasts three or four days, and half the audience don't know what you're talking about anyway." Although he was a registered Democrat in 1960, he may be the most conservative of the sixties comics; in *Hi-Fi/Stereo Review,* a critic praised him for creating "a special niche that distinguishes him from the neurotics and sickniks among other leading comics." Newhart was uneasy with the "well comic" image and maintained, "I find humor in the macabre because it's the only way of dealing with life." He proudly cites his famous submarine routine as evidence: "It deals with death in a very macabre manner." His man on the ledge also had a vaguely Charles Addams tinge.

The easygoing, famously failed accountant had a firm handle on the spin machinery of the day, and audiences were hip to it. The late fifties saw the first stirrings of media hustle, and Newhart was among the first to mock slick advertising and PR techniques. "I did a routine about Khrushchev's arrival in the U.S. and his coverage by TV," he recalls. "I really wrote it as a piece of inside material, but the people laughed. I was surprised, because I didn't think they knew that much about the business."

Unlike the other major comics of that time, Bob Newhart was a virtual Caspar Milquetoast; peeved was as angry as he got. Only Wally Cox and Jackie Vernon were as meek. However outlandish, crazy, or boorish the person on the other end of the line, Newhart was unfailingly polite and hesitant to criticize, say, Lincoln's decision to shave his beard, or Orville Wright's cuckoo plan to fly. Newhart is invariably the civil, unflappable listener. Or so he sounds to the guy on the opposite end of the line, all the while signaling us in subtle ways—eye blinks, coughs, nervous smiles, eyeball rolls, a lift of the brow, a blank disbelieving stare, his trademark stammer—that he realizes the guy he's talking to is a psycho. "The longer he blinked," said a colleague, "the funnier it got." Said Newhart, "All of my humor is based on the fact that I'm the only sane person in a world gone completely mad."

Newhart's placid reactions in routines were more complicated than they appeared. He simultaneously had to convey the message and personality of someone we can't see, communicate his own response to it, and telegraph his honest private reaction to us, the eavesdropping audience. Newhart was always playing two parts at once, but all we saw was the straight man. You can sense Newhart's artistry by trying to imagine listening to a Burns & Allen routine in which you don't hear Gracie's voice, just George conveying her lines to us.

It was comedy by inference, a rare performing technique, and Newhart managed it with a seamless ease, as in his routine about a teacher instructing would-be bus drivers: "*Okay, now, do you see that little old lady running up behind you out of the rearview mirror? Now, let's see how you handle it. . . . Well, that was all right, but you pulled out of the stop too soon. She gave up all the way down the block there. You see, what you want to do is wait and sort of hesitate, so that they still hope they catch you. . . . Now, let's try it again . . . much better. Class, did you notice how he slammed that door right in her face this time?*"

Because Newhart had never performed standard monologues, he didn't really address his audience. Berman related to the audience in sketches, at times confided in them, but Newhart was uncomfortable talking to us directly. This native unease, however, was indistinguishable from that of the hesitant characters he played in sketches, and the modest demeanor reflected in both the performer and the person has worn well over forty years.

Newhart slipped into stardom almost accidentally. Like Tom Lehrer, he didn't crave the adulation of flesh-and-blood multitudes, nor did he need to prove himself night after night in strange clubs in different cities. Once he settled permanently into television, in 1972, he could put up his feet and relax; he was home.

GEORGE ROBERT NEWHART, JR., was born in 1929 on Chicago's West Side into a middle-class Catholic family, the only boy among four children (one of whom became a nun). His father was part owner of a plumbing and heating supply company; his mother was a housewife. The Newharts were, he once said, "neither more or less hilarious than anyone else's family." His deadpan style was established early. "Even as a kid there was something about his poker face that made whatever he had to say funny," recalled his boyhood friend Jack Spatafora.

Newhart had what sounds like a totally unremarkable childhood, boringly uneventful. He failed to come from a dysfunctional home, was not funny-looking, and did not have to fight schoolyard taunts. No class clown, he was the runner-up in an elocution contest in high school. The oddest thing about the young Bob Newhart that anyone could recall for his biographer, Jeff Sorensen, was that in school his breakfast consisted of a Pepsi-Cola and a slice of vending-machine strawberry pie. If Newhart had any early show-business ambitions, they were neatly masked, although among some schoolmates he had the reputation for being a closet wiseacre. He once said, "I liken it to the guy with the lampshade on his head at a party, and I'm the guy in the back who says something to the guy next to him, who breaks up, and then the guy next to *him* asks, 'What did he say?' "

His most discernible talent was impressions, with Jimmy Durante an unlikely speciality ("Every comic starts out doing impressions," he says, "imitating somebody else until they find out who *they* are"), later perfected in an all-male high school production at St. Ignatius of *The Man Who Came to Dinner,* in which he played Banjo, Durante's role in the movie version. He majored in accounting at Loyola, where he took a public-speaking course but had an aversion to speaking in public, or even in class.

Instead, he wrote monologues that he hoped he might sell to comedians. Classmates encouraged him to deliver the routines himself, but he only wanted to write them. He took a bachelor of science degree in commerce in 1954 but flunked out of Loyola Law School in '56, after eighteen months. He joined a stock company in Oak Park, a Chicago suburb, acting mainly in comedies. A fellow actor then, Joe Coan, recalls that Newhart was a quiet guy who came in, painted sets, did a few bit parts, and kept in the background. "Nobody paid that much attention to him." When his public-speaking teacher came to see him in a tent-theater show, Newhart asked her how he had done, and she said, tactfully, that he was "improving."

The other actors felt Newhart was funnier at cast parties than onstage. "He was considered one of the lesser lights in the group," said Spatafora, noting that Newhart was always less actor than reactor, which accounts for his lack of success in movies, where quizzical takes and pregnant pauses are hard to build a career on. It was Newhart's lowest period. He called himself "a dismal failure" and fantasized about becoming a forest ranger and living in a tower by himself, reading books and playing flute and piano. "I wouldn't have to explain to anyone what I was doing," he said; his family would say, "Bob? We don't talk much about him."

In lieu of becoming a forest ranger, he worked as a shoe salesman, a copywriter, an unemployment clerk (where he realized he made only five dollars more a week than if he didn't work at all), and, to be sure, a bookkeeper. Each job provided him with material; to and from the office watercooler, he would jot down notes on people's conversations and behavior. He suspects that the year and a half he spent at law school honed his ear for language. "There's such emphasis in law school on the exact meaning of a word. That was helpful, like in the submarine-commander routine, when the guy says [addressing the crew after a sea disaster], '*I don't mean in any way to slight the contribution of the men who* [didn't make it back]. . . .' *Slight* is such a key word. You have this horrible situation and he uses a word like *slight*." In that same sketch, Newhart's commander gazes out blankly and says, matter-of-factly, "*Looking back on the mutiny . . .*"

Newhart fell into sketch comedy when, at the Oak Park Playhouse, he became friends with Ed Gallagher, a copywriter with the Leo Burnett Company. While he was working at U.S. Gypsum as a bookkeeper (he was never actually a CPA), he and Gallagher would call each other and, to break up the day—and themselves—devise funny bits over the telephone. Gallagher was the straight man. Newhart would dial him and say: "*You don't know me, Mr. Gallagher, but I'm a commercial airline pilot. I just picked your name out of the telephone book. We took off from Midway Airport half an hour ago, but the copilot and I got to horsing around in the cabin and we both fell out. The plane is still up there with fifty-seven people on board. I tried to call Midway and tell them about it, but they just hang up on me.*" Newhart's submarine routine evolved out of the airplane bit. Another time, he called Gallagher and began, "*So you say your office building is filling with soap bubbles and they're up to the third floor?*"

In early 1959 the informal team began taping their conversations ("It was Ed's idea. He said, 'We oughtta record these things'") and decided to turn it into a nightclub act at a time when comedy teams were the rage— not just Martin & Lewis, Nichols & May, and Flanders & Swann but also radio comedy teams like Rayburn & Finch in New York, Coyle & Sharpe in San Francisco, and NBC's Bob & Ray—a major influence on Newhart. "Ed and I would do what I called a poor man's Bob & Ray."

As Newhart & Gallagher, the new team struck a deal to sell their tapes to a chain of ten West Coast radio stations at ten dollars a station per week. They sent out tapes to a hundred more stations. Three replied, but almost immediately the original ten stations backed out, calling their stuff too sophisticated, leaving Newhart & Gallagher with three stations and $350 in the hole. Soon after, Gallagher moved to New York, abandoning the would-be act, forcing Newhart to reconfigure the two-man routines for one man and a telephone. Now he wondered, "Do I look for another partner or do I try stand-up? I didn't think anything was gonna happen; nothing was on the horizon. At one point I tried to sell [the pieces] to comedians. I figured, okay, I'll be a comedy writer, since I couldn't get arrested as a comic." He recalled recently, "I went to see Jonathan Winters in Chicago when I was just starting out. I watched him for an hour and thought, Why bother? Why even think of going into comedy?"

He showed a sketch to one comedian, who said, "'Well, I can't use that particular piece but if you think of anything else, maybe I'll buy it from you.' So a month later, I'm watching Steve Allen's show and he comes on and proceeds to do my piece. I'm sitting at home watching my own material being done and I'm not getting paid for it. So I thought to myself, well, if they're going to steal it I might as well do it myself."

It was a life-changing moment, but Newhart still didn't imagine himself as a career comedian. "I wasn't actively pursuing stand-up. I didn't know if I was gonna wind up in radio or writing commercials, or what. I was getting nervous because all my friends were getting married and having families and buying homes in the suburbs, moving up, and here I was still kind of muddling around in comedy." After failing at accounting and law, he felt he'd messed up his life—then, for a local Emmy Awards ceremony, Newhart devised his classic Abe Lincoln sketch in response to a request for him to perform something that would razz press agents. It got a rave in a Chicago newspaper.

His timing was perfect. As Spatafora observed, if Newhart had come along five years earlier, in an era when comics had to be loud and aggressive, he might easily have been drowned out and followed Cox, Vernon, Stanley Myron Handelman, and Jean Carroll into stand-up oblivion. But the combination of the arrival of a more leisurely style of comedy pioneered by Shelley Berman gave him a chance. TV's ability to zoom in on a comic's facial expressions made it possible for him to find an audience. Newhart's influences, besides Bob & Ray, were the writers Max Shulman and Robert Benchley, and primarily Jack Benny. "I've been compared with Jack for timing, which I think is innate, not something you learn. What I admired about Jack was his courage—that he would take his time. He wasn't afraid of silence." (After Benny's death, Newhart's son said, "My father doesn't get really demonstrative, but it was palpable how sad he was when Jack Benny died.") Newhart's own use of extended silences was almost radical. All comedy relies on pauses, but Newhart's many minutely timed pauses created a comic tension as audiences eagerly waited to hear what his funny callers had to say next.

Newhart's clever routines and historical switcheroos were perfectly in sync with the time. Equally important, he was in sync with a popular Chicago disc jockey named Dan Sorkin, who proved crucial to Newhart's career. Sorkin, one of Chicago's leading radio personalities, who went on to become an equally popular deejay in San Francisco at KSFO, is a deadpan personality himself. Sorkin did what he called "a satirical music show" at a time when Chicago was the hub of cutting-edge satirical comedy. "Danny was the guy who sort of pushed me along and encouraged me. You need someone at that point to say you're funny."

Sorkin, who thought the tapes that Newhart made were on a level with Berman, Nichols & May, and Jonathan Winters, said, "Bob was one of the freshest, most creative comedians I'd heard in years. Bob's stuff was already very polished." He compared Newhart's relaxed style to Sinatra's singing: "It sounds like anyone could do it but then if you try to do it you find it's not really so easy after all." Newhart became Sorkin's go-to guy for funny on-air bits: the deejay would call for his reaction to whatever happened to be in the news, and Newhart would ad-lib something, often posing as an expert in the field—a stock-market analyst, the owner of a big building that had burned down, a comptroller commenting on a budget scandal. Sorkin praised Newhart's ad-lib abilities, surprising given that his stand-up routines were so tightly scripted and that he never winged a word in his act or on TV.

Once they became good friends, Sorkin found Newhart a manager and got him a job in radio in Battle Creek, Michigan—not a great idea. Newhart also worked for a while at Chicago's ABC affiliate, WBKB, but none of the formats was right. Newhart's pieces were only five minutes long and nobody could figure how to use them; they even tried him as a man-in-the-street *interviewee* on a short-lived local TV show hosted by Sorkin, but he left after a few months. Spatafora recalled that when Newhart would do his little routines at churches and local clubs, audiences were unsure how to respond. Spatafora said the comic "was a little ahead of the local Chicago market." Newhart was to find easier audiences in New York and San Francisco, but his real success with live audiences came only after they had discovered his records.

In his Bel Air living room, Newhart is extremely, well, Newhart-esque—coughing, clearing his throat, letting his voice drop and trail off, chuckling politely. Sorkin attests that Newhart is pretty much the Boy Scout he appears to be: "There's not a phony bone in the kid's body." Spatafora recalled, "Bob never dated, he played cards." The agent Don Gregory, a close friend, can only add, "He's Mr. Nice Guy—he's so unstarlike, a very generous guy with a sense of humility—but he always had a tough cutting sense of humor. You'd go to dinner and he'd really rip you." Gregory recalls the time Newhart took him to the once-restricted

Bel Air Country Club and the comic turned to him and whispered, "I'm allowed one Jew a year."

Sorkin eventually arranged for Newhart to meet some visiting executives from Warner Bros. Records—James Conkling, the head of Warner's, and his vice president in charge of sales, Hal Cook. "Warner Records was about to go broke," Sorkin recalls. "I said, 'This is the funniest guy I've heard in my life.' He said 'Okay, great, we'll record him—where does he play?' " Sorkin insisted that they first listen to Newhart's tapes, but, as Conkling and Cook had to catch a plane, the best they could do was a quick meeting at a Warner Bros. Records warehouse near the airport. Newhart arrived by bus; he didn't drive.

As Conkling recounted the historic meeting in Jeff Sorensen's biography: "It was at the far end of the warehouse and it was sort of dark. There were no chairs or tables around. . . . Bob was pale, congenial, quiet—not cracking jokes at all. He seemed quite serious. Then he turned on the machine and played us his tapes. The first one was the Abraham Lincoln routine and it absolutely floored us. There were a couple of other very funny ones. And we said to ourselves right away that it would be ridiculous not to record him. At the time, about the only comedian on records was Shelley Berman, who was doing quiet well. And here we were, a new company looking for unique artists."

Conkling continued: "We immediately thought this could be a tremendous hit. I've auditioned thousands of singers and other performers, but I've never had anything else happen the way it did with Bob. He didn't even have to finish the Abraham Lincoln thing for it to be clear. He was an original, a real talent. Usually you have to see the artists three or four times, talk it over with other people—and then you're usually still not sure about them. I have never been so sure of something." George Avakian, Warner Bros. Records' artists and repertoire director, told Sorensen, "The astonishing thing was that the routines were already very polished and well developed."

Recalls Newhart: "When I recorded the routines, they had no laugh track or anything. They said, 'Okay, we'd like to record you at your next nightclub,' and I said, 'There's one problem.' " He had never played a nightclub. But Avakian wanted to record him live—still a new idea then—in order to capture actual sounds of laughter and applause in a nightclub.

The record executives weren't thrown by Newhart's relatively amateur status. But none of the Chicago clubs would book an unknown. As

Newhart recounts, "They [club owners] thought it a little strange. 'Who's interested in a guy pretending he's talking on the telephone?' " Furthermore, he says, "I had no following in Chicago at all. They tried to do it at Second City and Second City said, 'It really isn't our kind of material.' " Finally, after months of no takers, Warner's found a club in Houston, the Tidelands, that agreed to book him for two nights. Over a February weekend in 1960, the nervous, young would-be comic performed his routines to an audience that had never heard of him. When the crowd demanded an encore, Newhart was stumped. " I only had, like, eighteen minutes of material." He'd already pitched his best routines, so he went out, thanked the crowd, and asked, "Now which one of those routines would you like to hear again?"

Most of the material on the album came from the second night's show, because he was "terrified" the first night before a live audience. As Newhart recalls it, "We did three shows. The problem was, at the Friday-night show I had a drunken woman in the audience. She kept saying, 'That's a bunch of crap! That's a bunch of crap!' " Avakian later mixed bits from the two nights to get a series of strong tracks, and in April *The Button-Down Mind of Bob Newhart* was released. The odd name for the album caught the shirttails of a fashion trend, captured the essence of Newhart's advertising-based comedy, and epitomized the comedian's neatnik look.

By summer it was on top of the charts. "We couldn't press the records fast enough," recalled Conkling. The album, says Sorkin, "rescued Warner Bros. Records from bankruptcy." Warner's told him they were "shipping every copy we have to Minneapolis, because there's a deejay there who's been playing the driving instructor bit. So it started happening first in Minneapolis. Newspapers would report the times you could hear the different cuts on the air." Recalls Newhart: "A year before, I was working in a little TV station and a year later Ed Sullivan is calling and he wants six appearances." A columnist wrote: "Less than a year ago he was an accountant. Now he needs one."

Even as his record sales soared, he was still living at home and didn't yet drive; ironically, the cut that got the most airplay was "The Driving Instructor," in which Newhart tries to give driving lessons to a woman who almost totals the car: *"Um, just how fast were you going when Mr. Adams* [her first instructor] *jumped from the car? . . . Seventy-five? . . . And where was that? . . . In your driveway? . . . How far had Mr. Adams gotten in the lesson? . . . Backing out?"*

Newhart's new manager, Frank (Tweet) Hogan, shrewdly promoted the album by sending a copy to Bing Crosby and then telling columnists that Crosby and the cast of his new movie were playing the album between takes on the set. "Eventually, it became a kind of inside thing," said Spatafora, "that here was a very different kind of comedian performing on a record instead of in a nightclub, and you could get him for three ninety-eight." It was a historic leap in the art of comedy and promotion. Unlike the old-wave comics, who spent decades grinding out a following, town by town, Newhart—much like radio and TV personalities—became a star in months, the first comedian manufactured solely out of vinyl.

Gene Norman, who ran the Crescendo in Los Angeles and its upstairs comedy room, the Interlude, recalls, "I saw his album going up the charts, and I called his agency and I said, 'Do you have a guy named Bob Newhart?' and they said, 'We'll check. . . . Yeah, he's in Chicago.' I booked him for six weeks. By the time he got to my club he had the number-one album in America. Everyone who came to see him owned his album." The only act Newhart really had was his album. Norman recalls, "One guy would say the punch line whenever Bob got to it. Bob got flustered—he was inexperienced—and walked offstage and told the guy, 'Okay, you come up and do the act, you know it as well as I do.' So there I was, with a packed house. I conned him into going back out."

In the 1950s, as TV slowly sucked the life out of network radio, local radio raged into prominence. Hip radio personalities like Sorkin, San Francisco's Don Sherwood, and a guy in Phoenix named Steve Allen played comedy cuts regularly. The Bay Area in particular became a huge market for comedy albums. A fourth of the first hundred thousand Newhart albums sold were snapped up in San Francisco alone. Newhart's record was a special case, for not all comedy records then became must-haves—remember Woody Woodbury? Brother Dave Gardner? Eddie (The Old Philosopher) Lawrence? Newhart's routines were cerebral, not just verbal, and didn't depend on catchphrases, like Lawrence's "*Is that what's troublin' you, Bunky?*"

When you saw Newhart perform, it really wasn't much funnier than hearing him, maybe even less so. Comics like Berman, Caesar, Winters, Cosby, and Diller used their faces, hands, bodies; even highly verbal comedians like Woody Allen, Steve Allen, and Mort Sahl were funnier to see than to hear. In the flesh, they crackled with energy; Newhart was pure anticrackle, all nuance and underplay. Although his blank face adds a dimension, most of the humor in his routines was hooked to his voice, his stammer, his embarrassed chuckle, his half-finished sentences, his serial *um*'s and *uh*'s and *ah*'s. David Mirkin, one of the producers of Newhart's TV show, once said, "Bob is the best 'Oh' man in the business." Tim Conway observed of Newhart: "He learned to stammer and stutter at a very early age, and he's made a nice living out of it."

Half of the joke, in fact, is how unflappable his characters try to remain in the face of calamity, like his hesitant guard at the Empire State Building who tries to report a giant gorilla sitting atop the building swatting at airplanes, or the guy talking the man down from a ledge (*"Oh, hi. . . . You thinking about jumping, are you? Your first time, is it? . . . Me? No, no, I'm just on my way to work, as a matter of fact. . . . I usually walk around on the ledges a while. . . . I think it kind of helps me unwind. . . . You know, you're drawing a hell of a crowd for a weekday . . ."*).

In an interview on National Public Radio with Terry Gross, Newhart spoke of how he was part of "this shift in American comedy" in the 1950s and '60s: "The audience was largely college kids and they didn't have mothers-in-law, so mother-in-law jokes didn't mean anything to them. So [a lot of] the humor that was being done in nightclubs was irrelevant to them." He told Larry King in 2002: "We didn't all get together in a restaurant and say, 'Let's change comedy,' but that's kind of what happened."

Newhart counted on the alertness of his audience, plus a certain built-in self-congratulatory element. "The reason the telephone gets the reaction it does," he says, "is that the audience is supplying the unspoken part, so they're very much interactive with you. And at the end when they applaud, they're kind of applauding themselves for being clever enough to figure out what's going on—to get it."

The prime example is his routine about Abe Lincoln's handler patiently trying to talk him out of revisions to his Gettysburg Address, such as changing "four score and seven" to "eighty-seven": *"What else, Abe? 'People will little note nor long remember'? . . . Abe, what could possibly be wrong with that? . . . Abe, of course, they'll remember it. It's the old humble bit. You can't say, 'It's a great speech, I think everyone's gonna remember it.' You come off a braggart, don't you see that? Abe, will ya just give the speech the way Charlie wrote it?"* He notes: "In the Abe Lincoln routine, what I'm saying is not funny—it's what Abe Lincoln is saying." Jack Benny so loved the Lincoln monologue that whenever Newhart left out any lines, Benny would correct him. "The Abe Lincoln bit is probably truer today than it was then, with all the spinmeisters," Newhart says. "It's probably the best piece of writing I've ever done."

The Lincoln bit was a prototype for many Newhart routines in which historical figures confront modern life, like his Sir Walter Raleigh monologue in which Raleigh has reported a wondrous new product he's found—tobacco—to a dubious manufacturer, who responds: "*You can shred it up and put it in a piece of paper, and roll it up? Don't tell me, Walt, don't tell me—you stick it in your ear, right, Walt? Oh, between your lips! Then what do you do to it?* [Giggles.] *You set fire to it! Then what do you do, Walt? You inhale the smoke! Walt, . . . you're gonna have a tough time getting people to stick burning leaves in their mouth. . . .*" What makes that and other similar sketches work so well is that Newhart doesn't play Raleigh, as other comedians might have; he plays the disbelieving listener.

Stan Freberg, using a full orchestra and chorus, also reimagined American history in his album *Stan Freberg Presents the United States of America,* filling it with playful jabs at advertising, promotion, and press agentry. It was a much more elaborate theatricalized version of what Newhart did solo in his classic twisted history routines, such as "A Private in Washington's Army" and "Merchandizing the Wright Brothers" ("*You only went a hundred and five feet, huh? . . . That's all? . . . And the twelve guys still had to push it down the hill? . . . Gee, that's gonna cut our time down to the coast*").

Newhart survived the land mines of show business in better shape than most of the other major new comics of his time, with the possible exception of Steve Allen—another Chicago-born Catholic, though with a far more liberal bent than Newhart. Campaigning for the Kennedys in the 1960s was the extent of Newhart's political engagement. No social causes publicly stirred him. If Newhart ever hugged a tree, opposed a war, picketed a waste dump, manned a barricade, or tied a yellow or red ribbon, it's gone unrecorded. In a 1961 interview he said, "I don't feel like a crusader. I'm really not mad at anybody." In a two-hour A&E *Biography,* his two major life crises were revealed to be chain-smoking and getting a bad time slot.

He reflected the middle-of-the-roadness of middle-class America in the early 1960s. "I did what I thought was funny. I didn't have an agenda. I've always said I didn't consider myself an educator. I was an entertainer. That was my job, to make people laugh. I may have very strong personal views, but I'm not gonna inflict them on others. I don't think because someone likes my persona in a TV show or in a club that they should vote for who I like." In his inspired routine about how a private fire department would work in practice, he's not trying to make any political points.

A few critics found him too buttoned-down bland—"only pleasantly amusing," wrote Ralph J. Gleason, "never belly-laugh funny. He never ventures into the taboo areas." *Variety* at first panned his monotonal manner: "His style of delivery is similar throughout and that makes it hard to take for too long. His material is fresh and good but after about the first twenty-five minutes there's too much of it."

As the sixties bumped along, he felt increasing pressure to get a little raw: "There was a temptation, about the time of *Laugh-In,* to do more sexual things, more dangerous material, which I never succumbed to. I take great satisfaction that I do a clean act, which Jerry Seinfeld does also." Yet he's a major fan of Lenny Bruce and Richard Pryor—"the funniest comedian who's ever stood on a stage," Newhart raves. "Pryor's language is so brilliant. The words certainly don't bother me. I'd be offended if Richard Pryor said 'gosh darn.' In the world he came from, they say 'motherfucker' " (it's alarming just to hear Bob Newhart utter the word). During warm-ups of his TV shows, Newhart was a little risqué and shocked a few tourists.

Newhart was not the most prolific of the new comics. He scarcely had enough routines to scrape together for his first album; he half worried that he might have a hit and be forced to come up with new material. He was creative but highly self-critical and threw out a lot of pieces that he felt didn't measure up; some bits he would work on for a month, only to scrap them. He was forced to rely on collaborators to produce enough material to fill his later albums and the clubs he played before going into TV full-time. By the fourth album, he was working with writers to help shape routines, although he says, "Ninety percent of the routines have been me. The first two albums—it just poured out."

Like many of his comic-renaissance colleagues, he got out of clubs as soon as he could—in his case, almost as fast as he got into them, and for the usual reasons: travel, drunks, and the jangly atmosphere that made him tense up. "Those early TV guest shots on *The Tonight Show* and all the variety shows were paradise," says Newhart, but Jeff Sorensen comments that on TV the young comedian looked nervous and inexperienced. He learned on the job, and was a quick learner. After his second hit record, *The Button-Down Mind Strikes Back,* was cited for "Best Comedy Performance" and he for "Best New Artist of the Year" in 1960 (his first LP won a Grammy as "Album of the Year"), he played Carnegie Hall to rave notices, and Arthur Gelb wrote in the *New York Times:* "For a man who has been exercising his twin talents of writing and acting for such a short time . . . he is an extraordinarily polished performer. He is also hilariously funny." Marcia Wallace, who played the receptionist on the show, observed, "He's the Astaire of comedy—he just makes it look so easy."

Carnegie Hall virtuoso or no, he was eager to find a safer harbor, so when NBC offered him a half-hour variety show in 1961, he grabbed it, with a characteristically self-effacing disclaimer: "I don't think I'm going to be the savior of evening TV. But TV is just something I think I ought to do. It was a case of my either standing still or taking a big gamble. If I hadn't taken a gamble a few years ago I'd still be an accountant." The show, presided over by a seasoned producer named Roland Kibbee (who saw in Newhart a satirist in the vein of Fred Allen, with whom Kibbee had worked), was standard variety-hour fare: singers and sketches, opening with Newhart on the telephone performing a bit like those on his albums (e.g., a school for moving men, a knockoff of his school for bus drivers).

Newhart, who was accustomed to working alone, was a mediocre sketch comic and, because of his problems coming up with new monologues, the opening pieces proved a weekly headache. He refused to repeat routines from his albums, but he had such a defined personality that he could only play a limited range of characters—never a jerk, a dope, a letch, or a heavy. He was totally wrong for the broad comedy that the director wanted—or even for domestic skirmishes in the vein of Sid Caesar and Imogene Coca or Lucy and Desi. Nothing involving anger or zaniness fit him, and he didn't want to do parodies of TV shows like *The Untouchables*. As with Jonathan Winters, it was hard to know just *what* to do with him.

The Bob Newhart Show was uneven and, reports Sorensen, the star looked "high-strung, intense, and nervous," not at all like his smooth self of later sitcoms. In desperation, Newhart would fall into funny voices and accents. Despite its problems, the show had a nice self-mocking sensibility, advanced for its time. In one monologue, Newhart mentioned that, in an effort to convey warmth, he had considered bringing out a small child every week, or he might just "give the illusion of warmth by talking to members of the crew on a first-name basis."

But Kibbee and Newhart didn't mesh at all. "I started with the frivolous notion that we could be a team," Kibbee said later, "but [Newhart] is not a team man. It soon became a notion of his putting his career in my hands—or mine in his. That I was unwilling to do." Newhart's version: "Kib is a strong man. He had been writing comedy for twenty-five years and I'd been at it for only three or four. So he figured, rightly, 'Who's this guy to tell me?' Of course, I figured I'd been writing for Bob Newhart three years longer than Kib had."

Bob Kaufman, a writer on the show, said he left when Newhart resisted "hitting sacred cows. Newhart didn't want satire on the show . . . and was pretty timid about doing shows about the hate groups. Our sponsors gave us no trouble, they *liked* satire, but our star didn't." Newhart wanted to shape scripts so they became more "like me." His comedy, he realized too late, "depended too much on what you didn't see." He now says, "I was very naïve." He no longer had the luxury to try out new material, as in a club, but had to perform new pieces each week before a roomful of millions. Eventually, his worst nightmare came true: "I began to feel, 'I'm not a comedian, I'm a corporation.' And then you die a little every week." Kibbee didn't like Newhart rewriting material. "I said to Kib, 'We're writing the show for, like, eight people in Hollywood.' At times it was so inside." The show was a borderline hit, critically well received but only marginally popular. "One of the conditions for the second year," says Newhart, "had been to get rid of the announcer, Dan Sorkin. I said, 'Here's the guy who's more responsible for my career than anyone.' They felt he was uncomfortable on-camera. I said no, and that was it."

In mid-1962, just when the show began to find a groove, the network and sponsors pulled the plug, only to have it later win several Emmys and a Peabody Award—more awards than any of his later, more popular sitcoms. "It was never clear what NBC was unhappy about. No one ever told me." Newhart was relieved that now he could relax, but recalls thinking, "What's the use of trying? I guess I was bitter, all right." He compared doing the variety show to a novice pilot flying a plane. "I knew nothing about my craft. I was raw funny, not polished funny." To which he added a very un-Newhart-like bit of introspection: "Deep down I guess I didn't feel entitled to all that success."

He dreaded returning to clubs, partly because he was newly married and settled, but he also had "this mortal fear of drunks and hecklers. When I played the clubs I used to peer out from behind the curtains hoping to spot the belligerent ones. It didn't work; I never picked the right ones. The thing I'm most proud of is getting through the nightclubs. It was like walking through a minefield. It was so unlike me. Looking back, it's like, 'Oh, my God, I did that.' " But he finally conquered his fear of audiences. "You learn very soon in a nightclub that you have to be the boss. The stage is yours. If you give any indication you're not sure, the audience will take over. There was a bravado there you had to assume"—which took real acting, since Newhart's style is decidedly antibravado. When his wife, Ginny, first met him, she said, "I couldn't bear to watch his act. He was really uptight about the drunks. He'd hassle the maître d's, trying to get them to do something about it."

Newhart the worrier loosened up some after he got married (in 1962), or so say the couple's friends, among them Buddy Hackett, Dick Martin, and the professionally obnoxious Don Rickles, of whom Newhart observes, "*Somebody* has to be his friend." (Rickles calls Newhart "Charlie Everybody.") Newhart and his wife of forty years (they met on a fix-up arranged by Hackett) live in a spacious (but not gaudy by Bel Air standards) home behind an electric gate, where Ginny Newhart collects—what else?—antique telephones. Newhart, though umbilically tied to the telephone, actually dislikes the phone and never answers it if his wife is home. "I'm not a phoner."

After the variety show folded, Newhart tried to get used to being an unemployed star and watched other rising comics on TV to try to pick them off. "I used to sit down every Sunday night and watch *The Ed Sullivan Show*. I'd watch the new comedians and every week I'd say to the TV set, 'Well, fella, you're okay, but not socko. We know who's still number one.' Then one night I turned on the show and there was a guy named Bill Cosby. 'Good luck, kid,' I said. 'Take it and run with it a while.' " Cosby, like Newhart, later ran with it to sitcom pay dirt. Newhart wasn't surprised—he has a good eye for future sitcom heroes. "Someone asked me once who the next Newhart would be and I said Jerry Seinfeld—this was a year before his show went on. Somehow we all understood TV." He pauses. "When I'd watch the comedy shows more than I do now, I'd sit there and I'd think to myself, 'Who's he doing? He must be doing someone. Oh, yeah, he's doing Letterman, okay.' Then a guy would come along and you couldn't figure out who he was doing and they were the ones who lasted. They had the original voices."

Newhart used to worry that stardom might pull him away from his source material as a working stiff—"trying to relate again to things I used to relate to when I was an accountant. It's a danger all comedians face. You have to keep in mind what it was that first propelled you to be funny. What happens is, you become more affluent, you get an apartment in Hollywood, you start going around with a horsey set, and pretty soon you lose sight of people's problems. A comedian has to keep being involved."

Had Newhart's career not been salvaged by situation comedies in the seventies and eighties, he might not have survived as a stand-up comic. However clever his material, there was a sameness to it—the history switches, the corporate cogs—and, as he found out on the first series, the routines didn't play as well on camera. One critic complained that Newhart's targets were too narrow and his satire not fierce enough.

As the 1960s grew grittier and nastier, alongside the vitriolic stuff coming out of Sahl, Bruce, and Nichols & May, Newhart's routines seemed amusing but beside the point. His routines about noncorporate subjects—babies, big dogs, a Hitler look-alike—feel forced. By the mid-sixties, satire had turned its guns on racism, the women's movement, gay rights, Vietnam, the Cold War, and nuclear missiles. Rude bus drivers and the invention of baseball were considered neither relevant nor funny— an unfair charge, for Newhart's refusal to be drawn into the fray was always part of his strength and charm. "*Laugh-In* changed comedy, for better or worse. I fought the temptation to go along with it, to become risqué and kind of abandon what I was doing."

Newhart has always been, notes Sorensen, "a model of consistency," the down side of which is that his stand-up comedy remains about where it was in 1960. He doesn't claim otherwise, saying in 1985, "I've basically been doing the same thing for twenty-five years . . . and getting away with it." He briefly considered getting broader, a little like Jerry Lewis. It didn't work. The intensity of the sixties made him fear that he might fade away. "I always thought I was gonna be passé," he told me. "I never thought it would last forty years. I've had a great run. I thought it would last four or five years, and people would stop laughing. The comedian always feels that the next audience is going to be the one that's going to stare."

Yet if Newhart came along next week, the likelihood is that the squeaky-clean neighborly comedian would be a hit all over again. The only catch is that comedy's stand-up dynamic has changed since he broke in with his structured little sketches. "Comedy has become more conversational and less structured. There was a time when you went from one thing to the other. There's more interaction today with the audience. I'll do one or two of the record routines, then have conversations and observations—and that's the most fun." Between 1962 and '67, after his variety show folded, Newhart produced four new albums (*The Button-Down Mind on TV, Bob Newhart Faces Bob Newhart, The Windmills Are Weakening, This Is It!*); but in 1968 the pragmatic, unprolific Newhart quit recording albums, explaining, "You're giving your material away on a record. It's self-defeating because people become familiar with the material and tend not to show up for the live shows."

He found himself in 1964 on an ill-fated variety show called *The Entertainers,* with Carol Burnett and Dom DeLuise, which he quit two weeks before it was canceled. The only other idea the networks could come up with for him was a game show, which never aired, so he padded out the rest of the sixties as a guest on variety shows and, most significantly, as a frequent guest host (seventy-eight times) on *The Tonight Show,* which kept him sufficiently visible. He also made a handful of modest, indifferently received film comedies (*Hot Millions, Cold Turkey, The First Family*) and one major one, *Catch-22,* playing the ineffectual squadron commander Major Major. He found moviemaking a bore, missing the instantaneous audience reaction, his old antipathy toward audiences having shifted 180 degrees.

When Newhart first played Las Vegas, however, his low-energy style nearly caused him to implode like an old casino. "Part of Vegas is energy," he observed—what might be called the Sammy Davis, Jr., syndrome. "People don't care if you're good or bad if they can say, 'He or she really works hard.' For the money they pay, they want to see you sweat. And if you don't sweat they don't think you've entertained them."

Although he played Vegas regularly, he found it a treadmill. He was forced to adapt his six-minute routines to audiences suffering from TV-induced attention deficit disorder—even a routine as inventive as his piece about Superman trying to identify his lost suit at the dry cleaners: "*Let me describe my suit to you. The cape is a kind of royal blue with white piping, and the leotards are kind of an off-blue. . . . No, they're not my wife's, no. They're mine. I'm not married. . . . What's that remark supposed to mean? . . . How would you like somebody to come down there and knock that silly cigar out of your mouth? . . . Never mind how I can see it—I can see it.*"

GIVEN HIS UNIMPRESSIVE EARLY GO AT TV sketch comedy, Newhart was an unlikely candidate for a situation comedy. He turned down the first offer, in 1962, telling *TV Guide,* "It would be death for me to do the same character week in and week out, boring for me and the audience." Newhart was still resistant when David Davis and Lorenzo Music came to him in 1971 with an idea for him to play a psychologist. It was either do a sitcom or hit the road again, and a TV series struck him as the lesser evil. At least he wouldn't have to face the amateur comics with

Jim Beam on their breath, could stay home, and avoid travel. He had developed a fear of flying—the theme of the series' first episode.

If ever a man was born to play a sitcom dad, it would have seemed to be the sincere, understanding, and upstanding Newhart, but a TV dad was the very thing he refused to play, stipulating that he would do a series on one condition—no kids. "I hated precocious children and I didn't want it to be a show with kids always bailing the dumb father out of some scrape—'We love you, Daddy, but Daddy's an idiot.' I was resolved I wasn't going to do that kind of show." It proved a smart, even radical, move on Newhart's part, immediately separating him from the *Make Room for Daddy/My Three Sons/Brady Bunch/Partridge Family* pack. One critic called his show "a sitcom for adults." Apart from his dislike of sitcom brats, the childless show seemed hipper at a time (during the Zero Population Growth fad) when increasing numbers of people were opting not to have kids.

His only other stipulation was that he be a psychologist and not a psychiatrist, "because psychologists deal with people who are less disturbed. We didn't want to do any schizophrenia jokes." Newhart wasn't the first stand-up comic to star in a situation comedy, but he was easily the most successful up to then and paved the way for an endless line of stand-ups who would be catapulted into sitcom stardom. Stand-up comedy is now just a pit stop on the way to a long and lucrative TV/movie life.

Adapting a stand-up comedian to a sitcom is trickier than it looks. "It's fine [to use comics] but make sure they can act," advises Newhart. "The big advantage a stand-up comedian has in a sitcom is, first of all, he's a comedian, so he can time a joke. But more important, he knows himself. He knows what works and what doesn't work for him." Also, a comic with a clearly defined stand-up identity gives writers a hook on which to hang plots and jokes. His series thrived, he thinks, because he wasn't the focus but off to the side, just as he was in his routines. "What you realize is, if you're doing a situation comedy it's not me, me, me. You're the glue that holds the thing together. If *I'm* crazy then there's no show."

The original Newhart series worked because Davis and Music found the perfect character to fit his reactive comic persona. His job as a psychologist was to listen to other people's problems and respond calmly. Newhart mastered his character—at his most expressive he would blink nervously or emit a small, exasperated sigh, just like Jack Benny, and, as with Benny, we always knew exactly what he was thinking. One of the show's directors said: "The more he blinked, the funnier it got. He listens funny. You know him and you know what makes him uncomfortable. He was made most uncomfortable doing love scenes or any act of affection."

"Lorenzo Music asked me if I could run some of the speeches together a little faster because the show was running long," relates Newhart, "and I said, 'Look, this stammer got me a home in Beverly Hills and I'm not about to change anything.' "The little breaks in his sentences create a kind of comic tension. John J. O'Connor, former TV critic of the *New York Times,* put it best: "Without moving much, without shouting, Mr. Newhart can squeeze more out of an innocuous line than anybody else in the business." Tom Poston, who played a handyman on Newhart's second series, commented: "Bob Newhart is a great believer in the idea that there are many people who haven't lasted in this business because they had a tendency to overdo things." Music said that if the writers tried to sneak in a joke, he wouldn't do it. "He does attitudes."

Peter Bonerz, who played Newhart's dentist pal, Jerry, on the first show, says the key to Newhart making the transfer from comic to sitcom was the original concept: "To set him up as a psychologist is *perfect*. He's not a doer. As a psychologist married to a dominatrix, he can't *do* anything. He merely responds to all this lunacy around him. I can't think of a more perfect position to put him in—a professional listener."

The writers gave Newhart a sharp-tongued, sexy wife with a smart, liberated outlook, played by Suzanne Pleshette, worlds away from perky Donna Reed, Florence Henderson, and Mary Tyler Moore; the couple even slept in the same king-size bed, a scandalous departure from the coy toy twin beds depicted in the dollhouse sitcoms of the era. Newhart's patients, per his dictum, were not psychos, just lovably weird. The show's mentally healthy star did once see a shrink, because his wife was seeing one, but stopped after three sessions, afraid of meddling with whatever comic demons sparked his humor. He says, "You don't want to get too close to it because it may go away."

Jokeless and childless, *The Bob Newhart Show* debuted in the fall of 1972 and quickly became a hit, cited by critics for its intelligence and believability; the show still plays regularly in reruns alongside *The Dick Van Dyke Show, The Mary Tyler Moore Show, Taxi, Cheers, The Cosby Show, Happy Days, M*A*S*H, The Honeymooners, All in the Family,* and *I Love Lucy* in the pantheon of classic situation comedies. Yet it never won a major Emmy for best comedy series. "That frustrated me, because the people were so darn good," says Newhart. "I always said they made it look too easy." His own understated style was overlooked and underrated. "You don't look like you're acting. But when they have three cameras aimed at you, and you have to hit certain marks, that's *acting*. The satisfaction now is having his shows being seen by a new generation." James Wolcott wrote in *Vanity Fair,* "Newhart wears well. His modesty has a rumpled warmth. And no matter how dour or cranky he may act in his roles, some part of him reaches out for our company."

The cast was dismayed when Newhart decided to walk away from the hit show after six years; some felt abandoned. Jack Riley, a regular, said, "The sitcom wasn't that big a deal to him. He had Vegas, and we didn't have Vegas." Pleshette said bluntly, "If Bob would tell the truth, he'd admit he was afraid after *The Mary Tyler Moore Show* went off that we wouldn't have the lead-in audience." She added, "He's very protective of his real feelings because I think he's got *so* much inside him." He once admitted that he regretted quitting the first series, perhaps prematurely, while it was still a big hit. "Was I bitter? Yeah. We kind of worked in the shadow of *The Mary Tyler Moore Show*. Six years was enough. I didn't want to limp off."

The series had bailed Newhart out of a major career crisis, and nobody realized his close call better than he, who once said, "I'm like the guy who walks down the street, hears a crash behind him, and when he looks back he sees a safe has fallen and missed him by *that* much." Of Newhart's TV appeal, Bonerz says, "I think he's accessible as a comic and as a man. The thing about Newhart is, he's from the Midwest—he's a church-going American family man married to the same woman all his life. He eats beef! And he doesn't have an ax to grind. He's a family-values guy, so he's perfect for television. What's so awful about television is that it has to reach that normalcy gap every second of every day—and still be entertaining and still be edgy and yet still hit that middle line, and the middle line doesn't change much. So it takes a certain kind of genius, like Newhart, to figure that out."

Newhart is a tidy man who has led a tidy life. James Conkling never heard him utter a dirty word on or offstage. The sets on his shows, said Tom Poston, were "the most orderly in town." Poston makes Newhart sound like a man obsessed by orderliness, someone who "absolutely insists everyone do his job exactly right with the least fuss." Bonerz recalls a happy set: "The nice thing about that show was, it was truly a family. We always went to dinner after each episode." The quiet, modest star hated confrontations, and rarely vetoed a line, according to Dick Martin, who directed several episodes of *Newhart*. Yet the star had more input in the show than the cast probably suspected, says Bonerz: "The more I've thought about it, the more I recall instances when writers would just suddenly disappear. I get the feeling that he would suggest changes very quietly. He'd get on the phone and do it that way. He didn't rant on the set as many of the people I've worked with will do. He didn't kvetch, but I suspect he exercised a *lot* more control than I was aware of." Notes Tom Poston: "He's not a nebbish. He's got a spine."

Newhart's second sitcom, a lesser hit, was a sort of updated *George Washington Slept Here* (the 1942 movie starring his hero, Jack Benny). He played the owner of a quirky New England inn, married but once again tot-free. Newhart was the serene center of a weekly crisis involving demanding guests and a staff that he attempted to command. He was wounded when the later series in the eighties and nineties failed, leaving him with a slightly sour aftertaste for the medium, and he reluctantly but realistically decided to leave television. "You have to walk away at some point and realize it's someone else's time," he said.

Without a series, Newhart, for the first time in almost a quarter century, was left without a base. Back out on the road again, he found that his TV audiences wanted him to address them directly, now that he had become a welcome household guest. Drunks and bad lady drivers were no longer fashionable, so—to avoid being labeled sexist—he changed the little old lady Mrs. Webb to a little old man. His old routine about a no-frills airline is even funnier now, but audiences no longer pick up on some historical references that once got laughs.

At seventy-three, he now plays some thirty stand-up dates a year but hasn't created any new routines. He still recycles what worked, golden oldies. He told me: "I don't think in terms of sketches anymore. But I had an idea the other day about an unemployment agent for the Goths and Visigoths. She's talking to a Goth and she says, '*Well, would you like to stay in pillaging?*' And he says, '*No, no, you've got me confused with the Visigoths—* they *were the pillagers. We were the ravagers.*' " He couldn't readily remember an idea that didn't pan out in performance ("It's too painful"), but thought a moment and said, "Well, I did one I felt was very funny but it never worked. A guy who'd been taken by Martians and spent some time on Mars had returned to Earth and was being debriefed: '*Did you find Mars a more advanced civilization?*' '*Oh, yes.*' '*How much more advanced?*' '*Oh, about six weeks. They had the disposable razor six weeks ahead of us.*' " Newhart glanced up, blinked, and chuckled.

The Elvis of Stand-up

Lenny Bruce

Please don't lock up these words.

———

IT IS ALMOST IMPOSSIBLE any longer to get an accurate fix on Lenny Bruce—the comedian, not the martyr, or the myth, or the messiah, or even the man. Bruce's acolytes manufactured the Bruce we know best now, the Lenny of legend.

As time slips by and his legend becomes ever more encrusted and elusive, just how *funny* Bruce actually was has been fuzzed over by the mixture of sentiment, hype, and politics that turned him into a radical folk hero, a stand-up Joe Hill. Even his old records can't quite clear away the haze that has enveloped him. Much of the material that seemed so potent, brilliant, hip, and explosively funny has been denatured by time, even as his reputation has risen as a misunderstood rebel artist.

Hourly, Bruce's stature keeps rising, like James Dean's, Marilyn Monroe's, and Elvis Presley's. Since he died at forty, in 1966, the avalanche of books, movies, documentaries, tributes, poems, plays, and even a song has built an impenetrable brick wall between Lenny Bruce and his legacy. There is Lenny the saintly fallen idol and Bruce the suffering working comic.

The guardians of the flame—scholars, sycophants, friends, comedians—credit him with blazing the anything-goes comedy trail that his critics now see as an eight-lane superhighway of vulgarity cluttered with bumper-to-bumper little Lennys, renegades with the mouth and chutzpah but not the mind, the style, or the charisma. The handwriting Bruce scribbled on the wall is now mainly graffiti. Apart from Bruce's two heirs presumptive, Richard Pryor and George Carlin, the landscape is cluttered with Lenny's children straining for laughs with crotch jokes that make Bruce worshipers wonder, What the fuck hath Lenny wrought?

Bruce stumbled upon a rich, sensual mother lode of American humor unmined before him: locker-room rumors, green-room gossip, Stage Deli shtick, and watercooler snickers about stars, musicians, gays, blacks, hipsters, hookers, druggies. All of this came from years of knocking around burlesque houses and whorehouses masquerading as nightclubs.

Offhand cracks he had once played to the band became public property. His underground offstage life became his act. What had always been inside stuff—the raw and ugly, the unmentionable, the socially, culturally, racially, religiously, and sexually incorrect—Lenny Bruce embraced. He dared to re-create onstage the rotten, zany, uninhibited repartee overheard at places like Hanson's drugstore, the comics' favorite New York haunt and a font of showbiz street wisdom.

Bruce—the last performer in the United States to be tried for obscenity—insisted to his final day that his words were only vehicles for ideas and insights. They were never punch lines—although many Bruce jokes, images, and anecdotes relied on jarring language to make people react: be repulsed, laugh, leave, but, goddammit, do something. Which is why even the more publicly prudish comedians of his era—Steve Allen, Bob Newhart, Bill Cosby—became Bruce diehards.

There still remains the question of how many people were genuinely amused by Bruce, how many were just pleasantly shocked listening to a guy talk dirty onstage, and how many simply wanted to take a crash course in cool. Once Lenny became a cause célèbre, people and the press were forced to choose up sides, which is when he stopped being just a daring comedian and morphed into a comic gunslinger. Many who attended Bruce's concerts went to gaze with both curiosity and horror, as today they go to see Ground Zero or NASCAR pileups. And just maybe, as an added bonus, he would get busted. Hardcore Bruce fanatics ranged from prime ministers and professors to convicts and cross-dressers. He became the man that people loved to hate—"A vulgar, tasteless boor" (*Billboard*), "Diarrhea of the mouth" (*Cue*), "The man from outer taste" (*New York Daily News*), and "America's No. 1 Vomic" (Walter Winchell). Unlike any comedian before him, he roused primitive, conflicting emotions—repugnance, anger, pity, fondness, indignation, and howling delight.

When life came crashing in on him in the mid-1960s, Bruce was at the height of his powers. He had broken free of the traditional comedy cadre. He had proved that he could go higher—and lower—than anyone who had come before, not just in his language but in his ruthless candor. He merged the blushing blue humor of the seedy strip clubs of another time with the let-it-all-hang-out sensibility of the sixties, his own time. It was a radical head-on collision of old and new comedy, of Yiddish and bebop, of burlesque and bohemia. Satire and sin was an exotic cocktail for 1960, and it left him, his fans, and America with a horrible hangover.

Bruce's actual life in the limelight was shamefully short—maybe half a dozen good years, bookended by his breakout performance at the Den in the Duane in New York in 1958 and a final bedraggled gig at Bill Graham's Fillmore West in San Francisco in the summer of 1966, two months before his death. His entire career was telescoped into about an eight-year time span, though it now seems much longer. Bruce jammed several extra decades into his forty years. Those unlived years cracked Bruce's once leading-man-handsome face, which became a wreck of Presleyan proportions—haggard, puffy, and incurably sad. The swagger had been knocked out of him, replaced by a pleading mask. He wasn't yet forty but looked sixty, a brilliant comedian broken by his own demons, and by many other people's. He was ahead of his time, he advanced it, but finally he was a victim of it.

A surprising amount of Bruce's material was similar to material performed earlier or at around the same time by Nichols & May, Bob Newhart, Shelley Berman, and Stan Freberg. Newhart and Berman both dealt in the realm of advertising and agents; Newhart's Abe Lincoln and tobacco sketches had the Bruce imprint. Godfrey Cambridge did a "rent-a-Negro" bit reminiscent of Bruce's classic "How to Relax Your Colored Friends at Parties." Bruce did Bermanesque telephone routines. And Elaine May's starlet who once dated Albert Schweitzer has clear Bruceian overtones. His jazz musician interviewing for a job with Lawrence Welk was pure Freberg (Welk threatened to sue Bruce).

Lenny's most famous monologue, "Religions, Inc.," which Paul Krassner considers Bruce's turning point, sounds like vintage Bob Newhart (if Newhart were not a well-mannered Catholic). Bruce plays one of Newhart's image doctors, or maybe Bruce was really Newhart unbuttoned: "*Hello, Johnny!* [Pope John XXIII] *What's shakin', baby? It's really been an election month, hasn't it, sweetie? Well, listen . . . yeah, the puff of white smoke knocked me out! We got an eight-page layout with Viceroy. 'The new Pope is a thinking man.' . . . Billy* [Graham] *wants to know if you can get him one of those Dago sports cars? A Feraroo or some dumb thing. When you coming to the Coast? I'll get you the Sullivan show the nineteenth. Yeah, and send me some eight-by-ten glossies. It's good television. Wear the big ring. Don't worry, nobody knows you're Jewish.*"

Likewise, Bruce's classic routine about a German talent agency handling Hitler anticipates Mel Brooks, *MAD*, and Second City. After auditioning a few actors, the first booker says, "*My name is Ben Meltzer and I am the agent here. We are trying to find a dictator today. We have no script, a couple of pages. We don't know where the hell we're going with the project ourselves. We wanna just see how you guys move, you know?"* Later, the agent asks a promising actor, *"What's your name, my friend?"* Hitler: *"Adolf Schikelgruber."* Agent: *"You're putting us on."* Hitler: *"What are you guys talking about? I wanna go back to my painting."* Agent: *"We're going to make a lot of money with you, sweetie. We should give him a different act. Put a little rhythm section behind him. . . ."* He sings, *"Poland, how I love ya, how I love ya, my dear old Poland!"* (pre–Mel Brooks's "Springtime for Hitler").

A 1962 review in the *Saturday Review* notes Bruce's often conventional premises—airplanes, agents, doctors, TV, movies—all heightened by his audacious execution; he took his parodies to their limit. His early material wasn't so much about drugs or sex as about show business, not so different from comics today. On *The Sick Humor of Lenny Bruce,* eleven of the sixteen cuts are showbiz centered—riffs on *The Defiant Ones,* Dracula, Welk, the calypso fad (a Dr. Shalom Stein parses calypso lyrics, like Steve Allen's rock lyric recitations), tabloid TV coverage of a kid down a well, plus his famous prison-film parody, "Father Flotsky." There are hints of Winters and even a Berman-like airline sketch. Many ramble on too long; "Religions, Inc." lasts ten minutes and goes a little crazy.

Bruce was a comedic challenge to keep up with, a Jewish Robin Williams zigzagging in nanoseconds from issue to issue, not always with a payoff. He punctuated his act with jive-speak ("like wow," "man," "dig this," "cat"), Yiddishisms (*"schmuck," "putz," "faygeleh," "shmegegge," "shtup," "shvartzer"*), sounds, accents, and political invective.

> DICK CAVETT: *In the list of adjectives I would append to him, I would leave out profound. All the "only worthy successor to Swift" jazz is, I feel, crapola. He was a dazzling performer at his best, and I don't know why that isn't enough for people. I think the intellectuals who sucked onto him like lampreys, and told him it was beneath him to play any room but the Parthenon, contributed to his already dangerous delusions and tragic end. Anyway, he was gifted, an immense talent who pissed away his career on drugs. All the cruddy little establishment comics, and some of the big ones, who said he was nothing "because if you have to say 'shit' to be funny, et cetera," were themselves full of it. Most of what has been written about him is a waste of good ink, and his most zealous adherents and hardest-core devotees are to be avoided.*

One reason that opinions vary so widely about Bruce the comic—as opposed to Lenny "the dark prince," "the Earl of Angst," "the Duke of Dissent," "The Führer of Fifties Fury"—is that you might see him on a Friday night and wonder what all the fuss was about and then see him on Saturday and become an ardent fan, as happened to Cavett: "I had seen Bruce twice before, and I thought he was lousy and overrated and depressing. Since all the best people liked him, I decided to try again. Then I saw what they were talking about. He was quicksilver brilliant, funny, versatile, and likable. I met him for a moment afterwards and said, 'Are you going to do any more concerts?' He flexed his fingers like a pianist and said, 'No, my hands won't permit it.' "

Like Jonathan Winters, another mad genius, Bruce was less consistent than most of his fellow sixties rebels. But, also like Winters, he was more than the sum of his routines. He had far wider range than many may remember, lining up Hitler, Billy Graham, Ike, and assorted period icons to be picked off like tin cans on a fence. His humor, his appeal, was really *who* he was—his attitudes, his eloquent body language, his in-your-face interaction with the audience.

Part of Bruce's posthumous fame is that he died young and tragically—always a good career move—and that his personal life was so dramatic. Lenny lived loudly, with wine, women, and song, as well as drugs, men, and tangles with the law. His painful denouement was a running headline in the United States and Europe. He was a legend in his time, but for many of the wrong reasons. Since his death, he's been resurrected as a comic prophet—a kind of lifetime achievement award bestowed by those who failed to properly recognize him while he was alive. Bruce's deification is America's apology for hassling him and for hurrying his demise. Had he survived, he might have wound up languishing in eternal comic limbo, like Sid Caesar, Mort Sahl, Will Jordan, David Frye, Shelley Berman, and Dick Gregory. Some think he'd have become a radical sixties artifact, like Timothy Leary, Abbie Hoffman, Andy Warhol, Eldridge Cleaver, and Ken Kesey. In his own day, Bruce's core audience was fellow comedians, critics, and a coterie of hip cognescenti—never a huge demographic slice of America.

Tony Hendra, the writer, actor, and former editor of the *National Lampoon,* writes that Bruce had no true peers: "Lenny Bruce stands alone. And he is not just 'head and shoulders' above the rest. He is off by himself, in a world essentially closed." If you're not on TV or in movies in America, you barely exist—and yet Bruce only appeared on network television *six* times. Many traditional stand-up comedians leaped over Bruce in a single guest shot or sitcom while Bruce was still slugging it out in small subterranean clubs. Far more people heard *of* him than ever heard him. For the guy in the street, Bruce was too far out on the comic fringe, too rarefied, too hip, and, to be sure, too crude.

Bruce arrived as a one-man backlash against tired mainstream 1950s entertainers. Teenagers sat home perplexed watching *The Ed Sullivan Show* with their parents, who roared at aging headliners. Bruce mocked the whole sentimental show-business monolith. As Nat Hentoff put it: "Like Charlie Parker changed the definition of what jazz could be, Lenny Bruce changed the definition of what comedy could be. He cut much deeper than anyone of his generation."

Bruce's theatrical journey moved, *Gypsy*-like, from a mama's-boy performer doing off-kilter impressions of Cagney and Karloff on *Arthur Godfrey's Talent Scouts* in 1958 (*"Kiss me, Gregory, I've been Pecked"*), to a raunchy burlesque comedian introducing strippers, to the most bizarre comic since Lord Buckley. Buckley (thought by some Lennyites to have been an influence—less his content than his cadences) was a bizarre cat who rapped out demented routines and songs in a kind of revivalist scat (many thought he was black), à la Steve Allen's "Bebop's Fables." Robert Weide, who produced the definitive documentary about Bruce, *Swear to Tell the Truth,* discounts Buckley's influence, commenting: "You'll think I'm kidding, but certainly in the early days there's a strong Jerry Lewis influence. He's totally doing Lewis. I think his influences were more movies, also Sid Caesar and Mort Sahl."

A major influence on Bruce was the fabled Joe Ancis, a phantom figure who also crops up in the comic lives of Mel Brooks, Rodney Dangerfield, Buddy Hackett, and Will Jordan. Ancis was first a neighborhood buddy of Lenny Bruce and later a regular at Hanson's, the legendary gathering place for comedians on the way up or down—a sort of Lindy's farm club at 1650 Broadway, across from the old Taft Hotel, that housed a beehive of comics, chorus girls, actors, agents, flacks, and producers.

There, the comics shmoozed for hours over stale coffee and bagels, bouncing bits off one another until chased away by the owner. Milton Berle, Victor Borge, and Jerry Lewis would drop by and take a bow. Ancis, an amateur with no performing ambitions, consistently came up with offbeat notions, off-the-wall and off-color riffs, wild impressions and one-liners that fed the starving comedians' ravenous imaginations. Ancis was the jesters' jester, an unquenchable source of the *shpritz* who took requests ("Joe, do the one about the Marine" . . . "Do the gym teacher!"), but so mike-shy that he shrank at the sight of a microphone when Bruce tried to tape him. Buddy Hackett called him "the original version of Lenny Bruce" and claimed that Ancis was the source of Bruce's "whole way of thinking about things." How much Bruce took from Ancis is an imponderable that Lenny scholars still haggle over.

Albert Goldman, Bruce's biographer, claims that much of Bruce's humor can be traced to these "shingle men," fast-talking roofing and aluminum-siding salesmen like Ancis and Rodney Dangerfield who traveled in packs and spent time on trains cracking one another up with stories and shtick. They were drugstore Harold Hills, New York Jews rather than Iowa con men.

Few outsiders ever *saw* Joe Ancis, and no tapes exist of him in action at Hanson's, but Goldman describes him as "the funniest person in the borough" (the Bensonhurst section of Brooklyn). And one of the funnier-looking—"tall, tubular and thin, with a big, long nose and close-set squinty eyes," a Jewish Ichabod Crane. Mainly it was Ancis's skill at the *shpritz* that captivated and transformed Bruce. The *shpritz,* as defined by Goldman, is "serious rapping about intellectual themes" that embodies "all the tricks of stand-up comedy—the timing, mugging, dialects, and sound effects—plus hyperbolic physical clowning. Interior monologue and stream of consciousness are the fancy words for the *shpritz.*" Mel Brooks under full sail is the supreme living exponent of the *shpritz.*

Goldman insists that Ancis gave Bruce his Jewish soul, the *Yiddishkeit* that he was denied as a boy growing up in a marginally Jewish family. To hear Bruce, you would think he came from a family of rabbis, like Jackie Mason, but Goldman states: "Lenny had come to Broadway a veritable goy, without the slightest genuine knowledge of Jewish life, customs, beliefs, values, words, or mannerisms. He was this pretty little *shaygets* [gentile boy] from Long Island with an absolutely adorable nose. It was from Joe that Lenny got the flavor of the Jewish lower classes."

One of Bruce's signature routines was in fact "Jewish and Goyish"—that is, hip versus square: "*Dig: I'm Jewish. Count Basie's Jewish. Ray Charles is Jewish. Eddie Cantor's goyish. B'nai B'rith is goyish; Hadassah, Jewish. If you live in New York or any other big city, you are Jewish. It doesn't matter even if you're Catholic. If you live in Butte, Montana, you're goyish even if you're Jewish. Kool-Aid is goyish. Chocolate is Jewish and fudge is goyish. Fruit salad is Jewish. Lime Jell-O is goyish. Drake's Cakes are goyish. Pumpernickel is Jewish. Instant potatoes, goyish. Black cherry and macaroons are very Jewish. Balls are goyish, titties are Jewish. Baton twirling is very goyish. All Negroes are Jewish. . . .*" (Jackie Mason took a similar idea and later built it into his most popular routine.)

Bruce had tapped into a secret cache of underground Jewish humor, the sort of jokes that now zip around the world on the Internet. Bruce was a Jewish comic who embarrassed older Jews because he dared use Yiddishisms usually only heard on stages at the Catskills and Miami Beach—or anywhere two or more Jews gathered. At one performance, a woman said, "He looks like such a nice Jewish boy—until he opens his dirty mouth." The writer Sanford Pinsker comments: "An older generation of Catskill comics—who did material of the Jews, for the Jews, and, most important of all, in Jewish—knew instinctively that some things were tasteless, *shmutzike* ('dirty'), not funny, even at Grossinger's. But in front of 'mixed' crowds like those at nightclubs like the hungry i? Unthinkable!" He adds: "If Bruce was a phenomenon that only the 1950s could have created and only the 1960s could have loved, he was also some very old Manischewitz wrapped inside a new brown paper bag."

Jewishness had seeped into the routines of Shelley Berman and Nichols & May, and had infiltrated Jules Feiffer and *MAD* magazine cartoons. It had been a secret subtext in the humor of everyone from Milton Berle to Groucho Marx and Sid Caesar, but Bruce dragged it out of the comedy closet kicking and kvetching. He was followed not long after by Woody Allen, Allan Sherman, and Mel Brooks. Most comics had their Jewish names—Kominski, Kubelsky, Levitch, Chwatt—bobbed like noses to Kaye, Benny, Lewis, and Buttons. Feiffer was struck by Bruce's candor about his Jewishness: "It frightened me, because when I grew up, you didn't wear your Jewishness on your sleeve, because you were essentially among enemies." Rodney Dangerfield (born Jacob Cohen) once told Bruce: "All you guys who try to get away from being Jewish by changing your last name always give away the secret by forgetting to change your *first* name. What kinda *goy* has a first name Lenny?"

EXACTLY SO. Bruce was born Leonard Alfred Schneider in Mineola, Long Island, in 1925, and grew up in North Bellmore, where his British-born father, Myron (called Mickey), was a podiatrist who, during the Depression, worked as a shoe salesman. He had married Lenny's mother, Sadie Kitchenberg—a stripper/comic known as Sally Marr (a.k.a. Sally Marsalle and Boots Malloy), who had an act called "Legomania"—after she told him she was pregnant. By the time she *was* pregnant, with Lenny, they had split up.

Their son, although surrounded by relatives and pampered with toys, a typewriter, an encyclopedia, and a Wurlitzer, spent a lot of time alone.

"Lenny was a melancholy child," said his mother, whose day jobs were waitress and maid but who also ran a children's dancing school, as well as a school for strippers at the Pink Pussycat. "Lenny grew up free," said Marr. "No guilt." A leftover flapper, Sally was as peppy, liberal, and lawless as Myron was quiet, conservative, and judgmental. "She has to charm you, disarm you, tickle you, and make you laugh," says Goldman. "She sees everybody as an audience to be flattered, cajoled, and seduced"—much like her son.

Bruce writes that his father was rarely around after his parents' divorce, but Goldman contends that his mother relinquished custody of Lenny and was gone for most of the next ten years. Between eight and seventeen, he was mainly raised by his father and relatives with what his father called "an abundance of love." Bruce's last girlfriend, a comedian named Lotus Weinstock, said: "His father was more Lenny's conscience than anyone else. His father was the duality in Lenny—the conflict." The boy was raised mostly by him but mainly influenced by his mother, whom Goldman calls "a delinquent mother but a great date"—more older sister than mom. "Lenny was like a buddy of mine," Marr told Weide. Bruce rarely mentioned his father, who, embarrassed by his son's notoriety, all but vanished ("the missing man," Goldman calls him), while Sally happily grabbed any leftover spotlight.

Marr took her twelve-year-old son with her to burlesque houses where she worked as a wisecracking emcee. "He became a man at thirteen at the Star Theater in Brooklyn," his mother boasted on a *Playboy After Dark* show. You can catch two minutes of Sally in the last scene of the film *Harry and Tonto,* as the gabby old lady on the beach who picks up Art Carney. She was also celebrated in the 1994 show *Sally Marr . . . and Her Escorts,* starring and cowritten by Joan Rivers, who says: "There wouldn't have been a Lenny Bruce without her. I loved Sally. She really lived the life. She was a comedienne before you could be a comedienne in clubs. Her philosophy became his philosophy."

Lenny left home at about fourteen and lived for some two years with a homey couple named Dengler ("They were the mother and father I had always dreamed about") on their dirt farm in Wantagh, Long Island, his fondest boyhood memory. He had knocked on their door in search of work and ended up staying; he helped out by weeding, packaging eggs, and washing jars used to sell fresh produce at the Denglers' roadside stand. He left at seventeen to join the navy and was serving aboard the

U.S.S. *Brooklyn* when it saw action at Anzio and Salerno. After leaving the service in 1946 with a dishonorable discharge for admitting to cross-dressing desires (Officer: "Do you enjoy wearing women's clothes?" Bruce: "Sometimes . . . when they fit"), he worked on freighters and tried to write a seagoing *Studs Lonigan*. He even talked of becoming a social worker, which in a sense is what he became. After being fired for fooling around on the job in crayon and peanut-butter factories, and as a Roxy usher, he went to Hollywood to study acting at a dramatic workshop on the GI Bill of Rights, and then began entertaining at amateur nights in and around New York.

His first gig was at a Brooklyn nightclub that gave him twelve dollars and a spaghetti dinner. On the strength of that, on April 18, 1949, he won a shot on *Arthur Godfrey's Talent Scouts* radio show, the talent scout being his mother posing as a Brooklyn housewife. In a takeoff on Nazi films, he did stock impressions in nonsense German, partly to hide the fact that he wasn't very good at voices ("*Aw-right, Louie, drop de oogen ge shplugen ein schvei, you dirty rat*"). On the show, he acknowledges Sid Caesar's German doubletalk as the inspiration for his "Bavarian Mimic" bit, a curious act that earned him a first-place tie.

On the tape, you can hear the eager young comic trying to please. Godfrey chuckles merrily as he brings him out—"We have another lad here. . . ." Later, on Godfrey's daytime show, *Arthur Godfrey and His Friends,* Bruce pays proper homage to the host, who comments that Lenny's novelty act may help bring back vaudeville; Lenny coos, "Thanks to you, Arthur!" One offhand comment in his routine—"*Portable radios may produce a country of people with crooked necks and flat ears*"—signals the Bruce to come, as does a bit about a bebop addict. But it was his standard lineup of voices (Bogart, Cagney, Bette Davis) that got him a week at the Strand on Broadway and another at the Tick Tock Club in Milwaukee, capering in a straw hat. He bombed at the Strand—"I was ready for them, but they weren't ready for me"—with a stolen Sid Caesar routine, word for word and gesture for gesture; "I didn't get one goddamn laugh. The audience knew it was dishonest. It wasn't me."

While knocking around drag clubs and roadhouses playing to truckers, rednecks, aircraft workers, and college boys, he tried making a few grindhouse films, bizarre soft-core grade-Z backyard epics like *Dance Hall Racket, Rocket Boy,* and *Dream Follies.* After a minor nervous breakdown, he put his money into one last movie, *The Leather Jacket,* about a disabled bum with a hearing aid who tries to save enough money to buy a leather jacket, "his symbol of virility." Said Bruce of the project: "It'll be arty, sort of a *Bicycle Thief* with a motor."

His film career amounted to a bad joke, so he began playing honky-tonks—Duffy's Gaieties, Strip City, the Bamboo Room, the Cobblestone Club, and the less grungy Colony Club—squeezing in jokes between the girls and the band breaks. Inevitably, he married a stripper, Honey Harlowe (a.k.a. Hot Honey Harlowe, born Harriett Lloyd), whom he met in a Baltimore hotel coffee shop. On first meeting Bruce, she recalled, "He was my prince come walking in. Oh, boy, like a sheik." After a quick stint in the merchant marine, he found a screenwriting job that allowed him to arrange his hours to be with Honey more often. But after five troubled sex- and drug-ravaged years, six abortions, and one child, Kitty, they divorced. During the marriage, as Goldman tells it, they were scoring drugs, shooting up, or screwing every twenty minutes. At first, Bruce tried to reform her and turn her into a respectable singer ("The Singing Southern Belle, Honey Michelle"). The couple formed an act in which he did impressions and gently crooned "How Are Things in Glocca Morra?"; she sang "Granada." They teamed up on parodies of movies, like *The Bride of Frankenstein,* in which the monster picks her up in a pizza parlor.

He stole impressions from Will Jordan's treasury of voices, but Bruce's impressions were funny whereas Jordan's were only accurate. Many were rip-offs (his Sabu was a swipe from Jordan, his rubber-lipped Bela Lugosi was pilfered from Jack DeLeon), but he wasn't after mechanical precision. For him, the voices were just a vehicle, a way to make a larger comment; their very existence was a comment about the bankrupt nature of entertainment. He saw no difference between Sammy Davis, Jr., and Billy Graham; and long before Andrew Lloyd Webber, Bruce created a superstar Jesus Christ. Bruce's best voices were not stars but closer to Jonathan Winters's regional types—enumerated by Goldman as "his lispy spade voice, his screaming faggot voice, his gravel-throated Mafia voice, his hardy-har-har Long Island contractor, his old Jewish storekeeper, his Deep South shit-kicker, his babbling *pachuco.*" To Bruce, said Goldman, "everything became an impression." Indeed, his entire act was an impressionistic view of a seamy 1950s America, such as a funny bit on the teenage glue-sniffing fad.

As a strip-club survival tactic, Bruce began to loosen up onstage to hold the attention of horny guys who couldn't wait for him to bring on the girls and get off so that they could get off. He was forced to dirty up his act to compete with the strippers, some of whom he ridiculed onstage, often cruelly (*"You see here a lovely lady. Too bad she's diseased"*). It was in these shadowy dives that Bruce's satirical worldview intersected with hard-core showbiz. Tracing Bruce's origins, Weide observes: "If you look at him on the Arthur Godfrey show doing bad impressions, his roots were really in shticky show business. Even as he was hip enough to rebel against that later, he always had one foot mired in it. Sally told me that when she first took him into the strip joints, one of the comics was Red Buttons. That was his first inspiration. He was a movie brat and loved the radio—all those early routines are movie parodies. He didn't go into it saying, 'I'm gonna be this breakthrough comic who's going to bring social satire to the stand-up stage.' "

But the strip circuit was a humid proving ground—"no pressure," he recalled. "I could try anything. Every night doing it, doing it, getting bored and doing it different ways." Just to get the crowd's attention he devised shocker lines: "*Sitting ringside,*" he said in a Chicago club, "*are two boys who got their start right here in the Windy City—the wonderful Leopold and Loeb!*" Said Honey, "He did bits about everything that happened in our life." He smashed archaic mother-in-law jokes with his own version— "*My mother-in-law broke up my marriage. My wife came home and found us in bed together.*" You can hear the rim shots in your head.

Tony Hendra reports: "He would make 'phone calls' from the stage, pretending to call up the customers' wives; he would fall down in the middle of a routine and froth like an epileptic; he would turn the stage curtain into a huge floppy hand puppet giving him head." Hendra calls him "a satiric terrorist," as when he dialed a couple's baby-sitter to say that the child's parents had been killed in a car crash. Maynard Sloate, the co-owner of Los Angeles's Strip City ("Home of Big-Name Burlesk"), said, "He went totally berserk." To quell hecklers, he enticed them onstage and hurled pies in their faces. He called nightclubs "the last frontier" of uninhibited comedy.

André Previn met Bruce in 1954, when they shared a bill in San Francisco. "We became instant friends and hung out together," Previn writes in his memoir. One day, they passed a bookstore and Previn ogled a ninety-dollar set of Mozart's letters. He fretted that he couldn't afford the three volumes and they proceeded to a coffeehouse. Bruce excused himself—to get a fix, presumably—and later returned, opened his overcoat, and plopped the Mozart books on the table. "Here, man," he said, "I brought you a present. I stole them for you." Previn, aghast, said he couldn't accept the purloined letters. "Lenny's reaction was an eye-opener," Previn recalled. "He was truly and deeply angry. 'You're not thinking straight, man,' he hissed at me. 'If I had ninety dollars and spent it to get you a present, what would be the big deal in that? It wouldn't even make a dent in me! But to steal 'em for you—I'm already on parole, man, and if I had got caught, I would've gone back to jail! Now *that's* what I call giving you a present!' " Previn, chastised, thanked him and asked Bruce to sign the books. "He grinned from ear to ear, happy again. Here is what he wrote on the first volume: *$90* [crossed out], then *$50* [crossed out], then *$12* [crossed out], then finally 35 *cents,* to which he added: 'Take it, shmuck, no one's looking. Love from Lenny.' "

At Strip City in '53, Bruce became known as "Dirty Lenny." He found that the fastest way to get an audience's attention was to go ruthlessly for the comic jugular. "If I haven't managed any rapport in the first ten minutes," he said, "I'm dead. But when I'm swinging and I feel that warmth coming up at me, I want to ball the whole audience." Bruce transformed stand-up comedy even more than Mort Sahl, whose intellect was too high-pitched for most comics' ears to catch and whose political insights demanded hard specific knowledge. Bruce simply prowled his own psyche for material.

At Duffy's Gaieties, in '55, a former druggist named Rocky who ran the joint loved Bruce and let him work regularly, bumping other comics when Bruce needed a gig. He had full run of the place and sometimes introduced the girls while in the nude himself. It was at Duffy's that Lenny found his style—part strip-club patter, part Joe Ancis/Hanson's lunch-counter shtick. He did his version of Will Jordan's concept of Hitler's life as a Twentieth Century Fox musical. When Jordan complained, Bruce told him, "Why would you [i.e., a mere impressionist] be doing this? So I might as well do it." (The premise later turned up in *The Producers.*) Will Jordan has been seething for four decades.

"He had tons of stuff but not when he started," says Jordan today. "When he won the Godfrey show, he had to hire writers. That's how devoid he was. Back in '57, when I was at the Copa with Connie Russell, this guy told me, 'You've gotta see this guy Lenny Bruce.' I said, 'I know Lenny. You mean, the German mimic?' 'No, no, he's doing all these bits.' It was very filthy but never just a dirty joke—it was always something bizarre, about an abortionist, this wild grotesque stuff."

By 1957 word had got around the L.A. club scene that a wild man named Lenny Bruce was the guy to see—and book. He got a shot at bigger clubs, the Crescendo and the Slate Brothers, but both rooms proved too traditional for him. It was a tiny place up north in San Francisco, Ann's 440, that put Bruce on the comic map in '58 and where he often returned to break in material. Run by Ann Dee, a chubby sometime-chanteuse, the club was better known for its lesbians than its comedians; the featured attraction was a gorgeous French drag queen. Dee initially wanted to book Sally Marr, who suggested that she hire her brilliant boy instead. The night Dee caught him, he wasn't cooking, and dropped his pants in desperation, but when Dee met him later, she was so charmed that she booked him, confident he would draw her kind of kinky crowd.

Hugh Hefner first caught him at Ann's 440, taken there by the columnist Herb Caen. Hefner got him booked into the Cloister in Chicago at $850 a week—the big time at last. "I hadn't realized till then how much material I had—I could just wheel and deal for hours and hours," Bruce said. "I had a whole bagful of tricks which I'd developed in the burlesque clubs." He was soon playing major rooms like the Crescendo, whose owner Gene Norman recalls: "He was a wonderful sweet guy, the nicest guy, very warm and friendly. But I was never a great fan of his. I thought his shtick was a little rough. He got busted a lot there. When he asked me to record him, I said, 'No, I don't think so.' I didn't want to be identified with that. So Saul Zaentz [of Fantasy Records] came in and made the first album, *Lenny Bruce at The Crescendo*," which put him on the showbiz map.

Nat Hentoff said: "His records on Fantasy were considered family treasures in some homes. And he was continually changing and growing as a performer. I'd sometimes hear him four or five nights a week at the Village Vanguard, and each time was like the first time." In 1958 Fantasy recorded *The Sick Humor of Lenny Bruce*, playing off the careless branding of comics of that era as "sick," with a deliberately provocative cover that depicted Bruce picnicking in a cemetery. He wound up doing seven albums for Fantasy (*I'm Not a Nut—Elect Me; Lenny Bruce, American*, etc.). The first album includes impressions and safe routines about hi-fi and movie spoofs, revealing a decidedly tame Lenny, who readily admitted he wasn't a true improviser. "People often have the impression that I make things up as I go along. This isn't true. I know a lot of things I want to say; I'm just not sure exactly when I'll say them. In an hour, I'll ad-lib four minutes—ten minutes tops if I'm having a really good night."

The "sick joke" was a plague on the land in the sixties, and Bruce was a major carrier. Sick jokes were everywhere—a nonfatal disease you picked up from playgrounds and around watercoolers (Q. "*Can Billy come out and play?"* A. *"You know he has no arms and legs."* Q. *"That's all right, we just want to use him as home plate"*). Suddenly it seemed as if everything was "sick," from Tom Lehrer songs to Charles Addams cartoons. This was also the era of silly Tom Swifty and elephant jokes, but many innocent new comics were infected. Bruce rejected the tag while gleefully exploiting the craze with bits about a mine disaster (a rescuer shouts down a hole to trapped miners, *"Stop whining!"*). Posters advertised "A Wonderful Sick Evening with Lenny Bruce" with a picture of Hitler saluting. Bruce despised the term *sick* but conceded: "All my humor is based upon destruction and despair. I see traces of Mephistopheles. If the world were tranquil, without disease and violence, I'd be standing on the breadline."

When things began heating up for Bruce, he felt picked on by *Time,* which coined, or at least popularized, the label "sick comic" in its July 13, 1960, issue, writing that Bruce "uses four-letter words almost as often as conjunctions, and talks about rape and amputees." The sick label "was just cheap-shot shorthand journalism," says Paul Krassner. "It dismissed him, so it wasn't fair because it wasn't accurate. Bruce thought society was sick and that he was the cure. He wasn't immune himself, though, for as he said, *'Of course, I'm corrupt, too. If I wasn't I'd pick up your tab.'"*

By the time that *Time* finally got around to reviewing him in its "sick-nik" issue, it said dismissively: "Bruce somehow recalls the kid in *The Time of Your Life* who thinks he is a comedian but succeeds only in spouting his miseries. Although audiences unquestionably laugh at Bruce, much of the time he merely shouts angrily and tastelessly at the way of the world."

Bruce was a little too rough for the hungry i. The critic Grover Sales recalls: "The i had an upper-middle-class Yuppie image. He made Enrico Banducci and the audience nervous, but his material at the i was fairly tame compared to later on." Banducci tried to fumigate Bruce's material and recalls once seeing a man in the audience holding his hands over his wife's ears. Bruce joked that he didn't mind people walking out on him, except in Milwaukee, "where they walk *toward* you." Bruce offended even the open-minded Banducci with a routine about two kids from Cal who were killed by some sharks off the coast; Bruce defended the sharks.

Lenny told Arthur Steuer in *Esquire* that he needed to shock people into listening: "I don't use words to get laughs. I use them for color, like Picasso—a big bold stroke. And people *do* talk that way. I want the same license Tennessee Williams has. I don't have a big vocabulary. My conversation is the argot of the gangster, the hipster, and Yiddish. But I never use any of them for a punch line." He often tempered his language to the crowd: "If I get a lot of hostility, I cool it. The club could lose its license. I'm not getting paid to offend people. My job is to entertain."

In an early piece about Bruce at the hungry i by Don Stanley in the *San Francisco Chronicle* in 1958, the critic wrote: "Not since Mort Sahl captured the imagination of the city's hungry intellectuals has a nightclub comedian caused such local stir. He has pushed satire beyond the limits agreed upon by most comics and their audiences."

Bruce had dug his way up from the strip-club circuit and the more rarefied Ann's 440, where his mother took tickets. In '58 he was booked into New York's most offbeat club, a grim, windowless, claustrophobic cave called the Den in the Duane, in the basement of a lower Madison Avenue hotel. Hentoff said it had "as much charm as the corridors of the Motor Vehicles Bureau." The thirty-five-foot-long room was run by the respected Rollins & Joffe management agency, which represented Nichols & May and Woody Allen but chose not to handle Bruce, whose humor was too raw for the gentlemanly Jack Rollins. The dark, cramped cavern was the ideal place for Bruce, a creature of the night.

Lou Gottlieb of the Limeliters first introduced Bruce to Ralph J. Gleason, the influential *San Francisco Chronicle* jazz critic. He said, "This is the leader." Gleason became obsessed with Bruce, who was suddenly being discovered, analyzed, and boosted by jazz critics—Gleason, Hentoff, Gene Lees. He broke new ground and cracked up the band, grim souls who rarely laughed. *Variety* panned him at first, saying he was *only* trying to make the band laugh. Gleason wrote: "While Mort Sahl upset conservatives, Lenny upset everybody."

The two social satirists were highly competitive. Herb Sargent recalls, "Mort didn't like [Bruce's] language. He's very pure. Mort once was coming out of the Crescendo, and Lenny sees me with him and yells at me, 'Traitor!' " People confused Bruce and Sahl because Bruce occasionally savaged politicians. He also, like Sahl, infused his routines with Freudian jargon. Albert Goldman says, "It enraged Lenny Bruce when people compared him with Mort Sahl. Lenny Bruce was a hipster. Sahl was too ridiculously uptight to be a hipster."

Orrin Keepnews, the veteran jazz record producer, comments that he "was very impressed by the fact that [Bruce] was the first nonmusical legit comic who employed the [jazz] idiom; he understood the environment. A whole generation of people grew up wanting to be Lenny"—including musicians, with whom he hung out. Gleason compared Bruce's "modal improvisations" and abandonment of linear structure to John Coltrane, to which Hentoff added, "You could really feel his beat, and there was a fair amount of bop in it." Bruce told audiences, "Please don't applaud—it breaks my rhythm."

In 1960, when he finally cracked the Blue Angel, the room was wall-to-wall celebrities. The club's impresario, Herbert Jacoby, worried how Bruce's routines—about vibrators, blacks, racists, gays, rich drunks—would play. Bruce, too, doubted that he would appeal to a chichi Blue Angel crowd, but he sold out despite a then exorbitant seven-dollar minimum. After a few minutes of Lenny in their faces, about half of the Angel's regulars, real-estate brokers and former Stork Clubbers, walked out as Jacoby paced in back with a horrified look at the thinning crowd. Bruce drove Ethel Merman from the room during a lurid routine about Sophie Tucker propositioning a Latino houseboy, and as Merman tried to wend her way through rows of tables, Bruce cried after her, "And there's *another* old has-been. She does the same thing, probably. What's wrong, you old cow?" Critic James Gavin observed, "After Lenny Bruce, fewer New Yorkers regarded the Blue Angel as a home of polite sophistication."

Most of the notables on hand (Mel Brooks, Buddy Hackett, Sammy Davis, Jr., Shecky Greene, Wilt Chamberlain) loved him right from his opening line—"*Looks like some faggot decorator went nuts in here with a staple gun!*" The showbiz contingent was on the floor when he spun out his long signature piece about a two-bit comedian opening for Georgia Gibbs at the Palladium, Bruce's favorite routine ("*Well, folks, I just got back from Lost Wages, Nevada. Funny thing about Lost Wages . . .*"). It's a brilliant deconstruction of the hack mentality—of himself, of Catskills comics, of much of show business. Bruce's comic tries to sell himself to the Palladium booker in a monologue that Goldman calls Bruce's "ultimate statement about showbiz's desperate whoring after status, its preposterous smugness, its crybaby sentimentality, and its secret contempt for the public it fawns upon": "*I got my act tight now. I got twenty-four minutes of dynamite. I know every laugh. I can work all kinds of people, too. Work the Jewish people. I learned how to say 'toe-kiss,' all right? Now, when I work to musicians, I do a bit called 'Hep-smoke-a-reefer.' All right? Got them right in my pocket. Work to the eggheads, I do the Stevenson stuff. I got it down. Twenty-four minutes— wherever I go, I kill them. . . .*" Decades before Steve Martin stuck an arrow through his head, Bruce brought us comedy about comedy, not to mention swish impressions of John Gielgud and a vast gallery of gays, drunks, and Jewish/Irish/black/WASP stereotypes.

Kenneth Tynan, the critic whose lurid *Oh! Calcutta!* did for the revue what Bruce did for stand-up comedy, first saw Bruce at the Duane and was blown away: "A nightclub Cassandra bringing news of impending chaos, a tightrope walker between morality and nihilism, a pearl miscast before swine. . . . He is seldom funny without an ulterior motive. You squirm as you smile. What begins as pure hilarity may end in self-accusation. Among those who work the clubs, he is a true iconoclast. Others josh, snipe, and rib; only Bruce demolishes." Tynan called Bruce "an impromptu prose poet who trusts his audience so completely that he talks in public no less outrageously than he would talk in private." *The New Statesman* called him "the evangelist of the new morality." Jonathan Miller, pillar of the *Beyond the Fringe* foursome whose sketches ridiculed British institutions, agreed with Tynan that "Bruce was a bloodbath whereas *Beyond the Fringe* had been a pinprick."

Sales, who became a Bruce scholar, recalls going with Dick Gregory to see him. They walked in during the middle of the show. Sales writes: "Spotting Greg, Lenny peered at the audience for an unnerving interval. *'Are there any niggers here tonight?'* Greg stiffened like a retriever, with the rest of the audience. In 1962 nobody had ever heard that word onstage, not in a white nightclub." Bruce then rattled off a string of ethnic insults, trying to defuse brutal hate words like *nigger, kike, dyke, wop, greaseball, gook, frog, sheenie,* and *jigaboo.* Gregory told Sales: "This man is the eighth wonder of the world and if they don't kill him or throw him in jail he's liable to shake up this whole fuckin' country." As it played out, all three events transpired.

The showbiz establishment went ballistic over the infidel in their midst. Abel Green, the staid, aging editor of *Variety,* called Bruce "undisciplined and unfunny"; columnists wrote, "He airs the lowest thoughts I have ever heard on a stage" and "The most obnoxious act I've seen in a night club." Hy Gardner, the widely syndicated Broadway columnist, called Bruce "just a fad, a one-time-around freak attraction." Leo Schull, editor of the theatrical trade paper *Backstage,* wrote: "Like hula hoops and calypso, the witless Lenny Bruce will have a quick flash before the public." Bruce had the temerity to ridicule show business emperors like Jack Paar and princely figures like Sammy Davis, Jr. (Judge: *"What do you do, Mister Junior, to deserve forty thousand a week?"* Defendant [sings]: *"Racing with the moon . . . That old black magic . . . Hey, Dean, I gotta boo-boo!"* Judge: *"Strip him of his Jewish star, his stocking cap, his religious statue of Elizabeth Taylor. Thirty years in Biloxi!"*)

He was becoming known not only as one of America's most inventive comedians but also as its most dangerous. Steve Allen introduced him on TV as "a shocking comedian." Bruce then was fresh, clean-cut, and roguishly handsome (Paul Mazursky describes Lenny as a Jewish Turhan Bey—"the dark looks and the lips and the sensuous Tony Curtis look"), but also fearless. Once, called onstage at the Flamingo Hotel by Pearl Bailey to take a bow against his will, he pinched her butt and raced away, only to return with a fire extinguisher and hose her down. She accused him of a racial slur when Bruce left a note backstage accusing her of performing "Uncle Tom bits you did like a lazy Negro." The casino owners gave comics Shecky Greene and Frankie Ray $200 to hustle Bruce out of the hotel.

Bruce and Philadelphia deejay and Sinatraphile Sid Mark once made a home movie in Mark's living room when the comic came to dinner. "I had just got a projector," Mark recalls. Bruce said, "Great, let's make a movie, *Dracula Meets the Jews*—I'll be Dracula and you and your wife be the Jews." In Bruce's remake, Dracula doesn't suck blood but circumcises Jews with garden shears. Chicago deejay Dan Sorkin remembers the times Bruce came into the station: "He'd listen to the show after he'd been out all night scoring dope, but I was told by the station not to play his records. He never went on the air. He'd just sit there for the whole three-hour show, six to nine A.M. He just wanted to hang out. I'd ask, 'Don't you even want to promote your show?' I never knew which Lenny Bruce I'd be talking to; it depended on if he'd scored dope or not. If he had, he was a paranoid psychotic, crazy as a hoot owl. If not, he was lucid and just a joy."

Bruce's standard movie takeoffs hatched some of his vintage routines, such as his deconstruction of prison films, "Father Flotsky," which defined him as not just a comic but as a cultural force and as a wit to be reckoned with. His X-rated movie riffs were delicious vehicles for his observations about gays, Jews, Catholics, blacks, hookers, producers, and addicts. The only way to bring those worlds alive was to glorify the language of the people who lived those lives. Charles Champlin, the critic, noted: "Bruce was a relatively minor entertainer who did not so much change history as anticipate it." Richard Pryor's street people were built on Bruce's innovations.

Bruce took on the American Medical Association, then also a juicy target for Mort Sahl and Alan King, accusing it of concocting a new disease every year by changing the name of the grippe to something more exotic, say the Asian flu, so that drug companies could hustle pricey new pills; everyone benefits except the patient, who still has his cold. Nobody but Bruce could recycle ancient premises and crush them into comedic gold, like his used-car salesman trying to sell a car that has been damaged in a suicide pact (*"There's just a little lipstick on the exhaust pipe. Wipe it right off"*), or a German car *"that was just used a little bit during the war—taking the people back and forth to the furnace."*

Other "sick" comics' jokes were outlandish, but none revealed either a social conscience or a perverse psyche like Bruce's. Many comedians had parodied the Lone Ranger, but only Bruce blasted his phony modesty for not having the decency to stick around to be thanked. He doesn't just develop the idea, he pushes it as far as he can and ends up with a neurotic loner plying kids with silver bullets. The Jewish townspeople watch him gallop off and one asks, *"What's wrong with that putz? The shmuck didn't wait! Momma made a cake and everything! I got my hand out like some jack-off—he's on his horse already! What an asshole! I'm standing there with the mayor and a plaque and everything. I'm gonna punch the shit out of him if I ever see him here again!"* Another says, *"You don't know about him. He's going through analysis. He can't accept love. . . ."* Bruce then cuts to an aging Lone Ranger forced to beg for thank-yous.

Show business was Bruce's template. "Clearly, show business for Bruce stands for American society itself," says Goldman, "and indeed in no other country have entertainers come to be more profoundly symbolic of national values than here." His comic-at-the-Palladium monologue is so desperate for love that he'll lie, contrive, and pander like the shabby comic Archie Rice in *The Entertainer*. Unlike many rebel comics who gave up, Bruce kept destroying the ghosts of Show Business Past. "He loved it as much as anyone," comments Tony Hendra, "but what he could do was expose it, ridicule it, burn holes in its dress, puke down its tux, torture its overfed little pets to death. What Bruce understood was that America received its values from the screen, from its media. Bruce saw in celebrities the monstrous clichés, frauds, smiley façade, and shameless sentimentality of America."

Long before all the pop books on celebrity mongering, media spinning, and the nation's entertainment mania, Bruce was blowing up Madame Tussaud's wax statues. He wasn't alone, but he was the most daring and honest. He gouged below the flesh, striking bone, unlike the more gentlemanly needling of Lehrer, Freberg, Nichols & May, or even the early Sahl. Writes Goldman, "He regards the audience as an object of sadistic lust, he hates it and loves it; it is the enticing enemy, and he attacks it repeatedly." Pushing to see how far comedy can go, he even insulted his own crowd of fanatics.

Malcolm Muggeridge, writing in *Esquire* in 1965, observed: "Every time he used an obscene word or expression you could feel the audience shiver with delight. It was what they were waiting for, what they had paid for, what they wanted of him. He met their requirement generously and contemptuously, spitting out the filth, as though to say, 'Take that, you vile bourgeois scum!' " The critic remarked on "the spectacle of smart, rich people being lambasted and simply loving it. Please, please, Lenny, despise us again, spit on us again, insult us again!"

Like Andy Kaufman decades later, he tested the true psychological core of his audiences, wondering, How low will they (or I) go? Will they jump through any hoop for me? What can I do that will totally alienate them? Bruce had turned the corner from satirist into sadist. As it was for many troubled comics, the audience was his shrink, the stage a place to vent very private demons. Best of all, he got the therapists to pay *him*.

Herb Caen began tracking Bruce's trajectory from his days at Ann's 440 Club. In 1959 the columnist wrote: "They call Lenny Bruce a sick comic—and sick he is. Sick of all the pretentious phoniness of a generation that makes his vicious humor meaningful. He is a rebel, but not without a cause, for there are shirts that needs un-stuffing, egos that need deflating. Sometimes you feel guilty laughing at some of Lenny's mordant jabs—but that disappears a second later when your inner voice tells you, with pleased surprise, 'But that's true.' "

Five years after cheering him on at the start of his career, Caen wrote: "Confidential to comedian Lenny Bruce: We're all sorry you're having personal problems, but an endless airing of them does not constitute nightclub entertainment, sorry." Bruce, in a classic display of self-destructiveness, fired back in his act that Caen wore a garter belt. He sent him a letter calling him "a disgrace to the newspaper industry," copies of which he sent to local news desks. Grover Sales recalls, "He called Caen a cocksucking motherfucker. The place exploded." Caen's response in print: "Lenny Bruce should be doing this material on a psychiatrist's couch, not in a nightclub." Bruce was a master arsonist when it came to burning bridges. He once took out ads in *Variety* thanking "All the People Who Have Helped Me in the Business"—and then ran an enemies list of everybody who had ever screwed him over and why ("Murray Meltzer, who didn't hold me over at the Crescendo," etc.).

His language was blunt street talk, but he was hardly the first dirty comic; others, like Belle Barth, Rusty Warren, Pearl Williams, Redd Foxx, and the notorious B. S. Pulley, rose to underground fame using filthy language (in some cases wearing a Yiddish fig leaf). The difference was that Bruce was in the public eye. Barth and company hid out, mainly in the Catskills, Miami Beach, and the saloon gulags. Foxx and his comic brethren were walled off in black-ghetto rooms; Pulley (Big Jule in *Guys and Dolls*) was a harmless curiosity.

Bruce had a way of winning over reluctant fans: "People come in hating me in the parking lot. They'll come in a group, say four people, with this hostility—before you come onstage they're rumbling, and then one of the group will like me and start laughing, and that'll really bug the other ones. 'You think that's funny? You're sicker than he is.' I know I can get them really cooking and thinking my way exactly. But when they leave the club, then other influences work on them." He wound up winning a Grammy nomination for his *Sick Humor* album, by which time he had carved out an identity, the hardest thing for any comedian.

The *New York Times* commented in 1959 that Bruce was "scarifyingly funny . . . a sort of abstract-impressionist stand-up comedian paid $1,750 a week to vent his outrage." The review compared his act, as others had, to a Salvationist lecture—"quite often funny but never in a jovial way. His mocking diatribe rarely elicits a comfortable belly laugh. . . . There are also spells of total confusion." Gilbert Millstein, in a *New York Times Magazine* article mockingly headlined "Man, It's Like Satire," revealed that Bruce created all his material himself (still a radical idea then). "He sticks mainly to the American scene," wrote Millstein, "for which he seems to cherish an affectionate repulsion."

Once the obscenity arrests began, in '61, Bruce got hung up on semantics, such as his tedious routine "To Is a Preposition, Come Is a Verb" ("*If you think I'm rank for saying it to you, and you the beholder think it's rank for listening to it, you probably can't come!*"). Gradually, he became as interested in scoring legal, moral, and syntactical points as in scoring laughs ("I really want the Supreme Court to stand up and tell me that fucking is dirty and no good"). Like Sahl, he became a comic evangelist for his cause. When judges refused to let him perform in court, Bruce argued legalities in nightclubs. He felt he was building a new constituency, but he was gradually losing his fan base.

Bruce's creative godmother, Mae West, said, "It's hard to be funny when you have to be clean." She, too, was constantly hassled by the police for writing and starring in plays like *Sex,* and once served ten days in jail

(Belle Barth also was jailed on obscenity charges). Bruce might have won the day if he'd kept jabbing at the cops and the law with just his fiery brand of humor; but that cool, Lenny was not. Laughing at the law is easy to advise now, but in the 1960s the national mood was idealistic and combative. Barriers were falling, institutions in meltdown, old values and assumptions upended; every other Volkswagen sported the bumper sticker "Question Authority." Lenny was just doing his part, carrying his spear in the cultural wars, marching alone, his satirical banner in tatters.

He saw humor in everything—in racism (asking men in the audience if they'd rather sleep with Lena Horne or Kate Smith), in the Holocaust (holding up a fake newspaper with the headline "*Six Million Jews Found Alive in Argentina*"), in marital relations (a husband begging his wife to "*touch it, just once*"). Jokes for the john, pope jokes, assassination jokes— the world was his tainted oyster. The sole exception was his own drug and obscenity busts. He discussed them, endlessly, but without the essential comic distance. He liked to say, "Satire is tragedy plus time," though for him tragedy was satire plus time. Like Sahl, Bruce broke the first commandment of satire—never preach. As the critic Walter Goodman wrote: "The man was plainly courting a crackup. The sick comic was sicker than his admirers realized. After throwing needed light into America's dark places, by age forty Bruce had nothing left to lighten the darkness of his final years."

Not two years after being discovered and hailed as the era's comic genius, Lenny Bruce's decline and fall was well in progress. His collapse was speeded up by an obsessive and troubled relationship with his wife, whom he snitched on to police about her heroin habit. Bruce felt betrayed when she became a lesbian, but Honey protested that he turned her into one via their bedroom threesomes.

After becoming a revered and reviled star, Bruce had only a few years to revel in his success before everything toppled. Much of his reputation now rests on the two-record album of his February 4, 1961, midnight concert at Carnegie Hall, which was packed, despite a blizzard. It ended at two A.M., only after Bruce had exhausted the crowd and his repertoire; he moralized, he explored his hip operation, he ravaged his fertile mind and found bits still lurking there. The climax of his career, it was a magical night during which he could do no wrong. It was Judy at the Palace, Jolie at the Winter Garden. It was the end of the beginning and the beginning of the end.

In that show, Bruce loosely raps, with jokes tucked in along the way.

He always tossed in a lot of hamburger helper—meandering sentences, fuzzy ideas, stories that circle but don't end up anywhere. Throughout, he snaps his fingers to maintain the beat, punctuated with a repeated "*Hey, man.*" Of the twenty-seven cuts on that double LP, most examine the underbelly of showbiz—Vegas tits and ass, movie sex, a singer with hair under her arms, nightclubs, burlesque, Shelley Berman, Miami ("*Old Jewish ladies are mugging the Cubans, man*"), blacks and Jews; the more daring bits involve "dykes and faggots," the clap, and the KKK. He enacts more than he narrates. He ridicules the "bad taste issue" and people who don't dig him and those who are walking out. As Ronald L. Smith recounts: "At Carnegie Hall, he was at the height of his powers, mixing hysterical older bits with free-form raps. At the Curran Theater in November of that year, he spoke largely about his harassment, rambling and misfiring." In 1962 Herb Caen had called him "a marked man now, great as he is." By '65, Bruce had declared bankruptcy. A year later he was gone.

BRUCE'S BATTLES WITH the law began at the Jazz Workshop on October 10, 1961, over a single word, *cocksucker,* which a newspaper defined as "the vernacular of the pool room in connection with a certain sexual act that was a violation of Police Code No. 205." Bruce contended, "You break it down by talking about it," but Patrolman James Ryan was not persuaded. When the van finally arrived, the account went on, a police sergeant "opened the door with a small flourish and said, 'Mr. Bruce, if you will please enter the car.' " He was released on a bail of $367 and was back onstage in time for the one A.M. show. "He wasn't the same Lenny Bruce after that," says Sales.

As Gleason wrote days later in his column, the illegal word "is familiar to every schoolboy. As has been pointed out, it is used at the bar twenty feet away from where Bruce is performing. There was no objection from the audience and the performance was by no means an open public forum." The critic argued that Bruce's message was the same as those of semanticists like Korzybski, Stuart Chase, and S. I. Hayakawa—"Bruce was engaging in attacking the tendency in our society to attribute evil to words themselves."

Says Weide: "I do think 'they' *were* out to get him, to shut this guy up—DAs, cops, the power elite who were offended by Lenny. There were phone calls. The agenda was to shut this guy up and teach him a lesson. It was a very selective prosecution-persecution." The other comics whose acts were full of raunchy material relied mainly on coy double entendres. "It was sex stuff, but it was nudge-nudge," says Weide. "Language wasn't what they went after Lenny for—that was just the loophole. Although obscenity was technically illegal, blasphemy was not. So you couldn't go after a guy for talking about the pope but you *could* go after him for saying 'fuck.' " But as Weide asks: "Who was being harmed? You had to pay money and go into a club to see this guy. He wasn't out on the street with a bullhorn or yelling 'fuck' into the hearing aids of little old ladies." As Gleason noted, "His mistake was using a microphone." Despite all the travail, Bruce never served any jail time for obscenity arrests, nor did he ever pay any fines. He was convicted only once; every other guilty verdict was later dismissed or overturned on appeal.

Respected critics like Hentoff and Tynan lined up to testify on his behalf. "He is the evangelist of the new morality," Tynan said, "ousting all other favored contenders. He is the most original free-speaking, wild-thinking gymnast of the language." Goldman observes, "Obscene language was as necessary to his act as dynamite to a miner."

Bruce's 1962 courtroom wrangles soon ensnared him in legalistic knots and narrow interpretations of the law. His message got lost, until finally all he could do was plead that he was being misunderstood and that to fairly assess him the judge must see his act. "If I was there," snapped San Francisco Municipal Judge Axelrod, "I'd want my money back, I can tell you that." Krassner recalls that Bruce told him, " 'You have to understand, I'm fighting for ten years of my life.' So for Lenny it wasn't a legal abstraction."

Bruce began dressing like a pimp in court, wearing tight black pants, matching black linen jacket buttoned at the neck, and shiny black boots, a costume that he would alternate with an equally gaudy white-on-white outfit. He kept arguing that he wasn't being obscene, merely trying to prove (weakly, forlornly) that certain words are taboo only because some people don't get their context. He paid a hundred-dollar contempt fine for saying that Judge Axelrod "violated every concept of what a judge should be. He would listen to nobody. He was a king in his palace." Bruce grabbed the red-eye back to New York for a Carnegie Hall gig and didn't appear again in a San Francisco club for two years. When he returned, the room was full of plainclothes police. There were pickets, not protesting Bruce's appearance but the high price of the tickets ($5.50).

Bruce himself often questioned his crusade, and himself. He told

Newsweek: "Sometimes I look in the fun house mirror at the carnival. I see myself as a profound, incisive wit, concerned with man's inhumanity to man. Then I stroll to the next mirror and I see a pompous ass whose humor is hardly spiritual."

After Bruce was acquitted—he was found not to pose "a clear and present danger"—he vowed, "I'm never going to say any four-letter words again. I'm bored with the dirty-word aspect. I'm off for a bigger mission. I'm going to thwart pseudo-Christians and make them live their religion or back down." The more he was persecuted, the more, like Sahl, he adopted a savior complex. One critic wrote, "He is as dangerous as any religious fanatic, as Savonarola or any other revolutionary." Gleason printed letters from Bruce followers calling the comedian a messiah and noted that Bruce, who had a Jesus obsession, wanted to make a movie about Christ. He began to dress the part of nightclub evangelist. In his last years, he wore a long black alpaca Nehru jacket, what he called his "Chinese rabbi suit." He would turn up in court dressed in a black frock coat buttoned to the chin, like some sort of orthodox high priest; he once refused to raise his right hand in court while taking the oath.

Such Bruce comments as "Every day people are straying away from the church and going back to God" were an early flower-child manifesto. John D. Weaver wrote in *Holiday* in 1968: "Long before the Flower Children began to flock to the holy land of Haight-Ashbury, Lenny had worked the same wilderness, clearing the way for their sexual candor, their drug hang-ups, their freakouts."

By 1964 the preacher in Bruce had overtaken the comedian, and he was pleading his case to the choir. Any insights got all snarled up in his battles, or in semantic soliloquies on why *toilet* is thought of as dirty when toilets are not living things. Not exactly laugh-a-second stuff. Bruce had once told Krassner that the role of a comedian is "to get laughs every fifteen or twenty seconds." Years later, when Krassner pointed out to Bruce that he was only getting laughs about every twenty minutes, Lenny made his famous declaration: "I'm not a comedian, I'm Lenny Bruce."

Goldman lamented Lenny's fall: "Gone, now, are the metaphors of the show business manipulator; gone, too, are the story-telling devices of the personal narrative and the dramatic impersonations. All that remains are sketchy, often underdeveloped, sometimes incoherent, scraps of former routines. The new material consists of deep, psychologically primitive fantasies, hurled at a defenseless audience without the mitigating intervention of art." Like nineties comics with lame material, he began trying to get by on attitude.

His physical appearance began to slide, too. Of Bruce's 1962 show at Chicago's Gate of Horn, Goldman writes, a touch melodramatically: "The once handsome, animated, brilliant performer and commentator was now a fat, bent, shabby-looking street cat, a horribly dissipated, baggy-eyed, numb-fleshed junkie, with a tragic darkness in his eyes. Merely looking at Bruce these days is a disturbing experience. Whereas in the past Bruce would walk briskly out on the floor, wearing a chic Italian suit, now he comes on stiff-legged and stooped, wearing shabby clothes, his pale face a mask of dissipation." In his act, Bruce would portray Adolf Eichmann in the dock, reciting half-baked poems, and ending with an anguished wail. Or he would turn the lights on and off, beat the drums and cymbals, and crouch in the darkness, even exposing himself to bewildered spectators.

> MORT SAHL: Lenny used to sit there at the Crescendo and play sophomoric antiauthoritarian games. One night through the ventilator I heard him playing a prom—three or four hundred high school kids—and he had them chanting, "Lynch Mort Sahl!" If he could make a few people uncomfortable he enjoyed it. I used to go down and catch his show and he would come up and catch my show. This was before the liberals got hold of him. At the time, he didn't swear, he just talked about the movies. And he was pretty damn funny. He ad-libbed a lot, which very few do even today. Everybody held him up as Voltaire. Lenny wasn't a sick comic. What he was was truthful. He was this warm Jewish guy who loved kidding people—a funny comedian, a great impersonator, and a very sentimental guy. I did not find him profound; he was wholly ignorant politically. And I disagree with those who now put him on the cross. Even Lenny knew that only you can kill yourself.

Obscenity was the official charge against him in 1962 in Chicago (one of his offending lines was, "If we'd have lost the war, they would have strung Truman up by the balls"), but his real crime was sacrilege. When he antagonized the Chicago police, DAs, judges, and the public by making sacrilegious cracks about the Catholic hierarchy in a heavily Catholic city, they threw the Good Book at him. He ridiculed the revered Cardinal Spellman and Bishop Sheen; he insinuated that the Church was in cahoots with the mob; he taunted the pope for wearing a ring costing $10,000, which could house "forty Puerto Ricans living in one room." All in all, not the best defense, but eventually the charges were dropped.

Bruce was also persecuted in Philadelphia because, as in Chicago, he offended the city's conservative sensibilities. "He seemed to get a kick out of rubbing salt in wounds, and he was becoming intolerable," said Goldman. Sid Mark supplied Bruce with his own attorney after the comic was busted at the Red Hill Inn near Philadelphia. Mark says he was in the room when Bruce, the attorney, and the judge met there. Bruce told Mark to leave—he didn't want him to be involved or to testify in his behalf (Dan Sorkin, the Chicago deejay, had already been fired for testifying as a Bruce character witness). "He said, 'I'm leaving, but you have to work here tomorrow.' That's how thoughtful he was," notes Mark. "I was in the dressing room when it [a bribe] was all going down. He told me, 'I don't want you to be here to see this.' They had made a deal whereby he would plead guilty and give the judge ten thousand dollars [to let him off]. But when he appeared before the judge on live TV the following Monday and the judge said, 'How do you plead?'—and he said, 'Not guilty, and incidentally I can only come up with fifty dollars'—I knew he was in trouble." Even so, the case was dismissed, and the judge was disbarred and later killed himself.

The notoriety only egged him on. A Bruce lawyer said, "Lenny felt the publicity of a trial would help his career tremendously." Not quite. He wasn't allowed back into Australia after he told a stunned Sydney audience, "Tonight, I'm going to do something that's never been done before in a nightclub—I'm going to piss on you!" He was also banned in England—"as if he were a stag movie," one critic wrote. After being deported from England, he said, "It's chic to arrest me." In London, where he was embraced by the satirical establishment—Peter Cook, Dudley Moore, and Jonathan Miller (and by the Establishment Club itself, where he performed)—there were equally celebrated walkouts: the playwright John Osborne, poet Yevgeny Yevtushenko, actress Siobhan McKenna.

By 1965 he had been arrested nineteen times, with one obscenity conviction, later overturned on appeal. After he was acquitted in San Francisco, he felt free to do his act anywhere, but all the arrests triggered a domino effect: "I guess what happens," mused Bruce, "if you get arrested in Town A and then in Town B—with a lot of publicity—then when you get to Town C they *have* to arrest you or what kind of shithouse town are *they* running?" Krassner noted, "It became an actual news item in *Variety* when Lenny *didn't* get arrested one night." Toward the end, the only states Bruce could work in were California and Florida.

In despair, Bruce finally went to the FBI and asked them to investigate collusion between police and prosecutors in various cities. By now, the cops were tearing open his candy bars looking for drugs. During a Café Au Go Go gig, he was arrested for performing a bizarre fantasy about Eleanor Roosevelt baring her breasts for him (*"What Capitol Hill biggie's wife has a pair of lollies that are setting the Washington-go-round a-twitter?"*). Clubs were notified that they could lose their license for booking him; the Troubadour in Los Angeles posted a jittery disclaimer: "The Troubadour neither condones nor condemns Mr. Bruce's statements since it is our policy not to interfere or limit in any way an artist's performance on our stage." The LAPD sent a cop to the club who spoke Yiddish and who cited Bruce for using *schmuck* and *putz* (penis) in his act; in the report, he noted, "Suspect also used the word '*shtup*' [copulate]."

Through all his arrests, he never attacked the cops, who he realized were just doing their jobs, but the comedian in him was insulted by the fact that he couldn't testify in his own defense, to do his lines—well, justice. He joked, "In the halls of justice, the only justice is in the halls." Maury Hayden (a.k.a. the comic Lotus Weinstock), his last girlfriend and fiancée, said, "He had an obsessive faith in the Constitution." Weide adds, "He had this naïve, childlike view of the law, that you could just go up to a judge and reason with him and chum up to him. He got caught up in the technicalities." Observes Robin Williams of one case, "I think he just wanted the respect of this uptight goyish judge." As Lenny told his attorney Martin Garbus, "If only the judges knew me they'd like me." He was a hard man not to like. As the critic John Leonard wrote: "It's hard to imagine how Bruce was ever perceived as a threat to the republic. Imagine a comic who sold out Carnegie Hall at midnight in the middle of a blizzard not being allowed to tell jokes at the Café Au Go Go?"

MIKE NICHOLS: *Do you know when he stopped being funny? When he started getting persecuted, and when he started reading from the court transcripts in the show. It got sort of sad. You can get so obsessed with an injustice that you lose sight of what's funny—that's what happened to Lenny very late—and then it happened completely. But when he was himself he was really funny. He said a flamenco dancer is a guy applauding his own ass. That's so literally exact. He had that clarity of observation.*

Bruce's celebrated New York trial in 1964 was his last chance—he now had more courtroom gigs than club dates. But he felt he was at last in friendly territory. A celebrity on trial was still novel stuff, even for New York City, and the media—finally—turned out in droves. Hentoff wrote that Bruce had many fans among the assistant district attorneys, but the one assigned to prosecute the case, Richard Kuh, was not among them. Hentoff described Kuh as "a humorless, ambitious assistant district attorney" and a "dime-store Torquemada."

A petition signed by everyone from Richard Burton and Rudy Vallee to Reinhold Niebuhr and Theodor Reik was sent to Mayor Robert Wagner, and a laundry list of literati testified on behalf of Bruce—Hentoff, Feiffer, *Newsweek* drama critic Richard Gilman, and, astonishingly, the conservative gossip columnist and prim *What's My Line?* panelist Dorothy Kilgallen, who called Bruce a "brilliant . . . moral man" with "valid, important comments, whether or not I agree with them." Confronted with a routine about a man caught by his wife having sex with a chicken, the ladylike Kilgallen demurely replied, "Well . . . he got into some *other* animals, too." And in response to the district attorney's reading of a catalogue of obscenities, the nonplussed columnist parried, "They are words, Mr. Kuh. Words, words, words." She testified before the three-judge panel that Bruce "employs these words the way James Baldwin or Tennessee Williams employ them on the Broadway stage: for emphasis or because that is the way that people in a given situation would talk."

Gleason noted: "The people we expect to fight against censorship—the writers, the magazines, and the ACLU—all seem to be passing this one up." A few months before he died, Bruce wrote Krassner a letter. "Lenny was talking about death," says Krassner. "He died in August and in May I got a letter from him saying he was still fighting the New York laws, and he drew a doodle showing Jesus on the cross. And the speech balloon says, 'Where the hell is the ACLU?' "

Even a petition circulated by Allen Ginsberg and signed by a blue-ribbon celebrity intellegentsia (Max Lerner, Gore Vidal, James Baldwin, Lionel Trilling, George Plimpton, Lillian Hellman, Irving Howe, Dwight Macdonald, Alfred Kazin) couldn't help Bruce regain his name or his career. It was too little too late. (Bruce's legal team had hoped that a recent court ruling favorable to Henry Miller's novel *Tropic of Cancer,* in which it was established that a work of art should be judged in its entirety, not dissected word by word, would help their client.) Gleason noted, acidly, that the New York literary establishment didn't take out their fountain pens until Bruce was busted there; "Welcome aboard, fellas, it's nice to have some company," he wrote. "It's been kind of lonely out here on a limb all these years." Magazines covered the trial with unlikely star reporters—Feiffer for the *Village Voice* and Philip Roth for the *New York Review of Books;* Roth told a reporter he thought he was funnier than Bruce.

The attorney Ephraim London, a tall, professorial figure, faced off against Kuh, a stand-in for his outraged boss, DA Frank Hogan, who had gotten Edmund Wilson's *Memoirs of Hecate County* banned in the 1940s. Garbus has described Hogan's pursuit of Bruce as "a holy mission." Everything about Bruce offended Hogan's version of Catholicism, most of all the comic's ridicule of Spellman, Sheen, and, maybe holiest of all, Jacqueline Kennedy, whom Bruce had accused in his act of "hauling ass" to scramble out of the limo after her husband was shot.

London patronized Bruce, calling him "insane," and Lenny felt that the lawyer wasn't listening to him and told him so. When Bruce finally dismissed London, he made a desperate, last-ditch plea to Judge John M. Murtagh: "Please, Your Honor, I so desperately want your respect. The court hasn't heard the show. I can give you the show verbatim. Let me tell you what the show is about. Counsel doesn't understand my show. I tape-recorded every day of this trial. . . . There are two thousand one hundred and thirty errors [in the transcript]. . . . Let me testify, please, Your Honor. Don't finish me off in show business. Don't lock up these [six thousand] words." Murtagh responded, icily, "The court urges you to be represented by *counsel.*"

Bruce maintained all along that reading his words cold in court robbed them of their meaning, context, and, most of all, their humor (even though he had been convicted after doing his act in a Chicago courtroom). Bruce was thus forced to defend a cop's rendition of his act. "*His* act *is* obscene. I'm [charged] and have to hire lawyers, maybe go to jail— because of *his* act. There's something screwy about the whole thing." Arguing as eloquently as any free-speech defender, Bruce said: "The ideas I have are now imprisoned within me, and unless this court acts, will not be permitted expression." Garbus writes: "He was enraged that we would not let him take the stand. It was his naïve conviction that the law was a perfect and independent organism that could produce a magical justice if only it were left to operate unencumbered by those who practiced it."

A scratchy, at times unintelligible, tape of Bruce's act was played in the courtroom, but the comic highpoint arrived when London asked a witness of the Café Au Go Go act, "Did you see Mr. Crotch touch his bruce?" Spectators at the trial responded with "strangled laughter," said Goldman, who called the trial more theater than a search for truth. According to the biographer, defense witnesses failed to prove that Bruce was "a brilliant social satirist from the crude, unfunny bits mercilessly laid out in the transcript. . . . These liberal intellectual witnesses turned the case into the conventional issue of the blameless artist versus the uncomprehending world."

The issues were distorted and misstated, he insists, but perhaps saddest of all were the tapes themselves, which didn't reveal Bruce at the peak of his powers. In fact, even the *best* recordings of Bruce don't really capture him, partly because he was a careless performer when it came to mike technique. Gleason wrote in *Rolling Stone:* "Lenny always treated the microphone like an enemy. He would walk away from it, back off, come in too close and, in effect, do everything wrong. His early records, all of which he produced himself, were nightmares for the engineers." And Bruce recorded everything—performances, phone calls, interviews.

In the dark, grainy hour-long performance film *Lenny Bruce,* shot in 1965 at Basin Street West, Bruce doesn't look that wasted, nor does he seem crazy, just obsessive and rambling, dressed in what seems to be pajamas and a robe, standing before a stone wall that looks like a dungeon; the lighting was intentionally low to protect his weak eyes. Even here, just a year before his death, he has great vitality, manipulating voices, inflections, and body language for laughs. He seems fresh, even when he's rerunning old routines. There are a few hopeful laughs at first and then just polite sympathetic titters as he skips from topic to topic without segues. You're struck by how tame and harmless it all now sounds, and also by how sophisticated he is about the holes in the law: he wonders aloud if a tape recording of his act could be admitted in court, since he would, in effect, be incriminating himself. Claire Harrison, then a publicist and now a psychologist, remembers seeing Bruce at Basin Street West: "That was the night I thought he was gonna die. I thought he was falling apart. I never saw so much perspiration! He was a maniac onstage, but, like Woody Allen, he made his neuroses work for him." Bruce's final audiences were filled mainly with adoring intellectuals and hard-core Bruce addicts before whom he could do no wrong. At Berkeley, Bruce did an obscenity-free show, as if to prove, belatedly, that he could be as proper as Bob Newhart. The great irony of Bruce's downfall is that he was just as funny when he worked clean.

In his final two years, Bruce was teetering on the edge—literally. In 1965, in a bizarre accident, he was almost killed when he fell twenty-five feet out of a second-story hotel window in North Beach near Enrico's Coffee House. When police found him, he was shouting profanities and embracing Eric Miller, his sometime guitar accompanist and the foil in the "Colored Friends" sketch.

The *San Francisco Chronicle* reported that when he arrived at Mission Emergency Hospital, "the 38-year-old comedian put on a performance so sick that doctors slapped a bandage over his mouth while he was being treated." He broke both ankles, fractured his pelvis, was put on the critical list, and wore a body cast for six months. Eric Miller said that Bruce fell "because he got carried away explaining something about freedom to me." He said that they had talked all night and that Bruce fell while standing on the sill, crashing through the window. The story mentions no drugs, but Krassner says, "He had LSD and was leaning against the window and lost his balance and fell backwards." In midair, claims Krassner, Bruce quoted John Wilkes Booth: "Men shall rise above the rule!"

Peter Breinig, a former *Chronicle* photographer who says that he and Bruce once shared the same girlfriend, believes that Eric Miller "pushed him out the window. I think Miller was giving him a blowjob. That's what Miller told me." Breinig insists that Bruce had occasional homosexual forays, but neither Krassner nor Weide can verify it and Miller is dead. Banducci says: "Oh, yes, he liked boys, too. He went both ways. He talked about it. He kissed me on the mouth all the time and said, 'I wanna fuck you.' " Breinig adds: "Lenny swung any way that was convenient at the time. I *know* he and Miller had something going. For him, it wasn't a big deal. He just didn't give a shit. There are some guys who don't care what they fuck, but you couldn't call him a faggot. For him, fucking was fucking—you know, 'Let's get it on.' "

Clearly he was catnip to females of all ages and kinds. Bruce referred to himself as "cute 'n' kissy"; he hypnotized women with what Goldman called his "swami eyes." One woman a day was his minimum daily requirement. "The women would come and just pass out," recalls Sid Mark. "He could have any girl in the audience. He once scored one of the undertakers' wives in town and he did her in a coffin." Weide comments, "He was a terrible womanizer. If he could sleep with a friend's wife and get away with it, he would, just as a sport." Bruce slept with Krassner's then wife while his confidant was in Chicago interviewing Sahl.

A year before tumbling through the window of the Swiss-American

Hotel, Bruce was interviewed by the *Chronicle*'s Donavan Bess, who wrote that the comedian "seems much older than a year ago." (The newspaper photo depicts him hunched over a tape recorder playing back testimony.) Bess wrote: "His brown eyes glowed with joy just once, while reading extracts from U.S. Court decisions on obscenity. 'Beautiful!' he exclaimed. 'Magnificent writing!' He savored the eminent sound of 'Judge Learned Hand.' He exclaimed, 'That is his *name*!' "

The hassles, huge debts, and his inability to be hired made Bruce a doomed but not a mute man. He began making bizarre remarks, such as dedicating his autobiography, *How to Talk Dirty and Influence People,* to Jimmy Hoffa—"a true Christian, because he hires ex-convicts as, I assume, Christ would have."He considered going on welfare when the few job offers he got fell through. He tried to market his despair, planning to sell the minutes of his San Francisco trials and the tape that was played in court. He boasted to Melvin Belli, whose office served as Bruce's classroom while he boned up on pornography case law, that the tape would sell half a million copies; Goldman reports that Bruce's four records for Fantasy had, by 1962, sold only fifty thousand copies. Bruce claimed that *Playboy* and the *New York Times* refused to run ads for an album, forcing him to sell it via mail order. The Philadelphia DA ordered him to take a drug test and submit his routines for "review" before being permitted to perform there. An arsonist tried to burn down a theater where Bruce was to appear.

He took over his various trials from the lawyers, working out of a Greenwich Village hotel room piled high with stacks of trial transcripts and law books; it was his customized prison. Garbus said the room "resembled a storage space that had been ransacked by vandals." After that, he holed up in his cluttered office at home, plotting legal strategies, his room a waste dump of wadded-up paper, tape reels, and legal pads.

In 1965, beset by legal woes, Bruce asked a federal court for protection from harassment by the law, which he filed *in forma pauperis* (as a pauper) because he couldn't afford the fifteen-dollar filing fee. Krassner helped bail him out with $500. He had been hired by *Playboy* in 1963 to edit *How to Talk Dirty and Influence People,* which was excerpted in the magazine. Bruce and Krassner stayed at the YMCA in Milwaukee and worked on the manuscript. (Goldman, a rival for the Bruce-insider franchise, labeled Krassner a Bruce groupie "who wanted to be Lenny Bruce when he grew up . . . a competent editor [who published] slightly sycophantic interviews" with Bruce. Krassner dismisses Goldman's biography: "I resisted it. I skimmed it. It was so sensationalistic.")

Krassner says, "We fact-checked the most outrageous thing in [*How to Talk Dirty*]"—where Lenny pretended to be a priest in Miami, soliciting $8,000 for lepers, to whom he sent $2,000 and kept the rest for "operating expenses"—"and it checked out with the Miami Police Department. It was a matter of record. Lenny may have gone off on fanciful things now and then, but the book rang true. I didn't ghostwrite it." Bruce had backed out of an earlier as-told-to autobiography, saying, "I don't need a collaborator. I just need a typist."

SHELLEY BERMAN: *He was angry before anger was in. He spit in the face of the establishment. He was magnificent. Sahl turned me on to him. We used to go see him. He was a handsome guy. He was sleek and slender, dark hair and dark eyes, and he wasn't dressin' up for work. He'd wear a Levi top and Levi pants, boots, and he was different than we were. It is hard to talk about Lenny. If we join in the beatification of him, elevating him to martyrdom, we may not be adhering entirely to the truth. The thing that Lenny Bruce would've laughed at most was the attempt to enshrine him. He would've found that the most stupid bit of hypocrisy. He wasn't all that heroic. He began to believe he had a mission. The truth is, every comedian has a mission—to make the audience laugh. Someone else will decide for you whether you've accomplished a mission.*

Ron Fimrite, the *Sports Illustrated* writer, saw Bruce during his decline at the Off Broadway in San Francisco and recalls: "It was a sympathetic audience—there was hardly any sound at all. He droned on unmercifully. He was obviously psychotic by this point. He had absolutely no interest in the audience at all. It was awful and embarrassing—painful. *He* wasn't embarrassed at all. A few people walked out. I don't recall any hecklers, just stunned silence. You knew he'd talk about the trial but you thought it'd be entertaining. It wasn't even sarcastic—just bitter and angry—and this was the same guy who'd had me falling out of my seat just a few years earlier."

Krassner comments: "He wasn't a performer anymore—he'd become an icon. The crowd would yell for him to do this or that bit, but he'd take out the legal papers and read them verbatim." (A large chunk of Bruce's autobiography is taken up with trial transcripts.) Many who went to see Lenny by then were thrill seekers wanting to say that they'd seen him in person; the club Le B in south Miami Beach hired him simply to capitalize on his scandalous name.

The Crescendo's Gene Norman recalls: "At the end, he became his own lawyer, but by then he was crazy. I didn't want to play him anymore because he got too rough on the stage. Sally, his mother, said, 'Gene, Lenny loves you, you've gotta give him a chance.' So sure enough, I brought him in and he was terrible. He was disconnected, wandering all over the place. One night, a couple sat in front of the stage and at one point the man got up and said, 'You're disgusting.' They actually confronted him. He said to them, 'You can't laugh 'cause you can't come.' Jesus, I wanted to crawl under the table. Everyone heard it. Only by the grace of God the sheriff didn't bust me. But on top of that he was an enormously sweet pleasant man. I loved Lenny."

One of the major unanswered—also unasked—questions about Bruce's demise is why so few comedians came to his rescue. The day after he died, comics fell all over themselves praising his genius, but when he needed them—when his livelihood had died—most entertainers disappeared. Gleason wondered: "Why don't Steve Allen, Jonathan Winters, Shelley Berman, Irwin Corey, and the rest of them who know Bruce is a genius, make a public statement to support him? It might be a help. Where are these people?" Looking out for their own careers, maybe. Steve Allen did, in fact, book Bruce for one of his last TV appearances, in which Bruce warbled his own plaintive ballad, "All Alone."

Phil Berger notes in his book on seventies comedians, "Curiously, it was the showbiz types that Lenny always was putting down who came through with money at his death. Milton Berle was very generous. Sammy Davis, too." Buddy Hackett and Jackie Gayle remained loyal. Garbus writes that Sahl refused to take the stand for Bruce. "Sahl, who saw himself as an avant-garde political satirist, was openly resentful of the adulation and respect accorded Bruce by the liberal intellectual community, an audience he felt did not take him [Sahl] seriously enough." Bruce's steadfast inner circle also included the writer Terry Southern and the cartoonist and writer Shel Silverstein. Few editorials championed his cause, despite the First Amendment issues. *Variety* refused to accept his ad stating he was available for work.

An unlikely woman rushed to Bruce's rescue—a society matron named Judith Peabody. The sister-in-law of the governor of Massachusetts and from a prominent Boston Brahmin family, she was moved by a column Dick Schaap wrote in the *New York Herald Tribune,* headlined "Where Are Lenny's Friends Now?" He began, "It used to be fashionable to be for Lenny Bruce," and recounted how Bruce had been abandoned by his old allies. Peabody sent him a check for some $50,000 and invited him to her upper Fifth Avenue duplex, telling Goldman that it wasn't so much his cause as his humanity that deserved support. "He touched me very deeply," she said. "He was a beautiful man. Very kind, very thoughtful, very gallant, gentlemanly, funny, loving, appreciative. He was a tragic picture. Poor, overweight, tattered lovable creature!" She took him under her wing and visited him in his scruffy room at the Marlton on Eighth Street in Greenwich Village, with its soiled carpet, dripping faucets, and stuck windows. Bruce lived at the fleabag hotel when in New York and asked that it be repainted Dufy blue each time he checked in. Peabody ordered him, "Eat! Walk! Take care of yourself!" and took him out for strolls and tea at a nearby coffee shop.

After visiting him at the Marlton, Nat Hentoff wrote: "He became almost a Dostoyevskian character in his interest in the law as a redemptive force. Lenny was absolutely convinced that the Constitution would make him whole again. And then the gigs would come flowing back. . . . Maybe his case would go as far as the Supreme Court. Maybe he could do his act before the Justices. *They* certainly would understand the redeeming social value of his performances." As Bruce said when accused of offending society values, "I'm society, you're society—there is no 'they.' "

In his own memoir, Krassner quotes an unnamed former assistant New York DA, who confessed: "Bruce was prosecuted because of his words. It was the only thing I did in [Frank] Hogan's office that I'm really ashamed of. He didn't engage in any conduct that harmed someone else. We drove him into poverty and used the law to kill him." He was found guilty in the New York trial on November 4, 1964.

Of his drug problems, Weide says: "He wasn't a junkie in the technical sense—he wasn't a big user of heroin. He was a speed freak— methedrine was his drug of choice. What happened was, he would be up two or three nights in a row working on his briefs. He wanted to 'crack the code' that would absolve him. He had this terrible fear of going down in history as that awful vulgar pornographer. He'd say, 'Jesus, I got a daughter. I don't want her to grow up thinking that her father is this or that.' He'd be shooting speed just to stay up and literally not go to bed; people would have to bring food in to him. Then he would just crash and he'd be a wreck. Bruce had prescriptions for many of the drugs and carried frayed letters around in his wallet from doctors explaining his drug needs for treatment of hepatitis and pain. "You couldn't say no to Lenny," testified a doctor who provided him with clean needles and prescriptions for a virtual medicine cabinet of drugs.

JONATHAN WINTERS: *I'm drinking sauce in Chicago and he's got a rubber band around his arm. I said, "Lenny, don't do this," but the junkies don't want to hear this. The initial Lenny Bruce was a funny, capable, bright guy. He was a rebel, needless to say, nothing was sacred. But like alcohol [with me], the drugs took him out. He got dirtier and dirtier, and the next thing you know the whole act became a thing about the Feds, and who wants to come in and see that?*

Wilfrid Sheed, reviewing the performance film *Lenny Bruce* for *Esquire,* was one of the few who actually spoke positively of the comic's manic final performances: "Bruce was impressive in those last years. Every step down into paranoia and monomania seemed to add a new dimension to him. This is no Borscht Belt frippery, let alone a desire to shock, but a language of prophesy, of dirt, and sacrament. The punk stand-up comic became a man of real stature, under the zany harassment of polite society. Until, that is, it all became too much for him and he toppled over the edge."

In mid-February 1966, Bruce played Los Angeles for the first time in three years, and the *Los Angeles Times* reported: "Although the opening night crowd was quite small, they bunched down in front and Bruce was able to bring the brethren the sermon." During his last few months, joints like the Trolley-Ho off Sunset Boulevard were willing to risk a bust to fill the room for a few nights (Bruce, forever suspicious of club owners, made sure that a friend took tickets). John D. Weaver wrote: "He was back in the cheap rooms, working for a dwindling flock of admirers, a few hecklers, and cadres of vice squad officers who brought Yiddish interpreters along so they didn't miss anything juicy. It was painful to see the wreckage of Lenny's talents. Lenny stumbled around in dark, airless cellars, chanting a lewd litany that had long since lost its capacity to shock or to edify. The once-shocking words could be found in any popular novel." Added Weaver, "While Mort Sahl split doctrinal hairs about the grassy knoll and burned autopsy notes, Lenny was citing *Regina v. Hicklin.*"

Bruce once quipped, after getting a rare nightclub booking, "I feel like it's taking me away from my practice." After hiring and firing a carousel of attorneys, Bruce finally represented himself in a Los Angeles obscenity trial, which he lost despite the aid of ace lawyers like Garbus coaching from the sidelines. "The problem was Lenny," claimed Goldman, "who clasped the asp of persecution to his bosom and would not let go of it, even when its sting proved less than fatal." Had he lived long enough for his case to reach a more enlightened, mid-sixties Supreme Court, Bruce might have prevailed. Garbus writes, "In the final reckoning, Lenny was vindicated. But what he never quite understood was that . . . the law often works slowly. Justice has a rhythm of its own; it is, finally, a lethargic process that moves to the ticking of its own clock. Lenny just ran out of time."

At home, meanwhile, a growing harem of women tended to Bruce's needs—his ex-wife, mother, daughter, girlfriends, old lovers, and live-in groupies formed a caring female commune. They shared a common cause—"Lenny showed rare genius in getting all his girls to cooperate without visible friction," said Goldman. After Edmund Shea, a photographer friend, was also busted for drugs, he and Bruce would compare legal strategies when Shea stayed at his L.A. home. He remembers the odd layout: "His downstairs was totally separate from the upstairs—there was no internal stairway, so you had to go outside to go upstairs or downstairs. He lived upstairs. The idea behind it was that he was going to work and nobody could bug him from downstairs. He also had a funny little area out by the pool where he would go and nobody could see him." In his last months, Bruce turned into a bearded, pudgy man with shaggy, greasy hair, and dark, hollow eyes who kept alert living on Cokes, candy bars, and methedrine. Long gone was the sassy guy who, just a few years earlier, had skipped onto *The Steve Allen Show.*

When, in January 1966, Krassner, no stranger himself to sensation, ran an obituary of Bruce in *The Realist,* readers believed it. Krassner's and Gleason's phones rang for days with calls from distraught fans. The editor says he published the hoax with the permission of the "deceased," who resented that people who died got all the applause. Lenny, of course, was still technically alive, although his career was comatose. Seven months after *The Realist*'s make-believe obit, Bruce died for real. His death, on August 3, 1966, was as blood-chilling and controversial as his life, as mysterious as any Raymond Chandler novel. He was found dead on the floor of his bathroom in his Hollywood Hills home, a bunker fortified by barbed wire and a concrete gate, wired with security systems. Bruce's housemate John Judnich found him with narcotics gear strewn nearby, a kettle bubbling on the stove, and the electric typewriter humming, with an unfinished sentence from his latest defense on the page: "Conspiracy to interfere with the fourth amendment const—."

The coroner at first could not conclusively cite the cause of death. Foul play? Accidental overdose? Suicide? That same day Bruce had received a foreclosure notice on his home. Krassner writes, "Lenny's death was on the cusp of accident and suicide." Lotus Weinstock told Goldman that Bruce had almost OD'd on sleeping pills a few days earlier and had been talking of death and acting oddly, even for him, shredding a sleeve with a razor so he could plead poverty before a judge. Ten days later, the coroner ruled that Bruce had died accidentally of an overdose of morphine (not heroin, contrary to the legend). Goldman contends that it was a suicide, triggered by the foreclosure threat, but he concedes: "The argument against his having committed suicide is almost as compelling. It begins with the fact that Lenny loved life on any terms. Why should he sacrifice every future prospect of accomplishment and pleasure for a single moment of revenge?" Phil Spector's mordant conclusion: "Lenny died of an overdose of police." Dick Schaap wrote: "One last four-letter word for Lenny. Dead at forty. *That's* obscene."

To Bruce scholars like Weide, some aspects of his death look suspicious, but others don't. He says: "It definitely was no suicide—he was in the middle of a sentence. There was water boiling. What John [Judnich] said was that it was not his usual scene. I think it was a John Belushi situation. Someone in the house fixed Lenny at his request. Someone said let me tie you off, and then he keeled over and they panicked and ran. The business in Goldman's book about Bruce killing himself because he got a letter that day that his house was being foreclosed was just Goldman's sense of the dramatic."

> SHECKY GREENE: *Lenny was a poor soul. We were kindred spirits. I didn't see Lenny as everybody else saw Lenny. They all saw him as a genius. I saw Lenny as a fucked-up human being. I saw someone destroying himself, and I know, because I was drinking at the time and I saw what was happening to me and I couldn't control it. You see someone else who's losing control, you know he's killing himself. So what kind of genius is that if he gets on a stage and he gets a few laughs? That's not genius. I saw all that, and the people kissing his ass, and the women saying, "You're brilliant." I used to say to him, "Lenny, you're not fooling anybody." I also watched the demise of Lenny onstage, just talking about the case. I watched him in San Francisco, and all the police were there. For two hours he was brilliant. Guys were backstage taping everything he said, and fights going on. I said, "Lemme get away from this. This is craziness." In my career I never saw things like that. People were insane around him.*

Spector, who called Lenny Bruce and Abe Lincoln his two greatest influences, paid for Bruce's funeral. He also shelled out $5,000 for some lurid police photos of the dead and naked Bruce on the bathroom floor that a cop sold him, shots that some say were staged. Says Krassner: "When the cops came and found him, they pulled his pants down, as if to say, 'Even in his death, we'll have the last word.' "

Judnich, also Bruce's sound engineer, threw a microphone into the grave at his burial at an Orthodox Jewish cemetery in Los Angeles. His memorial service attracted SRO crowds, and the cemetery had to close its gates for the day. Later, Bruce fans tried to hold their own service at a nearby Catholic church, but were turned away by a priest when he learned the name of the deceased. An alternative service was held anyway, in the backyard of a disc jockey's home. His tombstone reads: "Lenny 'Bruce' Schneider . . . Peace at Last."

The Bruce obituaries came from every direction, not just from the anticipated mourners. Bruce's death, like his life, was momentous. Even the conservative *National Review* observed that "Lenny, like Whitman and D. H. Lawrence, was basically moved by a strange but sincere vision of the sacredness of life, and like them he used obscenity to express it." The writer, touched more by Bruce's humanity than by his humor, recalled seeing him in the Midwest, when he wasn't very funny: "He was not even saying outrageous things, as he usually did to give the impression that he was funny," but rather "preaching an ad-lib sermon for kindness to children." *The New Yorker* remarked on Bruce's "huge appetite for life, in its transiency, absurdity, and potentiality. What he wanted was to make it all more real, to startle his listeners into realizing how much they were missing as a result of their evasions. His questioning was never malicious; it was affectingly—as well as risibly—hopeful. Lenny Bruce was a chronic optimist." Banducci says, "Lenny wasn't doing it for immortality. He did it because he thought he could really save us." When some comedian called the departed Bruce "a real hero," Redd Foxx cracked, "You got to remember one thing: heroes ain't born, they're cornered."

Weide regrets that Bruce's playful side has been forgotten (he once wanted to do an X-rated *Candid Camera* that would include such stunts as showing a pretty girl on the street with her skirt blowing as men try to look up her dress), but his most surprising quality, says the filmmaker, was that "he had a sort of Andy Hardy/Norman Rockwell American-dream thing about him. His politics were not strictly liberal; there was a kind of conservative streak in him. Also interesting was his respect for the people who were tearing him down. He didn't call the cops pigs; he called them peace officers. He said they were just blue-collar guys trying to do a job.

"The thing that remains with me," Weide adds, "is the thing that's most overlooked about him—what I'm left with after all the self-destructiveness and the drugs and the legal problems—is a very warm-hearted—*haimish,* to use the Yiddish word—kind of guy who really had no intention beyond just entertaining people. Everything else was laid on him." Only weeks before his death, Bruce told Banducci, "I want to be remembered as a pioneer and a legend and not as a faded nightclub comedian."

STEVE ALLEN: *There are not many comedians to whom I would apply the word "genius." But I would in the case of Bruce. He was far more than just a successful nightclub stand-up comedian; he was like Jackie Mason, a comic philosopher. Lenny was never simply trying for a cheap laugh but was invariably making a philosophical point. There was a great difference between the vulgarity that Bruce employed and that to which the average nightclub comic will resort. Lenny seemed to me the first of the modern comedians. He broke entirely new ground. Lenny was an original, gifted, and, I'm afraid, part-crazy comedian. Everything he said was deep, biting, cutting, and usually brilliant. American comedy generally has nothing whatever to do with morals. But Bruce was, among other things, a moralist. While Bruce's humor was usually quite heavy and freighted with social philosophy, it often had a component of pure playful silliness.*

As Artie Shaw once cracked about the passing of Glenn Miller, "Death is the best publicity agent." Bruce was worth much more dead than alive. Record-company executives who wouldn't return his phone calls before his death now began circling his grave. Lawrence Schiller, who later researched Goldman's Bruce biography, set to work on a documentary about the comedian's life for Capitol Records, entitled *Why Did Lenny Bruce Die?* He later produced a book, *Lenny, Honey, and Sally.*

Suddenly it got very crowded on the Bruce bandwagon. A promoter of Bruce's 1961 Carnegie Hall concerts offered to sell tapes of the three-hour show for $50,000, and United Artists Records brought out its elegant two-record set. A year after his death, the 1965 performance film shot by John Magnuson of Bruce at Basin Street West, the only film of him that survives (its original purpose was to be viewed in court), was a hot cult item. By 1970 two movies were in the works—a TV movie, *The Lenny Bruce Story,* and *A Tough Gig,* which depicted Bruce from 1959 to his death. In 1974 Fred Baker released a documentary, *Lenny Bruce Without*

Tears; Sandy Baron did a one-man show, *A Celebration of Lenny Bruce;* there was even an animated cartoon version of his Lone Ranger routine, *Thank You, Masked Man.* In the end, Bruce became a figure of worship. After his death, Grace Slick wrote a song called "Father Bruce." The beatification of Lenny Bruce had begun. Eddie Izzard, the cross-dressing British comedian who played Bruce in a London revival of *Lenny* in 2000, hailed Bruce as "the Jesus Christ of alternative stand-up."

> JOAN RIVERS: *Lenny Bruce was the breakthrough for everybody. He talked about things that really happened. He dealt in hypocrisy and hurt and greed. So what does he get for this? He gets arrested for talking dirty and dies a broken man. Now people are calling him the Rabelais of his time. The day after he died, the* Times's *obituary included comparisons to Swift and Twain. And I said, "This poor slob couldn't get a cabaret card"—which you needed in those days.*

Out of the woodwork crept people who had once met Bruce in an elevator and now claimed a close personal friendship. In making his documentary, Weide had to weed out the imposters: "The three biggest things that everyone in L.A. has in common are: They all lived in Chaplin's old place, they were invited to Sharon Tate's party but couldn't make it at the last minute, and they were all with Lenny the night before he died. Lenny was responsible for that. If you got five minutes with Lenny, he truly made it count. So a lot of people really were deluded that they knew him better than they did." Sally Marr's career—mainly as Lenny Bruce's wacky mom—was revived after Lenny died. She popped up on TV shows like *Playboy After Dark* as an amusing curiosity, did a few small parts in movies, and spent a lot of time grandmothering comedians (even loaning them money) who wanted to be near Lenny's mom and muse.

Writing in 1968, Goldman predicted a boom market in Lennyana: "Live, Lenny was a pro. Dead, Lenny is a property." Goldman himself produced a biography as controversial as the comedian himself, a tantalizing stew chocked with trivia, hyperbole, and suspect conjecture. Sally Marr, who died in 1997 at ninety, rejected much of the book, insisting, like Gleason, that Lenny was a "drug user, not an addict," and could have quit any time he wanted to but didn't—a pretty fair working definition of addiction. She asked, "How come no one ever discusses the real Lenny Bruce who loved his home, was a good father and a good son?"

It was only a matter of time—five years, actually—before someone wrote a play about Bruce. Julian Barry's *Lenny,* a "musical drama" (originally an unproduced screenplay) starring Cliff Gorman, opened on Broadway in 1971. The 1974 Bob Fosse movie, with Dustin Hoffman, was far more successful. Orrin Keepnews scoffs: "Both the play and film were bullshit. They denied the humanity of the man. They made him into a monster. He was just your ordinary talented fucked-up person. He wasn't a very stable human being, but name me one comic who is?"

Sid Mark says of the film: "It should have been called *Leonard*. It wasn't Lenny. He didn't even carry himself like Lenny." The film, important now only because it imposed what would become the generally accepted view of Bruce, sanctifies the comedian but fails to humanize him. Fosse depicted the seedy, sweaty atmosphere of Lenny's life in grim, grainy black and white, but without capturing the colorful man who lived it. Says director Robert Zagone, "The only thing wrong with the movie is that Dustin Hoffman wasn't funny." Gleason wrote: "Hoffman plays Lenny like a wet lox most of the time, making of him a whining, sniveling, giggling, self-conscious performer . . . an incoherent slob . . . and losing altogether the charm and the vitality of the real-life Bruce."

How would Bruce have fared had he lived? Weide's vision: "I'd like to think he'd stay on top of the times and would be working, but I do have this more realistic fear—it's kind of the Brando/James Dean theory. Brando had it all over Dean as an actor, but Dean died tragically and so his posters still sell and teenagers have his pictures on their T-shirts. But Brando had the audacity to live and get fat, so he's just made fun of on *Saturday Night Live*. If HBO had been around then, Lenny would still be alive today—he'd have had a place he could have performed. If Lenny had lived he probably couldn't get booked on the Conan O'Brien show now. He'd be in Shecky Greene territory." David Steinberg imagined that Bruce would be doing Dexedrine commercials. Bruce always feared that he would soon be history. "I'm thirty-nine and already I can't relate to Fabian," he wrote in his memoir the year before he died. "There's nothing sadder than an old hipster."

WOODY ALLEN: *I was not his greatest fan. Of that rush of comics that came along—Mort Sahl, Jonathan Winters, Nichols & May—I thought Lenny Bruce was fifth or sixth in that group. I don't think there's any comparison between him and Mort Sahl. He was okay. Decent, but not great. I found him talented but pretentious. Sometimes funny. But nowhere near in the class of these others. If I say this, people say, "Oh, he's putting him down." I'm not putting him down. I don't think I could touch him—he towers over me. He's just not one of*

my favorites. But he's been the big influence. Most of the ripoffs are of Lenny
Bruce. I had no interest in his personal life whatsoever. I was interested in him as
a comic, but he didn't mean much to me personally. Bruce was not particularly
brilliant. He pandered. He was and is idolized by the kind of people who must
invent an idol for themselves. Many middle-class people and squares followed
him very avidly, because he was—at a time when it was forbidden—talking
dirty, and clearly on dope. And a huge amount of his audience was straight,
middle-class people who thought they were doing something wicked, that they
were suddenly "in the know," suddenly hip and rebellious. And they tittered and
snickered at all the marijuana references as if they knew just how it was and
they were souls in common with him.

No long-dead comedian has more influenced today's stand-up generation. Jon Stewart, of Comedy Central's *Daily Show,* says: "He should be
remembered for the incredibly lyrical way he used the language. He
didn't step over the line just to step over the line. There was method to
his madness. Nowadays too many comedians are just saying, 'Look what I
can get away with.' " Margaret Cho says she tapped into her own angst
through Bruce's routines.

But much of what Bruce fought for—the license to speak your mind
onstage—has been squandered by comics who haven't got a whole lot on
their minds. Bruce took the fall for Andrew Dice Clay, Eddie Murphy,
Sam Kinison, and countless Lenny wannabes. He was the patron saint
of the Bad Boy School of Comedy of the 1970s—John Belushi, Cheech
& Chong, Richard Pryor, *National Lampoon,* George Carlin, and Mel
Brooks. "What's lacking now is wit," says Weide. "It's too bad Lenny had
to sacrifice himself for Howard Stern. Stern doesn't rock any boats
because he's harmless."

There is also a savagery among many contemporary comics that was
foreign to Bruce, who may have ruined stand-up comedy unintentionally
by opening it up to anyone nervy enough to step on a stage. During the
last two decades, open-mike nights turned hundreds of stand-up clubs
into comedy karaoke bars. While he loosened things up for comedians to
say whatever they like onstage, most of Bruce's disciples (from Buddy
Hackett to Eddie Murphy) proved unequal to the task. Only Pryor, Carlin, Bill Maher, and the late Bill Hicks, a direct descendant, took up his
license to seriously discuss today's taboos. Bruce dwelled on sex, but he
got out of bed long enough to venture into religion, racism, politics,

hypocrisy, and social values. Most of Bruce's comic acolytes are still diddling in the bathroom and refuse to come out.

"Nightclub comics set free in the Bruce legacy," Lawrence Christon wrote, "can now *shpritz* their dull obscenities unendingly without fear of reprisal; practically none, however, seems willing or able to go after America's institutional thought and prevailing social currents. For that, the figure of Bruce seems to grow larger and larger as time goes by." Bruce freed comics' tongues, but not their minds. He finally triumphed, posthumously, but you have to wonder: Was it all really worth it—a great performer destroyed just for the right of future comedians to shout "fuck" in a crowded theater?

Color-Coordinated

GODFREY CAMBRIDGE

If I had to only talk about racial matters I'd go outta my cotton-pickin' mind.

GODFREY CAMBRIDGE, the portly but courtly black-on-white comedian, enormously funny and highly original, presented a comic persona he squeezed in somewhere between Dick Gregory and Bill Cosby. His razor-sharp racial barbs felt painless wrapped inside so much personal warmth. Cambridge, who died at forty-three after battling weight-related health problems, gave racial humor a more everyday face. If Dick Gregory confronted racism in his act, and Bill Cosby dodged it, Godfrey Cambridge teased it to death.

Cambridge was dry, droll, and immensely human. The critic Mel Gussow noted, "Some of his commentary is as acidulous as Gregory's, but not nearly as alienating." Gregory was always a little wary, and Cosby a bit cocky, but Cambridge struck no poses. A natural charmer, he spoke softly about his maddening life as a black man in white America, but he transcended the jokes with above-the-fray common sense.

He was a cultivated, intelligent comedian whose ample girth and heavy-lidded look belied the quick literate chap underneath, a reader of books fluent in several languages. The comedy writer Abe Burrows, who didn't fling bouquets lightly, noted: "Most comedians who do topical humor seldom make you laugh. They evoke respectful nods and appreciative grunts. Very little laughter. But Godfrey has the comic spirit."

The actor and writer Ossie Davis says, "Godfrey's comedy was intellectual, and it drew an urbane civilized conclusion from chaos and ridiculousness and bigotry. That lifted him above the street-corner humor and put-down and things that were the staples of black comedy, particularly those things that denigrated us as a people."

A rotund teddy bear of a man of equally immense charm and wit, he spoke with a precise diction that sounded almost British. Despite his refined demeanor, he had a very short fuse when it came to slights, racial and otherwise. He once destroyed a shabby dressing room with a fire ax after requests to repair it went unheeded. When a taxi driver splashed mud and refused to allow him, Ossie Davis, and Ruby Dee to enter his cab, Cambridge ripped off the door as the taxi idled at a stoplight. Davis later said, "He was frightening when the rage was upon him and undoubtedly, when provoked, the most violent man I ever met."

A former cabdriver himself who knew the hack manual by heart, Cambridge reported some forty cabdrivers who had passed him by, despite the fact that he carried a black attaché case that served as a kind of doctor's satchel, loaded with medications—an antidepressant, diet pills, a painkiller, and a hay fever remedy. Davis compares Cambridge to the writer James Baldwin—"on the verge of destroying himself until he finds that people are listening," at which point he stopped screaming. "What saved Godfrey was his humor." He didn't go out of his way to look for trouble, but as a heavyset black man, trouble often sought him out. As he once admitted, "People say I have a way of walking into a place like I just bought it. I've always had a kind of arrogance—of knowing just who you are. It's part of my West Indian heritage." He was a West Indian from Canada, and he didn't cope very well when confronted with the realities of life in New York, notes his ex-wife.

Davis thinks Cambridge was different from Gregory and Cosby in his sense of defiance. "His comedy didn't protect him. It was easier to get under his skin. He wasn't as successful at hiding behind his comic persona as others were. I knew that under certain circumstances Godfrey would possibly kill somebody. I don't know that other comedians were that vulnerable or explosive." When he moved to WASPy Ridgefield, Connecticut, Cambridge and his wife were hassled. In Detroit he roughed up a rude Howard Johnson's manager who failed to provide heat or room service.

When he fell through the rotting plywood floor of his new fourteen-room house in Ridgefield, Cambridge said, "I was displeased." He sued the Realtor for fraud but pleaded with the reporters not to turn it into a racial incident, saying, "Please, media, if this is a slow race day, don't make this a black and white story. Green is where it's at." In Ridgefield, a wealthy white enclave, his wife was once run off the road by a car, one of his two teenage daughters was threatened with death if she went to a school dance, and—in an incident right out of *Ragtime*—his car was doused with gasoline while parked in the driveway. He finally bought a pistol and erected a two-hundred-foot chain-link fence he was later forced to remove. "You hear stomping outside the windows. You hear gunshots on your property. People drive all the way up your driveway and then back out. The same strange cars keep driving by the house. You get worried."

Yet onstage he radiated great sweetness. He had a tart, incisive mind but refused to be prodded into taking stances. He mocked black stereotypes—in fact, racism itself—and his hilarious, Tony-nominated creation of Cousin Gitlow (*"Yo is de boss, boss"*) in Davis's *Purlie Victorious* put to final rest the shuffling Stepin Fetchits and Willie Bests of an earlier shameful time. But he equally resisted stereotypes of his own time. "When you see me comin,' don't look for no image," he said. "If I had to only talk about racial matters I'd go outta my cotton-pickin' mind." As one writer put it, "When they finally smash the Negro stereotype mold, they're likely to find the man who supplied the hammer is Godfrey Cambridge."

"All my life I ignored being colored," Cambridge told Gussow. "I never felt racial prejudice because I was the only Negro. It's terrible for someone to reach the age of twenty-one and realize he's a Negro, to spend all that time leading a sheltered life." But he also noted, "You can't duck a fight." He was exhausted by the various causes of the 1960s, saying, "I hate the word *relevant*. When I walk out there on a stage for an hour, I say, 'I'm gonna have me some fun.' I've got to be me. If they want a Dick Gregory or a Jane Fonda, then they're in big trouble."

He ingeniously skewered black clichés. Ashamed to buy a watermelon, he tells the grocer, *"That big squash over there, wrap it up—put handles on it"*; and when later stopped by a friend, he explains, *"That's my bowling ball."* He mused, *"Do you realize the amount of havoc a Negro can cause just walking down the street on a Sunday morning with a copy of the* New York Times *real estate section under his arm?"* He proposed integrating parties with his "rent-a-Negro plan." He cheerfully told audiences, *"It's so nice to go overseas and be hated solely because you're an American."*

Paul Mazursky, the director and former comedian, says, "He was underrated and very funny. He captured the essence of the black dilemma without being anti-white." Like his line chiding black upward mobility, about the executive who carried an attaché case with fried chicken in it, adding just the right mitigating personal grace note to what might otherwise have been a stereotype—*"I'm not goin' to give up everything just to live with you-all."* As one writer put it, "Godfrey is out to shatter all clichés, on both sides of the fence, and on the fence as well." But he also slipped in more pointed jabs: *"Skydiving is the ultimate solution to the Negro problem"*;

and of a separate-but-equal swimming pool in Mississippi: "*the pool for blacks had no water but the diving board was higher.*"

Cambridge took on race but took it further by kidding the very notion of confronting it, as in his comment about going to parties where "*everyone would want to talk about the race problem and I'd want to talk about my golf scores*"; and he despaired of ever finding a flesh-colored Band-Aid. Commented a critic, "Never once does he go for the easy racial laugh." He stated, "My freedom starts onstage." He even dared to say, in 1967, "I'm tired of these Sidney Poitier I'm-helping-white-people roles. I'm a man. I have love, hate, and I'm tired of being asked to understand. I have my own problems." He spoke of wanting to rewrite *The Dick Van Dyke Show* with himself as a contented suburban homeowner (exactly what Bill Cosby would do many years later).

At one point, he said: "I don't deal with race anymore. I cannot carry that concrete sack with me onstage every night. There's nothing worse than the prophet who delivers his message and then runs around saying, 'Did you get my message? I'll repeat it for you.' I got it! I just go in wherever I find stupidity. I don't feel my function is to go out and whip white people. If you need to feel guilty and you need a flagellant, go hire a Negro, pay him above scale, and have him whip you."

Not unlike Alan King's, his comedy act was a series of major complaints about the minor corporate insults embedded in the system. Cambridge quoted phone company rules to operators reluctant to return his dime; stapled IBM cards that ordered, "Do not fold, staple, or mutilate"; and complained to the New York license commissioner about laundries that sent back shirts with missing buttons. He took little guff and buffed up his life experience for his act. "I am Horatio at the bridge, defending the little man," he said. "I'm a screamer for the little man. I get my phone fixed because I'm Godfrey Cambridge. Why do I have to be Godfrey Cambridge to get my phone or car fixed? How about Joe Blow? I don't deal with race anymore."

GODFREY MACARTHUR CAMBRIDGE WAS BORN in 1933 in New York City's Harlem, where his parents raised him to be proud of their British Guianese origins. His mother liked to say, "If you're not West Indian, you're nothing." His father was an accountant who wound up unloading coal cars in Canada, and young Godfrey grew up in Nova Scotia with his grandparents before returning to Flushing High School on

Long Island. His class yearbook called him "Unforgettable Godfrey Wonder Boy Cambridge," with "a laugh, a chat, a pun, a friend to all who knew him, a smile for everyone."

He went to Hofstra University on a scholarship but left before graduating in order to act. After placing fourth in a national laughing contest, he earned ten dollars a night as a hired "laugher" at Broadway comedies. He had a great laugh, recalled the dancer Pearl Williams: "He laughed so loud it filled up the theater. He had such a big heart. He embraced so many people. When he laughed at a show, everyone just said, 'Godfrey's here.'" Following a series of equally odd jobs (popcorn-bunny maker, airplane-wing cleaner, maternity-hospital driver, hot-rod racer), he began performing in clubs and eventually worked his way up to headlining at the Aladdin Hotel in Las Vegas, the hungry i and Basin Street West, and Mister Kelly's. He wrote a book, *Put-Ons and Put-Downs,* and joined The Living Premise, an integrated improvisational comedy group in Greenwich Village.

Cambridge became a comedian while awaiting acting jobs and, following a sparkling debut in 1964 on Jack Paar's *Tonight* show, cut his first record, *Here Comes Godfrey Cambridge, Ready or Not.* We were ready. He won an Obie playing a white woman in Genet's *The Blacks,* the first of several antistereotypes for him; he starred on Broadway in *How to Be a Jewish Mother,* played a suburban white man who turns black, a Jewish cabbie in *Bye, Bye, Braverman,* and the slave Pseudolus in *A Funny Thing Happened on the Way to the Forum* in a Berkeley, California, production in 1965, three decades before Whoopi Goldberg did it on Broadway to huge hoopla.

He had begun as a low-billed comic at black rock-'n'-roll shows at which cops roamed the aisles with dogs, but within a few years had worked his way up to performing at the White House, where he was introduced as "a distinguished actor and social commentator." Cambridge was indeed a man of learning who traveled with a bag full of books (heavy on black writers like Eldridge Cleaver, LeRoi Jones, Gwendolyn Brooks, and Regis Debray), plus a shortwave radio, tape recorders, exercise bicycle, target rifle, stereo, and cameras. He read all the New York newspapers and twenty-five magazines; during the 1965 New York newspaper strike, he read German newspapers.

When an agent asked him if he could make his comedy act "more racial," Cambridge told him, "Hell, no. The more I broaden, the better I am. I want to do the little things that bug me. I'm not going to tour the

South. I'm a northern urban Negro and I don't know *nothin'* about Mississippi! I've never been farther south than Washington, D.C." Howard Storm, a comic who knew him well, says, "He was very easy to be around. You didn't feel he was watching you all the time."

But Cambridge was conflicted about race. "I don't think he was very happy being black," a friend said. "He was very bitter about being black," according to his ex-wife Barbara Ann Teer, founder of the National Black Theatre. "Not skin color, but being a gifted individual and not being able to get a job in his profession." Mainly he was frustrated at being overlooked for movie roles because of his size and skin color. When a director told him, "We can't use you because there's no part for a Negro," Cambridge said, "Use me and I'll make it Negro." Says Teer, "He wanted to be a very great actor," and would lose whatever weight it took (he once dropped 117 pounds in a few weeks). On a binge, he could down ten cheeseburgers, two steaks, mountainous sundaes, with a side of doughnuts. Teer describes him as "a lovable teddy bear, but very cynical, with that refined wit."

Teer says: "He'd lose eighty or ninety pounds in a month, and he had asthma. He had a lot of physical challenges that he constantly overcame, because he loved performing so much. He had two or three wardrobes for different sizes. Godfrey would eat two dozen doughnuts and two quarts of milk at a sitting. He ate out of an emotional pain. He'd eat and eat and get big and big and then he'd have to go lose it. It was up and down, up and down, a roller coaster. He treated his body as dramatically as he treated his life." She recalls, "When Godfrey asked me to marry him, he was very large, and I said I would not even consider it and he lost almost a hundred pounds. He worked very hard at it." He tried every diet, vowing, "I just have to lick it. I gotta be around to enjoy this money."

His marriage to Teer, she says, "had its moments, but he told a lot of jokes about me that I didn't like, and I would have to sit there and laugh. We got along pretty good, but his temper was one thing I could not deal with. You never knew when he would explode. He needed to be babysat. He was just not stable in his emotional life. He could blow up in a grocery store, or he'd blow up in a laundry if they broke a button off his collar. It kept him from getting jobs. It wasn't a secret. All that stuff he made into jokes. Everything he hated or that he was cynical about, he turned it into something humorous." When someone jumped out of the window one time and committed suicide, we were all sitting there and we heard this big clump sound, and Godfrey said, "When is their apartment vacant?" He was turned down for a role on *Hogan's Heroes* because he was "too fat," then taped the rejection notice on his refrigerator. Davis says, "His feelings could best be described in a joke he created, in which he was describing the white maiden in distress, and he was Superman flying to her relief, and when she saw it was Godfrey coming she turned and grabbed the monster."

Teer, who was married to Cambridge for three and a half years before they divorced, recalls: "Everywhere Godfrey went he was hassled. He was a very clear person about his likes and dislikes. If you bumped him the wrong way you would get his wrath. He was potentially a very volatile person if he thought you were disrespecting him. He was very misunderstood. If you're a genius and way ahead of your time and your creative ideas are not nurtured by the mainstream that you want to be a part of, you could be very sad."

Davis comments, "Godfrey deeply wanted to be loved and respected. I'm from the South and I never expected that, but Godfrey expected to be appreciated. He was a little hurt that it never happened. America never grabbed Godfrey and kissed him full on the mouth." He died in 1976 before that could happen while on the set of a movie in which he was playing the African despot Idi Amin.

Cambridge's deepest comic artistry was revealed in his unsettling "Uncle Arthur" character, a sadly self-deluded old black performer who rationalizes a lifetime of shuffling roles by explaining to his dubious fellow actors, "*Shufflin' is actually a way to make the white man suffer—while waiting for his food, it gets cold. Shufflin' is a sign of defiance.*" Arthur justifies his racist portrayal as "*historically accurate—dats how it* was *in dem days.*" Cambridge said of the piece, "It was the first time I trusted myself to use pathos as well as comedy." Harry Belafonte compared Cambridge to Ray Charles as "a great interpreter of the Negro soul."

Sibling Revelry

THE SMOTHERS BROTHERS

When you're on the ledge, and things push you there, it's real hard to keep the whimsy intact.

             —Tom Smothers

———

I T W O U L D H A V E B E E N H A R D to find two less offensive satirical comedians of the early 1960s than the Smothers Brothers. At a time when Lenny Bruce, Mort Sahl, Dick Gregory, and Nichols & May were taking wild swings at politics, racism, relationships, and American society, amiable Tom and Dick Smothers came on like lucky winners of the Dad's Club Talent Show.

Their comedy doesn't translate well onto disc or into print. Much of the boys' humor was the alchemy of their onstage attitude and their Cain-and-Abel relationship. The earnest Dick was forced to untangle his dimwit brother's rambling and confused mind, his convoluted introductions, or to scold Tom for absurdities and political incorrectness. To survive, he often told Tom just to shut up and sing. Tommy was the obtuse wide-eyed lad delivering book reports on a book he hadn't read, trying to slide by on cute, lopsided grins, quack facts, and dubious history about, say, the origins of the Venezuelan Rain Dance. Dick was the exasperated but devoted teacher stuck with a hopelessly muddled pupil.

They managed, miraculously, to keep this modest act alive through stagecraft, sly interplay, and good-humored banter. They are living refutation of the truism that comedians need to change with the times. As with a classic vaudeville routine, they're doing essentially the same act they did in 1959 at the Kerosene Club in San Jose, California. They've polished and updated routines, but the style, structure, and themes haven't changed. Notes the comedy guru Herb Sargent, "It's one joke, yeah, but it's a good joke."

It was never meant to be more than that, and it could get pretty silly, but the mix of clean-cut comedy and clean musicianship kept them popular. If you'd had to guess which sixties stand-up act might have the shortest life span, the Smothers Brothers would likely have been your choice. Yet here they are, more than forty years later ("For Smotherly Fun,

Come to Harrah's," laughs an ad), outlasting most of their more daring comic brethren, survivors of a midcareer breakup and the calamitous front-page TV finale that almost ended their careers in 1969.

Television produced precious little satire in the fifties and sixties—so little that it can be counted on the fingers of one hand. There was Sid Caesar, there was Steve Allen, there was Ernie Kovacs, and, briefly, there was *That Was the Week That Was.* Then there was the Smothers Brothers—or, more accurately, *The Smothers Brothers Comedy Hour.* Tom and Dick, the shyest of rebels, played innocent bystanders on a revolutionary journey, boys next door strumming perky folk-song parodies. But their TV show did not originate from next door.

It took nearly three seasons for CBS to get wise to what was going on in the network's otherwise orderly family and to send the brothers and their audacious radical friends packing. Tom and Dick seemed such *lovely* fellows, too, not front men for a TV revolution. Who would guess that they fellow traveled with such threatening desperadoes as Pat Paulsen, Steve Martin, David Steinberg, Mason Williams, and Pete Seeger? Tom's major comic influences were not exactly cutting edge: George Gobel ("He didn't do jokes—he did timing, and he played the guitar," says Tom), who mastered the art of the boyish simpleton conveying twisted wisdom, and Burl Ives, a back-porch balladeer.

Tom and Dick Smothers were the perky shills for the subversive satire that, between 1967 and 1969, turned their jaunty variety show into a comedy terrorist cell. The Smotherses were our jolly hosts, but also the secret instigators (Tom far more than Dick) of songs and sketches that aggressively took on Lyndon Johnson, Richard Nixon, the Vietnam War, and racism while singing the praises of drugs, sex, the counterculture, and everything else that wasn't nailed down. Looking at the shows now, which give off the happy-go-lucky, devilish air of its chummy hosts, they seem as innocent as old newsreels of the naughty Jazz Age. You can almost whiff the sweet aroma of pot amid the psychedelic sets and sideburns, the daisy decals and turtlenecks and peace pendants; it all feels like a Sunday-night frat party at Tommy and Dicky's place.

Nobody was more surprised at the satirical trench war that *The Smothers Brothers Comedy Hour* became than its genial hosts. "It was just a variety show with some satirical sketches to spice it up," notes Dick. Suddenly they found themselves locking horns with network censors over material that would scarcely have been noticed had it turned up in a nightclub rather than on prime-time TV. What began as sweet summer replacement lemonade hung around for years, laced with acidic LSD. The Smotherses were always deceptive, looking like a warm-up act for, well, George Gobel. Dressed in preppy sherbet-colored blazers or tuxes and bow ties, they gently kidded the self-righteous folk-song fad. That was it—the entire act. No politics; no social commentary; no messages.

They were folksingers who skipped into comedy, with no satirical agenda whatever. Tom even once said, "Comedians are afflicted emotionally. People like Jonathan Winters walk the thin line. We don't want to be that good. We're too normal. We're not even ethnic." Like Allan Sherman's ingenious parodies, which mocked folk music a different way, by viewing them through a Jewish American prism, they tapped the pop trend at its height. Following in the wake of the Weavers, Peter, Paul & Mary, Joan Baez, and the countless slicker commercial versions, ersatz ethnic balladeers serenading the nation with "John Henry," "Tom Dooley," and "Witchita Lineman," Tom and Dick went after the folk-song craze from their perch at San Jose State College. The widely popular Kingston Trio, out of nearby Stanford University, cast an imposing shadow ripe for Smothering.

The brothers Smothers were at the time members of Phi Sigma Kappa fraternity at a college then known for, and proud of, its reputation as a party school, and not a whole lot else. Tom, the older by two years, was a half-hearted advertising major who dropped out before his senior year; Dick, an education major, dropped out in his junior year. By then (1959), they were local stars at the Kerosene Club, one of the popular beer-and-pizza cellars that edged the campus. The team was originally a threesome, the Smothers Brothers & God, with God played by bassist Bobby Blackmore.

The Smothers Brothers built their act on a meticulously market-tested routine as classic as Laurel & Hardy, Abbott & Costello, Burns & Allen, and Martin & Lewis. It was an updated reprise of the good-natured buffoon (Tom, on guitar and banjo) trying the patience of his wiser, long-suffering partner (Dick, on bass fiddle, guitar, and banjo). They found endless ways of revamping folk songs—ironically, the very stuff of sixties grassroots revolt—"*Hang down your head, Tom Crudely,*" Tom would sing, and Dick would interrupt to correct him; or Dick would explain the history of a song and Tom would break in with dopey responses ("*When John Henry was a li'l baby, sittin' on his daddy's knee / His daddy pick him up, threw him on the floor, and said, 'This baby's done wet on me.'*"). Dick would roll his eyes and shout, "*When you talk like this you act like a stupid fool, Tom!*" and Tom, stung, would shout back, "*That's my job!*"

Tom later said, "The comedy just sort of edged its way in." At first, he did most of the talking, but Dick's role gradually expanded as he spoke up more and found amusing ways to attack his brother's inanities. On the road, the youthful duo refined their act by watching old comedies on TV during the day. Tom noticed how little the stooge actually spoke. "Oliver Hardy did ninety percent of the talking," says Tom, "Stan just said, 'That's right, Ollie.' In Abbott & Costello films, Abbott dominated. If you didn't have Bud Abbott it would just be Lou Costello as a screaming fat boy. In our first years, I was doing too much of the comedy, so when we came back in 1980 we balanced the act a different way and I think that's the thing that's given it a longevity." Their blood link gave the Smothers Brothers a built-in warmth and charm, and they were also blessed by the happy accident of a catchy rhyming name.

The trio went directly from San Jose to San Francisco's Purple Onion, but after six months Bobby Blackmore married and moved to Australia. Tom says, "We didn't think we could pull it off, because he was the lead singer." The first time Tom and Dick worked as a duet was at the Limelite in Aspen, Colorado. "We sounded like Bud and Travis." They stayed a year at the Purple Onion. "I nailed the character there," Tom told me (we're former college classmates). "I understood what worked and didn't work; I'd never worked as a comic before. Onstage, improvising, I could discover where the little jokes were." Not everyone, however, was immediately amused. Stanley Eichelbaum, the *San Francisco Examiner* critic, recalls: "The Purple Onion manager called me and said they had a hot folksinging trio from San Jose called the Smothers Brothers. I walked out and I said, 'Send 'em back to San Jose!' " No way.

Of their network TV debut not long after, Tom recalls: "We were working the Blue Angel with Pat Harrington. He mentioned us to the Paar show booker, and so we went up to an NBC guy's office and we did a song for him. He said thank you and we left. Someone fell through a week later and they needed an act." When they appeared on *The Tonight Show,* in January 1961, Paar conferred his blessings ("I don't know what you guys have, but no one's gonna steal it") and hung a star on them.

They were always confident. Says Tom: "We were just so road competent, since we'd been working so much, that we had no fear." But they soon had to disguise themselves in public. "Everyone suddenly knew you.

The power that show had then! Today, you can do fifty *Tonight Shows* and nobody gives a hell. Back then, ninety percent of the TV sets were tuned to the three networks. We were the last ones—Cosby, Winters, Newhart, Carlin, people who [in one appearance] could saturate 'em. You don't get to do that anymore." They made thirteen appearances with Paar before Johnny Carson took over the show.

After their innocent beginning as just winsome folksingers, Tom began to introduce the songs and get unscripted laughs. "I knew I could say things funny back when I was fourteen or fifteen. So when I was introducing the songs I'd naturally use that technique and I'd try to make it funny. I'd make it up every night at the Purple Onion, four shows a night—we only did fifteen-minute sets. I'd make a new one up every show, but I was running out of ideas. After a week, Dick said, 'Tom, why don't you repeat some of that stuff?' I said, 'I can't do that—people will know. That's lying.' You could sing a song again and again but I always thought that the talk had to be new every time. All of a sudden it got a laugh again, and I thought, 'Oh, my God.' It was never *ever* written. We made eleven albums and the only album that was written was *Aesop's Fables, the Smothers Brothers Way.*"

The unthreatening Smotherses had struck satiric gold, partly because their pop timing was perfect. People were just beginning to grow weary of all folksingers, who were reproducing on street corners like lab mice. However deftly worked out, the act was tepid stuff for so tumultuous a time, but Tom and Dick had a guileless boyish quality that nightclubbers had rarely encountered; and that persona was their ticket to TV stardom—and eventual trouble, stirred up by their audience's parents. Murray Kempton once wrote that "if they had not originally been so appealing to nice old ladies" they could never have backed a minor TV revolt. Eventually, they did in the old ladies by also attracting TV's lusted-after younger viewers who felt that the Smothers Brothers were cool, savvy, and honest—a blast.

Although Steve Allen noted that it was questionable how much "pure satire" was on the Smothers Brothers show ("To do a joke about George Wallace is not necessarily to have created satire"), he remarked that "both Tom and Dick had a social conscience. Consequently, some wonderfully pithy things got said on the program, things that seemed daring in terms of what television had been doing during the previous eighteen years."

Their 1967 CBS show was crucial to the success and the thrust of sixties satire because at that time it was the only regularly scheduled show headlining news-driven satire. Such contraband humor might be smuggled occasionally onto other variety or late-night shows, but *The Smothers Brothers Comedy Hour* became the anti–*Ed Sullivan Show,* and even had the good fortune to follow the real *Ed Sullivan Show* at nine P.M. on Sundays.

It all ended noisily in '69 when CBS stepped in and deleted a David Steinberg monologue, a "sermonette" about Solomon and Jonah that was to have run not only on Easter Sunday but the week of President Eisenhower's funeral. The piece was deemed "irreverent and offensive" by the network, which refused to air it when executives said they weren't shown a script. CBS could thus hide behind religion, not politics, by blaming the allegedly sacrilegious sketch by Steinberg (an ex-rabbinical student). A single Steinberg line, from his Jonah piece, caused CBS brass to explode: "*The gentiles, as is their wont from time to time, threw a Jew overboard, and Jonah was swallowed by a giant guppy.*" The next line went, "*The New Testament scholars literally grab the Jews by the Old Testament.*" Jack Gould in the *New York Times* called it one of their best shows of the season and said that the flap over Steinberg's routine "was not worth all the managerial jitters." Tom says, "Just because a show's entertainment doesn't mean it can't have an edge."

Steinberg recalls today, with some pride: "I was the reason they got thrown off the air. It looks so tame, but at the time it was just astonishing to do. I had no idea I was going to create this stir." He adds: "When they were number one they were number one in prime time—and that was *huge.* There was no competition. You were doing the biggest show in America. They were funny and topical and combative. They were already against the war and attacking Lyndon Johnson. They established the political tension more than anybody else by just being innovative." The groundwork for such innovation had been laid by *That Was the Week That Was,* the 1964 satirical show from London.

CBS, to counter the impression that it was being pushed around by the Smothers Brothers, cited their failure to comply with network policy to preview shows as its pretext for closing them down. But the series had been living on borrowed time for months, ever since Pete Seeger (back from a long TV blacklist) sang his anti–Vietnam War parable "Waist Deep in the Big Muddy." The song generated seventy-five letters of protest, a deluge by network standards, and the affiliates began to bail out. The CBS brass was also trying to please Congress's conservative and censorious Senator John Pastore, who loathed the show. Even more dangerous to the show were its sagging ratings opposite NBC's inoffensively satirical upstart, *Rowan and Martin's Laugh-In.*

THE SMOTHERS BROTHERS, sons of an army major who died in a World War II prisoner-of-war camp, worked the sibling rivalry angle for all it was worth—Tom's pouty *"Mom always liked you best"* became their calling card. The act was (is) full of standard comedy-team ploys—malapropisms, tongue-tied passages, exasperation, confusion, false starts, interruptions, and arguments—all of it culminating in a comforting song. Dick would shout, *"Take it, Tom!"* and Tom would shout back, *"No!"* Or Dick might snap, *"You know why I'm mad most of the time? Because it's difficult being an only child."*

Tom describes his character as "a man-child," and maintains that it's evolved. "Like George Burns said, you've gotta do comedy with respect for what your age is. So I don't still do *'Mom liked you best,'* I don't scream as much. I didn't get caught in the bracket that Jerry Lewis did. He's either yeh-yeh-yeh or he's this pontificating person." Tom says he never took any heat, as Lewis did, for doing a slightly retarded character. His defense is that he actually had severe dyslexia as a kid and didn't realize it until he was thirty-nine.

"I was left-eyed and right-handed," he explains, "the last one chosen in spelling class. I got a ninety-four on an IQ test in college; I took it again and moved it up to ninety-six. I was always the last one to finish a test. When people called my character dumb, I said, 'Okay, *I'll* show you dumb,'" which served him well as a wannabe comedian. "I used it to dominate a room by playing this character; it was always socially driven. And then when I'd get onstage, I thought, 'Hey, this is a pretty good comedic character.' I have a good sense of timing. The Smothers Brothers has always been about timing—it hasn't been content, for sure—except for the sixties when we had our television show, which was all content."

In their spiffy red blazers, they looked harmless, and indeed they were, until their writers and performers radicalized them. "We weren't avant-garde or on the cutting edge," admitted Tom. Their well-scrubbed collegiate façade fooled CBS for a time, but also, ironically, annoyed liberals. Tom recalls: "The prowar people didn't like how we dressed. It was like we were hiding behind it. They could see everybody *else* coming. We kind of violated that."

A TV executive once instructed them, "We want you to be controversial but at the same time we want everyone to agree with you." A station owner told Tom that he was "incompetent to make social comments." One CBS memo said it was fine "to satirize the president, so long as you do it with respect." The boys did their respectful best to conform. Ever the polite sons of a military man, they wrote a sincere note to Lyndon Johnson after he dropped out of the 1968 presidential race: "Please accept our apology on behalf of *The Smothers Brothers Comedy Hour* for our over-reaction in some instances. . . . If the opportunity arose in the coming election to vote for you, we would." Even as renegades, they were trying to behave patriotically. As one of their writers, Carl Gottlieb, said: "They were a product of their time, they came out of the Eisenhower era, but their consciousness had evolved beyond that."

If their show had been headlined by almost anyone else, it wouldn't have lasted a month, but the Smotherses kept the tone as good-humored as they were. Slowly, such shady types as John Hartford, Howard Cosell, and Janis Joplin infiltrated the show. To network honchos, it was as if the Hardy Boys had joined a Communist cell. The simpler truth was that there were no TV variety shows for viewers under forty. Ed Sullivan was serving up Alan King as cutting-edge comedy, and *McHale's Navy* and *Hogan's Heroes* were considered antiwar satire.

"We'd watch TV and be appalled," said Mason Williams, the songwriting musician who also wrote for the show and was its "moral strength," according to Dick, who said, "Tommy listened to [Williams] a lot. And he listened to all the young writers." Tom was only twenty-seven, but "some of the writers made him seem conservative, they were so radical." Rob Reiner was one such writer who got in Tom's face. "Rob was pretty radicalized. He'd say, 'You're coppin' out!' " Williams recalled: "There was nothing on TV for me or anybody we knew to watch. There was a void. You could sense there was a revolution in the works. A whole segment of society wasn't reflected on TV at all." Perry Lafferty, an ex–CBS vice president for programming, says, "Their show had a feeling of now. Most TV had a feeling of then."

To Marvin Kitman, *Newsday*'s TV critic, *The Smothers Brothers Comedy Hour* underscored the absence of political satire on television. Blood may have been running in the streets, but on TV, viewers still lived in a placid land ruled by benevolent comedy dictators Bob Hope and Johnny Carson, who never challenged showbiz authority. "That made every [Smothers Brothers show] exciting," writes Kitman, who called their show "the

Palace Theater of political comedy acts," adding, "There was risk in political comedy in the old days. You weren't just shooting arrows in the air. The targets got upset. They would bleed when hit."

The Smothers show broke sociopolitical ground on TV: Leigh French spinning drug jokes as a dippy hippie girl and as the hostess of "A Little Tea with Goldie" (their radical answer to *Laugh-In*'s vapid Goldie Hawn); upsetting a ladies' show by demonstrating how to use a gas mask; and Harry Belafonte singing "Don't Stop the Carnival" over clips of the violent 1968 Democratic National Convention in Chicago. If it was often heavy-handed stuff, it was a heavy-handed time. Ron Clark, who wrote for the show, recalls: "Tom had a lot of input—not that he would sit down and write, but he would certainly direct them in certain areas he wanted them to go. On no other show could you be that political—hard-hitting sketches about President Johnson. They got away with it because they were very charming. They all looked like good little college kids."

Tom says: "I wasn't very political at all—it turned me around, absolutely. When you're on the edge, and things push you there, it's real hard to keep the whimsy intact." He got so radicalized that he began publicly chiding Bill Cosby for not being more outspoken on civil rights issues, a stance that led to blows one October night in 1976 at the Playboy Mansion. As Tom recalls it, "At the time I was very volatile and thought everyone should take a stand. I guess I [had once] said something that really pissed him. For a couple of years after that, I'd say, 'Hiya, Bill, how ya doing?' and he wouldn't shake hands with me—you know, like, 'Fuck off.' "

On the night in question, hoping to ease tension, Tom congratulated Cosby on his newest TV show, not realizing it had just been canceled. "I liked your show," said Tom, "it was a really good effort." Cosby didn't respond. "He just looked at me like, 'Fuck you,' and I said, 'Well, fuck *you,*' and turned around and walked away. I'd been gettin' this kind of thing from him for a long time. It started when he was hosting *The Tonight Show.* He had that kind of dismissive way of introducing people, kind of like Letterman, and I nailed him—you know, comedic one-upmanship—and I remember he said, 'Maybe sometime I'll knock you upside the head one of these days,' and I said, 'Yeah, go ahead, give it a try.' "

Tom continues: "A couple of months later . . . boom, there it was. I should never have turned my back on him. He didn't have the balls to do it when I was lookin'. . . . He slipped behind Hefner and sucker-punched me. He hit me right in the head with his fist—knocked me down. . . . And I was down there a minute or two and he was standing over me screaming at me, 'C'mon, I'll kick your ass,' stuff like that. . . . I've never seen him since then. I always thought, maybe if he turns around sometime I might give him a shot." Cosby's version, says his spokesman David Brokaw, is that "Bill told him three times to stop talking so much—he was taunting him and just being obnoxious—and when he wouldn't stop, Bill tried other means to get him to stop."

As Bill Maher described the Smothers Brothers phenomenon when he introduced them at a 2000 tribute at the U.S. Comedy Arts Festival in Aspen, Colorado: "CBS thought they had nothing to lose putting [the show] up against *Bonanza,* against which nine shows had failed." The network figured it was a nice innocuous show (the reason the hosts got creative control), a transition until something bigger came along. But nothing did. The Smothers Brothers *became* the big show and in the process, in one writer's phrase, they lost their showbiz virginity. Cloaked by Tommy's blank-faced Charlie Brown innocence, and Dick's sincere wisdom and counsel, the show hurled some potent political grenades. Dick: "*We've come a long way since that first Thanksgiving in Plymouth, when the Pilgrims sat down at the table with the Indians to eat turkey.*" Tom: "*Boy, I'll say we've come a long way. Now we're in Paris, sitting down at a table with the Viet Cong, eating crow.*"

The team itself was almost a microcosm of the country—Dick the staid establishment authority figure, Tom the loopy, well-meaning youth spouting unwitting (and witty) truisms. They seemed unintimidating and cozily suburban. As Ken Fritz, their onetime manager, put it: "They were big brothers to little people, contemporaries to teens, sons to the people who had sons, grandsons to people with grandsons."

At the Aspen retrospective, Tom remarked: "We were not political until we got the show. It took two years for us to be politicized. We just started seeing the war as something wrong. Also segregation. A lot of things were happening." The comedy show began as simply another pleasant variety hour; the commentary simply "crept into it," as Mason Williams said. A major mouthpiece for the show's political satire was Pat Paulsen, the thin, hangdog, shifty-eyed mock presidential candidate who resembled a shriveled-up Richard Nixon; Paulsen one year actually got two hundred thousand write-in votes for president. Paulsen was an ongoing and, eventually, overworked running gag, but because he, too, seemed utterly harmless, he got away with satirical murder in prime time. "Hard times make for good comedy," says Carl Gottlieb.

By 2003 standards, the show's censorship battles seem almost comical. Bob Einstein, another writer-performer, noted at Aspen that the sketches looked "so inane" to him now that nobody today "would ever believe anyone would censor them." Even so, there was pressure from the super-sensitive White House and its allies, such as *TV Guide* publisher and Nixon crony Walter Annenberg. CBS's new president, Bob Wood, also wanted it gone. Says Tom: "Annenberg was trying to kiss ass with Nixon—'What can I do for you, sir?' He was humping for an ambassadorship to England, and he got it." Station licenses were threatened, said Avery Schreiber, whose show with Jack Burns replaced the Smothers Brothers and was in the same risky vein.

James Sullivan, who covers comedy for the *San Francisco Chronicle,* attended the Aspen tribute to the Smothers Brothers. He said that clips from the show resembled old *Laugh-In* excerpts—"silly in a period piece sort of way. But a lot of the stuff was daringly political. Maher [formerly of ABC's *Politically Incorrect*] was host for good reason." He noted that nobody even makes an effort to do intelligent political humor anymore on TV; the whole art form has atrophied. "The stuff that did fly on the show," Sullivan reports, "was the free-love and pot-smoking jokes, lifestyle jokes. Nixon didn't care about that stuff—he cared about the Vietnam War material."

Despite the creative tension, it was a fairly loose cast and crew, though at one point during the Aspen panel, when Tom told Einstein to stop talking so much, Einstein cried, only half jokingly, "Tom was a tyrant then and he's a tyrant now!" Says Einstein: "I remember Tommy was into everything but memorizing his lines. He was so brilliant that he got laughs even if he missed the mark. He was into directing, watching the monitor, looking at wardrobe, hearing music. Dick always surprised me because I never saw him study anything and he never missed a beat. I'd give him a note while he was getting a hot oil massage from his secretary and he would come out and nail it."

Einstein called Tom "the most ego-less performer I have ever met in this business. I have never met anyone who cared so much about seeing other people do well. And that's where the crying shame of them getting thrown off the air is. Tommy was just a genius at letting his staff run wild, and we'd try all kinds of things—he fostered this creative atmosphere." Tom agrees: "I gave Pat Paulsen and everybody first shot at everything; I was never competitive. That's probably why the show was so good—I allowed everybody to be who they were."

Neither brother, however, is quite what he appears: Dick raced fast cars; Tom now runs their California winery, Remick Ridge Vineyards in Sonoma. Dick is livelier offstage (says his brother, "Dick's very funny, except onstage"), Tom more earnest and intellectual. They often finish each other's sentences. Tom has said: "We're as different as two people can be. We had different friends. He's pragmatic, precise. There's a bit of abrasiveness in our relationship at all times. I brought him into show business reluctantly. He introduced me to wines, to golf, to just about everything else I do besides performing." Tom, now sixty-six, says of his more placid kid brother: "Dickie was the thing that kept me grounded. If I started to go into sort of a gay joke or something, he'd say, 'Man, that's dumb.' He was like the governor on a car. If I was doin' too much drug stuff [jokes] he'd always jump on me."

The very concept of a comedy team seems archaic now. "It used to be the thing," responds Tom, "but I think it takes more time, it's more difficult, there's a compromise involved. It's a more complicated dance. Nobody has stayed together as a comedy team more than fifteen years." Only Bob & Ray lasted as long, but Bob & Ray didn't have to endure the rigors of nightclubs and network television, nor were they related.

The team has had few major rows, Tom says—"Just over bits and stuff. He never said 'I told you so' or 'You shouldn't have done that.' Dick wasn't as passionate and had a more conservative viewpoint. His political awareness was slower coming around." While Tom was the creative force, and the more political and driven partner, they were generally in sync, unlike many comedy couples. Dick said, "It's sort of like the Dorsey brothers, Tommy and Jimmy, who fought constantly over tempo. The nuances is what we fought over, not the content."

Dick once said: "Tommy was the bumper on the show. Tommy was the protector, Tommy was the fighter for the writers. He stood up for them." Tom: "I kinda ran the show pretty much. I wasn't into performances much. I was watching content and direction and evolving the show—hands on." He refused to use a laugh track. If he was doing the show now, he says, "I'd be more judicious in my editing. I'd have me in it a little less and pay much more attention to my own performance. I'd make everything much briefer, and I can say what people say now about *Saturday Night Live*—that we didn't know how to get off."

Their show wasn't that far out. Reflecting the brothers' basic traditional tastes, it was frequently far in. Nobody presented the all-American menu better than they did. "The thing I'm maybe most proud of on the show was the eclectic booking we did," says Tom. "Bette Davis and the Who. George Burns and Herman's Hermits. Kate Smith as Sergeant Pepper. Lana Turner and Buffalo Springfield. Dickie and I had one foot in the old world—Jimmy Durante and Bette Davis, Jack Benny and George Burns—and we also had the Mamas and the Papas. I didn't know that I was mixing generations. That was just my taste. I was a little too old to be a young hippie. Steve Martin was twenty-one and I was thirty."

Their show also was known for developing writers and for booking whoever grabbed its hosts' fancy. TV exiles found a home at the Smothers urban ranch, from Jackie Mason (after his debacle on Ed Sullivan's show) to the emerging outlaw comics—George Carlin, political impressionist David Frye, Don Novello (a.k.a. Father Guido Sarducci), The Committee (the Second City offshoot from San Francisco that traded heavily in political satire), and Mike Nichols and Elaine May, whose sketch on TV censorship was yanked but the next day was quoted in the *New York Times*.

May, playing a presumably CBS censor, tells Tom, "*I think the word* breast *should be cut from the dinner scene. I think that* breast *is a relatively tasteless thing to say when you're eating. I wouldn't mind if they were having cocktails or even a late supper, but dinner is a family meal.*" Tom scribbles a note and says, "*Take the word* breast *out of the dinner scene.*" May: "*Tell them to substitute the word* arm." Tom: "*But won't that sound funny? 'My heart beats wildly in my arm whenever you're near'?*" They compromise on "*My pulse beats wildly in my wrist whenever you're near.*"

The writers were crypto-anarchists, outthinking and outplotting every CBS censor's manual on comic subversion. To put censors off the scent, the writers inserted meaningless phrases, like "Rowing into Galveston," into a script. They implied it had nasty overtones, raw bait for toothless sharks, just to see if they would bite, and they usually did. Potentially troubling lines were smuggled into scripts by using even more outrageous decoy lines—"just so they'd have something to pull out," Tom says, leaving the slightly less offensive lines alone. He once played a game of table tennis with a censor to determine if a line was in or out.

Once the show generated headline buzz, Tom learned how to pluck the media like his banjo. He said that whenever the network tampered with anything, he'd "run to the press and start screaming. They'd say, 'Poor boy, are they treating you badly?'" The brothers were hot copy, welcomed by TV critics with open arms. Jack Gould wrote in the *New York Times* that the Smothers Brothers (and *Laugh-In*) might actually drag TV into the "mainstream of modern concern" and that "the Establishment may possibly have more to fear from the contagion of laughter than from stern protest."

Lafferty, a fan of the show ("I thought most of what they were doing was wonderful") who was caught in the middle, observes: "It was like a mosquito buzzing around CBS's ear. It wasn't that big a thing, but Tom *made* it that big a thing and he wouldn't let up. It got to a point where both sides had drawn a line in the sand and that was it. You see it coming and you say, what a shame you can't stop this collision." Adds Mike Dann, another ex–CBS programming executive: "Tommy liked to be met head on."

Tom would carry the cause directly to the censors, who would simply tell him, "You cannot say this"—whereupon he would dig in his heels. As he explains it, "I'm a contrary guy anyway—I'm a screamer, I can be volatile—but when you get hit by a drunk driver, you become a mother for MADD [Mothers Against Drunk Driving]." When Tom saw the crisis brewing at CBS, he sold his homes and other costly items in case the ax fell, so that, he said, "[I] might make decisions that would not be fully courageous if I was having to cover some expenses. I got rid of the big houses and all that kind of stuff so I could afford to be fired and go straight at them." He rubbed the network's nose in it by turning their censorship troubles into a running gag on the show. Steinberg comments: "Tommy liked pushing the censors and the network. He loved to upset the suits. He felt comfortable in a fight." Tom figured, "The more they said don't do it, the more you realize it must be important."

Their cuter, cuddly rival, *Laugh-In,* had far less trouble. "We made it easier for *Laugh-In* and they made it easier for us," remarks Tom. "George Schlatter [*Laugh-In*'s producer] would say, 'I don't know how you guys got away with that.' " Tom says today: "*Laugh-In* was naughty and nice but no threat. It was quick, in and out, a different tone. When Nixon goes on *Laugh-In* [to say "Sock it to *me?*"] you knew they'd give it the Good House-keeping Seal of Approval." One of *Laugh-In*'s comedy writers, Paul Keyes, was a Nixon speechwriter (the Smothers Brothers became part of the Kennedy circle). *Laugh-In,* with its marshmallow zingers and *Hellza-poppin* pace, stole the spotlight from the brothers' show, a clear triumph of style over substance.

Tom is convinced that Nixon's election killed the show. "He was inau-gurated and eight weeks later we were fired, even though our option had been picked up," he says. "If Humphrey had won we'd still be on." Tom reflects: "I always say I was at the scene of the accident. We had a prime-time show while Kent State was going on, the '68 convention, the Martin

Luther King and Bobby Kennedy assassinations, and for us not to reflect that, it would have been absolutely a crime. The whole country was kind of fermenting. It was a growing-up process." He adds, "There was no doubt that we were going to change the world."

Though he concedes that he might have been less confrontational, he says: "I was so young then, and so pure and idealistic, and absolutely bulletproof. You think you can go through anything. I know how I feel now and it's not nearly as pure or as reckless. I don't know what self I would be—but smarter." Tom said that a guy he knew who had been in jail told him, "You're lucky you aren't dead." Tom recalls, "There were drug setups on us and all kinds of shit. They were trying to discredit me, 'cause I never shut up. It was a scary time." A certain self-righteousness seeped into his remarks during the show. "I look at myself now and I cringe," he says. "I was so desperately sincere."

But none of it seemed daring or courageous to him at the time. "Only looking back do I see how radical our career became. Now we get all this residual respect. In spite of ourselves, we're having a kind of renaissance. All the concerts we're doing are filled up. Forty years of performing, and from '61 we were on TV constantly—our sitcom, the shows—and then the winery got a lot of attention." They were among the first celebrity winemakers, marking the mellow end of their wild youth in 1979.

Because of its notoriety and its impact, Tom says, "people thought that the show was on ten years but it was only three seasons." After CBS pulled the plug (replacing them with *Hee Haw* and *The Leslie Uggams Show*), they did a summer show for ABC, *The Summer Brothers Smothers Show,* which he calls "a scathing show," and which he also produced. When the Smotherses were fired, said Bill Maher, "they wore it as a badge of honor, as well they should. They sacrificed their show because they wouldn't sacrifice their principles." Later, they sued CBS and won a $276,000 settlement, but it ended their careers on TV—and almost everywhere else. Yet Tom says, "We became bigger celebrities by being fired than by being kept on."

After their TV career died, they began treading water. They even decided to split up for a while, and neither was sure he could make it on his own; Tom briefly considered running against California senator S. I. Hayakawa. "We took a break," he says. "We weren't gettin' anywhere. We were blacklisted from Nevada"—because, he claims, of the TV show, naming Howard Hughes (with his government defense contracts) as the culprit. "There were no jobs in Vegas. Bill Harrah would give us two weeks a year, but everything was falling apart." They did a few bad films, dinner theater, and then reunited in 1978 for a sweetly innocuous musical, *I Love My Wife,* first on Broadway for a year and then on the road.

The team scrambled back to prominence with showbiz grunt work. Dick was content to retire and race autos: "I had other things, but show was everything for Tom." Tom was the brother with the more dominant performing gene. "We started diggin' ditches," he told me. "We had to work discos and comedy clubs, we opened for Lola Falana. We had no agent, no one cared, we were dead in the water. We got very little eye contact in Hollywood—we were like an embarrassment, an auto wreck. It took us all of the eighties to come back. Then we got this commercial for Magnavox in '88"—with Tom doing yo-yo tricks, as if signaling a return to his innocent middle-American youth.

"We'd been out of the public eye long enough by then," he continues, "that people were saying, 'Oh, yeah, those guys are still good, and they're still relatively young.' Then we got the twentieth-anniversary show [in 1988] and got this residual respect when we made the comeback" (CBS eagerly invited them back for a reunion special in 1988). He pauses. "This is the longest we've gone without a TV show—nine years. They say we're too old, but Cosby's still gettin' work and Newhart's still gettin' things. Hey, it's a great act." They performed more than a hundred dates in 2001.

"We're kind of the last living comedy team," Tom said in 1996, when the touring retro act included singing "The Impossible Dream" in front of a symphony orchestra. Their aging fans now treat the boys as long-lost relatives. "We were brothers, we were family, so there's always a lot of emotional attachment to that, regardless if we wavered and sometimes were not so good—like wine. We're in our forty-fifth year now. Dickie says it's like an old marriage—a lot of fighting and no sex. We're constantly working on our relationship, so it is like a marriage. It's a struggle all the time." Dick lives in Bradenton, Florida, Tom in Sonoma County, north of San Francisco near their winery; they have half a dozen marriages and nine children between them.

The apolitical Rex Reed, reviewing their 2001 New York return, was uncharmed, writing in the *New York Observer:* "Their frat-house humor always eluded me, but now that they're old enough to own a senior bus pass, it eludes me even more. They're products of the angry '60s—subversive comics who became peace-movement celebrities. . . . Now, with nothing left to be subversive about, they show home movies and clips from their old TV shows. If you're an aging flower child who's been living in a space capsule since 1969, this is an act for you. For me, the Smothers Brothers are as dated as Chubby Checker, the Automat, and a good ten-cent cigar." *The New Yorker* took a longer view: "If the brothers have become fossilized as sixties media revolutionaries, remembered mainly for anti-war barbs, pot jokes, and counterculture hipness . . . their gig here reminds us how gloriously old school, in the best sense of the word, these two pros are, with their impeccable timing and true wit."

At the Aspen tribute, Bob Einstein recalled the show's brief moment in the sun's glare: "I don't think any of us ever dreamed you would be fired. I mean, we were so hot! We had the youngest demographic in the history of television as far as teens watching TV on a Sunday night. We were beating *Bonanza*." Said Tom: "After the cancellation, I became the poster boy against TV censorship. And I lost my sense of humor for about three years after that"—until he saw Jane Fonda on TV discussing Vietnam. "I saw this dreadfully stern person," he said, and realized he had lost comic perspective about "the big picture." He told Mason Williams, "There's something wrong with me. I don't feel funny anymore."

Rather than remount a battered satiric soapbox handed down from Lenny Bruce, Dick Gregory, and Mort Sahl, Tom eventually climbed down. He became more mainstream and began performing again, but without the pamphleteering. "So I owe Jane Fonda a big debt of gratitude," he reflects now. "I was on the soapbox for three years." After the controversial TV show, audiences on the road expected them to be more biting. "Our act never was politically oriented. We'd still make social commentary, but people would say, 'Why don't you say more?' I'd say, 'Why don't *you* say more?' I was tired. I said what I wanted to say. I don't have to keep saying it to verify my validity."

Despite their breakthroughs, nothing has changed on prime-time network TV. Tom maintains that if he and Dick had a TV show now they would have all the same censorship problems. "If you look at television today, there's no political satire in prime time. People say, 'Wouldn't it be great if you were on television today—you could say anything you want.' That's not true at all. All the political-social commentary isn't done in prime time but on the fringes—*Saturday Night Live,* Dennis Miller, HBO after midnight. There's an illusion that there's all this freedom of speech. Sexual innuendo and violence is allowable, but political satire is as taboo today on CBS at nine P.M. Sundays as it was forty years ago." Revved up, he goes on: "It's a false sense of freedom. All it is is a lot of expressions of violence, sexuality, self-indulgence, narcissistic reflections, and dirty talk—and people say, 'God, look how free we are!' And yet within all that freedom of violating the social code, there's hardly a scintilla of intelligence. No social commentary whatever. Sahl and Bruce now would be on cable, where one percent of the country see you."

For all the entertainment industry's financially driven championing of the First Amendment, the still easily riled Tom has a long memory: "The Hollywood people, like Jack Valenti and all those guys who go to Washington to defend the rights [of filmmakers]—when we were thrown off the air, no one in the industry said a *word* about the First Amendment. I had to get the ACLU to defend me. *No* one stood up. We got thousands and thousands of telegrams and all that stuff, but in terms of the industry, the Jack Valentis and the producers—silence. And this was a *genuine* First Amendment issue. That's always the case, even today. Tell me about John Rocker and Fuzzy Zoeller, Marge Schott, Jimmy the Greek—where is the defense of the First Amendment there? It's supposed to cover all that, but there's all this political-correctness shit."

Like older comics who were groundbreaking in their day, Tom Smothers is shocked by the language of contemporary comedians— "Those guys where every other word is *F, F, F* . . . Sometime I think I'll turn to my brother onstage and say, 'Mom liked you best,' and he'll say, 'Fuck your mother!' " He laughs. "Then they can say the Smothers Brothers have set foot in the twenty-first century. Dick and I never worked dirty. We were raised in a different time. *I* thought Lenny Bruce was shocking, too."

He concedes that in the sixties the issues were more sharply defined, which helped comedians frame satire and identify the black hats more easily. "The protests and the struggles were certainly better, clearer. There was more substance to it. And it wasn't so splintered with self-interest. The comedy was much brighter, perceptive, and more political. It wasn't just the war. The sixties was a social revolution; everybody was defined by how they looked. But I still think it's easy to be funny. Good comedy transcends time." In 1996, back home in San Jose for a command performance (their alma mater later gave the dropouts honorary degrees in 2000), Tom said, "I didn't really work that hard at it. I had a little gift, and it's just about always worked."

It turns out that the most ironic of all the Smothers Brothers' jokes is that, without really trying, these two mild-mannered folk-song satirists eventually became not just folk heroes, but, in their own unassuming way, eloquent urban protest singers.

Bawdy and Soul

Mel Brooks

It was like I was screaming at the universe to pay attention, like I had to make God *laugh.*

———————

MEL BROOKS'S 2,000 YEAR OLD MAN was the ultimate comedian, *shpritzing* about everything in human history. The godfather of the comedy renaissance, this gnomish, world-weary Jewish geezer was Methuselah reincarnated as a Seventh Avenue dress cutter. The cranky, dumpy, street-smart 2,000 Year Old Man could not have come out of any other era. While he's a throwback to a prehistoric, dialect vaudeville archetype, he's also astute, contemporary, and fearlessly vulgar. He's Lenny Bruce at ninety-seven.

Brooks's ancient golden oldster transcends America's postwar satirical revolution. Under his big black Frank Lloyd Wright cape you discover not just Bruce but the go-for-broke spirit of Jonathan Winters, Mort Sahl, Woody Allen, et al. Something of every comedian in the era was embodied in Mel Brooks's elfin soul. Brooks and his partner, Carl Reiner, were a one-shtick pony, but their 2,000 Year Old Man routine was a three-ring circus.

They and their smart-ass, flamboyantly Jewish mouthpiece were a joyous accident, a couple of happy-go-lucky showbiz buddies who performed their routines for friends at parties until, in 1961, the pair was prodded into a recording studio. They came out the other end with an immense Grammy-nominated hit, several sequel albums, and a permanent place in comedy history. Their 1996 update finally won a Grammy. Not coincidentally, *2,000 Years with Reiner and Brooks* also jump-started Brooks's sputtering career, and his life.

Brooks wasn't a stand-up comedian, but his cartwheeling improvisational style and audacious wit propelled satirical comedy forward in the 1960s more than many formal stand-up acts. His irrepressible energy and spontaneous brilliance—his mere presence—lit a fire under the era's already simmering satirical revolution. As somebody said of him early on, "Mel Brooks stood on the corner and the world turned."

He was capable, in full lunatic flight, of improvising a paragraph that

Woody Allen might have labored over for hours—for example, his defense of sharks on a 1970 David Susskind TV panel: "*One time, a shark followed my brother Irving home on the Brighton local, and upon being admitted to the apartment house, the shark entered his apartment—apartment 4B—and ate his entire family and a brand-new hat. Apart from that, the shark is a pussy-cat.*" Mike Nichols says of him: "When he was cooking, when he was doing the 2,000 Year Old Man, or *Young Frankenstein,* Mel is great. Like all truly great anythings, it comes and goes. To make jokes as good as his calling Paul Revere an anti-Semitic bastard for crying, '*The Yiddish are coming! The Yiddish are coming!*' is to make a great classic joke."

Brooks, once described as having "bullied his way up" to become Sid Caesar's writer, was, then as now, a manic Jewish gremlin who would not be denied. "I've always used my wit to bring my enemies down," he said. He began as a Borscht Belt junior *tummler* at fourteen and went on to be a comic tumult for life. At the Hotel Tamiment, in Pennsylvania's Pocono Mountains, he latched onto Sid Caesar and rode his coattails into TV, battling his way up from hanger-on to gofer to staff writer. He was the loudest mouth in a roomful of raucous gagwriters working at *Your Show of Shows.* His friends both enjoyed and endured his fanatical aggression; one of his producers once said, "He's the sanest maniac I've ever met."

It was at Tamiment that Brooks and Sid Caesar met and became inseparable; a few years later, after the war, Caesar hired him, over the fierce objections of the TV producer Max Liebman. Liebman himself had discovered Caesar while putting on lavish shows at Tamiment, and later put together *The Admiral Broadway Revue,* the 1949 stepping-stone to *Your Show of Shows.* The comical twosome became a Mutt and Jeff duet—the squat, nattering Brooks was Sancho Panza ("Sid's boy," he was called) to the bruising, brooding Caesar, who became his protector and meal ticket. To Liebman, Brooks was a loud cutup and pest—"a Catskill camp follower and Caesar's private court jester," to quote Brooks's biographer, William Holtzman. The Caesar comedy writer Lucille Kallen thought of Brooks as a Damon Runyon character who introduced himself as "your obedient Jew" and was always popping Raisinets, his vitamin of choice.

Carl Reiner was a performer and writer on *Your Show of Shows* when he met Brooks, a young antsy staff writer who was the runt of the litter. Brooks's humor was channeled into sketches, most famously the movie and musical parodies for which Caesar's shows are best known. Some of those sketches found homes years later in Brooks movies—*The Producers, Blazing Saddles, High Anxiety, Young Frankenstein.*

The Producers, the 1968 backstage farce, began as an idea for a comic novel about a poor misunderstood Viennese youth named Adolf who yearned to be a dancer. The film includes the definitive Brooksian song-and-dance moment, "Springtime for Hitler," which finally found its way to Broadway in 2001 when Brooks (urged on by his wife, the actress Anne Bancroft) turned *The Producers* into a full-blown blockbuster for which he wrote all the songs (*"It's springtime for Hitler and Germany. / Deutschland is happy and gay. / We're marching to a faster pace. / Look out, here comes the master race"*).

"Some things are meant to be—this show was meant to be," he said. Brooks claimed that the idea originated with the producer David Geffen, but it was on its way to becoming a show in the early 1960s, when Brooks worked briefly on a play tentatively titled *Springtime for Hitler.* The musical was a sparkling capstone to Brooks's career just when he had fallen into a funk in the 1990s, after a series of failed film farces (a time when "he was not funny, so full of angst," said Bancroft). It displayed his passion for musicals and his gift for inspired nonsense. Like him, the show is sassy, brassy, and insistently funny.

THIS NEVER-SAY-DIE COMIC LEPRECHAUN was born Melvin Kaminsky in 1926. He took his stage name from his mother's family name, Brookman. His father died at thirty-four, when Melvin was two years old. "I can't tell you what sadness, what pain it is for me never to have known my own father," he told an interviewer. "He was lively, peppy, sang well. If only I could look at him, touch his face, see if he had eyebrows!" Brooks has almost none.

Kenneth Tynan, in a *New Yorker* profile of Brooks, wrote: "To be Jewish, Brooklyn-born, fatherless, impoverished, and below average stature—no more classic recipe could be imagined for an American comedian." Little Mel was a munchkin from the start. "I was adored. I was always in the air, hurled up and kissed and thrown up in the air again. Until I was six, my feet didn't touch the ground. Giving that up was very difficult later in life."

Growing up in the Williamsburg section of Brooklyn, he became a grade school *tummler.* "I was a bright kid and I was bored, so I'd try to yock it up," he recalled. "I was always funny. They'd ask me in school about Columbus and I'd say, '*Columbus Cleaning and Pressing, Fifth and Hooper.*' The class would laugh and I'd get hit by the principal, kicked down the stairs, bleeding in the gutter—I couldn't stop laughing." He once said, "I always felt it was my job to amuse those around me."

The young Mel was "the undisputed champ of corner shtick"—meeting at Feingold's Candy Story to quaff egg creams, girl-watch, and crack jokes with buddies like Speed Vogel (later a pal of the novelist Joseph Heller), whom Brooks roomed with after divorcing his first wife. Brooks, Heller, Vogel, and Zero Mostel would meet Tuesdays for a big Chinese dinner as The Group of the Oblong Table, with comic chaos from wonton soup to fortune cookies. Brooks once said of those dinners, "I'm sure we're funnier than the Algonquin Round Table, but we're not as bright."

At Tamiment, he had been a "pool *tummler*," the guy at the Jewish resorts who keeps the guests laughing around the swimming pool—"a busboy in baggy pants," someone put it. His main bit was to walk out on the diving board—he was fourteen—wearing a black derby, a heavy black alpaca overcoat, and carrying two suitcases and yell, "*Business is terrible! I can't go on!*" and leap into the pool. He would sink to the bottom with the heavy suitcases and remain there until the lifeguard dove in and fished him out. He told Terry Gross on her public-radio show *Fresh Air,* "You started by just tending the rowboats or being a busboy and you prayed to end up in a variety show on Saturday night." If he had gone into movies, he told Gross, "I would have played the bellboy in hotel movies in the thirties. In the forties I'd've been a good-natured soldier—they'd have called me 'Brooklyn.' In the fifties I'd've been the band boy in a rock-and-roll group. I would've been called Winky or Blinky or Nod."

Brooks wasn't influenced by comedians, Jewish or otherwise. Rather, he absorbed the humor and theatricality of the Jewish theater he saw as a kid. He joined a stock company at fifteen, where he met the impressionist Will Jordan, who recalls, "He's exactly the same as he was in 1957, except now I know that he's Mel Brooks, but he talks to me exactly as he did then." At a summer-stock company, adds Jordan, Brooks "would do Jolson and things equivalent to the 2,000 Year Old Man. He did Gregory Peck's father as an old Jew. The humor was attuned just as good as it is now."

Brooks became a drummer in a Borscht Belt band (he'd taken lessons from Buddy Rich) and one night went on for an ailing comic; he hung on all summer and never played the drums again. Brooks told Gross, "The owner of the resort, Pincus Cohen, would say, 'Melb'n, the comic is sick and we know you're cute and funny so jump on the stage and amuse the guests.'" His first night, he imitated a maid who had locked herself in a storeroom, which was the talk of the resort. After saying, "*Good evening, ladies and Jews,*" Brooks bellowed like the imprisoned maid, Sophie.

"There was a lot of great material lying around in the Catskills waiting to be noticed," he recalled. He delighted the guests—the henna-haired ladies in the tearoom, the yentas on rubber life rafts in the pool, the old guys baking in the steam room and rocking on the porches. They all wound up inhabiting his 2,000 Year Old Man. "In the Catskills," he recounted, "I didn't know what I was doing. I was billed as the crazy Mel Brooks. I used to imitate Thomas Jefferson. They would say, 'Very good.' Who the hell knew what he sounded like? The band always laughed. I never had the Jews but I had the band. It was like a tearoom, people eating pound cake. They all said, 'Melb'n, you stink but we love you!' " He told an interviewer, "I decided then to do people's comedy—comedy everybody knew, instead of 'jokes,' and I've been doing it ever since. I didn't want to do those ancient jokes, so I decided to go out there and make up stuff, just talk about things we all knew, and see if they turned out funny. Look, I had to take chances or it wasn't fun being funny." Taking chances is Mel Brooks's comic credo.

His anything-for-a-laugh persistence wore even him out. "I was terrible," he said of his *tummeling* days, when he would dash on with a theme song: "*Da-da-da-dat dat daaa! Here I am. / I'm Melvin Brooks! / I've come to stop the show. / Just a ham who's minus looks / But in your hearts I'll grow! / I'll tell you gags, I'll sing you songs. / Just happy little snappy songs that roll along. / Out of my mind, / Won't you be kind? / And please . . . love . . . Melvin Brooooooooks!*" He has readily admitted, "I just browbeat my way into show business." He joined a New Jersey theater group, the Red Bank Players, and ran it for a while. Brooks, the abrasive but irrepressible comic hustler, was born with the Sammy Glick–Duddy Kravitz gene. Beneath all the moxie, however, was a needy and insecure clown.

A typical Brooks sketch was his very first for *Your Show of Shows*—a takeoff on *Jungle Boy,* with Sid Caesar in a loincloth trying to survive in New York City by eating pigeons (Interviewer: "*Don't the pigeons object?*" Caesar: "*Only for a minute*") and battling deadly cars (Interviewer: "*You're afraid of a Buick?*" Caesar: "*Yes, Buick can win in death struggle. Must sneak up on parked Buick. Punch grille hard. Buick die*").

He had a hard time convincing Max Liebman of his comic gifts. The producer's first reaction to him was, "Who's this meshuggener?" "Max hated me," Brooks told *Playboy* in 1975. "I was a pretty snotty kid. But I hated him right back. He didn't like my fast mouth. When I'd sass him back he'd throw a lighted cigar at me—right at my face!" But Liebman couldn't fire him, because he'd never hired him. One day onstage, Brooks cried, "Pepper Martin sliding into second! Watch your ass!" and flung himself at Liebman headfirst, between his legs, and sent him flying.

Another time, the comic enfant terrible (who was notoriously late to meetings) crashed through the door of an important conference with David Sarnoff, RCA's chairman of the board, and Pat Weaver, the head of NBC, whipped off his straw hat, sailed it across the room and out the window, leaped up on the conference table, and cried, "*Hooray! Lindy has landed at Le Bourget!*"—followed by a chorus of "La Marseillaise." Not surprisingly, his comic heroes were the Ritz Brothers. Amid such madcap capers, says Brooks, he learned a lot working for Liebman—"I went to Max Liebman University for four years." Off-campus, he wrote sketches for *New Faces of 1952*. In the show's *Death of a Salesman* parody, a revue classic, the father is a burglar who's anguished when his son gets straight A's and has no interest in becoming a crook ("*Steal something, anything! I know you can. I know, deep down inside, you're rotten*").

The one who laughed the hardest at Brooks was Caesar, who paid the little madman fifty dollars a week out of his own pocket just to keep him around as his pet comic muse, a sort of freelance fool. "I'd wait in the hallway outside where they were writing the show. Sid would stick his head out and say, 'We need three jokes.' So I'd give him three jokes, but Max wouldn't let me in." Liebman kept telling Brooks that he wasn't ready yet (he finally crashed the party in 1951). "He saw me as some kind of adventurer and didn't think I was very talented. I was a street kid and didn't have any sophistication. Max was a classy guy who wanted to do a real Broadway revue every week. He wasn't interested in street humor."

Brooks stirred up the writers' meetings during creative silences by bursting in, brandishing his cigar or a bagel, bubbling over with inspired but mostly unusable ideas. Of rumors that everyone there hated him, he said: "Everybody hated everybody. There was tremendous hostility in the air. A highly charged situation, but very good. We were all spoiled brats competing with each other for the king's favor, and we all wanted to come up with the funniest joke." At the king's table sat Brooks, Neil and Danny Simon, the head writer Mel Tolkin, Lucille Kallen, Joseph Stein (who later wrote the libretto for *Fiddler on the Roof*), their typist, Michael Stewart (the future *Hello, Dolly!* librettist), Larry Gelbart, and a few lesser-known geniuses. Woody Allen, contrary to legend, was not part of this original hallowed circle, but worked on two later Caesar specials. All comic roads in the 1950s led, if not to Rome, to Caesar.

"Seven rats in a cage" was Brooks's description of Caesar's writers. "The pitch sessions were lethal. In that room, you had to fight to stay alive." His major contribution to the show, he said, was "energy and insanity. I was totally willing to be an idiot. I would jump off into space, not knowing where I would land. Pain. Humiliation. In those pitch sessions, I had an audience of experts who showed no mercy. But I had to go beyond. It wasn't only competition to be funnier. I had to get to the ultimate punch line, the cosmic joke that all the other jokes came out of. I had to hit off the walls. I was immensely ambitious. It was like I was screaming at the universe to pay attention, like I had to make *God* laugh."

Of his personal jester, Caesar said, "He was funny and ingenious and he liked my type of humor, so he hung around me." Brooks was smitten early: "I saw the movie *Stars and Spars.* I studied what Sid did and I said, This guy is *really* funny, *uniquely* funny." Steve Allen observed that almost anything Brooks did might just as easily have worked for Caesar, adding, "Sid is the only other comedian who could have done the 2,000 Year Old Man. Mel's and Sid's minds in those days seemed two halves of the same brain." Alan King agrees that Brooks had everything it takes to be a stand-up comic—"except the guts. He was only funny around his friends. He's not very comfortable in front of an audience."

Neil Simon knows why Brooks never became a stand-up comic: "Mel is not that controlled. Mel is one of the funniest people I ever met in my life. Mel could sit and do one of those 2,000 Year Old Man records with Carl Reiner. But one album could be the result of twenty nights. He's not the kind of guy who could get up and do monologues. His mind was so splintered into brilliance that, if Mel was there, it wasn't a joke, it was just a comic explosion. The movies Mel did were very Mel Brooks kinds of things." So Caesar became the comic that Brooks might have become. "He was such a great vehicle for my passion," says Brooks. "Sid had this terrific anger in him—he was angry with the world, and so was I. Maybe I was angry because I was a Jew, because I was short, because my mother didn't buy me a bicycle, because it was tough to get ahead, because I wasn't God—who knows why?"

Brooks once followed Caesar down the street and, to get his attention, threw a punch at the comedy star, who towered over him. "He was indefatigable in trying to sell his ideas to me," said Caesar, who told him, "Mel, I will let you live. If you feel that strongly about your idea, I'll use it." Brooks had another favorite tactic—interrupting Caesar's preshow nap by opening the door and whispering some of his lines that had been rejected, hoping to get them into Caesar's brain subliminally. The other writers kept a Mel Brooks doll handy to hang in effigy when he grew too exasperating. He was once thrown out of the *Your Show of Shows* theater by two ushers who tossed him into an alley. "I said, 'You're crazy. You can't do this to Mel Brooks. I'm potentially very important.' "

After both worming and barreling his way onto the staff, moving up from "additional dialogue by Mel Brooks" at fifty bucks a week to staff writer at a thousand dollars a week, he felt added pressure to prove his worth. He would run through the streets to work off his adrenaline. He couldn't sleep nights. Kallen recalled Brooks at a script meeting imitating "everything from a rabbinical student to Moby-Dick thrashing about on the floor with six harpoons sticking in his back." He leaned heavily on Tolkin, who became a surrogate father to him. The droll, Russian-born Tolkin got Brooks to read Tolstoy and Gogol, which partly quieted him and gave him a life philosophy (and a name for his son, Nicholas, after Nikolai Gogol): "Gogol said that life is so tragic, so stupendously sad, that we'd better laugh a lot and enjoy ourselves," said Brooks. "The Russian novelists made me realize it's a bigger ballpark than the *Sergeant Bilko* show. I wanted to achieve more than Doc [Neil] Simon and Abe Burrows did. I wanted to be the American Molière, the new Aristophanes."

Brooks left *Caesar's Hour* to write for Imogene Coca's new show, which was in need of help. Now feeling his oats, he antagonized the other writers, at one point telling the show's head writer—it was Kallen—"Don't you tell me what's funny, you just type." A colleague once described his writing style as shouting at a secretary. The other writers told the producer that it was either Brooks or them. A friend said of him, "He's a tremendously warm and loving guy, but he has to have his way." A détente was reached, but the show folded soon after, in time for Brooks to rejoin *Caesar's Hour* in its second season, in 1955.

Everyone assumed Caesar & Co. would go on indefinitely, but when *Caesar's Hour* was canceled, it sent Brooks into a tailspin for two years. Just when he had felt himself ready to take off, "the roof fell in," said Brooks. "There I am, strolling around in silk shirts and thinking I'm cut out for greatness. Television's too small for me. How am I going to get out of this lousy racket? And suddenly I *am* out of it. The show is off the air. One day it's five thousand dollars a week, the next day it's zilch. I couldn't get a job anywhere. It was a terrifying nose dive."

What saved Brooks's career, and maybe his sanity, was the 2,000 Year Old Man, who was conceived in the writing room at *Your Show of Shows* but was never performed on the show as such. He and Reiner, and occasionally Tolkin, had done a similar Q-and-A routine at parties. "We spent our days inventing characters for Caesar," Reiner told *The New Yorker,* "but Mel was really using Caesar as a vehicle. What he secretly wanted was to perform himself. So in the evening we'd go to a party and I'd pick a character for him to play. I never told him what it was going to be, but I always tried for something that would force him to go into panic, because a brilliant mind in panic is a wonderful thing to see. There was no end to what he could be—a U-boat commander, a deaf songwriter, a convention of antique dealers." Brooks's 2,000 Year Old Man led this secret life for ten years before he was recorded in 1960. The unruly routine was at first considered too inside, too special, too Jewish, too surreal, too intellectual, too everything.

Brooks later recalled the character's genesis, in 1953: "He [Reiner] brought in a new tape recorder. Just to try it out he made up this thing. He said, '*Ladies and gentlemen, there's a man here who claims to be two thousand years old. He says he was actually at the site of the Crucifixion of Jesus Christ. Sir?*' And he turns to me, knowing that I would give him something, and I said, '*Oh, it was a terrible t'ing,*' and he said, '*Did you know any of his followers?*' I said, '*Sure, dey all came in deh store, and dey never bought anyt'ing! You can't make a living from t'ese apostles.*' And from there on in, he never let me go—he kept annoying me with this 2,000 Year Old Man."

Reiner's recollection: "I knew I would get a funny answer, because Mel had gotten up in the office many times without questions and just regaled us; he did a Jewish pirate who had trouble getting sailcloth at a good price that I'll never forget as long as I live." Brooks said, "We did it at parties for our own amusement." Parties would even be built around it. The team became a cult act on the celebrity circuit. George Burns insisted the team record it or threatened to steal it himself. Steve Allen volunteered to finance the album, telling Reiner, "You guys listen to it; if you don't like it, burn it or throw it away. But at least get it down." "And the next thing you know," said Reiner, "it's up for a Grammy."

The skeptical Reiner and Brooks permitted Allen to make a few calls on their behalf to Dick Bock, the head of World-Pacific Records, a small, West Coast jazz label, who took Allen at his word that the world's-oldest-man routine was hilarious. (Later, Bock unwisely sold the rights to Capitol Records for $40,000.) Before an invited audience, Brooks and Reiner spent two hours ad-libbing. Reiner remembered, "We thought it might be considered a little anti-Semitic, using a Jewish accent." Brooks said the character was a combination of his mother, his Uncle Joe, "and a lot of *Yiddishkeit* clichés that only people who grew up in the Bronx and Brooklyn would know." Reiner said, "We had no idea people like Cary Grant would get it," but he later heard that Grant bought albums for friends and even took a record to Buckingham Palace to amuse the Royal Family. "He told us they loved it."

Allen assured Brooks that the routine wasn't too inside or too Jewish at all. "Ten years of Sid Caesar's brand of comedy on television [i.e., steeped in borscht and sour cream] had made American audiences—or at least a segment of them—hip enough to laugh just as much at this material as we all did." Allen was right, and the old Jew later appeared on such mainstream TV shows as *The Hollywood Palace, The Colgate Comedy Hour,* and *The Ed Sullivan Show.* "Jewish humor" was becoming American humor.

On that first milestone album, Reiner asks the 2,000 Year Old Man, "*Can you give us the secret of your longevity?*" and Brooks replies, "*Well, deh major thing is that I never ever touch fried food. And I never run for a bus. There'll always be another.*" Without Brooks, those are mildly funny lines, but with Brooks delivering them in his skeptical American-Yiddish manner, they become irresistible and hilarious. Reiner: "*There were no buses at that time. What was the means of transportation then?*" Brooks: "*Mostly fear.*" Reiner: "*Fear transported you?*" Brooks: "*Fear, yes. An animal could growl, you'd go two miles in a minute.*" Reiner: "*What language did you speak?*" Brooks: "*Basic Rock. That was before Hebrew.*" Reiner: "*Can you give us an example?*" Brooks: "*Hey, don't t'row t'at rock at me!*"

It was Allen who first talked Brooks into wearing the 2,000 Year Old Man's trademark cape and black fedora on his TV show, but Mel Brooks looks funny just as himself—the frantic, closely set eyes in a face once described as "a small mudslide," the troll-like body, the gravelly Brooklyn rasp that's half bravado and half bored. Of the dialect he uses, he explained: "I really wailed. I could hear my antecedents. I could hear five thousand years of Jews pouring through me. Within a couple of decades, there won't be any more accents like that. They're being ironed out by history. It's the sound I was brought up on, and it's dying."

A Brooks crony, the comedy writer Ron Clark, witnessed two 2,000 Year Old Man recording sessions. "They sit for a while and go over subject matters and decide what areas to cover," recalls Clark. "Then Carl has all the questions and knows how to feed him. He'll know where it's going but he doesn't know where the jokes are, and Mel gets off on tangents and will do a five-minute riff that Carl is surprised by. It's all based on his *tummeling* in the Catskills."

At the time he created the ancient sage, Brooks was not yet thirty-four and was "on the brink of [financial] disaster." Reiner said, "It gave him an identity as a comic performer for the first time." The record crossed comedy lines and jumped all age, culture, and ethnic gaps. While the content was contemporary and smart, the style was as traditional as Weber & Fields. Holtzman described it as "a brisk twelve and a half minutes that plays like an ingenious jazz improvisation on a standard melody."

The 2,000 Year Old Man is the perfect open-ended sketch and a textbook example of the art of fifties and sixties improvisation—even if the finished recordings were edited from several performances before invited audiences. The routine relies totally on the team's mental agility and chemistry. It's almost heresy to imagine Brooks performing it with any other straight man. Reiner was a solid straight man to Caesar, but with Brooks he is the second-banana supreme—egging on the feisty little egomaniacal Jewish bimillenarian, cutting him off when he's run out of jokes, smoothly shifting to a new subject that piques his interest. Reiner became the subtle rudder, guiding his partner's churning comic mind. Without batting an eyelash, and with a continuous air of respect, curiosity, and fascination, Reiner feeds and nourishes his partner's deadpan hunger. The comedian Richard Lewis put it nicely: "Carl drives the truck and Mel carries the explosives."

Brooks always praises Reiner's skills as his inquisitor: "Carl is sculpting the piece as it emerges. As I rave on about Jesus and Joan of Arc and all these people, he's making a little playlet out of it." Says Holtzman: "Carl guides the tempo, and the moment he senses a given theme is nearing depletion, he moves on. Sometimes he intentionally interrupts, teasing with just the tip of ideas. He is by turns doubtful and gullible. His timing is magnificent, his tone unshakable. Whenever the interview hints of becoming a checklist of historical gags, Carl adroitly steers it to more personal territory." At a 2001 TV tribute to Carl Reiner, when Reiner won the Kennedy Center's third annual Mark Twain Award for Humor, Jerry Seinfeld said, "When I watch the 2,000 Year Old Man, I watch Carl Reiner."

Brooks has said that Reiner "chases me like I'm a mouse," trying to corner him with high-minded queries, which he reduces to the humdrum level of his own earthbound life. Nothing daunts him. How did he feel about Joan of Arc being burned at the stake? *"Terrible."* As Joan of Arc's boyfriend, he told her, *"I'm gonna wash up. You save France."* Shakespeare, he recalls, *"was not a good writer at all. He had the worst penmanship I ever saw in my life."* Brooks diminishes the history of civilization to lousy handwriting, a nectarine, a guy named Murray, Saran Wrap (Q. *"You equate that* [Saran Wrap] *with man's discovery of space?"* A. *"T'at vas good"*). When Reiner asks, *"What work did man first do?"* Brooks replies, *"Hittin' a tree wit' a piece of stick was already a good job. If you could get it."* History's original Zelig, the 2,000 Year Old Man recalls an Eleventh Commandment cut from the final draft: *"Thou shalt not squint."*

The interview format, a stand-up staple since minstrels' Mr. Bones and Mr. Interlocutor, was the ideal showcase to display Brooks's restlessly inventive mind. Whoever Brooks plays, it's usually a close relative of the 2,000 Year Old Man, Brooks's *alter-kacker* ego, such as the annoyed off-screen narrator of an abstract 1963 animated cartoon parody, *The Critic* (*"Dis is cute, dis is cute, dis is nice. Vat da hell is it? It must be some symbolism. I t'ink it's symbolic of junk!"*).

Reiner would never tell Brooks what character he wanted him to portray. Whatever the character—Israeli wrestling champion, celebrated sculptor, Jewish pirate—Brooks would be off and riffing. It became a game, like those that Nichols & May and Bob & Ray played, with Reiner trying to provoke Brooks with a preposterous premise that he suspected Brooks would knock out of the park. Reiner said, "The best things are the ones that aren't terribly well planned—accidents, almost." Much of the act is a dazzling display of Brooks's verbal prowess. His basic twist—contrasting the old world with the new in the tired voice of an old Jew—is not just funny but biblically correct. Maurice Yacowar states that "Brooks's Yiddish is a declaration of independence" from gentile America.

On their 1973 album, *The 2,013 Year Old Man,* the old man says he was breast-fed for two hundred years by various women he talked into it, and that it took him another two hundred years to get his "public hair." *"You mean pubic,"* corrects Reiner. *"No, no—my public hair—on my head, my arms, the hair the public sees."* Reiner wonders if the ancient skeptic ever believed in anything, and Brooks replies, *"Yeah, a guy named Phil."* When the subject of masturbation comes up, Reiner asks Brooks if Onan was ostracized. *"No, but he was circumcised."* When Reiner asks what was man's greatest invention, Brooks shoots back instantly, *"Liquid Prell!"* Asked if he has any kids, the 2,013 Year Old Man kvetches, *"I hed forty-two t'ousand children, an' vould you believe, not* one *comes to visit."* A *Newsweek* reporter asked him to name the greatest comedy team in history: *"I would have to say Wilt and Neville Chamberlain. What a hysterical team. First Neville would read the Nurem-berg pact, then Wilt would stuff him through a basket."*

After the first album, Brooks was a star and no longer had to intro-duce himself as, "Hello, I'm Mel Brooks, I write the Sid Caesar show." He had a new advance man, the wizened wise man. "I can say anything I want. And then if people question me, I say, 'Don't blame me. Blame the old Jew.' " Discussing his early life as a party entertainer known by every-body in show business but no one else, Brooks told Brad Darrach: "For thirty-five years I was an underground funny. I was a comic's comic, then I was a comedy writer's comedy writer. When I'd go to where they were working, famous comedians would turn white. 'My God, he's here!' But I was never a big name to the public. And then suddenly I surfaced. The record came out. Sold maybe a million copies. Saved me."

If the 2,000 Year Old Man saved his career, a thirty-three-year-old woman, Anne Bancroft, saved his life in what became one of the least likely, most celebrated marriages in show business. They met in 1961, right around the time the album hit. He arranged to be at a rehearsal of the *Perry Como Show,* and after she'd sung "Married I Can Always Get," he burst into applause, rushed over to her, and, legend has it, cried, "Hi, I'm Mel Brooks. I would kill for you!" They became instant and constant friends, and married three years later on Brooks's lunch hour in a civil ceremony; he twisted one of her silver earrings into a wedding ring. When she took Brooks home, her mother told her, "You could do better." An explosive Jew and an emotional Italian (born Anna Maria Louisa Ital-iano) seemed a sure match for disaster. "We have plenty of fights," he once conceded, "but, I mean, we're *married,* right? But for me, this is it." (Before Bancroft he was married to Florence Baum, with whom he had three children; he and Bancroft have a son, Max.)

Ron Clark, who wrote *High Anxiety* with Brooks (he and his wife are close to Brooks and Bancroft), agrees that the comic can be a bit intimi-dating to strangers. "Mel can get into different moods—he doesn't want to talk to outsiders, whereas Carl will talk readily. But once you know Mel he opens up." Brooks acts as unlicensed physician to his friends. Remarks Clark, "He's so good at it that people, myself included, if I get a strange pain, I would call him first. And if he can't solve it, he refers you to a very good doctor."

The massive success of the 2,000 Year Old Man gave Brooks the license to venture as far afield as his teeming, somersaulting comic brain could take him—which resulted in *The Producers,* still his most beloved film. Will Jordan insists that Brooks and Lenny Bruce both stole his Hitler-as-a-musical idea. Jordan and Brooks had once hung out, trading voices, lines, ideas, and shtick, often entering parties as a gay couple. "I'm sure he doesn't even realize he stole it from me," says Jordan, "but it's the concept that's important and I'm very proud of it." Pre–*The Producers,* Jordan recalls running into Brooks and complaining to him how Lenny Bruce had lifted the Hitler bit: "Mel sat there screaming at the story. But here's the part that really kills me. I saw them on interviews describing at length how they wrote the Hitler routines. So in order to cover for your theft you invent a whole history of how you wrote a routine!"

In time, Brooks spun out his elaborate movie parodies (*Silent Movie; Robin Hood: Men in Tights*), and movies of pure comic anarchy (*The History of the World, Part I; Life Stinks; Space Balls*) that displayed him at his silliest and most self-indulgent. But he also engineered two glossy, controlled nonparodic comedies, *The Twelve Chairs* and *To Be or Not to Be,* the latter a remake of Ernst Lubitsch's Jack Benny–Carole Lombard classic. His parody TV series *When Things Were Rotten* proved a fast flop, but he and Buck Henry created the hit 1960s TV spy spoof *Get Smart.*

Brooks's friends were surprised that he could ever be organized enough to direct a movie. He once called his directing style "calculated chaos," remarking, "Something a lot of people don't realize about me: I am a very well-trained maniac." As a cinematic satirist, Brooks is a kind of comic-kazi, strafing his movies with everything in his battered arsenal of gags. His general instruction to casts is, "Go bananas!" Brooks's favorite comic precept, which he regularly breaks in all of his over-the-top films, is: "Never, never try to be funny! Comedy is a red rubber ball, and if you throw it against a soft, funny wall, it will not come back. But if you throw it against the hard wall of ultimate reality, it will bounce back and be very lively." His most quoted dramatic theory is: "Tragedy is if I cut my finger. Comedy is if you walk into an open sewer and die."

Without the structure of a genre or specific classic film to anchor his humor, he often cruises on crude gags, puns, antique groaners, juvenilia, and sheer chutzpah. He has readily admitted, "There are critics who regard me as a vulgar primitive—I never quarrel. I got nothing against cheap jokes—if they work." He shrugs and says, "When you work in the

mountains, cheap jokes never leave you. I'm a purveyor of cheap jokes."
The composer Charles Strouse (who worked with Brooks on the 1962
Ray Bolger musical *All-American,* and with whom Brooks first discussed a
musical about Hitler) once called him "a comic brawler who keeps swinging wildly, and when he connects he knocks you out." Alan King adds,
"There's a sense of danger, like with Robin Williams. How far are they
gonna go?" In a tribute to Brooks on PBS's *Newshour,* the Princeton classi-
cist and critic Daniel Mendelsohn noted, "People love Mel Brooks because he's so *outré* and crazy. So much of what Mel Brooks is about is
tastelessness."

Brooks once explained that the comic method behind his madness is
to thwart dying: "In order to keep death at bay," he said, "I do a lot of '*Yah!
Yah! Yah!*' And death says, 'All right. He's too noisy. I'll wait for someone
who's sitting quietly, half asleep. I'll nail *him.* Why should I bother with
this guy? I'll have a lot of trouble getting him out the door. This will be a
fight. I ain't got time.' Most people are afraid of death, but I really *hate* it!
My humor is a scream and a protest against goodbye." Gene Wilder, a
major player in the Brooks laugh factory, said: "I see him standing bare-
chested on top of a mountain, shouting. 'Look at me!' and 'Don't let me
die!' These are the two things that rule his life." Brooks has said: "Look at
Jewish history. Unrelieved lamenting would be intolerable. So, for every
ten Jews beating their breasts, God designed one to be crazy and amuse
the breast-beaters. By the time I was five I knew I was that one."

Herbert Gold wrote in a 1975 *New York Times* profile of Brooks:
"Woody Allen and Mel Brooks do not threaten total revolution, but they
play with nihilism. Where Lenny Bruce shocked, Mel Brooks consoles."
Billy Wilder compared Woody Allen's comic style—"lighting ten thousand safety matches to illuminate a city, each one a little epiphany"—to
that of Brooks, who "wants to set off atom bombs of laughter." The director Barry Levinson, who worked with Brooks on *High Anxiety,* adds:
"They're total opposites. Mel is a peasant type. His films deal with basic
wants and needs, like power and money. Woody's films are about inadequacies, especially sexual inadequacy, and frailty and vulnerability." The
film critic Andrew Sarris wrote that Allen and Nichols & May represented the intellectual Jewish camp and Caesar and Brooks the philistine.
Holzman notes, "Brooks was less the social critic than the social vandal,
his comedy less commentary than graffiti."

It is this very outlaw sense of derring-do that made Mel Brooks a chosen son of the comic renaissance. He brought to the era an outsize outrageousness, an explosive Marx Brothers freneticism, a lightning, leaping mind, and a blend of little-boy naughtiness and old-timer wisdom. He had a crazed affection for pop culture, an acute eye and ear for parody, and a tilted view of life that saw the world through a cracked bottle of seltzer. His 2,000 Year Old Man was the funniest comedian who never lived.

Curing the Body Politic

Dick Gregory

I found somethin' that made me feel better inside than comedy.

BARELY BATTING a heavy-lidded eyelash, Dick Gregory could turn racial turmoil in America into a fun evening. He was so sweetly and serenely reasonable, so nonthreatening, so downright amiable, that you didn't realize until you were walking out of a club that he had heightened your sense of civil rights. Like Huck Finn's runaway raftmate, Jim, Gregory won you over by his understated wisdom, compassion, and unassuming common sense.

A polished comedian perched on a stool in a nightclub, he coolly inhaled a cigarette and blew thoughtful smoke rings while benevolently blasting the hottest topic of the day—racism—as if discussing the weather. Behind this sly comic façade, he was a brilliantly funny smooth-talker, and still is, now peddling health cure-alls and social remedies in lieu of jokes after virtually vanishing from the public eye a generation ago. Since the 1970s, Gregory has languished in the celebrity twilight zone of "Whatever happened to . . . ?" where he floats in time with such other ghostly comic souls of his era as Mort Sahl, Tom Lehrer, Shelley Berman, David Frye, and Vaughn Meader.

When Bill Cosby was asked, in 2001, on National Public Radio's *Talk of the Nation,* where Dick Gregory fit into the history of American comedy, Cosby asserted that "Dick Gregory *is* history. Dick Gregory is not with those people [comedians]. Dick Gregory stands alone." He added, however, "Dick does not get the tip of the hat publicly."

One of the toughest sociopolitical comedians of the 1960s, Gregory simply said what he wanted to say and then moved on. He wasn't bumped aside, like Shelley Berman; he didn't scamper into movies like Woody Allen, or slip into cozy sitcoms like Bob Newhart and Cosby. Nor did he burn himself out like Lenny Bruce or wear out his welcome like Mort Sahl. Like Bruce and Sahl, however, he used his comic tools to build a playing field much larger than comedy. He voluntarily quit show business at the top—at first for civil rights activity, which led him, circuitously, to health issues, which merged, ultimately, into humanitarian concerns and fears for the planet. Social and physical concerns—he views them all as part of some larger, cosmic tragicomedy.

Making people laugh failed to fulfill Gregory. It was too easy; he felt like a trained (but troubled) seal. The world, he decided, needed to hear more candor, a harsher, more urgent message. Eventually the preacher in him edged out the performer in a friendly takeover. Gregory gave it all up to become a professional propagandist, even though he was far more effective as an astutely dry political comedian delivering firebombs about blacks and whites coexisting in America. Gregory wasn't kidding.

It was an epic American journey. Gregory, born in a St. Louis ghetto, became the first black comic to permanently cross over into the major all-white clubs of the 1960s. He had played a few black clubs before being called (while working his day job at a car wash) to fill in for Irwin Corey. He made his big leap forward in a single bound at the flagship Playboy Club in Chicago on January 13, 1960. It was not just a major career move, it was a major sociological move for black stand-up comics, who, prior to that, had performed mainly in ghetto rooms. The idea of a black comic in a white club was virtually unheard-of; in many clubs (extending to Harlem's Cotton Club), blacks weren't even welcome as customers. That he was a curiosity on a nightclub stage seemed not even to have occurred to him. He behaved as if he belonged up there, unapologetically, as if his presence was inevitable.

There seemed nothing all that noisily revolutionary about it at the time, when the civil rights movement was ignited and provided the thrust that zoomed him to fame. Had he appeared in calmer times, or tried to make it with only traditional jokes, he likely would have been turned away. But Dick Gregory's arrival as the first major breakthrough black comedian seemed a logical step in the racial revolt of the fifties and sixties—a case of being not just in the right place at the right time, but, more crucially, of being the right man for the job.

There had been black comics on the fringes: Timmie Rogers ("Oh, yeahhh!"); Slappy White, an ex-hoofer with snappy patter who was among the first black comics to work the Catskills; and, to be sure, the bright-eyed and sassy Nipsey Russell, with his rhyming couplets and uptown veneer, who observed that "aside from Billy Eckstein and Lena Horne, black performers were variety entertainers, not headliners." Black comics had to stay in costume or character. Black comics who spoke directly to a mixed audience were regarded as uppity niggers stealing a white man's act; Redd Foxx and Moms Mabley were ruthlessly honest and seasoned veteran comics forced, for decades, to work below society's racial radar, heard only on raw "party records."

Gregory was perceived as a keen satirical social commentator, a full-blooded, card-carrying member of the comedy renaissance, not just as a black comic. "Gregory avoided most of the superficial mannerisms and traditional subjects that perfectly defined old-time African-American humor, concentrating on the irony and satire," observes black historian Mel Watkins. Asked why he, rather than Redd Foxx, Slappy White, Timmie Rogers, or Nipsey Russell, had broken through, Gregory suggests it was because he stayed in Chicago: "Had I been in New York, I don't think I would ever have made it—New York was too goddamn fast," he says. "So many comics of that era came out of Chicago. Chicago is not a city. It's the number-one *town* in America. New York is so intimidating. You can go and get rave reviews on a play in Chicago and go to New York and die."

The other black comedians were bright, skillful, and funny, but, as Watkins puts it, "the temper of the times assured that, before the comics reached mass, mainstream audiences, much of the edge in their humor was blunted." They were unable to bridge two cultures and to interpret the headlines as adroitly as Gregory. For all their funky street-life and semipolitical material, the others worked in the black nightclub tradition on the "chitlin circuit."

Watkins notes that Gregory was "more of a candid satirist than an entertaining funny man," like the others, and thus fit in better with his times. Rogers, White, mimic George Kirby, and most of all Russell (who became a regular on *Hollywood Squares* and on Jack Paar's show) each helped dismantle the stand-up-comic color barrier a few bricks at a time. Gregory vaulted across it in a flash, leapfrogging over black comics who had spent decades in the trenches. Consequently, their reactions to Gregory were a conflicted mix of envy, resentment, and grudging respect.

Gregory's material was black enough to regale black audiences and white enough to pass as mainstream comedy. He joked about giving up smoking (*"I been readin' so much about cigarettes and cancer, I quit readin'"*), about Khrushchev (*"Wouldn't it be funny if Khrushchev didn't really hate us, but his interpreter did?"*), and about growing up poor (*"Kids didn't eat off the floor. When I was a kid, you dropped something off the table—it never* reached *the floor"*).

The widely heard radio news commentator Alex Dreier, an early Gregory supporter, wrote in the liner notes on the comic's first album,

Dick Gregory in Living Black and White: "Dick Gregory is neither Ralph Bunche nor Amos 'n' Andy. Gregory's humor is not 'negro humor' in the traditional sense. Nor is it 'shock' type humor. It does not jar you, nor does it 'shake you up.' It doesn't depend on dirty little words, or dirty big thoughts." To potential white LP buyers, Dreier said comfortingly: "No matter what his subject, Dick Gregory will not make you angry. Nor can the most vitriolic race-baiter anger him. This record carries no message, unless the message is this: There is no problem so serious that it cannot be leavened with humor. This is Dick Gregory's credo."

Although he had done some blue material in black clubs, Gregory wisely torpedoed his black-and-blue jokes in white rooms. He studiously avoided being pegged the new Redd Foxx, a fine line that Bill Cosby, too, later walked in his raceless ride to the top. "If you use blue material," Gregory wrote in *nigger,* his 1964 memoir, "you slip back into being that Negro stereotype comic." As Watkins notes, Gregory eradicated "all traces of the minstrel image" of earlier black performers. "Gregory was to most of his black forerunners what Mort Sahl was to Milton Berle." Both Gregory and the comedian Godfrey Cambridge gave off more wily, candid, and contemporary vibes, despite droopy-lidded expressions reminiscent of the Sambo era, a shrewd disguise to mask their potent social message.

He also became the first black crossover comedian, Gregory adds, "because of the way I talk. White folks heard this genius, but it wasn't threatening. I don't speak perfect English—never tried to. I think that's what wasn't threatening." His security onstage produced easy laughter. "When you go out on the stage worrying about the laughs, then you get in trouble. They sense a certain insecurity. They gotta see that *fun* look." He insists, however, that he made no conscious attempt to be nonthreatening to whites and that his "fun look" wasn't painted on.

To cross the color barrier, he had to tell more white than black jokes, and he tailored his act accordingly. "I bought white man's joke books to figure out what whitey was laughing at—you know, mother-in-law jokes and Khrushchev. Then I made a mixture—twenty percent black, eighty percent white." Not just any black jokes, either. "When I hit in 1961, there wasn't a healthy race joke in America," he once said. "They were all derogatory to one race or another. It was in 1961 that a little ol' nigger born in 1932 gave the country a new way out—healthy racial jokes." Gregory said he started earning $5,000 a week "for saying out loud what I'd always said under my breath."

He didn't make fun of himself or whites but tried to get both sides to laugh at themselves. It was his calling card: "If I've done anything to upset you, maybe it's what I'm here for," he told audiences. Gregory worked both sides of the comedy street, using old jokes as a decoy, interspersing harmless gags (*"My wife's a terrible cook—she can't even make corn flakes"*) with biting social commentary (*"There's no difference between the North and the South. In the South they don't mind how close I get so long as I don't get too big; in the North they don't mind how big I get so long as I don't get too close"*).

Although one critic noted that "Dick Gregory's humor is, by and large, designed for a white audience," he managed the transition without compromising his integrity. He never watered down his punchy commentary for whites. He never Tommed, although some claimed that his act for black clubs was earthier and harder-edged. Like all comics then, both black and white (save Mort Sahl), Gregory performed in an executive suit and tie. He was clean, never mean. Unlike the nattering Nipsey Russell, he spoke quietly and slowly, nor did he flash ingratiating grins. But clearly this was no Stepin Fetchit.

Gregory has said in retrospect, "I was doing things to people's minds I wasn't even aware of. For the first time they could see an intelligent black man standin' flatfooted and tellin' 'em about their business." For years, he notes, black entertainers had to be animated—dancing, or, at the very least, singing, but never speaking. The black historian Donald Bogle writes: "During a period of [social] upheaval . . . Gregory projected intelligent self-assurance. He was not servile. These were things that black people wanted stated."

On his first record album, Gregory comes across as a sharp but congenial voice, bright but not brash. Yet in performance his delivery had just enough street flavor to give him credibility on both sides of the racial divide. He talked the lingo but he didn't have the pugnacious, insolent glare of a Redd Foxx (what Watkins calls the "Bad Nigger" persona) or the beleaguered and bedraggled look of a Moms Mabley—"the first female stand-up," says Bogle, and whom the writer-actor Ossie Davis calls "the mother of all black comics."

Gregory, one of Moms's most gifted stepsons, radiated positive, cool vibes. He was very Playboy Club, very *GQ* in his natural-shoulder three-button black Italian silk suit. He suavely fingered his cigarette as he meandered smoothly through his routines, in full control. He was a comedian whom Hugh Hefner could book without squirming, one who would further Hef's "Playboy Philosophy" of being on the cutting edge of the social—not to mention the satirical—revolution. (Following Gregory's success, Hefner booked several other black comedians.) Gregory even drew praise from the conservative columnist Robert Ruark, who had blasted Lenny Bruce and all "sick comics" but welcomed Gregory as a wit "in the best classic tradition of Will Rogers."

In his *Dick Gregory in Living Black and White* album, taped at the Playboy Club in the early 1960s, the comic chats abouts whites who ask him if he knows Joe Louis (foreshadowing Lenny Bruce's advisory to whites on how to relax their colored friends), and jokes that "*Ralph Bunche is in Israel trying to explain Sammy Davis.*" He stirs in jokebook hamburger helper ("*With my luck, last week I bought a suit with two pairs of pants and burned a hole in the coat*" . . . "*I got so drunk I took my wife to another apartment*") with more thoughtful ones ("*In my home town they make us take a test to vote— nuclear physics in Russian*"). He wisely took care to end with, "This is the greatest country in the world," and he fumigated the room against any lingering odor of racial animosity by slipping in a little uplift: "You got to learn how to make the bad things pleasant. 'Cause I believe one day this'll all be over. . . ."

While he was cool, he wasn't collegiate (although he'd attended Southern Illinois University for three years on a track scholarship), as was the next great black comedian, Bill Cosby. Unlike Cosby, he had a refined ghetto wisdom. Cosby noted, "There had been people like Slappy White, but here you saw this black man in a Brooks Brothers suit. Dick brought an intellect into the arena." He was not so much a black comedian as perhaps a gray one, or maybe off-black. Typical of Gregory's talent for blending white and black humor was the Polish joke he told to a group of southern tourists, but with a racial spin: "*When I drink I think I'm Polish. One night I got so drunk I moved out of my own neighborhood.*" He could get off a stinging rebuke to white racism and get away with it ("*You gotta say this for whites, their self-confidence knows no bounds. Who else could go to a small island in the South Pacific where there's no crime, poverty, unemployment, war, or worry—and call it a 'primitive society' *").

He was an effortless comedian who incorporated some of the artful stagemanship of Shelley Berman, Chicago's hottest comedian at the time. Gregory smoked onstage, like Berman, and he discoursed, like Berman, from a stool, a natural, relaxed prop for him—"The stool was where you sit and you talk and you had a drink." He was unhurried, again like Berman, and Gregory similarly took you into his confidence, made you an ally and not an adversary. He let you savor him, and he was hard to resist when drawling lines like, "*Wouldn't it be a helluva joke if all this were really burnt cork and you people were all being tolerant for nothin'*"; or, "*Lookin' for a house can be quite an experience. Especially when you go into a white neighborhood, offer forty thousand dollars for a twenty-three-thousand-dollar house, and then get turned down 'cause you're lowerin' the property values.*"

No matter how vitriolic his comments, such as discussing why advertisers have no sway in Harlem ("*We're the only ones who know what it means to be Brand X*"), they weren't laced with rancor. Gregory didn't seem out to politicize us, just to get our ear for an hour. He made racism, in a strangely ironic way, manageable. Long before Rodney King, Gregory seemed to be saying, "Why can't we all just get along?" He might have been seething underneath, but on the surface he generally appeared bemused by the hostilities and hypocrisies of the racial divide. Here or there, a joke might betray a hint of bitterness, like his line about an integrated swimming pool that had a blind lifeguard.

Gregory, curiously, wasn't subjected to much abuse in clubs, laughing off hecklers with lines like, "*When you're working to a crowd that can get in for thirty-five cents and a bottle of beer, let's face it, they'll heckle God.*" One of his favorite antiheckle devices when he played redneck dives and was subjected to taunts of "nigger" was to smile and say, "*According to my contract, the management pays me fifty dollars every time someone calls me that, so will you all do me a favor and stand up and say it again in unison?*" In the dedication to *nigger*, he wrote: "To Momma, wherever you are—if ever you hear the word nigger again, remember, they're advertising my book."

He carefully prepared himself for audience abuse, much as Branch Rickey had prepped Jackie Robinson by hurling hatred at him to steel him against bigots. For six months, he had his wife shout abuse at him. One day, he asked her what she would do if someone called her a bitch— "And she said, 'I'd just ignore them.' The way she said it was the attitude I wanted . . . the tone of voice . . . and once I had that tone the rest was easy." The tone was not cocksure, but bemused: "*Where else would I have to ride in the back of the bus, have a choice of the worst schools, the worst restaurants, and the worst neighborhoods—and average five thousand dollars a week just talking about it?*" . . . "*I voted for Kennedy; I hear he's gonna air-condition the cotton fields.*" And perhaps his most-quoted zinger—"*I sat-in six months once at a Southern lunch counter. When they finally served me, they didn't have what I wanted.*" They're all definitive Gregory jokes, provocative and witty without being belligerent.

He had discovered a cardinal rule of humor: "Once I got them laughing, I could say anything." A joke like, *"Way things are, ten years from now you'll have to be my color to get a job,"* reveals why he was called "the Negro Mort Sahl." It wasn't just a catchy billing. He had Sahl's ability to succinctly sum up a situation, an event, a national attitude, in lines that were terse and epigrammatic. Unlike Sahl, he didn't tear off on tangents but ambled nonchalantly forward: *"I was thinking of taking a bus tour of Alabama—only my Blue Cross has expired. On the other hand, better it than me."* (In 1964 Sahl said churlishly of him, "Dick Gregory has one joke—the back of the bus.") The onetime "black Mort Sahl" says Sahl had only a minimal influence on him. "Mort had an influence, but when I'd go see Mort, most of the time I'd feel embarrassed because he would say things I didn't understand. It was very intellectual. My stuff was country next to his." Watkins quotes Gregory saying, "Lenny Bruce shakes up the Puritans, Mort Sahl, the conservatives, and me—almost everybody."

Gregory has a vivid memory of his first gig: "I went to this black club in Chicago and I saw this other comic come out and the whole audience shut up. And I said, Wow, what power. I'd always been the life of the party and so I went back the next night and I told everybody I was this big comic from the East Coast, and they hired me, and then I learned something: I knew about comedy but I didn't know about *timing*. The difference between goin' up there as a guest and coming back workin' is altogether different. I learned the timing, the breathing, the whole piece."

He also learned that "the more power you have, the funnier you are to the audience. You could walk out [as an unknown] and tell some jokes and if they're not so funny, people aren't going to laugh. The president could come out and tell the same jokes and people fall all over the table. I now bring a new dignity and a new power and I get a different type of immediate laugh." He watched the pros and picked up on their tricks before playing Chicago joints like the Fickle Pickle, a coffeehouse, and the Esquire Lounge, on the city's South Side, for ten dollars a night. When he wanted a two-dollar raise, they fired him, so in 1959 he opened his own club, the Apex, in a black suburb of Chicago, but it folded quickly.

Gregory always had his eye on the big white clubs—"where the bread was." He had discerned that whites laughed easier in a black club than in a white environment, so he shrewdly decided, "I've got to go up there as an individual first, a Negro second. I've got to be a colored funny man, not a funny colored man. I've got to act like a star who isn't sorry for himself—that way, they can't feel sorry for me. I've got to make jokes about myself before I can make jokes about them and their society. No bitterness, no Tomming. Then you can settle down and talk about anything you want." In a cagey bit of comic sleight-of-hand, he interwove black jokes into a basically "white" act, but because Gregory was black it was perceived by the white media as "black humor."

Gregory told me that as a young entertainer he was incredibly naïve. "One of the great pains I had in show business, when I started out in these little black nightclubs, was, I did not know black comics were not permitted to work white nightclubs. I didn't know *nothin'* about show business when I was growin' up in St. Louis." He says he had never even *seen* a black comedian as a kid. When Gregory was a kid, the major black comics were Mantan Moreland, Pigmeat Markham, and Moms Mabley. "Where would I see 'em in St. Louis? They didn't have black clubs in St. Louis. They only had the Showboat, with jazz musicians."

He was most influenced by the white comedians he heard on the radio—Bob Hope, Red Skelton—and, later, Lenny Bruce, whom he salutes: "Two thousand years from now he'll be one of the names that will still be remembered. He's to show business what Einstein was to science." Gregory once said, "I looked at the white comics for a rhythm, then the black comics had a whole new rhythm, and then *my* rhythm changed."

He changed his act for white clubs. "I tried to go back to the black community, and it was painful, because I had to change stuff I was using. I could look at the *New York Times* and the best-sellin' books and go do something funny about that, but that don't play in the ghetto. But now I've noticed something that's very interestin'. Today there's nothin' you can do in a white club that I couldn't do in a housing project—because of TV. Things are moving that fast! When I was out there, who ever heard of NASDAQ? Where in the black community could you go and talk about a Bill Gates? Now they know as much about Bill Gates as they do about Tiger Woods!"

His act grew progressively whiter the farther downtown he traveled. Nat Hentoff wrote that when Gregory opened at the Blue Angel in '61, an "angry trio"—Slappy White, Nipsey Russell, and Timmie Rogers—taped Gregory's act, watching him with undisguised disdain. "We wanted to find out which of our material not to use anymore," White bitterly told Hentoff, who wrote that Gregory "is more a mechanic than a spontaneously creative comedian. He would probably be decimated in an ad-lib duel with Redd Foxx, Moms Mabley, or Nipsey Russell." Maybe, and maybe not.

The black comedians that Gregory most talked about, says Robert Lipsyte, the comic's coauthor on *nigger,* were Mabley, Russell, White, and Foxx. "He respectfully saw them as his ancestors, and he never put them down. We went to see them sometimes." Lipsyte never detected any resentment on the part of older black comics for the upstart in their midst. They seemed to embrace him, he recalls, but "I couldn't tell if it was genuine admiration or showbiz. I went on marches with him and I was kind of amazed at the enormous appreciation and respect that he got."

While Gregory cites no major black comic influences, Dick Shawn unwittingly smartened him up fast. "I never went into white areas in St. Louis, and I never felt comfortable in Chicago in white areas," he told me, "but once I went downtown to a major nightclub to see Dick Shawn. I thuoght I was *so* funny, man, and everything was clickin'. Then I see Dick Shawn"—whose polish awed him—"and I say, 'My God!' I walked home and I told my wife, 'Baby, I'm gettin' out of show business.' All that day I was depressed."

Gregory hung out in the men's room until Shawn's show started, for all he could afford was a 7UP at the bar. After the first show, he ducked back into the men's room and told the attendant, 'Man, I wish I had me some money to see the next show.' The guy said, 'Why? He do the same show.' I say, 'What?' He say, 'Yeah, that motherfucker been doin' the same thing for twenty years.' I did not know that in those big clubs you did the same thing year after year after year, until you had *perfected* it. When you're workin' those [white] clubs, nobody got that kinda time to sit through two shows. Next time they see you is in two years." He howls. "The next day I got back into show business!" He comments, "Right now, I can go and wipe out young comics because I still have all this stuff in my head. I can stand up flat-footed and go three hours."

More jobs followed at the grandiose Regal (Chicago's Apollo) and other black rooms, as well as a few small blue-collar white clubs, where he tested his black-on-white formula. So he was ready when the call came, unexpectedly, from the Playboy Club to replace Irwin Corey, who wanted to take a Sunday night off. Corey says he suggested Gregory. (The hungry i's Enrico Banducci told Abby Wasserman that he first met Gregory while going through a car wash in Chicago with Corey: "This guy was wiping the window. He said, 'Aren't you Irwin Corey? I'm a comedian, too.' I said, 'Why don't you bring him into the club?' ")

The club that night was full of frozen-food-industry conventioneers from the South, whom Gregory quickly disarmed, much to the relief of nervous Playboy Club executives. As Gregory moseyed out onstage, his cool demeanor didn't betray the turbulence beneath: "*Good evening,*" he said, with his unblinking, poker-faced stare—what a *New York Times* writer would later describe as "the deceptively disengaged air of a gourmet about to pick apart a squab." "*Glad to see all you fine Southern people here tonight. I know a lot about the South. I spent twenty years there one night.*" He bent racial stereotypes back on themselves, like his classic line about going to a restaurant and being told, "*We don't serve colored people in here.*" "*That's all right,*" was his reply, "*I don't eat 'em. Just bring me a whole fried chicken.*" By the end of the set, the southerners were eating out of his hand, and by the end of the week, he had an offer from Jack Paar to appear on the *Tonight* show, a major turning point not only in his career but for all black entertainers.

Unbeknownst to their audiences, white clubs had unwritten rules regarding black performers. According to Gregory, "No black person was permitted to stand flat-footed and just talk. Now, you could dance and stop and tell a joke, and you could sing and stop and tell a joke, but you could not stand flat-footed and tell a joke." This was the nature of the taboo the night Gregory took the stage at the Chicago Playboy Club. He recalls every detail of that milestone event: "They had found out [after booking me] that that room had been rented out to this southern delegation of frozen-food people, and they had sent word that I didn't have to go on. But I was so nervous from tryin' to get there on time that I just went ahead and jumped up on the stage at eight o'clock. At midnight, I was still there and I walked offstage at two o'clock in the morning."

Word reached New York that Dick Gregory had scored a triumph, which led to his appearance on *Tonight* and to another racial cultural footnote from Gregory: "Billy Eckstein was the cause of me makin' it on the Paar show," he told me. "Eckstein was drunk and he was cussin' Paar out to me. Now, Paar was my man. And I just *knew* that I would be on the Paar show one day. Paar would go off [at one A.M.], and at five o'clock in the morning I'd still be at the mirror doing what I was gonna do on the Paar show. Until Billy Eckstein told me, 'Hey, man, that motherfuckin' Jack Paar, he ain't *never* let a nigger sit on the couch.' And I never *noticed* that if you didn't sit on the couch, your salary didn't move. If you didn't sit on the couch, you wasn't one of the Dody Goodmans, one of the regulars. I was so embarrassed, so humiliated, I never told my wife that I could not do the Paar show. It was just a personal thing."

He goes on: "Then they gave me this write-up in *Time* magazine. Paar read it and he's on the phone Monday. My wife took the call and she's so happy. It was Paar's man. So I got on the phone and I said, 'No, I don't want to do this,' and I hung up and started cryin'. I said to my wife, 'Well, that was my big break.' The phone rings again, and this time it's Paar himself, and he said, 'How come you don't want to work the show?' I said, 'Look, the Negro never sits on the couch.' He said, 'Sammy did,' and I said, 'Mr. Paar, I have watched every show. Sammy has sat *in* for you.' "

Was this a Paar-show policy? A gentlemen's agreement? Conscious bigotry? "I have no idea. So he told me to come in and I sat on the couch and my salary went to five thousand dollars! I got letters from white folks sayin' they never heard a black person talk about their family"— as Gregory did on that appearance with Paar, who offered him six more appearances. The upshot, as Mel Watkins writes, was that Gregory "had become the first black comic superstar since Bert Williams and Stepin Fetchit."

Gregory approached his act like a senior executive: "I always had a profound respect for the audience. The suit I would wear I never wore onstage. I always looked at that nightclub the same as I would if I worked in a steel mill. It's not a party." He was such a persnickety performer that his timing was thrown off once when he sent a hungry i gofer out for a pack of Winston's but had to make do with a different brand onstage. "Look," he told the gofer, "the timing of the drag that I am using on this cigarette is part of my act. I can't suddenly change." He used his cigarette as comic punctuation, the way George Burns meticulously deployed his cigar. "Once I quit I never realized how much the cigarette was a part of my act. Before I got ready to wipe you out, I took a puff, and when I took a puff, doctor, that was *everything*."

Since Gregory's act seemed so inborn and unlearned it's surprising to find that he had gagwriters, most of them white. The jokes sounded original and organic, not purchased, but in fact a lot of them were written by hired gagmen like Bob Orben, the joke-book giant. The writers would retool old gags to fit fresh headlines with a black perspective, but they were very "jokey" jokes. Many were nonracial—jokes about women drivers ("*How can your wife spot a hair on your jacket and miss the garage door by a mile?*") and vaudeville gags dating back to Bert Williams ("*My luck is so bad that if I didn't have bad luck I'd have no luck at all*"), even mother-in-law jokes ("*My mother-in-law is in the hospital. My Valentine's Day gift to her*"); and he wasn't above a joke about Cadillac-owning blacks.

Robert Lipsyte, who collaborated with him on his autobiography, recalls that Gregory had an erratic offstage working procedure: "He'd get to the dressing room early with a pile of newspapers and a yellow legal pad and he was kind of writing and scratching up to the last minute. He'd be ripping things out of the paper. He has this kind of litany. I sat there many times. I would never know when I could grab him for an hour or two, so I stuck to him. He'd say, 'Can you believe this shit? Can you be-*lieve* this fucking shit?' He'd be reading something in the newspaper, and he would write it down and somehow he would meld that with the same dumb joke that Orben had sold to Bob Hope, and he would kind of weave that in in an amazing sort of way, like saying Eisenhower was the white Joe Louis." Sometimes, says Lipsyte, he'd partly wing it onstage. "On a night that he'd do two or three shows, over a period of three or four nights in a row, I'd watch a routine evolve, get dumped, grow, change, so that by the third night it was this polished gem that would last in the repertory for a month or two."

Gregory usually had a couple of writers traveling with him at all times—Ed Weinberg, who later wrote for *Taxi, The Mary Tyler Moore Show,* and *The Cosby Show*, and a young black writer, Jim Sanders. Gregory totally trusted his writers. "When I'm out partying, it's their job to see to it. Then we'd come together every evening, and sit around, but we didn't act like [we were writing]. We'd like just be playin', and I'd say, 'Hey did you see how stupid that . . . blah-blah-blah . . .' And at a certain time, the writers would disappear."

He continues: "Now here was *my* genius: when they turned their stuff in, I never read it until thirty minutes before I was ready to go on. If it didn't stick enough in my head for me to memorize, I didn't use it, but the funny parts I would just build on. It was almost like I was improvisin', but I wasn't. A lot of comics feel if I pay you twenty-five hundred dollars for a piece of material, I gotta use it. Bob Orben came to me and said, 'You pay me so much money, you're wastin' your money, 'cause you never use my stuff.' And I would say, 'Bob, I use it every night, but you don't recognize it.' " He distinguishes between writing and adapting: "I never wrote. I would *create*, I would *invent*."

The Village Gate's Art D'Lugoff recalls Gregory fondly: "His home was the Gate. I could combine him with almost anybody. I enjoyed being in his company. He was a real gentleman, personally very nice. Here's what kind of a mensch he was. One evening, there was a snowstorm, there must've been ten people in the audience, and he was sitting in the back. Dick sort of looked over at me and said, 'Don't worry, Art—this one's on me.' *Nobody* ever did that. A lot of major artists who worked there didn't care; to them the club owner is an SOB." While he would readily drop a club engagement for a civil rights rally, he said that he always made it up to the club or played a later date for free. "No nightclub owner has ever lost on me."

Gregory walked a fine and dangerous line between ingratiating and jiving, persuasive and aggressive, sympathetic and servile. *Time* praised him for being able to joke about blacks and whites "in a sort of brotherhood of humor"—an equal-opportunity satirist who could joke as easily about the PTA as the NAACP. Gregory wasn't just witty and disarming. Some critics said that white audiences laughed to neutralize their guilt, but something else was at work: Gregory was helping to defuse black-white anger by getting whites to laugh at his racial jokes.

Juan Williams, in the tribute on NPR's *Talk of the Nation,* told him: "What was distinctive about you was, you had humor that could penetrate on the racial level but without making white people feel tortured or uncomfortable, but make them have some clarity about the stupidity of segregation." Gregory answered, "I was takin' a situation that had finally come into your living room, on the television, and brought it up on the stage—but not say it in your face."

RICHARD CLAXTON GREGORY GREW UP poor in St. Louis, on relief. His father, known as "Big Presley," deserted his mother whenever she had a child (she had six), until he finally left for good. Dick had the good luck to inherit his mother's optimism. She told him, "Man has two ways out in life—laughing and crying. There's more hope in laughing." Even so, she sometimes smacked him at the dinner table for his smart mouth. He later wrote an essay in school, titled "Shame," in which he confessed that he was "ashamed of my mother, ashamed of my family, ashamed I didn't have a daddy." Years later, however, in his autobiography, he would write more sentimentally, Cosby-like, of "googobs of kids in my bed, man. When I get up to pee in the middle of the night, gotta leave a bookmark so I don't lose my place."

He went to an all-black grade school where children were seated according to a cruel pecking order—light-skinned and crisply starched in the front rows, darker-skinned and shabbier in the back rows. The scrawny Dick rarely made it up to a midrow seat. "When I was eleven, I was the size of a kid of six," he recalled. During the Depression, he got work sandbagging levees on the Mississippi River during floods (he weighed only thirteen pounds more than the bags), picking up heavy steel casings in a munitions factory, peddling wood, coal, and cardboard, and delivering groceries.

Undaunted, at school he developed into a popular, active kid—writing, staging, and starring in shows and winning a citizenship award. He also ran track, where he set a state record in the mile (4:28), but it was disallowed because it was clocked at an all-black meet. Nevertheless, it got him athletic scholarship offers from twelve colleges. When Gregory learned that his track record was not official, says Lipsyte, "he went crazy. He was furious and he went down to City Hall and complained. The day he went down to City Hall, there was a march of black school kids protesting school conditions. So he became a monitor in the march. He ended up being interviewed on TV; the march was called Communist-inspired. And that was really the beginning of his civil rights involvement."

Gregory was driven to succeed, a confident and convincing guy—like Cosby—whose almost sleepy demeanor belied the charm that he used to get himself elected senior class president in high school before enrolling at Southern Illinois University. He left in his senior year, before they could flunk him out— but not before a white history teacher wrote "negro" on a blackboard; Gregory walked up and changed the *n* to *N*. After college, he was fired from a post office job for placing letters addressed to Mississippi in the "Overseas" slot.

Once Gregory had made it, when he played big cities, such as Kansas City, he would swing into affirmative action, paying barbers and bellhops a hundred dollars to bring their families to see him. "I just wanted to make sure Negroes were accepted in the club, so that's what I'd do." He instructed blacks, "Make like you don't know me. Don't come as a friend of mine, and let me know if you feel any racism. In all my contracts it said if the club advertised in the white papers, it had to advertise in the black papers."

Some accused the young Cosby of trying to become a Gregory clone. "I don't know if Bill Cosby was tryin' to do me. Bill Cosby is to storytelling what I was to one-liners. I could never hold an audience for five minutes with one joke, like Bill—that face, his demeanor." Gregory was always a big booster of Cosby, who told NPR's Terry Gross, "Dick taught me. He wasn't afraid to share what he had discovered. He would come down from the mountain and tell you where the gold is."

Cosby recalled for Gross the night Gregory came to hear him at his sixty-dollar-a-week gig at the Gaslight Club. Gregory gave him advice and didn't bug him about becoming more racial, as many blacks did. But on one occasion Gregory was critical of Cosby's color-blind act and was quoted as saying, "I think anyone who looks at a Negro comedian like Cosby—who is brilliant and has a sharp mind but doesn't mention anything about the racial situation—would have to feel he was ducking it."

Lipsyte, who worked with Gregory in 1963, recalls: "In those days he drank and smoked a lot and was overweight. He would kind of roll back in a chair or in his stool onstage, and very often in a kind of brusque, snapping-finger fashion, he'd have the waiter bring him a scotch. He made sure that there were black waiters. He'd always have to be served by a white waiter—of course, set up in advance—and he would treat the white waiter in a very officious fashion. He would take the drink and dismiss the waiter, and there would be a kind of hush—people were very uncomfortable. Then he would look out with this beatific smile across his face, and he would say, '*Governor Faubus oughta have seen that.*' Bang! That absolutely snapped it. The audience was then totally on his side. He had brought them in, he had anointed them as liberals—you're good people for being here and I did this as some sort of a lesson. Once he did that, he owned them."

As Lipsyte analyzes his technique: "He understood that comedy is friendly relations. He has this parable about falling down the stairs, lying crumpled at the bottom of the stairs, your legs broken and your head bleeding. If you begin screaming in pain people will run away from you and you're not gonna get help. If you begin laughing, they'll come to see what's going on and take you to the hospital. He saw comedy as a way to bring attention to situations that otherwise people would run from."

In 1962, almost immediately after he had arrived, Gregory began speaking out at civil rights events. The movement nearly bankrupted him, costing him an estimated $250,000 in travel and telephone expenses, and a fortune in lost bookings. Against the advice of almost everyone, he decided to risk his career for civil rights. "Everybody—my manager, my press agent, nightclub owners—they told me to stay out of it. They said nobody would laugh at a guy who was running around being *serious.*" He gave 120 benefits for CORE, NAACP, and other groups during the sixties and seventies.

What turned Gregory's head around was hearing an old black man at a rally tell how he had registered black voters in Mississippi and later gone to jail for killing a black man who had been hired by whites to burn his house down. While he was in jail, the old man's wife had died. "That destroyed me," said Gregory. "I realized that what I'd been doing wasn't worth a damn. Here was a little old nigger, the kind of kinky-haired verb-buster everyone looks down on, and the man was fighting the system for me. I was never the same after that."

Gregory drew a sharp line between performing and politics: "I never walked up on that stage to win one person over. When I walked up on that stage I walked up as a comic. If I walked up on that stage and won everybody in the audience over and didn't get one laugh, I'd walk off defeated. And if I was marchin' and they were laughin' at me, I would have been defeated. When America goes to war, she don't send her comedians. In the history of great movements, it wasn't comedians, it wasn't entertainers, it wasn't athletes. . . . So I never mix the two together."

He took his fearless attitude from John Wayne. "Lemme tell you something. I went to movies as a little boy because I was ashamed of bein' poor. When I would walk home, man, I *was* John Wayne. I'd walk through alleys. I didn't give a damn. When Clark Gable says, 'Frankly, my dear, I don't give a damn,' for two years that was my line! When I got into the civil rights movement, and three hundred cops couldn't wait for me to land, for the first time I felt like John Wayne. And I loved it! It terrorized these folks. And so it didn't make no difference what they [his advisers] was sayin'. I didn't even hear it. I found somethin' that made me feel better inside than comedy."

Gregory told his wife and family that his social activism now came first. "My wife and I made a personal deal. I loved America, and I'm talkin' about the whole wave-the-flag and the star-spangled banner, America the beautiful . . . I said to my wife, do me a favor: let's never make a decision in the civil rights movement based on how this will affect our family, because if we was at war, we wouldn't do that. So when it comes to liberatin' the black folks, let's don't let this interfere. And another thing, never worry about how will this decision affect my career. Let's always worry about how will my career affect the movement." Just after his wife told him they needed $18,000 for his child's tuition, he donated it all to raise money for buses for a demonstration. He lived simply, he says. "I didn't have stock, I had no big investments, I wasn't worried about tomorrow."

When Lipsyte was hired to coauthor Gregory's autobiography, he first met the comedian in his hotel room, where Gregory was wearing shorts and crying on his bed. Gregory had just read about the four schoolgirls who had been killed in the bombing of a Birmingham church the day before. "His head went back on the pillow, and he began talking softly to the ceiling, for hours," wrote Lipsyte in *Esquire* in 1967. "How could the white man be so evil as to kill children?" he asked. " 'They were just little girls,' he kept saying. 'They weren't even demonstrating for civil rights.' Softly, he wondered if there was any point staying in show business while a revolution was under way. If America went to war in the morning, he'd fight, he said. He wouldn't satirize the war from the Blue Angel." Added Lipsyte: "I left early in the morning, confused. He was not the cool, slangy hipster I remembered from a nightclub table, and he seemed to be far more than the 'concerned human being' people described."

Gregory proved an infuriating collaborator at first. He was four or five hours late to meetings, unable to remember Lipsyte's name (he autographs everything, "To you"). Interview sessions, says the writer, "often degenerated into diatribes against white America." Lipsyte now says, laughing, "He was fucking impossible!" Two weeks into the project, after waiting six hours for him to arrive, Lipsyte says he told Gregory that he "didn't need money badly enough to put up with an irresponsible, selfish fool who was trying to hang me in reverse prejudice. In fact, his color was the only thing I *didn't* have against him. I listened to him for a while, then finally I thought, Fuck him, and it was at that point that he said, 'Finally, you sound colored.' " He'd passed the test. Gregory invited him to join him for a sandwich in the hotel drugstore, where the comic's tone changed and he kept repeating Lipsyte's name, telling him, "Let's go back upstairs, I think we're ready to write a book. A real book, one they're not expecting."

In retrospect, Lipsyte says: "It was like a hazing experience. Then we began to work, and of course it was a major wonderful experience of my life, that year we spent together. The beginning of any real racial or political education for me began with him." Gregory explains now, "I was lookin' for a white man to write it because I wanted to put my life in his head and have him spit it out. I wanted white people to read it. Black people didn't need to read it."

The book's original title was *Callus on My Soul,* which Lipsyte hated, but in 2001 Gregory resurrected it as the title of a subsequent memoir. "He had a fantasy about opening the world's greatest restaurant, which was gonna have one table, and the name of the restaurant was gonna be Nigger—and when he said that, I said, 'That's what we should name the book,' and he said, 'Yes!' Our editor said absolutely not, and the head of the publishing house said we're not going to publish it, and Greg said, 'Okay, we'll take it [the book] back.' And they said, 'Okay, we'll do it.' It was a very controversial title, and black friends and colleagues of mine hated it." (Gregory later wrote a sequel, *Up from Nigger.*)

NPR's Juan Williams told Gregory, "You embraced the word *nigger,* you challenged it, you took it on," and Gregory replied: "I said, let's pull it out of the closet, let's deal with it, let's dissect it. It should never be called 'the N word.' How do you talk about the swastika by using another term? I will never use 'the N word.' Put it out there and stop hidin' it."

Once they began, Lipsyte says, working with Gregory was strife-free. "The only argument we had was when, after I started writing the book, he wouldn't read any pages. He said, 'I know you're a great writer, I know it's gonna be terrific.' I was really nervous. Suppose he didn't like the style? We forced him into a room and locked the door and the editor and I sat outside and we wouldn't let him out. Finally he came out after three or four hours, and he was shaking his head. He said, 'No, I can't let this go through.' My heart really clutched, and I said, 'What?' And he said, 'You've hyphenated *motherfucker*—it's one word. And that was it." When the book was optioned as a movie, Gregory threatened to tear up the contract unless Lipsyte got a cut of the film rights. "Well, man, it was your words," he told the writer.

Lipsyte says that all the suspect stories Gregory related checked out, "I have never in my life had such a stand-up subject. He can be hyperbolic and we know that he's a conspiracy theorist, there are also self-legends, and things I really was not sure about in the book. I went over things I felt were touchy he might want to take out, and he said, 'No, it happened and I told it to you.' Anything he said to me or that I wrote could stay in the book. All the stories he told me were true." By the time the book came out in 1964, Gregory had, according to his agents, "blown his career," had his car repossessed, and was $35,000 in debt. The book did not do all that well, says Lipsyte. A critic in *The Nation* said that Gregory's account of his work in the South was "sentimental, mechanical, undiscovering. . . . A little vein of sentimentality, just apparent at first, begins to bleed copiously."

Some of his declarations then sounded less like the restrained Dick Gregory and more like the strident H. Rap Brown, with long-winded lectures that showed a new threatening caustic tone: "Man, we will burn this country down house by house and brick by brick if you don't stop these insults. This country is so sick, the riots have actually helped. . . . I can't understand why you get so upset over niggers chasing white ladies when you made the dumb, stupid mistake of bringing *your* movies into my black community, not showing me nothing but white ladies making love. And any time you showed me a black woman it was *Beulah.*"

Lipsyte calls Gregory "an amazing conspiracy theorist. It wasn't long before JFK was assassinated and we were having whispered conversations with strange people in the basements of West Village town houses. Or we'd go to Chicago and meet the Blackstone Rangers or Malcolm X. He saw a major conspiracy against blacks and poor people in America." Gregory maintained that the FBI had a file on him that was ten inches thick, and that his phone was tapped (he says he once heard agents talking to each other). Washington columnist Jack Anderson said that Gregory was on an FBI list of potential assassins.

Some clubs wouldn't risk booking him, afraid he might be jailed during an engagement, or just leave in midrun for a demonstration. Many owners decided he was too much trouble to bother with, so he transferred to the college circuit. By 1968 he was fully radicalized, with a bushy head of hair and a beard, which was when he began his fasts for racial justice. He grew gaunt, with sunken cheeks and bulging eyes. He started issuing statements, proclamations. He ran for mayor of Chicago (and got 22,000 write-in votes) and then for president. Ralph J. Gleason wrote that in this period Gregory's press conferences were more exciting than his stage show.

Some cynics in show business and beyond accused him of using the civil rights movement to *advance* his career, a charge that pretty much dissipated when he was shot in the leg during the Watts riots. He was living at the time with his wife and five small daughters in a large apartment in Chicago full of half-packed suitcases and piles of papers he couldn't bring himself to throw out. "Gregory is almost a stranger in this apartment," wrote Lipsyte in *Esquire,* "but the children seemed easy with him" as he corrected their homework and handwriting. He was always on the go, as he still is, an early Jesse Jackson who would fly anywhere he felt needed, often existing on two hours sleep a night, squeezing in club and TV appearances when he could, and usually retaining his good humor; on *The Mike Douglas Show,* Gregory said he was "the only Negro in America who has no rhythm."

When Eliot Asinov interviewed Gregory in 1968, the comic was leaner and shaggier than the writer remembered—also preachier. After a few local jokes and potshots at Lyndon Johnson and Ronald Reagan, Gregory shifted into harangue mode, whipping himself into a frenzy about American racism but lacing the tirade with caustic wit, like his story about a black man dying of thirst who is told by a white man with a glass of water, "*Nigger, that's the trouble with you—you ain't got the education to make your own glass.*" Gregory might leaven his new hectoring tone with humor, but there had been a sea change in his temperament, and he had a new firebrand message. On the campus lecture circuit, he was smothered in hugs and beads by adoring hippie girls moved to tears by his oratory, which mixed humor and anger. When a distressed coed said, "You say you're nonviolent, but you keep threatening to burn my house down," he answered, "Sure, I'm nonviolent. I'd just make sure you weren't home." He insists he wasn't angry, but his sixties rhetoric suggests otherwise.

To officials in the civil rights movement itself (like Whitney Young of the National Urban League), who felt he was more valuable on a stage than on a soapbox, his reply was, "I'm a Negro before I'm an entertainer. These critics who feel I'm destroying myself as an entertainer, all they know is show business." Countered Young: "We can find marchers and fasters and people who can run for political office. But we don't have many Dick Gregorys. Think of the thousands of people he could reach with his humor. He could be devastating." Gregory's standard reply: "Humor can no more find the solution to race problems than it can cure cancer. We didn't laugh Hitler out of existence."

On NPR's *Talk of the Nation* salute, Cosby praised Gregory's sacrifices and his sincerity: "They let him use his celebrity, but instead of gettin' on the plane or the bus and goin' back, Dick stayed! He allowed himself to be more than just a one-day photo op." Gregory was so accessible he was in the phone book, and racists would call him at home. Added Cosby: "His dressing room door was always open. Lenny Bruce wasn't on the line. Mort Sahl didn't march and get his hands whipped by the police. They didn't—nor did Bill Cosby—give up salary to go down and spend time in jail after facing police dogs." According to Cosby, whenever Gregory gave up a gig for a speech or a rally, Cosby would send a check to his home. Whenever Gregory was not available, Cosby always was. Said Gregory, "Bill Cosby said [his agent] Joe Glazier offered him all the dates I was walkin' out on, and they said how crazy I was."

Leaving show business was not a problem for Gregory, explains Lipsyte: "He began to see that comedy without purpose was just another way of black guys dancing for white people. Comedy used in the service of what he felt was righteousness—remember, this was a God-fearing man—and civil rights was a much higher order than just getting laughs. People who do that, if you ask them why, they kind of look at you with a certain level of disdain. 'This is what you're *supposed* to do—why aren't *you* doing more?' He saw it as a natural progression. Yeah, it was great to be making a fortune at Playboy Clubs, but he was talking to boozing traveling salesmen who were trying to feel up the Bunnies. There was something higher than that."

In a 1960s interview, Gregory said, "To be a comic is another form of being a whore," because, he theorized, comics simply peddle humor, which occurs naturally in life. Stirring people to action also fed his increasingly hungry ego. At one point, in 1968, Gregory went so far as to declare, "I'm probably the voice of America today. I don't think there's anyone in the country that's stronger than me today." Gregory never made that final leap into out-and-out megalomania, but he clearly basked in the adoration that went beyond being a popular comedian—rousing crowds, quelling riots, and, in 1966, making a run for mayor of Chicago. He now had a shot at history, the ultimate booking. Not even *The Ed Sullivan Show* could top a gig in posterity.

He cleverly used his accumulated stature and goodwill to gain attention in the civil rights fight. Lipsyte recalls now: "This funny man, this comic, goes down South, but he makes sure that Huntley and Brinkley are there with a camera crew, and he's probably saved a lot of civil rights workers from, at the least, getting their heads broken, because the cameras were there. He's very canny, very shrewd, and there's also a kind of madness there—a messianic madness." The comedian told a *New York Times* interviewer, "Baby, I'm going to change the world." Lipsyte agrees that Gregory, like Sahl and Bruce, had a savior complex: "He really did think he had a divine purpose and mission."

Yet even during the most militant moments in the civil rights movement, Gregory could step off the racial battlements and duck into a club for a quick show, shedding his angry rhetoric and slipping into his affable onstage guise to do what he called his "standard, safe [Cosby-like] kids things": "*We all have problems. My wife can't cook—how do you burn Kool-Aid? Yes, well, my daughter, she doesn't believe in Santa Claus. She knows doggone well no white man is coming into a colored neighborhood after midnight.*" By the end of the hour, all his anger was drained away, but ultimately his heart wasn't in it.

Lipsyte has a theory that comedy was never Gregory's ultimate goal—glory was: "I could just be projecting here. He started out as an athlete, not as a comedian. He may have had Olympic aspirations. I don't know that he was wedded to comedy as the only path to stardom. He often told a story about his mother reminding him that a voodoo lady in the neighborhood had seen a star glimmering on his forehead when he was born. He felt he was destined for great things, whether they would come through comedy or some other kind of leadership." One of his role models was Paul Robeson, who believed that "the artist must take sides."

Joan Rivers once spent an evening out with Gregory when he was at the height of his success, going with him to see some black comics. She remembered: "He had just met Eleanor Roosevelt and kept talking about how she would not have had anything to do with him six years before, when he was a chauffeur. The anger and bitterness in him were so great you could see he would not last long as a comic. He could not keep himself from making a statement—and you cannot make statements through comedy." And yet, what better way?—*"You know the definition of a southern moderate? That's a cat that'll lynch you from a low tree"* . . . *"Shouldn't be no race problem. Everyone I meet says, 'Some of my best friends are colored,' even though you know there ain't that many of us to go around."*

His segue from activist comic to Citizen Gregory was a natural progression. "Lemme tell you when this started affecting my career. One day in 1973 I decided I would not work clubs that sold alcohol"—the devotion to his health crusade effectively ended his comedy life. "I was doin' a thousand dollars a night at colleges, and even the racist colleges that wouldn't want me would fight to get me 'cause I was such a bargain!" He laughs. He didn't just "speak out"—he also took action personally. On one occasion he freed a falsely accused black man from a southern jail; he integrated an Atlanta restaurant; and he was not above berating black churchgoers for not doing more than praying. He was beaten up and shot at. In Birmingham, he served forty days in jail for parading without a permit. His response: *"Birmingham is a nice place to demonstrate, but I wouldn't want to live there."* He joked that the judge had it in for comics.

Gregory left the scene thirty-five years ago, and a decade ago ill health forced Richard Pryor offstage; since then, no black comic has emerged with seriously committed sociopolitical chops. "There are no white ones, either," says Gregory, "but there will come a time. My concern with black comics is, the only ones they'll let through are the ones who use profanity, and they will never work white nightclubs because black profanity and white profanity is different. It bothers me when the only way a black comic can get on *Def Jam* is with profanity; with profanity, you can't invent." Cosby remarks, "What Dick threw down, these young comedians couldn't pick it up." Most of the black comedy that Cosby sees today he calls "minstrelized embarrassment." Times have changed enough now that Gregory says, "*Amos 'n' Andy* could come back on and nobody would mind."

After he gave up performing in nightclubs, Gregory devoted himself full-time to speaking on a broad spectrum of issues, from drug and alcohol abuse to prison reform and overpopulation (the last of which he preached more than he practiced: he's the father of ten children). "Dick's at the top of his form," says his manager, Rusty Michael. "He's never home. He does a lot of college, corporate, and nonprofit speaking. The lectures and the act are part of the same thing." He's even spoken out on behalf of animal rights for PETA—"He did a thing for the circus elephants," says Michael.

Gregory's vegetarian regimen, which evolved out of his vow of nonviolence, led him to forty-day fasts to protest the Vietnam War and other causes. (At one time he weighed 98 pounds, down from a high of 288; his average "meal" during a fast was a juice smoothie.) All of these concerns led ultimately to his health fadism, and then to running (up to ten miles a day; he says he once ran from Chicago to Washington to call attention to starving African nations and claims that in 1976 he ran from Los Angeles to New York in seventy-one days), and finally to his becoming a practicing "breatherian," whose adherents claim to live on air—at which point even some of his most devoted early fans dismissed him as a little wacko.

Lawrence Christon suspects that "Gregory is borderline certifiable. Something must have happened to him in all those years; maybe fasting did something to his brain chemistry. His performances became loopier and loopier. I was interviewing him once, and he said, 'You know what laughter is, it's these carbon pellets that bounce up and down.' You'd think that all the black activists would like to have Dick Gregory on board, because he's been on the bus, so to speak, but they don't have him because he's too weird."

Fasting may turn out to be Gregory's most lasting legacy. In a 1999 article on the increased popularity of fasting, Gregory was linked with such world-class fasters as Gandhi, Cesar Chavez, and Jesus. In 1975 he predicted food riots, and lived for a while on kelp and sesame, pumpkin, and sunflower seeds, and a mixture called Gensa 4×3 that he claimed would wipe out world hunger. He says that his longest fast lasted eighty-one days, and he lived for two and a half years on fruit juice to protest the Vietnam War. In 2001, after a bout with cancer, he weighed 127 pounds but still went on a four-month liquid fast to protest police brutality. "I eat ninety percent fruit. I always hated vegetables!" He's a fruitarian, or perhaps, as some have surmised, a bit of a fruitcake. Robert Weide, who is making a documentary on Gregory, calls him the Jackie Robinson of health food—"He broke the color barrier of the New Age."

Fasts never threatened his life. He says, laughing, "The closest I came to dying was when I was drinkin' a fifth of scotch a day and smokin' four packs of cigarettes." Gregory swore off smoking and mother-in-law jokes at about the same time. He gave up cigarettes the day the surgeon general's report came out and refused to perform on any TV shows with tobacco sponsors, further snuffing out his performing career.

Looking back, he says: "Lemme tell you how I sum this up: comics, entertainers, and athletes, they work so hard on their craft, they command large *audiences*. People like me, people in this movement, command *respect*. There's a difference. I tell people, had I behaved myself I would probably have been one of the richest black men in the world, because I had enough smarts in the business. I can call Buckin'ham Palace and I can call the White House today and somebody's gonna call me back. That's the difference." He says it doesn't bother him that he's out of the limelight; legends don't need the limelight. "Once you become an institution . . . When it's over, it's over."

He never actually tired of comedy, which he calls "a luxury item," conceding, "There's nothin' that ever took the place of it." Although Gregory rarely performs his comedy act now—just twice a year in St. Louis and a couple of dates in New York at the Black Spectrum, a club—he's still on the road nine months a year, speaking out on health and social issues, fusing comedy and his concerns. And always leading off with a gag: "I'll walk out and say, '*I called my wife and she asked me if I took my liquid ginseng, so I popped two liquid ginseng, and not until I was gettin' ready to walk out here did I realize I took my Viagra by mistake. So I have to talk fast.*"

In one of his rare comedy appearances, in 1996, he spoke for two and a half hours, jabbing and joking as he ticked off gags about dental surgery, the CIA's role in drug trafficking, Queen Elizabeth, Michael Jackson,

Boris Yeltsin, Oprah Winfrey, Connie Chung, Rose Kennedy, moving from antiquated boffs about Lorena Bobbitt and Malcolm Forbes to sharp lines about a dim-bulb brother who acted as his own lawyer and "got his traffic ticket reduced to second-degree murder"; he called *USA Today* "two degrees below a coloring book." One reviewer asked, "Who else would mix nutritional tips with dumb-relative jokes, or sexual and racial humor with a consistent undertone of progressive political analysis?" Wearing a tux with African accents, he directed most of his comments to the blacks in the crowd, warning them off fried foods and starches ("*We ought to get white folks to eat and drink what we do, and they'd be wiped out in three months*"). He paced the stage, holding up newspapers and magazine covers to illustrate his points. "The talk was pointedly radical, but short of pontificating," said the critic Peter Stack.

Tracking down Dick Gregory these days is a marathon event for even the most intrepid detective. Once you locate him—say, at his home in Plymouth, Massachusetts ("*I think the white folks is comin' back and I'm gonna get a handful of Indians and stop 'em there this time!*")—the merry chase has just begun. His wife, a gracious woman who acts as combination travel agent, message center, and dispatcher for her constantly on-the-road husband of some fifty years, has come to accept his peripatetic nature. "We home when we home," he says with a laugh, quoting his own seldom-home father. "Strangely enough, it works just fine," Lillian Gregory once said. "Since the first day I met him, Dick has been on the go. It's his nature. When he comes home for a spell, we have a little celebration and it's all very joyous. Dick is a good father and we're a very close family. He calls every day, no matter where he is."

His phone bills have run as high as $3,000 a month. Gregory only accepts calls before seven A.M. or after eleven P.M., and, in lieu of "Hello," answers the phone with "God bless you." He dislikes being pinned down to a time and place for a long conversation, dropping teasing promises of possible future meetings, and enjoys playing hard to get. After we spent months attempting to arrange an interview, he suggested meeting in Los Angeles, where he was to speak to a primarily African-American gathering of salespeople who peddle All That's Natural, a health supplement that is supposed to relieve everything from Alzheimer's disease and arthritis to deafness and athlete's foot, PMS, sunburn, carpal tunnel syndrome, and—oh, yes, cancer.

When Gregory finally arrived, he was irritable. "I told you to be out here and we'd do it, and we *will* do it!" he exploded, his eyes and neck veins bulging. "I been up since three fuckin' o'clock. These folks are payin' me to come here! *You* ain't payin' me! You respect me like I respect you!" When he finally stepped to the mike, becalmed, he easily captivated a crowd of three hundred people, packed into a small, hot room, who welcomed him with a loud reverential greeting. The pep-talk rally had the flavor of a revival meeting ("Show him you love him—Mister Dick Gregory! Mister Dick Gregory! Mister Dick Gregory!"). The guest speaker strode forth like a biblical patriarch with a gray beard, a wiry prophetlike figure who could have been cast as De Lawd in *Green Pastures* if he'd had a rod and a robe. The aging comedian, newly energized, began slowly, first praising his audience for their selfless work on behalf of All That's Natural, then gradually segueing into a speech-cum-routine that was funny and full of earthy allusions to bodily functions. Dick Gregory, though much leaner, a little meaner, and much older, still has all of his comedy licks.

His theme, more or less, was to respect your body and listen to it. He boasted that he hasn't taken an aspirin in fifty years and walks eight miles a day. He reassured the crowd that the product they were pitching was the greatest thing since, well, Serutan. "I wouldn't be here if this was a trick." Ten times he tried to wind down, saying, "So I leave you with this . . . ," but the old stand-up comic in him couldn't quite get off the stage. When he finally exited, his parting words of wisdom were, "Laugh, take deep breaths, walk, and drink plenty of water."

After the meeting, a revived, relaxed, and suddenly chummy Gregory said he was now ready to be interviewed. Finally, in a corner of a deserted lobby of the Radisson Hotel in Culver City, at eleven-thirty P.M., he eagerly retraced the journey that took him from leading the American comedy revolution of the 1960s to advocating the joys of regularity in a small room in a warehouse on the outskirts of Gardena. Once cornered, the elusive Gregory became an amusing, compelling man who revels in repeating the well-thumbed stories of his life, his sturdy principles, and his faith that he has found the right path for him.

He leans in close and, in a confidential tone, begins most answers with, "Lemme tell ya . . ." He often takes the long route to get to a short idea, conveying anecdotes in a warm, slangy dialect. He skips from *A* to *Z* in a single answer, making points, both pertinent and pretentious, with great emphasis, unspooling a reel of rich social and cultural lore along with a certain amount of hokum. This Gregorian chant, delivered with great certainty, is half Ebonics and half King's English. One moment he's dropping pearls of wisdom, the next moment he's dropping his *g*'s and joshing, all of it coated with his performer's innate gift of gab.

He can be amiable and open, but, like any celebrity, he's accustomed to being listened to and kowtowed to. On C-Span's *Book Notes* in March 2001 to promote his new memoir, *Callus on My Soul,* a single Gregory answer consumed the show's final thirty-five minutes. The patient host, Brian Lamb, wisely let him ramble. While he's made an art out of being prickly and elusive, he's equally likely to treat a stranger like an intimate long-lost friend. Upon parting, Gregory walked me to my car at one A.M. and bestowed a bear hug and a kind of benediction: "I really enjoyed this. Say hello to the family and stay in touch, Brother!"

Lasting Impressions

DAVID FRYE, VAUGHN MEADER, WILL JORDAN

Nobody wants to be a mimic. . . . We all want to be ourselves.
                                                    —WILL JORDAN

THE 1960S WAS NOT just a golden age of stand-up comedians, it was also a renaissance for impressionists. There were so many good mimics around then that a TV show, *The Kopy Kats,* had to be created to hold them all. Even so, mimicry—a stand-up comedy subspecies falling somewhere between ventriloquism and voice-overs—has never been a high show-business calling. This is partly the fault of impressionists themselves, riddled with identity crises and self-esteem trauma. Many impressionists, no matter how brilliantly inventive, admit that a Marlon Brando imitation is a one-way ticket to Palookaville.

Impressionism is just an unlucky comic form. This disrespected art— the most underrated form of satire—deserves far better, but mimicry is considered a fluke talent, a mere trick, a technical skill, a kind of comic special effect, not the rare, precise, fragile craft that it is. Audiences regard mimics with amusement but also a faint condescension, as if to say, "Hey, that's a terrific Kirk Douglas, but what do you do in real life? Who do you want to be when you grow up?" The best Kirk Douglas, or even Tom Brokaw, imitation in the world won't take you very far in show business, and it may be your undoing. The back alleys behind nightclubs are littered with the broken careers of comics who flashed across the sky as mimics and then fell into oblivion. In the stand-up world, imitations are the sincerest form of obscurity.

Consider the plights of David Frye, Vaughn Meader, and Will Jordan, the foremost impressionists of the fifties and sixties, who took the art to new levels only to hit a brick wall. They are the three most conspicuous examples, but similar first-rate mimics from that era came to similar disappointing ends. Whither George Kirby, the superb black impressionist who served time on drug charges, Marilyn Michaels, whose great impressions of Barbra Streisand and Judy Garland are distant memories, the masterful and droll John Byner, and Frank Gorshin, who, says his former manager, suffered from a numbing lack of self-confidence? Only Rich Little enjoyed a long and lucrative career, but, for all his skill and late-sixties fame, he was an old-school mimic, not someone who advanced the art, despite his lifelike renderings of Jack Benny, George Burns, John Wayne, and Johnny Carson.

What made Frye and Jordan a vital part of the comedy revolution is that they were more than performing parrots, mimics who broke loose from the usual list of movie-star suspects. Frye went political while Jordan leaped to the head of the class by revealing that there were vocal lives after Edward G. Robinson, James Cagney, Jimmy Stewart, and Peter Lorre. He landed with a single perfect impression—his signature takeoff of Ed Sullivan, which inspired a legion of Jordan imitators until his original masterpiece was considered an imitation of the forgeries, a crushing experience from which he never recovered.

*

DAVID FRYE, the master political impressionist whose Richard Nixon catapulted him to glory in the mid-sixties, is in virtual hiding. Calls to his home with requests for an interview go unreturned, but Al Gore's voice on Frye's answering machine in 2001 reveals that he still has an uncanny ear.

Before Frye, nobody had ever imitated politicians (apart from FDR and JFK), but Frye did devastating political impressions and also managed (like Gorshin before him) to *look* like his subjects. Frye did such unlikely voices as those of Senators George McGovern, Ted Kennedy, and William Fulbright, and a raft of rarely mimicked stars—Raymond Burr, Jack Palance, Rod Steiger. Moreover, he made biting satirical comments that took him beyond mere mechanical reproductions.

It was Frye who came up with the definitive Richard Nixon, an animated version of Herblock's swarthy shifty-eyed cartoon—jowls wagging, wary darting eyes looking up from under shaggy brows, arms stretched maniacally into a V—that comics still palm off as their own. Frye's Nixon looked, sounded, and thought like Nixon. To his full-length presidential portrait he added the trademark Nixonian line that captured forever all of Tricky Dick's menacing paranoia: "*Make no mistake about it—I AM the president*"—also the title of Frye's first and most famous (1968) album, which sold a quarter of a million copies in three weeks.

If Frye (born David Shapiro in Brooklyn in 1936) had created nothing more than a stage Nixon for all time, he would have served the country well. But Frye also came up with voices and matching faces for Lyndon Johnson (lidded eyes peering menacingly through steel-rimmed glasses, drawling, "*Ah come here as uh simple barefoot boy from Texas who has become yore king*"); Hubert Humphrey (chin thrust up, grinning gleefully, chirping, "*I want to say that I'm just as pleased as punch to be running for the presidency of the United States! Under Lyndon Johnson, I ran for many things—coffee, sandwiches, and cigarettes*"); and, most unexpected of all, William F. Buckley, Jr. (tipped way back in his chair, eyes bulging wildly, snakelike tongue flicking in and out, chanting Latin phrases in Buckley's undulating, patronizing, patrician voice).

Frye worked from photos, explaining that once he had the physical look, the voice emerged from it. To get into the mood before a show, into the voices and psyches of his many subjects, he would go into a stall in a club's men's room and work on characterizations. One time, someone told the club owner about a crazy guy in the john speaking in tongues. Will Jordan, considered by cognoscenti the king of mimics, still calls David Frye the greatest living impressionist: "David, right from the beginning, was doing extreme faces. He told me he became a mimic when he saw me do Ed Sullivan."

Frye imploded when his best voices left office, died, or were slain. Phil Berger says that when Bobby Kennedy was murdered in 1968, Frye, "with tears in his eyes, booze in his hand, told comics at the Improvisation that it blew one of his key bits." Berger describes Frye as "an intense, dark, driven, brooding little man"—not unlike Nixon—"whose moods capsized in a shot glass." Frye lost it one August night in 1973 onstage at the Venetian Room in San Francisco. The critic John L. Wasserman wrote: "It wasn't even a bad show, but just a painfully embarrassing montage of a man falling apart in front of one's eyes. He was often unintelligible, forgot his routines, repeated lines, was alternatingly insulting and obsequious toward the audience, garbled his impersonations, and generally made a shambles of the entire affair."

Whatever happened, Frye faded from view, and fans and colleagues from the era assumed he had died or gone back to selling air-conditioning units. He did neither but quietly vanished. Arsenio Hall recalls Frye coming over to his table during the height of Hall's fame, telling him, "I remember when I used to be you. I had that same look you have in your eyes." When someone wanted to call security, Hall said, "'No way! Don't you remember him? He's David Frye!' I saw him on *The Ed Sullivan Show* when I was a kid. Man, I used to try to do Nixon like him! They didn't even know who he was." As with Meader and JFK, as with Jordan and Ed Sullivan, David Frye's fortunes were linked in some star-crossed way with Richard Nixon, who rehabilitated himself and had an afterlife— unlike, unhappily, David Frye, his satirically altered ego.

*

THE EVEN MORE SORROWFUL BALLAD of Vaughn Meader—who claims, "David Frye patterned his whole act after me"—gets updated every decade, as in a brief article on the back page of the *New York Times Magazine* of November 21, 1999. To mark the anniversary of John F. Kennedy's death, the *Times* reported that Vaughn Meader was alive and well and living in Waterville, Maine. As Ronald L. Smith writes, "Periodically, Meader is unearthed, checked for vital signs, and buried again."

Meader was forced to perform incognito for years after the Kennedy assassination, first as a bearded country singer named Johnny Sunday and then, more openly, as Abbott Meader. He soared to stardom in 1961 on the basis of that one precise but ill-fated voice. His stardom both began and (literally) ended overnight. One twist to the single-bullet theory that didn't make it into the Warren Report: the same bullet that killed JFK also murdered Vaughn Meader's career.

Meader rose to fame with his 1961 album *The First Family*, a series of seventeen sketches that spoofed the Kennedys' wealth, clannishness, offspring, and "vigah"; it was quickly followed by volume II. In one sketch, Jack and Jackie are in bed, and she says: *"Family, family, family. Jack, there's just too much family. Can we ever get away alone?"* Jack: *"Tomorrow, I, ah, promise—tomorrow we'll get away together. No more family for a while. Now, ah, turn off the light.* [Click.] *Good night, Jackie."* Jackie: *"Good night, Jack."* Jack: *"Good night, Ethel. Good night, Bobby."* Voices: *"Good night, Teddy. Good night, Peter. Good night, Pat."*

The LP's wild success was as much a measure of the Kennedy allure as a response to the album itself, which was smartly written and enacted but hardly biting, and only added to the Kennedy legend. The album could not have been more adoring, one writer commented, than if it had been written by Ted Sorenson; the album's actual creators were Earl Doud and Bob Booker. *The First Family* was clearly boosted by the presence of Mort Sahl and Dick Gregory, who helped make political humor trendy. Camelot fever had a lot to do with it, too: nobody did any Eisenhower or Truman albums, and spin-off record spoofs of Lyndon Johnson and Nikita Khrushchev bombed. Yet all the big record companies shied away from *The First Family,* and it seemed the project might die until the tiny Cadence label took a chance. One major record executive had said he wouldn't touch it with a ten-foot pole, so the following Christmas Earl Doud sent the executive a gift-wrapped ten-foot pole.

The day the LP was released, Meader got a call from Ed Sullivan's show, and the media soon descended upon him. He had become a kind of Beanie Baby. "It was a freak—and magic," he told me, looking back. "You can't duplicate it. Then it got totally crazy. It was just a whirlwind, a blur. I was having the time of my life. Who wouldn't? Just wine, women, and song. But it doesn't last."

Prior to the explosion, Meader was a run-of-the-mill stand-up comic and failed "hillbilly" singer and piano player. "Before I was a comedian, I had a country band in the army, but the music never seemed to get across." So he put together a monologue with a topical slant: "*A politician down in Louisiana said, 'These literacy tests don't prove nothin'.'* " He did other impressions (Fats Domino, Nat Cole); nobody noticed.

When the JFK album sold seven million copies (more than the original cast album of *Oklahoma!*), Meader shot to the top in four weeks. But he was strictly a vinyl phenomenon, a fad, not really a rounded comedian, and most of his otherwise routine act was just foreplay for the Kennedy bit. In person, without the supporting cast on the recording, or the sharp material, he lacked any bite.

Meanwhile, he recalls, "There were commercials poppin' up all over the country with people doing the Kennedy voice" (his manager turned down half a million dollars in commercial endorsements). Meader now asserts: "They think that's how Kennedy sounds: that's not how he sounds, that's how *I* sound. Anyone who did Kennedy was really imitating me"—complete with finger-jabbing gestures. "More than the voice, the sound, it was the meter, the cadence, the speech rhythms, the stops and stutters."

Supposedly the Kennedys "tried to shut [me] down," as they did Mort Sahl. Meader contends that the FCC was called and radio stations were asked not to play the album when the Kennedys were in Palm Beach, Florida, over Christmas, so as not to upset Joe Kennedy. "This is historically documented," says Meader, who adds that JFK's press secretary, Pierre Salinger, "freaked out" and hurried to the White House in horror to issue a correction when he first heard the Kennedy album on the radio—the mock-press-conference segment, in which JFK is asked if a Jew could ever become president and he replies, *"Well, I, ah, don't see, ah, why not, but as a good Catholic I could, ah, nevah vote for him."* Despite such publicity, Meader's follow-up concert tour proved "disastrous," said *Billboard;* "a major disaster," seconded *Variety.* His career seemed on the verge of taking a slide, so Meader had an inkling, well before JFK's death, that he had better wean himself away from Kennedy.

While contemplating how he might escape the Kennedy label, the president was killed. Meader heard about the assassination from a cabdriver in Milwaukee. The driver asked him, "Hey, did you hear about Kennedy?" and Meader, ready for yet another Kennedy joke, said, "No, how does it go?" Back at his hotel, he drowned himself in a bottle of liquor. "Everything got canceled and everything stopped." The LP was immediately withdrawn from record stores.

A few months later, Meader, at twenty-seven, valiantly attempted a comeback at the Blue Angel with a disjointed monologue that included one-liners, parables, topical comments, parodies of "Ol' Man River" and "On Top of Old Smokey," and digs at farm parity and Liz Taylor's marriages. He took a few stabs at what he termed "political satire," but his heart wasn't in it. "I could feel the audience's pity washing over me." He describes his post-Kennedy act as "spooky. I could see the humor in it but I couldn't convey it. In one bit, I had a kid playing football who becomes a kid throwing a grenade in Vietnam. I put a deathly pall on the place. At the Troubadour in L.A., Rod McKuen refused to follow me."

His world fell apart. "Friends dropped me," he said. "I was no longer a commodity to them." He "got barroom heavy" and then got into drugs. He began drifting, heading south at first and then out west. In 1967 he wound up in San Francisco, where, bedecked in tiger robes, sandals, and beads, he threw himself into the Summer of Love. He hung out with hippies and characters like Margo St. James, the former hooker who was trying to unionize prostitutes. Meanwhile, there were rumors that he had gone crazy and killed himself. Not quite, although in 1968 he overdosed on angel dust and was seen running naked and half-crazy through the streets. "I seemed to be a living reminder of a tragedy," he said while working his way back.

Meader left San Francisco in '68 to live in a log cabin in Maine, where the columnist Bob Greene discovered him. "I've been sitting in the woods for a long time," he told Greene. "It's peaceful, I go fishing, people let me alone, and the ones I know accept me for myself." Around that time,

Meader was mugged and stabbed by a cabdriver in Chicago after falling asleep on a chilly morning in the back of the taxi.

After that, he tried to rehabilitate himself by meditating and reading the Bible, running in the park with his eyes closed, mumbling, "Blind faith, blind faith, blind faith." He pulled himself up and out, moved to Maine with a new wife, and began writing songs. In 1972, reduced to giving talks to Knights of Columbus groups in Kentucky, he got a $7,500-a-year government job in Louisville but had to resign when it was disclosed he had used drugs in the sixties and danced at the Hookers' Ball.

In Louisville, he started a country-western band, the Honky-Tonk Angels, but gave it up when lured back by the man who created James Whitmore's one-man shows on Will Rogers and Harry Truman, and who wanted Meader to do an evening with John F. Kennedy. He agreed to do it in a weak, insolvent moment, then changed his mind. "It was a case of 'Do Kennedy and we'll get you four weeks in Vegas.' But I just could not do that. I wouldn't be able to look in the mirror in the morning." Someone even wrote a show featuring Meader as Kennedy in heaven, and just a few years ago a guy called him with an idea for a show in which Meader would play Kennedy as an old man reflecting back on the Camelot era. JFK devotees practically regarded him as a way of channeling Kennedy. He says, "People had this Kennedy thing. They *still* got it."

Meader hung around Los Angeles doing voice-overs (Walter Winchell in a Tony Curtis movie about the mobster Louis Lepke), but never again enjoyed doing impressions. In the late seventies, though, he was reported to be developing a Jimmy Carter impression while earning a living playing piano at recording sessions. In 1980 he was a state convention delegate for Ted Kennedy from his hometown of Waterville, Maine ("I feel like the Rip Van Winkle of politics"), and wrote a campaign song, "I'm Getting Ready for Teddy." When Teddy came to Meader's hometown, campaigning for the Democratic nomination, he told the crowd to support him "so Vaughn Meader can have a job again."

Finally, Meader settled into his original groove as a country singer called Johnny Sunday, a drunk who turns evangelist, and played honky-tonk piano at New England ski lodges and lounges. He rose as high as warm-up act at the Lone Star Café in New York, where displaced and ersatz Texans gathered. Rudy Maxa tracked him down there in 1979 and wrote that Meader, on piano and guitar, had a "strong rich voice" and wrote clever lyrics, noting that the rowdy Lone Star crowds had no idea who he was, creating a new schizoid dilemma for Meader—how to escape his past while using it to get himself heard at cafés and record companies. Said Maxa, "Meader wants to be successful again."

He now makes a modest living in Maine, performing with his trio at places like Bob and Sue Crory's Country Club Lodge, working in exchange for room and board. He sings standards as well as his own gospel/country songs, with titles like "My Life Ain't Been a Bed of Roses," "You Can't Keep a Good Love Down," and "I'd Rather Rise Than Fall in Love." In the winter, he lives in Florida for health reasons. Aside from emphysema, he sounds hale, hearty, and content at age sixty-seven, except for a lingering resentment about *First Family* residuals he feels he's owed. "I couldn't track down the royalties. I hear that *First Family* albums are sold on the Internet and I haven't seen a penny from 'em." On a later album, *The First Family Rides Again,* about the Reagan clan, on which Rich Little impersonated Reagan, Meader did a Kennedy cameo.

When he began performing again in small rooms, he says, "There wasn't too much recognition. My beard grew and my teeth fell out. But everywhere somebody would say, 'You know who that is?' and then it would start." When he plays and sings now at a little restaurant in Gulfport, Florida, they pin his old *First Family* album to the front of the piano "so they can tell people who I am. That's not who I am, but that's fine."

After his zigzag journey, Meader has nearly come to terms with what happened to him. "It's like the movie of our lives is already in the can and all it's doing now is running." It could be a great movie, and indeed Tom Hanks has optioned it. "I don't know if I ever came to terms with it. I don't know if the *country* ever came to terms with it. Maybe I just hardened myself, cut if off. It probably hit me deeper than I let myself know. Something happened psychologically. I just covered it with denial. I could do other stuff and I tried to run away from it but it just stayed there—my association with the Kennedys. It had a bigger impact on people than I ever imagined at the time. I was just doing a gig."

*

WILL JORDAN WAS the Al Hirschfeld of mimics, a man who so dominated the field of vocal caricature that by 1960 he had become its guru. The top cat on TV's *The Kopy Kats* was so good that other mimics on the show would gather to watch him at rehearsal. He was the Lon Chaney of voices, a mimic whose vocal acrobatics included such dazzling feats as Bela Lugosi and Boris Karloff playing Dean Martin and Jerry Lewis.

Woody Allen, on a TV special, pronounced him "a genius," the Renoir of the impressionist school of comedy.

According to Jordan (who won't divulge his real name), he just fell into the impressions by accident in high school. He ran in the same circle as Mel Brooks and Lenny Bruce, hanging out in the late forties and early fifties at Brooklyn soda fountains, perfecting his voices and his lines, many later allegedly lifted by Brooks, Bruce, and others. Jordan was touted for superstar status among his colleagues at Hanson's drugstore, the legendary hangout for comics. The comic Adam Keefe recalled, "We all used to look for Will to see what he's got today."

Jordan recalls: "I could stand in front of Hanson's for hours and just keep doing crazy bits—what would happen if Jack E. Leonard gave Ed Sullivan a blood transfusion? A lot of sick stuff—long before Lenny— that you couldn't do on stage, but Lenny could." Jordan found voices nobody ever considered mimicking, such as Dwight Eisenhower.

Bruce-like, he got into his subjects' psyches. William Holtzman writes that Jordan's repertoire was "not just prodigious but highly liter-ate. Where other impressions were technicians, carbon copies, Will used the impression not just as an end in itself but as a point of departure. He took his knack for mimicry, a second-class comedy in the eyes of some, and made it the cornerstone of a sophisticated act." At the chic Blue Angel and Le Ruban Bleu, he burbled with bizarre shtick, earning the nickname "Ill Will."

Jordan broke through in 1954 when he chanced upon Ed Sullivan, a totally original impression out of nowhere and a milestone for two reasons: it revealed that everybody was fair game and that a truly in-spired mimic could go beyond reproducing a voice, reshaping himself into the personality itself. Jordan went where no mimic had ever gone before when he molded the essential, complete Ed Sullivan—the mush-mouthed, teeth-baring, eye-popping, arm-folding, no-neck, shoulder-hunching Sullivan—"the character you now think of as Ed Sullivan," emphasizes Jordan; two years earlier he had first showcased Sullivan on a 45-RPM record, "The Roast of the Town," but it only made a national impression when it became visual on the Sullivan show.

Jordan created Sullivan by "thinking of an ape. I put my tongue in my upper lip. I rolled my eyes up to show the whites—the kind of grotesque face kids make all the time. You must stay in the Ed Sullivan character, but you've got to make it *funny*. Sullivan of course is *not* funny, but there was just something about him that called for satire." To make his Sullivan funnier, Jordan turned him into a revolving robot with a pinched voice, bared teeth, and elongated sounds ("*Thenk yew all virr-r-y virr-r-y much, la'ies and gennulmen, and now let's re-e-e-ally hear it feer a t'rrific star of the recent MGM musical . . .*"). "The basis of the bit," he says, "was the shoulder shakes, the eye rolls, the belches, the knuckle cracks, the 're-e-e-ally big shew.' That's the basis of the bit, and that's mine. And of course the whole idea of even *doing* Sullivan was mine." "*Re-e-e-ally big shew*" remains a part of the language.

"The reason it went over," Jordan explains, "was because it wasn't anything like the real Sullivan. It was a partial invention of my own. He never said 'really big,' he never said 'shew,' he never cracked his knuckles, he never rolled his eyes up, he never did spins, he never frowned. Most of those Ed Sullivan gestures are mine." The Sullivan case is a long-lost cause, for by the 1970s Jordan's impression had effectively entered the public domain; everyone's uncle could mimic Will Jordan's Sullivan. Talking with Jordan is like taking a master class in mimicry: "I want to clarify the difference between an invention and an exaggeration. I did not exaggerate Ed Sullivan's mannerisms. He didn't have any. I *invented* them. Jackie Mason exaggerates the mannerisms that I made up. Jackie Mason is doing a satire on my impression." Mason turned Sullivan into a whirling dervish mouthing gibberish.

Jordan opened up the field, at one point earning $6,000 a week, unheard-of for a mere mimic, thanks mainly to the Ed Sullivan bit, which Sullivan further exploited by having Jordan on his show several times, even teaching him how to "do" Ed Sullivan. In a case of nature imitating art, Sullivan revealed to Jordan that he often felt compelled to talk like him because people expected him to.

Ed Sullivan was Jordan's signature piece—his hook, calling card, and bread and butter—and he watched in horror as other comics, greater and lesser, stole it without batting an eye. "That was my entrée to stardom. That was the big bit. They all knew the value of it." He says that one prominent comic "stole it word for word and later he got top writers to make it better and longer than mine."

Jordan later confronted the more famous comedian: "I said, 'How could you do that to me?' He just screamed at me, 'You're small-time and you'll always be small-time!' That was his answer." Jordan says that Jerry Lewis later stole it and Sammy Davis, Jr., stole it from Lewis. "I told Sullivan about it. But Sullivan had no loyalty. He hired everybody that stole it." Later, Jordan was booked into a Catskill resort, only to be canceled when a booker told him, "We had Jack Carter here last week, and he did Sullivan, so we can't use you."

Many comedians ransacked Jordan's trunkful of voices, he says. "Jonathan Winters stole a bit from me, too. I don't want to underscore this too much, but he stole my Sabu. Winters was doing sort of a gay Indian." Lenny Bruce also kidnapped Jordan's mincing Sabu voice. One night at the Gaslight Club in Greenwich Village, Jordan saw David Frye's show, which also included a Sabu bit, and afterward he said to Frye, "That's my '*ooo*,' you took my '*ooo*.' I don't ever want you to do it again."

He concedes, "Now, I didn't own Ed Sullivan, I didn't own Sabu, but I hope I would own the mannerisms and the phonetics. You get very little sympathy from the public when you say you invented '*ooo*.' But I *did* invent the '*ooo*,' and the '*ooo*' is what makes it funny. Without that '*ooo*' you have nothing. You have the real person, a charming little boy from India. But when I imitate Sabu it's much funnier than Sabu, because I'm translating it into a form that *makes* it funny." Jordan had, as mimics say, "cracked the code" and found the key that rang the cash register.

Jordan maintains that Lenny Bruce stole not just routines and concepts from him, but also certain lines—"little things, which will sound very small-timey, but they're the things that define a personality and a style." The most valuable bit Bruce stole was Jordan's "Adolf Hitler Story" done as a Twentieth Century Fox musical. Around 1959 Jordan learned that Bruce was stealing from him, pilfering at first, but then he came back with a truck for "the Hitler bit."

Larceny, both grand and petty, is the central theme of Jordan's life, and has become a forty-year crusade: "It's terrible. It can really abort a career that never happened. How could I possibly prove it? I admit that my material probably wasn't as funny as Lenny's, but here's the point— my material is not for sale, it's not for rent. The only way you can get it is by illegally stealing it from me. I don't give anything away because I don't have that much to give away. I need those things to survive. I don't really think the public has any idea to what lengths people will go to connect in show business. Bob Hope said, 'Why don't you come up with another impersonation?' I said, 'Bob, you can come up with another joke, but suppose I said, Don't talk like Bob Hope anymore.' "

Jordan kept working, but the brass ring had slid from his grasp by the early 1960s, when a kind of terminal mimic's block set in. He said, "I've just frozen up. I can't write anymore 'cause I know it's going to be stolen. I know that's foolish. . . ." Jordan's former manager thought that his client had a hand in his own undoing because he "considered mimicry so easy, so unimportant"—and eventually grew to hate the Sullivan impression. "He did Sullivan only under absolute duress, if they were screaming and yelling," his manager told Phil Berger, who writes that Jordan began hearing "echoes everywhere" in other mimics—inflections and gestures—that he felt were his rightful comic vocal property.

Holed up today in his cramped apartment in New York, Jordan readily admits: "I'm full of explanations and complaints. I made a lot of mistakes. I'd have played it entirely different if I had it to do over. Larry Storch did what I should have done—he dropped the impressions and returned as a comic. Storch was my idol and inspiration. He was the first one to do Cary Grant." He goes on: "I kept trying to do comedy, first-person monologues like Alan King or Jackie Mason, and it kept failing. Winters did sound effects, but he wasn't a full-blown mimic and was strong enough to drop that. I didn't have the stick-to-it-iveness. I was lazy and chicken or I'd have given up the impressions right away and gone out as a comedian, like Don Rickles. But they were calling me the greatest mimic who ever lived."

Jordan states the classic mimic's dilemma: "Nobody wants to be a mimic. I never met a mimic yet that wants to do it. We all want to be ourselves, but the public loves mimics. You do it because you get the instant recognition. Mimics were always considered secondary acts."

Jordan was drawn to the more elusive voices—virgin vocal territory like Paul Newman, Ray Milland, and Robert Shaw, whom he prides himself on capturing even though most people can't remember Shaw, let alone his voice. He laments that mimicry standards have fallen. Jordan has absorbed the history, theory, and practice of mimicry and can trace the lineage of impressions, comedians, even cartoon voices: "Sid Caesar was just an imitation of Danny Kaye, as was Dick Shawn. Rickles is really Jack E. Leonard and Milton Berle. Bullwinkle was an actor imitating Red Skelton, just as Mel Blanc was imitating Art Carney as Barney Rubble, and as Alan Reed was imitating Jackie Gleason. Top Cat was Arnold Stang imitating Phil Silvers." To demonstrate the small but critical difference between Gorshin's impression of Alec Guinness and his own, he stands up and mimics Gorshin's Guinness. "Now—compare that with my authentic Guinness. The walk is Stan Laurel's walk." He mimics the walk, a perfect representation of Guinness's saunter.

Jordan sinks back down into a leather recliner in his tiny, smoke-filled apartment, cluttered with books, photos, newspapers, and a rare collection of old stills of stars before they fixed their noses. He says he works only four or five gigs a year, usually as Sullivan in salutes to the Beatles or Elvis Presley, but remains on call for cartoons and commercials. At seventy-two, he looks none the worse for showbiz wear and tear, much as we remember him from forty years ago—an anonymous blank slate of a face behind big black Jack Benny glasses. Jordan says he felt hurt when he wasn't hired to do Sullivan in a Walter Winchell biography, or for a tribute to Sullivan called "A Really Big Show," or as a voice-over in *Pulp Fiction*. "Not to brag," he says, "but why would you hire *anyone* else to do Ed Sullivan?"

To survive, he does film looping—once as Bert Lahr, who died during the making of *The Night They Raided Minsky's*. "The other mimics were surprised I'd beaten them out. I wasn't a better mimic. I simply imitated the outtakes. Lahr didn't sound like the Cowardly Lion, he sounded like a dying Bert Lahr." Jordan nails a voice by replaying the same phrase a hundred times to find the voice placement. He frets over voices that got away: "So many voices I still can't get—Orson Welles, Basil Rathbone."

Of all the impressionists during the comedy renaissance, Rich Little went on to have by far the biggest career, due in part to Jordan, who insists that Little, too, robbed him blind. "Between Adam Keefe and Rich Little, virtually every single routine I've ever done appeared on the Johnny Carson show. The way actors walk, Little took that from me. The whole thing about Gable and Eisenhower sounding alike, Little took that from me. Only about fifty percent of his voices are accurate. He's a horribly ungrateful person. It's strange for me to criticize him, because I discovered him."

Jordan saw him in 1959 in Ottawa, and in 1961 he says he gave a tape of Little to Mel Tormé, who was then producing Judy Garland's TV show. "He's never thanked me or in any way tried to repay me. But let's not get into that, because that's bitterness and sour grapes and it gets you nowhere." Yet Jordan can't help getting into it, because it gnaws at him daily. He adds, "I met Little not long ago, and asked, 'Why are you doing this to me? These are my routines. You're making fifty thousand dollars a week—I can't even get a job.'" Little responds through his agent, David Martin, who states: "Rich feels it would serve no purpose to fuel the fire or to debate his [Jordan's] memory." Martin adds, "It sounds as if everyone who made a buck stole from Jordan."

These days, Jordan indeed performs all too rarely—at the occasional industrial show or special event—but he realizes this is another time. He loves doing his really obscure stuff at old-time radio conventions, which he describes as "far and away my best audience." Today's stars bore him. He says that 90 percent of today's celebrities have no mannerisms, citing Robert Redford and Tom Hanks. To paraphrase Norma Desmond, there are no more *voices*. So Jordan stays stuck in his own era, burnishing his vintage collection of Robert Shaw, Ray Milland, and Peter Lawford. "That's where I'm very ashamed of myself. I'm terribly aware of being antiquated"—but he just can't let go of those resonant old voices.

Occasionally, a call comes in for a Nigel Bruce (he tosses off a remarkably real Bruce, quavery and weathered) or for Gene Autry's *speaking* voice. He says he hasn't lost any of his technical virtuosity. "That's sort of my hidden weapon. While there are only four or five performances a year, I'm working better than ever. A singer starts to lose it. A mimic and a comedian—I don't think you lose it when you get older. That little bit of senility helps the comedy. It helped George Burns. He was better when he was ninety-five."

What ignites Jordan is his burning sense of injustice. "One of the things that keeps me going is my anger and my frustrations and—it's an awful thing to say—my desire for revenge. It's kind of an ugly thing, but you know, revenge is what's keeping me alive. I want to make the point of what I was. It's almost like I'm two people: I'm this old guy, but I'm also representing that other guy back in 1954 who never got a fair shake."

Schnook's Progress

Woody Allen

I could always be funny. That I had control over.

H E WAS NOT POOR, unhappy, unloved, or itching to make people laugh. By all accounts, the scrawny, freckled, red-headed, bespectacled Brooklyn boy loved sports, movies, magic, jazz, radio shows, and comic books, hated school, and was bored and ignored by his family. So far, so normal.

There is no real clue in any of this that the kid just described would one day be the subject of intense critical scrutiny, tabloid scandal, half a dozen biographies, scads of doctoral dissertations, and a documentary film of his musical tour of Europe. Or that he would one day escort First Lady Betty Ford to a Martha Graham Dance Company concert, publish three volumes of humorous pieces (originally in *The New Yorker*), and inspire legions of would-be comics to take the plunge into stand-up comedy.

In the early 1960s, when he was still flinching pitifully before a microphone, nobody would have imagined that this frail-seeming little fellow, who looked like a helpless twerp that a magician had pulled from the audience, would surpass almost every other stand-up comedian of his day. No comic of that era had a bigger impact than Woody Allen, who—along with Mort Sahl (his own idol), Lenny Bruce, and Mike Nichols and Elaine May—redefined the meaning of stand-up comedy. He helped turn it into biting, brutally honest satirical commentary on the cultural and psychological tenor of the times.

A lot of people who grew up on Woody Allen movies are not aware that he ever *was* a stand-up comedian. The busy auteur filmmaker covered his tracks well. His thirty movies, made over three decades and two generations, seem as far removed from his early career of cracking jokes in dank nightclubs as his few years as a stand-up star were from his humdrum boyhood. Allen might have gone on being one of the funniest stand-up comics in history had he wished, but he couldn't wait to get out. Something about stand-up—the hours, the travel, the nightly performing pressures, the robotic repetition—resists long careers; few comics have stuck with stand-up and not made a beeline into TV or movies at the first opportunity. For Allen, as for the hundreds of others now who use comedy clubs as sitcom waiting rooms, stand-up was an entry-level position in show business.

Allen just may have been the most radical of all the renaissance comedians—not only in his choice of subjects, but in his onstage character. The comedian physically embodied his jokes. As he once said, "*I am the premise.*" The Woody Allen he first gave us represented the interior Woody Allen—his obsessions over women, his Jewishness, his life of the mind, and his ego- and life-threatening traumas (Los Angeles, nature, gentiles). He made us *believe* that the schnook spinning jokes onstage was really Allen.

So totally did we buy it that, when he ran into personal troubles in the 1990s, involving an affair with his longtime lover Mia Farrow's adopted daughter (now his wife), certain Allen fans stopped going to his films. For some it was a moral choice; for others, it was a case of Allen just not seeming funny anymore. It was during *l'affaire* Soon-Yi, in fact, that Allen began insisting that the nebbish he had built a career on was nothing like himself. This troubled long-time followers, who felt he'd deceived them all those years and that the ultimate joke was on them. Devoted Allenites felt used, had, disappointed. If he *wasn't* that funny, dithering, helpless little guy up there, just who was he? The two looked alike, dressed alike, sounded alike, thought alike, and, presumably, behaved alike.

Though he has since distanced himself from the stage-and-screen Woody, as if he were some guy he'd hung out with in his youth who now embarrasses him, they were once inseparable. It's a tribute to Allen's artistry that the persona he manufactured and nurtured over the years seemed so alive, so authentic. The mundane truth, of course, is that the fictionalized Allen, as with most autobiographical artists, is only a piece of the real person. Allen is decidedly *un*-dithery; you have to be highly disciplined and focused to produce a movie a year for thirty years.

Yet like his screen counterparts, he was indeed a mass of neuroses (twenty years in therapy), and he still appears to be, to judge by *Wild Man Blues,* Barbara Koppel's 1998 documentary film that follows Allen and his jazz group across Europe. In it, Allen looks startlingly like the stage-screen Woody, befuddled and frightened by anything unfamiliar. He once told Roger Ebert that he needed a night-light in his bedroom until he was in his forties and said that he considered suicide every day. But Allen says his glum face inaccurately reflects his mood. "I always have a deadpan face. It seems sad in repose, but it just seems that way. I'm not really sad." And yet he could also say, "I don't think being funny is anyone's first choice."

He noted in the late sixties that "everybody unequivocally confuses the real Woody Allen with the onstage character. When I started performing, I thought of myself as exactly the opposite. I've always offered myself as a lover, a sportsman, a raconteur, a defender of the faith—all the good things—and not in any way a bumbler. But the audience would always laugh." It was this very discrepancy between his self-image and his physical image that was the source of the laughter.

Despite his dinky appearance, fragile looks, timid demeanor, and apologetic voice, one of his role models was Bob Hope, whose own cowardly bravado he would emulate in his jokes and movies. Woody pursues women, but they never take him seriously, the theme of *Play It Again, Sam* and the thread of many Allen stand-up stories and films. His apparent ineptitude was another of his secret weapons. He has always enjoyed overturning expectations, choosing to play the schlemiel.

"Even when he was growing up, Allen was more formidable than he liked to show," John Lahr wrote of him. He was in fact a decent athlete (a would-be boxer, a leadoff hitter in baseball, a medal-winner in track), and, image to the contrary, he had no trouble with women and claims he began dating in kindergarten, asking little girls if they wanted to share a soda with him. "He could always get the girls," says one of them, Diane Keaton. "Incomprehensibly," noted Anne Beatts, the comedy writer, "many women found this posture sexually stimulating. Countless bespectacled thin-chested young men got laid throughout the sixties and seventies by passing themselves off as a 'Woody Allen type.' " His biographer Marion Meade writes: "Woody represented a new breed of man, the quintessential misfit, the heroic frog who turned into a prince." Girls sent him their phone numbers, photos, and statistics; one pleaded for a sock.

Allen's love life, like almost everything else about him, has been the subject of microscopic analysis. An alleged womanizer in his heyday, he told Tony Schwartz, "I've never been a big believer in going to bed with women that I don't have some feeling for," drawing a smile from his friend and early costar Tony Roberts, who countered, "Put it this way, Harpo Marx probably chased the most girls. I chase the second most, and Woody is a close third."

Allen has painted a spartan portrait of himself holed up in his study dutifully batting out jokes, essays, and screenplays, emerging only long enough to mix himself a chocolate malted. But, wrote Schwartz in the *New York Times* in 1980, "the catch is that what Allen says is often at variance with the way he really lives, and with what some of his close friends say about him. Many of Allen's contradictions are the sort you'd expect to see him lightly parodying in his films. He insists, for example, that he cherishes his privacy, but he eats dinner several nights a week at the city's leading hangout for celebrity and gossip columnists [Elaine's]."

He plays his clarinet Monday nights in very public saloons, first at Michael's Pub and now at the Café Carlyle, where he slips in and out quickly. "He seeks his privacy so publicly," remarked Schwartz, "tries so conspicuously to be inconspicuous." His street "disguises"—an old fishing hat and a brown floppy hat—instantly draw New Yorkers' attention, but, says the director Sydney Pollack, "he refuses to stay off the streets, no matter how many people recognize him. It's a pain in the ass for him. But he needs to move around in life all the time." Walking with him, said a friend, is like accompanying the Statue of Liberty down the street.

Schwartz revealed further mixed messages: "He professes simple tastes but he lives in a luxuriously furnished Fifth Avenue duplex penthouse overlooking Central Park, is driven around in a Rolls-Royce, employs a full-time housekeeper who doubles as a trained Cordon Bleu chef, and even gets his rumpled looking clothes custom-made by Ralph Lauren." Friends said the Rolls embarrassed him; he would have the driver let him out a block away from his destination and walk the rest of the way, like a kid driven to school by his parents.

Allen told Studs Terkel in a backstage interview at Mister Kelly's in 1965, "I am very shy and uncomfortable onstage and offstage." To Terkel's rejoinder, "You're shy and yet you're outgoing. You're real but you're a cartoon figure at the same time," Allen replied, "Everything is based on absolutely true events, but it's all exaggerated. I'm not kidding when I'm onstage—I have a series of trials and tribulations all day, and I've never had an easy time coping with people or events or mechanical objects." After her telephone interview with Allen in 1981, Leah Garchik wrote: "Allen's voice was small, serious, and self-assured. Although he dwelled on his feelings of failure, his voice didn't sound whiny, not even depressed."

The stand-up and the cinematic Woody Allen began to diverge around 1975, when Russell Baker observed in his *New York Times* column that Allen's movie character had stopped being believable or sympathetic since Woody had begun to get the girl. After seeing *Love and Death,* Baker wrote: "Allen has been traveling under false colors. He is not a schlemiel at all, but a Valentino in schlemiel's eyeglasses, and he has made fools of us; he's lured us into feeling superior and then has sneaked away to get the most desirable girl in the house." Indeed, the once bumbling would-be Bogie of *Play It Again, Sam* was suddenly surrounded by gorgeous women in his films; by *Stardust Memories* in 1980 he was fending off Charlotte Rampling, Marie-Christine Barrault, and Jessica Harper, with whom he was briefly involved off-screen. Critics and freelance cynics began grumbling that he was casting his films with his female fantasies, which of course would be a very "Woody Allen"–ish thing to do.

The waiflike Allen's mere presence on a nightclub stage in the early 1960s was in itself funny, even startling. He exuded what one writer termed a "wistful futility"; critics referred to his "lemur-like" visage. Apart from Wally Cox, there had never been anybody in nightclubs who remotely resembled Allen, a pipsqueak with the chutzpah to invade the territory that had for decades been the province of brassy guys in tuxes. Even Mort Sahl, who altered the stand-up dress code and elevated the intelligence quotient, was brash and frenzied. Woody Allen was none of that. He looked like a bookworm in a green corduroy suit who, blinking at the light, seemed to have just crawled out from the library stacks, unprepared to meet the world.

Yet something unlemur-like happened when Allen stumbled onstage and began to talk. People paid attention, if only out of curiosity. Audiences took pity on him. Anyone who saw Allen in those first weeks at the tiny room upstairs in a Greenwich Village club called the Duplex must have thought, There seems to be some mistake, and wondered what time the real comedian came on. He wasn't a wuss, like Cox and Jackie Vernon, who traded on meekness. If you felt sorry for him, it was only because he was so uneasy onstage. But the strength of his jokes sustained him over those first shaky months, when Ralph J. Gleason wrote warily, "Woody Allen might be worth hearing more than once."

His presence was easily overlooked at first, but he was not without valuable funny physical attributes. Foster Hirsch, the film critic, writes: "Allen's face is his fortune. Your immediate reaction is to laugh. The thin lips, the slanted, jagged nose, the sallow complexion dotted with freckles and framed by stringy red hair. And the eyes—staring, glassy, stunned, bemused, knowing, and accented by the arching eyebrows and the black, willfully old-fashioned horn-rimmed glasses. Woody's owlish, lopsided face creates an immediate comic aura. Like [Buster] Keaton, he uses the stubborn, immobile mold of his features as a defense against misfortune. 'Keep away!' the deadpan mask announces. Allen's face, like those of the great silent comics, issues a fixed statement to the world." Hirsch, in his 1981 study of Allen, called it "a great cartoon of a mug"; in 1976 there actually was a comic strip called *Inside Woody Allen,* drawn by Stuart Hample, with gags supplied from Allen's file; it ran for eight years in 180 newspapers, a helpful promotional device.

His jokes fit his image like a glove. On going to the track, he cracked: "*Mine was the only horse with training wheels*"; on making love: "*During sex, I think of playing ball, and as she's digging her nails into my neck I pinch-hit for Willie McCovey*"; on oral contraception: "*I asked a girl to go to bed with me and she said no*"; on water skiing: "*My wife was in front of me, rowing frantically*"; on his grandfather: "*He was a very insignificant man—at his funeral, the hearse followed the other cars.*"

Allen, seated in a screening room at his Manhattan Film Center in 1999, told me: "The funny part of it is, I never thought of it as a character, although comedians do. I just went out and told stories that were interesting or funny to me. I was surprised right from the start—and I don't say this with any false modesty—that there was any interest in it at all. I was *shocked* by the fact that audiences embraced me. When I would go on at a hootenanny or something, ten comics would go on before me, and every one of them would kill the audience. And I also killed the audience. [But] for some reason, there were certain ones that stuck to the ribs more, who the audience focused in on. So I always thought it was a lucky accident. For some reason they saw something in me."

Unlike many comedians, Woody didn't put spectators on the defensive, and he spoke conversationally. He seemed to be groping for words only to stumble upon the perfect phrase; he knew exactly what he was doing. He didn't try to overpower the room and impress you with his "personality"; he let you discover him. He appeared to be normal, not larger than life but lifesize, barely. His presence, or lack of it, made you lean closer and let him gradually unburden himself of his doubts, fears, and worries. He even "hid" in his clothes, as someone put it. The utter absence of showbiz veneer and shtick was the best shtick any comedian had ever devised. This uneasy onstage naturalness became a trademark.

In a 1964 *Life* profile, William Zinsser commented: "He is a person who walks out onto a stage and immediately makes his presence unfelt. . . . Even his lank red hair looks defeated." He fidgeted onstage and twisted an arm around his head, as if trying to strangle himself. He would furiously rub his eye, adjust his spectacles twenty times, finger his jacket buttons, smack his lips, and scrunch up his body. His entire onstage manner seemed to be an elaborate apology for taking up our valuable time, as if to say, with every gulp and grimace, "Listen, if you have anything better to do, don't feel you have to sit here on my account."

Most of the major comedians of the fifties and sixties renaissance boasted that they didn't tell jokes; Allen, on the other hand, did tell jokes, but they were jokes he'd labored over and subtly tucked into little stories, supposedly from his offstage life, that produced now-classic Woody Allenisms—about his ex-wife (*"The Museum of Natural History took her shoe and based on the measurements they reconstructed a dinosaur"*); about his parents (*"Their values in life are God and carpeting"*); about the Berkowitzes, who shot a moose in the woods and, on the way to a costume party, realizing it wasn't dead, took the moose along—it placed third and was the life of the party (*"The moose mingled. Did very well. Scored."*)

As different as he was thematically and stylistically, Allen was a highly traditional comedian whose jokes involved hairpin turns of logic and hilarious images. His thrust was no more avant-garde than Henny Youngman's, including the wife jokes: *"For a while, my wife and I pondered whether to take a vacation or get a divorce. We decided that a trip to Bermuda is over in two weeks but a divorce is something you always have. With the divorce, though, my wife got absolutely everything. In the event that I remarry and have children, she gets them."* Or: *"My wife cooked her first dinner for me. I choked on a bone in the chocolate pudding."* Almost unique among stand-up comics, Allen could be funny about sex without ever being dirty (*"The difference between sex and death is that, with death you can do it alone and nobody's going to make fun of you"*; *"Bisexuality instantaneously doubles your chances for a date on Saturday night"*). "Sex and food," he noted, "are always good for laughs."

After his first wife (*"the dread Mrs. Allen"*) sued him for "holding her up to scorn and ridicule"—always a risk in marrying a comedian—he toned down the take-my-ex-wife wisecracks. One of them, about buying orgasmic insurance for his wife, also got him into trouble with Ed Sullivan. As Dick Cavett tells it, "Ed went into a spinning, bubbling, screaming apoplexy," crying, "Attitudes like yours are why kids are burning their draft cards!" Allen apologized and Sullivan restored his stripes. "From that day on," Allen told his biographer Eric Lax, "I had no better ally in show business. He had me to dinner, he plugged me in his column, and had me on the show all the time." His decision to escort Betty Ford to a Martha Graham concert in a tux and tennis shoes was pure PR; as Lax noted, Allen hadn't spent years working for press agents for nothing.

Allen, who expresses "tremendous affection" for the Borscht Belt school of comics, explained his method: "I always said I was doing wife jokes and coward jokes and the same jokes Bob Hope or Henny Young-man were doing—exactly. I'm doing the same thing as 'My room's so small you have to step outside to change your mind.' I would just do my version of it—it could be the identical joke. But I'd say it in a way as if I'm conversing with someone—other than like some guy who's sitting across from you at Lindy's giving you the one-liners with a cigar."

Woody Allen is the only comedian of that jazz-linked comedy era, other than Steve Allen, who actually *is* a jazz musician. However, his delivery wasn't jazz inflected or in any way improvised. Because he was totally a manufactured stand-up comic, unlike most of his tradition-shattering colleagues of the day, Allen never improvised a syllable on-stage. "I put very little premium on improvisation," he told Studs Terkel. "The fact that someone makes it up on the spur of the moment doesn't mean anything to me." (And yet, strangely, in his movies he encourages actors to improvise, explaining that "dialogue in a movie sounds better half-improvised.")

Allen never considered his comedy as "intellectual" as the critics did. "I have a *slight* intellectual component," he once said. "Mort Sahl and Nichols and May are genuine intellectuals. Great humor is intellec-tual without trying to be." Even so, he flashed what one critic labeled "intellectual brand names"—Sartre, Eliot, Socrates, Proust, Goethe, Wordsworth, Malraux, Arendt—that lent an intellectual gloss, and then comically juxtaposed them with his own humdrum urban life. He spun out his bizarre little "verbal cartoons," as he called them, studded with sublime jokes, as if they had actually happened to him ("*Once I tried to tip a process server*"), in a voice unlike the usual comic's voice of the time: heavily inflected with New York Jewish cadences—kvetching and kid-ding, whining but winning. The crazier a story, the more earnestly he told it; his demeanor was always dead serious. Allen appeared to be a man to whom nothing ever happened and yet was a guy to whom extraordinary things happened—like the meeting he called with the appliances in his house that he suspected were conspiring against him.

So Allen used his inner, not his actual, life to conjure up the vignettes that wound up in his monologues. It was his way of dealing with a world he saw as, if not overtly hostile, then totally alien (*"A huge dog came after me. It was the kind of dog that chases automobiles—and brings them back"*). He felt inept in everything but in comedy, where he felt "completely at ease," as he said in 1962, after he had broken through. In one year he estimated he had written twenty thousand jokes for various comics (Sid Caesar, Art Carney, Herb Shriner, Garry Moore, Peter Lind Hayes), until his fee reached a high of $1,500 for a five-minute segment.

He had supreme confidence in his ability to write funny lines and to translate any personal experience into humor: "If I got beaten up by a bunch of hoodlums, three weeks later I think I could describe it to an audience and make it funny." (In a classic Allen joke, he is mugged by his doorman.) He told Richard Schickel in a 2002 TV documentary: "I was instantly successful [writing jokes]. If you can do it, there's nothing to it. I can't draw, and I was astonished when the kid next to me in class would draw a rabbit. For him it was nothing, and *he* wonders why *I* can't do it."

His act was peppered with what one writer called "fragments of auto-biography" and what someone else called "a legend of defeat": *"As a boy I was ashamed to wear glasses. I memorized the eye chart, and then on the test they asked essay questions"* . . . *"I don't think my family liked me. They put a live teddy bear in my crib."* At interfaith camp, he was *"sadistically beaten by boys of all races and creeds."* He translated his worst nightmares into jokes, depicting himself in movie clichés, like his gangster-film vignette about having his house surrounded by police because of an overdue library book (*"They drove me down to the main branch and took away my glasses for a year"*). All his jokes played into his image as that ninety-eight-pound wimp (*"For my birthday, they wheel out a big cake with a girl in it who pops out and hurts me and gets back in"*). Observed Zinsser, "What he does is to sock his listeners with jokes and also cater to their emotional needs." He became an ideal hero in the cynical age of the nonhero. John Lahr wrote, "He started mass-marketing his anxieties."

Like the early Sahl, Allen routinely mocked trendy cultural pretensions, with his cracks about sports cars, therapy, and fashions. And like Nichols & May, he ridiculed intellectual trends, dropping in references to artsy movie houses that serve *"pre-Columbian coffee,"* and jokes about *Commentary* (he imagined a merger of *Commentary* and *Dissent,* titled *Dysentary*), the mere mentions of which, in an Allen monologue, were grounds for laughter.

Au courant as his jokes and stories were, they were rarely politically or socially relevant, putting him at odds even with the breakthrough comedians of his own time. ("He is not only an interesting new comedian," commented *Time* in 1962, "but a rare one, as well: he never mentions John F. Kennedy.") Allen had no agenda, and rarely uttered a joke about civil rights, the women's movement, the Cold War, the Vietnam War, or Watergate. He said he was more interested in "the real issues"— life and death and sex—and that topical humor didn't interest him.

Allen was a living Jules Feiffer character, something Feiffer was quick to notice: "It's hard to believe that Woody Allen could have gotten that early character of his without having read about Bernard Mergendieler," says the cartoonist, referring to an early recurring character in his *Village Voice* strip. "Now we know it's not Woody at all—he didn't draw it from his own character, he drew it from mine." Allen once even said that the kind of beatnik girl he was attracted to in his teens (long hair, black leotards) was "almost what you'd call a Jules Feiffer type of girl."

Allen let his Jewishness drive his comic persona unlike any major comedian before him. "Until the 1950s, there was never any Jewish humor in the American media," Albert Goldman, Lenny Bruce's biographer, says in *Jewish Wry,* a study of Jewish humor. "So many Jewish comics and never a Jewish joke!"—Myron Cohen notwithstanding. Allen didn't tell Jewish jokes, but he was the classic nebbish, a Jewish version of Chaplin's luckless Little Fellow in his hapless pursuit of The Girl. (In the late eighties, Jerry Seinfeld emerged as the anti-Woody: a secure, non-neurotic, totally assimilated Jewish guy with no self-esteem issues who was attractive to, cool about, and adept with women.)

While Lenny Bruce, Allan Sherman, and Mel Brooks were steeped in Jewishness, Shelley Berman dipped a toe into it, and Elaine May mimicked Jewish mothers, Allen most personified the urban Jewish guy—and many non-Jews easily identified. Allen was a stereotype—intellectual and ineffectual—but a huggable one. Many women found him adorable, while men either felt superior to or identified with him. But Allen didn't wallow in his Jewishness the way Brooks did—he ran from it (into the arms of blonde shiksas) and he razzed it. Brooks's Jews were caricatures, but Woody was closer to the real thing. In the sixties, Jewish humor exploded, not just in acts but in books like Dan Greenburg's *How to Be a Jewish Mother,* Bruce Jay Friedman's *A Mother's Kisses,* Harry Golden's Lower East Side memoirs, and in Allan Sherman's chicken-fat-drenched songs. Suddenly it was hip, even profitable, to be Jewish, but Allen transcended Jewishness. His humor was universal, even though the only gentiles in his world are those he makes fun of or ogles. You didn't have to be

Jewish to love Levy's rye bread—as the famous ad campaign of the sixties went—and you didn't have to be Jewish to love Woody Allen.

Yet Allen has little more than a joking acquaintance with Judaism. "There's a common misconception about my being Jewish," he once said. "What it is, really, is that I'm not gentile." He has identified himself as "Jewish, with an explanation." In the Jewish quarterly *Tikkun,* he wrote: "I have frequently been accused of being a self-hating Jew, and while it's true I am Jewish and I don't like myself very much, it's not because of my persuasion. The reasons lie totally in other areas—like how I look when I get up in the morning, or that I can never read a road map." Allen told his Boswell, Eric Lax: "I was unmoved by the synagogue. I was not interested in the seder or Hebrew school. I was not interested in being Jewish. It just didn't mean a thing to me. I was not ashamed of it nor was I proud of it. It was a non-factor to me. I cared about baseball, I cared about movies."

In the typical Allen joke, he mixes the ornate and the ordinary, what one critic calls "the mayhem of madcap juxtapositions"—to wit: "*Not only is God dead but try getting a plumber on weekends*" . . . "*I don't believe in an afterlife, although I plan to bring a change of underwear*" . . . "*When we played softball, I'd steal second, then feel guilty and go back*" . . . "*As a kid I never believed in heaven. It was hard enough for me to visualize Kansas.*" Or this exchange in *Play It Again, Sam:* Allen: "*What are you doing Saturday night?*" Diane Keaton: "*I'm committing suicide.*" Allen: "*What about Friday night?*"

All the jokes came out of his own life's actual wide-ranging interests—Kafka and the Knicks, Tolstoy and Kid Oliver, Martin Buber and Humphrey Bogart, the Mafia and Fellini. He took a dance class from Martha Graham to understand the psychology of women (and maybe meet a few). Humor is Allen's way of confronting, deflecting, and escaping from life's grim realities. Comedy is also, for this former boy magician, the ultimate trick to deceive the fates. He told *The New Yorker*'s John Lahr: "I like being in Ingmar Bergman's world. Or in Louis Armstrong's world. Or in the world of the New York Knicks. You spend your whole life searching for a way out. You just get an overdose of reality, and it's a terrible thing. I'm always fighting against reality. I've always felt that people can't take too much reality."

ALLAN STEWART KONIGSBERG, called "Red" as a kid, was born in the Bronx in 1935 into what he calls "a lower-lower-middle-class" family bustling with stray relatives from Europe and squabbling parents. "They did everything except exchange gunfire," said Allen. His family was "loud and demonstrative," like the one in *Radio Days,* and Allan retreated into the refuge of his bedroom. His movie ardor was fed by reading his cousin Rita's fan magazines, and he was startled that his classmates didn't even know who Cesar Romero and Jennifer Jones were.

The Konigsbergs moved a lot. "I was not poor and hungry and neglected," he told a reporter in 1969. "We were well fed, housed, and clothed." They had enough money to pay for a cleaning lady and even a low-budget nanny. His father, Martin, had countless short-lived jobs—taxi driver, jeweler, singing waiter at Sammy's Bowery Follies. Allen said his father "would promote or hustle everything. I guess he had to make a living." His mother, Nettie, kept the books for a florist. A younger sister, Letty, has produced several of his recent films. "I liked her from the moment I met her," he said of Letty, who was a kind of worshipful Phoebe to his sensitive misfit Jewish Holden Caulfield. "We had a spectacular relationship," he says, and remain close.

The young Allan never understood his parents, nor they him. In the last scene of *Wild Man Blues,* his parents still seemed to think their son squandered his talents; his mother sounds disappointed that he never became a pharmacist. "They're preposterous," he once said. "My father is a comical gnome who looks like Fernandel. My mother looks like Groucho, and she talks like him, too." On a more forgiving occasion, he said, "They were people of the Depression. They were surviving. They had no time for foolishness. They were affectionate but harsh. They were typical cliché Jewish parents. You were always presumed guilty, me especially." In *Wild Man Blues,* his mother says, "I didn't think he'd turn out to be this successful." When he proudly shows her a plaque he received in Europe, she admonishes, "Don't think you are what you are by yourself. You had a lot of help."

In an interview last year at the 92nd Street Y with Gail Saltz, a New York psychoanalyst, Allen remarked: "It was a loving family. But we were constantly battling one another, making jokes with one another. Not even jokes all the time, but hostile remarks. But there was not a constant spate of aggressive criticism." His mother was "critical and acerbic in a less gifted way than Groucho. My mother used to say I was a sweet kid for the first four years of my life, and then I turned sour. No traumatic event happened. I'm only theorizing that it was an awareness of mortality. At a certain age it becomes clear what you're involved in. You never recover." Even so, he adds, his partners were "very, very proud" of him. "My father used to go down to the cinemas and come back and tell me there was a huge line."

Lahr writes that Allen's parents "were not so much hostile to him as indifferent," and quotes him as saying, "I never felt that either of my parents was amusing in the slightest way. I loved my parents but I had no interest in currying favor with them. I spent my time in my room. I ate all my meals alone." He sometimes ate in the basement. His folks nagged him to get a haircut and settle down. Allen eventually bought them a home near his, plus a place in Florida, and insisted on buying his father new suits. Joked Allen: "When I was a child they'd give me a quarter to leave them alone. Now I give them money to leave me alone."

From eleven to sixteen, Allen lived in the Coney Island section of Brooklyn. "There were no books, there was no piano," he recalls. "I was never taken to a Broadway show or a museum in my entire childhood. Never." His parents did take him to movies. Lahr says Allen dwelled "in the kingdom of self," which led to his need to amuse himself. He went to P.S. 99 and Midwood High School ("*a school for emotionally disturbed teachers*"), but reading was always a chore. He didn't begin reading books other than comic books until his late teens, primarily to keep up with those literate beatnik girls he was so attracted to, but after that he read voraciously, mainly philosophy.

His boyhood passion was magic (which he still practices, mostly card and coin tricks), the source of his play *The Floating Light Bulb,* about a stuttering boy who takes refuge in magic. One of Allen's youthful ambitions was to be a gambler or cardsharp, and he often made money off friends with crooked dice and various card cons. "Never play cards with Konigsberg," pals warned. His twin obsessions were girls and gangsters, a favorite theme in his routines and films (*Take the Money and Run, Crimes and Misdemeanors, Bullets over Broadway, Manhattan Murder Mystery, Small Time Crooks*).

Allen's capsule summation of his early academic career: "At ten I was very shy, a terrible student, a problem at school. At twenty, I was finally thrown out of school." His sister said, "Nothing worked for him." An accelerated class didn't help. School for him became a Dickensian memory—"an abysmal horror," he called it, "a humorless, joyless, educationless experience provided by nasty and unpleasant teachers." He played hooky, interrupted classes, was rude to teachers, and did no homework. His book reports were full of Bob Hope–isms ("*She had an hourglass figure and I wanted to play in the sand*").

Allen claimed he learned nothing in school ("I paid attention to everything but the teachers") and everything from movies, radio, comic books, fan magazines, and TV. The Konigsbergs' TV set was the first on their block. One childhood friend said that Allen was "consumed with sex and fame as an adolescent" and "had this powerful need to be recognized." He once recalled, "When I was very young, I wanted to go to Las Vegas and play the big hotels with the best jokes I could manage."

So beneath a façade of ordinariness, something in Allen was churning away—a restless intellect, a hunger for adventure and achievement, a taste for comedy, a quest for fame and sophistication. Though hardly a reader, at the age of nine he picked up a copy of *You Can't Take It with You* at the school library and was instantly seduced by the wit of Kaufman and Hart's play. He soon had read all of Kaufman's comedies; Allen and his boyhood pal Mickey Rose would stand outside Kaufman's house, waiting for a glimpse of him. Groucho Marx, of course, was another early hero (and later an Allen fan), whom he came to know. In a sense, Woody Allen was the long-lost last Marx Brother.

By fourteen, Allen had become addicted to jazz and was taking clarinet lessons from a former Fats Waller sideman, Gene Sedric, who taught him to play by ear. He got hooked on Sidney Bechet (after whom he named his daughter Bechet) upon seeing him at Jimmy Ryan's. Years later, in the mid-sixties, Allen would form the New Orleans Funeral and Ragtime Society after sitting in with Turk Murphy's band at Earthquake McGoon's in San Francisco when he was appearing at the hungry i. Murphy invited him to sit in, but it took Allen two years to get up the nerve. "I used to stand outside the club just to listen to the music," he said.

As a kid, when not listening to jazz, he spent long summer hours in air-conditioned movie houses like the Midwood Theater, where he saw *The Road to Morocco.* The image of Bob Hope and Bing Crosby atop a camel crooning "Like Webster's dictionary, we're Morocco bound" was a kind of epiphany for him. As he told Lax, he knew "from that moment on exactly what I wanted to do with my life." Allen was blown away in particular by Hope's breezy delivery. "Hope was the one I emulated. I learned from his glib and brilliant delivery. Even as a teenager, when I went out on a date, I would try to pattern my personality after Bob Hope." Discussing his movie character with Richard Schickel in 2002, he happily confessed, "I do Bob Hope all the time. The reason people don't see it is that I'm not as good." Allen had such reverence for Hope that, when asked to emcee the Academy Awards, Hope's longtime position, he turned the offer down even though he ached to do it, explaining, "I know I could kill that audience but I can't bring myself to do it."

Comedy was always his way of coping. "It was a very painless way to get through life," he said. "If you were never at a loss for a wonderful comic remark, then it was great. I was always able to come up with those gliding Bob Hope one-liners." He began writing gags as a preadolescent and by the age of sixteen was sending them to Broadway columnists under the name "Woody Allen," a pseudonym that he felt had "a slightly comic appropriateness and is not completely off the tracks"; at school he was still Al. In time, "Woody" became as valuable a trade name as Bing, Frank, Groucho, Marilyn, or Judy. His first joke sales were to Nick Kenny, a corny columnist at the *New York Mirror,* for Kenny's "Cheer-Up Club" for shut-ins, but he first landed on Broadway, so to speak, in Earl Wilson's widely syndicated show-business column of November 25, 1952: "*Woody Allen figured out what OPS* [Office of Price Stabilization] *is— Over People's Salaries.*"

Wilson paid seventy-five dollars an item and sometimes credited Allen in print (though more often he put the lines in celebrities' mouths or attributed them to himself as "Earl's Pearls"): "*Taffy Tuttle* [Wilson's mythical showgirl] *told Woody Allen she heard of a man who was a six-footer, and he said, 'Gee, it must take him a long time to get his shoes on*"; "*It's the fallen women who are usually picked up*"; "*Woody Allen boasts that he just made a fortune downtown—he auctioned off his parking space.*"

Allen was a seventeen-year-old high school kid when a publicity firm, David O. Alber Associates, hired him to knock out jokes for its clients Guy Lombardo, Arthur Murray, and Sammy Kaye. "I gave them fifty jokes a day," he recalled, some twenty thousand lines over two years. "They kept saying they didn't need that many, but it was easy—I wrote most of them on the subway from Brooklyn and then sat around their office reading the paper until six o'clock. They used to give me talks about the way I dressed. I came over in my school clothes. I was such a little digger ant. I wrote and wrote and wrote. It was a big deal to me."

He was two decades younger than anyone else in the Alber office. In his act, he later said, "*I was hired by an ad agency to sit in the office and look Jewish.*" He was even then a comic prodigy, at least among press agents, and earned sudden respect from his hard-nosed boss when he attracted the attention of Bob Hope's manager, Jimmy Saphir. Mike Merrick, then a press agent and later a Broadway producer, told Lax: "Nobody ever said, 'This kid is going to be a genius.' But he was overwhelmingly likable. He was sweet, he was curious, and we thought he was a character, in the positive sense. He was the antithesis of a smart-ass. He was completely unassuming. He was always saying 'Wow!' or 'Gee!' " Said Allen, "I was succeeding in a way unheard-of in my environment. I thought I was in the heart of show business."

As a Midwood High freshman, Allen first fantasized about performing comedy while watching a student variety show in which a student did card tricks, someone sang, and a girl performed a Dorothy Parker monologue; the emcee was comic-to-be Morty Gunty. Allen said: "I came away with stars in my eyes. I thought it was the greatest thing I had ever seen. I just wanted to be a comedian in the worst way." Next to his photo in *The Epilog*, Allen's high school yearbook, there's a blank space. "Of seven hundred and twenty students in the class of '53," notes Marion Meade, he was "the only one who did not participate in a single extracurricular activity." He was too busy learning magic and performing his first stand-up gig at the Israeli Social Club's amateur night every weekend in Brooklyn.

Allen spent a little while at both City College of New York and New York University, which kicked him out. "I never actually failed a college course. It was always a very indefinite D"; he even got a D in film production and would amuse himself by writing his English essays in Max Shulman's rococo comic style. "My teachers all loathed me," he claimed. "I never *ever* did homework. I'm amazed to this day that they really expected me to go home and work on those sleazy projects they had outlined." He still resisted reading. "It's strictly a secondary experience. If I can do anything else, I'll duck it. I'm a very slow reader. But it's necessary for a writer, so I have to do it. I read for survival, not pleasure." He'd much rather watch a movie or a Knicks game.

He would take the subway to NYU but often neglected to get off at the campus stop. "Usually I just closed my eyes and shot by. It was such a *pleasure* not to show up." He stayed on the train until it reached Times Square, where he would get off to haunt the movie houses and Tannen's Circle Magic Shop. He also was mesmerized by Birdland and the Paramount Theater. "It was just absolutely astonishing," he would later tell Lax. "When I cut school and went to the Paramount for the first time, the movie ended and suddenly the lights went on and Duke Ellington's band came rising out of the pit, playing 'Take the "A" Train.' I just couldn't believe it. It took the top of my head off." It is this same sense of awe about Manhattan that infuses his lacy film valentines to the city of his youth.

He saw about five movies a week but was also an avid baseball fan, roller-skating to Ebbets Field to watch the Dodgers; he played second base for a Police Athletic League team. Allen loved most sports, from fishing to boxing—he wanted to fight in a Golden Gloves tournament but his father refused to sign the entry form. "I was a very, very atheletic kid, a popular kid," he says. "I was always the first one to be chosen for teams. I had no reason to be fearful or insecure." Despite his passions for sports and jazz, he patterned himself primarily on his writing idol, George S. Kaufman, whose eyeglasses, untamed hair, high forehead, slender frame, taciturn manner, two-fingered salute, and wisecracks suggest the aging, dour Woody Allen. "I tried to look like him. I cultivated a sardonic manner. I was aloof and didn't communicate with people."

In 1954, through a distant relative, Allen met the Broadway comedy writer Abe Burrows, the coauthor of *Guys and Dolls,* who said in his memoir, "Wow! His stuff was dazzling." Burrows told his wife, "I have just read a couple of pages of [his] jokes, none of which I could ever have thought of." Burrows wrote him letters of introduction to Sid Caesar, Phil Silvers, and Peter Lind Hayes, who instantly made out a check to Allen for fifty dollars just for the jokes Burrows had included as examples in his letter.

On the strength of the gags he had placed with columnists, Allen was accepted into the NBC Writer's Development Program in 1955 and later won a job on *The NBC Comedy Hour* in Los Angeles at $169 a week (he was only nineteen and his mother had to sign the contract for him). While writing for Herb Shriner, he was so naïve that he once actually stood in line to attend Shriner's show. He then joined the staff of *The Colgate Comedy Hour,* where his mentor was Danny Simon, Neil's older brother and a comedy-writing guru, of whom Allen has said, "Everything I learned about comedy I learned from Danny Simon." When Danny Simon read Allen's jokes, he said, "I think this kid is my next brother." Simon taught him how to structure jokes, the importance of straight lines that set up but don't tip off a joke, about questioning a comic premise, to only use jokes that move a scene along no matter how great a gag it might be, and always to ask the question, "And *then* what?"

Allen wrote the Buddy Hackett sitcom *Stanley* with Sid Caesar refugees and worked on everything from *Candid Camera* to *The Pat Boone*

Show. Boone later recalled how Allen, in total deadpan, would "set up this crazy premise, pepper it with a lot of little jokes, and lead up to some preposterous payoff that obviously I couldn't use on the show. I would dissolve in laughter. As I think back, I realize Woody was actually polishing his own routines for what would become his stand-up comedy act."

He was fired from Garry Moore's show for "nonfeasance"—he played hookey from writers' meetings and chafed at having to write sketches involving Carol Burnett pratfalls. In 1958 he cowrote a couple of Sid Caesar specials with Larry Gelbart. Even writing for Caesar at nineteen, he later said, made him feel "like a paid hack." By then he was twenty-one, but, as Gelbart recalled, "He looked to be all of six years old. His previous writing credits, I assumed, must have been learning the alphabet. He seemed so fragile, a tadpole in horn-rims." When he won a Sylvania Award for writing, Allen was too timid to attend the ceremony at Toots Shor's. "It was a big honor for me," John Baxter quotes him as saying. "And I went to the door at Toots Shor's and I couldn't go in, and I never did go in. I went home and felt so relieved when I got home. I've repeated that problem or syndrome many times." His last TV writing job was an Art Carney special, *Hooray for Love,* in 1960, for which he wrote a parody of Bergman's *Wild Strawberries* that possibly seventeen viewers appreciated.

During the summers he wrote for shows at the Hotel Tamiment, where the composer Mary Rodgers remembered that he "already had a reputation for being a genius." Jane Connell recalled that he was "confident of what he had to offer, and though he was very shy he never kowtowed to anyone." Max Liebman, who produced Tamiment's shows, remembered, "Woody would listen, nod, then go away that night and come in the next day with reams of paper. I got the impression he'd been working half the night. But it wasn't right. It wasn't what I wanted for the show."

He finally met Bob Hope, and in a letter was kiddingly casual about at last writing for his idol ("Working for Bob Hope on assignment. Must do sketch for Hope and Kathryn Grayson. Ah so"). Hope called him "half a genius." But Allen couldn't adapt to stars' whims, as when he and Gelbart were summoned to Sid Caesar's home to join the comedian for a writing session in his sauna. Allen declined to get undressed, saying he couldn't be funny naked, and waited outside.

Allen much preferred writing alone, up to fifteen hours a day, talking to himself and laughing, fueled by homemade malteds, but he was able to work anywhere—even on vacations, which he abhors; he famously loathes sunshine ("*I don't tan, I stroke*"). "I like to goof around," he said in 1973, "but if I'm not creating something funny after half a day goes by, I start to feel guilty." Although he was in psychotherapy much of his adult life, his true therapy is writing. "I've never had a problem working in my darkest hours," he said. As he told the director Stig Bjorkman, "I could always write. Even as a little child. . . . I've always said I could write before I could even read."

Writing was his first language. His monastic regimen in the sixties was to rise around ten-thirty, shower, have a light breakfast, and work for about six hours before knocking off to practice the clarinet for an hour. After that, he would often see a show and then write from midnight to three A.M. For monologues or plays—anything spoken—he used a typewriter, but wrote his comic essays on his bed in longhand. "It's like working with a finer tool," he explained. "Your concentration is focused." He would scratch down jokes wherever they occurred, on napkins or matchbook covers, and throw them in a drawer until it was time to get new material. "I take them and lay them out in the room, and I see which jokes are worth going for." He writes screenplays with the same efficiency. "I can write in any place, under any conditions. I've written in hotel rooms. I've written sitting on the sidewalk. I've got scenes written on the backs of envelopes. Writing is a complete pleasure for me. It's a sensual, pleasurable, intellectual activity that's fun. Thinking of it, plotting it, is agony."

He worked on jokes as he later did screenplays, complete with a back story and motivation. Allen described for Larry Wilde how the thought process works: "Suppose I'm going to write about trying to move a piano. I try to take it as far back as I can go. The first thought that occurs is getting stuck with the piano, and then I start retracing this. Why am I moving it myself? Because I don't want to spend the money on moving men. Why do I want to move? Because I don't like my apartment. What other apartments have I lived in? What was my apartment in Brooklyn like? Why was it poor? Because my parents couldn't afford very much rent. What did my parents do for a living? I find this can go back forever."

Marshall Brickman, who wrote four movies with Allen, experienced how Allen's mind works. In planning a scene, Brickman told Lax, "I would try to *reason* it out: Well, what would the character do? Maybe if *that,* then *therefore.* Woody would look at me and say, 'Yeah, but would it be funny if the guy had a rabbit suit on?' He would always have some sort of intuitive leap that would have within it the thing we wanted. It's a big talent to surprise and remain within the framework and also be interesting."

THE COMEDIAN-TO-COME FOUND his lifelong manager-mentor in 1962 when he went to see Jack Rollins, who had just discovered Mike Nichols and Elaine May. Allen badly wanted to write for them, but Rollins only handled performers, and he limited himself to very few of those. Yet Rollins instinctively believed Allen had the goods. "We smelled that this shy little guy could be a great performer," he said.

"Woody was the shyest little bunny that ever was," Rollins told me. "He came up to our office and said he'd like to write for Nichols & May. But they didn't use writers. Woody said, 'Well, would you consider managing me? I'm a writer.' We said we don't manage writers, we manage performers. We were the hottest New York agency [for comics] at the time. A month later, he came back. We looked at his material and we thought it was terribly funny and original. We said we'd take six months and see if we could do something for him."

Rollins goes on: "During that time we got this magic wave of comedy coming from him, without me being able to tell you what it was. There was something about him that came across to Charlie [Joffe] and myself. Something about the guy made us break up. He'd do it in a monotone like a writer, not trying to presume to perform, and to us it came across hilarious. He undersold everything. And we got the idea, 'If it hits us, is there something there?' " One night at dinner at Rollins's home, Allen enacted a routine about the prospect of the *New York Times* running comic strips, and it cracked up everyone at the table, further convincing Rollins and Joffe that here was a latent performer. Whenever he read his own material, says Lax, "the shyness left him."

To Rollins and Joffe, it wasn't just that Allen wrote funny jokes; his jokes were of a different kind from anyone else's, full of surreal concepts and funny images—like his routine about a damaged-pet shop that sold bent pussycats and straight camels and where he bought a dog that stuttered—"*When cats gave him a hard time he would go 'B-b-b-b-bow wow.'*" Or his joke about being raised in a home so strict that he had to be home by nine-thirty on prom night—"*So I made a reservation at the Copacabana for five o'clock and I took my date and we watched them set up.*" Rollins adds: "What occurred to us, in a selfish way, is that we stood so much better a chance if he were a stand-up act." Once Allen mentioned that he had sometimes thought of getting up onstage, they seized on the notion and began the project of building themselves a custom-made stand-up comedian.

According to the Allen saga, he had to be dragged onstage at first, but a glimpse of Mort Sahl made it easier. He told an interviewer in 1973: "I guess I was ready. Somewhere in the back of my head I suppose I'd always thought about telling the jokes as well as writing them, but I'd never had the nerve to talk about it before. Then Mort Sahl came along with a whole new style of humor, opening up vistas for people like me."

Sahl made it safe for avant-garde comedians like Allen, who five years earlier never would have presumed to play a nightclub. Sahl's message to would-be comics was that you could be smart *and* wildly popular. Said Allen: "He was an authentic intellectual and talent, a true fresh new thing that came along. He cut a great figure in those days. He was witty and attractive. I didn't have the confidence, [but] I thought, my God, this guy's a genius, and I was inspired to want to do it. I never achieved what he achieved. And I don't think anyone has. I think he's the greatest mono-loguist we've had." He adds, "Seeing Sahl, I felt I had two options—to kill myself or quit the business. There was nowhere to go after that."

Rollins resumes the oft-told tale: "So Woody wrote himself this little act, and since he had zilch experience we would place him at these small cabarets to let him work." The quiet, quizzical writer first set foot on a professional stage in October 1960 for a one-night tryout at the Blue Angel after Shelley Berman's last Sunday-night show. Berman introduced Allen as a young TV writer who would be performing his own material. The audience was with him right away, laughing so much that, reports Lax, the new comic "drew back into his shell. After the first wave of acceptance, he became quieter and quieter." The one-nighter was judged successful enough to encourage Rollins to open him in a longer run at the Duplex, where he began his on-the-job stand-up training in earnest.

"He was so bright," Rollins goes on, "that in the next six or eight weeks he began to absorb how to perform—began to learn on the job, how to sell his material a little better. What happened was, a little clique developed, and he was encouraged. I wouldn't call his material highbrow. There was nothing he ever spoke of that you had to have special knowl-edge about, not at all. But it was material that wasn't normally used by the commercial comics, and the approach was so different."

Rollins, with his sad, baggy eyes and bald head, is, at eighty-seven, the

Yoda of stand-up, whose credo is: "It's not what you do onstage, it's what's left onstage afterwards." Allen didn't look like a comic, but his beleaguered looks worked for him—the perfect setup for what followed, an image that played against his Casanova fantasies. Gelbart offers the unusual observation that "he was Elaine May in drag. He just styled himself completely after her—his intonations, his voice. He was doing Elaine May. I'm sure of it. Eventually Diane Keaton would do Elaine May."

Rollins recalls: "We put him in these little clubs that paid nothing, and because of his lack of cachet as a performer, he would come out, and not only was the material offbeat and strange to people, but he would present it like a kid doing show-and-tell at school. It was a monotone and on top of that it was offbeat. Not a laugh. We'd put him in for a week—he'd barely finish out the week. It was very hard for us to get a platform."

Allen hated leaving "a nice, safe, warm typewriter and going out into the freezing cold to stand on a bare stage and make a fool of myself. I'd stand out in the cold at night, shivering and trying to get a cab to go downtown and wondering why I was doing it. That took more courage than I knew I had. I worked at my own expense, financially and emotionally, going down to some godforsaken, mostly empty, club at eleven P.M. and then nobody would laugh. I wanted to die." Allen didn't lack for funny jokes, or discipline, or drive. What he lacked was the thing most comedians have even if they have nothing else—nerve.

At first, his material was too cerebral. He told me: "I didn't understand the concept of the performer. I thought, having been a writer all my life, that it's just the material they're responding to. I felt if I came out on the stage and read the material, they would laugh if the material was funny, as if you ran onstage and memorized an S. J. Perelman essay. Jack Rollins explained to me that it's the *man* that's funny. . . . [But] I didn't come from that school, the performance school. So I had to get less literary in my performance. You have to come out and say hello and talk to them and relate to them and hook in—and if they like you, they find your stories funny, they go with you. That took me a while to realize. It's experience." He adds, "Then a funny thing happened. I began to get comedy ideas that could only be expressed in monologues."

He found that "what audiences want is intimacy with the person. They want to like the person and find the person funny as a human being. The biggest trap that comedians fall into is trying to get by on material. That's just hiding behind jokes. . . . It's all so ephemeral. Such a thin line of luck and intangibles."

He goes on: "It's not the jokes that do it, it's the individual himself. The comedian has nothing to do with the jokes. It's just a great, great fallacy that turns out so many mediocre comedians and causes so much trouble. The best material in the world in the hands of a hack or someone who doesn't know how to deliver jokes is not going to mean anything. You can take the worst material in the world and give it to W. C. Fields or Groucho Marx and something funny will come out."

It didn't take him long to learn the rudiments of performing: "You gain strength, like a kid learning to walk. You suddenly come out onstage and you instinctively engage the audience. You find you can do it. They like you and they're paying to see you and you don't have to get the audience on your side. They've paid their admission. They're *on* your side. You don't have to win them. You can only lose them."

Rollins recounted to Phil Berger how, in his dressing room before a show, Allen "would walk like a small caged lion, up and back, up and back. He'd wear out a path, working off the energy." Rollins was impressed with his manic work habits and spirit: "He was the most uncomplaining guy. He's one of the seven wonders of the world, this kid. I mean, I adore him as a human. This guy will never, never place his troubles, his burdens, his neuroses—and God knows he is neurotic—on other human beings' shoulders. He stoically went through it." Rollins and Joffe "badgered me and got me up onstage," adds Allen. "They wouldn't let me stop. Many times I said, 'This is not really for me.' They came every night and they pushed and pushed, and they said once you emerge as a performer, everything else will follow. And they were right."

WOODY HAD MARRIED Harlene Rosen in 1956, when he was twenty and she was a seventeen-year-old Hunter College freshman. "She looked like Olive Oyl," Jane Connell recalled, adding that the couple were "more like little kids, brother and sister, than passionate lovers." To his fellow married writers he explained that he needed someone to go to the movies with, but wound up leaving her for the actress Louise Lasser (later the star of TV's *Mary Hartman, Mary Hartman*). Jan Wallman, who ran the Duplex, said: "I was very fond of Woody's wife, who was very supportive and used to show up every night, and all of a sudden she's supplanted by this weird girl, who just took Woody over." Allen later said that he knew his first marriage was a mistake after a few days but stuck it out for six years.

Allen's frazzled feelings about performing took a toll on his marriage. Recalls Rollins: "The main thing we faced at the time was Harlene"—or "Mrs. Woody," as she was known. "She was his wife and was protective, and rightfully so. She said, 'What are you doing to my husband? He's not suited for this. You're cheapening his gifts. Here's a man who's a brilliant writer and you want to turn him into a cheap comic.'" Byrna Goldstein, Allen's childhood sweetheart, told biographer John Baxter: "He was leading a very schizophrenic lifestyle when they were together. She put up with a lot of very hairy creative insecurities and neurotic shtick and then didn't get any of the gravy. She was the one who got him where he is, and was with him until months before his ship came in."

Rollins finally suggested that if the process was proving too painful, perhaps Allen should call it quits. "We said to her and to Woody, it's very easy for us to be in the back of the room, where Charlie and I would fall down laughing at the total stillness and the audience wonderment. This would amuse us, but it was really very cruel of us—for him to be up there and take a beating every night. We'd say, 'If you have no connection to this idea, please stop it, but we think you can break through and that you have it. But you can't do it in two months—you gotta live through this hell.' Sure we had doubts—we didn't know if he *would* break through, but he wouldn't know unless he gave it six months."

Allen remarks today: "It was Jack Rollins who had all the knowledge—he was a great coach, a great teacher, a great manager. He was responsible for all those people—Nichols & May, Dick Cavett, Robin Williams, Letterman. Jack had turned down many comedians, and I turned out to be one of those selected, so it was an honor just to be handled by Jack Rollins—it was a confidence booster immediately. He said, 'Our job is to see that you become a household name. Just go out onstage, do your thing, and don't worry what they're gonna think. Let me worry about that. You just gotta get out there every night, in every condition, and every place. Just work.'" Allen says he instructed him to "take my time onstage and enjoy my time up there. When you're out there for forty-five minutes, you really have to make it an enjoyable experience. And so I listened to him and just went out and did what he said. And it worked."

Rollins verifies that Allen did indeed need to be pushed onstage and would throw up afterward. His stage mannerisms were really survival tactics, he says. "He needed something to hold on to and it often took the form of wrapping a mike cord around his neck." Allen paced the dressing room muttering, "I hope they like me, I hope they like me," and followed each show with anxious calls to an analyst he was seeing several times a week. Joffe calls Allen "the shyest man I have ever known—to this day" and recalls that when Allen first met the agents, "he'd ask if he could call home, and when he left we'd find a dime sitting there."

The agents' mere presence in a club lifted Allen's spirits. He says, "When you'd go into a room, Jack had created an up feeling. He had the right magazine people there. He'd told them, 'You gotta see this kid!' So there was an air of excitement. Then it was up to me." After shows, Rollins and Joffe would stoke their clients by talking comedy till four in the morning in delis and parked cars. Rollins once counseled Howard Storm, "You were working like a stand-up, that's why they weren't laughing. Just talk about your life."

In hashing over the act, line by line and laugh by non-laugh, Rollins told Allen that he was too inside. As Allen puts it, "I was writing for dogs with high-pitched ears, but the people couldn't hear me." They edited his monologue by taking out or clarifying obscure references, such as "Bird lives." "Jack had the brilliant gift of being a hundred percent truthful and candid and still being encouraging at the same time—to tell me how bad I did and the mistakes I made and how I screwed this up and how I went into my shell and rushed my stuff—but when he finished you felt sensational and ready to meet the world. He was everything—he was parental, awe-inspiring, an analyst, a friend, a press agent." He also credits Rollins with prodding him forward into filmmaking, stretching him beyond his stand-up limits.

Despite all their step-parenting, recalls Joffe, after a year or so Allen felt he'd had it and didn't want to do it anymore. "We said all right, we understood, and it was like a shock to him." Allen wanted to be talked into continuing and hated to quit on his handlers. Joffe says, smiling at the memory, "I remember I got a call when I got home about three in the morning, and Woody said, 'Did you actually mean that?' and we knew we had him." Joffe adds: "We took some of the biggest agents and they saw Woody getting huge laughs at the Village Gate," but when they brought the superagent Abe Lastfogel to see him, Lastfogel's judgment was: "Too Greenwich Villagey, too Jewish, too corduroy." Nobody wanted to book him. "We knew other managers and agents were laughing at us behind our backs. They thought we were crazy."

Joffe, unmarried then, even accompanied Allen on the road. He continues: "Woody was the easiest client we ever managed because he was so prolific and he kept giving us the tools to help build his career. That's the other thing about Woody—he had guts. He had the nerve to try things. He wasn't ambitious in terms of stardom or money, but in terms of the work. For him, getting a piece accepted by *The New Yorker* was more important than if he scored in Vegas. He had to have time to write for *The New Yorker,* and he always had to have an hour a day to play his clarinet."

People who saw Allen in those early days at the Duplex can't forget his onstage idiosyncrasies. Ron Clark, the comedy writer, says: "He had a very unusual delivery that was totally non–show business—you know, mumbling. And that was interesting, because when you're used to these guys snapping their fingers, then suddenly there's this guy and out of his mouth comes some very funny things. That was him—and he's still scared to death." Enrico Banducci recalls, "He was doing Mort Sahl— 'Right? Right?' I told him, 'One Mort Sahl is enough.' " Don Asher, the house pianist at the hungry i, remembers, "Midway through his opening performance, pale and trembling, he turned from the audience, bent his elbows on the piano, and sunk his face in his hands."

Lawrence Christon says Allen was a basket case when he saw him in Las Vegas, opening for Petula Clark. "He was so nervous, he was scratching his hair so vigorously that I saw him literally pull his hair out. He made the discomfort part of his act. But it crosses the line when you start to squirm and see this person is in real pain." Marshall Brickman, who met Allen in 1963 at the Bitter End while singing with the Tarriers, saw more than just a bundle of tics: "This comedian came on and he was just stunning. It was like discovering a great author you'd never read." Allen had some help in those days, according to John Baxter, who names two Toronto writers who supplied Allen with jokes, Hart Pomerantz and Lorne Michaels, later CEO of *Saturday Night Live.*

In his 1974 memoir, Dick Cavett gives a detailed description of the early Allen dying in front of a puzzled Blue Angel audience: "About a third of the way through, the audience began to murmur and talk. Woody plowed on, his face largely concealed by the mike, and ended, more by excusing himself than finishing, and left the stage to polite applause. I recognized immediately that there was no young comedian in the country in the same class with him for sheer brilliance of jokes, and I resented the fact that the audience was too dumb to realize what they were getting. . . . Woody had been casting pearls over the heads of swine." A few such pearls: kidnappers smoked out of hiding by police who, in lieu of tear gas, perform Camille's protracted death scene; a defrocked Mother Superior who ran a floating nunnery; a disco featuring "topless" rabbis who didn't wear yarmulkes; at the psychotherapy groups he attended, he was captain of the latent paranoid softball team that played the bed wetters; and his mother died of an overdose of mah-jongg tiles.

Cavett was also humbled by Allen's work ethic: "He can go to a typewriter after breakfast and sit there until the sun sets and his head is pounding, interrupting work only for coffee and a brief walk, and then spend the whole evening working. One day like that represented more work than I had done in my life. When Woody told me that he spent a day getting a joke right, I couldn't imagine what he was talking about."

Allen told Lahr: "In my teens, I would meet some comedians, and they all seemed to have a million distractions. I thought to myself, The guy who's gonna come out at the end of the poker game with the chips is the guy who just focuses and works." He once said: "I feel like Picasso, who once said that when he sees an empty space, he has to fill it. Nothing makes me happier than to tear open a ream of paper. And I can't wait to fill it! I love to do it." His mantra: "You have to just work. You can't read your reviews. Just keep quiet. Don't get into arguments with anybody. Be polite, and do what you want to do, but keep working."

He prepared for Las Vegas by laying out routines on the floor and then, as Lax describes it, "walking around them like a gardener in his vegetable patch, picking what was ripe." When his longtime secretary, Norma Lee Clark, first went to work for him, he brought her a suitcase packed with hundreds of jokes scrawled on scraps of paper; it came to two hundred typewritten pages.

He was a tough self-editor. When Allen wrote for other comedians, they would use about eight of every ten jokes, but he would only use about one in ten himself. "I'm much more cowardly. I pamper myself more. In order to get a half-hour act it takes me a long time." He once estimated that his club act contained "forty-five minutes of unrelenting jokes." The toughest thing he learned was the "enormous compactness of the jokes. You can't *imagine* how much writing it takes to get that much material. I would write a routine for myself, after two nights I might have two jokes, and in order for that to build to a thirty-minute routine it would be six months, because the things are so incredibly dense." When he was stuck, he would change rooms, take a hot shower, go for a walk, listen to some jazz, or call a girlfriend to talk the problem out.

Gradually, Allen found his audience. "You saw it coming along little by little," Rollins relates. "At first, there was a look of complete bewilderment on the part of the audience. They didn't boo. But they were just quiet. They didn't know what was going on. Then he began to get a few titters from a small group of bright people who saw what we saw in him. It was satisfying—thank God, there's *somebody* in this world who agrees with Charlie and me. At least there are two people and not *no* people. Then it became twenty people and then two hundred and then two thousand."

When the *New York Times* finally put its imprimatur on him, Arthur Gelb wrote: "The most refreshing comic to emerge in many months is a slight, bespectacled, unhappy-looking, former sketch writer of twenty-six named Woody Allen. He has hunched shoulders, an air of harassment, and a carefully cultivated nebbish quality. Mr. Allen approaches the microphone on the unadorned platform at The Bitter End . . . as though he were afraid it might bite him." Gelb picked up on the comic's nudnik air, calling him "a Chaplinesque victim with an S. J. Perelman sense of the bizarre and a Mort Sahl delivery (despite the fact that he steers clear of topical material)."

To Allen, it was mainly a question of learning a few basics. "The simple fundamentals of working in clubs can be learned in a month. This business about needing 'ten years of experience' has no meaning to me. I learned all about the controllable externals in a couple of weeks, and I think those instincts are either inborn or—give up, it's hopeless."

By 1965 Allen had mastered the medium and become a different comic from the trembling fusspot who had first set tentative foot on a stage just two years earlier. As Ralph J. Gleason described it: "Woody Allen scampered through the aisle at the hungry i, leaped onstage, grabbed the microphone, and was funny before he opened his mouth. From then on, he couldn't do anything wrong. The audience broke up on cue every time. Everything worked and Woody spun around the stage surfing on those waves of audience laughter, in complete control."

Larry Gelbart witnessed a similar sea change: "Years after, when I saw him perform at a Democratic rally in Washington, D.C., the transformation was total. He'd become a performer who exuded confidence and authority, doing joke after joke about how little he had of either of those qualities. He was no longer a male Elaine May. He was Woody Allen. And Woody, the writer, was supplying Woody, the comic, with absolutely stunning material that showcased his gift for defying and deflating that which disturbs him the most: life, sex, no sex, not enough sex, too much sex, and, of course, that old standby, death."

Although he's remembered as a verbal comedian, Allen's nervous tics embellished his neurotic stories and funny appearance, turning him into a kind of low-key physical comic, a stand-up Harold Lloyd. Once he'd made it, he hung on to the amateur mannerisms until they seemed mannered shtick. He would mug, gulp, and overstress words to cue laughs. He later confessed, watching a tape of himself, "All that fooling around with cords and stuff is fake." His habit of rubbing his eyes on a punch line was a ploy to distract audiences—"so that it doesn't sound so much like a joke." Paul O'Neill, in a lengthy 1967 *Life* profile, observed: "He lifts one foot, twisting, and rubs the knee against his thigh. He twists the other way, and lifts the other foot. He rubs his hair into his eyes . . . scratches his back . . . twists the microphone cord in agony and finally stuffs it into his mouth and chews."

Of the later stars who are Allen's gifted comic children—Joan Rivers, Albert Brooks, Garry Shandling, Steven Wright, Richard Lewis, Rita Rudner—none matched his dazzling imaginative flights. Shandling remembers the day in 1966 he first saw Allen on a kids' TV show explaining how baseball bats are made. "He said that originally bats were made of halvah, and that after a batter would strike out he would have to eat the bat," recalls Shandling. "It was like someone who sees a beautiful woman and says, 'One day, I'm going to marry that girl.' I said, 'Who is this person? He's the funniest person I have ever seen.' "

Even so, Allen firmly believes that his influence was minimal: "The only mild, mild influence I had at all was presumably telling the truth about myself. I was being in some way honest. They thought the person coming out was being honest and talking about my wife or my ex-wife or my friend or my shrink or my parents, in a certain new way. Even though it's not at all real if you look at it. The big influence of the day was Lenny Bruce. My feeling is that every comic who came after him was influenced by him. *He* was the guy that they all wanted to be and they all revered and looked up to."

Of the astonishing dozen years that produced so many influential and lasting comedians, he questions if it was all that great: "There were a few exceptional talents that came along at that time. It doesn't look that different from now, except that now they have them all on television. A couple of years ago I was home watching those myriad comedians that appear on television and I thought to myself, 'Oh, God, we were all so wonderful, and these guys are nothing special.' And then someone wanted to show some of my old television specials and I screened a lot of old TV stand-up monologues and I realized that *I* was nothing special."

He misses nothing about the stand-up life that he led for eight years and abandoned for good in 1972, earning $85,000 for two weeks at Caesars Palace—except, of course, the laughs. "The idea of working to a live audience was a very exhilarating experience. I'm *tempted,* but it requires so much work to put it together. The only problem with stand-up comedy is not living at home for six months, which is a very, very difficult life. And working all night long, six nights a week, two shows a night, three on Saturday and three on Sunday."

Once upon a time, Allen loved the action in Las Vegas—the hours and the gambling—where he could indulge his boyhood hustling instincts. He'd spend a few hours a day at the blackjack tables. Allen did well in Vegas but was never a Cosby or a Diller. At Vegas, the casino management was stunned when he first appeared in his standard corduroy suit. How well he did, he said, didn't much matter to him. It was strictly for the money, so he could afford to make low-budget movies.

Although he turned down sitcom offers in the seventies, Allen did host some TV specials—a mixture of monologues, sketches (Woody and Liza Minnelli parodying *Bonnie and Clyde,* Woody as a Chaplinesque silent comedian), and serious interviews, not spoofs, with Billy Graham and William F. Buckley, Jr. He's embarrassed watching his old stand-up TV appearances, and intensely critical of his recordings as well, telling Lax: "I was absolutely convinced that as the years went by, if all else failed, I would always be able to listen to the records of my nightclub act and think, 'That was good stuff.' But it sounds pretty terrible to me when I listen to it. I sound pretty repulsive and obnoxious. And I'm not being falsely modest here. I'm just trying to be honest about it."

He added: "If I were to come out in front of an audience now, I'd come out as an equal to them and talk to them as an adult. I'd still try to be funny, but I would never do the same kind of material. I would not posture myself as someone who couldn't get women. All that bullshit about being short and unloved. But in those days I was currying favor." Watching himself bantering with Johnny Carson, he comments to Lax: "My acting is not bad but what I'm doing is nauseating. It's bad rehearsed material. I'm no longer like a human being. . . ." He continues reviewing himself: "When I'm not in my stand-up mode, when I'm sitting down on a panel or something, I'm less loathsome. Less mannered. But it's so patently material. In those days it was a little less obvious as material. It's disgusting now. It doesn't hold up well at all. It's not about anything. I'm just a *tummler,* a guy up there making jokes."

ALLEN REALIZED EARLY THAT "the public can tire of a comedian," and so he decided to venture beyond stand-up and try something he had always dreamed of doing. By 1965 he was already planning to move on. His 1967 Broadway comedy, *Don't Drink the Water,* was a series of travel gags loosely linked to form a mechanical, second-rate version of a Neil Simon comedy, lacking Allen's playful, off-center touch.

His next try, in 1969, *Play It Again, Sam,* was a far more original, tightly constructed, funnier Broadway comedy, but it was, again, essentially a dramatized Woody Allen monologue, with Allen present onstage, narrating the story. Walter Kerr put his finger on the problem: "He's still out front, *telling* us about this funny thing that is rumored to have happened to him. It's all hearsay. He hasn't got the hang of creating lines that require *scenes* at all." Clive Barnes called it "a slender but hilarious evening. He is far from being just a gagman, but a theatrical talent that could, should, and probably will do better."

Yes, but not on Broadway. He had yearned for years to write bantering George S. Kaufman comedies, but by 1969 he was bashing New York theater: "I have great contempt for the theater—for the presumption of the theater. TV is idiot stuff, designed by idiots for idiots. But the theater puts on such airs. That's why it's dying today. And it should." (In 2003 he returned to the theater to direct two of his own one-act plays off-Broadway, entitled *Writer's Block.*) He had more of an instinct for movies and their fantasy worlds, which he entered easily, like his female surrogate in *The Purple Rose of Cairo.*

Rollins and Joffe steered Allen into stand-up and just as shrewdly maneuvered him out of it and into films. He got the chance in 1964, when Shirley MacLaine took the producer Charles K. Feldman to see him at the Blue Angel. Feldman was so inspired by what he saw and heard that, after the last show, he invited Allen to write and appear in a movie he was putting together. It turned out to be *What's New, Pussycat?*—a lame 1965 "mod comedy" with Peter O'Toole and Peter Sellers that Allen once described as "the result of a two-hundred-page manuscript that blew out of a taxicab window and never was put back in its original order." The movie was a hit, even though Allen's original screenplay bore little resemblance to what appeared on the screen. While it gave him an entrée into films, he paid a steep creative price for the experience. The finished farce, a hodgepodge of misfired gags, was for Allen a crash course in Hollywood dealmaking and wobbly star vehicles. "The worst nightmare one could think of," he later called it, but the movie introduced filmgoers to Woody Allen, who wrote a funny role for himself as a dresser in a Paris strip club; Allen meanwhile killed time in Paris writing his first piece for *The New Yorker*.

Casino Royale (1967) was an equally embarrassing escapade for Allen ("I still don't know what it's about"), as was a deadly 1969 film version of *Don't Drink the Water* with Jackie Gleason and Estelle Parsons that he never bothered to see. He called *Casino Royale* a "moronic enterprise from start to finish." It was followed by an even patchier animated comic-book movie, *What's Up, Tiger Lily?*—in which he dubbed a cheesy Japanese action film with cartoony dialogue about the search for the world's best egg-salad recipe. He tried to sue to keep it from being released, but when the movie got good reviews he dropped the suit.

Suddenly, Woody Allen was everywhere—besides Broadway and films, he was headlining at Caesars Palace, batting out brilliant *New Yorker* pieces, making comedy albums, and popping up in advertisements for everything from Smirnoff vodka to Foster Grant sunglasses; he made funny faces on the cover of *Esquire*. He was quickly becoming America's first beloved nerd.

Behind his befuddled image, however, Allen was always a dedicated careerist. Marion Meade notes: "He diligently embarked on what would become a lifetime of self-marketing, manipulating the media to his own advantage. His coquettish handling of the press—coyly standing in the paparazzi line of fire, pleading for attention while feigning reluctance." After Judith Crist wrote a bad review of *What's New, Pussycat?*, Allen sent her the original script, invited her to dinner at his home, and made it a point to charm her.

The self-confident Allen, whose approval so many people now shamelessly seek, marketed himself to select critics, despite his claims that he read few reviews. Tony Schwartz reported that he often sent complimentary notes to critics and would see a number of them socially for lunch and dinner. After John L. Wasserman praised *Sleeper*, Allen wrote him: "It just knocks me out that I can really please you. Think you'll be in New York this year? I look forward to eating scrambled eggs with you again." In another note to Wasserman that betrays either his inner PR man or his profound insecurity, he sounds like a spurned lover: "John! I thought I recognized you at [the] press conference but figured—no—couldn't be—he'd come over and speak to me! What goes? You *were* there I find from tear sheets. How come no personal chat? After all—I am a friend. What obtains? You vanished. Do you have amnesia?—Mr. W. Allen (the comic)."

Now, at thirty-one, he felt ready to make a truly Woody Allen movie, written and directed by and starring himself. When he delivered *Take the Money and Run,* it was a funny, polished comedy that steadily paid off in laughs that haven't diminished over time. It remains one of his most inspired movies, a mock documentary of one Virgil Starkwell, an inept but most-wanted bank robber. Allen said Starkwell was the criminal he would have become had he fulfilled his fantasy life of crime. It built a perfect bridge from stand-up into filmmaking in that the movie is really an illustrated Woody Allen routine full of sight gags lifted from his monologues, like the scene in which a chain gang escapes, still manacled at the ankles—an image taken from his old joke about prisoners who escaped "posing as an immense charm bracelet." Several of his early films—*Bananas, Sleeper, Everything You Always Wanted to Know About Sex*—are mainly monologues dressed up as movies.

Originally, Allen wasn't going to star in *Take the Money and Run* and sent the script to, yes, Jerry Lewis, whose performances he had always enjoyed. "I can't say I was a fan of his films, per se," he now explains, "but I thought that he was a hilariously talented man. The movies were always too infantile for me. But his own work was quite good." He drove up to the Catskills to see Lewis, but in the end decided against him, worried that the star's famously colossal ego would cause as many problems as had Peter Sellers's during the making of *What's New, Pussycat?* and *Casino Royale.* So Joffe suggested that Allen play it himself. The producers, who had just formed Palomar Pictures and were looking for cheap, offbeat projects, let Allen make it, for under $2 million.

Allen was unfazed by the prospect of directing. "It never occurred to me that I couldn't. Directing a film is just common sense. Like the Marx Brothers' *A Night at the Opera,* it's all laughs, no message." He added: "Directing and acting at once are much easier than most people think. The less you know about directing the better off you are." Learning movie grammar—crosscutting, panning, close-ups—came instinctively to Allen, who said, "I knew what I wanted to see on the screen." He told Lax: "It's a mystique promulgated by the film industry that technical background is a big deal. It's common sense when you look through the camera. You can learn all about cameras and lighting in two weeks."

Allen's untutored entry into film directing was another mark of the serene self-confidence that had pushed him to submit quips to Broadway columnists at sixteen, to write for Sid Caesar at nineteen, and to take to the nightclub stage with no experience whatever at twenty-three. He later confessed: "I didn't really know what I was doing. Everything was dependent on funniness. So everything was subjugated to the joke. If the movie was funny, it was successful; if it was not funny, it wasn't. And I could always be funny. That I had control over."

When *Take the Money and Run* was first screened by Palomar executives, they sat stony silent, and at the end of the first reel one executive asked, "Are the rest of the reels like this?" They were hesitant to release it, but Joffe talked them into playing it at a small East Side art house, the 68th Street Playhouse, where it broke a box-office record. Vincent Canby of the *New York Times* raved: "The nicest surprise of *Take the Money and Run* is that it shows [Allen] has been able to complement visually the word-oriented humor of the writer-performer." Canby said the movie looked effortless. "It has a loose-leaf form. Scenes, perhaps entire reels, could be rearranged without making a difference in total impact."

When Allen began, with *Annie Hall*, to make riskier, more complex, layered films that mixed comedy with somber themes, some of them (*Interiors, Another Woman, September*) were ridiculed as third-rate Bergman. As usual, he plowed resolutely forward, continuing to turn out a movie a year. Says Mike Nichols: "Woody is great, but to me the amazing thing about him—the unique thing about him in this country—is the way he just . . . goes . . . on. There's such a lesson in that in itself. I'm impressed and moved by it because it's the only way to approach work. He doesn't look back, he doesn't look down, he just looks ahead." He remains his most unforgiving critic, telling Richard Schickel last year, "I think I'm going to write *Citizen Kane* every time, and then when I see the film I'm so humiliated. I feel I've failed almost every time." He added that he has to fight the urge to make every film funny.

He later expanded on the theme before an audience at the 92nd Street Y: "I regret that my muse was a comic muse. I would rather have had the gifts of Eugene O'Neill or Tennessee Williams than the gifts I got. I'm not kvetching. I'm glad I got any gifts ay all. But I would like to do something great." He added, "I'm not overly humble. I feel I had grandiose plans for myself when I started and I have not lived up to them. I've done some things that are perfectly nice. But I had a much grander conception of where I should wind up in the artistic firmament. What has made it doubly poignant for me is that I was never denied the opportunity. The only thing standing between me and greatness is me."

Beginning about 1990, there were grumbles that moviegoers were growing tired of Allen parading his neuroses; critics began calling his treatment of women misogynistic, and his copyrighted "loser" image as a lover was harder to buy (despite his crack that now he *"just struck out with a better class of women"*). When the sixty-year-old Allen persisted in casting himself opposite women in their twenties, he lost a slice of the audience.

Jules Feiffer is one such disaffected Allen fan: "The early Woody Allen I adored, until he began taking himself too seriously and Vincent Canby told him he was the greatest director in American films. He peaked with *Hannah and Her Sisters*. A few were brilliant, like *Crimes and Misdemeanors*, but the later work I just can't stand. I began hating his stuff with *Manhattan*, where the fadeout is on poor Woody who has dumped his teenage girlfriend. As a father of a teenage daughter going to the Dalton School [like the film's Mariel Hemingway character], I wanted to punch him in the nose. The self-indulgence and the spiritual nastiness peeked through more and more. And as he got older, that twitchy nervousness, which was appealing originally, became an unpleasant tic that makes me very uncomfortable to watch now." The Allen mystique was shattered forever in 1992 by the tawdry Soon-Yi scandal, which burst into a tabloid nightmare that destroyed his lifelong well-guarded cocoon.

Allen has controlled his movie universe as few U.S. directors have. His films are known within his production company only by initials, such as WAFP (Woody Allen Fall Project), with each secretive upcoming release treated like a sculpture unveiling. Actors are only fed pages of their scenes. Publicists are sworn to secrecy. "I have control over everything, and I mean everything," he told Lahr. "I can make any film I want to make. Any subject—comic, serious. I can cast who I want to cast. I can reshoot anything I want to as long as I stay in the budget. I control the ads, the trailers, the music." Yet he maintained just last year, "Films are not a religion to me. I'm not a workaholic. That's a myth about me."

Despite a few inspired exceptions like *Everyone Says I Love You,* a charming demimusical in which actors sing old standards in their own untrained voices, and *Sweet and Low Down,* another music-centered film (a homage to Django Reinhardt about a troubled jazz guitarist), many of Allen's recent movies—*Deconstructing Harry, Celebrity, Small Time Crooks,*

The Curse of the Jade Scorpion—disappoint moviegoers who remember when his films were wall-to-wall laughs. The newer films tend to be thin comic exercises rich in production values and low on wit, with seductive Manhattan scenes, a jazzy nostalgic soundtrack, and all-star casts. But the jokes rarely pay off now, as if someone has let the air out of Woody's whimsy. If the actors were delivering the same lines in a club, they'd be drenched in flop sweat.

In June of last year, a *New York Times* writer surmised: "After more than thirty years as the on-screen embodiment of angst-ridden, urbane New York, his long moment as cultural icon may be over." The *Times* piece quotes a twenty-four-year-old law clerk remarking that the sixty-seven-year-old comedian's "sense of humor is frozen in the seventies. He appeals to an older crowd." A month after *Hollywood Ending* opened, the movie had earned only $4.7 million in domestic ticket sales. But his films rarely make money in the United States.

People who meet Allen privately are invariably disappointed by his unamusing demeanor. Unlike his role models, Groucho Marx and Bob Hope, and unlike most comedians, he rarely utters a wisecrack. "I'm just not a funny man in real life. I don't make anyone laugh." He's said, "I don't like being around people who are amusing. I like to hang around serious people. I'm certainly not the delight of any party." Allen has a notorious reputation for showing up at dinner parties and spending the entire evening watching basketball on TV, as he did at writer Blake Green's home in San Francisco in the early seventies. She recalls: "He was eccentric, nervous, and awkward. He wore his little hat and was rude in that New York way. He went berserk at the sound of the knife on the china plate, and I had to change the plate for him." Liv Ullman said that at a dinner at which Allen was seated across from his filmmaking idol, Ingmar Bergman (himself an Allen fan), the two men never exchanged a word.

Allen's somber, all-business attitude hovers over movie sets and the bandstand; in three decades of playing clarinet to audiences who come expressly to hear and see him, he has yet to utter one word, funny or otherwise, and barely communicates with his fellow musicians. Claire Harrison, a former publicist turned psychologist, vividly recalls working with Allen when he came to San Francisco to promote a film: "Woody's was the most difficult press tour I ever did. Nobody made me more uncomfortable—even worse than Andy Warhol. He never said a word and all he would eat were chocolate milkshakes." She says he phoned his therapist every day. "He made his neuroses work for him. God knows what he'd have been like without his neuroses. When I saw *Wild Man Blues*, I said, 'My God, the man has not matured!' "

Forty years after arriving as the darling of American comedy, Woody Allen is still starstruck by his own success and not ready to let go of his history. He told his biographer: "It's amazing when I think back on the awful days in that little school, and coming home and sitting at the oilcloth-covered kitchen table, that one day I would actually be in a movie with Charles Boyer or direct Van Johnson or take Jane of *Tarzan* fame to dinner, because she's the grandmother of my kids. It's so unimaginable to me, and has retained its power to amaze me. Sometimes when I look in the mirror I'll see myself back there and I'll say, 'You're Allan Konigsberg from Brooklyn. Shouldn't you be eating in the basement?' "

Father Goose, Inc.

BILL COSBY

I've always wanted my act to get the same response as when people are listening to me at the dinner table.

DICK GREGORY CRACKED the color line, Godfrey Cambridge crossed it, and Bill Cosby whited it out. Nobody from the fifties and sixties comedy renaissance has had a longer run than Cosby, who combined the storytelling artistry of Hans Christian Andersen with the feel-good marketing skills of Oprah Winfrey. Now in his fifth decade as a stand-up star, he is still on his feet talking. Like certain others from that golden era—Woody Allen, Jonathan Winters, Joan Rivers—Cosby is an elusive, complex soul who is only coincidentally what he appears.

Blessed with a strutting self-awareness and an early drive to be a millionaire, Cosby knew where he was going the moment he realized he could make people laugh. When the jokes aren't working, he cranks up the persona. When his career coasted, his legend kicked in. Unlike most of his comic sixties peers, Cosby had few doubts about either his skills or his personal worth. For a black kid seemingly mired in the grime of an inner-city ghetto, Cosby emerged with enormous self-esteem and a golden gift of pleasing others. As the comedian Adam Keefe recalled of their early days in Greenwich Village: "It was like he'd already made it. Super cool. Like he had an air of success about him. Of not only success, but social position." Only three years in, a profiler wrote, "everyone accepts him as though he had been in show business all his life."

Cosby had a talent to entertain, but he also had a talent to parlay that talent in ways that went beyond his innate comic gifts. He told stories, not jokes, with a sunny optimism that people loved basking in. His winning manner told you, This guy can be trusted. It was part show business but more homeboy social savvy—the Bill Clinton thing, what George W. Bush calls "the charm offensive." Cosby was a canny manipulator on the make; the word *cocky* attached itself to him early. While he liked entertaining, he loved the rewards of celebrityhood more—money, for sure, also status, power, and entrée into America's royal circles.

Cosby became a crucial bridge—a black comic who ignored race in his act and, by ignoring it, made it all the more apparent; he got more mileage out of being black by avoiding the subject and going generic with his short stories. It was the elephant in the room, but the elephant eventually vanished. Whether that was brave, naïve, or shrewd—or all of the above—it made Cosby different in a way that erased skin color. Dick Gregory, Godfrey Cambridge, Redd Foxx, Flip Wilson, and Richard Pryor faced down racial rancor in the sixties, while Bill Cosby went blithely on his comic way, as if there were no rancor. More than that, his beaming face said there was nothing more to discuss. Woody Allen calls himself "Jewish, with an explanation"; Cosby is black, without an explanation.

Gregory got extra comic points by making his liberal white audiences feel better about themselves for accepting a dark-skinned Negro comedian. Cosby scored even more points with whites by not mentioning race at all. He made it all go away, if only for an hour or two, focusing on human-race issues. It was a harmless but meaningful deception, and it worked wonders. Cosby played to audiences of all hues, who gave themselves credit for ignoring his blackness. Friends of his say he was scratching a lot of feel-good backs, a showbiz back rub that became a lifelong love-in.

He wasn't nearly that bold in the beginning. In fact, his plan was to be the next Dick Gregory. He told Gregory jokes until he realized—after urgings from his manager, Roy Silver—that it was better to be the first Bill Cosby than the Dick Gregory sequel. That piece of elemental advice, which Cosby at first rejected, turned his career around. It uncovered a vast, untapped national audience and made him an unparalleled success in clubs, at concerts, and on television. His self-effacing public shtick, his essential Cosby-ness, never transferred to movies, where decades of warm, fuzzy TV goodwill oozed away on a big screen. Like so many video comedians who couldn't make the leap to movies—Dick Van Dyke, Mary Tyler Moore, Bob Newhart, Phyllis Diller—Cosby is inaccessible on a big screen. In movies, he was a lesser version of himself; that early boyish guile, which later turned into fatherly sitcom charm, evaporated in movies. Cosby fails when he can't confront his people one-on-one.

Unlike all the other renaissance comics, Cosby sold lovability more than ideas. Compared with his neurotic, urban comedian contemporaries, Cosby was a stroll in the country, a life-affirming barefoot boy with cheek of tan. Only Cosby (and perhaps Bob Newhart, the only other major stand-up comic from that time to make it on television) was certifiably cuddly. Like Newhart, and unlike every other black comic then or since—from Gregory, Cambridge, Wilson, and Pryor through Whoopi Goldberg, Eddie Murphy, and Chris Rock—Bill Cosby struck gold in Middle America. His characters have more in common with Red Skelton's Mean Widdle Kid than with Richard Pryor's Mudbone. Cosby (a sort of inner-city Mark Twain) knew how to get out the heartland vote. The comedian Greg Proops, in his 1990s BBC documentary on American comedy, said: "He was clean and bright and never swore or mentioned race. He gave black people a face and a voice in mainstream America's consciousness, and he did it with style."

Cosby didn't discuss male-female relationships and only dipped a toe into social issues. He didn't satirize. He didn't parody. He didn't comment on American political life in the sixties. He spooned out Campbell's Soup tales about his boyhood. Even so, the notion of a black stand-up comic in the sixties doing color-blind material was radical in and of itself. Listeners to Cosby might think that he grew up next door to Norman Rockwell, and that his pals Fat Albert, Dumb Donald, and Ol' Weird Harold played football with Bill on the village green—not in the projects of North Philadelphia, where he grew up.

It was a boyhood that white America found particularly charming coming from a black man. Cosby sold it, and few questioned it. His memories were rich and real but smoothly edited to leave out the ugly parts. Even though he came of age, comically, during the radical sixties, Cosby was the most conservative of cutting-edge comics, one who believed his own tales of growing up in a pastel Booth Tarkington world of fishin' holes and firecrackers. "He is in the great American tradition," wrote Ralph J. Gleason, "of making humor out of the contrast between the world as seen by children and the world as seen by adults"—much as Charles Schulz did in *Peanuts.* "Bill Cosby is the child that each of us was, the child that lives within us," wrote Steve Allen, seconded by a critic who summed him up best: "Cosby reaches people where they live—at home."

Cosby was playing off the first glow of sixties nostalgia for a slower-paced, more innocent America, as families teemed toward Disneyland to escape social unrest. He was a godsend, a welcome relief from political power plays. He was wholesome, happy, and sweetly droll, issuing mellow messages rather than the dark, troubling, crazy, even nihilistic bulletins issuing from other comic social commentators—not to mention the mournful folksingers and drug-addled rockers.

His success in itself was a major social comment. That has always been Cosby's message. Reagan-like, he made folks feel good about America; his unspoken racial message was really a sentimental portrait—the Family of Man, headed by Papa Cosby. The humor was just the icing on the cake; *Cosby* was the cake. He was doing family values before the Republicans stole them for their own act—funny hokey-pokey about his brother Russell and other pals (later reprised in the Jell-O commercials). His best-sellers about fatherhood, marriage, and aging, a series of children's books, and even a revival of Art Linkletter's *Kids Say the Darnedest Things* have given Cosby the deed to his Upper East Side town house. Wrote *Ebony* in 1968, "Bill Cosby may be the most subversive charmer of youth since the Pied Piper"—of youth's parents, actually.

The real-life Cosby kid excelled early as a high school track and football star at Germantown High School in a Philadelphia neighborhood known as "The Jungle." After finishing his secondary education in the navy, he went to Temple University on a track scholarship, but left college three years later when he began making faster tracks in New York City as a stand-up comic. A rapid year later, in 1963, he recorded his first album, *Bill Cosby Is a Very Funny Fellow . . . Right!* which won a Grammy. He soon had four albums in the Top Ten simultaneously, a feat that impelled him to boast, "I don't think even Elvis Presley ever did that." Phil Berger, the comic historian, noted: "Cosby was a natural. No beginner's kinks in his style. He was the flimflam man from the start. Cosby was self-contained. He'd be at the Café Figaro [in Greenwich Village] playing chess. Or on the street corner talking to girls. Or at the basketball court on Sixth Avenue, across from the Waverly Theater. And he was always ready to work. One afternoon, he dropped into the Café Wha? in a sweatsuit and did a fast twenty minutes, just after having shot baskets."

IF SUCCESS CAME EASILY to Cosby, he only made it seem so. In fact, William Henry Cosby, Jr., grew up in a home with two younger brothers but without a bathtub. The family's middle-class beginnings were shattered when his father's life collapsed. An ex-navy steward and welder, Bill Sr. was a menacing, violent man whom Bill Jr. feared. His father began to drink and stay away from home; Bill recalls him beating up his mother three times. The family was forced into a housing project, the Richard Allen Homes. Here, Cosby shared a bed with one of his brothers as trains rattled past and shook the walls. His mother, a major influence, cleaned homes, but the Cosbys still wound up on welfare. He often heard his mother crying. "Her tears alone would shake us up," he told his biographer. "No spankings. No beatings. She'd start crying and you'd start crying."

This dismal home life provided the very raw materials for Cosby's amusing quasi–fairy tales. He portrayed his father as "The Giant" and fashioned a fantasy family life onstage to replace the one he had grown up in. He even paints his scary dad with affection, joking, "*I remember Dad used to send me to the store and move away.*" At the age of eight, Bill worked in a deli; soon he had three jobs—shining shoes, hauling boxes in a grocery store, and selling fruit. When just eleven he would make breakfast for his brothers before heading off to school, and after school came home to supervise his younger brothers. "He kept us in line and whipped us when we got out of line," recalled Russell, who later worked for big brother Bill.

While Cosby has been accused of sidestepping the painful truth of his youth for one filled with high jinks and glib moral lessons, it was because he created something cheerier and more habitable in his head. When asked if he had had a happy childhood, he said, "It will be, onstage." Cosby traces his comic roots to the family dinner table, an audience he broke up consistently. "The largest, most sustained laughs you can come by," he told Lawrence Christon in 1982, "is in a natural environment with friends. I've always wanted my act to get the same response as when people are listening to me at the dinner table. That leads to a secure feeling; it means the absence of the storyteller's death statement, which is, 'You had to be there.' " Cosby *took* you there.

He discovered early that a little deceit and play-acting paid big dividends. He often fooled his mother into thinking he was sick, or cadged an extra cookie out of her. Cosby said, "You know that if you can get her laughing you can get around her," and, as his biographer Ronald L. Smith observes, "He found that a little charm goes a long way. Soon he was able to con the teachers and, with a little joking around, con his classmates, too." He could jolly a higher grade out of teachers, one of whom once pronounced, "William, you should be a politician. You lie so well." Bill, nicknamed Shorty, recalls how he "got to feeling that as long as people were laughing, they were my friends. So to get myself across and to be an important person, I made them laugh. Through humor I gained acceptance"—the central theme of many comedians' lives.

Apart from his mother, Anna, who read Twain to her sons, he was strongly influenced by a sixth-grade teacher, Mary Forchic Nagel, who taught a class for the "unreachable and unteachable." She instilled pride and purpose in her students, and saw in Cosby something not only reachable and even teachable but unique and funny. She wrote on his report card: "He would rather be a clown than a student and feels it is his mission to amuse his classmates in and out of school." She added that he was "a boy's boy, an all-around fellow, and he should grow up to do great things." Although she gave him his first gig by asking him to repeat a riff of his for his sixth-grade class, Mrs. Nagel wasn't about to give him a booking on her time: "In this classroom," she told Cosby, "there is one comedian and it is I. If you want to be one, grow up, get your own stage, and get paid for it." She pointed him toward theater, but he was too shy to volunteer; he wanted to be chosen.

His early comic influences, like those of most comedians of the era, came from radio, "a source of wonder for Cos," says Smith, especially the ethnic characters on Fred Allen's "Allen's Alley" (he liked imitating the southern windbag Senator Claghorn). He was drawn to stories and characters even then. When television came along, he was addicted to *Your Show of Shows* and fantasized becoming a Sid Caesar second banana. He loved the physical comics—Red Skelton, Jerry Lewis, Jonathan Winters, Jackie Gleason ("I'm amazed by his moves, they're funny and graceful"). He was "never much for the talk comics, not even Bob Hope."

Watching TV in a North Philadelphia ghetto, the teenage Cosby was especially impressed by a genial storytelling comedian named Sam Levenson, who spun wry homilies about growing up in a Jewish ghetto in New York City and teaching Spanish to Brooklyn schoolkids. Levenson, as both comic and teacher, became a role model for Cosby—who also grew up in cramped quarters, coped with siblings, and had a firm but loving mother. Here was the germ of Bill Cosby's act, only minus the junkyard rat hunts, the angry, alcoholic, absent father, the thin soles and faded pants, the bill collectors, and the meager dinners.

Admitted to Central High, a school for gifted students, Cosby found himself in over his head and read comic books in class. When a teacher who took a comic book away said, "You'll get this back at the end of the school year," Bill sassed her back, "Why? Does it take you that long to read it?" He transferred to the more racially mixed Germantown High, but dropped out when forced to repeat the tenth grade three times; in 1956 he joined the navy, where he became a hospital corpsman, won awards in track (and set a record in the high jump), and finally earned a high school degree that took him at twenty-three to Temple University on an athletic scholarship. His football coach at Temple, Ernie Casale, saw that his fullback had the comic goods when Cosby imitated him giving a locker-room lecture: "This was the first time I'd heard him in front of a group and he did such a terrific job you could tell that something was gonna happen with that guy." Cosby later developed the pep talk into a routine about his old Temple team, heard on the album *Why Is There Air?* Casale thought that Cosby might have been a great college player had he focused on football; he had attracted the eye of a New York Giants scout.

What intruded on that plan was Cosby's need to earn some money. He heard about a bartending job at a little joint called the Cellar, where he was paid five dollars to mix drinks and mix it up with the customers. The Cellar lacked an actual stage, so Cosby would just stand on top of a table and tell jokes that he'd heard on TV or had stolen off comedy records, relying heavily on a young black comic named Flip Wilson. As Smith writes: "Cos put his 'con man' experience to work, and he earned tips as the funniest, most charming bartender the place had ever seen."

Gradually, he built the jokes into longer segments, then moved up from the Cellar to the Underground, a saloon in the same building, where he had an actual stage and the time to construct tales about his student and football life at Temple. His breakthrough routine was about playing football as a kid ("*Cosby, you go down to Third Street, catch the J bus, have him open the doors at Nineteenth Street, and I'll fake to ya . . .*"). It staked out his future. "He was an athlete and he had no fear," observed Frank Werber, a manager at the hungry i. "When he went onstage in his first concert with us, the mike was dead and for seven minutes he hassled with that thing and then did a series of bits on the dead mike that had the audience collapsing. He was never nervous."

At the Underground, he filled in for the house comic, a boozy old-timer who missed enough shows to give Cosby his shot in 1960, earning him a few bucks. Meanwhile, a cousin of his hosting a local TV show hired Cosby to warm up the audiences before airtime. At a local burlesque house, he made six dollars a night "telling Ivy League jokes to six sailors and a junkie, doing a Shakespearean routine. They didn't want some college darkie talking about Hamlet between bumps and grinds, so I got fired. I went to a beatnik dive full of ugly Negro girls and ugly white men—sort of a lonely-hearts integration. But they laughed. I was getting closer."

While he never got dirty, he wasn't above reciting some Lenny Bruce routines, which he would later call a "tribute." "He was very shrewd, even when he was a bartender in Philadelphia," said Lawrence Christon, who had lengthy discussions with Cosby about comedy for the *Los Angeles Times*. "He said that if you threw out a story you got more tips. He wasn't telling jokes, more of a raconteur. There's a lot of racial anger in him but he didn't want to get into that arena."

A Temple classmate, Herb Gart, who had been managing folksingers, offered to help Cosby find club dates, steering him to a Greenwich Village room, the Gaslight Club, which was looking for new talent in the summer of '62; Cosby won a spot. He started to dress and look like a certified comedian, sporting a pinky ring and smoking a cigar, mimicking Alan King, his mentor. King recalls: "I started a correspondence with Cosby when he was at Temple University. This kid was writing to me and I wrote back and I developed a pen pal. He wanted to be a stand-up comedian. I said, if you're ever in New York, come see me, and all of a sudden one day my secretary says there's a black man outside. That was the first time I knew he was black. He said I was a role model." They've been friends and tennis partners ever since.

Cosby wound up playing six sets of comedy a night at the Gaslight, sandwiched between folksingers. Often on weeknights he opened to a half-dozen paid customers, earning twelve dollars a night. He literally ate and slept comedy—living in a room over the Gaslight and eating there.

As Gart told Smith, "Dick Gregory was hot with political material, Flip Wilson and Redd Foxx were not doing clean things. And here was Cosby, doing clean, nonpolitical humor. He's never been a 'stand-up comic.' He's always been a storyteller. Other than Myron Cohen and Sam Levenson, who did that? And they more or less did slightly extended jokes, whereas Cos could literally go on for half an hour about the situation at the dinner table." Cosby attributes his story-weaving skills to his grandfather. "As a kid I watched this man. He told stories. My father did, too, but mostly to my mother. Between the two I learned how to tell a story."

Even more than race and political strife, Cosby avoided jokes. He diligently worked the hearth-and-home beat, adding a little Woody Allen–ish whimsy—an outcast saber-toothed tiger who lisps because he's missing one saber tooth; the wolf man who tells his barber, "*Just a light trim around the legs*"; a praying mantis he teaches to be an agnostic.

Gart wasn't an experienced manager, but he had a keen ear for comedy and gave Cosby sound advice about working clean and the mechanics of delivery. He had him study such unlikely comics as the bizarre Lord Buckley and opera parodist Anna Russell as models of comic efficiency. Although Cosby never panicked onstage and never got defensive, many early bits bombed, mostly from his lack of experience. His school days proved to him he could always charm his way out of a corner. Once, when a table of front-row spectators was staring at him in silence, he calmly slid off the stage, sat down with them, and finished the routine from their table, prying a few smiles out of them. He learned to work a room by addressing people in the crowd directly, at times challengingly—forcing, prodding, as if daring them not to laugh at him.

Cosby was doing well enough, but he hadn't yet mined the mother lode of childhood ore that would create his career. He was funny and likable but strained and unformed, still just a guy memorizing comedy records and TV routines, everyone from Mel Brooks and Carl Reiner to Brother Dave Gardner. But he was moving up. By 1963 he was a regular at all the downtown Village clubs—the Bitter End, the Café Wha?—though he still had no central theme, no idea who he was, comically. He was flopping and fishing, but always with confidence and savoir faire. "If the comic isn't secure," he once observed, "the audience will smell it. The audience can smell a weakling, and *they* will go for the kill." Comedy, he said, is really "control over other people." He had confirmed to himself that he was truly a funny guy. That was his salvation. "There is such a thing as natural ability," he said, "but to think you can get by on that alone is a big mistake, just like some athletes think they can get by without studying their game. You've got to study yourself and know just where the laugh is coming from."

Fred Weintraub, the owner of the Bitter End, who briefly managed Cosby and helped shape him, told me: "He'd come into town weekends and play the Café Wha? He was goin' nowhere fast. He was a poor imitation of Dick Gregory. He was bitter but was trying desperately to be nice. Gregory was ahead of him, and was much more brilliant than Cosby, and much more racial. Then Bill came to me and he said, 'I'm not goin' anywhere, will you manage me?' " Cosby wasn't appealing very strongly to audiences of any color then, and once recalled, "When I first began telling racial jokes, the Negroes looked at the whites, the whites looked at the Negroes, and nobody laughed."

Jack Rollins had declined to represent Cosby. "I didn't want to handle him," he says. "I thought he was arrogant. I didn't want to be near an arrogant comedian. I had to at least start off liking people I was to try to manage. He was too slick, and a little corny. There was no substance. I like a comic with some weight." So Weintraub took Cosby on: "We'd go over the routines in the afternoon, and I kept saying to him, 'Talk about yourself and your family, talk about Fat Albert.' Basically, the idea was to make him human, to make him a sweet and appealing black guy to a regular audience. I helped change his persona. He wanted to be a 'black comedian.' I must have told him a thousand times, 'There's one Dick Gregory. You gotta be Bill Cosby.' " He didn't argue? "Nah, he was smart and he wanted to be successful. He wanted to date white girls." Weintraub adds: "You have to understand—the people who make it are all very smart. The ones who make it could almost manage *you*. They know where they're going." Very early, Cosby's goal was to become a millionaire. "I like money," he told a TV critic flatly. "I can be bought. I'm using anything I can as a means to get a million bucks."

Cosby listened to Weintraub—at first. "At the beginning they all do. Then all of a sudden they know everything." He believes that white audiences took to Cosby because of his looks. "He was clean-cut. He was a college boy. He was not threatening to the audience at all, and they liked the fact that he was talkin' about what they could understand. Everyone wanted to like him."

Enter Roy Silver. Every comedian needs a Roy Silver, someone who can make the crucial phone call and can keep the comic honest. Silver at the time was just starting to manage a strange young folksinger named Bob Dylan. He quit handling Dylan to focus on Cosby, while Weintraub concentrated on handling the moneymaking Serendipity Singers. Silver, like Weintraub, was convinced that Cosby should "work white."

Silver disagrees that Cosby was a natural who had some kind of magic that makes people laugh. He details the effort it took to maneuver Cosby from amiable stand-up comic to superstardom, and feels he deserves a few bows himself for helping to make Cosby happen, attending every show with a tape recorder and spending all night sweating over each word: " 'Why was a line funny in the first two shows but not the third? Was your timing off? Didn't you punch it right? Was it just a dead audience?' Line by line like this, for weeks, till we knew we had a thirty-minute set that was working, going over every single line—edit and cut, edit and cut."

There were long painful nights, tensions, and many battles. "Being 'almost there' brought frustration," Smith recounts. When the act wasn't working, Cosby would throw in a "saver," a racial joke, and when the laugh came he would glare at Silver and, says Smith, on the way offstage, "push past Silver and bark out a quick 'Up yours!' The men would scream at each other, and Cos would ball up his fist and shove it in Silver's face, ready to punch some sense into him."

Don Asher, the hungry i's house pianist, has his own Cosby memory: "He was a soft-spoken guy and spoke onstage in that put-on drawl, but I remember some arrogance—how he treated underlings. He could be abrasive." Silver recalls their first meeting in 1962: "I heard there was a young comic in the Village named Bill Cosby. So I took a walk one day over to the Gaslight. He said, 'Can I help you?' I knew he was Bill Cosby immediately because he was snotty. I knew he was very special. His being black was not a consideration in any way. He was Bill Cosby."

Very few blacks were booked into major clubs then, but Silver says: "I was determined to make him a star. I gave him the no-black [material] concept. Some of his act was good, some of it was not. It wasn't per se racial—it was much sweeter than what anyone else was doing. The act had echoes of Lenny Bruce and Bob Newhart, such as bits about the Lone Ranger and General Custer. His early black jokes fell somewhere between Gregory and Godfrey Cambridge, racial but congenial, as in, '*One morning I woke up and looked in the mirror. There was a freckle and it just got bigger and bigger.*' "

Mel Watkins observes that white audiences who had "abided" Dick Gregory's more biting wit were "consoled by the playful brilliance of Cosby." In 1991 Cosby told Arsenio Hall on Hall's late-night TV show, "When I started out in the Village, I did racial material, what I called guilt material." In an *Ebony* interview in the early sixties he said that he gave up racial humor in order to be unique, not to duck any issues: "I was telling racial jokes then. You know, the biting, witty kind about the Negro's role in America. But pretty soon critics began to regard me as a sort of hip Nipsey Russell and a Philadelphia Dick Gregory. Well, I decided then and there that I had to be original if I wanted to fulfill my aspirations of becoming a big man in show business."

It was his answer to, in *Ebony*'s words, "skeptics who would like to brand him as a deserter to the cause." He later explained himself: "I'm not Dick Gregory, and he's not Martin Luther King. So we all serve our purpose the way we know how." Sounding a little like Colin Powell, he told Rex Reed, "People accept me because I'm not controversial. Most of them don't even think of me as a Negro." He was not an easy client and took Silver's advice "with great hostility. He was real pissed that I would do that [insist that he delete racial jokes]. I never used the word *commercial,* but I wanted him to be special, somebody who had the ability to transgress all hostility and race." Cosby had no qualms about his own persona, saying, "Right now I like me just like I am, an all-around winner." What finally convinced him to abandon racial jokes was a comment by a shrewd friend, who told him, after hearing his Stephen Foster routine, "You know, if you turned white tomorrow, you wouldn't be funny."

To "leap over" Dick Gregory, the former high jumper finally decided to become the un-Gregory, regaling audiences with his memories of things past, which got him labeled a "nostalgia act," a tag he resented. "It's larger than nostalgia," he argued. "It's not all, 'Oh, yeah, I remember that.' Man, nobody's gonna laugh at that. You got to pay the people off." Cosby took care that each story was studded with laughs and buttoned up snugly with a memorable tag line. He'd end stories with "*That's the truth.*"

Says Silver: "We recorded ten albums—and I made Bill Cosby a major star when I put him on *The Tonight Show.* I'd tried six times. They said he wasn't funny enough." Finally, Allan Sherman put Cosby on the show when Sherman was guest-hosting. Silver had to drag his stubborn client off the outdoor courts on Waverly Place, where he found him shooting hoops, to convince him to appear on the show. "Screw 'em," Silver says Cosby told him. "They're all fucking assholes. They already turned me down. Why should I put myself through that again?"

As Silver continues the saga: "I took Bill down to *The Tonight Show* and Cosby just sat there, and finally [Sherman] said, 'What do you wanna do?' and Bill stood up, steam coming from his nose, and he did his routine without a single trace of inflection. He was *hostile.* Allan said, 'Gee, that was great—you'll do it tonight.' I was amazed. I called everyone I could think of, cashed in my chips. There we were, walking that line that separates the men from the boys. We were a step away. We both knew that this was the start of something big."

Twenty years later, Cosby recalled that night on TV to Johnny Carson: "I came out and I was going to do my karate routine. And I hadn't really thought it would be funny. But I guess the people were so conditioned to see a black person come out—they said, 'Okay, he's gonna talk about the back of the bus and the front of the restaurant'—and I walked out and I said I wanna talk about karate." In the now classic bit, he plays a novice karate instructor, who says, "*The big slab of callus you got on your hand . . . makes your hand look like a foot. Don't laugh. This is good. Keep your hand in your pocket for nine days, then when somebody attacks you, you take a swing at 'em and even if you miss, the smell'll kill 'em."* He shows how to frighten attackers even without knowing karate—that all you needed was the shout to ward them off. *"Watch out or I'll shout again. Matter of fact, you give me your dough!"* It was another textbook example of a comedian who, with one appearance on *The Tonight Show,* became a star overnight, or at the very least made a big enough splash to open a few weeks later at the premier clubs—Mister Kelly's in Chicago and the hungry i in San Francisco.

Ralph J. Gleason wrote, "His timing is the best of any performer I have seen since Pearl Bailey first hit the stage." Steve Allen christened him "nothing less than the most gifted monologuist of our time. He is the Art Tatum of comedy." Allen noted how Cosby would begin in an easy ambling manner, chatting up the audience, slyly winning them over, and then subtly slide into a routine before anyone was aware of it.

Managing Cosby was anything but a barrel of laughs. "I was with Cosby for nine years," says Silver, "and for me it was a project. He tolerated you. We didn't hang out. We weren't buddies or anything like that. I was just the right guy at the right time—that's what it came down to. Then we split [in the late sixties]—it was never amicable. I haven't spoken to him since. He listened to me, but he was changing before me. He got very big very fast and everyone was pulling on him." Many comics, indeed most entertainers, explains Silver, like to think they did it all themselves. "Grateful? No—not even close. He trusted me because he saw that I was very smart. I would hammer away at him and ultimately he would acquiesce. I even put him together with Camille [his wife]. It got so hard because he became a star." Silver says Cosby would queer deals in meetings because of his attitude. "He was just tough. He wasn't fun."

Cosby began taking heat from the press, which was always after him to explain the absence of racial issues onstage. (Godfrey Cambridge was also accused of "not being black enough" in his act.) Cosby's argument: "It would be easy to get onstage and talk about 'The Problem.' " Labeling racial jokes "a crutch," Cosby commented: "I'm tired of those people who say, 'You should be doing more to help your people.' I'm a comedian, that's all. My humor comes from the way I look at things. I am a man. I see things the way other people do. . . . A white person listens to my act and he laughs and he thinks, 'Yeah, that's the way I see it, too.' Okay, he's white. I'm a Negro. That must mean that *we are alike, right?* So I figure I'm doing as much good for race relations as the next guy."

In a 1969 *Playboy* interview, he expanded on the subject: "The fact that

I'm not trying to win converts onstage bugs some people, but I don't think an entertainer *can* win converts. I don't worry how to slip a social message into my act; I just go out and do my thing." His attitude reflected a new kind of stereotyping that expected all black comics to toe the racial line. Smith comments: "The idea of letting a black comedian do what every other comedian was allowed to do—well, that was too radical." Cosby had no interest in appearing on TV as "a show Negro" to do the racial shuffle, adding, "Now, if you need a comedian, call."

It was the start of Cosby's touchy relationship with the press, which wanted it both ways—first praising him for not relying on racial matters and holding him up as a model black citizen, and then chiding him for ducking black concerns. The comedy critic Laurie Stone noted: "Cosby signaled to the audience that some blacks have made it so successfully that they don't have to call attention to race." The comedian was the message. Donald Bogle contends: "To his great credit, Cosby—the master of nonethnic anecdotes—never came across as a black man trying to be white. He managed to hold on to his ethnic grit—through his rhythm and his *attitude*. Still, it might strike some as odd that Cosby—with his seemingly politically neutral persona—became a star in the politically restless 1960s."

IN 1963, when Cosby was performing at the Crescendo in Los Angeles, he met Carl Reiner. Reiner was there with the producer of *The Dick Van Dyke Show,* the tough-guy actor Sheldon Leonard, who wanted to talk to him about a TV series he had in mind. It was the era of *The Man from U.N.C.L.E.* and *Get Smart* on TV, the James Bond movies and Bond ripoffs like *Our Man Flint.*

Leonard had something trickier in mind—a comedy-adventure series about a spy team, one white and one black. *Variety,* however, wondered if America was ready for integration on a weekly dramatic basis; the last TV show to costar blacks and whites had been *Beulah* in the 1950s. *I Spy* was not quite the groundbreaker it claimed to be; the bland sitcom *Julia,* with Diahann Carroll, had debuted a year before and Cosby sprang to its defense (maybe anticipating the heat that would later come his way): "Everyone says Diahann Carroll's not black enough in *Julia*—right? By the same token, TV isn't a real reflection of the white world either. Do white mothers behave like Lucille Ball? Do all Marines act like Gomer Pyle?"

Cosby had zero acting training but charm and smarts to burn. When Leonard asked him if he'd done any acting, Cosby quipped, "You didn't see me when I did Othello in Central Park last year?" Leonard had envisioned using Cosby as a funny Tonto to Robert Culp's Lone Ranger, but Cosby's leading-man presence asserted itself and Leonard cast him as a partner, not a sidekick, playing the trainer and traveling companion to Culp's globe-trotting tennis star, the cover for their spy games. ("Bob Culp and I fought the international Communist conspiracy on an equal basis," in Cosby's words.) "He blows a hundred scenes a day but he's wonderful," said Culp. "He's the fastest natural study I've ever seen." Proclaimed Cosby: "I think I have a personality talent. I have the intelligence and the talent to be a big star. This isn't conceit; I just know what I can do." Ron Miller, the TV critic, says, "He was never a stranger in a strange land. He immediately knew what he was doing. His success in *I Spy* was kind of an amazing thing." As the critic Elvis Mitchell writes, "Cosby stole the show because he was a much more charismatic and subtle actor."

The black-white pairing became the 1965 show's biggest selling point and its major threat. TV's past was strewn with black sacrificial lambs like *The Nat King Cole Show* and *Amos 'n' Andy,* both of which caused a huge racial ruckus that drove them off the air; the latter's banishment was greatly due to Cosby's attacks on it, even though he had one major theme in common with *Amos 'n' Andy*—it never mentioned race, either.

I Spy proved a colossal hit, a quality show with movielike production values that became the springboard for Cosby's long career in comedy and on television. *Newsweek* said: "At twenty-eight, Cosby has accomplished in one year what scores of Negro actors and comedians have tried to do all their lives: he has completely refurbished the television image of the Negro. He is not the stereotyped white-toothed Negro boy with a sense of good rhythm. He is a human being, and a funnier, hipper human being than anyone around him." The *Saturday Evening Post* credited him with "launching a racial revolution" and becoming "the Jackie Robinson of television."

Cosby dryly cracked, "This is the first time they called [a Negro] up to play a spy instead of a problem." Only four TV stations in the Deep South refused to carry the show. "None of the bogeymen we had foreseen ever materialized," said Leonard. "We have more sponsors than we need." Culp said the show was "doing more [for Negroes] than a hundred marches." The essential Cosby came through, a critic noted: "Mr. Cosby may never get to play more than himself, but since he's an ingratiating fellow, he'll do fine. Gary Cooper went farther on less." Ralph J. Gleason, brushing aside the hype and the raves, wrote, "He has taken a really dumb TV series and made it into a personal vehicle which has put him in orbit."

When the press pounded Cosby about The Cause, Sammy Davis, Jr. (who had been similarly castigated), spoke up: "Bill Cosby carries as much weight on his shoulders as any Negro I know, and he wears it as well and as lightly as any man could. He may not be a front-runner in the cause—that's not his nature—but he's totally committed. He gives freely of time and money. The cats on the street corner dig him, and he represents something very important to me." Had he been born ten years later, Davis might have snagged the *I Spy* role. Cosby did what Davis, Nat Cole, and Lena Horne had been unable to do. "It was catapult time," as he said.

Gradually, the scripts began to play off Cosby's droll, lightly acerbic style, and even Culp began tossing in Cosby catchphrases ("*Is that a fact?*"; "*Isn't that wonderful*"; "*Does that shake your tree?*"), enriching their comic chemistry. The dapper, swinging duo put in a lot of time at Playboy Mansion soirées and got on well together off-camera. Even though the show supposedly focused on Culp (the opening silhouette depicted him in action shots, and he presumably was the "I" in *I Spy*), Cosby's flashier role won him awards that might have triggered tension on the set; Cosby graciously remarked when he won his first Emmy (of three in a row), "I extend my hand to a man by the name of Robert Culp. He lost this because he helped me." If Culp hadn't been so generous toward him, Cosby said on a different occasion, he might well have fled the show and focused on his booming stand-up career. Cosby became the show's featured de facto lead. Wrote Stanley Karnow in the *Saturday Evening Post* in 1965: "Cosby's role is not fashioned to fit a Negro. At times, his fresh charm and casual humor so overshadow Culp that the show commits the heresy of subordinating the white man to the Negro."

I Spy gave Cosby heightened moral authority, which forced him to take, or evade, political positions on such urgent issues as: why he rarely got the girl, and when he did, why not a white girl. The London *Sunday Times* diligently tabulated that Cosby only got the girl six out of seventy-eight times, "and she was always black." But in response to the *Times* article, "Why Cosby Never Gets a White Girl," he promised in 1968: "As long as I'm on the screen, whether television or films, I will never hold or kiss a white woman." Off-screen, he loved being a sex symbol to white women, as he told Rex Reed: "It should've happened a long time ago, with Belafonte and Poitier. It's funny, but psychologically it just didn't happen. Those guys still play Negroes when they act, but I refuse to do that. I don't sing, tap dance, juggle, or say 'Sir.' I am not a Rochester."

Even so, the liberal media intensified their scrutiny and kept badgering him: Why didn't his character reflect the black man's position in society? To which a *National Review* critic had the best answer: "Cosby is not primarily a Negro [on the series]. He is primarily a guy." Behind his own rational responses to the ongoing barrage of touchy questions, which implied he was Uncle Tom's nephew, Cosby seethed ("I find the ultra-liberals a total pain"). Smith says it was all the star could do to keep from punching reporters who hoped to goad him into a news-making controversial moment.

I Spy gave him the freedom to speak more honestly to the stand-up audience and to play off them. Standing onstage and delivering happy 'hood stories now seemed passé. He began to do what he had done in the beginning—charm his fans face-to-face, reveling in their adoration. He called it "total communication" and he still exploits his charm as hard as he can, winning audiences by just sitting in a big chair onstage, wearing a sweater, and wielding a long cigar. In a backstage interview with me at Harrah's Club at Lake Tahoe in the late 1960s, he puffed his stogie and, godfather-like, called for members of his entourage to step lively. The Temple University locker-room jester had become a king in his court.

He no longer needed smoky, boozy nightclubs. He moved to Madison Square Garden and the Westbury Music Fair, playing to families, explaining, like a newly crowned emperor, "I like to see my people." He might patronize his subjects, but he didn't want them "crammed into a small club and paying a hefty cover charge. The parking is better and people don't have to drive into the city. Plus, they're not drinking." When his nurturing old club, the Gaslight, fell on hard times and tried to sell tapes of early unpolished Bill Cosby, he allegedly snapped them all up.

It was about this time that he first began to rumble about leaving show business to teach. "I'm going to retire at thirty-seven, go back to school, get my degree, and become a junior high school teacher. This acting is going to be only a small part of my life," he vowed in 1965. "I'm not interested in having a yacht and six Ferraris"; he had owned one Ferrari, also a Mercedes and a Cadillac. "I want to go back to Philadelphia and teach junior high school in a lower-class section—as low as you can get." Maybe Watts. Or maybe he'd open a sporting goods store.

By 1967, however, Cosby's classroom dreams had gone totally corporate. He was now the millionaire he had longed to be, with a Rolls-Royce and significant investments. After shooting ended on *I Spy* that year, he played twenty-five comedy dates one month, chasing money by the hour, earning $25,000 a gig. He made a halfhearted run at a singing career that crashed with the release of a much-mocked album, *Silver Throat Sings,* launched a chain of Fat Albert hamburger stands, and did a series of five-minute radio commercials for Coca-Cola. He also supported a large extended family ("I've put together a hell of a one-man antipoverty program"). All the while he was on a binge of jewelry purchasing (for himself) that would choke the Home Shopping Network.

At a concert in Kansas City on the April 1968 night that Martin Luther King, Jr., was killed, Cosby attempted to do his usual show, but forty minutes in, he couldn't continue. The audience greeted the announcement with a standing ovation. This event radicalized him politically to the extent that he joined the Memphis march that King had led and attended the funeral in Atlanta, temporarily silencing any criticism. That week he came to the decision, like Dick Gregory before him, that comedy, for an American black man, demanded commitment.

In 1969, after *I Spy,* he kept his pledge to become a schoolteacher—on TV, at least. *The Bill Cosby Show* was a docile, even insipid, series (preachy and simplistic, critics called it) that opened just out of the Top Ten in the ratings and further established Cosby's image as comedian-cum-teacher. In it, Cosby imparted antiquated moral lessons, such as telling a football player, "The important thing is not winning. It's knowing what to do when you lose. Humility in victory; pride in defeat." He took over a nephew's paper route on the show, proclaiming, "There's no labor a man can do that's undignified—if he does it right." The series further laid the groundwork for Cosby's career as a truism-chocked raconteur.

That first Cosby show, which lasted only two seasons (it was finally done in by *Bonanza*), was far too risk-averse for the late sixties, when harder-edged series like *All in the Family, The Jeffersons, Sanford and Son,* and *Diff'rent Strokes* made sharper points about political and social issues; Cosby's saintly character, Chet Kincaid, was a sort of stand-up high school teacher, not unlike his hero Sam Levenson. Cosby pursued his own undergraduate degree from Temple, finally earning his B.A. on the strength of his "life experience" and body of work. He later got a doctorate in education in 1976 (from the University of Massachusetts in Amherst, where he had a home) for a thesis on Fat Albert that some critics sneered at. Cosby liked referring to himself, only half jokingly, as "Dr. William H. Cosby, Jr." The thesis was titled "An Integration of the Visual

Media Via Fat Albert and the Cosby Kids into the Elementary School Curriculum as a Teaching Aid and Vehicle to Achieve Increased Learning."

While black columnists still grumbled about Cosby hiding out on racial issues, he had begun supporting black colleges (Spelman College alone has received at least $20 million, and millions more have gone to other schools and charities), and he insisted that half the crew on his shows be black; some episodes had all-black casts and episodes featured black comic icons like Moms Mabley and Mantan Moreland; he also wrote in parts for Dizzy Gillespie, Joe Williams, and Lillian Randolph, the onetime *Beulah*. In the sixties, Cosby and Redd Foxx opened a club, but they split over black power posters Cosby wanted to display.

Whatever his humanitarian credentials, Cosby kept colleagues at arm's length. "He's a very private guy and can even be prickly," said one. "He's pleasant and professional, but he doesn't like to talk about his private life at all. It all becomes a riff." Interviews with him are rare, due to unhappy early experiences at the hands of interviewers—some of them drunk, he claimed; some who just used his jokes to spice up their articles; some, like Earl Wilson, who sat in the star's hotel room eating sandwiches and asking incoherent questions. He also was not greatly loved by publicists. One former press agent recalls that when he came through San Francisco, "He was kind of intimidating. He was like Big Daddy, the head of this entourage. He never once looked me in the eye. He didn't need me."

In 1972 Cosby put up $800,000 of his own money in the first of several aborted attempts to carve out a career in movies, with a film about a black family's struggle in the post–Civil War West. *Man and Boy,* despite off-camera financial and personnel problems, did reasonably well, although it didn't exactly establish its star as a leading man for the screen. By now, Cosby *was* a part-time educator—narrating a documentary on inner-city schools, hosting an antidrug special, and playing Aesop on a show in which he spun animated fables to an audience of two kids. A lackadaisical variety hour called *The New Bill Cosby Show* quickly came and went in 1972–73 sinking Cosby to near the bottom of the TV ratings. "It was such a disaster that it almost finished him off," says Ron Miller. When a kiddie-centered show called *Cos* materialized on TV in '76, "it gave further proof that he was finished on TV," says Miller. Opposite *60 Minutes,* it lasted a month.

His appeal was wearing a little thin. His record sales had dwindled. He was being overtaken by the rougher comedy of the seventies, when more radical, harder-edged comics appeared—Richard Pryor, George Carlin, and then the first whoops of the "wild-and-crazy" school of Steve Martin, John Belushi and *Saturday Night Live,* Robin Williams, Cheech & Chong, *The National Lampoon,* Flip Wilson, and Eddie Murphy. Cosby's competitors punched up the rhythms and lingo of street life, larded with sex jokes, drug jokes, and bathroom jokes. To keep up, Cosby took a few tentative steps into the blue zone (a raunchy album was titled *For Adults Only*). In Las Vegas, his cushy familial ramblings veered off into occasional crude insights on married sex life and urinating in front of his daughters. He injected a little profanity, uneasily. His fans weren't buying it. As Smith writes, "They didn't want Cosby to tarnish his image. They didn't want a Pryor Cosby, they wanted the prior Cosby."

Just as Pryor's wildfire died down, along came an all-new heir to the black comedy throne, Eddie Murphy, who was aghast that Cosby had actually called him up and, in his most fatherly manner, told him, "You can't go onstage and say 'fuck you.' " Said Murphy: "That was the most bizarre thing that's happened in my career, Bill Cosby calling me up and reprimanding me for being too dirty. Wow." Both Pryor and Murphy had broken out of stand-up and into a string of funny, moneymaking movies, while the legendary Cosby foundered. Cosby and Murphy engaged in a simmering feud that stemmed from Cosby's damning Murphy with faint praise in a *Playboy* interview. Murphy responded on *Saturday Night Live* with a devastating impression of the pompous, cigar-waggling Cosby, right down to the wire-rim spectacles and satisfied smirk. Of the parody, he said, in a typically Cosbyesque tone of indulgent condescension and avuncular wisdom: "I didn't mind it. There are always these positions younger people take, looking at older people and thinking, 'Hey, you're not that good; I can do better.' That's how you get pupils to surpass their teachers." (Indeed—in the fall of 2002, Murphy starred in a movie version of *I Spy,* which barely made a ripple. Wrote Elvis Mitchell in the *New York Times:* "The old show took something negligible and made it sui generis; this new version is just plain generic.")

Suddenly unsure of who he was for the first time in his life, Cosby was trying a little of everything and the pressure began to show. When a reporter commented, "Bill, my readers think you're spreading yourself too thin," Cosby, flashing his celebrated arrogance, said, "Madam, I just don't care what your readers think, see?" During a show in Las Vegas, when he heard a stagehand sawing wood backstage, he stomped offstage, stopped the sawing, and returned to bid adieu to his stunned audience.

Not knowing what his mood might be, coworkers walked on eggshells around him. Craig Tennis, a former *Tonight Show* talent coordinator, described Cosby as "mercurial, veering from cordiality to rudeness for no apparent reason." Anxiety at the show heightened when Cosby, booked as a guest, rejected pre-interviews so he could wing it. Tennis added: "Bill changes from moment to moment. I've seen him come on completely unprepared and yet work himself into a monologue that is warm, original, and killingly funny. At other times he's been cold and aloof, maddeningly playing the superstar, talking down to the audience."

Desperate to seem relevant, he started speaking out more often—against black English and interracial sex but in approval of interracial love. The *Village Voice* pronounced him passé: "Cosby has become unfunny in recent years," wrote a critic who called him "a monotonous young fogy capitalizing whenever he can on his splendiferous teacher thing . . . clubby-kissing the ruling-class hand of Johnny Carson, making spokesman commercials for such established products as White Owl cigars and Pan American Airlines. He has evolved into a kind of self-parodying sap." Cosby grew incensed over what he saw as changing public taste: "People don't want 'Mr. Nice Guy.' They want Archie Bunker, a lovable bigot." Smith says Cosby had "a smoldering dislike for *All in the Family.*" He also had a running feud with Harry Belafonte. They battled over the airing of *The Cosby Show* in South Africa and also over the rights to Nelson Mandela's life story, culminating in a lawsuit that Belafonte won.

Cosby wanted to move with the times, but didn't know how. He tried to sharpen his edges with jokes about flatulence and masturbation. He tried a rhythm-and-blues parody album titled *Bill Cosby Is Not Himself These Days, Rat Own, Rat Own, Rat Own,* with takeoffs on such R&B idols as James Brown. He appeared in several instantly forgettable films (*A Piece of the Action, Let's Do It Again, The Devil and Max Devlin*). In the wake of his only hit movie then, *California Suite,* he and Pryor were rapped by Pauline Kael for playing stupid black stereotypes; Cosby responded with an ad in *Variety* that insisted black actors had as much right as whites to play clowns and offered Chaplin, Keaton, and Laurel & Hardy as evidence: "If my work is not funny—it's not funny. But this industry does not need projected racism from critics."

Driven into a corner, he protested, "I don't have time to sit around and worry whether all the black people of the world make it because of me. I have my own gig to worry about. If a white man falls off a chair, it's just a guy. If a Negro does it, it's the whole damn Negro race. I don't want to be a crusader or a leader." He finally got into a black-issue brawl with Tom Smothers, who for years had ragged him and says that they'd had "a running disagreement from just about the time we first met." It finally got physical in 1976 at the Playboy Mansion: Cosby, rankled by Smothers's constant gibes, decked him when, he says, Tom refused to lay off.

In a slightly desperate attempt to revive his tottering career, he costarred with Robert Culp in a violent 1972 movie about two private eyes, *Hickey and Boggs.* But it faced a firing squad of criticism; again, his TV home audience had refused to follow him into movie houses. To recover, Cosby rang his trusty school bell again with a cartoon show, *Fat Albert and the Cosby Kids,* a long-running Saturday-morning hit that borrowed heavily from the comic's old standby routines.

Distracted and feeling out of fashion, stung by writers who called him "the white man's Negro," Cosby redesigned his outer self with a semi-Afro, sideburns, and mustache. With the rise of earthier black comics ("He was out of date after Eddie Murphy," decreed one writer), Cosby finally gave up trying to be with-it and retreated to his market-tested home turf, the family, finding an awesome side career as a commercial spokesman for such virtuous all-American products as Coca-Cola, Jell-O, Del Monte, and the Ford Motor Company. Uncle Bill was back. It was still rare to see a black TV pitchman, but Cosby again transcended tradition by merchandizing his own brand of 100 percent wholesomeness. While many celebrities worry that commercials can stain careers, hawking big-name products greatly enlarged Cosby's.

Ron Miller comments: "The reason for his later TV success was really the Jell-O commercials. That gave people the idea that he had this great rapport with kids. The pilot for *The Cosby Show* was one of the most fantastically well-executed pilots there's ever been. Cosby was really the creative force behind the show. He built it from his own persona. *The Cosby Show* was rejected by ABC but he took it to NBC, which [in 1984] was really in the ratings toilet, and they put it on opposite *Magnum PI,* the hottest action show on TV at the time, and from the first episode it trashed *Magnum* and went straight to the top. It was so titanic in the ratings, it was getting a fifty share. It just carried the whole network."

His placid view of family life ran counter to the entire sitcom mindset of the mid-1980s. Once more, Cosby had the field all to himself. "The great thing about Cosby was, he always had a great feeling for the universals," said a writing colleague. *The Cosby Show* unified the best of Cosby's familial humor, flawed theories of child raising, and being a parent. It made him the titular head of America's household just when his career was entering the twilight zone and he was embarrassing himself in movies like *Ghost Dad* (a *Topper* remake); *Mother, Juggs and Speed; Let's Do It Again; A Piece of the Action;* and *Leonard: Part 6.* At one showing of *Leonard,* a critic noted that schoolkids were booing and hurling insults at the screen as the comic "ran through his bag of tricks." Cosby, on movie screens, was an aging black Bob Hope, stumbling through lame comedies at half speed.

The new TV series salvaged a sagging career and reestablished him as America's Father Emeritus. The show, full of retro images, was a black *Father Knows Best,* and it had the advantage of coming along after the other black family sitcoms had worn out their raucous welcomes. Once daring to perform color-blind routines during a period of racial, social, and political activism in America, Cosby flew in the face of 1980s situation comedies whose lifeblood depended on situations steeped in racism, sexism, ageism, and infantilism. His functional, grounded, loving, well-to-do Huxtable family (Cosby played a physician married to an attorney, two devoted parents) was almost suspiciously normal. The show made *The Brady Bunch* and *The Partridge Family* seem progressive.

John J. O'Connor commented in the *New York Times:* "At a time when so many comedians are toppling into a kind of smutty permissiveness, Mr. Cosby is making the nation laugh by paring ordinary life to its extraordinary essentials." Music to Cosby's ears. But the show took a barrage of hits for its comforting white-bread flavor and goody-two-shoes philosophy. *MAD* magazine satirized it, and even Johnny Carson quipped, "Now I hear they're trying to get Prince and Tina Turner for a remake of *Ozzie and Harriet.*" Says Miller: "He came under a lot of criticism for the show being a Disney version of black life." But Cosby was a powerhouse star again, with television's highest "TVQ" rating (for familiarity and likability). The series was so popular that NBC charged sponsors $400,000 a minute, nearly as much as each show cost to produce.

Cosby exercised total control over the show, sensing it might be his last hurrah. He insisted on having thirteen weeks to prepare the program, not the usual six, and he hired a noted black Harvard psychiatrist, Dr. Alvin Poussaint, to serve as adviser. Cosby told writers, "I don't want sitcom jokes. I don't want jokes about behinds or breasts or pimples or characters saying, 'Oh, my God!' every other line. We want to deal in human behavior." He wanted a TV family that resembled his own—educated, cultivated, with professional parents. He explained to reporters, "All we're trying to show America is that in a lot of ways behavior is the same all over. Why do they want to deny me the pleasure of being an American and just enjoying life?"

Some in the media kept peppering Cosby for being untrue to his roots—and indeed to his true feisty, often churlish self. A *TV Guide* interviewer called him "by turns combative, defensive, challenging, threatening, and hostile—one of the most arrogant celebrities I've ever met." Several magazines happily reprinted excerpts from the damaging piece as payback for Cosby's insistence on talking to them only in exchange for cover stories. He once blew up on *The Phil Donahue Show* when audience members asked him his opinion on certain racial issues. "It's none of your business," he snapped. He said, justifiably, that he was sick of having to discuss race because he was black. "When Bob Newhart comes on here, let's have him talk about it."

In the mid-nineties, on the annual TV press tour, he had a tent built and filled with pillows outside a hotel. Recalls Miller: "He was dressed like a Turkish caliph, smoking a cigar, surrounded by all these people. That's him. He likes to be this gigantic sultan. Everyone tells me that's the way he is." Privately, he enjoys the company of fellow sultans like Donald Trump and has been known to berate lackeys publicly, such as a kid at a celebrity tennis tournament who dared hand him a bottle of water that wasn't cold enough; he sat in an elevated umpire's chair, as if surveying his kingdom from on high.

His private life and racial issues are off-limits to interviewers, although he went on at passionate length in a 1985 *Playboy* interview about civil rights and black life in America. When a writer asked him what his precise problem was with the media, he said, "I guess I let people know when I think a question or a statement is rude or dumb." He particularly targets interviewers who want to perform amateur psychoanalysis on him ("They like to use phrases like 'the dark side'—*tah-dah-h-h!*") and "neoliberals who feel I should be a martyr—the kind who feel I should take my show, tell everything like it really is, and get canceled in three weeks. That person has no idea what life is all about. And neoliberals have a lot of racism in their hearts. Why else would they tell you to go out and get your brains blown out?"

The Cosby Show ran eight years and may exist in reruns forever, but when the sitcom cycle reversed itself yet again, Cosby found himself bucking slick, coarse, "reality"-charged shows, like *Roseanne, Married . . . with Children, Beavis and Butthead,* and *The Simpsons,* which was positioned opposite him. *The Simpsons* didn't flatten Cosby, as some thought; his series was already running out of gas by then. Cosby, at the time, charged, "The mean-spirited and cruel think this is 'the edge' and their excuse is, 'That's the way people are today.' But why should we be entertained by that?" Nonetheless, Cosby's show slipped in some teenage sex, menstruation, and sexist bachelor parties demeaning women. Ardent Cosby lifers were unamused, though one viewer said the show gave him a headache because he "learned too much." In the end, *The Simpsons'* caustic wit was a much-needed antidote to Cosby's sugar pills.

Cosby's bitter indignation surfaced in a speech at a TV Academy Hall of Fame dinner: "I thought I had given you something with *The Cosby Show,* but I see you've learned nothing." On *Good Morning America* he called other black sitcoms minstrel shows—"the only thing is, you don't have to put the makeup on now." He blamed the networks for asking black actors to put "hands on hips, shake yo' head, mo' def, everybody put the hat on backwards, everybody walk the hip walk."

As in his routines, he's only on solid ground when he stays home. Whenever Cosby strays from family material onstage, the stories are less closely observed or less deeply developed (a routine about going to the dentist sounds secondhand). The housebound stuff is still his bread and butter: "*My mother was an authority on pigsties—'This is the worst-looking pigsty I've ever seen!'* " Or on how the FCC should clamp down on parents who deal in hideous carnage when yelling at their children: "*Mothers can talk up some violence, man! 'I will beat you to within an inch of your life!'* " After a routine on natural childbirth, he tells how he turned to his wife, kissed her, and said, "*Darling, I love you very much. You just had a lizard.*" In a Cosby story, his kiss and the "Darling, I love you very much" are every bit as crucial as the lizard. He often mentions his wife, Camille, whom he married in 1964 and paints as a saint ("*Women* fall in love with Camille").

In the act, he still relies a lot on sounds, voices, mugging, body language, and his trademark woozy baby-talk voice that seduces the crowd. Throughout, he seems to be enjoying his own performance more than the audience is. His stand-up delivery often is more strident than his laid-back sitcom persona, sliding into a kind of ersatz black dialect. He was uncomfortable with the noisy sitcoms of the seventies that twitted but also exploited black comic stereotypes, and he refused to make "blaxploitation" films, explaining, "I prefer doing things I can feel good about."

Cosby preferred to settle for becoming an institution. After teaming up with Sammy Davis, Jr., in a ballyhooed Broadway show that flopped, he peeled back again to niche-market himself. Following Pryor's and Murphy's leads, he recorded some concert videos. In one, 1983's *Bill Cosby Himself,* he revealed his physical comic skills in a perceptive routine that depicted the numerous walking styles of drunks, as well as in a vintage Cosby bit about a kid in an airplane seat in front of him. Throughout, he splices in his own folk wisdom—*"My wife and I were intellectuals, until we had children"* . . . *"One of the things you learn when you become a parent is the horrible thought that your children will be your children for the rest of your life. That's why there's death"* . . . *"I don't like my daughter anymore, but she's too cute to throw out"* . . . asking the doctor after his child's birth, *"Can you put it back? It's not done yet. It needs to cook more."* Aided by his Ph.D. credentials, the doctor of homilies could hang out his shingle as a comic pediatrician, a partner in the office of Spock, Seuss & Cosby.

The video displays his effortless, if calculated, way of winning an audience. He can coast or he can soar, as in a 1987 video, *Cosby: 49,* in which he ponders the dangers of turning fifty. Easing into a chair in sweater and khakis, sucking on his signature cigar, he seems to be in our living room, his lifetime aim. He muses about how he now "makes noises my father used to make," tries to kick away a pain in his leg when his underwear cuts off the circulation, needs to rest after getting dressed, and observes, *"I'm growing hair on places I don't need hair."* Cosby blends and balances all his old nuanced tricks, such as searching his head for his spectacles and portraying his grandmother threading a needle by (as *he* must now do) squinting through trifocals (*"That bottom strip on the trifocals is so you can read your medicine"*). It's a beautifully crafted performance.

To revive himself, Cosby took to digging up old TV graveyards. He concocted a pallid revival of *You Bet Your Life,* which limped through one season (Cosby was no rapier Groucho), and a new *Kids Say the Darnedest Things,* but these Cosby kids didn't and it, too, failed to charm the critics. Remaking classics is a thankless grind. Inevitably, *I Spy Returns* became a 1994 TV movie with Cosby and Culp trying to squeeze into their old swinger suits. Like most reunion shows, it was a misbegotten move. Then came *The Cosby Mysteries,* another one-season wonder with detective Cosby trying to follow in the footprints of aging stars turned video sleuths (Peter Falk, James Garner, Rock Hudson, Angela Lansbury, Dick Van Dyke). Again, Cosby's stand-up charisma failed to cross over.

In 1996 he reunited with his longtime TV wife, Phylicia Rashad, in a remake of a British sitcom, *One Foot in the Grave.* Retitled *Cosby,* it featured Cosby as a grumbling unemployed airline mechanic ("a correctible fool" in the Archie Bunker mode). But as Cosby noted, the show lacked Archie's lovable bigotry. Complained the head writer Richard Day, who left the show, disgusted by the star's temperament and tinkering: "Cosby took a dark, interesting show and turned it into something bland. . . . Of all the stars I worked with—Roseanne, Garry Shandling, Cybil Shepherd—I had the worst experience with Cosby." The show got off to a good start anyway, ahead of *Frasier* and *Mad About You* in the ratings, and ran a couple of seasons on leftover *Cosby Show* goodwill.

Cosby, who had left his stand-up career behind for TV, reemerged onstage to polish up his legacy, further burnished in 2002 when he won a presidential Medal of Freedom. In his TV talk-show appearances, he morphed, notes Smith, "from an impish, childlike performer to a more adult figure, coming out in a vested suit, walking his special stately walk, and enunciating though the cigar flaunted between his teeth." He still likes to glide through concert performances, reclining in a big wing chair (suggesting a royal bearing, too imperious to stand) and blowing smoke like a CEO of comedy. He can charm a crowd by wandering the aisles during an evening of extemporaneous musings and then exit with a classic bit, like an aging Sinatra ticking off his greatest hits.

"Bill Cosby Chuckles His Way into Old Age," read the headline over a review of a 2002 performance in San Francisco, where James Sullivan wrote that the sixty-six-year-old Cosby "rambled in that incomparable mouth-of-marbles style of his, dissecting all sorts of nothing"—the Weather Channel, a trip to the mall, falling down, and twenty minutes on removing a splinter. He described the voice, "like a crusty, half-napping old man's," and the heavy mugging—the sly disarming grins, the dumbstruck stares, the many long pauses. "At this point, it's not as though he spends any time preparing," said Sullivan. The comic's "seemingly unscripted monologue" was, said the critic, "like having a dinner date with Cosby, with no need to keep up your end of the conversation."

During the show, a small spotlight played on an empty chair where a sweatshirt was draped, on which was printed "Hello Friend," his late son Ennis's favorite phrase and the name of a Cosby family foundation. Ennis was murdered in a roadside incident in 1997, at a time when Cosby's life was also clouded by scandal, when a twenty-two-year old woman claimed to be his illegitimate daughter and demanded financial support from him. The charge was never proved, and the woman went to prison for extortion, but Cosby was forced to admit the extramarital affair.

Christon remarks: "When he's sitting in the chair, he's coasting. When he's on his feet, he's creating pictures and taking you places, like Garrison Keillor. The image of someone sitting in a chair onstage is very static. You can't be an inert image in front of people when you're live. Maybe he's tired. Maybe there's an element of self-congratulation. All he has to do is show up and people are going to love him. I've seen him onstage when he's pretty flat and he just sits there, as if people owe him something." Adds the critic: "The last time I saw him, he was just terrific. He was very sharp and reenacted the entire tableau of his daughter's graduation and it was hilarious. Most of the audience was white and they were just loving it. When he's on, he's one of the most commanding performers." Mike Nichols says, "He's remarkable for doing something that's almost impossible, which is staying funny for decades and decades—really funny. However he does it, more power to him."

It isn't easy to lift funny lines out of a Bill Cosby routine because the themes and stories are intertwined, and a part of the man, carried along by his smooth conversational flow. Cosby likes to say that he learned how to "make people laugh" (almost literally) by mastering certain technical performance devices; but, in fact, people were laughing because they enjoyed his company. He once challenged other comedians to steal his lines—"If anyone else can get laughs with my stuff, they're welcome to it." It was a safe bet. He knows all too well that, even with his lines, you have to *be* Father Goose, Bill Cosby himself, to make the audience laugh.

Girl Squawk

JOAN RIVERS

*Humor doesn't come out of the good times. It comes out of the anger,
pain, and sorrow. Always the anger.*

———————

WITH FORKED TONGUE and sharpened talons, Joan
Rivers bit and clawed her way to comic success and has
clung to it for dear life. Her climb, and her desperation
to succeed, fueled her jokes, which have grown increasingly abrasive with
every leap forward and tumble backward. She still operates with a fear-
driven ferocity, as if it could all be yanked away at any moment.

When Rivers first arrived, she was a major departure (on the surface)
from the reigning female comedian of her day, Phyllis Diller, a fashion
disaster who ran herself down for our listening pleasure. Rivers was an
attractive young woman, especially for a comedienne of the mid-sixties,
neatly turned out in black dress and pearls, blonde hair carefully coiffed.
She always looked exactly like what she was—a Jewish princess, albeit a
tarnished, failed one in her family's eyes. She was smart, clever, quick,
and likable. She had not yet set free the untamed shrew within.

Her refusal to conform to the dream of her Larchmont, New York,
family—she left home, a brief early (annulled) marriage, and a job as a
Bonds Stores fashion coordinator to work in dives—originally sparked
her aggressive comedy. The experience of learning through pain created
the Joan Rivers that audiences came to know and love, or loathe: the
manic motormouth, forever on the attack, loaded with envy and spite.

Examined more closely, Rivers is actually the well-groomed comic
granddaughter of Yiddishe mamas like Belle Barth and Pearl Williams,
female titans who roamed the Catskills and Miami Beach and who reveled in subversive humor at the expense of both men and themselves.
Rivers was their glossy, Barnard-educated descendant who ridiculed herself. When that wore out and she became a star, she turned her death ray
on others, verbally abusing women who were thinner, richer, and more
famous while serving audiences as their new bitchy role model, styled by
Oscar de la Yenta. Decades before Dr. Laura and Judge Judy, there was

Joan Rivers, offering hard-nosed counsel on how to deal with male desires by using female tricks and treats.

It was a calculated decision to shift from insightful jokes to a full-scale frontal assault on women who don't realize that it's marriage and money that matter most. Rivers was also pushed by market forces. She had come of age in the era of cutting-edge satire—had worked at Second City and was admired in the sixties and seventies for her sassy, incisive wit. But clever was not enough in the greed-is-good 1980s, when American humor grew coarser and angrier. Her career became an explosive elixir, one part clever to two parts cruel and crude. To remain au courant, Rivers turned into a comic paparazza ambushing celebrities for our fun and her profit, not so much girl talk as all-out girl-illa warfare.

Following a series of career setbacks—a failed play (*Fun City*) and a movie that she produced, wrote, and directed (*Rabbit Test*), not to mention an ugly feud with her former savior, Johnny Carson—her survivor instinct goaded her to go after bigger game than herself or mere mortals. Sniffing the wind, she ditched her pepper spray and, armed with rubber bullets, stalked celebrities—women, in particular, the more unattractive, ungainly, and trampy the better. She proceeded from "I was so fat as a kid" to "Liz Taylor is so fat that . . ." The noisier and nastier she got, the richer and more famous she became. The inept Jewish princess of Larchmont was now the brassy Queen of the Vile.

Just as Phyllis Diller formed a bridge from the fat female comics of the forties and early fifties, Rivers built her own bridge away from Diller as a sleeker, better-groomed Phyllis Diller. She was just as self-deprecating, but set new comic records in ball-busting. She was too presentable to destroy herself as persuasively as Diller, who worked hard to look gawky and goofy. So Rivers made jokes about how she *used* to look "(*I was so ugly that they sent my picture to* Ripley's Believe It or Not *and he sent it back and said, 'I don't believe it'* " . . . "*My mother used to say, 'Take candy from strangers'* "). An early sixties review in *Newsweek* noted: "Like Phyllis Diller, Joan was the butt of her own jokes, but in all other respects they are opposites. Joan is no grotesque. She is chic, blonde, and pretty, hip, intellectual, and restrained[!]"

Rivers, caught between generations, still tried to have it both ways—making crass jokes about herself while maintaining a classy façade. Was she the lady or the tiger? "Ladylike ways do not work for my audience," she says, and compares herself to a wild-animal tamer who warns, "If you come near me, I'll kill you." Eventually, the tiger got more laughs, devoured the lady, and Rivers was off and roaring, ripping everything in her path. By the nineties, she became the comic brawler she had flirted with for decades. Now, instead of a hatpin she wielded a cleaver. Yet even the comedians, writers, agents, critics, and club owners who didn't care for her act (and in some cases her), respected her tenacity, her cunning, her material, and how she had prevailed almost in spite of herself.

BROOKLYN-BORN JOAN SANDRA MOLINSKY grew up in a family that displayed an archetypal disapproval of her desire to become a comedian at a time when a female comic was on a level with showgirl, if not call girl. They uprooted her at the age of nine from the New York City borough that was a classic breeding ground for comedians and transplanted her to a more refined milieu: Larchmont.

Here, in the sedate upscale heart of Westchester County, she writes, "elegance was my mother's religion and the home her temple. Everything in her domain had to be absolutely correct. The atmosphere in the house was stiff and formal . . . etiquette was paramount." Joan even had a governess. Her hoity-toity mother and *haimish* father were locked in what Rivers called "a toxic mismatch"—a sort of Jewish translation of Jiggs and Maggie: a warm, funny, corned-beef-eating family doctor who had none of his wife's status-grubbing pretensions and whose grateful patients brought him gefilte fish, homemade jam, and cakes. Despite her battles with them, "I adored my mother, perhaps because in so many ways I am my mother." Like both parents, she has been shadowed all her life by "the fear that you will be thrown back to where you started"—in her case, a fat, multiflawed flop.

The Molinskys—Joan had an older sister, Barbara, whom she felt was prettier and smarter and who became a lawyer—indulged her whim to become an actress as a postcollege fling before settling down. But when she tried to break into stand-up comedy, they all but disowned her. Joan describes scenes that sound like something out of *The Jazz Singer,* with her European-born parents, Meyer and Beatrice, rending their clothing over their daughter's shameless ambitions to become a common clown.

Before she finally moved out, there were bitter shouting matches, threats, and slammed doors. After playing cheap clubs and even strip joints, she would skulk home to Larchmont at three in the morning, like a shiftless drunk. As with Lenny Bruce, her brief time in burlesque houses toughened both her act and her resolve. She was a nightclub-comic version of *Private Benjamin;* someone later called her "the material girl of stand-up." The teenage Joan was an obedient daughter who attended the Brooklyn Ethical Culture school, Adelphi Academy, and made Phi Beta Kappa at Barnard, graduating with honors with a B.A. in social anthropology; later she conducted a poll in nightclubs on women's issues for one of her old professors, Margaret Mead. "*I would be an anthropologist now,*" she joked, "*if I could bring my hairdresser and makeup man with me.*" She graduated in 1954, a fact that Barnard kept classified as a favor to her; but a reporter who managed to unearth the '54 yearbook found that the only unsmiling senior photo was of Joan Molinsky.

Rivers tentatively tried acting, once appearing in an off-Broadway play with Barbara (pre-Barbra) Streisand before joining the Second City. When the second-class status of women in the improv company grated on her, she left to become one-third of Jim, Jake, and Joan. After the trio failed, Rivers wrote for *Candid Camera* and for comics like Diller, Phil Foster, and Topo Gigo, the winsome Italian puppet-mouse. Around this time, the early sixties, she struck out on her own and began doing stand-up at a protected haven in Greenwich Village called the Duplex, where her fellow new faces included Woody Allen, Milt Kamen, and Dick Cavett. Inspired by Mike Nichols and Elaine May, Cavett and Rivers briefly considered becoming a team.

In a 1963 gig at the Showplace in New York (heard on a private recording), performing to what appears to be about eight people, Rivers sounds ragged but brazen and uncowed. Even then, she laughed at her own jokes and peppered her lines with "*Oh, please!*" Rivers jabbers in rapid bursts to a friendly crowd that guffaws obediently. She had already begun to master her bratty bravado, zinging rotten Times Square movies and taking a swipe at Shirley MacLaine, as if shadow-boxing for her later title bouts with Elizabeth Taylor. Like Diller and many other female comics—Lily Tomlin, Bette Midler, Sandra Bernhard—she developed a frenetic gay following who dug her bitchy infra digs.

Rivers went from that scattershot style to combing her girlhood for fat and ugly jokes, treading in Diller's footprints. "I was fat," she explained, "and you have to be *something* if you're fat. I was funny. No Miss Pom-Pom ever made it." The fat-girl gags provided her with a convenient persona, poking retro fun at her slender, stylish twenty-six-year-old self. She said she was no threat to men—or women—in the audience, declaring, "I'm the girl that women know will never steal their husband." Diller made that same claim ("I was thirty-seven and ugly—no woman was in jeopardy"), but Rivers looked like Cinderella next to her homely, klutzy comic stepsisters.

While invariably compared to Diller, Rivers lacked Diller's crucial confidence and self-esteem. "Diller is rarely in doubt, always on top," said one writer. "You never felt sorry for Diller; Rivers seemed needy." Diller took digs at her stage husband "Fang," Rivers at "Edgar" (her actual husband). In Bill Cosby's liner notes for her first album, he calls her "an intelligent girl without being a weirdo . . . a human being, not a kook." Diller, the kook, mocked upper-class pretension and values; Rivers both kidded and embodied them.

Diller, says Rivers, "was a whole different era. She was able to break through because she was a funny-looking woman. No one who thinks they're pretty ever becomes a comedienne. Everyone always thinks back to Martha Raye and Cass Daley. I liked Eve Arden; she was very chic and very smart and funny. I never wanted to be 'Brooklyn.' " A *Time* critic compared her in 1966 not to Diller but to Woody Allen and Shelley Berman—"she is an unindexed handbook on how to be neurotic about practically everything," adding, "her style and femininity make her something special." If Diller's model was Hope, Rivers's was Woody Allen; she even aped his nervous head bobbing, nudging audiences into agreement. "Woody was talking about real things, as I was," she says. "He was a writer, which I basically was. And he was doing his own material, and talking about things that affected our generation that nobody else talked about, like his psychiatrist."

The first inkling that Joan Molinsky had an innate comic gift was when she was twelve, at a family friend's big summerhouse on Montauk, Long Island. Over pot roast, she stood up and regaled dinner guests with an ad-lib soliloquy about the lives of the faculty at Adelphi Academy. As she recounts it: "The whole table was enjoying me, giggling and laughing, faces crinkling up, eyes squishy. I could see their dental work. And my father was laughing and proud of me." The latent professional comic within stirred: "I felt timing inside me," she says in her memoir. "I knew instinctively the right moment to pause, the instant to hit a line like punching a button to detonate laughter—and it was laughter *with* me, not at me." It changed her life. "I couldn't wait until I got my childhood over with so I could get into showbiz. 'C'mon, feet, grow!' "

Her earliest public success as a performer came at Adelphi, where she performed a monologue at the school's annual variety show. "I could hear the wonderful quiet that settles in when you are doing something well and seriously—total silence, cotton-soft—broken by flashes of laughter." For a moment, she felt, "I was the supreme princess, somebody dazzling, somebody else." At camp, she had stationery and pencils monogrammed with the princessy-sounding "J. Sondra Meredith," her patrician alter ego, in place of the ungainly Joan Molinsky.

One wintry morning in 1958, in a scene right out of *Stage Door,* the would-be actress went to a photo shop in Grand Central Terminal to have head shots taken of herself wearing an array of expressions. She pored over the trade papers at Howard Johnson's before making the rounds of seedy agents' offices. Between calls for off-Broadway plays, she figured she might make a few bucks as a comedian, leaving her days free to look for real theater work. Rivers thought, "Certainly cheap stand-up comedy would be easy, only a minor skill, not like *acting.*" She saw stand-up as showbiz temp work. "They were just nightclubs. Comedy to me was such a garbage profession, so if they didn't like me, it wouldn't kill me."

She checked out Hanson's drugstore, the landmark comics' luncheonette at Seventh Avenue and Fifty-first Street, and sneered at the low-rent comics eating and cackling in the booths in their white-on-white shirts with blue suede shoes, Comedy and Tragedy cuff links, and pinkie rings. "What did they have to do with theater?" she sniffed, her Westchester nose tilted upward. Rivers hung out instead with acting hopefuls like Linda Lavin and Dom DeLuise at the B&G, a coffee shop across from the Taft Hotel, and dropped by agents' offices, where she amused the secretaries with shtick in the hope of being remembered. She'd ask, "Should I give you my résumé or should I save you a step and just throw it in the wastebasket?" She crawled on all fours to drop a rose on a secretary's desk. She scribbled in their appointment books: "This is your last warning: get Molinsky a job or you'll be wearing cement booties."

In her gritty autobiography, *Enter Talking,* Rivers tells how the agents steamed uncanceled stamps off envelopes and cheated actors by skimming cream off the performer's fee before taking their legitimate cut. She heard of a helpful comic named Lou Alexander, a megastar at the Silver Slipper in Glen Cove, Long Island. Over dinner ("I was impressed that he received a free meal, with Jell-O for dessert") she noticed what a sharp dresser he was in his black mohair dinner jacket, patent leather loafers with tassels, and ruffled shirt with French cuffs and big initials over the breast pocket—the standard stand-up comic uniform of the 1950s. He said she was free to use any of his lines but shouldn't expect success like his (forty bucks a show) to happen overnight. "The end of the rainbow is beautiful," he told her, "and there should be room for a woman." Maybe two. She thought, "I was certain I could walk right in that door, because not many girls wanted to be Jerry Lewis."

Rivers assumed that stand-up would be a pushover, since Alexander had the audience howling with dreadful jokes. "If that garbage is what they think is funny," she told herself, "I'll give it to them. No problem." She set to work creating an act by watching TV and copying down jokes, then rehearsed in her bathroom, lest her parents overhear her, before going to see a prominent agent, Irvin Arthur. Arthur told her she wasn't ready and suggested she see Jack Rollins, who, as she says, "could take a grain of sand and make it into an industry" (Harry Belafonte, Nichols & May, Woody Allen). "Jack Rollins was God to nightclub comedians. His word alone could get an act a booking. He almost lived in nightclubs, looking for newcomers he could form and mold."

Rollins's suite at the Plaza Hotel, decorated with early American antique sideboards and hutches, primitive sculpture, and oil portraits of clients, was palatial compared to the ratty agents' holes she was used to. Rollins always made time to see anybody, she writes, and he greeted her in scholarly-looking half-glasses, a cigar in his mouth. "He spoke to me for five minutes and was intrigued that here was a woman comic—and of his type, preppy and un-theatrical. There were no ruffles and suede shoes on Jack Rollins's performers."

Rollins took her to a studio to hear her perform, and then said, "You shouldn't be doing other people's material. Do your own because you're naturally funny." He told her to come back when she knew who she was, comically. "You're not ready for me yet. You'll make it in three years." She was perplexed: "The only comedy I could imagine then was what I was stealing. Writing a funny joke about what I thought and felt, talking about myself onstage, was unimaginable to me."

Rivers's devoted boyfriend, a wannabe actor named Nick Clemente, got her an audience with an agent named Harry Brent, a Broadway Danny Rose type who lived in a tiny apartment with a hot plate and toaster on the bureau; his big client was the Catskill comic Dick Capri. Brent, who also booked himself as an accordionist at weddings and bar mitzvahs ("Just to keep my hand in"), offered Rivers some Fig Newtons and Ritz crackers as he nibbled from a bowl of sunflower seeds and proudly showed off a framed bounced check from Dean Martin.

She performed her act while he blew cigar smoke, and he agreed to take her on, saying, "I'll do it because I think there's a place for a girl comic, but it's going to be a lot of work. You have gowns?" He said she needed gowns, and a new name: "People remember names. A guy named Jackie—right away, you know he's funny, cute. A girl named Jackie, you gotta laugh." Brent promised to coach her, so each day after her typing job, Joan would turn up at his apartment to work on her act—mainly jokes cribbed from Robert Orben's *The Emcee's Handbook* and *The Working Comedian's Gag File*. She jotted down favorite lines in old Barnard blue-books; during breaks, Brent told stories about his close ties to "Joey" and "Sammy." A few of her feeble early jokes, with built-in rim shots: "*Tonight I am brought to you by the product all America is talking about—Brand X. . . . I don't have to be up here. I've had other job offers, but I'd have to sell hats. . . . On my first job, I made eighty dollars. I sold my car to the bandleader.*"

Looking back, it's amazing that Rivers ever made it beyond Brent's apartment. But he taught her the fundamentals—how to segue from bit to bit, how to wrap up with a song like "I'm Just Wild About Harry," and what sort of "gowns" she would need. Holding up her black prom dress and green bridesmaid dress, he said, frowning, "There's no pizzazz here. Gotta pick up the light onstage. Get sequins, maybe feathers." Brent also helped her to baldly steal a Shelley Berman routine about a hung-over dinner guest.

"I thought a lot of his ideas were idiotic, but I did not want to hurt his feelings," she writes. "And Harry Brent, no matter how ridiculous, was a professional." More important than his advice, he believed in her. When he renamed her "Pepper January," she said fine but once outside she told her boyfriend, "I'm going to commit suicide." She took the name in the scant hope it would get her work, which it did. Her guiding principle then was anything for a laugh, and it still is. "All my career I have been a snob who sold out a thousand times," she confesses.

Brent got "Pepper January" her first paying job, as an emcee at a Boston strip club called the Show Bar that paid $125 a week for two shows a night. She had no idea how to emcee, but Harry gave her a crash course. She took a room in a scary hotel across the street with hookers, bums, musicians, pimps, and strippers; the room smelled of peanuts. The Show Bar was equally shabby, with a stage at the far end of a lunch counter. The dressing room, which she shared with three naked women in the show (one of whom sprayed herself with gold paint before going on), reeked of stale perfume, sweat, talcum powder, and deodorant, with an iron pipe for a clothes rack; a bare bulb dangled from the ceiling.

Rivers relates how she "hung up my big-skirted June Allyson Jewish Princess dresses" and returned to her room to dine on crackers from a vending machine while she watched TV until it was time to go on. In a moment out of *Gypsy,* she recalls a stripper named Dyna Mite asking her, "Honey, are you sure you're in the right place?" Hoping to sound like a pro, Rivers asked the girl painting her flesh gold (named Aurora Borealis), "What are the lights like onstage?" "You got two choices," Aurora said, "on and off." Rivers was later surprised to learn that one of the strippers had attended Connecticut College for Women, where she had also gone for a time.

After being announced (*"Boston's world-famous Show Bar, the bar that shows it all, presents, direct from New York City, the one and only Pepper January—comedy with spice!"*), Rivers saw, among the expectant faces staring up at her, a rich guy from Yale she had dated. Immediately, flop sweat set in as her opening jokes were met with silence, followed by cries of "Get the fuck off! Bring on the girls!" and "Take it off!" She quickly introduced Dyna Mite to the grinding chords of "Night Train" and ran offstage.

Rivers, however, was undaunted. She thought, "I can turn them around, I know I can." She went with her best bit—the purloined hangover routine—which was received with cries of "Let's see the broads! Beat it!" She feared they might pull her off the stage physically and decided to heed their advice, scurrying back to her dressing room. The strippers told her she might do better if she took a few clothes off or maybe peeled a banana.

Pepper January was fired before the eleven o'clock show and wound up sobbing in her crummy hotel room, asking herself, "What am I doing? I'm ruining my life! What am I doing talking to men with their hands in their pockets? If I can't even cut it at this level, maybe I *am* a loser." But, like Diller, she was determined to make people laugh: "You must want it so badly you will suffer anything, *anything,* just to get on a stage in front of people—be willing, again and again, to pick yourself up and keep going after you have been hit on the head by a sledgehammer." She once said all comics are crazy and that comedy is "a medium for revenge." For Rivers, comedy became a blunt instrument to batter old foes, rivals, and, when necessary, audiences into submission.

She vowed never to admit defeat to her parents, who presumed their daughter's shameful affair with comedy was over now and that the deluded girl would return to her senses. Rivers had a minor epiphany the next morning in her fleabag Boston hotel: watching TV while waiting for her boyfriend to pick her up, she was reinspired by the revue comedian Charlotte Rae, who did a routine on TV about her eating compulsion. Rivers reached for a blank telegram form and began jotting down bits of Rae's funny confessions. "In the midst of my anguish," she recalled, "I was responding to the true voice of a woman speaking to women, but I was too dumb and naïve to realize this was the answer for me."

Comics never forget; they also internalize every failure, slight, and humiliation. "After years of being pampered," Rivers admits in her memoir, "I am [still] angry because of the Show Bar. Whenever I ask for an extra bottle of champagne or a new bar of soap in my dressing room, what I really want is the respect that comes with it. I am punishing Caesars Palace for the indignities I suffered getting started—for the nights I had to get dressed in filthy toilets, for all the disgusting dressing rooms. . . ." She cites a clause in Totie Fields's contract that called for twelve cups of coffee in her dressing room—because twenty-five years earlier Fields couldn't get even one cup of coffee.

Rivers now joined the ranks of the comedian drifters at Hanson's, haunting agents' cubicles hustling jobs. "The comics I met in those offices were, like me, on the bottom of the cage." To be an actor required specific gifts, but "to be a comic, you needed nothing. You could be a derelict and be a comic, and that was my level—all of us sad sacks together, aspiring to be admired and famous like the Bob Hopes and Milton Berles— and stealing their jokes for our sorry little acts." She explains now, "I didn't trust my own material. I didn't know what else to do. If it was on TV I took it. You find out very quickly [stolen jokes] don't work for you."

Just in time, Rivers met a comic soul mate, Treva Silverman, who wanted to be Elaine May and later wrote for *The Mary Tyler Moore Show*. The women worked on comedy routines together, calling each other up with lines and ideas. "At last I had a person in my life who understood what it was like for me to be a female in the fifties." May was their comic role model—"an assertive woman with a marvelous, fast mind and, at the same time, pretty and feminine. We did not know any other women like that." Silverman helped Rivers find her comic direction. "The brilliant, schizophrenic insanity," the record producer Ben Bagley said, "came from her work with Treva." Rivers still stole lines but also did clever sketch material and witty songs written by members of her new circle, revue ditties like "I'm in Love with Mr. Clean." Part of her still yearned to be an authentic actress, but when she was turned down for *Our Town* because of her age (twenty-six), she figured comedy had a better future—no age limits. Stand-up is harsh, but it doesn't demand ingenues.

She had staked her claim in stand-up comedy, but her new agent, Tony Rivers, decided she needed a brand-new name. "I can't send you out as Joan Molinsky" (Brent had retained ownership of "Pepper January," sure that it would pay off one day). So she took Rivers's own name, which somehow made it easier to perform when she played Brooklyn joints like the Club Safari, Bill's Place, the Monkey Club, and the Swiss Terrace. "'Joan Rivers' was like a party dress I put on." At a dive in Springfield, Massachusetts, Rivers was fired after the second show and, when she cited an AGVA (performers' union) rule that she was entitled to full payment, the stage manager said, "Ask AGVA can you work with two broken legs?" She won the case, but Harry Brent dropped her, perhaps fearing for his own creaky legs. At Bill's Place, Rivers was encouraged to push drinks between shows and cash in her swizzle sticks for dimes. People babbled away during her act; drunken couples jumped up to jitterbug. Finally the boss shouted over the PA system, "Get her off! Get her off!" The indignities kept piling up.

During an audition for a snazzy Manhattan room, One Fifth Avenue, the manager ate lunch and gabbed on the phone, but he let her perform at a Monday amateur night, where at last people finally laughed in all the right places. Rivers recalled: "I experienced the intoxication of playing a roomful of people like an instrument, of sensing that every person was riveted, was catching every nuance, quiet when they should have been quiet. I felt myself opening and expanding, every fear dropping away. I felt able to be silly, fool around, cross my eyes, and get a second laugh, which let me invent and go even further—and they followed me to that new level—and I was free and soaring. It was everything I thought comedy was going to be and should be."

On the strength of that momentous night, her father got her booked at his New Rochelle beach club, but she shamed the family by bombing before guests who whispered during the show and left early to beat the traffic. Afterward, her father called her a tramp and told her to abandon her career or leave home. She left the house, slowly, expecting them to run after her, but nobody did. That night, she checked into the YWCA in New York City at one A.M., written off by her family for associating with (as her father wrote her) "low-lifes—a despicable bunch of failures, ne'er-do-wells, parasites, procurers, mistresses, fairies, and possible dope peddlers! The crowd you are consorting with cannot bring you anything but evil results. It's disgusting what you're doing with your life. Come to your senses!" In a caring father's P.S., he added that she could come home anytime. She stayed instead at women's residences and dined on Orange Juliuses, sandwiches at Chock Full o'Nuts, and $1.49 Tad's steaks. She told a wealthy suitor that if he gave her $10,000 he could have half her income for life. When he only laughed, she thought: Love me, love my talent, and shed him.

With Nichols & May hotter than ever, Rivers decided to turn her boyfriend, Nick, into half of a comedy team, but one night in Atlantic City was enough; it ended with Nick slugging the club owner when he demanded that Rivers "work blue" or not get paid. In despair, Rivers threatened her family that she was going to become a hooker, which she considered for about an hour during the darkest day of her young life. Her family, alerted by Nick that she was about to hit the streets, captured her. The posse included two aunts who forced her to come with them or be committed to Bellevue. Broke and broken, she drove back to Larchmont the next day.

In December 1959, Rivers found a glimmer of her stage identity—just a "fetus," she said, but recognizable as a living comic being. She was accepted into a showcase run by Actors Equity for new performers, *Talent '60,* which earned her her first review in a New York newspaper—well, anyway, four words: "Joan Rivers was appealing."

After again retailing secondhand goods to Irvin Arthur, he said, "You should write material yourself, you're a funny girl." Rivers observes, "It did not occur to any of us then that you could say something in conversation and then use it onstage," adding, "I never heard my private sense of humor echoed on any stage." Arthur liked her enough to hire her as a secretary, as a result of which she became pals with the comic Milt Kamen, who became her mentor. Kamen told her to get quieter instead of louder when she began losing an audience—and to dredge the humor out of herself. "Milt was the first one to take me seriously as a comedian." He advised her to avoid following in the steps of Mort Sahl—in Kamen's view just a collection of jokes. (Rivers had a severe crush on Sahl then; backstage at the Second City, she practiced signing her name "Joan Sahl.")

She devised a routine that, she said, "tapped into who I was—a sassy, unmarried girl trying to get married." It was called "The Diary of Joan Rivers," a sixties Jewish version of *Bridget Jones's Diary,* about a desperate unmarried girl. The routine was a smash when she performed it for her first core audience—five hundred gays on Fire Island, who, she writes, were "smart, realistic, literate, and up-to-date, with a taste for camp and the outrageous" and who shared her bitchy attitude: "Gay audiences have been the most loving, the most generous, the most forgiving, the most loyal, and they would keep me alive in show business until I could go it alone."

Rivers's tiny successes coincided with the opening of a host of small Greenwich Village clubs, all of them in need of new cheap talent—places like the Phase 2 on Bleecker Street, whose owner recalled Rivers as "a clumsy, clumpy girl who hadn't made it as an actress and probably wouldn't make it as a comic either." He took a chance, but one critic wrote, "There are two main things amiss with Miss Rivers's approach: her material is tired and her delivery frenetic." She was still waggling her head and wore a pained expression. He noted that audiences wanted to help her as she recited the comic melodrama of her life, adding that "her frantic and strained efforts are only nerve-racking and do not disguise, but rather point up, the material's essential aridity." Some people might still agree with him.

Don Gregory met Rivers when he was producing revues at Phase 2. "I didn't like her act," says Gregory. "She didn't do 'Can we talk?' then and all that stuff. She was always a little pugnacious, and that doesn't engender much rapport with an audience, or laughs. It wasn't until she became a yenta that she caught on. Sure, she clawed her way up, but they all clawed their way up and did it with a lot more grace and style. I've been around performers all my life, but she goes beyond anyone else." He recalls, "I fired her in the kitchen and she hit me in the stomach. In her book, she said I was stealing money. When I confronted her about her made-up version, she said, 'Yeah, but it's a better story that way.' She's grotesque."

The columnist Murry Frymer, then an editor at *Newsday* and a fledgling comedy writer, met Rivers in 1964 at Phase 2: "I found her very obnoxious. She had that yenta edge, but she was talented in her way. She copied all of Woody Allen's mannerisms. After each joke, she'd go, 'Yeah-yeah-yeah.' I was very unimpressed but all the writers were kowtowing to her; that's what pissed me off. She wanted fast one-liners and paid three dollars for them. The writers were like panhandlers!" She asked Frymer to hold her shoes while she changed.

A booker with Jack Paar's *Tonight* show saw her and liked what he saw.

Paar would play the bewildered foil to in-house female zanies Dodie Goodman, Genevieve, and Peggy Cass, and Rivers saw herself as the perfect female cutup for his harem of eccentrics. She was ecstatic. Her long-delayed big break at long last, a chance to legitimize herself with her disbelieving family, who were big Paar fans. The booker, Bob Shanks, told her, "Just be yourself—everyone's on your side—just talk to Jack. It's going to be fine."

Rivers recounts: "I walked onto the show like gang-busters—Miss Fun! Here we go!" She discussed her mother's anxiety about getting her married off, her life as a temp, and her boyfriend whose father was in the Mafia. It was meant to be a conversation, but it was all shtick, some of it very funny. She told a joke about a Mafia school where the math lesson is, "*If Johnny has ten fingers and they cut off two, how many does he have left?*" and a bit that went, "*You've never seen a gay Italian because anytime they turn gay, they make them into nuns. That's why so many nuns have mustaches.*" Paar sat there, she said, "with wide-eyed fake innocence," and then squelched her by asking, "Do you realize Italian people are watching this show?"

Everyone else, she says, liked her—the booker, the studio audience, the producer. Paar ignored her in the elevator afterward and crossed her name off his return-guest list. "Never again," he said. As Rivers recalled it for me: "I was too strong for him. Also, I told things on that show you just didn't talk about in those days—about being an office temporary and stealing stamps and selling them at half price. And I was a college girl, and Westchester girls didn't say they slept with married men." The real problem was that Rivers didn't play the lovable ditz for Paar; she was too fast, too brassy—too Joan Riversy. The experience set her back years, not just psychologically but comically. For a while she lost faith in finding humor within her own experiences, and in show business itself.

Howard Storm met Rivers when they were young comics at the Duplex; he later appeared in her play *Fun City,* and directed such sitcoms as *Rhoda, Mork and Mindy, Lavern and Shirley,* and *Newhart.* He recalls: "She's always just been a very ambitious person, and it made me very uncomfortable to be around her. People who are extremely ambitious have problems. When you want it so bad that you'll do anything, you gotta wind up hurting yourself. It's like it's out of control. Childish needs. She struggled but, hey, we all struggled." When Storm told her Rollins was going to represent him, "she actually cried. So I talked Jack into taking her on and he later did, but he couldn't stand her." Asked for his view of Rivers, Rollins pauses a long time before saying, "I can't tell you unless you let me go off the record." On the record, he would only remark, "I was hoping it would happen for her, but, I mean, the screaming . . . who needs it?" He managed Rivers, screaming and all, for two years.

She worked hard to invent original material but was constantly depressed (*"I'm so depressed I just called the suicide prevention center and they put me on hold"*; *"People say money is not the key to happiness, but I've always figured if you have enough money you can get a key made"*). She considered actual suicide for a day and swallowed a bottle of baby aspirin with a box of Oreos. Even her suicide attempt flopped. Facing rejection everywhere, she grew used to the pain ("My old friend misery was a warm, consoling coat").

Rivers got a tryout at the Bon Soir, which, happily, was filled with gays and showbiz types. Even when her week's booking was extended to three weeks, her family remained skeptical; and when Jack Rollins came to see her again he predicted that she would be big in three *more* years. "I was only trying to be a funny girl—anything for a laugh, if it fit the character or not," she writes. "There was no focus, no theme. There was no core to me, nothing that made me all the same girl. The minute there was no laugh, there was no me—and the audience knew it instantly." Yet she had moved up a few notches and could sit at the Stage Deli as a near equal with Milt Kamen and Orson Bean, dissecting jokes.

In 1961 Rivers tried out for Second City, where they needed a replacement for Barbara Harris. After a five-hour wait, she says, director Paul Sills and producer Bernard Sahlins called her in. Asked to improvise something, Rivers was unaccountably befuddled, unprepared to improvise for an improvisational company. "Don't you have a script?" she asked, naïvely. "We don't work with scripts," Sills said, but asked her to improvise the scene in the room, which triggered a furious tirade:

"In this room there is a cheap ugly little man sitting behind the telephone without the manners to get off and watch somebody who has been waiting five hours." She blasted their arrogance, insensitivity, and disrespect, recounting, "I was insane now, screaming, 'I don't care about you. Don't care about your goddamned show. You can go to hell and William Morris can go to hell!' "—at which point she chucked a glass ashtray across the room. Sahlins told her to calm down and tell them about herself. In what sounds like a showbiz fairy tale, Rivers says they asked her to join the company (apparently drawn to her emotional outburst, however unfunny), gave her a ticket to Chicago, and told her to report the following Tuesday. She arrived there with fifty dollars, a five-month contract, and an Equity card. "Something is wrong," she thought. "They should be rejecting me." As she once said, "The paradox of my life is that I can be very pushy, but at the same time, I am truly timid."

She was shunted into the role of secondary female. Nobody in the company, she says, talked to her, heightening her fears and loneliness. "I was not their typical Second City girl—compliant, very pretty, uninterested in being funny." She found the group ingrown and wary of outsiders, especially of female New Yorkers with no improv pedigree, but things clicked into place when she played a hooker. She told a john who asked her to disrobe, "*I don't know what kind of women you deal with. I always stay dressed when I hook my rugs. Now, what do you want? A six-by-ten? We're having a special on throw rugs.*" She began to swing during the improv scenes—"I was astonished, electrified, relieved. . . . So *this* was improvising, and it was *inside* me." Rivers became friendly with one of Second City's resident geniuses, Anthony Holland, and they deftly began playing off each other. She learned to trust what came out of her mouth, because it often got a laugh. On off nights, feeling intellectually inferior, she read the classics to keep up with the company's University of Chicago–trained actors and audiences.

As Rivers told Jeffrey Sweet in his oral history of Second City: "I was never truly happy at Second City but it made my whole career. By working with these people, I learned self-reliance and that I didn't have to talk down in my humor. I could make a living making bright people laugh. You [talked about] Tennessee Williams or Chekhov and they understood it." Her stand-up affinity for talking to audiences grew out of bantering with actors onstage. She noted later, "I was really born as a comedian at Second City. I owe it my career. Finally in Chicago I came to believe, totally—for the first time in my life—that my private sense of humor . . . was applauded by audiences who truly thought I was funny."

But it was dog-eat-dog offstage. Her Second City cohorts looked down on her nervy hunger for laughs, regarded as a cardinal sin by the group's core disciples. They disdained overt jokes, searching instead for comedy that emerged from life. Rivers readily confesses to her star-crazed obsessions: "I was obscenely pushy. I wanted to be a star and 'J. Sondra Meredith' at twenty-eight was not a team player. That is what drive is. Thank God I *am* driven. Being driven is my energy source. It is my fun. I have always liked a good fight . . . especially if you have right on your side." She's conceded that she "lived in an Italian opera" and said, "If my life ever becomes steady and even, I will go crazy with boredom. I am addicted to drama." A major grudge holder, she once created a TV movie, *The Girl Most Likely to . . .* , a *Carrie*-like story in which a girl rejected by everyone has her face redone after a car accident and proceeds to methodically slaughter all her enemies.

The First City didn't care how funny she might have been in Chicago, where people were calling her the next Elaine May. New York agents and managers considered it "an out-of-town credit and therefore meaningless. They acted as though I had been on a long vacation"—a sort of USO tour of the Midwest. Nor was the New York branch of Second City interested; her reputation as a "troublemaker" had preceded her.

She now began to work more free-form, letting her jokes arrive impromptu, taping shows and refining them later, a lifelong habit. Jan Murray, the veteran comedian, recalls, "She'd be in her room all day writing jokes. No social life, nothing. You never saw anyone so dedicated, who worked harder, so she deserved it. She was a professional, you gotta hand it to her. Even when she was making it, she was smart enough to play clubs for seventy people and work out her material."

WHEN RIVERS CAUGHT Lenny Bruce for the first time at the Village Vanguard, a light went on for her. Like most comics then, she genuflected to Bruce's insights and guts—"The father of us all," she called him. (Years later she would cowrite and star in a one-woman show about Bruce's mother, *Sally Marr . . . and Her Escorts*.) Recalling Bruce now, she says: "He was an epiphany. Lenny told the truth. It was a total affirmation for me that I was on the right track long before anyone said it to me." Bruce supplied "the revelation that personal truth can be the foundation of comedy, that outrageousness can be cleansing and healthy. It went off inside me like an enormous flash. That night I realized the importance of getting down to basics: what are we really talking about? He also was hysterically funny, with total control of his audience. The children were lining up to be fed. I was seeing Jesus."

Once the scales fell from her eyes, Rivers dropped her modish sketches and began digging into her soul for more basic material. She built a ten-minute routine from her own life. "I had found the key," she exalted. "My comedy could flow from that poor, vulnerable schlepp Joan Molinsky. At last I had been hurt enough, upset enough, to expose her onstage—and in my act from that night on, the pain kept spilling and spilling and spilling." Ridiculing herself "wasn't necessary to survive as a comic—it was necessary to survive as a person. All comedy goes back to, 'I'll do the joke before you so you can't hurt me.' That's still my cover. The insecurities are still there. If I verbalize them and get everybody to laugh, then it's okay. My audiences are group therapy."

When finally she was accepted into the New York branch of Second City, she refined her new authentic self and unveiled it twice nightly after each Second City show. The genesis was "Rita," an anxious, lonely, unmarried girl in an old model-and-tailor Second City sketch that fit her snugly, and which unfolded into the Joan Rivers that her fans liked when they first heard her—smart, sharp, and vulnerable, in lines like, "*The way my mother sees things, she has two daughters that aren't, as the expression goes, moving. She is so desperate to get me married, that if a murderer called, she'd say, 'So he has a temper.' When a boy does come to the house, to impress him she leaves a Bible open on the coffee table and writes 'How true!' in the margin.*"

Instead of performing in snappy little East Side satirical revues, Rivers spent her nights downtown working for free in dark pub rooms. In time, the smarty little uptown satirical revues went into decline, replaced by solo satirical acts setting up shop on dinky Village stages. "We young comics were being liberated to go our own way, to develop our own very personal comedy," she noted. Like folksingers, comics were writing and delivering their own stuff—raw and unpolished, but authentic. While the Larchmont princess felt out of place among the ragamuffin Village crowd—she had no interest in free love, gay love, starving, and funky outfits—her jokes were more at home there: "*A friend of mine was taking the pill and was in great trouble because they said, 'Take one a day,' and didn't tell her where to put it. Every night she put it in her ear, and the next thing she knew she was eight months gone.*" She ended her act, "*If you like me and know any agents, please remember that my name is Joan Rivers and I put out.*"

She was only moderately successful at the Bitter End, but its owner, Fred Weintraub, liked her and kept her on. He recalls: "She was too brash for the audience and went over the top sometimes. It was never the material. Audiences resisted *her*." When she asked him to manage her, he said, "No way. I'll manage you as a writer but not as a performer. I don't see you ever making it as a single." Art D'Lugoff, who ran the Village Gate, was similarly unamused. "I didn't like her approach of putting down people for being fat or having a big nose or because of their haircut. She got furious with me. She has a talent, she's done well, there's an audience for what she does, but she's not my cup of tea."

Rivers had her reasons for being so brash. As she explained to me: "I *had* to be to get the audience's attention. I wasn't that gorgeous—there was no gasp at my beauty when I came onstage—nor was I wild-looking. I was this girl standing there in her little black dress. I still come on and take command—'You pay attention to me. I'm talking to you!' " Asked how she might describe herself to a Martian, she replies, "A mouthy woman who takes the hypocrisy of current society and sets it straight."

When Rivers got booked for her first full week's run at the Duplex, she sent fifty postcards to everyone from her past. Almost nobody came to see her. One night, with only five people sitting in the back, agent Roy Silver showed up. Silver, the new manager of the white-hot Bill Cosby, remembers: "A card came into my office that said, 'Hi, I'm Joan Rivers and I'm appearing at the Duplex.' So I said to Jack Rollins, 'Who is this girl?' He hated her—everyone did. I said I'm gonna take a chance, one of my gambles."

Silver goes on: "There were three acts on the bill—Joan Rivers, Joanne Worley, some other girl. I was the only one there, me and three gay guys, and Joan went right into the toilet. Ooh, God, heavy. She was crying afterward, and I said, 'Do the same act again the next show, I want to see how you function under tough circumstances,' and she said, 'I can't. I've done it.' Right into the toilet again for the second show. When she got through, I said, 'Okay, I will manage you, under one condition— you must listen to me. I will meet you every night at the Bitter End at six o'clock, and if I say to you, 'This is out,' it's out. I will say to you, 'This works, this doesn't work.' And I started to edit. . . . I saw her fail in a lot of appearances, but I knew she was bright."

Silver was told by bookers that Rivers was damaged goods after her failure on the Paar show. Even so, he worked with her, watching her every night in the manner of his mentor, Jack Rollins, advising her what to cut and what to enhance—such as a routine about her mythical hairdresser, Mr. Phyllis. Rivers kept finding saviors, each more blessed than the last. "Roy was the element I had lacked," she believed, "the outside ear, the editor, able to give my nonsense a real shape, the hard polish of a pro. For the first time in my life, I was physically, systematically, constructing a stand-up comedy act, instead of machine-gunning jokes. Roy's instincts were right. He kept saying, 'Take it away from the *Partisan Review* crowd.' He cut out every piece of esoterica, a lot of the homosexual references, a lot of the ethnic references. Now I was looking for universals."

The Duplex crowd ate her up, but she still felt in need of a foil, a partner to play off, and finally realized that she could make the audience her partner—interacting with women at tables as invisible "straight men," bouncing setup lines off them like, "*Are you married? Single? I'm the last single girl in Larchmont. My mother's desperate. She has a sign up, 'Last Girl Before Turnpike.'* " Eugene Boe, a nightclub critic for *Cue,* gave Rivers her first rave review: "Joan 'Second City' Rivers, in the late show at the Duplex, is a very funny femme in search of an act. Her monologue contains some of the sharpest, smartest talk to proceed out of the mouth of a babe since Elaine May. Female comics are usually horrors who de-sex themselves for a laugh. But Miss R. remains visibly—and unalterably—a girl throughout her scream-of-consciousness script." Twenty-five people rushed to see her, including Jack Lemmon, who fell asleep.

Jan Wallman, a blonde, buxom, no-nonsense woman whom Rivers describes as "looking like a clipper ship under full sail," managed the Duplex in Greenwich Village between 1959 and 1962, and again from '65 to '68. Downstairs was a gay bar, upstairs was a tiny room called Upstairs at the Duplex. The room was unchic and unnoticed, attracted few critics, yet drew enough savvy regulars to test untried talent like Rivers, Allen, Cavett, and Lily Tomlin. Rivers called the club "a special cocoon" that was a second home to emerging talents. It was an insider's club for new comics and singers unready for prime time, or even prime rooms. Only adventurous agents, raw comics, and Villagers knew about the Duplex. Rivers recalls the club with great fondness, and even more so the woman who ran it: "[Jan] defended us, told drunks to be quiet when we performed, booked us even when the audiences hated us, and on Thanksgiving invited us all to Thanksgiving dinner at her apartment."

Wallman had liked her right away. "She had the fastest mind in the business and the most dedication," says the former impresaria. "Joan developed the most [of any new comic]. I never knew anyone in my life, in any field, who worked harder than Joan did. Driven! She was so quick. She started as a singer-comedienne and I made her stop doing that; I took the piano player away from her. She always wanted to sing. She still can't sing. I told her to stick to stand-up. She would bounce ideas off me; we were very close friends. At that point, she was still feminine and girlish— softer. It wasn't until later that she got that tough, coarser side. It sold."

Several other comics at the Duplex were trying to break through then—Bill Cosby, David Brenner, Rodney Dangerfield. Joanne Beretta, a singer, said, "You knew they had to make it, because if they didn't they'd kill themselves. You could smell the desperation in the air." Dangerfield was even more driven than Rivers. "Compared to Rodney, I was Little

Mary Sunshine," she says, laughing. "His jealousy festered right on the surface. He constantly knocked Dick Cavett and sneered at all the 'intellectual comics.' " Dangerfield said she needed a hook, like his million-dollar catchphrase "*I don't get no respect,*" and eventually she found her own perfect phrase—"*Can we talk?*" It was a reflexive line she transformed into a hook that defined her, served as an excuse to unburden herself and to establish an instant rapport with audiences, and gave her an identity that critics and headline writers could bounce off of.

Still, she couldn't find the missing link—a major agent. When a William Morris agent came to the Duplex to see Rivers, he wound up signing a singer on the bill, Linda Lavin. Silver pestered *The Tonight Show* again but was told to go away. Seven years in the business and Rivers was still doing temp work, driving her dilapidated car, wearing a dress from her Second City days, and living at home again. She landed a writing job on a Phyllis Diller TV show while working nights at the Duplex. When she again invited Irvin Arthur, he ducked out quickly, but Rivers stopped him at the door to ask what he thought. "What can I tell you?" he said. "You're too old [she was thirty]. Everybody's seen you. If you were going to make it, you'd have done it by now." But he was kind enough to add that he'd told the same thing to Peter, Paul & Mary.

The never-say-die Silver tried to con a booker at *The Tonight Show,* Shelley Schultz, who had rejected Rivers several times, telling Schultz, "Never mind Joan Rivers. I've got another girl. Her name is Joan Molinsky. You'll love her." He sold her as another Selma Diamond, the razor-voiced comedy writer and a Carson favorite. When Shultz saw it was just Joan Rivers again, he angrily left them in the waiting room. Months later, however, a call came from Carson's people offering her the "death slot," the last ten minutes of the show, reserved for writers; someone had dropped out and Schultz was desperate—Rivers called it "a mercy booking." On February 17, 1965, the defeated Rivers went in, set to fail again, and listened in the green room as Johnny Carson introduced her as a comedy writer—"She's funny. Let's bring her on. . . ."

This time she wasn't nervous, and she felt relieved seated on the couch alongside her old chum Milt Kamen. She played off Kamen, who laughed; and then, more important, Carson laughed, cuing the audience that it was okay to like her. "This was the new Joan Rivers," she later wrote. She told Johnny about the night her car failed and she got out, clutching her wig under one arm, and began walking for help in the rain as the hairpiece fell on the highway and was nearly run over by a car—an actual incident that put her over. "I went on automatic. Those years were paying off—the night after night after night of working to drunks, to Catskill audiences, to guys with their hats in their laps, to cheaters— those layers and layers of knowledge and experience, an accumulated sixth sense, was carrying me through. I had learned to listen to the audi- ence and feel its vibrations, learned not to be hesitant. I had the timing right and did not rush and could wait for the laugh I knew would come— and I knew, too, that if it did not come, I would not be destroyed."

Carson was with her all the way. Sarah Blacher Cohen observes, "She was very much aware of the contrast between her Jewish acerbic self and the genial, gentile Johnny Carson." Recalled Rivers in her memoir: "He was there from the first second. He understood everything. He wanted it to work. He knew how to go with me and feed me and knew how to wait. He never cut off a punch line, and when it came, he broke up. It was like talking to your father—and your father is laughing, this warm face laughing, and you know he is going to laugh at the next one. And he did and he did and he did. . . . Carson did not know that it was 'too late.' I had not been a nuisance to him. He just noticed I was funny. At the end of the show, he was wiping his eyes. He said, right on the air, 'God, you're funny. You're going to be a star.' "

Watching the taped show at home later with her family was a let- down. Nobody called afterward—"The girl on the screen making Amer- ica laugh seemed utterly remote from me," she writes. Her mother conceded, "If it did go well tonight and it means something, you've done it all on your own"; her father instantly countered, "What are you talking about? We've always encouraged her." The next day, Silver told her his phone had been ringing all morning "with offers you won't believe." Rivers felt vindicated, if not yet famous, as everyone suddenly boasted how they had known all along that she would make it. "My father had known it all along. Irvin Arthur had known it. Jack Rollins—'Hey, it's just a matter of time.' Well, the time had arrived—without him. It was all over. Thirty-one years of people saying 'No.' And suddenly it was all over. Ten minutes on television and it was all over."

AFTER THAT hallowed network moment, everything finally fell into place for Rivers, who got over any remaining self-confidence problems and gradually began ratcheting up the level of jokes so that, by the early seventies, she sounded like a hard-boiled Erma Bombeck: "*Face it, my dar-*

lings, it isn't easy being a woman. No man's ever made love to you because you cleaned the linoleum. . . . Any woman who does anything but take care of herself is a fool. . . . Why change the sheets? Tell him they come three colors—white, gray, and black. . . . I got a waterbed—my husband stocked it with trout. . . . If God had meant us to cook, he would have given us aluminum hands." Anne Beatts remarked that when earlier women comics like Jean Carroll and Phyllis Diller said they were lousy housekeepers, people laughed, but when Rivers said it, "we believed her."

Along with her success came critical attention, some of it unwanted, from the women's movement, for which she became a lightning rod. Sandra Archer wrote of her in 1972, when Rivers was headlining in Las Vegas, "She dresses like a lady but tells 'men's' jokes." Archer felt that Rivers was a throwback to an earlier, prefeminist, period, noting: "The rage Joan Rivers has runs through her jokes and every movement of her body. She is a very bitter woman who uses her humor to disguise that bitterness. Every woman in the audience listens to her and says, 'Is she ever right!' Joan Rivers is talking about the Big Secret . . . that romance dies with the diaper . . . that bitter knowledge that life fell short for us."

Lawrence Christon comments: "Her whole act is predicated on the politics of envy. She's a very good Jewish version of getting down and dirty. You know, get the ring before you do anything and a trick pelvis will get it every time. She's great at dishing—what upper-middle-class women say when they get together. She really does tell the truth about being avaricious, though some people think that's a Jewish stereotype."

Ronald L. Smith is more generous: "I don't think people give her her due for all the things she did accomplish in comedy. Her comedy first turned inward and then outward. Then she had the problem that a lot of comedians have—they want the audience to love them so much that the audience dictates what they want from the comic. And what they were saying was, 'Be more vicious—attack! Attack! Go overboard!' And then as soon as she goes overboard, they say, 'Oh, you went overboard!' When a comic is giving you some truths, you don't turn around and bite him for it. Didn't they learn anything from Lenny Bruce?"

Her initial acceptance as a bright new spokeswoman was tempered later by the shrill tone of her act. An hour exhausted you. One critic, writing in 1976, called her "a male chauvinist pigette," and said: "Rivers perpetuates stereotypes. She has not fundamentally changed since she was here in 1965." Rivers found herself trapped in a comic time warp—a quasi feminist with old-fashioned comic values, outspoken on topics that younger women professed not to care about anymore. She sounded closer to her mother's generation, had turned decidedly conservative, and wound up a Nancy Reagan crony hawking costume jewelry on QVC. Gucci, Hermès, and Cartier were her constant companions. She was a streamlined Sophie Tucker, who used to sing, "When Am I Getting the Mink, Mr. Fink?" For Rivers, women's lib was a license to do rougher material. "Comedy should always be on the brink of disaster," she argues.

Rivers insists that turning more ruthless was not a cold-blooded career move. "It wasn't a conscious decision," she told me. "Nobody makes a conscious decision as an artist. These things evolve, and, thank God, you change. I'm much more biting now. I don't take shit from anybody now. I expect truth in my life—other than that, *nothing*. I'm less tolerant of the audience not recognizing the hypocrisy of things. The only good thing that comes with age: I'm going to tell it to you as I truly think it is because what are you gonna do to me? Fire me? I've *been* fired. Knock me down? I've *been* knocked down. That changes what you say. I'm very tough onstage and I take no prisoners. I just slam people up against the wall and I say: Look at it *really* and understand what's going on here!"

Christon liked Rivers until her act turned rank. "At the beginning, she was fresh and then after a while, when you play up a certain approach, you get locked into it. The great comedians have a broad range, they have a view of humanity and they touch on some deep level of humanity. She's not universal in that way. And then once again, the sexual politics overtook her, when it wasn't fashionable anymore." It got tougher for her to please the critics and the show-business hierarchy, but her devotees whoop like naughty, revved-up Chippendale's audiences. A few examples of how far she would go for a laugh should suffice: to a woman in the audience, she said, "*If he wants the ring back, you swallow the stone. No man will go through shit for a diamond. I got that from Nancy Reagan.*" To another woman: "*So what size Tampax do you wear? Before deciding whether to wash pantyhose, you sniff the crotch, right? I always do.*" Rivers insists that she's only attacked for being too dirty because she's female. "People don't want to hear it from a woman," she has often said, but will lap it up from a Richard Pryor or a George Carlin.

Even if her vigilante attitude repelled as many people as it attracted, she insists: "You have to be abrasive to be a current comic. These are tasteless times, all restraints are gone. And I've ridden right on that crest. All great comedy is tasteless. That's the whole point. You take something and go the other road with it"—even the low road. Rivers, who called herself a "Ramboette," cheerfully owns up to her aggressiveness—"Nothing has come to me. I have to be aggressive." She once said her only taboos were religion and deformed babies, since updated: "That was then. The only thing I wouldn't do is hurt anyone—ever, ever. I'll know what the line is and nobody can tell me what it is. It's a little harder to shock, because we're so desensitized, but there are still secret compartments in our lives."

Rivers quotes Buddy Hackett, who said, "If it's funny, it's not dirty," and she remains "a major fan" of Howard Stern. "Howard is beyond brilliant. He's so truthful." She dismisses her critics like flies: "All we're here for is to amuse. Over and out. You paid your money, you chose to see me, I want to give you a good evening. I want you to walk out saying, 'God, wasn't that fun!' I don't give a damn how I got there." She targets specific markets, but tries to please everyone. "The older ladies think I'm going to do housework jokes, so I always throw them in. They pay—they deserve six housework jokes."

The critics have stayed on her case. Laurie Stone, writing in the *Village Voice* in 1988, found the most talked-about female comedian in America to be, at root, hypocritical: "Her work hasn't developed. Her mode is attack, and without some larger context, this kind of comedy devolves to bullying, dyspepsia. . . . Inside Joan is a tangle of confusion about self-worth, work, and males that eventually takes over her show. Women are always bitches and sluts. The only proper use of brains is scheming to marry. Joan might seem to be satirizing feminism, but [she] means these words. Her message is that relentless, that resistant to her own experience. She calls herself ugly, refusing to see that, through diets, trips to the surgeon, and haute couture, she looks glamorous. She lies about the meaning of work, which, right before our eyes, is saving her life. She's like a woman who has orgasms and *says* she fakes them."

Although she told *People* in 1983 that she felt she was sexy ("Women never see me as a threat, but men find me attractive"), Rivers sulked in a *Playboy* interview that "men have taken my self-esteem and flushed it away. I have very low self-esteem, because the press refuses to allow me to have it. . . . No man, except for my husband, has ever said anything nice about me, backed me up, or come to my rescue. Not one man has ever told me I'm beautiful—in my entire life. Not even Edgar. They've said other things—'You're perky' or 'You're fun' or 'You're good in bed.' I think that's what's made me the aggressive wreck I am today."

Rivers arrived at the tail end of the stand-up comedy renaissance, in the mid-sixties, and what seemed witty, daring, and outspoken in 1965 was archaic ten years later. When her jokes about finding a rich man and staying thin, gorgeous, and sexy after marriage collided with the liberated comedy of Lily Tomlin, Roseanne Barr, and Sandra Bernhard, her routine sounded like excerpts from the *Total Woman* handbook. Her jokes by then had shifted to her *wifely* inadequacies: "*Yesterday, I started to give my husband, who is English and very conservative, a hug and a kiss and he said, 'Not here, not here,' and I started to cry because we were in bed*"; "*I have no sex appeal. If my husband didn't toss and turn, we'd never have had the kid.*"

When merely being funny and famous wasn't enough for Rivers, she turned comic assassin, a sort of female Don Rickles, except that, unlike Rickles, she issues no mushy apology once the evening's ritual slaughter is ended. Rivers went from good-naturedly wicked, like Rickles, to sav age. She stopped delivering jokes and began inflicting them. That old conspiratorial twinkle was gone, replaced by a spiteful glint. Always frantic, she's turned almost manic, mowing down everyone in her path. When she filled in for Johnny Carson, viewers tuned in to the show as they now do to Jerry Springer's show—to see the carnage. Those who wondered how far she might go saw that she was going all the way, a comic stripper who skips the tease and takes it all off. She had turned into, yes, Pepper January: *comedy with spice.* Make it cyanide.

Rivers views herself as a "spy infiltrator"—someone who sneaks inside the covert female psyche and brings back all the dirty little secrets. But those early eighties albums now sound fatally dated, stuck in that "get-the-ring-first" groove that underscores her abrasiveness. She used women in the audience to set up jokes and then scored off them in a voice that wasn't just grating but hoarse, semihysterical, at times even contemptuous and mean (she spies a woman's ring and cries, "*A piece of shit and four prongs!*"). Sometimes it descends to junior high girls' room jokes ("*Is Christina Onassis the ugliest woman in the world? Arf! Arf!*" . . . "*Madonna's living proof that one size fits all. Her legs are named Seven and Eleven because they never close*").

Rivers wasn't influenced by earlier women comics, she says. "There *were* no women to copy or not copy, so I could say anything I wanted. I was having an affair with a married professor at the time, and I talked about it, and that was my first good routine. Truth! Truth! I was the first one who brought her life onstage and talked about it. I was the first woman to talk about orgasms on the stage, the first to talk about my gynecologist on the air . . . subjects women had never spoken about before." As for other female comics, Rivers envied only one: "I'd love to be Carol Burnett—she had that great voice and she was a throwback. She got to do all the fun sketches, and then stand there and sing a sad song, a great Fanny Brice moment. I think she's had *the* most wonderful career and had *the* most fun."

She claims little knowledge of Elayne Boosler, her successor to the title of groundbreaking female comic. Rivers said that female comics seldom came to see her. "They don't think that what I'm talking about is pertinent to their lives today. And it isn't. It's pertinent to *my* life." Despite Diller and Rivers, nothing much has changed in the stand-up war between the sexes. Says Boosler: "Now it's, 'Take the bitch—please!' " It's still a no-win situation for women comics. If they desexualize themselves, as the comic Abby Stein said, "we systematically destroy everything that made us funny to begin with." Carol Siskin's take on the self-deprecation issue: "It's called self-deprecating only when women do it."

Like Diller, Rivers considers herself to be outside, even beyond feminism, bristling at any mention of women's lib: "My life is liberated. Leave me alone! I have no time to join a movement, because I *am* the movement." Also like Diller, she enjoys having it both ways, as a sort of libertarian feminista. "I always tell feminists that my life is a feminist life—just turn around, you idiots. What do you want from me?" She maintains that there's no such thing as women's humor—"I have fights about this all the time. If something is funny, it's funny" ("*I sort of half-believed in women's lib. I went to a bra burning and burned one cup*"). Rivers still firmly believes that women remain sex objects. "Any woman who's intelligent knows it's true. People used to say to me, 'You don't have a [contemporary] woman's point of view,' and I'd say, 'I don't need one—I'm a woman.' "

It's risky to suggest to Rivers that perhaps the world has moved beyond the sex wars she still fiercely wages. "Nonsense!" she cries. "Here we go—don't start that nonsense. That's such bullshit. All animals have a biological thing going and a genetic thing going and we are there to find a man and impregnate ourselves and continue the species. Do . . . not . . . trust . . . women. We all try to help each other as much as we can, but I'm sick and tired of helping you because you're a woman. I'm helping you because you're smart—that's it. Next."

Coming to her defense in 1983, James Wolcott wrote: "Rivers was dismissed as a masochistic throwback to the uptight '50s . . . often lumped with Phyllis Diller as that dying species of comedienne whose consciousness was too retro to allow her to thrive in the looser, hipper, feminism-awakened '70s. But, curious thing, the careers of many of those hot new items have since tapered off into irrelevance, and where is Joan Rivers?—aloft, in full, fizzy flight. If Joan Rivers's career proves anything, it's that it is better to be unfettered than hip."

Once Rivers quit making fun of herself, her husband, and fictitious people (Mr. Phyllis and Heidi Abramowitz, a tramp who is the Jewish American anti-Princess and perhaps Rivers's secret sleazy alter ego— "*She had more hands up her dress than the Muppets*"), she began attacking the rich and famous: Bo Derek ("*She studies for her Pap test. . . . She lost at cha-rades to Ray Charles*"), Margaret Thatcher ("*Who picks Margaret Thatcher's clothes—Helen Keller?*"), Jackie Kennedy ("*She looks like E.T without makeup*"), Leona Helmsley ("*She made her money in exact-change ambu-lances*"). She joked about Rod Stewart's acne ("*You can play connect-the-dots on his face*"), Barry Manilow's nose ("*If he were on hard drugs, he could inhale Peru*"), and stomped all over the British royal family. You almost wound up feeling sorry for her victims.

Her ascent neatly coincided with the rise of America's celebrity fetishism. "Maybe I started it," she suggests. "We're a very gossipy cul-ture. All we want to know now is private lives." Going after celebrities turned her career around. "I think it made a difference in people noticing me, but I always did it. The Elizabeth Taylor fat jokes turned the corner for me." To some, attacking celebrities was shooting goldfish in a bowl. Mort Sahl once said, "It's a given that entertainers are fatuous."

Rivers maintains that she has survived in show business "joke by joke." She catalogues and cross-indexes some fifty thousand jokes filed on three-by-five cards in twelve drawers. Herb Sargent remembers when she was a guest host on *Saturday Night Live:* "She came in with a stack of cards and said, 'Which ones would you like?' and pulled them out of her file."

Many of her original fans felt that she had lowered her aim and her standards to make a bigger racket and also to make the cash register ring louder. When John Stossel on *20/20* asked her if she ever worried about hurting people's feelings, she looked wounded, as if only Joan Rivers were off-limits. Rivers made a pragmatic choice that getting filthy was where the spotlight was, at a time—the wild and woolly seventies—when being called "outrageous" and "controversial" was a media benedic-tion. When she took to punctuating jokes with cries of "*Grow up!*"

and "*Oh, stop!*" (as Jay Leno does now, to slough off crude lines), they were really preemptive strikes that shout: "Admit it, you're just as bad/dirty/tasteless as I am."

Christon despaired of Rivers when she moved from her Fat-and-Ugly to her Purple Period, writing in his *Los Angeles Times* "Comedy Corner" column: "Joan Rivers has co-opted the healthy anarchy of comedy into an aggressively personalized tastelessness. She has never forgotten what it feels like to harbor a loser's spite. She represents the women who don't think they can make it on their own, a gold digger's Voltaire. There's an underlying cynicism that verges on the grotesque. Famous people aren't people to her; they're consumer items. She shreds and discards them without savor, and with a unique cruelty. But who we laugh at says as much about us as it does about her. Joan Rivers slams at human defense-lessness and helplessness. She turns laughter into sneers." He cited her comment, "If Adolf Hitler came back with seven good minutes, he'd be working today," as an indication of "the moral vacuum she's working in."

Unlike Diller, who was happy catering to older traditional audiences, she worried that she might soon be a dinosaur. In 1983 she boasted, like an outlaw striding into town, "Right now, I'm the meanest bitch in America." To cling to her hard-won title, she began doing catty fashion commentary with her daughter, Melissa, for the E! cable channel.

Rivers has by now pretty much divided the public into those who swore by her and those who swore off her. She needed to talk but not everyone wanted to listen. "Will Joan Rivers Please Shut Up?" read a headline above a 1980s review by Peter Stack, who called her "a one-woman beauty parlor of slutty talk" and wrote that she now dressed "like a San Fernando Valley shopping mall floozy in spike heels and a wrap-around split-leg gold gown." She finally had the "gown" that Lou Alexander once envisioned for her. Stack listed her topics—"proctology, gynecology, disposable douches, flatulence, vomit, toilet bowls"—and concluded, "The crowd wanted trash and she gave it to them." "Everything trashy is good for me," she says. "The *National Enquirer* is my bible. That's the kind of stuff people want to hear about."

Rivers promises, "If it hurts anybody, I take it right out. I'm not out to hurt. My career has not been built on these people; my career has been built on me." She truly doesn't think that she's mean-spirited. "When I hear that from people," she once said, "I stare at them, because I don't know what they're talking about." At the end of her act, she used to half joke, "If I've offended one person, or made one person cry, or upset someone . . . well, tough." Her standard defense is, "It's *all* in fun," and adds that she never goes after anyone who can't answer back—namely, celebs.

Of her most famous clay pigeon, Rivers said, "Elizabeth Taylor is a very close friend of Roddy McDowall's. I said to Roddy, 'Does it upset her?' And he asked Elizabeth, who said, 'She doesn't get me where it hurts' "—not exactly a ringing endorsement. "If she had said, 'I wish she wouldn't,' the jokes would have come out. Out!" So the jokes continued about Taylor's thighs going condo, of her "walk-in belly button," of mosquitoes landing on her with cries of "Buffet!" and of Liz standing before a microwave yelling, "Hurry!" Mean or not, her Taylor lines are undeniably clever and funny (*"I take Liz to McDonald's to watch her eat and make the numbers change"*). When Rivers was attacked for making jokes about Karen Carpenter's fatal anorexia (*"I don't feel that sorry for anybody who is so thin she can be buried in pleats"*), her response was to turn on the audience for not buying Carpenter's records—and besides, pleaded the comic, she herself is a former bulemic.

She took pride in renewing her act every six months, or at least rotating celebrities, adding twenty new lines a week by trying out material in small clubs en route to *The Tonight Show* or Las Vegas, where she insisted on remaining an opening act even after she became a star. Her purse is always crammed with scraps of paper with jokes and ideas scrawled on them. At The Horn in Santa Monica, where she used to break in new material, former owner Jules Hock remembers Rivers behaving as if she had been in show business a week: "Joan was one of the most enormously insecure people I've ever met. I once said to her, 'It's such a grueling schedule every day, why do you do this?' and she said, 'I never take any of this for granted.' " She quotes Jack Benny, who told her, "No matter how big you are, you have to get to the stage through the kitchen." She still talks like a comedian on the way up, or on probation. She says, "It's all quicksand. If I stop working, I'll be gone in a week."

Once she peaked, Rivers was always armed in battle-ready regalia, claiming that "all the powers that be were waiting for me to fail" when she was chosen as Johnny Carson's regular fill-in host in 1983. "It was a risk because I was a woman, because I was urban, because I was East Coast, and because I was Jewish. Everything you don't want in a talk-show host. And I said I'm going to make this work." And she did, infusing the show with a sort of the-cat's-away wildness. As James Wolcott put it: "Her karate style of attack chops away a lot of the flimsy showbiz clutter that Carson has come to tolerate. When Joan Rivers pinch-hits for Johnny . . . it's party time." It all went beautifully until she left to start her own talk show on the Fox network—after seeing a list, she said, of ten possible replacements for the departing Carson, none of whom was her. Carson loyalists and soreheads somehow read her move as an act of betrayal, but it was merely Rivers's survival instinct kicking in.

She argues that Fox wanted her because her ratings were higher and her demographics younger than Carson's, facts that she said his staff hid from him. She had once called Carson her Moses ("He parted the seas and took me home") and pledged to put her hand in the fire for him. In the end, she didn't inherit the Carson throne, one strongly suspects, not because she was a woman, urban, East Coast, or Jewish, but because she was Joan Rivers, whose slash-and-burn style was the very thing that made her a perfect reliever for the cool, reliable starting pitcher, Johnny Carson.

Because of the Carson feud, her husband's suicide, and her well-chronicled battles to make good, Rivers became a soap-opera heroine to her fans. She was even the subject of a TV movie, *Tears and Laughter: The Joan and Melissa Rivers Story,* with mother and daughter playing themselves as plucky survivors in a heartless world. She still says, "There's never been any love for me at any network. It's a cold, hard business. I've always been a person of the people. Nobody likes you—but you fill up ten-thousand-seat auditoriums."

Rivers has always battled what she calls "the show business establishment," which she accuses of confusing her Calamity Jane stage image with the true, refined Joan Rivers. Hollywood especially has shied away from her. Over a long career, the slights and grievances have piled up. In her memoir, she notes that *Interview* magazine once gave a party to mark an edition featuring a Rivers cover story and failed to invite her. "Socially, I am an outsider." Like Jackie Mason, another bruised infighter who likes to show his battle scars, she now says, "The only time the critics were nice to me was when the Fox series folded and I was dead."

Many people blamed her abrasive offstage reputation on her husband's hardball managerial tactics (Jules Hock says, "Joan had a lot of problems, but mostly her problems were Edgar"), but she told the writer Nancy Collins in 1983: "People think he's the son of a bitch, but I'm the one who says, 'You tell them to go to hell.' Edgar just makes the calls. He's much nicer than I am—charming, well-read, very sweet." They met when he hired her in 1968 to rewrite a Peter Sellers script and were married four days later. Roy Silver hadn't then managed her long—"ten minutes," he says. But a crucial ten minutes. "What happened was," as he recalls it, "Joan went down to Bermuda with Edgar Rosenberg and fell in love and dumped me. It was Edgar's idea, but I knew she had no loyalty." Rosenberg killed himself in 1987, in part depressed over the cancellation of his wife's talk show, which he produced. Rivers credits him with making her a star. "My husband pushed me to headline. He kept saying, 'You're ready, you're ready.' "

Don Gregory's take: "Edgar was prodded by his wife; then he also became tough. He had to justify his existence—one of those husbands who make a living off their wives and become tigers." Jan Wallman is more generous: "Edgar had a big influence on her career and he was very good to her. She was a very emotionally needy person and she needed that support. They had a very strong and good marriage and she loved him very much. The press was very unfair to him."

RIVERS, NOW SIXTY-NINE, is still haunted by her lean years—and by what may lie ahead. She can't forget seeing an aging Danny Kaye singing to sixty old-timers. One of her idols is Mae West, another comedian who went on too long; Rivers went to West's funeral in 1980 and lamented afterward that "there wasn't a star to be seen." As she approached sixty, Rivers, like Diller, went public with her facelifts and made them part of her act since there was no hiding the fact, her eyes tugged so taut that she looks Eurasian. She wrote a book on the wages of aging, commenting, "You become invisible as a woman at a certain age."

Yet Rivers still attracts men of all ages: she was reported in late 2001 to be dating an investment banker about thirty years her junior, after breaking up with an octogenerian Lehman Brothers heir. Ralph Schoenstein, who has worked with her on some of her humor books, testifies to Rivers the nurturer: "She's very empathetic about family things. She was always giving my wife jewelry. She was very generous. She has no airs. She doesn't stand on ceremony. The woman has absolutely no pretense. She'll tell you everything immediately. Joan isn't cool—she's completely open. It's all grist. It's her old thing—'Can we talk?' "

Rivers, he goes on, works all the time. "She's a whirlwind, very focused. The jewelry show is taped in Westchester, then she'll play Atlantic City and then fly to London to play there." The ads for her now read, "Rare stand-up comedy appearance!" Since 1997 she's done a nightly two-hour talk show on WOR in New York. Reports one listener, "She is as feisty and right-wing as ever. She is also still insulting, in the Bob Grant [the archconservative radio host] mode. She sounds like Grant's sister act. This bitter little cookie from Westchester is still hustling." Last fall, she and Melissa began a column in *The Star* tabloid. Schoenstein, who helped Rivers write *Bouncing Back,* her saga of rebirth, says, "She's got guts. After the *Tonight Show* thing and after she lost her own show, she couldn't work in a bowling alley in Newark. And then her husband committed suicide. Look at the heights she was on. She got blackballed. I like her message, which is to stay in the arena and do things, not go to Florida and check out." He says that Rivers volunteers for God's Love We Deliver, helping to deliver meals to AIDS sufferers on Christmas and whenever asked.

Rivers sounds, if hardly mellowed, semicontent with her life, snubs and all. Looking back, she wouldn't alter her approach: "Nothing! I was what I was, I couldn't change it, so I did the best with what I had." Her only stated regrets are career might-have-beens: "I always say, 'Maybe I *should've* taken that sitcom, because so many people become so enormously wealthy out of that. I remember getting the script and saying, 'Never.' I put the kibosh to it. It was terrible. [She had her prime-time shot in a 1968–69 variety series, *That Show with Joan Rivers,* which ran eighteen months.] I always went with things I loved to do rather than with perhaps the right move. I should've taken the Oprah spot. I was offered that by ABC, and I thought, 'How boring—I can't do it.' I couldn't have done eighteen years of interviewing victims. I'm the only one *against* the victim culture—that's a big part of my act." Yet she sees herself as a show-business victim unappreciated in certain industry circles. "I still have trouble getting agents. Nobody can pigeonhole me: 'She acts but she can't direct'; 'She directs but she can't write. . . .' Nobody gets it. I'm a slut—I'll do anything!" She laughs her husky laugh. "I'm the lowest girl in the whorehouse."

In the twilight of her career, Rivers still feels herself a newcomer, an outsider: "I'm never called to do a movie. I'm never called to do a situation comedy. I am not called—ever. Nobody ever thinks of me. So therefore you do everything a little bit harder. Nothing is by chance." Her Upper East Side duplex once reflected her philosophy as stand-up's Ayn Rand, strewn with pillows embroidered with Rivers precepts—"It's Just as Lonely at the Top, Only You Eat Better"; "It Is Better to Be Nouveau

Riche than Never Riche at All"; "Vacations Are for Amateurs"; and "Don't Expect Praise Without Envy Unless You're Dead."

Rivers says that, for all her success, she isn't an icon: "I think I broke a lot of taboos, and I'm continuing to do so, but I was never revered. Never. I am never honored anywhere, but meanwhile I keep chugging along. I never held myself up as the mother of us all. Don't put me in the shadows and make me the grand old lady. Screw you! I'm funnier than you still and I'm going to get out there and get the job you're trying for. If there's that job in Vegas, I want it, too."

She believes that her onstage character is still evolving. "I'm starting to get funnier. I'm more physical on E!; I do really stupid things I'd never have done ten years ago. I'm different now than I was four years ago. I still don't think I've got it. But I love the person I am onstage." The onstage Joan is someone she trots out for the paying customers, displaying her sparkling wit like those faux baubles in "The Joan Rivers Classics Collection" peddled on QVC, where she also hawks skin creams.

In 1987 she told me she hadn't changed at all: "No, I'm as shallow as ever! Your style changes. There's early and late Georgia O'Keeffe and early and late Joan Rivers. When I did my TV show, the critics said I was *too* nice." And if she has changed, so what? "We're all so many things. Why can't you be in a man's world and wear a Victoria's Secret nightgown?"

Nancy Collins, who has interviewed Rivers several times, once wrote about her "near schizophrenic split between the public and the private person," confirming the comic's claim that her onstage persona is just "a character." Although this notion is at odds with the theme of Rivers's autobiography—that she was a comic nobody until she put "the real" Joan Rivers onstage—Collins states that "the Joan Rivers you see in private is quiet, thoughtful, and soft-spoken." And the comic concurs: "In real life, I just get very quiet." Joan Rivers once said that she would never invite her onstage self to dinner, but she's recently changed her mind—a little. "Maybe to cocktails," she says now, "but not dinner."

Acknowledgments

FOR COMING TO MY AID at various bumps and potholes in the road, not to mention downright dead ends and crashes, I am grateful for the help of friends and for the kindness of many strangers. Sincere thanks go to Morris Bobrow for his feedback on interview tapes and general thoughts about comedy and comics and titles; to Abby Wasserman, for providing letters of Woody Allen to her brother John L. Wasserman; to the late Steve Allen (and to his helpful son Bill), for providing unpublished manuscripts of chapters on several comedians, and for photos and other editorial aid; to Sedge Thomson, for supplying his on-air interviews with Steve Allen and Mort Sahl; to Ronnie Schell, for his contacts in the comedy community and for inviting me to a meeting of Yarmy's Army comics and writers; to Lawrence Christon, for various leads, perceptions, and encouragement; to Robert Weide, for supplying videos of his documentaries on Mort Sahl and Lenny Bruce, and for his incisive comments on and rare photos of same; to *Playboy* librarian Mark Duran, for digging up old *Playboy* interviews with comics from issues unavailable elsewhere, and to *Playboy*'s photo researcher, Liz Georgiou; to Associated Press photo researcher Martha Schmidt; to critic and friend Ron Miller, for his insights into the TV careers of various comics; to Max Schmid, for providing links to Jean Shepherd's friends, and to Jim Clavin, for his thoughts and leads on Shepherd; to Bob Sarlatte, the only comedian I actually know personally, for his canny and funny inside-comedy views; to *San Francisco Chronicle* librarians Johnny Miller, for knocking some sense into a recalcitrant microfiche machine, and Judy Canter, for locating old photos, and to *Chronicle* photo editor Gary Fong; to Pat Akre at the San Francisco Public Library; to Ron Reisterer, *Oakland Tribune* photo editor, and to the *Tribune*'s Frosene Phillips, for lending a hand; to Mary McGeachy, for her publicity advice; to Brenda Besdansky, for her recollections of Catskill life and comedians; to Ben Fong-Torres, for books and *Rolling Stone* articles; to Warren

Debenham, for loaning records and rare volumes from his vast collection of albums and books on all things comical; to Grover Sales, for supplying Lenny Bruce CDs and insights; to Lillian Gregory, for help in locating her globe-trotting husband, Dick, and to Gregory's manager, Rusty Michael, for getting me to him; to Murray Horwitz, for coming up with crucial telephone numbers and for his comedy savvy; to Richard Grant, for arranging an interview with Joan Rivers; to Christopher Porterfield, for leading me to Dick Cavett; to Marshall Jacobs, for his wry recollections and tapes; to Matt Cullison, for providing transcripts connected with the Second City's fortieth anniversary celebration; to Jane Klain and her efficient interns at the Museum of Television and Radio, Alix Sternberg and Kelly Buttermore; also to MTR's Alan Glover; to James Gavin, for sending rare videos of *Playboy After Dark* shows and other clips; to the singer Wesla Whitfield, for her little-known cassette-dubbing skills; to Lainie Kazan, for offering memories and phone numbers; to David Freeman, for plugging me into Paul Mazursky, and to his wife, Judy Gingold, a helpful sounding board for titles; to Ben Thum, for his ideas about Jewish comedians and for smuggling me into the New York Friars Club, and to Mel Bernstein for taking me to lunch there; to Michael Krasny, for his jokes and insights on Woody Allen, Mel Brooks, and other Jewish comics; to Suzanne Chase, for providing an entrée to her neighbor, Shecky Greene; to Pauline Tajchman, for her unswerving technical and moral support, for listening to endless progress reports, and for her thoughts on specific comics; to Leah Garchik, for helping to cut the Woody Allen chapter down to size; to Pantheon managing editor Altie Karper, for cheerfully shepherding the manuscript along; to Ed Cohen, whose demon copyediting kept me from hanging myself many times; to painstaking production editor Ellen Feldman; to Bonnie Schiff-Glenn and Margaux Wexberg at Knopf, and to publicist Pamela Mullin, for enduring nagging questions; to designer Archie Ferguson, for devising such a lively cover; and to Randy Poe, friend and comic soul mate, for providing inspired insights and intuition, for lending his sharp stylistic and journalistic eye, for wielding a keen knife on the more long-winded passages, and for his love of the subject—but mostly for his wisdom and wisecracks.

Finally and foremost, a low bow to my editor, Robert Gottlieb, for recognizing a vague idea as a viable book, for providing his sensible perspective and perceptions, and for his patience in helping to shape an unwieldy manuscript into a manageable book. Bob's pencil laser-surgery was almost painless. Some editors you tolerate; a rare few, like Bob, you learn from. His edits saved me from various excesses, often leading me through a thicket of tangled verbiage to a clearing. Whenever I would wince at a cut, sixteen pages later it would become clear exactly why he had made it. All in all, he made the last lap of this four-year trek a walk in the park.

Bibliography

Adams, Edie, and Robert Windler. *Sing a Pretty Song.* William Morrow & Co., 1990.

Adams, Joey, and Henry Tobias. *The Borscht Belt.* Bentley Publishing Co., 1966.

Allen, Steve. *Mark It and Strike It.* Holt, Rinehart and Winston, 1960.

—————. *Bigger Than a Breadbox.* Doubleday, 1967.

—————. *Funny People.* Stein & Day, 1981.

—————. *More Funny People.* Stein & Day, 1982.

—————. *Hi-Ho, Steverino!* Barricade Books, 1992.

—————. *Make 'Em Laugh.* Prometheus Books, 1993.

Allen, Steve, with Jane Wollman. *How to Be Funny.* Prometheus Books, 1993.

Asher, Don. *Honeycomb.* California Living Books, 1979.

—————. *Notes from a Battered Grand.* Harcourt Brace Jovanovich, 1992.

Baxter, John. *Woody Allen: A Biography.* Carroll & Graf, 1999.

Berger, Phil. *The Last Laugh.* William Morrow & Co., 1975.

Bjorkman, Stig. *Woody Allen on Woody Allen.* Grove Press, 1993.

Bogle, Donald. *Prime Time Blues.* Farrar, Straus & Giroux, 2001.

Bowen, Ezra. *This Fabulous Century: Shadow of the Atom (1950–1960).* Time-Life Books, 1991.

Bruce, Lenny. *How to Talk Dirty and Influence People.* Playboy Press, 1972.

Caesar, Sid, with Bill Davidson. *Where Have I Been?* Crown Publishers, 1982.

Cavett, Dick, and Christopher Porterfield. *Cavett.* Harcourt Brace Jovanovich, 1974.

Claro, Christopher, and Julie Klam. *Comedy Central: The Essential Guide to Comedy.* Boulevard Books, 1997.

Cohen, John, ed. *The Essential Lenny Bruce.* Ballantine Books, 1967.

Cohen, Sarah Blacher. *Jewish Wry.* Indiana University Press, 1987.

Coleman, Janet. *The Compass.* University of Chicago Press, 1990.

Collier, Denise, and Kathleen Beckett. *Spare Ribs*. St. Martin's Press, 1980.

Collins, Ronald K. L., and David M. Skover. *The Trials of Lenny Bruce*. Sourcebooks, 2002.

Feiffer, Jules. *Sick Sick Sick*. Signet, 1963.

Franklin, Joe. *Joe Franklin's Encyclopedia of Comedians*. Citadel Press, 1979.

Freberg, Stan. *It Only Hurts When I Laugh*. Times Books, 1988.

Fromer, Myrna Katz, and Harvey Fromer. *It Happened in the Catskills*. Harcourt Brace Jovanovich, 1991.

Galanoy, Terry. *Tonight!* Doubleday, 1972.

Gavin, James. *Intimate Nights*. Limelight Editions, 1991.

Gelbart, Larry. *Laughing Matters*. Random House, 1998.

Gilliatt, Penelope. *To Wit*. Scribner's, 1990.

Goldman, Albert, with Lawrence Schiller. *Ladies and Gentlemen—Lenny Bruce!!* Penguin Books, 1974.

Guthrie, Lee. *Woody Allen*. Drake Publishers, 1978.

Halberstam, David. *The Fifties*. Villard Books, 1993.

Hendra, Tony. *Going Too Far*. Doubleday, 1987.

Hirsch, Foster. *Love, Sex, Death and the Meaning of Life: The Films of Woody Allen*. Limelight Editions, 1990.

Holtzman, William. *Seesaw: A Dual Biography of Anne Bancroft and Mel Brooks*. Doubleday, 1979.

Horowitz, Susan. *Queens of Comedy*. Gordon and Breach, 1997.

King, Alan, with Chris Chase. *Name-Dropping*. Scribner's, 1996.

Krassner, Paul. *Confessions of a Raving, Unconfined Nut*. Simon & Schuster, 1993.

————. *Impolite Interviews*. Seven Stories, 1999.

Lahr, John. *Astonish Me*. Viking Press, 1973.

————. *Show and Tell*. Overlook, 2000.

Landesman, Jay. *Rebel Without Applause*. The Permanent Press, 1987.

Lax, Eric. *Woody Allen*. Vintage Books, 1991.

Lehrer, Tom. *Too Many Songs by Tom Lehrer*. Pantheon Books, 1981.

Leonard, Sheldon. *And the Show Goes On*. Limelight Editions, 1995.

Martin, Linda, and Kerry Seagrave. *Women in Comedy*. Citadel Press, 1979.

McCrohan, Donna. *The Second City*. Pedigree Books, 1986.

Meade, Marion. *The Unruly Life of Woody Allen: A Biography*. Scribner's, 2000.

Miller, Douglas T., and Marion Nowak. *The Fifties: The Way We Really Were*. Doubleday, 1977.

Morton, Robert, ed. *Stand-Up: Comedians on Television*. Harry M. Abrams, 1996.

Museum of Television and Radio. *The Vision of Ernie Kovacs*. 1986.

Novak, William, and Moshe Waldoks. *The Big Book of Jewish Humor*. Harper & Row, 1981.

Patinkin, Sheldon. *The Second City*. Sourcebooks, 2000.

Reed, Rex. *Do You Sleep in the Nude?* New American Library, 1968.

Rico, Diana. *Kovacsland*. Harcourt Brace Jovanovich, 1990.

Rivers, Joan, with Richard Meryman. *Enter Talking*. Delacorte Press, 1986.

Sahl, Mort. *Heartland*. Harcourt Brace Jovanovich, 1976.

Schaap, Dick. *Flashing Before My Eyes*. Morrow, 2001.

Sennett, Ted. *Your Show of Shows*. Collier Books, 1977.

Sherman, Allan. *A Gift of Laughter*. Atheneum, 1965.

Shore, Sammy. *The Warm-Up*. Morrow, 1984.

Silverman, Stephen M. *Funny Ladies*. Harry M. Abrams, 1999.

Simon, Neil. *Rewrites*. Simon & Schuster, 1996.

Smith, Ronald Lande. *The Stars of Stand-Up Comedy*. Garland Publishing, 1986.

———. *Cosby*. Prometheus Books, 1997.

Sorensen, Jeff. *Bob Newhart*. St. Martin's Press, 1988.

Stark, Steven D. *Glued to the Set*. The Free Press, 1997.

Sweet, Jeffrey. *Something Wonderful Right Away*. Avon Books, 1978.

Terkel, Studs. *The Spectator*. The New Press, 1999.

Tobias, Henry. *Music in My Heart*. Hippocrene Books, 1987.

Wasserman, Abby, ed. *Praise, Vilification, and Sexual Innuendo, or How to Be a Critic: The Selected Writings of John L. Wasserman (1964–1979)*. Chronicle Books, 1993.

Watkins, Mel. *On the Real Side*. Simon & Schuster, 1994.

Weaver, Pat. *The Best Seat in the House*. Knopf, 1994.

Wilde, Larry. *The Great Comedians Talk About Comedy*. Citadel Press, 1968.

Yacowar, Maurice. *Method in Madness: The Comic Art of Mel Brooks*. St. Martin's Press, 1981.

Young, Jordan. *The Laugh-Crafters*. Past Times, 1999.

Interviews

Edie Adams (10/8/99, in San Francisco); Steve Allen (6/2/99, in Van Nuys, California); Woody Allen (8/16/99, in New York City); George Andros (11/8/99, in San Francisco); Don Asher (4/22/99, in San Francisco); Enrico Banducci (5/28/99, in San Francisco); Bruce Bellingham (8/14/00, by telephone); Shelley Berman (5/1/99, in Bell Canyon, California); Brenda Besdansky (11/17/99, in San Francisco); Peter Bonerz (12/9/99, in Hollywood, California); Ray Bradbury (1/3/02, by telephone); Peter Breinig (5/25/01, in Sausalito, California); David Brenner (11/23/99, by telephone); Joy Carlin (11/30/99, in Berkeley, California); Jack Carter (12/14/99, in Bel Air, California); Dick Cavett (9/23/99, in New York City); Lawrence Christon (1/28/00 and 4/7/00, by telephone); Ron Clark (12/13/99, in Venice, California); Janet Coleman (11/29/00, by telephone); Irwin Corey (9/24/99, in New York City); Bill Dana (1/5/00, by telephone); Ossie Davis (3/14/00, by telephone); Ron Della Chiesa (2/23/01, by telephone); Phyllis Diller (6/2/99, in Los Angeles); Art D'Lugoff (9/17/99, in New York City); Eddie Duran (2/21/00, in San Francisco); Stanley Eichelbaum (7/13/99, in San Francisco); Bob Elliott (12/10/01, by telephone); Mimi Farina (8/3/99, by telephone); Jules Feiffer (5/8/00, in New York City); Ron Fimrite (5/3/99, in San Francisco); June Foray (8/27/01, by telephone); Stan Freberg (6/4/99, in Los Angeles); Budd Friedman (8/23/99, in Los Angeles); Murry Frymer (7/9/99, by telephone); Gary Gates (9/23/99, by telephone); Hal Gefsky (8/25/99, in Beverly Hills); Larry Gelbart (1/11/00, by telephone); Herbert Gold (5/10/99, in San Francisco); Paul Goldenberg (9/24/99, in New York City); Sydney Goldstein (8/10/99, in San Francisco); Garry Goodrow (9/21/99, in New York City); Blake Green (9/24/99, in New York City); Lenny Green (3/28/00, by telephone); Shecky Greene (12/14/99, in Los Angeles); Dick Gregory (6/20/00, in Culver City, California); Don Gregory (9/7/99, by telephone); Alvin Guthertz (4/26/99, in San Francisco);

Patrick Hallinan (1/25/02, by telephone); Larry Hankin (12/8/99, in Santa Monica, California); Claire Harrison (6/2/99, in San Francisco); Karen Hirst (2/18/00, in San Francisco); Jules Hock (10/31/00, by telephone); Murray Horwitz (2/4/00, by telephone); Joe Hughes (7/6/99, by telephone); Charles Joffe (6/4/99, in Los Angeles); Will Jordan (9/20/99, in New York City); Larry Josephson (1/5/02, by telephone); Lainie Kazan (10/27/99, in San Francisco); Orrin Keepnews (8/5/99, by telephone); Alan King (2/1/00, by telephone); Robert Klein (1/12/00, by telephone); Tom Koch (1/21/02, by telephone); Artie Kogan (12/9/99, in Encino, California); Hans and Ginny Kolmar (7/1/99, by telephone); Barry Koron (3/2/00, by telephone); Michael Krasny (8/27/00, in Greenbrae, California); Paul Krassner (8/24/99, in Venice, California); Steve Landesberg (12/13/99, in Los Angeles); Mal Z. Lawrence (8/14/01, by telephone); Tom Lehrer (4/20/99 and 8/4/99, in Santa Cruz, California); Marcia Lewis (2/8/00, by telephone); Naomi Lewis (12/28/01, by telephone); Richard Lewis (8/28/99, in Hollywood); Robert Lipsyte (11/6/00 and 12/24/01, by telephone); Jerry Mander (3/2/00, by telephone); Sid Mark (2/2/00, by telephone); Jackie Mason (5/19/00, in New York City); Paul Mazursky (12/15/99, in Beverly Hills); Vaughn Meader (2/11/00, by telephone); Russ Merritt (6/10/99, in Berkeley, California); Ron Miller (4/17/01, in Los Altos, California, and 7/5/01, by telephone); Art Mogull (12/10/99, in Los Angeles); Ed and Mary Etta Moose (6/11/99, in San Francisco); Michael Morris (11/6/00, by telephone); Stanley Mosk (7/15/99, by telephone); Jan Murray (12/8/99, in Beverly Hills); Alan Myerson (12/11/99, in Santa Monica); Bob Newhart (8/25/99, in Bel Air, California); Mike Nichols (9/22/99, in New York City); Gene Norman (12/21/99, by telephone); Louis Nye (2/16/00, by telephone); Terrence O'Flaherty (6/26/00, by telephone); Robert Osserman (10/30/01, by telephone); Don Pitts (3/1/00, by telephone); Randall Poe (5/6/99, in New York City); John Porter (2/27/02, by telephone); Bud Prager (2/23/01, by telephone); Wanda Ramey (6/28/00, by telephone); Dean Reilly (2/21/00, by telephone); Joan Rivers (5/30/00, by telephone); Jack Rollins (9/23/99, in New York City); Freddie Roman (8/11/01, by telephone); Asher Rubin (4/12/00, in San Francisco); Joan Ruderman (8/13/02, by telephone); Rita Rudner (11/21/00, by telephone); Grover Sales (4/19/99, in Belvedere, California); Herb Sargent (9/21/99, in New York City); Bob Sarlatte (2/28/00, in San Francisco); Ronnie Schell (6/3/99, in Beverly Hills); Jim Schock (6/26/00, by telephone); Ralph Schoenstein (2/10/01, by telephone); Avery Schreiber (2/10/00, by telephone); Paul Sills (2/1/00, by telephone); Roy Silver (12/15/99, in Los Angeles); Neil Simon (5/4/00, by telephone); Bobby Slayton (12/10/99, in Venice, California); Ronald L. Smith (2/27/01 and 12/10/01, by telephone); Tom Smothers (1/17/00 and 12/13/01, by telephone); Jeff Sorensen (2/20/01, by telephone); Dan Sorkin (4/21/99, in Oakland, California); David Steinberg (1/10/00, by telephone); Michael Stepanian (8/23/00, by telephone); Howard

Storm (12/29/99, by telephone); James Sullivan (2/16/00, by telephone); Barbara Ann Teer (1/28/01, by telephone); Lily Tomlin (3/18/02, by telephone); Jan Wallman (9/18/99, in New York City); Rusty Warren (12/12/01, by telephone); Abby Wasserman (3/26/01, by telephone); Robert Weide (2/1/00 and 8/4/00, by telephone); Fred Weintraub (8/27/99, in Los Angeles); Wesla Whitfield (3/14/01, by telephone); Alan Whitney (1/9/00, by telephone); Robin Williams (5/22/00, in San Francisco); Jonathan Winters (8/26/99, in Montecito, California); Faith Winthrop (2/4/00, in San Francisco).

Index

Page numbers in italics refer to illustrations.

About the Author

Gerald Nachman has, for more than forty years, covered theater, movies, cabaret, and television for newspapers and magazines, among them the *San Francisco Chronicle,* the *New York Times,* the *New York Daily News,* the *New York Post,* the *Oakland Tribune,* the *San Jose Mercury,* and the *Los Angeles Times.* His previous books include *Raised on Radio;* two collections of humor pieces, *Out on a Whim* and *The Fragile Bachelor;* and *Playing House,* a book on marriage. He lives in San Francisco.